BEYOND
RACISM

*Published in Association with
the Southern Education Foundation*

BEYOND

RACISM

Race and Inequality in Brazil, South Africa, and the United States

edited by

Charles V. Hamilton, Lynn Huntley, Neville Alexander,
Antonio Sérgio Alfredo Guimarães & Wilmot James

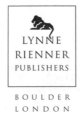

LYNNE
RIENNER
PUBLISHERS

BOULDER
LONDON

Published in the United States of America in 2001 by
Lynne Rienner Publishers, Inc.
1800 30th Street, Boulder, Colorado 80301
www.rienner.com

and in the United Kingdom by
Lynne Rienner Publishers, Inc.
3 Henrietta Street, Covent Garden, London WC2E 8LU

Library of Congress Cataloging-in-Publication Data
Beyond racism : race and inequality in Brazil, South Africa, and the United States /
edited by Charles V. Hamilton ... [et al.].
    Includes bibliographical references and index.
    ISBN 1-58826-026-7 (alk. paper)
    ISBN 1-58826-002-X (pbk. : alk. paper)
    1. Blacks—Brazil—Social conditions.   2. Racism—Brazil.   3. Equality—Brazil.   4.
Brazil—Race relations.   5. Blacks—South Africa—Social conditions.   6. Racism—
South Africa.   7. Equality—South Africa.   8. South Africa—Race relations.
9. Blacks—United States—Social conditions.   10. Racism—United States.
11. Equality—United States.   12. United States—Race relations.   I. Hamilton, Charles V.
F2659.N4B49   2001
305.8—dc21

                                                                    2001019797

British Cataloguing in Publication Data
A Cataloguing in Publication record for this book
is available from the British Library.

Printed and bound in the United States of America

⊗ The paper used in this publication meets the requirements
    of the American National Standard for Permanence of
    Paper for Printed Library Materials Z39.48-1984.

    5   4   3   2   1

12837799

fco

Contents

Preface

Lynn Huntley

After two centuries of such dramatic and spectacular progress, the divide between the rich and the poor, the powerful and the marginalized, that continues to exist—and in fact, to widen—puts to serious question the nature and quality of our humanity. That these inequities—amongst nations and within single nations—still correlate so strongly to racial differences demeans us all.

—*Nelson Mandela*

This volume is a unique collage of perspectives on the causes and consequences of gross disparities in power and well-being between "persons of European or African descent or appearance" in Brazil, South Africa, and the United States. The awkward phrase in quotation marks describes people who, in common parlance, are often labeled "white" or "black." Its use signals that perceived "race" is a subjective idea, variously understood, constructed, and maintained to forge group and individual identities and apportion rights and privileges in these three nations and others around the globe. Although all human beings are the same beneath the skin, and "race" as a scientific matter has little meaning, perceived differences in race, color, or phenotype have long furnished the method and rationale by which disparities in power and well-being between and among these groups have been perpetuated.

Much of the existing literature about "race relations" in Brazil, South Africa, and the United States mines the subject in country-specific terms. It is useful to focus upon the exceptionality of discrete nations. Such close-up examinations of culture, history, resources, governance, and other variations that comprise the world's tapestry of diversity are vital to understanding disparities and the processes by which they are sustained or can be dismantled.

This volume adds a comparative and transnational perspective to country-specific analyses. When one sees familiar problems dressed up in different national garments, new questions, factors, explanations, trends, linkages, and implications emerge. A comparative lens enriches by adding fresh thinking and perspective to our understanding. We may be enabled to see in the experiences of other nations and peoples that to which we have become blind in our own.

Though different, Brazil, South Africa, and the United States share a family resemblance. All were colonized by Europeans who sought to preserve for themselves and those who looked like them rights and privileges denied by law or custom to nonwhites. They created in each country a hierarchy of power in which white skin color, race, and other characteristics perceived to be European were valued. People of African descent or appearance were devalued and deemed fit to serve only as cheap, exploitable sources of labor. In this sense, use of perceived race or color to disadvantage some and benefit others was functional for Europeans. It allowed them to have their own form of "affirmative action," monopolize power, and destroy or marginalize the darker-skinned competition.

Overlapping with the color/race hierarchy in each country was a gender hierarchy with white men at the top. Women of all derivations were denied equal treatment and rights. Women of African descent were doubly disadvantaged—by race and gender—and subject to rank sexual exploitation by white men in order to create more people marked by their skins for enslavement and/or subordination.

As the twenty-first century begins, the over 125 million people of African descent who reside in these nations remain disproportionately numbered among the poor and disadvantaged, a legacy of the inequality and material disparities so diligently constructed in the past. It is a legacy that each of these nations is now forced to confront. For even as racism and discrimination are deeply etched features of life in each nation, as entrenched are efforts by people of African descent or appearance and their allies to end racism and discrimination and attain their place as full, equal, contributing members of society. Archbishop Desmond Tutu said it best: "Freedom will break out. People are made for it just as plants tend toward the light and toward the water."

This volume provides an overview of how "race" is constructed in these countries and samples some of the key ideas and strategies being used to move toward more egalitarian social orders. There is a lack of symmetry in these efforts. The countries are at different phases of development and evolution as modern states. A comparison does not imply similarity where it does not exist; it may underscore differences.

South Africa, the newest substantive democracy in this trilogy of nations, has had less than a decade of postapartheid governance. But it is a nation rooted in racism and discrimination. Race in one form or another has been at center stage since the first Europeans landed. South Africa's long history of efforts to overcome apartheid and "Free Nelson Mandela" is known around the world.

The volume describes some of this history, but its primary focus is on current efforts to redress the inequality that is racism's legacy, trends in the political and economic arenas, and the debates, perspectives, and dynamics that will likely shape the nation's future. Written by leading scholars and activists, the pieces on South Africa provide an insider's view and explore *quo vadis* for this nation. South Africa has come to embody fond hopes that human beings can overcome and move beyond racism to construct fairer, more open, and nonracial societies built less around difference and more around common aspirations. It remains to be seen, however, whether this nation—with its grand experiment with racial reconciliation—can marshal the resources needed to address staggering social problems that mar its prospects for a bright future. And, to a large extent, South Africa's prospects revolve around the extent to which the white minority, which still exercises enormous sway in the economic arena, can adjust to and cope with the imperative to share power, resources, and space with those who only a few years ago were treated as "disposable people."

By way of contrast, the people and government of Brazil are just beginning to publicly acknowledge that appearance or racism contribute to the nation's color-coded power hierarchy and help to sustain disparities and inequality. Brazil is one of the world's ten largest economies and has the largest population of people of African descent or appearance outside the continent of Africa. Still largely invested in its image of itself as a "great racial democracy," and awakening from a period of military governance that ended in 1985, national and public efforts to define, identify, and combat racism and discrimination are at an early stage. Brazil has only recently begun to look outward and recognize that, like its companions South Africa and the United States, it must find ways to expand opportunities.

The pieces about Brazil offer a glimpse of the impact of miscegenation and raise important questions about the effects that the absence of a de jure system of racial discrimination after the abolition of slavery had on identity formation and mobilization for social change. In Brazil, miscegenation and efforts to "whiten" the population were deliberately promoted, and on the surface, social relations appear to be more "cordial" than in the United States or South Africa. The pieces invite the reader to think about the intersection of race and gender in the three nations and explore the close linkage between racism and sexism that too often goes without note. The volume considers whether eased social relations in Brazil have real substance or are merely a measure of the harshness of police repression, the daily fight for survival, underdevelopment, and resignation to suffering by the mass of poor Brazilians. The reader will also be forced to grapple with the age-old canard of whether it is "race *or* poverty," rather than "race *and* poverty," that causes the color-coded disparities in status. The emerging literature about racial inequality and the black movement in Brazil is presented, bringing new questions to traditional analyses of social relations in that nation.

Although the United States is often cited as the world's oldest democratic state, in fact it was not until the demise of legalized discrimination against African Americans, women of all races, and other groups that the government could claim to have even begun to make real the nation's promise of fairness and justice for all of the governed. As the twentieth century ended, the nation had a variety of laws, public policies, practices, and experiences in trying to dismantle its system of second-class citizenship for blacks, women, and other vulnerable groups. African Americans have benefited from the civil rights movement's transformative impact in many ways, but, as a group, remain disproportionately mired in poverty and disadvantage. The volume considers the history of this movement, the responses to contemporary efforts to reverse many of the civil-rights-era policies and advances, and the nature of coalition politics among many American stakeholder groups. Women of all races, Latinos, Asians, immigrants, and others are reshaping the nation's historically dominant bipolar intergroup-relations paradigm.

The sections of the volume related to Brazil are in some ways the least elaborated due to the relative lack of social upheaval, limited debate and policy development to combat racism, the durability of denial, and the as yet small intellectual and activist community striving to promote truth-telling in order to effect transformation. But Brazil is an important counterpoint to the other two nations. It illustrates the complexity of racial identity, the role of color and other appearance-related factors in the practice of racism, and how race, poverty, and gender-based disadvantages intertwine.

South Africa, Brazil, and the United States are three nations with many critical choices to make about what they wish to be and the paths that must be followed to achieve national redefinition. They are nations that are wavering between old patterns and new possibilities, between white supremacy and sexism and promotion of human rights for all, and between insularity and aspirations to world and regional leadership.

Brazil and South Africa are among the world's most unequal societies measured by wealth and income maldistribution. But inequality is also pronounced in the United States. And there are emerging transnational trends and developments that are increasingly interacting with national efforts and prospects for movement beyond racism and toward human rights.

The technological revolution and the globalizing forces that it has unleashed have spawned some of these trends. Worldwide migration is at record levels. This is especially evident in the United States, which is projected to become a "majority minority" nation by the middle of the twenty-first century, and in South Africa, the preferred destination of many diverse African peoples from elsewhere on the African continent. The migration of peoples into all three countries and internal demographic and migration patterns pose new problems and imperatives with which these nations must grapple.

The emergent global economy is growing stronger each day. Depending upon where one looks or when, global economic integration may strengthen, disrupt, or limit the capacities of government to respond effectively to social welfare needs or plan for orderly national development. It may exacerbate or lessen the divide between the "developed North" and the "developing South." It may also create new incentives for the people in all of these countries to overcome racism, reduce inequality, and broaden investment in the human capital of diverse peoples. There is growing evidence that capital does not long remain in venues where social disorder and tensions are high, and a trained and healthy work force, expanding consumer base, democratic and participatory government, and other trappings of stability are wanting. Globalization may furnish incentives for Brazil, South Africa, and the United States to take more seriously the need to enhance the education and productive capacities of marginalized and poor people, including people of African descent, not only out of altruism or a concern for fairness, but rather, enlightened self- and national interest.

The international human rights and global women's movements will also likely gain newfound influence as time goes on, since global problems call for solutions of commensurate scope. Domestic efforts to advance the well-being of people of African descent, women, and other vulnerable groups in each country may benefit from this international engagement. Certainly in the international effort to overturn apartheid, one can sense the potential power of international human rights and women's rights movements.

Capital and people are flowing across national boundaries at unprecedented rates. The idea of democracy has taken hold in all three nations. In the cases of Brazil and South Africa, where so many are so poor and have limited material stakes in the mainstream of society, the effort to combat racism and inequality is increasingly seen and understood to be a central part of democratic consolidation. In the United States, as well, where high levels of voter apathy and special-interest politics are reshaping political dynamics, efforts to mobilize members of historically excluded groups to participate in electoral politics may result in gridlock and/or a progressive shift toward more inclusive and substantively representative government.

These points are explored in this volume's comparative papers on education, international human rights remedies for discrimination, economic costs of racial discrimination, and affirmative action. This is an exciting and fluid time at which to consider how nations and their peoples can effect social, political, and economic transformation.

While it is clear that there is no one solution to the problem of racism and discrimination—it is but a variant of prejudice that can have many subjects—it is also clear that there are as many diverse solutions. What is too often lacking is the will to do that which is needed to effect change.

There are several areas that the volume's editors would have liked to mine more fully, but could only touch upon lightly. The concerns of women, e.g., the struggle for equal rights, pay and education, violence against women, reproductive health, work and family issues, and the differential impacts that racism and sexism have on this half of humankind are subjects of enormous complexity and importance that cry out for in-depth examination and treatment. Likewise, the role of police violence, imprisonment, and repression directed toward men of African descent—especially in the United States and Brazil—are issues of great importance, among others, on which the volume cannot adequately focus.

Nor are we able in this volume to tackle issues related to development and economic policy in an in-depth way. Economic growth must be the point of departure upon which efforts to reduce inequality among groups must be based in each nation. However, as several pieces in the volume note, growth without targeted and complementary efforts to help excluded groups gain the ability to take advantage of enhanced opportunity or resources is unlikely to eliminate racially identifiable inequality. This is why comprehensive antipoverty *and* antidiscrimination measures must be mounted simultaneously to lessen inequality. Dr. Bernard Anderson, a former assistant secretary in the United States Department of Labor, underscored this need with these words:

> The relationship between economic growth and the reduction of income inequality is not just theoretical but is based on actual United States' experience. African Americans bear a relationship to the American economy much like that of the caboose on the train. When the train speeds up, the caboose speeds up, and when the train slows down, the caboose slows down. But in the natural order of things, the caboose never catches up with the engine. . . . Economic growth reduces income inequality, but economic growth alone won't produce a desirable level of parity in the distribution of income.

Finally, a word about the Comparative Human Relations Initiative, under whose auspices this volume was developed, is in order. The Initiative is a multiyear, multidisciplinary effort begun in 1995 to bring people from Brazil, South Africa, and the United States together to learn from each others' experiences in combating discrimination. It held a number of meetings of activists, scholars, and policymakers in the three nations. Partnering with nongovernmental organizations and leaders in the three nations, the Initiative published several reports that comprise the *Beyond Racism, Embracing an Interdependent Future* series, and three books, *Grappling with Change, Between Unity and Diversity,* and *Tirando a Máscara, Ensaios sobre o racismo no Brasil* (*Taking Off the Mask, Essays on Racism in Brazil*). This comparative anthology is part of this body of work.

Special appreciation is due to the Ford Foundation, Charles Stewart Mott Foundation, Rockefeller Brothers Fund, Levi-Strauss Foundation, and the Coca-Cola Foundation for their support. The other editors of this volume—Charles V. Hamilton, Wilmot James, Neville Alexander, and Antonio Sérgio Guimarães, consultant Steve Suitts, and my colleague Janet Keene—have labored long and hard to bring this volume into being and deserve special commendation.

Significant progress has been made in the twentieth century toward eradication of white supremacy, an ideology that was the order of the day as the century began. We hope that this volume will make a contribution to critical thinking, renewed resolve, and serious continuing efforts to rid Brazil, South Africa, and the United States of the antiquated and false ideas that link color, race, gender, and other superficial traits with intelligence or merit. All human beings have rights simply by virtue of our sentience. We are all the same beneath the skin.

Lynn Huntley
Director
The Comparative Human Relations Initiative

1

Race and Racism in Historical Perspective: Comparing the United States, South Africa, and Brazil

George M. Fredrickson

FOR MORE THAN fifty years, scholars from various disciplines have been comparing the history of group relations in societies that have traditionally used skin color as a marker of rank or status. None of these societies have attracted more attention than the United States, Brazil, and South Africa. The bulk of this work has compared or contrasted the American case with only one of the others; only rarely have all three been treated at the same time. This scholarship has yielded some significant insights but has also generated much controversy, resulting in periodic revisions and reevaluations.

New historical knowledge and methods have not been the only reasons for the protean nature of the comparisons. Color-coded group relations in all three of these societies have been changing in palpable ways in recent decades, sometimes relatively suddenly as in the United States in the 1960s and South Africa in the late 1980s and early 1990s. Long-term trajectories, projected on the basis of an understanding of earlier conditions and trends, have often failed to make such changes fully comprehensible and have obliged comparative historians to reevaluate the past in the light of the present. In the case of Brazil, an accumulation of evidence suggesting that there are now significant levels of prejudice and discrimination against people with African ancestry has forced the reconsideration of a past that hitherto had seemed almost idyllic in contrast to the blatant racism that historians had found in South Africa and the southern United States.

Like all history, comparative history is influenced by the location of the historian in time and space. When Americans write about race in Brazil or South Africa, even if they do not make explicit comparisons with the United States, their work often searches implicitly for analo-

1

gies or contrasts with the current state of black-white relations in their own country. A similar concern with what is locally relevant is likely to inspire the cross-national work of Brazilians and South Africans. The comparative history of "race" in these societies is clearly not a purely disinterested manifestation of scientific curiosity. To varying degrees, it reflects current interests and ideologies in its search for a "usable past."

To be useful and illuminating, historical comparisons must be based on some fundamental similarities. Juxtaposing radically different entities yields only obvious contrasts rather than the more subtle differences that raise questions of causation that historians and social scientists can fruitfully explore. Comparisons involving the United States, Brazil, and South Africa rest on three pillars. First, all of these societies resulted from the process of European expansion and colonization of the non-Western world that began around 1500. Between the early fifteenth and the mid-sixteenth centuries, the Portuguese in Brazil, the English in North America, and the Dutch in South Africa established settler colonies that displaced, marginalized, or subordinated indigenous populations. Second, each of these areas of colonization imported non-European slaves to meet labor needs that the settlers themselves were unable or unwilling to undertake and for which indigenous groups were (at least temporarily) unavailable or deemed unsuitable. Most of these slaves came from Africa, although in the Dutch colony at the Cape of Good Hope the East Indies and South Asia provided a substantial share of the unfree population. A slaveholding mentality therefore developed in which whiteness or European ancestry meant freedom and a dark skin, signifying origin outside of Europe, provided a presumption of servitude. (Literal slavery turned out in the long run to be less important as a matrix for race relations in South Africa than in the United States and Brazil, but coercive master-servant relationships between settlers and "natives" provided a similar paradigm.) The third pillar, therefore, is that each society developed at an early stage a color-code to determine status. European preeminence and domination were unquestioned assumptions. Some black or brown slaves did become free, but they were relegated by law or custom to an intermediate status between the masters and the slaves—victims of discrimination if not of enforced servitude. Hence an ethnic hierarchy was established by the colonial state and the original white settlers that would persist after these colonial regimes became independent states and after each of them abolished slavery before or after achieving nationhood.

Significant variations—both from place to place and over time in each place—have nevertheless been found in the way racial groups were defined and how their subordination was justified, as well as in the nature and rigidity of the racial order and in the way historical developments or changing conditions have adjusted, weakened, or strengthened the primal hierarchies. If there is one dominant assumption in current comparative studies in race and ethnicity, it is that race is a social and cultural construction and not a fact of nature or a primordial given. But it would be a mistake, in my opinion, to ignore the weight of the past and to assume that race is constantly being reinvented from scratch. The legacy of earlier racial attitudes and hierarchies is difficult, if not impossible, to overcome or fully transcend when racial orders are being reconstructed or reinvented. The burden of history can be lightened, but it would be utopian to think that it can be entirely eliminated.

Serious work on the comparative history of race relations began in the 1940s and 1950s with studies of slavery and its consequences in the United States and Latin America. Frank Tannenbaum's *Slave and Citizen* (1946), and Stanley Elkins's *Slavery* (1959) contrasted a relatively mild slavery and easy access to freedom in Brazil and other Latin American slave societies with a harsher servitude and more rigid color line in the United States. Their explanation for the difference was based primarily on the implications for slavery and race relations of the cultural antecedents of the European colonists. A relatively tolerant Iberian Catholicism and patrimonialism was pitted against an intensely ethnocentric and exclusionary English Protestantism, which not only set higher standards for conversion and "civilized status," but also unleashed an unfettered capitalism that exposed slaves to more brutal treatment than the allegedly more paternalistic regimes of colonial Latin America.

Revisionists writing in the 1960s and 1970s had little trouble undermining the case for a relatively mild or benign Latin American slavery—the high mortality rates that necessitated a constant influx of new slaves from Africa to Brazil and Cuba could only mean harsh or unhealthy conditions. Some even suggested that in North America, where the slave force more than reproduced itself even before the end of the slave trade, masters normally treated their slaves better, in a physical sense at least, than did slaveholders in Brazil or Cuba—if only because it made good economic sense to do so or because the growing of tobacco and cotton was less lethal to unfree laborers than the production of sugar and coffee.

Critics of the Tannenbaum-Elkins thesis did not deny, however, that emancipation during the slave era was much harder to obtain in the United States and that the form of black-white relations that survived the abolition of slavery was unique in its overt ideological racism and state-sponsored segregationism. The Brazilian state sought to "whiten" its population after the end of slavery by the encouragement of European immigration but did not extol race purity and seek to promote it by banning intermarriage and regulating interracial social contacts as did many of the North American colonies or states. The two striking peculiarities of race relations in the United States, scholars continued to affirm, were that there were only two basic racial categories—white and black—and that race was determined on the basis of a strict descent rule, meaning that those with any known African ancestry were considered black. In South America and the Caribbean, there were generally three or more official categories—usually black, mulatto, and white— and those who were of mixed but mostly European descent could, at least in the Iberian societies, hope to be incorporated into the white status group despite acknowledged African ancestry.

To explain the contrast between the rigid race relations in the United States and the more fluid pattern that existed elsewhere in the Americas, the revisionists played down the cultural antecedents of the colonizers and stressed material and demographic factors. According to the anthropologist Marvin Harris in *Patterns of Race in the Americas* (1964), the relative size of the nonslaveholding white population was the critical variable in determining whether mulattos would be routinely emancipated and assigned an intermediate status, as was the case in Brazil by the nineteenth century, or mostly kept in servitude and regarded as outcasts if they somehow gained their freedom, which was apparently what happened in the Old South. Planters needed auxiliaries to provide security against slave resistance and ancillary economic services. If enough lower-class whites were at hand to perform these functions, incentives to grant freedom and intermediate status to mulattos were weak or absent. Harris's thesis was so plausible and persuasive that most subsequent comparativists adopted it to help explain the origins of the seemingly unique black/white dichotomy that emerged in the United States.

Also deemed significant by some revisionists was the sex ratio among whites at the time African slavery became the predominant labor system in a particular colony. Where white women were present in relatively significant numbers, as in colonial Virginia and Maryland, miscegenation was less common, or at least less openly acknowledged, than in colonial Brazil where Portuguese women were in short supply and mixed offspring were more likely to be recognized by their fathers and emancipated. Three-category systems did not mean that race prejudice was nonexistent in Brazil and other parts of Latin America. Whiteness was everywhere privileged over blackness, even if brownness—especially light brownness—was less of a liability than in the United States.

Comparative race relations was also a serious preoccupation of historically oriented sociologists between the 1940s and the 1960s. Unlike historians of the Americas, their work sometimes attempted to incorporate the experience of multiracial societies outside of the Western Hemisphere. Most of them were preoccupied with demonstrating or testing the theories of ethnic conflict and accommodation developed in the 1920s and 1930s by Robert Park at the University of Chicago. According to this theory, racially or ethnically diverse societies went through a predictable series of phases that led ultimately to the assimilation of minorities. Applied to black-white relations in the United States and elsewhere by sociologists like E. Franklin Frazier (see his *Race and Culture Contacts in the Modern World*, 1957) this meant an evolution toward the obliteration of group differences through cultural, social, and ultimately biological assimilation (although it was generally recognized that this process could take a long time and was subject to temporary reversals). Frazier and others cited Brazil as an example of a society that was far ahead of the United States in its evolution toward the amalgamation of races. Because of its overwhelming black majority, the model could not readily be applied to South Africa, unless its ultimate destiny was the assimilation of white to black. In some formulations, this optimistic view was linked to the prevailing concept of modernization. When applied to race relations, modernization meant that status based on "ascription" or birth was inevitably replaced by status based on achievement as a society grew more industrialized, urbanized, and interdependent. These sociological studies ranged far and wide and were, for the most part, too general and aprioristic to be applied very fruitfully to individual cases.

The Founding of New Societies (1964), a multi-authored comparative study edited by the political scientist Louis Hartz (who also wrote a lion's share of it), first brought the United States, South Africa, and Latin America (along with Canada and Australia) into juxtaposition. Race relations was not the main theme of this study of settler societies, but its insistence that each of these societies was a "fragment of Europe" that perpetuated cultural characteristics and political tendencies brought by the original settlers had implications for relations with nonEuropeans that were compatible with the comparisons of the Tannenbaum-Elkins school. Iberian patrimonialism, Dutch Calvinism, and the incipient liberalism of the middle-class English colonists of

North America provided the ideological contexts that put black slaves at the base of a complex status hierarchy in Latin America or at the bottom of a simple white-over-black pattern of dominance in the United States and South Africa. Hartz was the first to argue that the growth of democracy for whites, when combined with a belief in black inferiority, intensified prejudice and discrimination.

More recent studies of patterns of race in the United States, while not explicitly comparative, have suggested that the two-category system and descent rule were not firmly established in the colonial period but became hard-and-fast only in the mid-to-late nineteenth century. In the antebellum Deep South before the 1850s, mulattos generally occupied a privileged position relative to blacks, especially in Louisiana and South Carolina. Although their status was maintained by custom rather than by law, this three-tiered system had some resemblance to the one that prevailed in the Caribbean plantation societies. Furthermore, some states defined as Negro only those with a black grandparent, making it possible for a few families with known African ancestry to become white. Discrimination against mulattos surged in the 1850s as a result of the sectional controversy over slavery and the racism that it evoked, but the "one-drop rule" to determine who was black was not legislated until the Jim Crow era around the turn of the century. (See Joel Williamson, *New People*, 1980). "Mulatto" persisted as a United States census category until 1920. Furthermore new studies have shown that some European immigrant groups, especially Irish, Italians, and Jews, were not initially regarded as unambiguously white and had to struggle to obtain full membership in the dominant race.

This new work on the construction of whiteness and blackness means that the stark contrasts posited by the pioneering comparisons between the United States and Brazil will need to be modified somewhat. The assumption that "patterns of race" are fixed early and set in stone now seems ahistorical and essentialist. The current controversy in the United States about the identity of mixed-race people and how they should be enumerated in the census has led to an increased awareness of the contingency and artificiality of racial designations. Systematic comparative work involving the United States and Iberian America has yet to take account of this new understanding of the evolution and reconstruction of racial categories and hierarchies. But the view that there are persistent differences in the precise way race is defined and constructed in the United States and Brazil is likely to survive this reexamination.

A new direction in comparative studies was set in 1967 by a remarkable work that still possesses considerable value. Pierre L. van den Berghe compared the historical evolution of racial orders in the United States, Brazil, South Africa, and Mexico in his book *Race and Racism*. A sociologist who had done his initial work on South Africa, van den Berghe deserves much of the credit for making that country a major reference point in the discourse about comparative race relations. At the same time, he manifested a stronger sense of societal transformation than Hartz and his colleagues and developed a more pessimistic or realistic view of postemancipation black-white relations than had been suggested by comparative sociologists in the Park tradition. He argued that the abolition of slavery occasioned a shift from a "paternalistic" to a "competitive" form of race relations, which meant that racism was likely to be intensified rather than diminished by emancipation. It was the fear of economic and social competition in rapidly modernizing societies that, according to van den Berghe, produced Jim Crow laws in the United States and "native segregation" and apartheid in South Africa. Because they were less modernized and retained strong elements of paternalism in their social attitudes and arrangements, his Latin American cases had not manifested these harsh, exclusionary tendencies. He coined the useful phrase "*herrenvolk* democracies" to distinguish the combination of rigid racial hierarchies with the norm of equal rights and full political participation for all whites, which he believed had developed in the United States and South Africa, from the more traditional social hierarchies based on class and culture that allegedly muted the effect of race per se in Mexico and Brazil. His treatment of Brazil did not challenge the prevailing view that class and culture modified racial attitudes and practices—that money and education could whiten mulattos to an extent that would be inconceivable in the United States. But it did raise the possibility that this paternalistic tolerance would decline as Brazil became more "modern" and competitive.

Since the 1970s, historians and to a lesser extent sociologists and political scientists have followed van den Berghe's lead by taking a hard comparative look at South Africa. Ambitious bilateral comparisons of race relations in the United States and South Africa by John Cell, Stanley Greenberg, and myself appeared almost simultaneously in the early 1980s. Following the recent trend in U.S.-Brazilian comparisons, these studies emphasized demographic and material factors more than cultural predispositions inherited from the European past—for example, a Dutch or English Calvinism that drew sharp lines between the saved and the damned that might have reinforced a distinction between white and black. In my own work, *White Supremacy* (1981), I found that dif-

1940s and 1960s toward establishing a manufacturing base under statist and authoritarian auspices. The development of militant unions in both countries during the 1970s can be attributed in part to the opening provided by business opposition to the heavy hand of the state. Confronted with the fact that their living standards were declining due to frozen wages and rising prices in Brazil and changes in the residence patterns of both countries that forced proletarians into peripheral townships or shantytowns far from their places of employment, workers took advantage of dissension among elites to organize themselves and push their demands.

Seidman's work raises important new questions for students of comparative race relations. She compels further attention to a factor emphasized earlier by Stanley Greenberg in his comparative study of South Africa and Alabama—the way that conflicts between business and government can sometimes be exploited by those seeking progressive social change. She also makes us more aware of the crucial role played by black unions in the struggle against apartheid in South Africa and the extent to which their class-based ideology prepared the way for the triumph of "nonracialism" under Nelson Mandela. I paid relatively little attention to labor movements in my comparative study of black ideologies in the United States and South Africa, because there was no American analogue to COSATU (the predominantly black federation of unions that provided much of the muscle behind the struggle for black liberation in the late 1980s and early 1990s). What may make Brazil and South Africa different from the United States is the role that an interracial but predominantly black and brown labor movement has played or could conceivably play in the struggle for racial justice and equality.

The history of race-based movements in Brazil is just beginning to be written. Michael Hanchard's *Orpheus and Power: The Movimento Negro of Rio de Janeiro and São Paulo*, published in 1994, was the first book-length study in English on this subject. It is evident from this work that black consciousness is on the rise among black and brown Brazilians and that efforts to unify them into a single Afro-Brazilian community are not entirely unavailing. But the most significant manifestation of this impulse—the Movimento Negro—has failed to gain mass support. Comparative studies of Afro-Brazilian, African-American, and black South African liberation or identity movements might prove enormously revealing. Hanchard's work shows, for example, that the debates between integrationists and black nationalists in the United States and between nonracialists and Africanists or advocates of

"Black Consciousness" in South Africa have their Brazilian analogue in the ongoing Afro-Brazilian argument between the *americanistas* and the *africanistas*.

Hanchard finds that an Afro-Brazilian "culturalism," based on an affirmation of African survivals and identities, has been subject to co-optation by the government and the white establishment. An official willingness to promote and celebrate the African strain in Brazilian national character and culture, which dates back to the 1930s, has served to distract attention from the economic and social plight of Afro-Brazilians and inhibit direct protest against poverty, discrimination, and police brutality. (Could people who seem to have so much fun at Carnival really be victims of oppression?) Butler's comparative study of São Paulo and Salvador provides further evidence that constructing and celebrating a distinctive cultural identity may be an impediment to political mobilization aimed at racial discrimination. It is in São Paulo, where Afro-Brazilians have generally sought inclusion in mainstream Brazilian society, that active and sometimes militant mobilization has occurred. In Salvador, where an Africanist identity thrives, Afro-Brazilians have remained, for the most part, politically passive. The history of black cultural nationalism in the United States and South Africa might also be interpreted to support an argument that black movements seeking justice through inclusion in a common democratic society are normally more militant and ultimately more effective than separatist identity movements, which may encourage escape or evasion rather than a direct confrontation with racism.

Anthony Marx has recently produced the first systematic comparison of how racial orders were constructed in all three countries—*Making Race and Nation* (1998). A political scientist, Marx has focused on the role of the state as the critical variable. His basic argument is that the United States and South Africa developed policies of racial exclusion and oppression primarily because of the imperatives of state or nation building as perceived by political elites that happened to be white. Stability and prosperity—the state's main goals—were threatened by crises resulting from sectional or ethnic divisions among the enfranchised white citizenry, leading in both cases to what amounted to civil wars. The North-South conflict in the United States and the Anglo-Afrikaner struggle in South Africa created a problem for nation builders that had no analogue in Brazil, where the white population has never been seriously split along regional or ethnic lines. Legalized racism, or in the case of the United States the acquiescence of the federal government to the Jim Crow laws of the southern states, was viewed as the price of national cohesion and a necessary device for building a modern nation-state. In other words, blacks were scapegoated to promote white unity. When, by the 1960s in the United States and by the late 1980s and early 1990s in South Africa, white unity had been firmly established and black resistance had come to constitute a threat to the health or survival of the state, ruling elites in both countries chose to abolish discriminatory laws and fully enfranchise blacks to promote the same goals of national cohesion and prosperity that had earlier led their predecessors to institute the opposite policies.

Marx's work suggests that we need to pay a lot more attention than van den Berghe did to the autonomous role of the state if we want to understand the variable development of race and racism. As I found in my own work on white supremacy in the United States and South Africa, disunity and conflict among whites and efforts to resolve them were a recurring factor that helped to account for changes or adjustments in race policy from the colonial period to the present. But, like any explanation that privileges a single factor, the state-as-actor thesis may risk oversimplifying a complex and multifaceted process. Furthermore, the model applies most directly to government-sanctioned racism, and offers less insight into the de facto prejudice and discrimination that still bedevils all three societies and serves to disadvantage blacks economically and socially.

A fuller and richer comparison of the historical trajectories of race and racism in the three societies would need to deal more fully with two other factors. Max Weber, in his efforts to categorize disparities in social power, pointed to three interacting types of differentiation: class, status, and party. "Party," for Weber, meant access to, and influence over, the state—the factor that Marx stresses. But class—unequal access to the market and the means of production—and status—the culturally constructed norms for the differential apportionment of honor and prestige—act upon the state as well as being influenced by it. Weber's term for what we call race is "ethnic status," the social rank and prestige that comes from belonging to an historically dominant ethnic or racial group. Following Weber, I believe that a three-way comparison should take more fully into account the developing economic situation and the kind of class relations to which it gives rise and also the cultural and psychological weight of a status order based on a presumption of white superiority. Another way of advocating this tri-causal model is simply to call for explanations that acknowledge the interaction of the state, the economy, and the prevailing hierarchy of sociocultural identities without giving a priori primacy to any one of them.

Anthony Marx has, with compelling originality, made a case for the state or "party" as an actor in the development and transformations of racial orders in Brazil, South Africa, and the United States, but his contention that racism can be regarded as a constant rather than a variable because it was present in all three cases is debatable. "Ethnic status" in a color coded form assumed a castelike character in the United States and South Africa that it has never had in Brazil. The banning of interracial marriage in much of the United States from the colonial period to the late 1960s and in twentieth-century South Africa has been unthinkable in Brazil throughout most of its history. In fact, as Thomas Skidmore demonstrated in *Black into White* (1974), twentieth-century Euro-Brazilian intellectuals and political leaders have frequently endorsed intermarriage as another way (along with European immigration) to "whiten" Brazil. A form of racism is clearly involved in this preference for the mostly white over the mostly black, but it is a more tolerant and permissive variety than the fixation with race purity and rigid color lines that characterized U.S. or South African racial thought and policies before and especially during the eras of Jim Crow and apartheid. Unlike Afro-Brazilians, southern African Americans and black South Africans were commonly viewed and treated not merely as social inferiors but as permanent aliens or social outcasts, ineligible even for second-class citizenship. A substantial number of Americans and South Africans of European descent probably still hold this view, consciously or subliminally. American and South African national identities were conceived on the basis of a commitment to white racial purity and exclusiveness that has no real analogue in Brazil.

That Brazil followed a trajectory different from that of the United States and South Africa in its postemancipation racial policies can therefore be explained as the product of the special character of its ethnic status hierarchy as well as by the fact that European political unity was never threatened to an extent that impelled nation builders to find a scapegoat. There is, I believe, a measure of truth in the traditional view that Brazil, while still a Portuguese colony or a Luso-tropical empire and before it aspired to be a modern nation-state, established a pattern of racial classification and interaction that differed significantly from that which developed in the United States and South Africa. The mulatto or *pardo* stereotype was quite dissimilar from that of blacks or *pretos* for a very long time, and to some extent still is, in ways that sanctioned race mixture and offered some mulattos access to many of the advantages of Euro-Brazilian status. The multiplicity of color categories and the permeability of the boundaries between these categories meant that a system of Jim Crow segregation or apartheid would have been virtually impossible to implement in Brazil even if there had been a strong political incentive to do so. It was simply too difficult to determine who was what. South Africa also generated a "colored" middle strata, some of whose members succeeded in passing for white, but this category originated in the intermixture of the white, brown, and yellow-skinned peoples resident in the Western Cape in the seventeenth and eighteenth centuries. It was an internally diverse group that was invented by white census takers in the mid-nineteenth century and then left in an ambiguous intermediate position when the confrontation of Europeans and Bantu-speaking Africans became the central theme of South African history. No mulatto category developed out of the frontier interactions that led to white dominance over most of South Africa in the course of the nineteenth century. The offspring of the black-white sexual unions that occurred on the frontier normally became African tribesmen rather than "coloreds."

The sharp black-white dichotomy that, for most practical purposes, came to characterize the U.S. and South African patterns was therefore not replicated in Brazil. If Brazil had been unfortunate enough to have a sectional civil war in the nineteenth century, it is quite conceivable that the resulting reunion would have unified *brancos* and *pardos* against *pretos*, in a way that might have had some parallels with the black-mulatto division during the Haitian revolution. The state may be an actor in the construction of racial orders, but the raw material it has at hand to construct national citizenship is conditioned by preexisting patterns of stratification or exclusion that may differ significantly.

The independent effect of economic class formation on black-white relations can begin to be assessed by problematizing Anthony Marx's contention that a major goal of national unifications is to foster economic development and prosperity. The obvious question is prosperity and economic development for whom? The United States, South Africa, and Brazil have at some point in their histories become developing industrial capitalist societies. But they did not all develop at the same time or at the same rate. The United States was the pioneer and South Africa and Brazil came later—in the case of Brazil much later. One does not have to be a thoroughgoing Marxist to acknowledge that the rise of industrial capitalism creates class divisions between wage earners and the owners of the means of production. If race can serve as a political unifier among white regions or ethnic groups, it can also serve to mitigate class conflict among whites. According to the cruder versions of Marxism, employers encourage racism among white workers in order to prevent proletarians from unifying across the color line. But a more sophisticated class analysis of "split labor markets" acknowledges that white workers may actually benefit from the exclusion of other racial groups from equal opportunity in the labor market. Skilled workers in the United States often excluded blacks or Asians from their trades not merely because they were prejudiced against them but also, and perhaps more important, because it served to protect their wages and increase their bargaining power with employers. In South Africa in 1922, white workers revolted against efforts to increase the proportion of African workers in semi-skilled jobs in the gold mines. Their strike was put down by force, but a subsequent government enacted the industrial color bars that made white workers a privileged class with virtually guaranteed access to skilled jobs and high wages. In both the United States and South Africa, capitalists, whose natural inclination was to hire the cheapest labor available, found that the price of peace with class-conscious white workers was an exclusionary policy that privileged white employees. Again, however, as in the case of the political explanation of racism, such job discrimination would have made no sense if a preexisting racial hierarchy had not divided the labor market between those who got there first and were best able to defend their interests and those who arrived later and were deemed to be low-wage menial workers by nature.

Brazil's later industrialization, as Gay Seidman has pointed out, put workers without a tradition of labor organization at the mercy of authoritarian governments and rapacious employers, both of whom wanted economic development that benefited the privileged few at the expense of the many. In this case, however, the unions, which needed all the support they could muster against the powerful forces arrayed against them, did not draw a color line. When the business community and the government split over the specifics of economic development, this fledgling interracial labor movement found some room to operate.

The Great Depression and the New Deal in the United States provided a comparable stimulus for labor organizing in general and made possible the integration of the great Congress of Industrial Organizations' unions. Prejudice among white workers persisted, especially in the South, but the desperate campaign to provide jobs and decent wages in a period of high unemployment and general impoverishment made some key labor leaders aware of the organizational advantages of racial inclusiveness. In South Africa, the white working class declined in size and importance beginning in the 1940s. More and more formerly poor Afrikaners used their state-supported advantage in education, employment, and access to capital to attain a middle-class status and standard of living. Thus the industrial working class became almost exclusively black by the 1960s, making it possible for the African unions that eventually gained legal recognition to become key participants in the struggle against apartheid.

American unions, although they did contribute money and personnel to the civil rights struggles of the 1960s, could not play a similar role. Although most of them were integrated, they remained predominantly white, and their leadership had to take into account the persisting prejudices of many of the white rank and file. Furthermore, the labor movement in general was beginning to decline in membership, militancy, and political clout. Hence militant "workerism" could not play the same role as a counterweight to power and privilege based on class and race that may have been decisive in South Africa and could become so in Brazil.

Even if one takes the existing class structure as a given, the success of the economy has major implications for race relations. Capitalism may foster inequality, but in my view it does not inevitably promote racial inequality (which is not to say that free-market capitalism is capable of rectifying structural inequalities based on a history of racial disadvantage). The production for profit of goods and services to be sold in a free market does not by its nature mandate racial discrimination. If anything, the logic of capitalism is based on a color-blind notion of economic man as entrepreneur, investor, consumer, and worker. As the U.S. experience of the past forty years clearly shows, racial reform is much easier in times of prosperity and rising expectations than in periods of economic decline and scarce resources. Many people believe that South Africa's experiment in nonracial democracy is dependent on whether the economy grows fast enough in the next few years to provide millions of new jobs to currently impoverished and unemployed Africans. The struggles of blacks and other poor Brazilians for a better life obviously requires a vibrant and growing economy, as well as one that distributes the rewards of economic growth much more equitably than it has done in the past.

To fully assess what history can teach us about the prospects for racial equality in the United States, Brazil, and South Africa, one other variable that seems of prime significance to me is the degree to which the prevailing conceptions of national character and identity in the three countries can be used or reconstructed to encourage the incorporation of blacks into the mainstream. Long-standing notions of what a nation stands for, what its highest aspirations are, and what it hopes to achieve are very difficult to change. It is a major element in the dominant belief systems and views of the world that history has bequeathed to the citizens of the countries being compared. Blacks in the United States have benefited historically at certain times—most obviously in the 1860s and the 1960s—from the commitment to individual liberty, equality, and opportunity to be found in the language of the Declaration of Independence (even if the framers of the document can be justly accused of hypocrisy or mental reservations). But does that liberal, individualist tradition still suffice in the circumstances of the late twentieth century—declining mobility for those at the bottom of the economic and educational opportunity structures and increasing cultural diversity? Do we now have to come to terms with the more community-oriented belief systems and practices of those minorities that may eventually become a majority in the United States? It is my personal belief that the best hope we have for a more just society is to continue the struggle to make our reality match our abstract commitment to individual human rights. But we can only do this if we are willing to make cultural and ethnic identity one of the "self-evident" rights that we recognize. Cultural freedom for the individual—the right to be different without being penalized for it—would seem to be as permissible a deduction from the right to "the pursuit of happiness" as is the religious freedom and diversity that is so thoroughly ingrained in American law and political culture.

In Brazil and South Africa, the prevailing racial or ethnic ideologies and conceptions of national purpose are oddly similar to each other in that they both de-emphasize race in favor of color-blind democracy and show a greater propensity than seems currently possible in the United States to substitute a conflict between capitalist and socialist or social-democratic ideologies for those that emphasize racial and ethnic divisions, either openly or covertly. Of course South Africa's racial democracy is proclaimed and enforced by the black majority, while that of Brazil is a myth created and promulgated by a white elite. In the latter case, at least, full exposure of the falsity of the claim could be followed most profitably by efforts to make racial democracy a reality rather than by jettisoning the ideal itself, just as in the United States a struggle based on fulfilling the human rights principles of the Declaration of Independence is likely to be more efficacious than one that rejects them out of hand because of their Euro-American origin.

In South Africa, where a new national identity is being forged, there is a Scylla-and-Charybdis problem. On one side is a fundamentalist version of nonracialism that obscures the reality of ethnic diversity and inhibits efforts to accommodate it. On the other is the danger of accentuating differences to the point where group consciousness and antagonism threaten the precarious unity of this "rainbow" society. Secessionist tendencies among Zulus and Afrikaners remain serious threats to the nationalist project. Furthermore, the failure of an ostensibly class-based nonracialism to deliver the goods to the African majority, at a time when the International Monetary Fund and the World Bank make social-democratic redistributive policies difficult and costly to implement, could easily result in the intensification of racial and ethnic conflict. Africanist and "Black Consciousness" groups are biding their time to see if the African National Congress can really bring white privilege to an end or whether nonracialism is simply a facade for the elevation of black elites into the ruling economic and political circles that were formerly limited to whites.

All these complexities and theoretical speculations do not hide the fact that in all three countries, race matters. By any measure of well-being and opportunity, blacks are still greatly disadvantaged in all three societies. South Africa has the greatest economic and social inequalities—this is the legacy of apartheid—but has the government with the greatest incentive and commitment to do something about them. In the United States the statistical disparities are much less than in South Africa and somewhat less than in Brazil. But the relative deprivation of African Americans may be the greatest because they live in a country in which the majority enjoys one of the highest standards of living in the world, whereas both Brazil and South Africa are among those nations in which the overwhelming majority is desperately poor. In Brazil, blacks are overrepresented among the poor and in South Africa they are virtually all of them. Nevertheless, inequality correlated and associated with race is the common problem, and "affirmative action" of some kind is clearly called for in all three cases.

Precisely what works in one context may not work in the others. Varying circumstances in the United States, Brazil, and South Africa may call for somewhat different strategies to overcome racism. Those concerned with social and political action against racism may get a better sense of what might or might not be effective in a particular context from comparative historical studies. My survey suggests that racism should be combated on two fronts simultaneously. First, attitudes need to be changed through education and the experience of interacting with members of other groups in an atmosphere of equality and trust. Affirmative-action programs, properly conceived and implemented, can contribute significantly to the struggle against prejudice as well as enhance the economic opportunities of individuals who would otherwise be denied a chance to reach their potential. Second, economic disparities among historically racialized groups need to be attacked by government policies and voluntary action aimed at the redistribution of wealth and privilege. The most effective of these policies should not be race-specific but would be directed at the eradication or reduction of poverty whatever the color of its victims. The state in its efforts to achieve unity, prosperity, and justice will have to be the central player in these efforts, but the civil society can also make a significant contribution. Comparative historical study cannot hope to provide answers to many of the immediate, practical questions asked by those resisting racism in these differing and constantly changing arenas of group conflict and accommodation. Only those on the ground who wrestle day-to-day with the current realities of race and racism in Brazil, South Africa, and the United States can hope to do that. But comparative historians can at least point in promising directions that seem to be consistent with past experience. Their work may help policymakers and activists to see what they are up against, what untapped material and cultural resources they may possess, and what changes are conceivable if certain initiatives are pursued, assuming that the will exists—or can be created—to sustain the long, hard struggle for racial justice and universal human rights.

References

Andrews, George Reid. 1991. *Blacks and Whites in São Paulo, Brazil, 1888–1988*. Madison: University of Wisconsin Press.

Blumer, Herbert. 1965. "Industrialization and Race Relations," in Guy Hunter, *Industrialization and Race Relations; A Symposium*. London and New York: Oxford University Press, pp. 228–253.

Butler, Kim.1998. *Freedoms Given, Freedoms Won: Afro-Brazilians in Post Abolition São Paulo and Salvador*. New Brunswick, NJ: Rutgers University Press.

Campbell, James T. 1995. *Songs of Zion: The African Methodist Episcopal Church in the United States and South Africa*. New York: Oxford University Press.

Cell, John Whitson. 1982. *The Highest Stage of White Supremacy: The Origins of Segregation in South Africa and the American South*. New York: Cambridge University Press.

Degler, Carl N. 1971. *Neither Black nor White: Slavery and Race Relations in Brazil and the United States*. New York: Macmillan.

Elkins, Stanley M. 1959. *Slavery: A Problem in American Institutional and Intellectual Life*. Chicago: University of Chicago Press.

Fernandes, Florestan. 1969. *Integração do Negro na Sociedade de Classes* (1965), translated by Jacqueline D. Skiles, A. Brunel, and Arthur Rothwell as *The Negro in Brazilian Society*. New York: Columbia University Press.

Frazier, E. Franklin. 1957. *Race and Culture Contacts in the Modern World*. Boston: Beacon Press.

Fredrickson, George M. 1995. *Black Liberation: A Comparative History of Black Ideologies in the United States and South Africa*. New York: Oxford University Press.

———. 1981. *White Supremacy: A Comparative Study in American and South African History*. New York: Oxford University Press.

Greenberg, Stanley. 1980. *Race and State in Capitalist Development: Comparative Perspectives*. New Haven: Yale University Press.

Hanchard, Michael George. 1994. *Orpheus and Power: The Movimento Negro of Rio de Janeiro and São Paulo, Brazil, 1945–1988*. Princeton: Princeton University Press.

Harris, Marvin. 1964. *Patterns of Race in the Americas*. Westport, CT: Greenwood Press.

Hartz, Louis. 1964. *The Founding of New Societies: Studies in the History of the United States, Latin America, South Africa, Canada, and Australia*. New York: Harcourt, Brace & World.

Marx, Anthony W. 1998. *Making Race and Nation: A Comparison of South Africa, the United States, and Brazil*. Cambridge: Cambridge University Press.

Seidman, Gay W. 1994. *Manufacturing Militance: Workers' Movements in Brazil and South Africa, 1970–1985*. Berkeley: University of California Press.

Skidmore, Thomas E. 1974. *Black into White: Race and Nationality in Brazilian Thought*. New York: Oxford University Press.

Tannenbaum, Frank. 1946. *Slave and Citizen: The Negro in the Americas*. New York: A. A. Knopf.

van den Berghe, Pierre L. 1967. *Race and Racism: A Comparative Perspective*. New York: Wiley.

Williamson, Joel. 1980. *New People: Miscegenation and Mulattoes in the United States*. New York: Free Press.

PART I

COUNTRY PORTRAITS

2

The Second Republic:
Race, Inequality, and
Democracy in South Africa

Wilmot James and Jeffrey Lever

Laws are always of use to those who possess and harmful to those who have nothing; from which it follows that the social state is advantageous to men only when all have something and none too much.
— J. J. Rousseau

South Africa belongs to a class of societies in which Brazil and the United States are also included: countries that are products of the wave of expansion unleashed in Western Europe from the fifteenth century onward. It has in common with Brazil and the United States interesting population diversity, immigrants from all continents, and a dynamic urban, industrial life. Unlike the United States, the majority of the South African indigenous population did not succumb to the combination of force of arms and an army of germs, but survived and flourished (Diamond 1997). South Africans today are in a large majority indigenous. By the end of the twentieth century, a sophisticated modern economy had brought millions of people of diverse origin into the closest of contact and, after much suffering, had created the only industrial democracy on the African continent.

South Africa shares also with Brazil and the United States a history of white supremacy that endured and hardened into the twentieth century (Marx 1998; Greenberg 1990; Seidman 1998; Friedman and Villiers 1996). Under the name of apartheid, it only gave way to democratic government in 1994. A liberation struggle supported by increasing levels of international encouragement in the 1980s led to the undoing of white supremacy in government and public affairs, leaving, first, Nelson Mandela and his government between 1994 and 1999, and, second, Thabo Mbeki and his government elected on June 2, 1999, with the task of building a decent society out of a history where the progress of a white minority depended on the deliberate repression of a black majority.

The difficulties and challenges of this historical undertaking are born of the unusual combination—for Africa and the Global South—of having democratic institutions and strong elements of an advanced technical base resting upon very uncertain social foundations. The benefits of economic and scientific advance have spread only to the minority. An urban industrial society has arisen that resembles a nineteenth-century Dickensian squalor. As in the England of that time, there is talk of "two nations," one rich, one poor (Mbeki 1998). Unlike England, each nation bears the badge of its economic status on its outward appearance, for the rich nation is white and the poor nation black—in crude outline, that is.

A closer look reveals more complex patterns and a demographic profile of great intricacy, albeit submerged under gross racial typologies that come down from the country's and its people's tempestuous history (Thompson 1990). Racial and ethnic designations do not neatly or consistently coincide with class, gender and lifestyle inequities, nor does the meaning of "race" or what it is people understand by "ethnic" remain untouched by history.

South Africans and Their Labels

The categorization of the South African population has undergone a number of changes since population censuses were first introduced in the nineteenth century. From the beginning, classification on the basis of ethnic labels has been the rule. These categories reflected patterns of settlement and immigration that have constituted the current South African population. In their matter-of-fact usage they imply rigidity regarding the population structure that belies a fluid process of population formation. The use of these categories is unavoidable given the fixity that they have come to acquire both in popular consciousness and official business.

The most recent population count in 1996 came up with an unexpectedly low figure of 38 million inhabitants (according to the 1996 census).[1] Of these, it is estimated some 29 million are "African," 5 million "white," 3 million "colored," and nearly 1 million "Indian." Here, then, are South Africa's four "racial groups," otherwise referred to as "population groups," "ethnic groups," and even "national groups." The African majority section of the population comprises the descendants of Iron Age farmers speaking eleven variants of the Bantu language family that dominates the linguistic map of sub-Saharan Africa east of Cameroon (Hall 1986). Formerly known under various labels (the awful "Kaffir,"[2] "Native," "Bantu," or the more benign "black") by the European settlers, today it is this African majority that, by virtue of electoral dominance and economic deprivation, is the focus of developmental aspirations. Here the issue of racial inequality is most acutely posed.

The country's whites (formerly "Europeans") descend from a melange of Dutch, German, and French who fused to comprise the country's Afrikaner population by the nineteenth century, and from a conglomeration of Britons, continental Europeans, and Jewish people. The Britons, as the dominant political power in the region, placed the stamp of the English language on the country's economic, educational, and governmental life.

It is questionable whether one can speak of *the* colored population at all. In this essentially residual category are to be found people of the most diverse descent, including the remnants of the area's most truly indigenous groupings: the pastoral Khoi-Khoi ("Hottentots") and the hunter-gatherer San ("Bushmen") (Elphick 1977). To be "colored" in South Africa today is merely to say that one can trace some ancestry from Africa or Asia, or both, and speaks either English or Afrikaans as a home language. That the very notion of a "colored people" exists is due to the complex sociology of three centuries of European domination and more recently the classificatory mania of the apartheid regime.

Finally, South Africa's Indian population, established first in the region around Durban, derives from the importation of labor for the sugar fields of Natal in the nineteenth century from the Indian subcontinent. This population was, however, drawn from several corners of India and came to comprise both Hindu and Moslem sections. Their seeming outward homogeneity (to the other South Africans) was a myth. It is as appropriate to call these South Africans of Indian descent a "racial group" as it would be to conceive of the variegated peoples of India as likewise one race.

Nevertheless, the broad differences of descent patterns, of partial endogamy (enforced by law for some of the nation's history), and the linguistic variety of the contemporary South African population make continued "racial" consciousness inevitable for the near-term future (Alexander 1979). The fourfold path of South African racial demogra-

phy is both a biological fiction and a social reality. That it could have
been otherwise is at least conceivable. The introduction of compulsory
group categories as part of the apartheid program of the National Party
government both entrenched and further reinforced the myriad of social
processes by which populations sort and label themselves. Introduced in
1950, the Population Registration Act deepened the ethnicization of the
South African population by bestowing an obligatory category on all
South Africans. One became perforce after this date a "White," a
"Colored," an "Asiatic," a "Native," with numerous subcategories
appended to allow for the developing, if depraved, ethnic sophistication
of government ideologues wishing to conceal a colonial-type domination under a welter of culturalist terms.

In response, major opposition groupings in the apartheid era promoted various conceptions of a de-ethnicized South African nation.
Most prominently, the African National Congress (ANC) adopted the
stance of "nonracialism" (Karis and Carter 1997). A future South Africa
rid of apartheid was to consist of juridically equal citizens whose
descent and appearance would be a matter of at most private concern.
By the 1980s, when even the National Party declared its opposition to
continued racial discrimination, it was clear that a future political dispensation could not rest on the enforced "racial" classification of the
country's population. In July 1991, the Population Registration Act was
repealed as part of the wholesale destruction of racially based legislation. All new South Africans would cease to have a racial category
endorsed on their certificates of birth. The ensuing years of negotiation
and constitution making proceeded accordingly upon a consensus
expressing revulsion regarding official ethnic classification.

In this climate it could be expected that South Africa's democratic
constitution would contain no reference to the population categories
that had been inflicted upon the nation previously. Finished in 1996, the
constitution is devoid of the old apartheid terminology (Constitution of
the Republic of South Africa 1996). The bill of rights included in the
constitution declares that "everyone is equal before the law" and that
"the state may not unfairly discriminate directly or indirectly against
anyone on one or more grounds, including race" (Constitution 1996).
Yet pressing political realities, as the last clause hints at, could not altogether ignore the group contours of South African society. "Unfair" discrimination was outlawed, but not discrimination per se—thus making
possible policies of affirmative action and redress on group grounds.
Various provisions of the constitution allude to the reality of population
divisions within the wider society: terms such as "communities" and

"race" appear here and there. Most notably, the phrases "reflect broadly the racial and gender composition of South Africa" (Section 174[2]) and "broadly representative of the South African people" (Section 193[2]) indicate fleetingly a deep-seated concern with patterns of "racial" inequality bequeathed to the new order by the old regime.

The constitution also contains, in chapter 9, provision for an elaborately named Commission for the Promotion and Protection of the Rights of Cultural, Religious and Linguistic Communities (Constitution 1996). Though yet to be established in practice, the formulation assumes—some argue reinforces and politicizes (Alexander 2001)—a division of the population into nomenclatures reminiscent of a sociological cultural pluralism. The nature of the transition, where white social power remained while their political power diminished, created sufficient insecurity in these and other quarters to warrant a body that would mediate the results of a racial past and, it is presumed, smooth a route toward a nonracial future.

As in other societies, therefore, the transition to democracy has not led to the complete submergence of the need to name and classify. With the design of new legislation to hasten processes of occupational mobility on behalf of the previously subordinated population, explicit definitions of the segmented South African population are reappearing. The notion of "historically disadvantaged" is being given more pointed content: official documents now include, for example, such appendices as: "Glossary of terms . . . Black is a generic term that refers to African, Coloured and Indian" (*White Paper on Affirmative Action* 1997). Opposition parties to the ruling African National Congress have decried what they call a "re-racialisation" of the South African scene (Democratic Party 1998). But with the current drive to audit, in order to address and eliminate racial inequality, it seems likely that such racial naming will remain prominent in a society constitutionally committed to nonracialism.

Colonial Conquest and the Land Question

By the end of the expansion of Anglo-Afrikaner power at the turn of the nineteenth century, the descendants of the European settlers had engrossed almost the total surface area of what became in 1910 the Union of South Africa. Some 7.3 percent of the land remained formally reserved for the African majority. The pastoral Khoi-Khoi and the nomadic San had fared worse. The latter had been altogether excluded from formal land occupation. The Khoi-Khoi's descendants, amalgamated to a considerable degree with other elements of the South African population as part of the colored group, retained scattered land holdings in the Cape, some of which were officially held by one or another missionary society. The largest of these holdings consisted of the five Namaqualand reserves in the semiarid northern Cape Province. While their area was considerable—around 2.5 million acres—their carrying capacity was minimal, with around 25,000 persons inhabiting them by the second half of the twentieth century (Boonzaier 1996: pp. 123–125). Finally, the immigrant Indian population had managed to buy a limited area of agricultural land around Durban and by the 1930s were owner-farmers of some 105,000 acres (Hellman 1949: p. 172).

The alarming implications of a society in which a physically and culturally distinct minority owned or controlled, by way of the state, almost all the land in the country were not lost upon the political leadership of the white section. The central problem was clearly the relationship between the numerically preponderant African population—still largely rural and involved in agriculture—and the dominant white landowners. The history of South Africa in the twentieth century was to be shaped by the search for a master policy that would combine land and politics in one grand plan. Land and space were to be configured so that the white minority could retain the lion's share of occupancy while disposing the rest of the population around it in ways that would combine white material advance with black fragmentation (Brown et al. 1998).

The result was, as it were, foreordained. Short of an equitable, mutually agreed partition such as that compelled by India and Pakistan in the late 1940s, there was no way to bring about a semblance of justice and stability on the land question. Every effort of the white minority to bring about a spatial reordering worsened rather than ameliorated the situation. Inequality deepened while the problems became ever more intractable. In both town and country, whole communities were abruptly disrupted, dispossessed, relocated, and embittered as a result. Systems of land and housing tenure proliferated, counterproductive to any rational form of agricultural advance or small-scale capital accumulation for the masses of people. The cities attracted and repulsed in equal measure, heightening a pervasive sense of relative deprivation. Clinging to bankrupt policies, the country's political elites bequeathed a land issue whose resolution remains difficult in the extreme.

The steps to this colossal failure were many and complex. The 1903–1905 Native Affairs Commission met in the aftermath of the

Anglo-Boer War, when the unification of the four South African territories into one political entity was imminent. A common line on the "Native Question" was highly desirable for the colonial elites, whose delegates formed the membership of the commission. There an uneasy consensus emerged around the notion of "segregation." The "basis of Native policy should be the territorial separation of the races" (Tatz 1962: p. 9). The slender reed on which this massive outgrowing of populations was to lean was the remaining areas reserved for African occupancy—a few large blocs of land such as the Transkei and many scattered areas consisting in cases of not more than a handful of conjoined farmlands. In part these were areas historically the residence of the African indigenes under the wilting system of traditional authorities. Their survival was a matter of great moment for the ideology of segregation—and later of apartheid. Here were authentic "homelands" of black people that the white polity generously was to preserve and indeed extend.

Much of South African history for the twentieth century can be written around the story of the homelands, also variously known as the reserves or Bantustans. They provided the single consistent justification for the elaboration of the order of racial inequality under successive white regimes (Greenberg 1990). In 1913 the Native Land Act decreed that no African could henceforth purchase land outside these African reserves. In order to enhance their viability, they would be extended. This enlargement of the reserves took more than seventy years to come to fruition and resulted in the increase in the area of South Africa allocated to exclusive African ownership from some 7 percent in 1900 to around 13 percent by the late 1970s.

The Native Land Act has rightly been seen as a watershed for the country, reverberating at many levels, both symbolic and concrete. In the famous words of the African writer Sol Plaatje, an eyewitness to these events, "Awaking on Friday morning, June 20, 1913, the South African native found himself, not actually a slave, but a pariah in the land of his birth" (Plaatje 1982: p. 21). The first and most severe consequence of this act was to evict hundreds of thousands of African dwellers on white-owned land, without any compensatory measure. These people were forced to surrender their tenure of such land based on various arrangements ranging from outright renting to sharecropping and labor tenancy—in return for the unasked right to occupy land in the now "scheduled" black areas.

The 1913 Land Act set a pattern of dislocation and deprivation that was to characterize all succeeding decades until the 1990s. The act, for example, had not touched over three hundred small freehold areas owned by Africans outside the reserves. These "black spots," as they came to be known, were largely to disappear under a persistent assault by the National Party government after 1948. More immediately, however, the act set in train processes that led to the destruction of both informal African tenure in the white rural areas and to the further overcrowding and degradation of the land held by Africans within the reserves themselves (Onselen 1996). Later measures set the seal on these processes: the Native Land and Trust Act of 1936 made all new land bought for African occupation in the reserves the possession of the state, indirectly under the control of traditional authorities rather than the household occupants (Platzky and Walker 1985: p. 89). The result has been the sustained fossilization of a land tenure system, which has allowed neither for private ownership and capital formation nor for vigorous promotion of viable small-scale farming.

The land acts of 1913 and 1936 finalized the size of the land that white rulers were prepared to surrender to the majority of the population, but not its eventual location. Under the policy of the National Party after 1948, continuing attempts were made to reconfigure the outlines of the African reserves and, in the process, to relocate massive numbers of people. It has been estimated that around 2.7 million African people were forced to leave homes in a variety of urban and rural settings to relocate in the areas to which the white government consigned them. In addition to various urban removal measures, these "forced removals"—from white farms (the single largest category), former African freehold areas ("black spots"), and official reserve areas that had shifted to white ownership—figure prominently in the sordid annals of this period of South African history (Platzky and Walker 1985).

Overshadowed by the dimensions of the white-black land struggle, the smaller colored and Indian populations were not allowed to escape unscathed as white politicians and bureaucrats strove to order the map to the tastes of their white constituents. Here the drama was played out mostly, if not altogether, in the nation's urban areas. Official urban segregation in South Africa began again with the African population, who from the later 1800s were subjected to various town ordinances establishing "locations" or "townships" where they might reside while in the city milieu (Davenport 1991). The urban Indian population was next. Successive steps beginning before 1900 (in the Transvaal) began to restrict urban tenure by Indian South Africans to segregated neighborhoods. Various measures culminating in the Pegging Act of 1943 and the Asiatic Land Tenure and Indian Representation Act of 1946 sought to prevent an increasingly prosperous stratum of Indian traders and professionals from buying land in central business districts and traditionally white-occupied suburbs (Pachai 1971: p. 189). Directed against the smallest and in a sense most politically isolated group in South Africa, these measures were to wreak immense harm on the fortunes of Indian South Africans. But their historical import is probably to be found in the fact that they had established a precedent and a model that could be taken further after 1948 when the National Party government came to power with a program of sweeping urban segregation, including the ghettoization of colored and Indian people.

The passage of the Group Areas Act in 1950 began a drawn-out process of dispossession and relocation. By the time the process had almost exhausted itself in the 1980s, it is estimated that 860,000 people had been forced out of their homes in the nation's towns and cities, the majority of them colored (Western 1981; James 1992: pp. 41–57). (This act was also used to remove an estimated 80,000 Africans from areas where they had enjoyed at least a tenuous urban status) (Platzky and Walker 1985: pp. 10–11, 100). For the tens of thousands of Indian and colored owner-occupiers, traders, and tenants involved, the measure was an economic and personal disaster whose consequences are still with us today.

The sharpest edge of apartheid segregation began to blunt from the late 1970s onward. Various factors contributed to this reversal. Increasingly turbulent African urban masses forced upon a reluctant government a measure of liberalization that resulted in more secure urban tenure through such schemes as ninety-nine-year leasehold arrangements in African townships. Squatter settlements, a pervasive feature of urban South Africa, no longer were bulldozed as soon as erected. Colored, Indian, and black South Africans began in various ways to settle in white areas despite official harassment. In 1985 the government bowed to the inevitable and formally abolished the control over the movement of the African population embodied in the so-called pass laws (Greenberg 1987).

In land and settlement, therefore, the reversal of apartheid began under apartheid. Spatial integration speeded up from the 1980s onward in the face of an official rearguard action. Nevertheless, these movements in the interstices of society could not undo the work of decades. An active program of positive land and tenure reform awaited the 1990s. In 1991 the de Klerk government repealed the most important land segregation laws with the passage of the Abolition of Racially

Based Land Measures Act. Henceforth all South Africans could in principle now work, reside, and own land wherever they chose. It was, however, only with the accession to power of the ANC-dominated Government of National Unity in May 1994 that the full weight of the state was thrown behind a major land reform program.

A new Ministry of Land Affairs assumed the responsibility of what on paper was quite radical land reform. The broad objectives of the policy were threefold: redistribution, restitution, and land tenure reform (*White Paper on South African Land Policy* 1997). Within these parameters, the policy aimed at achieving the ANC's preelection promise in its Reconstruction and Development Programme manifesto—to convert 30 percent of South African landholdings to black ownership (African National Congress 1994). Redistribution entailed the purchase of white-owned land or the disposal of public land to the targeted black constituencies. Restitution intended to restore or compensate the victims of the major land dispossessions of the twentieth century, in particular the 1913 and 1936 Land Acts, the removal of "black spots," and the Group Areas Act. Land tenure reform aimed at bestowing secure tenure on the millions of South Africans in the former homelands, on white-owned farms and in the huge number of informal settlements around the urban areas (Brown et al. 1998).

The program has proved complex and frustrating. The Department of Land Affairs itself is understaffed and inexperienced. Its incapacity to proceed with due haste is widely considered the major obstacle in the way of a more effective implementation of the policy. But other major obstacles also loom large: public authorities either have good reason to hold onto land under their control or are loath to cooperate for a variety of reasons. The principle of "willing-buyer, willing-seller" and the acceptance of market prices put land out of reach for the majority of would-be individual purchasers (*Mail & Guardian* 1998). In these circumstances only very limited gains have been registered. Some 26,000 group and individual claims have been made for restitution to the newly formed Land Claims Court; only a handful have as yet been disposed of. Redistribution has run up against very limited budgets and the small size of the state subsidy that may be granted to households for land purchases (15,000 Rand, or R15,000—the same amount households in the urban areas may claim). The hopes that had been nourished for the large-scale release of public land have proved more or less illusory. The director-general of the Department of Land Affairs recently stated that "although the state owns 19 percent of the entire surface of the country, most of it is made up of military bases, nature reserves, dams, coastal zones and land in the former homelands" (*Mail & Guardian* 1998).

By mid-1998, it was estimated that less than 1 percent of South Africa's land had been redistributed. More promising had been the progress on the housing front—a separate program under a different ministry than land policy, but obviously a related issue. Although burdened by administrative incapacity, bureaucratic quagmires, and limited state funding, significant progress is being made on fulfilling the ANC's promise to build 1 million homes by 1999. By February 1998, the government had awarded some 778,000 housing subsidies (at a maximum of R17,500 per household) since 1994. Of these, 600,000 awards had been converted into completed houses. With a delivery system now clearly in place, low-income housing could only but improve (Goldin and Heymans 1999: p. 110). The main beneficiaries have been the poorer, urban African households; their ranks, however, are estimated at around 3 million.

The nation remains thus underhoused, with the majority of the African population and a sizeable section of the colored population either in shacks or in altogether substandard dwelling conditions. Private land ownership outside of the urban areas remains a largely white affair and the legacy of racial inequality in this sphere seems likely to prove one of the most intractable to solve, short of wholesale appropriation of land. The latter, radical option is supported only by the Pan African Congress (PAC), which received about 1 percent of votes cast in the 1999 general election. Zimbabwe's route of radical and terroristic land reform measures has demonstrably disabled that country's economic progress, leaving a deep impression on South African policymakers. We have settled, therefore, for better or for worse, on the slow road of market-oriented land reform.

State and Social Inequality

With the transfer of power to the Government of National Unity in May 1994, the ownership of the state itself moved to new hands under the title deeds of a democratic election. This state had accumulated great assets: in land, industry, buildings, and a manifold of commodities. Its taxation power, public service jobs, and powers of spending through tenders, contracts, and agreements were also under new ownership.

The state's immense wealth—for which there appear to be no figures at all—was still only a limited slice of the country's accumulated riches. A protectionist state had overseen the heaping up of wealth in private hands—which were mostly white. Here again there are no figures generally agreed upon. A recent government document states:

> The highly unequal distribution of assets contributes to differences in incomes along race and gender lines. Apartheid prevented Africans from owning land. It limited the access of Black people, and especially Black women, to loans, markets and infrastructure, making capital accumulation difficult. Unfortunately, no definitive evidence exists on the ownership of assets by race, gender or class. Estimates suggest that Whites own over nine-tenths of all assets in South Africa. (*Green Paper on Employment and Occupational Equity* 1996)

The figure of nine-tenths may be too high if we take into account the issue of state assets and the increasing indirect participation of black South Africans in asset ownership through pensions and similar investments. Nevertheless, few will question that this estimate reflects an underlying reality. Private property has accumulated massively for the white minority and modestly for the black majority. It is worth noting that within the white minority, ownership itself is quite highly concentrated and control of the country's major enterprises even more so. The number of white farm owners, for example, has declined by half since the mid-1900s, from around 120,000 to 60,000 in 1985—and of these reduced numbers, a mere 18,000 produced nearly 70 percent of the nation's agricultural produce at that time (Cooper 1988: pp. 49–54).

Similarly, the ownership and control of the nation's industrial and commercial enterprises are remarkably concentrated, so much so that South African scholars saw it as conclusive evidence of the monopoly-capitalist nature of the South African economy (Innes 1984). Depending on the criteria applied, it has been estimated by a leading business analyst that the country's major conglomerate, the Anglo American Corporation, may control as much as 45 percent of the shares on the Johannesburg Stock Exchange, although the corporation itself has put the figure at 30 percent (McGregor 1987: p. 353).

Precisely how this accumulation and concentration of white wealth came about in the twentieth century after the completion of colonial conquest has been the subject of an extended debate in South African social science (Saunders 1988). On the one side, Marxist-inclined analysts argued that capitalism—and by implication the white business community—sustained or even called forth the racial order that culminated in apartheid (Greenberg 1990). In the words of a recent labor document indicative of this thinking: "Employers collaborated with the apartheid regime from the outset, supported apartheid in all its manifestations and benefited from apartheid capitalism with its exploitative and oppressive nature" (COSATU).

In truth, South African economic progress in the twentieth century has been a compound of oppressive exploitation and rational technical advance. The country's deep-level gold mines, worked until recently by over half a million black migrant laborers, but with one family, the Oppenheimers, dominating the structure of ownership and control, are a telling example, with deep underground operations grafted onto primitive labor and repressive social organization (James 1992). In a crude but valid sense, white wealth is a product of white political power over land and African labor (Saunders 1988).

And yet it is much more also. That liberal orthodoxy claims apartheid was economically irrational and set the country on a suboptimal growth path may be in part a self-serving dogma. But it is also the case that "capitalist economic growth in South Africa has been 'development,' not 'underdevelopment.' It has laid the material basis for a large-scale modern state" (Bromberger and Hughes 1987: p. 204). Unlike one cousin, Portuguese colonialism, South Africa's developmental drive has been brutal, but it left a worthwhile material infrastructure. Unlike another cousin, Stalinist forced industrialization, South Africa's racial development resulted in the growth of strong, if partial, economic institutions such as banking and monetary systems.

What is lacking in South African social science is a detailed grasp of not just the overarching structures but the myriad of microprocesses by which the white and, to a more limited extent, the Indian business strata and allied professionals have both accumulated and developed. The latter indeed are remarkable in their persistence: hounded from central business districts and forced into the "Group Areas" ghettoes, the South African Indian business community has yet survived and expanded.

Their more fortunate white counterparts were able to capitalize on numerous opportunities that white control of the state itself made possible. The colonial enterprise constituted a whole series of programs of affirmative action of a special kind. With the accession to power of the National Party in 1948, nascent Afrikaner elites were able to pursue a twofold program of occupational advance in the public service and financial advance in the private sector (O'Meara 1996: p. 61; Giliomee 1983). The Afrikaner component in the civil service doubled in the two decades after 1948. In the private sector,

the special relationship of the Afrikaner businessman to political control was of great importance. The Handelsinstituut (trade institute) is,
for instance, consulted on legislation pertaining to economic matters
and is represented, along with other interest groups, on government
commissions, tender boards, and marketing boards. Afrikaner capital
also benefited occasionally from government favoritism through the
allocation of fishing quotas and mineral concessions and the award of
government contracts and accounts. In 1977, for instance, 98 percent
of the Department of Information publishing budget of 3 million dollars went to the Perskor group, an Afrikaans publishing house that had
several cabinet ministers, including the minister of information, on its
board. Afrikaner firms have also been aided by a system of interlocking directorates between the state corporations and Afrikaner private
capital. (Adam and Giliomee 1983: p. 168)

Within the wider white community, the tax regime for most of the century has enabled the successful to pass down their wealth to their children and often, by use of generation-skipping trusts, to their grandchildren. There are no land taxes on farming land, no capital gains taxes,
and an "inadequate system of estate duty . . . Estate duty has never been
taken seriously by Inland Revenue in South Africa" (Davis 1992: p.
118). A recent, official commission of inquiry into the taxation system
has found a "huge disparity of income and assets between the various
groups in South Africa" but has stopped short of recommending any
radical new wealth taxes in the face of international evidence of their
apparent ineffectiveness (Katz Commission of Inquiry 1997: p. 1).

The democratic state also inherited an apparatus that skewed one of
modernity's greatest assets—education and training—in favor of
whites. Compulsory schooling for whites to secondary-level education
had been introduced in the 1920s, whereas the same step for Africans
was taken only in the 1990s. Intervening in this period was Bantu
Education, introduced by the apartheid government in the 1950s, having
the brazenly articulated intention of subjecting all African children of
school-going age to an education that trained them only to be unskilled,
servile labor. Mission and private schools for Africans, from whence the
educated elite of Nelson Mandela's generation came, were closed down.
Mixed schools were not an option. Mathematics and science, when they
were offered, were by exception under unusual circumstance.

A racial hierarchy of schooling emerged, with whites as recipients
of the best education, equivalent to First World standards, followed by
Indians, colored people, and Africans, below even Third World standards. Each group had their education administered separately; teachers
trained at their respective racial colleges and universities, financed by

Table 2.1   Education of Persons over 20, 1995

	African	Colored	Indian	White	Total
No Education	2,640,000	182,000	34,000	8,000	2,864,000
Some Primary	4,495,000	690,000	84,000	35,000	5,304,000
Some Secondary	7,413,000	1,001,000	448,000	2,632,000	11,494,000
Some Tertiary	822,000	102,000	74,000	952,000	1,950,000
TOTAL	15,370,000	1,975,000	640,000	3,627,000	21,612,000

Source: Central Statistical Services, *1995 October Household Survey.*

apartheid's wicked formula of providing the best for those who already had and the worst for those who had little. In 1994, when matters had already improved some, government was spending R5,403 per white school pupil but R1,053 for every black child in the Transkei, a former homeland now part of the Eastern Cape, the poorest of South Africa's nine provinces. (In 2000 about R7.50 equaled US$1.) The cumulative consequence of this unequal system was a desperately undereducated African population.

The figures are as unsurprising as they are alarming. Africans make up 92 percent, coloreds 6 percent, Indians 1 percent, and whites 0.2 percent of South African adults who have no education at all. In turn, most of the undereducated Africans are to be found in the more rural and poorer provinces of the Eastern Cape, Mpumalanga, the Northwest and the Northern Province. The majority—61 percent—of the formally uneducated are women (Robinson 1998: p. 62). On the other hand, whites and Africans are fairly even in the percent that have some level of higher education, though obviously the former are in a demographic minority and the latter in the majority.

Of the challenges facing the democratic government, education is probably the most formidable. A more equitable and better-performing system had to be created out of a desperately unequal, segregated, and inferior legacy. The scale of required reforms was staggering. Access for African children, especially in rural areas, had to grow exponentially; new schools needed to be built; teacher pre-service and in-service training improved; new curricula and teaching materials developed; and a single administration crafted out of eighteen separate administrations.

There is no question that matters have improved greatly. Access to schooling for African children has jumped beyond expectations. Since 1994, 2,500 schools have been renovated and 1,000 new ones built (Goldin and Heymans 1999: p. 110). *Curriculum 2005* lays the groundwork for improved content, new materials, and revised teacher training. The entry of African matriculants at colleges and universities is spectacular. A recent study by University of Cape Town sociologist David Cooper (1999) argues that change at the university level is nothing short of revolutionary, with black students entering universities and technical colleges at a rate that will mirror the demographic ratios of society. A single administration now exists, though the old bureaucracies and their staff have not entirely disappeared.

A recent report of the President's Education Initiative Research Project shows, however, that the good ideas and initiatives are trapped in a system that fails to work properly, compromising quality on a large scale (Taylor and Vinjevold 1999). The first democratic ministry of education failed to rise from the admittedly regressive weight of the past. The growth in sheer numbers should not conceal the fact that the schooling system, nevertheless, struggles to enroll all eligible pupils, fails to retain the majority of them to secondary level, and offers them a quality of schooling that varies from excellent for a minority to abysmal for the majority. The rapid expansion of tertiary educational involvement by Africans has meant their enrollment in the less technical directions since most schools for African pupils fail to qualify them in mathematics and science. The technical and commercial elite remains predominantly white and Indian as a result.

It is not surprising to find that the racially based endowment of the nation rears its head in other places, as in the jobs people tend to hold and the personal income they receive. As the main allocation mechanism of current income, the country's occupational structure, together with unemployment rates, is perhaps the most telling single datum for assessing racial inequality. In some ways the reconfiguration of South Africa's occupational and employment hierarchy is the most pressing issue facing the country, as current legislative moves suggest. Table 2.2 indicates how the most remunerative positions requiring the more advanced skills were distributed in each group in 1995.

As can be seen, whites and Indians dominate the upper levels of the occupational hierarchy, while coloreds and Africans are found mostly in the bottom rungs. Respectively, 40.1 percent and 38.8 percent of those who fall into the category "elementary occupation" are African and colored.

The need to raise the skills of the South African work force, and in particular its majority African segment, is urgent, and government is taking a hand (beyond the formal educational sector) with such measures as a Skills Development Act. Even this problem pales in compari-

Table 2.2   Distribution of Race Groups by Selected Occupational Levels, 1995

	African	Colored	Indian	White
Senior Management	2.9%	2.0%	10.7%	14.6%
Professional	2.0	1.7	6.7	8.4
Technician/related	9.6	6.6	11.9	18.5
Clerical	7.8	10.8	20.9	22.5
Service	11.2	11.6	13.3	10.6
Craft	10.2	14.3	16.0	15.0
Operators	14.0	12.3	12.7	3.8
Elementary Occupation	40.1	38.8	6.0	1.6

Source: Adapted from Central Statistical Services, *1995 October Household Survey*, Table 2.1.

son, however, with the unavailability of jobs at lower skill levels. Unemployment figures vary according to the criteria applied and the specific survey involved. Again, one of the most trusted sources, the Central Statistical Services(CSS) *1995 October Household Survey,* came up with unemployment rates for those fifteen years and older and willing to work of nearly 37 percent for the African population (compared to over 22 percent for the colored, 13 percent for the Indian, and 5.5 percent for the white groups). These figures are probably valid as orders of dimension and relative size, though their absolute accuracy has not gone uncontested. Many job seekers in the formal economy find low-paid and often very irregular work in the country's large informal sector—just whether such persons should qualify as unemployed is debatable. But both the size and ethnic complexion of this sector is yet another indicator of the country's vast material inequalities, with an estimated 78 percent of the 1.7 million persons active here found to be African in the CSS survey.

About 38 percent of people employed in the formal and informal sectors are women. In the formal sector, 37 percent of women are found in unskilled positions, 20 percent in clerical work, and 16 percent in technical and other professions. However, in the informal sector women outnumber men by a ratio of two to one (Robinson 1998: pp. 53–59). This sector is the principal source of livelihood for the African majority, and it is women who keep up the roof of life's cave both by being the principal source of income and by taking up the social welfare slack when government does not reach the rural areas of South Africa's poorest provinces, where most African women tend to be.

The distribution of skill and employability has been affected by historical emigration and immigration tendencies. On the one hand, white English-speakers who could more easily assimilate in the countries of the Commonwealth, the United States, and Canada, led skill emigration. Draft-dodgers, conscientious objectors, exiles, and those seeking a better life elsewhere made up an impressive list of South Africans who added their value to others' progress, representing as it were apartheid's brain drain. Since 1994, white emigration has proceeded apace, prompting politicians of the democratic regime to both despair and exclaim their anger at how those who benefit from South Africa's relatively low-cost training and development leave at precisely the time when they are needed most and when the going is tough for all.

On the other hand, South Africa has had a declining ability to replace skilled emigrants with skilled immigrants. In the 1950s and 1960s, apartheid's racist and anti-Semitic assisted-immigration schemes brought Anglo-Saxon and Protestant Europeans in numbers large enough to maintain some balance in population size and skill figures. After the Soweto revolt of 1976 and the unraveling of apartheid in the 1980s, the figures began to fall, leaving a net loss of skill that even the turn to Eastern Europe in the late 1980s and early 1990s could not reverse.

Indeed, immigration in the late 1980s and 1990s swelled the ranks of the unskilled and semiskilled. South Africa has always had the benefit of Africa's unskilled and semiskilled labor in the form of coal and gold mine employment that reached a peak of close to 350,000 foreign workers from Lesotho, Mozambique, Malawi, and elsewhere in the 1960s, but the dismantling of apartheid and the introduction of democracy in 1994 attracted a high number of Africans who slipped into the country without proper documentation. There are no proper figures of the scale of this phenomenon. The Central Statistical Services arrived at a figure of 500,000 while the Department of Home Affairs, the ministry responsible for immigration, used a figure of 6 million based on a study conducted by the Human Sciences Research Council, which subsequently has been challenged for its methodological veracity (Crush 1998).

Whatever the real figure, African immigration has created tension and in some instances havoc in the employment market. In their various studies, the Southern African Migration Project documented that many African immigrants are itinerant, female entrepreneurs who add economic value as small-scale traders by creating rather than taking away jobs and by performing jobs South Africans have little interest in doing (Southern African Migration Project 1998, 1999). But there is little doubt that pockets of intense competition over access to jobs and the social services that South Africa does provide are the cause of heightened xenophobia and outright conflict in places where particularly visible cultural differences and language make foreign Africans in South Africa conspicuous.

Beyond employment and unemployment, income differentials have a class and racial character. Income data are notoriously difficult to collect on an accurate and comprehensive basis. South African figures are no exception. However, it is well known that South Africa shares with Brazil the dubious distinction of having one of the highest Gini coefficients—a measure of income inequality between the richest and the poorest—in the world (Wilson and Ramphele 1989; O'Connell and Birdsall 2001). The measure is higher than that of India or the Russian Federation and, as in other areas of South African life, thoroughly racialized. While the share of national income earned by the black population has been increasing with time, the white minority still secures the larger portion of the earnings potential of the nation.

In class terms, the top 10 percent of the population earned 50 percent of national income while the bottom 10 percent earned less than 1 percent. The poorest half of the population, almost entirely African, earned a mere 8.9 percent of national income.[3] Development Bank economist Stephen Gelb observed recently that the South African Gini coefficient has been falling and that the income differentials within "racial" groups has been rising (Gelb 1999: p. 160). Nevertheless, the growing importance of class differentials does not yet alter in any substantial fashion the racial character of inequality or the concentration of deep levels of poverty in African households.

Tables 2.3 and 2.4 provide the latest available overviews by race and are probably as accurate as any. These figures confirm the expected fourfold hierarchy in material inequality. They also indicate the distribution of household income by province; for Africans, the highest income is achieved in Gauteng (where Johannesburg is located) and the lowest in the Northern Cape; for coloreds, Gauteng is highest and the Free State lowest; for Indians, Gauteng again is highest and the Northern Cape lowest; and for whites, the Northern Province has the highest and the Free State lowest. Of course, these averages are a mix of population density and the strength of regional economy, as in the case of whites who have a mix of low population density and a strong, large agricultural economy in the Northern Province.

Racial inequality in household incomes is further illustrated by these facts: 22 percent of households earning R500 (US$60) per month

Table 2.3   Average Annual Household Income by Race, 1990 and 1995 (R1000s)

	African	Colored	Indian	White
1990	20	38	45	117
1995	48	64	87	113

Source: Central Statistical Services, *1995 October Household Survey.*
Notes: Earning and spending in South Africa for 12 main urban areas; Rand expressed in thousands; 1990 figures adjusted to 1995 values.

Table 2.4   Average Annual Household Income by Race and Province, 1995 (R1000s)

	E Cape	Free State	Mpuma-langa	North West	Northern Province	N Cape	Kwa-Zulu-Natal	W Cape	Gauteng
African	17	14	20	21	26	13	24	22	37
Colored	24	16	30	25	43	18	41	33	53
Indian	58	—	78	—	—	34	61	54	111
White	90	72	82	93	140	79	98	98	118

Source: Central Statistical Services, *1995 October Household Survey.*
Notes: Earning and spending in South Africa: selected findings of the Sentrale Statistiekdiens (Pretoria) 1995 income and expenditure survey, 1997. Rand expressed in thousands.

are African, in contrast to 3 percent for colored, Indian, and white combined; the average white household income is six times that of the average African household income; the poorest 40 percent earned a mere 9 percent of the nation's income while the richest 20 percent earned nineteen times that of the poorest. South Africa not only has one of the highest income disparities between rich and poor, but the disparity also cuts along racial lines, posing the problem sharply (Robinson 1998: pp. 53–59).

It is not surprising that household incomes are lower for female-headed compared to male-headed or dual-parent ones. This is particularly the case for African households. IDASA's Shirley Robinson (1998) writes, "African female-headed households are generally poorer than urban households are. Nonurban households are likely to be the most vulnerable to poverty as 37 percent is represented in the lowest income quartile and 28 percent in the second lowest income quartile" (p. 57). South Africa's notorious Gini coefficient is buried in the heads of women, particularly African women in the rural areas of the poorest provinces.

Finally, health and welfare indicators, though sometimes highly variable, confirm the general trend—with some significant exceptions where conditions among the poorer section of the colored population may be worse than among Africans. Health provision is skewed toward the richer section of the population, as Table 2.5 indicates. For example, over half the nation's qualified doctors are in the private sector, while medical aid schemes cover only some 20 percent of the population. Health patterns are themselves in great part a function of living conditions, and here again the picture displays the usual marked racial inequalities.

As we know, health indicators are direct products of living conditions. Life expectancy is linked to the quality of nutrition and habits of lifestyle; infant mortality to maternal health and nutrition; and the incidence of tuberculosis, the one disease incidence noted in Table 2.5, to quality of housing and the nutritional status of populations. Indeed, exposure to life-threatening disease is mediated by critical factors such as access to freshwater supplies, sanitation, and primary health care. As Table 2.6 indicates, these resources are distributed racially and spatially, leaving Africans and African women in particular in the worst position

Table 2.5   Some Key Health Indicators

	African	Colored	Indian	White
Life Expectancy Age	64	64	70	73
Infant Mortality				
Study A	53%	52%	29%	17%
Study B	49%	36%	11%	10%
Distribution of TB patients	70%	28%	1%	1%

Source: South Africa Survey 1996/1997, Life expectancy: p. 14; infant mortality data is per 1,000 births in two studies, pp. 450–451; TB rates, p. 454.

Table 2.6   Indicators of Living Conditions

	African	Colored	Indian	White
Indoor Water:				
Urban	56%	80%	98%	99%
Rural	12%	44%	81%	78%
Indoor Sanitation:				
Urban	42%	70%	97%	99%
Rural	5%	38%	72%	98%

Source: Adapted from *South Africa Survey 1996/1997,* pp. 803–804, 806–807, 779.

of all. It is in recognition of this that the democratic government gave priority to these items and has already made considerable inroads in altering the balance. For example, progress in swamp clearing and clean water supplies have benefited 3 million people, most of whom reside in rural areas.

It is in the area of infrastructure that the democratic government has made the greatest strides. Beyond water, sanitation systems, new road networks, and telephone and electricity connections have incorporated more and more of those excluded in the past. Nearly 2 million electricity connections had been made by 1998, up from 100,000 in 1991, and a million new connections to households by the mid-1990s. It is perhaps safe to conclude that, under even modest economic growth, improvement in infrastructure and basic living conditions is one of the more tractable issues facing the democratic regime, as the electrification program demonstrates.

Racism and Democracy

With the abolition of most racially based laws in 1991, racism in South Africa was officially deinstitutionalized. What remains is the phenomenon that some scholars have referred to as "modern racism": sporadic, everyday incidents and rearguard actions in association and community life (Fakier 1998; James 1998: pp. 60–61). Just how pervasive this racism may be is hard to ascertain given its protean and now furtive existence in a formally nonracial state. At the public level, there is an ideological consensus on the old ways of racial discrimination. Even the white right wing (except for its most die-hard remnants) concedes that its former dreams of an orderly white paradise in which blacks will appear only as docile workhands are now both impractical and illegitimate. But it would of course be naive to conclude that racism (construed as objectionable treatment on grounds of one's "racial" membership) and racial hostility have disappeared. Formal juridical equality has in some ways inflamed grass-roots "racial" consciousness under circumstances of continued material inequity and new forms of resource competition. Affirmative-action policies necessarily drive home the relevance of ethnic background, particularly for those, mainly the "minorities," who feel aggrieved by them.

In view of the country's history, perhaps most remarkable is the absence of sustained mass-based racial conflict. The symbolism of a united nonracial population, so aptly projected by the country's first democratically elected president, Nelson Mandela, has worn more than a little thin recently. Yet it retains basic ascendancy. Among the most visible incidents of what might be called communal racism on the part of the formerly dominant white population have been clashes at a small number of high schools, mostly in the smaller towns or in the poorer, lower-middle-class suburbs of the major cities. Here, however, racist resistance has been interwoven with issues of the language (with black pupils preferring English to Afrikaans), the ability to pay school fees, and adolescent tensions. Likewise, some tertiary campuses have experienced racial flare-ups as white students have opposed black campaigns on matters such as fees. The latter, however, have also been features of campus life at the almost exclusively black tertiary institutions.

It seems fair to suggest that consciousness of race remains high in South Africa but that overt racism has declined considerably. There are continuing reports of rather anomic outbreaks of interpersonal violence, such as the shooting of a black child by a white farmer early in 1998. This incident, in turn, had to be viewed against a spate of killings of white farm occupants that took on worrying dimensions in 1997. It is an open question to what extent high levels of crime (as in the farm-killings) are in some sense racially based or at least racially justified in the minds of perpetrators. Similarly, the extent to which the economically dominant white section practices informal racial exclusion of an odious kind is not easy to gauge.

Democracy has brought to the fore perhaps the most dangerous communal cleavage of a racial kind that may shape future South African society. This division is constituted by the political, cultural, and economic realities that separate the majority African section from the three minority groups, the whites, colored, and Indian segments. Public opinion surveys consistently reveal an almost stable pattern of differences on social and political matters (Mattes 1995). The two most prosperous sections—whites and Indians—have increasingly convergent (and conservative) political views, with colored people in a middle position. The division is exacerbated by one of the least debated but most consequential social inequalities: the problem of language. Under the constitutional camouflage of equal treatment for the country's eleven official languages, there is a decided advantage in education and business for those with high English-language competence. In this regard, many, perhaps most, home-speakers of one or other of the nine southern Bantu languages (in other words, the African majority) suffer an almost automatic handicap that the country's poor schooling system seems unlikely to eliminate in the medium term.

The historic compromise forged in the pre-1994 negotiations has resulted in both a cultural and economic accommodation to the prevailing contours set by generations of white dominance. In the economic sphere, the decision to accept pro tem the pattern of asset ownership— forswearing the ANC's well-known pledge in its key visionary document, the Freedom Charter of 1955, to nationalize the country's "monopoly industries"—has meant that the new regime had to shift its fundamental strategy of socioeconomic transformation. If assets could not be transferred at one fell swoop to the people, then other means had to be devised to undo racial inequalities. Since 1994, the efforts of the new government in this regard have largely crystallized around four major goals: poverty alleviation, a steady move to the equalization of state social spending, and, probably of most import, the state-supported restructuring of the occupational and ownership structure of the economy. Given the limited public funds available, the scope for dramatic changes in the profile of racial inequality by way of the first two is also limited.

By 1994, the African National Congress had replaced its former quasi-socialist rhetoric with more endearing phrases for both international and local business elites: the Reconstruction and Development Plan (RDP) and affirmative action. Conceived as a kind of superministry of development coordination, the RDP as institution has suffered the fate of similar ventures elsewhere. The RDP ministry closed down in 1996 and the RDP has all but disappeared as an overarching blueprint of socioeconomic transformation (Goldin and Heymans 1999). Nevertheless, the reform process in the economic arena is far from dead, although transmuted into a host of business plans whose nature does lend them to high-profile political marketing.

By mid-1998, the most compelling slogans with more than symbolic import for the continued siege on white economic dominance were those of affirmative action and black empowerment. The ANC policymakers early on had adopted affirmative action as a useful concept to promote its goals of black advancement while appearing as less than militant revolutionists. In 1994, the ANC activist and constitutional court judge Albie Sachs lucidly sketched the policy dilemmas facing the ANC prior to its assumption of power. A middle way had to be found between a mere political transition to universal franchise and the strategy of a revolutionary confiscation of white-owned assets in a postapartheid South Africa. Sachs wrote:

The solution we chose was that of affirmative action. The phrase had no Cold War associations. It was sufficiently open to take on a specific South African content and meaning and yet concrete enough to have an unmistakable thrust in favor of the oppressed. Whatever form might emerge or whatever definition be given, everyone knew what the essence of affirmative action was: it meant taking special measures to ensure that black people and women and other groups who had been unfairly discriminated against in the past, would have real chances in life. (Sachs 1994: p. 1)

The idea of affirmative action was of course no newcomer to South Africa. Many firms had been paying at least lip service to such a policy since the 1980s, in a form of "anticipatory socialization" (Adam 1997: p. 231). Particular emphasis had been placed on the rapid creation of a black managerial stratum through various company training and advancement programs. The success of these ventures had been very limited, as a penetrating analysis of the 1980s by sociologist Blade Nzimande (elected in 1998 as general secretary of the South African Communist Party) demonstrated (Nzimande 1991). Progress in the 1990s had not been markedly better, and a survey in 1997 claimed that "in the three-year period to 1997, the number of black senior managers increased by only 2.3 percent, with a paltry 1.6 percent increase among middle managers" ("Employment Equity Bill" 1997).

Skeptical of the capacity of the normal hiring and promotion processes to move toward demographic representativeness, and with the data to back up its beliefs, the ANC-dominated government has increasingly focused on how to engineer black occupational advancement through affirmative-action policies. Matters will no doubt be more easily arranged in the public sector. A 1998 *White Paper on Affirmative Action in the Public Service* envisages affirmative-action programs for all civil service departments that will mandate plans, including numeric targets for the increased employment of the "historically disadvantaged groups."

More controversial is a similar scheme to be implemented in the private sector through the provisions of an Employment Equity Act, described as the "first major piece of race-based legislation to enter the statute books since our country became democratic" (*White Paper on Affirmative Action in the Public Service* 1998; Brassey 1998). The measure seeks to achieve "employment equity" for "designated groups" (blacks, women, and handicapped people) in all private enterprises employing more than forty-nine workers. Employers will be required to submit employee profiles together with plans to increase representation of the designated groups at all levels to the Ministry of Labour, which will have wide powers to monitor and induce compliance. No specific quotas are stipulated, but employee representatives such as trade unions will have the right to negotiate and register complaints on the process ("Employment Equity Bill" 1997).

On paper a measure of major import, the Employment Equity Act may of course fall far short of its goals in a system where governmental ambition outreaches its current capacity. In any case, black economic advancement that rests upon jobs alone cannot be considered in any sense adequate in a modern industrial society. The ownership structure of private property, and especially of productive assets, cannot be sustained in the long run if it is largely monopolized in white hands. Few deny the necessity of change; the question remains as to who will pay the price, and how. Land reform will contribute to this transformation, but only to a limited extent. And for an increasingly urbanized population the demand is for the widening of human and economic capital in the nation's cities and towns.

Dramatically higher rates of participation by black people in the nation's modern business sector have thus emerged as a priority with much greater clarity than ever before. The means to this goal are at hand: the promotion of black entrepreneurial investment in the equity market is the most publicized of them. Since 1994, black-owned or controlled enterprises have increased their share in the capitalization of the Johannesburg Stock Exchange from 1 percent to around 5 (Segal 1998: p. 80). The growth of black business will benefit greatly from the new form of the state: "affirmative procurement" means that black-owned firms receive preference from the state regarding tenders, procurements, and licenses. White-owned firms are encouraged to seek black partnerships, and government policy induces the private sector to look where possible to the use of black subcontractors.

To what extent these new developments will lead to the fulfillment of the economic aspirations of the emerging black elites is by no means clear. It is unlikely, for example, that the leading black business pressure group, the National African Chamber of Commerce, will see its "3-4-5-6" formula—30 percent black representation in directorships, 40 percent in black equity ownership, 50 percent for black external procurement, and 60 percent of black representation in management— fulfilled by its target year of 2000 (Makanya 1995: p.162). The progress registered by black business firms on the Johannesburg Stock Exchange must be qualified by the fact that "most black economic empowerment deals are little more than investment syndicates taking small equity in firms, only a handful of which are start-ups" (Segal 1998: p. 82). Black participation is most evident in the media and publishing sector, but lacking in major manufacturing. The operational capacity of black-owned firms remains heavily dependent on white management, and much of the money made by empowerment deals has ended up enriching white advisers and brokers. In short, a numerically significant black entrepreneurial stratum outside of the small business sector has yet to consolidate.

South Africa thus enters the new millenium with its profile of racial inequality on the material level that was built up over three centuries of white domination largely intact. But the relative success in installing a modern urban industrial economy—for Africa—has meant that the floor on which this inequality rested is subject to shifts over time. Significant segments of the wider black population have moved upward, and the political transition of 1994 has accelerated this trend. Politically, the white minority is now for the first time a true minority group, and economic transformation is now more feasible under a regime of juridical equality and a broad, integrative social thrust.

For the medium term, much depends on the ability of the economy to grow and create jobs. South Africa's growth in gross domestic product was 3 percent in 1996–1997, 1.5 percent in 1997–1998, and was estimated to be 1 percent for 1998–1999.[4] While these growth figures are considerably higher than those achieved in the early 1990s, they fall well below that required by the Growth, Employment and Redistribution (GEAR) macroeconomic framework accepted by government, if not the trade unions, as the guiding light of economic and fiscal policy. It is a matter of debate for economists why it is that South Africa is underperforming and why a loss, and not a growth, in jobs is accompanying even modest growth. It seems as if the so-called fundamentals for growth are not yet in place.

Much, too, depends upon the relative stability of political and social life, at present subject to the battering of crime, an economic downturn, and the material discontent of broad layers of the population. Short of the mass exodus of the dominant white group, a sharp and sudden reversal of racial inequality was always an unrealistic prospect. The issue remains the extent to which the system can generate business optimism and the economic competence that will attract investment and increase growth. If in the process the state can pursue its current reforms while maintaining a reasonable measure of efficiency, then the diminution of racial inequality becomes feasible.

The Second Republic

When the Government of National Unity came into power in 1994, it embarked on a massive and ambitious agenda of social change. Crudely put, we could say that one part of the agenda was to create and entrench—by constitutional and other means—rights-protection of individual citizens, and the other part, to deal with the socioeconomic inequality bequeathed by apartheid. On balance, the first period of democratic government was necessarily devoted more to rights-protection, though these noble and important checks against the abuse of apartheid became increasingly in question as government struggled to enforce a human rights regime in the face of a seeming explosion of criminal conduct, much of it rooted in apartheid's other legacy, black poverty.

Nelson Mandela's leadership gave additional emphasis to reconciliation between the "racial groups," and he appeared particularly concerned about Afrikaners and their place in the new democratic order. The extreme expression of Afrikaner anxiety was the demand for a Volkstaat, made both by the extraparliamentary paramilitary group named the Afrikaner Weerstandsbeweging (Afrikaner Resistance Movement) and by the parliamentary Freedom Front. The latter was willing to wait a hundred or so years to achieve its goal. A less extreme view is to seek some form of "group" protection through the recognition of so-called minority language and cultural rights.

Though Mandela in his presidential conduct made many—some say too many—overtures to the Afrikaner community, he and his government were insistent that every South African be juridically equal and that no concessions on a group basis were to be made. The presumption of jurisprudence was that strong and enforceable protection of individual rights was enough of a check against potential abuses against a group, particularly one that was seen to be historically responsible for the abuses of apartheid. But the insistence on individual rights required a reading of South African history on the basis of individual and not group responsibility.

The Truth and Reconciliation Commission (TRC) was established by Nelson Mandela in 1994 to find individual causes for egregious human rights abuses committed during apartheid. Its origins were rooted in two important conferences organized by Alex Boraine under the auspices of what was then known as the Institute for a Democratic Alternative in South Africa (IDASA) and the thinking of some members of the ANC, in particular that of Kader Asmal, Dullah Omar, and Albie Sachs (Boraine and Levy 1995, 1997; Asmal, Asmal, and Roberts

1997). South Africa's Interim Constitution contained a clause, negotiated at Kempton Park, that compelled the granting of amnesty to those who committed serious human rights abuses on both sides of the struggle. A law passed in 1994 established the commission and defined its brief, and the final constitution passed in 1995 confirmed its role as one of the many commissions established to support democratic consolida tion in the country.

The TRC was one of many rights institutions — including the Electoral, Gender, Human, and Youth Commissions — whose work dominated South African public life until 1998, when its voluminous report was submitted to then president Nelson Mandela (*Report of the Commission on Truth and Reconciliation* 1998). Over a period of four years South Africa heard the evidence of the many victims of apartheid's atrocities (much less so from victims of the ANC, PAC, and the other liberation organizations' war against apartheid) and the confessions of the perpetrators, again mostly, if not entirely, from the apartheid security machinery side (Krog 1998: p. 42; 1999). The unflinching premise of the TRC's work was that amnesty was to be granted on the basis of individual responsibility and truth telling, which is why the cause of blanket amnesty was rejected. On the other hand, by virtue of South African history, most perpetrators were Afrikaners, a fact leading some commentators to mistakenly proclaim that the TRC was an Afrikaner witch-hunt, alienating some leading Afrikaner establishments.

The point of the TRC was to establish individual culpability and so confirm a central principle of the rule of law. It was also to collate a South African memory and so present and cultivate new values of what were to be tolerated as proper, decent, public and private conduct among citizens and officials of the state. Beyond that, the TRC was part of a larger set of initiatives designed to promote democratic values and practices, the observance of human rights and the rights of women, and the setting in place of properly functioning democratic institutions. More than anything else, these initiatives were the mark of the Mandela presidency, the creation and consolidation of what in some quarters are called the democratic "software," reinforced doubly by Mandela's concern with reconciliation between the former enemies and the peaceful coexistence of South Africa's main population groups.

Barely under the surface lurked, now seen, now unseen, the question of the political economy of racial inequality. The issue clearly and increasingly occupied the mind of South Africa's deputy-president Thabo Mbeki who, in becoming South Africa's second democratically elected president, made it a recurring theme of public policy. On becoming president he elevated the delivery of social and public service to a position of preeminence. He linked black poverty to white wealth; and he declared that social and political stability could be achieved only by growth. Finally, he insisted that South Africa's future is part of a putative renaissance of the African continent (Mbeki 1998).

The complex problems of South Africa belie easy answers. The challenge—to find an appropriate fit between democracy and durable social and economic institutions—is as old as Alexis de Tocqueville (1956), but in a new setting with its own peculiar racial heritage. And yet, as the other chapters in this collection demonstrate, we are not alone in grappling with what W.E.B. DuBois once described as the major problem of the twentieth century, the problem of the color line. As we also began this essay, it is an effort to undo centuries of the imprint of colonialism and white supremacy. We hope that somebody will one day describe the twenty-first century as the end of color lines.

Notes

1. Preliminary estimates of the size of the population of South Africa. Prior to this census it had been thought that a figure of around 41 million was likely. Some population surveys continue to report 41 million.

2. Originally a neutral term from the Arabic for the Xhosa-speakers of the Eastern Cape, this word was later generalized to all black people and became a term of abuse that is now offensive in all senses and combinations.

3. Figures provided to authors by economist Francis Wilson of the University of Cape Town.

4. Figures supplied to authors by IDASA's economist Warren Krafchik.

References

Adam, Herbert, and Hermann Giliomee. 1983. *The Rise and Crisis of Afrikaner Power*. Cape Town: David Philip Publishers.

Adam, K. 1997. "The Politics of Redress: South African Style Affirmative Action." *Journal of Modern African Studies* 5, no.2.

African National Congress. 1994. *The Reconstruction and Development Programme.* Johannesburg: ANC.

Alexander, Neville. 1979. *One Azania, One Nation*. London: Zed Ivess.

———. 2001. "Prospects for a Nonracial Future in South Africa," Chapter 16 of this volume.

Asmal, Kader, Louise Asmal, and Ronald Suresh Roberts. 1997. *Reconciliation*

Through Truth:A Reckoning of Apartheid's Criminal Governance. Cape Town and New York: David Philip Publishers.

Boonzaier, Emile. 1996. *The Cape Herders: A History of the Khoi-Khoi of Southern Africa*. Cape Town: David Philip Publishers.

Boraine, Alex, and Janet Levy, eds. 1995. *The Healing of a Nation?* Cape Town: IDASA.

———. 1997. *Dealing with the Past: Truth and Reconciliation in South Africa*. Cape Town: IDASA.

Brassey, M. 1998. "None So Silent as Those Afraid to Speak." *Sunday Times*, July 12.

Bromberger, Norman, and Ken Hughes. 1987. "Capitalism and Underdevelopment in South Africa," in James Butler, Richard Elphick, and David Welsh, eds., *Democratic Liberalism in South Africa*. Middletown, CT: Wesleyan University Press.

Brown, M., J. Erasmus, R. Kingwill, C. Murray, and M. Roodt. 1998. *Land Restitution in South Africa: A Long Way Home*. Cape Town: IDASA.

Central Statistical Services. 1997. *1995 October Household Survey*, Pretoria.

Constitution of the Republic of South Africa, Act 108 of 1996.

Cooper, D. 1988. "Ownership and Control of Agriculture in South Africa," in J. Suckling and L. White, eds., *After Apartheid: Renewal of the South African Economy*. London: Centre for South African Studies.

———. 1999. Unpublished study in possession of authors. Cape Town.

COSATU submission to the TRC hearings on business and apartheid.

Crush, Jonathan, ed. 1998. *Beyond Control: Immigration and Human Rights in a Democratic South Africa*. Cape Town: IDASA.

Davenport, Rodney. 1991. "Historical Background of the Apartheid City to 1948," in M. Swilling, R. Humphries, and K. Shubane, eds., *Apartheid City in Transition*. Cape Town: Oxford University Press.

Davis, Dennis. 1992. "Taxation in a Post-Apartheid South Africa," in R. Schrire, ed., *Wealth or Poverty: Critical Choices for South Africa*. Cape Town: Longmans.

Democratic Party. 1998. "The Death of the Rainbow Nation: Unmasking the ANC's Program of Re-racialisation." Democratic Party, February 4.

Diamond, Jared. 1997. *Guns, Germs, and Steel: The Fates of Human Societies*. New York: W. W. Norton.

Elphick, Richard. 1977. *Kraal and Castle: Khoi-Khoi and the Founding of White South Africa*. New Haven: Yale University Press.

Fakier, Yazeed. 1998. *Grappling with Change*. Cape Town: IDASA.

Friedman, Steven, and Riaan de Villiers, eds. 1996. *Comparing Brazil and South Africa*. Johannesburg: Centre for Policy Studies and Foundation for Global Dialogue.

Gelb, Stephen. 1999. "Economic Growth, People and the Environment," in Gitanjali Maharaj, ed., *Between Unity and Diversity: Essays on Nation-Building in Post-Apartheid South Africa*. Cape Town: David Philip Publishers, p. 147.

Giliomee, Hermann. 1983. "The Afrikaner Economic Advance," in Herbert Adam and Hermann Giliomee, eds., *The Rise and Crisis of Afrikaner Power*. Cape Town: David Philip Publishers.

Goldin, Ian, and Chris Heymans. 1999. "Moulding a New Society: The RDP in

Perspective," in Gitanjali Maharaj, ed., *Between Unity and Diversity: Essays on Nation-Building in Post-Apartheid South Africa*. Cape Town: David Philip Publishers.

Government Gazette, "Employment Equity Bill," December 1, 1997.

Government Gazette, "Explanatory Memorandum to the Employment Equity Bill," December 1, 1997.

Green Paper on Employment and Occupational Equity. 1996, Section 3.2.9.

Greenberg, Stanley. 1987. *Legitimating the Illegitimate.* Berkeley: University of California Press.

———. 1990. *Race and State in Capitalist Development.* New Haven: Yale University Press.

Hall, Martin. 1986. *The Changing Past: Farmers, Kings and Traders in Southern Africa, 200–1860.* Cape Town: David Philip Publishers.

Hellman, Ellen. 1949. *Handbook of Race Relations.* Johannesburg: SAIRR.

Innes, Duncan. 1984. *Anglo: Anglo American and the Rise of Modern South Africa.* Johannesburg: Ravau Press.

James, Wilmot. 1992. *Our Precious Metal: African Labour in South Africa's Gold Mining Industry.* Bloomington: Indiana University Press.

———. 1992. "Group Areas and the Nature of Apartheid." *South African Sociological Review* 5, no.1.

———. 1998. "Contours of a New Racism," *SIYAYA* 2 (Winter).

Karis, Thomas, and Gwendolyn Carter, eds. 1997. *From Protest to Challenge: A Documentary History of African Politics in South Africa, 1882–1990.* Bloomington: University of Indiana Press.

Katz Commission of Inquiry. 1997. Fourth Interim Report.

Krog, Antjie. 1998. *Country of My Skull.* Johannesburg: Random House.

———. 1998. "Truth and Reconciliation Commission," in Wilmot James and Moira Levy, eds., *Pulse: Passages in Democracy Building.* Cape Town: IDASA.

Mail & Guardian, "Land Reform Targets Are Far, Far Away," June 6, 1998.

Makanya, M. 1995. "An Overview of Affirmative Action in South Africa," in A. Van der Merwe, ed., *Industrial Sociology: A South African Perspective.* Johannesburg: Lexicon.

Marx, Anthony. 1998. *Making Race and Nation: A Comparison of South Africa, the United States, and Brazil.* New York: Cambridge University Press.

Mattes, Robert. 1995. *The Election Book.* Cape Town: IDASA.

Mbeki, Thabo. 1998. *The Time Has Come.* Johannesburg: Mafube Publishing.

McGregor, R. 1987. "The Origin and Extent of the Lack of Competition in South Africa," in Jeffrey Butler, Richard Elphick, and David Welsh, eds., *Democratic Liberalism in South Africa.* Middletown: Wesleyan University Press.

Nzimande, B. 1991. *Black Advancement, White Resistance and the Politics of Class Reproduction.* Ph.D. dissertation, University of Natal.

O'Connell, Lesley, and Nancy Birdsall. 2001. "Race, Human Capital Inequality, and Income Distribution," Chapter 10 of this volume.

O'Meara, Dan. 1996. *Forty Lost Years: The Apartheid State and the Politics of the National Party.* Athens: Ohio University Press.

Onselen, Charles van. 1996. *The Seed Is Mine: The Life of Kas Maine, A South African Sharecropper 1894–1985.* Cape Town: David Philip Publishers.

Pachai, B. 1971. *The South African Indian Question, 1860–1971.* Cape Town: David Philip Publishers.

Plaatje, Sol. 1982. *Native Life in South Africa.* Johannesburg: Ravau Press.

Platzky, L., and C. Walker. 1985. *The Surplus People: Forced Removals in South Africa.* Johannesburg: Ravau Press.

Report of the Commission on Truth and Reconciliation. 5 vols. Cape Town, 1998.

Robinson, Shirley. 1998. "Demographics and Quality of Life," in Wilmot James and Moira Levy, eds., *Pulse: Passages in Democracy Building.* Cape Town: IDASA.

Sachs, Albie. 1994. *Affirmative Action and the New Constitution.* Cape Town: African National Congress.

Saunders, Christopher. 1988. *The Making of the South African Past: Major Historians on Race and Class.* Cape Town: David Philip Publishers.

Segal, S. 1998. "Black Economic Empowerment," in Wilmot James and Moira Levy, eds., *Pulse: Passages in Democracy Building.* Cape Town: IDASA.

Seidman, Gay. 1998. "Oppositional Identities in Brazil and South Africa: Unions and the Transition to Democracy," in Ran Greenstein, ed., *Comparative Perspectives on South Africa.* New York: St. Martin's Press.

South African Institute of Race Relations. 1997. *South Africa Survey 1996/1997.* Johannesburg: The Institute.

Southern African Migration Project. 1998. "Trading Places: Cross-Border Traders and the South African Informal Sector." Cape Town: IDASA, Policy Series no. 6.

————. 1999. "The Lives and Times of African Migrants and Immigrants in Post-Apartheid South Africa." Cape Town: IDASA, Policy Series no.13.

Tatz, C. M. 1962. *Shadow and Substance in South Africa: A Study in Land and Franchise Policies Affecting Africans 1910–1960.* Pietermaritzburg: University of Natal Press.

Taylor, Nick, and Penny Vinjevold, eds. 1999. *Getting Learning Right: Report of the President's Education Initiative Research Project.* Johannesburg: Joint Education Trust.

Thompson, Leonard. 1990. *A History of South Africa.* New Haven: Yale University Press.

Tocqueville, Alexis de. 1954. *Democracy in America.* New York: Vintage Books.

Western, John. 1981. *Outcast Cape Town.* Minneapolis: University of Minnesota Press.

White Paper on Affirmative Action in the Public Service. 1997.

White Paper on Affirmative Action in the Public Service. April 1998.

White Paper on South African Land Policy. April 1997.

Wilson, Francis, and Mamphela Ramphele. 1989. *Uprooting Poverty, The South African Challenge.* Cape Town and New York: David Philip Publishers.

3

Combating Racism in South Africa: Redress/Remedies

Mamphela Ramphele

SOUTH AFRICA'S TRANSITION to democracy continues to be undermined by the legacy of racism and the deep structural inequalities that are part of the postapartheid landscape. The country faces a major challenge in living up to its own constitutional commitments to socioeconomic rights. Insistence on the inclusion of these rights against the cautious comments of many analysts was premised on the correct view that no true democracy can be established in a society in which reasonable access to basic needs that define citizenship could not be guaranteed to all. Failure to make these commitments would have legitimated the continued existence of different classes of citizens: first- and third-class citizens.

Levels of inequality in South Africa are rivaled only by Brazil in terms of measures for which statistics are available, embodied in what economists have coined the Gini coefficient.[1] Inequality is structured along a hierarchy of privilege defined by race, class, gender, age, and geographic location. African women in rural areas tend to predominate in the lowest levels of this hierarchy. A major contributor to this profile is the legacy of migratory labor that simultaneously generated super profits for those industries such as mining that relied heavily on the system, while systematically impoverishing rural African people. The system of migrant labor sought to isolate the labor power of African men from their family obligations and turned them into labor "units" to be exploited without regard to their family obligations.[2] The fabric of families of many poor black people has been severely undermined as a consequence of this legacy, leaving young people vulnerable.

In this chapter I will set out what I believe to be the minimum requirements for a redress strategy for postapartheid South Africa to create a conducive environment for the development of the human potential of all citizens. I will also explore some of the difficult questions related to redress issues. For example, how does one balance equity considerations with those pertaining to merit? How does one accommodate the various categories of persons designated under the constitution for redress action, and what priority rating should be given to race rather than gender? How affordable is redress in a climate of diminishing resources? Should there be a cut-off date for redress action after which society would be allowed to function as a meritocracy? My analysis will be based on the experience of addressing these questions in the context of the University of Cape Town's approach to issues of equity and excellence. I will conclude with a few comments on the pitfalls of redress strategies that are driven by compromise with either the left or the right of the political spectrum.

The First Four Years

There is much to be proud of in terms of South Africa's track record in dealing head-on with the legacy of the past. We have a national constitution that is the envy of many. We have not shied away from confronting our hideous past. Through the Truth and Reconciliation Commission (TRC), we have sought to come to terms with the worst abuses of human rights, which left deep scars in the body politic of South Africa as well as on many individual souls. The five-volume TRC report, imperfect as it is, is there as a record of how far we had descended into a spiral of human rights abuses.[3] We have bravely embarked on major policy development and implementation to give life to the commitments we made in our constitution. We have an excellent judicial system that has taken the best from the past and enriched it with international experience to establish a firm foundation for an independent judiciary.

Yet we remain far from our own set targets. The track record of government has been patchy. Some cabinet ministers have done a marvelous job under trying conditions: lack of experience, archaic governance systems, and reactionary bureaucrats who were bent on undermining transformation of the civil service to bring it in line with the new democracy. Others have been less successful. Poor performance can in part be attributed to inexperience, but it is largely related to the failure to appreciate the need for an intellectual basis for good institutional governance.

There has also been a failure by a significant proportion of white South Africans to come to grips with the need to actively participate in the dismantling of the system of privilege based on racism and sexism. There are many white people who fail to see that the level of their privileges is in many ways directly related to the systematic deprivation of the majority of South Africans of the most basic needs and opportunities for normal human development. Vested interest in the privileges most white people have come to feel perfectly entitled to poses a major threat to genuine transformation to a more equitable society.

South Africa has also had to contend with the reality of a global economic environment that is fueled by instantaneous electronic communication. This global economy has begun to challenge the very foundations of the sovereignty of nations to order their own economic affairs without serious constraints by outsiders. Being categorized as part of the emerging markets adds to the vulnerability to volatile markets, which are increasingly driven by the desire for quick, large profits for fund managers regardless of the consequences for ordinary citizens. The very nature of the legacy of apartheid, which left a large proportion of citizens without basic education and skills, has made the country even more vulnerable in this knowledge-driven global competitive environment. The data below is demonstrative of this.

Table 3.1 demonstrates that Africans who comprise 76.6 percent of the total population of South Africa are overly represented among those without any education (92 percent), whereas there are hardly any white people without basic education (0.6 percent). It is thus not surprising that almost half of the population with higher education qualifications would be white people—an overrepresentation given the size of the white sector as a proportion of total population (10.8 percent).

Table 3.2 is an elaboration of the level of overrepresentation of white people among those South Africans with various university

Table 3.1   Education Levels of People over the Age of 20, 1995

	African	Colored	Indian	White	Numerical Total
No Education	92%	6%	1.4%	0.6%	2,864,000
Matric	51%	6%	5%	37%	4,131,000
Post Matric	42%	5%	4%	49%	2,000,000

Source: South Africa Survey 1996/1997, published by the South African Institute of Race Relations, 1997.

degrees reflecting the legacy of differential investment by the country
in skills development.

   In Table 3.3, the numerical breakdown of the skills base of the population puts the issue of the skewed nature of the skills base more stark-
ly. For example, in 1994, of the 26,443 total number of South Africans
with engineering qualifications, a full 24,413 (92.3 percent) were white.
This is by no means a reflection of white people's superior talents in the
field of engineering but a clear demonstration of differential access to
opportunity. It is not surprising that it is difficult to find people with the
requisite skills to perform the vital functions our new democracy craves
so much.

A Proposed Framework for Redress

Given the context in which South Africa is making its transition to
democracy as well as its entry into the highly competitive global envi-

**Table 3.2   A Proportional Breakdown of Some Key Degrees Held by South
           Africans, 1994**

Degree	African	Colored	Indian	White	Unspecified	Total
Accounting, Management & Administration	1.3%	2.6%	7.5%	6.6%	3.5%	5.8%
Agriculture, Forestry & Food Technology	0.9%	0.1%	0.1%	2.6%	1.0%	2.1%
Architecture	0.1%	0.2%	0.3%	1.4%	2.1%	1.2%
Commerce	5.9%	7.2%	11.2%	13.4%	15.4%	12.4%
Economics	0.1%	1.1%	0.1%	0.7%	0.8%	0.6%
Engineering	0.7%	1.6%	2.5%	7.4%	4.1%	6.1%
Law	5.3%	4.9%	7.0%	6.0%	7.3%	6.0%
Medicine & Optometry	2.0%	3.2%	8.7%	5.7%	5.6%	5.4%
Natural Sciences	5.3%	9.3%	9.7%	10.3%	7.8%	9.5%

   Source: South Africa Survey 1996/1997, published by the South African Institute of Race
Relations, 1997.

Table 3.3   A Numerical Breakdown of Some Key Degrees Held by South Africans, 1994

Degree	African	Colored	Indian	White	Unspecified	Total
Accounting, Management & Administration	655	358	1,667	21,681	778	25,139
Agriculture, Forestry & Food Technology	444	17	13	8,596	229	9,299
Architecture	38	29	70	4,558	459	5,154
Commerce	2,902	984	2,493	44,056	3,433	53,868
Economics	58	153	16	2,413	181	2,821
Engineering	330	214	564	24,413	922	26,443
Law	2,612	672	1,539	19,613	1,640	26,076
Medicine & Optometry	966	438	1,950	18,706	1,253	23,313
Natural Sciences	2,582	1,278	2,168	33,675	1,747	41,450

Source: South Africa Survey 1996/1997, published by the South African Institute of Race Relations, 1997.

ronment, any framework for redress to deal with the racist past will have to pass stringent tests for attention to details as well as internal consistency between the short-, medium-, and long-term strategies. Requirements for such a strategy would have to include:

- Defining a shared vision of a transformed South Africa beyond the generalities of the constitutional provisions. What are the basic essential elements of a more equitable nonracial, nonsexist society?
- Stating the principles that must not be compromised in striving toward the envisioned future. How would ordinary people assess these principles and live by them as well as hold leaders accountable in their performance according to them?
- Requiring society to measure progress toward attainment of the envisioned future in the short, medium and long terms. What corrective action is to be taken to keep performance to set targets?

- Setting a cutoff date for special measures to allow society to function with less and less reference to racial categories defining our legacy.

Defining a Shared Vision of a Transformed Society

A shared vision is an absolute requirement for the new South Africa. The deliberate enforcement of "separate development" in South Africa has left us with a legacy of a deeply divided society. The preamble of our constitution encapsulates some of the ideals of the future we have committed ourselves to, but it has not yet been distilled into a "one-liner" that can inspire ordinary citizens into believing that everyday action taken by individuals can make a difference to the attainment of the shared vision.

It is worth borrowing from the experience of successful enterprises all over the world, as documented in a book appropriately entitled *Built to Last*, in which the authors examine the successful habits of visionary companies. They make a crucial point: "One of the most important steps you can take in building a visionary company is not action, but a shift in perspective" (Collins and Porras 1997: p. 40). A shift in perspective has yet to occur in the minds of many South Africans—black and white. There are at least three key focus areas in which this shift in perspective has to occur.

First, we need to confront the legacy of inferiority and superiority complexes on the part of black and white South Africans. There are white people who genuinely believe that black people are a lower form of the human species. They may concede that some among black people are closer to their own civilized status, but on the whole they have a serious and deep-seated view of the inherent intellectual inferiority of black people. Claude Steele, an African-American social psychologist, captured the impact of this prejudice aptly: "I have long suspected a particular culprit—a culprit that can undermine black achievement as effectively as a lock on a schoolhouse door. The culprit is stigma" (Steele 1992: p. 68). This stigma, he says, borrowing Ervin Goffman's words, is capable of "breaking the claim" that one's human attributes have on people. Black people in such an environment find themselves under constant "'suspicion of intellectual inferiority" (p. 74). The impact of living under suspicion is devastating to the self-esteem of many black people. This is still the reality of the experience of many black South Africans. A shift in perspective is sorely needed to liberate those trapped by this stigma.

To add insult to injury, the very essence of apartheid education denied many black people access to the foundation of a scientific culture that is essential for functioning effectively in the knowledge society at the dawn of the new millennium. Edward Wilson, an experimental psychologist, captured the essence of the problem thus:

> Without the instruments and accumulated knowledge of the natural sciences, human beings are trapped in a cognitive prison. They are like intelligent fish in a deep, shadowed pool. Wondering and restless, longing to reach out, they think about the world outside. They invent ingenious speculations and myths about the origin of the confining waters, of the sun and the sky and the stars above, and the meaning of their own existence. But they are wrong, always wrong, because the world is too remote from ordinary experience to be imagined. (Wilson 1998: p. 48)

The double burden of being a suspect for intellectual inferiority and having to cope with the ignorance imposed on one by the denial of educational opportunities is an enormous one. Many black people have managed to triumph over this dual burden, but an increasing proportion of young, poor black people are being crushed by it. It is a cruel irony that the Verwoerdian social-engineering project has proven to be such a success so many years after his demise. It is a legacy that is likely to continue to undermine the ability of black people to compete effectively in the modern global environment they find themselves in. The same problems of living with the legacy of ignorance and lack of opportunities to develop appropriate skills are evident in many facets of our national life: sports and the arts, management and leadership in both the public and private sectors, technical skill areas, and so on.

White people who continue to hold the views that stigmatize their black compatriots are adding to this burden. The failure to distinguish intellectual inferiority from ignorance is criminal. It is like binding the feet of one's competitor and then proclaiming oneself the winner of a race run against the bound victim. But white people who hold these views are also in need of liberation from their superiority complex, which constrains their ability to enjoy and share the future with their compatriots. The positive impact of the Black Consciousness movement on the self-image of a significant proportion of young black people, especially in the 1970s, has enabled many to continue to play an important role in shifting the perspective of segments of the society.[4]

To a lesser extent, women are also regarded as a weaker form of the human species, not only physically but intellectually, by many men—

What should the vision of the South Africa determined to stamp out inequity and promote prosperity for all encompass? Collins and Porras have a few pointers for those seriously searching:

- it must be compelling—it must get people's juices up;
- it should fall outside the comfort zone—it must be doable but require heroic effort;
- it should be bold and exciting in its own right;
- it must be consistent with the country's core values (i.e., Constitutional principles). An example might be: "To be a prosperous African country building on the strengths of our diversity." (pp. 111–112)

Whatever vision is adopted by South Africans, it has to be a clarion call to action to build a more equitable nonracial, nonsexist society on a sustained basis. Uprooting poverty must be at the heart of any redress strategy. There can be no unified South African society unless the huge levels of inequalities between those experiencing grinding poverty and those who live in the lap of luxury are systematically addressed. A major focus has to be on strengthening the vital segments of our society that promote human development: the family, the education system, and civil society. All three were targeted for undermining by the racist system, especially among black people.

Principles to Guide Strategic Action

The very foundations of our society have been undermined by the legacy of the past. South Africans have to spell out some basic principles to underpin strategies for action to attain its envisioned goals. A few examples that have relevance for a successful redress strategy follow:

Enhancing equity must be at the core of any redress strategy. Given the legacy of inequity in South Africa, creating a culture that promotes equity at all levels of society will demand concentrated effort by all involved in redress strategies. One cannot redress inequity on a sustainable basis without actively promoting equity at every step along the way. It is in this context that issues of race, class, and gender have to be dealt with in an integrated way to minimize the emergence of, as well as the enhancement of, islands of privilege. For example, the promotion of black men in the private sector has the potential of exaggerating existing sexism in our society. There is also a risk in white women taking advantage of their relative privileged position to increase their level of advantage over other women. The complexity of managing an integrated redress strategy is not to be underestimated. There would have to be some tough calls on a number of cases where equally qualified people have to be considered for appointment to which only one person can be chosen. But such challenges should not discourage serious attention to detail and to approaching difficult decisions with integrity and transparency.

A human-centered approach has to be at the core of redress strategies. The interests of individuals must not be compromised in the name of "the people." Social engineering processes that disregard the legitimate aspirations of individuals in a democratic society are not sustainable in the long term and tend to create a culture that stifles creativity rather than enhances it. Human creativity is at its best when individuals feel appreciated. One cannot expect people to perform at their best by constantly being made to feel guilty or inferior.

Congruence and consistency between short-, medium-, and long-term goals. To minimize undermining the long term, the means have to accord with the ends. Undermining central tenets of the vision in the short term tends to weaken the very foundations of the future. For example, promoting human development has to be undertaken at all levels of society to get the multiplier effect of healthy families, good schools, well-run higher-education institutions, socially responsible private-sector organizations, and clean, efficient government.

Integrity of leaders, institutions, and the process is crucial to allay fears. To avoid targeting segments of society for discrimination in the name of redress, rooting out corruption, nepotism, and incompetence are the key to success.

Upfrontness in setting targets for redress and reviewing progress on a regular basis to ensure corrective action whenever problems are encountered. Covering up incompetence or errors made undermines the public's confidence in social institutions.

Fairness to all involved to ensure continued buy-in. One cannot expect those previously advantaged to willingly participate in action that is likely to put them at a severe disadvantage. For example, how can one expect white males to contribute effectively to the training and development needs of black people and women if their own future job security is at risk? A sensitive, balanced approach is critical.

Public accountability by government, the private sector, as well as organs of civil society will enable South Africans to evaluate progress toward the attainment of set goals. Transparency in reporting successes and failures as well as the nature of corrective measures taken is crucial in this regard.

Specific Redress Measures

Appropriate measures to redress the imbalances of the past have to be based on an audit of the status quo. A few examples of national data are used as a basis for the analysis in this chapter.

The report on poverty published by the office of the Reconstruction and Development Program in October 1995 indicated that 53 percent of the population lived in the poorest 40 percent of households and spent less than R385 per adult per month. The poorest 20 percent of households spent less than R225 per adult per month.

Table 3.4   Unemployment: Strict and Expanded Definitions, October 1995

	Strict Definition	Expanded Definition
African	1,641,000	3,665,000
Asian	43,000	57,000
Colored	225,000	347,000
White	90,000	135,000
Total	1,999,000	4,204,000

Source: South Africa Survey, 1996/1997, published by the South African Institute of Race Relations, 1997.

Note: Strict definition of unemployment refers to people 15 years and older who are not employed but are available for work and who have taken specific steps to seek employment in the four weeks prior to a given point in time.

Table 3.5   Unemployment: Expanded Definition by Race and Gender

	Male	Female	Total
African	1,592,000	2,073,000	3,665,000
Asian	28,000	29,000	57,000
Colored	151,000	195,000	347,000
White	54,000	92,000	135,000
Total	1,824,000	2,380,000	4,204,000

Source: South Africa Survey, 1996/1997, published by the South African Institute of Race Relations, 1997.

Note: Expanded definition of unemployment refers to people 15 years and older who are not employed but are available and have the desire to work, irrespective of whether or not they have taken active steps to find work.

The report also highlighted income disparities between black and white people. These disparities partly reflect the skewed skills base referred to earlier, but they are also reflections of the legacy of racially based job reservation and inequities in the remuneration system. A few examples follow:

- 36 percent of employed workers earned less than R1,000 a month in 1995.
- The single largest proportion of African and colored employed workers (46 percent each) earned less than R1,000.
- The single largest proportion of white employed workers (31 percent) earned between R4,000 and R7,999 a month, while 18 percent of Asian, 5 percent of colored, and 4 percent of African employed workers were in the same category.

It is thus not surprising that according to the 1996 Human Development Report published by the United Nations Development Program, South Africa had one of the largest income disparities in the world. The poorest 40 percent of households in South Africa earned only 9 percent of the country's income, while the richest 20 percent earned nineteen times more than the poorest 20 percent.

Redressing the above inequities is essential to the attainment of our envisioned goal of being a prosperous African country drawing on the strengths of our diversity. Such measures must be within the equity framework and principles encapsulated in our constitution and elaborated above. The very use of the term "redress" is an acknowledgement that something went wrong in the past and needs to be put right in order that a better future for all can be possible. Targeted action to enable those previously excluded to take advantage of opportunities that open up is an essential part of redress strategies. The Afrikaans expression *regstellende aksie* ("action to put right the wrong that was done") best captures the essence of what is needed.[5]

The issue of setting time frames for redress tends to be controversial from both ends of the spectrum. Institutions that feel under pressure to deliver on expectations to redress imbalances of the past tend to mistrust targets and time frames as proxies for quotas. This mistrust of targets is all the more puzzling when it comes from the private sector, which has business plans with clear budget targets as an essential part of the culture of successful enterprises. Some of those who stand to benefit from redress measures also tend to be unwilling to contemplate setting cutoff points beyond which redress measures would not be appropriate for society to enforce. But any commitment to an open-ended redress strategy in perpetuity is likely to undermine the consolidation of a common society with a shared vision. Why would white males want to continue to live in a society that would be weighted against them in perpetuity? Or why would self-respecting young black people and women want to live in a society in which their ability to compete openly is seen as inadequate regardless of their class position and educational attainment?

Redress measures encompass three essential components:

* increasing access to opportunities for all with a special focus on those most disadvantaged;
* promoting the development of the human potential of all; and
* transforming the culture of all societal institutions toward one that is more human-centered and affirms the richness of the diversity of South Africa's people.

There have been major strides across the South African society to institute redress measures that incorporate *regstellende aksie* with respect to designated groups as set out in our constitution. The government has taken the lead in creating a national policy and legislative framework for such action through such measures as the Education White Paper of 1995, the Higher Education Act of 1997, and the Employment Equity Act of 1998. Various policy measures have also been instituted to encourage the private sector and the rest of civil society to focus on the issue of redress in all aspects of society. For example, the insistence on broader representation of ownership of the means of production is being enforced by the preferential awarding of government tenders to those who comply. Success has been mixed. A more systematic approach is called for.

Increasing Access to Opportunities

Increasing access involves both the removal of barriers to access for all in the spirit of equity, as well as taking positive measures to enhance access to those previously disadvantaged. Outlawing racism and all forms of negative discrimination is a necessary condition for combating racism in the field of access to opportunity, but not a sufficient one. Active steps need to be taken to examine the premise used for defining access, as follows:

- Are the criteria used essential to the basic requirements of the area or field being accessed or have optional variables become additional hoops over which entrants have to jump? For example, is it essential to have six As to make a success of medical training, or can one succeed with lower test scores? The same questions apply in the job market. Is the experience often demanded of applicants essential to success or is it simply being used to keep outsiders out?
- How reliable are traditional measures used to predict the success of new entrants into a training area, a new job, or a particular skills area? For example, the Matric results of many disadvantaged schools do not necessarily correlate with the performance of the matriculants at tertiary level.
- What additional tests or assessments should be used to evaluate the potential to succeed in those who have been denied the opportunity to develop their full intellectual or sporting prowess? On a more positive note, what additional score should be attached to experience in a different cultural milieu in a selection process? How should the potential for value added that such a person would bring to a given institution be measured?

Increasing access also entails taking additional measures to prepare those targeted to enable them to compete effectively with their compatriots as well as with their peers internationally. More systematic orientation to the new environment, an identification of possible stumbling blocks to performance, more active assistance to put the new entrant at ease, and so on, are essential to an enabling environment.

Given the reality of poverty as a major barrier to access, targeted resource allocation to address possible barriers has to be undertaken in an agreed and transparent manner within the limits of resource constraints. For example, talented sports people who have no access to training facilities or basic equipment cannot be expected to compete effectively against their financially better-endowed compatriots. Nor can access to education become a reality without financial support.

Developing the Human Potential of All

To attain the vision to be a prosperous African country requires that as many South Africans as possible be net contributors to the prosperity of the country. To the extent that so many South Africans have undeveloped potential, to that extent is the country as a whole disadvantaged.

Undeveloped human potential is expensive to carry into the future. Not only is one concerned about the opportunity costs of underutilized human capital, but also about the actual costs resulting from poor performance, frustration, and criminal activity.

The poorly developed scientific culture among the majority of uneducated poor people is also a major contributor to the difficulties South Africa faces with regard to dealing with the HIV/AIDS crisis. The lack of knowledge about human anatomy, physiology, and reproductive health is a major constraint to effecting cultural change that would have beneficial outcomes in curbing the epidemic. The difference in the response of the gay community to the first wave of the epidemic compared to that of the heterosexual community most affected by AIDS's second wave, is instructive in this regard. The gay community, which has a profile that includes a significant proportion of highly educated people, responded positively to health education campaigns with a resultant major change in the morbidity and mortality rates from AIDS. The December 1998 brutal mob murder of a Kwa-Zulu Natal woman who dared to break the silence around AIDS in her township, is not only tragic but frightening in its implications. Her crime was public acknowledgement of her HIV-positive status and joining a health education campaign against its spread, which sadly was seen as bringing disrepute to her resident township. The chickens of cultivated ignorance are coming home to roost with a vengeance.

An important starting point in the development of human potential is creating a climate of success. Appropriate placement of people in positions in which they can succeed and feel challenged to incrementally move to more complex levels of performance is critical. Claude Steele refers to successful models of "wiseness" in schools dealing with disadvantaged students in which the common approach is acceptance of the student as a talented person who is then assisted to excel (Steele 1992: pp. 75–76).

The University of Cape Town's faculty of engineering has developed a successful model of enabling young people from disadvantaged backgrounds to excel. The record over the last ten years speaks for itself, as demonstrated in Table 3.6.

The results in Table 3.6 are remarkable given that the University of Cape Town had its first African male graduate in 1982 (civil engineering) and first African female graduate in 1984 (electrical engineering), and the prevailing wisdom of the time, which was reflected by a comment made to my predecessor, Stuart Saunders, by a prospective spon-

Table 3.6   African and Female Qualifiers in Engineering, 1988–1998

	African	Female
1988	9	10
1989	13	14
1990	12	15
1991	10	18
1992	21	22
1993	20	28
1994	36	21
1995	52	26
1996	74	34
1997	80	30
1998	96	48

sor that Africans could not think in three dimensions and thus were incapable of understanding engineering principles.[6]

Second, attending to the requirements of individuals with different learning abilities and strategies is the most cost-effective approach to ensuring success. Slower learners are not necessarily less intelligent. Enabling people to function in environments that build their self-confidence is likely to lay strong foundations for better performance on a sustained basis. Again, the University of Cape Town's Deep Foundations Program,[7] which uses a multimedia educational approach, is set to become an important model for using information technology to create learning environments that put learners at the center and build their self-confidence. Multimedia education also challenges teachers to become more innovative in their approach to curriculum design and teaching methods.

Third, affirming and rewarding good performance enhances excellence. Transparent regular assessments on the basis of clearly set out criteria are essential tools. A focus on the diversity of the talents of those involved is key to the overall strategic thrust. Tolerance of mediocrity to buy peace is dangerous. Poor performance has to be identified early, its causes analyzed, and corrective action taken. Poor performers sap the morale of the team in any setting.

Transforming the Culture to Reflect and Affirm Diversity

This is an often neglected area, given the subtlety that tends to pervade institutional cultures. For insiders there is often an unwritten code about what is and isn't proper, what value to attach to certain cues given by other participants, how important certain issues are to future prospects within the institution, what support is available, where and under what conditions, and so forth.

An equity framework requires spelling out basic fundamental values of an institution to enable all the participants to have a set of shared common assumptions about, and expectations of, their institution, fellow participants at the various levels within the organization, and their own role within it. Many failed appointments or "job hopping" practices are a reflection of the failure of organizations to pay attention to this crucial issue.

Indeed, part of the problem of postapartheid South Africa is traceable to a large extent to the failure of the society to spell out what the values of a democratic nonracial, nonsexist country are, let alone what role citizens should play in strengthening and entrenching such shared values. Democracy has been used and abused by criminal elements who assert their own individual rights to freedom and dignity as a means to create space for themselves to undermine the very foundations of the society. It is also not clear that the South African society has unambiguously declared itself intolerant of crime, corruption, and all actions that undermine democracy. It is not enough to outlaw discrimination and other unacceptable actions. There has to be the political will to enforce compliance.

At the institutional level, one has to pay attention to the microclimate within each social institution to promote a culture that enhances the development of the full potential of all the participants. The principles spelled out above have to be meticulously adhered to, especially by the leadership, which must lead by example.

Concluding Comments

There are many difficult questions that remain. How does one balance redress considerations with requirements of merit? How does one accommodate the various categories of persons designated under the constitution for redress? Should race considerations be privileged over all others? Can South Africa afford redress given the limited resources at our disposal?

I have already alluded to the imperatives of equity that in my view compel South Africa to ensure that in combating racism, it should not entrench existing contours of privilege nor increase the levels of inequality between the poor and the rich. The last five years have seen an increase in the number of black men who have risen into the ranks of the rich and even super rich as beneficiaries of black empowerment deals. Research indicates that levels of inequality between South Africans were not only between black and white people, but that inequalities between black people were also significant.[8] There is a growing gap between the poor and rich in the black community, with gender and geographic factors playing an important role in the differentials. The poorest sector of the South African population is black, female, and rural-based.[9]

There is an absolute imperative to combat the white male dominance of the ownership of the means of production—the black empowerment emphasis is intended to do just that. But does the focus have to be on empowering black men rather than black people? This is a controversial issue that has been the subject of many analyses, private and public.[10] There is an inevitability about capital accumulation creating a larger gap between the haves and have-nots. The question of the color of the haves is not an irrelevant one.

Empowerment in the private sector has historical precedence. The shift from an Anglo-dominated capital base to a more balanced one between English- and Afrikaans-speaking white males was a result of a deliberate empowerment strategy by the then owners of capital. Anglo-American Corporation's role in the creation of Gencor, the precursor of latter-day Billiton, was crucial in this regard. Since 1990, white capital continues to fall over itself to embrace black partners in the name of empowerment. Some of the deals are well thought through and likely to make a difference to wealth creation in the wider society. Sadly, a significant proportion is focused on the personal enrichment of individuals.

Opinion is divided on the extent to which such personal enrichment contributes to the greater good. Some would argue that the presence of rich black people helps to bolster the self-image of black people who are overly represented among the poor. The trickle-down effect of this wealth is also seen as a positive benefit. Others would argue that the culture of the super rich with an emphasis on conspicuous consumption in the midst of such poverty heightens the sense of deprivation among the have-nots, who feel cheated out of the fruits of liberation. The question remains: Why should a few black people be made rich on behalf of the black community, which on the whole continues to experience grinding poverty?

The focus on black men as desired partners also reinforces a major inequity in a society in which black women are overrepresented among

4

Whiteness in the Rainbow: Experiencing the Loss of Privilege in the New South Africa

Melissa Steyn

I didn't want to be racist, but the present Government, with its policies like affirmative action, is making me one now. The workplace is
making me racist.
—Comment by a white man at a conference, Gauteng, August 1998

When President Nelson Mandela, in his inaugural speech of May 1994,
referred to the new South Africa as the Rainbow Nation,[1] he provided
South Africa with a term on which profound acts of collective self-redefinition could be pinned. The rainbow metaphor was taken up in the
popular discourses of the country and became a rallying expression for
aspirations, hopes, humor, and cynicism in the transforming country.

Ironically, a pertinent aspect of the old South Africa could also have
been communicated by the metaphor. As the colors of the rainbow all
are absorbed into white light, the fates of all the people of this diverse
country were subsumed within the interests of the white population,
through the power historically centered in their hands to define both
self and other. White was the norm, all Others were peripheral—culturally, economically, politically.

The transition to the new South Africa, with the negotiated transfer
of power, heralded the relativization of "whiteness" in relation to the
other social groupings within the country. The white population is now
marked as one group among many, one band within the rainbow. In
some social domains, such as the political arena, its privileged status
has been removed; in other domains, such as the cultural, its hegemony
has weakened but still prevails; in yet other domains, such as in the economic sector, its dominance is relatively unaffected and remains pervasive. The shakedown within and between each of these domains is far

from settled; the space within which the identities of new South Africans are being reconfigured is unmapped and shifting. From this perspective, the democratic election was really the beginning of a psychological revolution now underway as social groupings stake out claims relative to each other in their attempt to fix new identities.

This chapter explores the subjective experience of white relativization. Given that the privileged position of whiteness has been ideologically supported by centuries of Eurocentrism, the taken-for-granted reality of "whites"[2] has undergone a sea change. They need to make sense of their new positioning—to explain what it means to be white in the new South Africa, to shape their intentionality toward other South Africans, the African continent, their heritage, their future. The old ways of accounting for the fundamentals of their social positioning no longer work unproblematically; in fact, the old narratives of whiteness have become part of what the new accounts have to explain and reframe. In other words, for white South Africa, encountering the new political dispensation in the country is also a challenging self-encounter. The old certainties that provided moorings for social and personal identities have given way to a world of ambivalence and ambiguity; where old self-(mis)knowledge no longer applies.

Founding Narratives of Whiteness

The experience of whiteness described in this chapter is contextually grounded in the relatively sudden change that South Africa is undergoing. Although the particulars of the self-encounter of whites in South Africa may be unique, a study of how whites here react to the relativization of their position has relevance for comparative study. The shifting fault lines of global power and demographic changes occurring internally within previously white countries point to possibilities of analogous experiences and responses.

Although inflected differently in the specific historical circumstances of each country, globally, white identity shares certain "founding narratives" (Allen 1994; Brantlinger 1985; Memmi 1990; Nedervcen Pieterse 1992; Said 1979; Stam and Shohat 1994; Steyn 1998a). These accounts regaled the inherent superiority, and consequent entitlement, of Europeans over Others. A light skin acted as the "natural" marker of European distinction (Guillauman 1995). This European self-image was constructed by taking the believed inherent deficiencies of the Other as collateral. Africa, particularly, acted as Europe's negative mirror image (Nederveen Pieterse 1992). Such self-ennobling beliefs were in part enabled by, and in part the products of, the relative economic advantage of Europe as it expanded its colonial influence over its Others. Whiteness accrued to people of European extract as they settled amongst Others across the globe in unequal power relations. The reproduction of these ideologically informed self-constructions helped to constitute, explain, and sustain this social position of relative advantage for subsequent generations of European descendents.

The following quotation from the superintendent general of Cape education in 1890, Sir Langham Dale, illustrates the interconnection of ideology, whiteness, and the articulation of resources. Talking about education policy at the time, he maintained:

> The first duty of Government has been assumed to be to recognise the position of the European colonist as holding paramount influence, social and political; and to see that the sons and daughters of the colonists, and those who come hither to throw in their lot with them, should have at least such an education as their peers in Europe enjoy, with such local modifications as will fit them to maintain their unquestioned superiority and supremacy in this land. (Quoted in Maurice 1980)

The manner in which whiteness has been exercised has varied according to different historical processes. Marx (1998), for example, provides an excellent comparative analysis of some of the factors that shaped the racialization of the United States, Brazil, and South Africa. In each case, however, the ends have been the same—enduring social advantage and control by whites (see Lipsitz 1995, 1998; Wander, Martin, and Nakayama 1999). Within South Africa, whiteness was championed by successive regimes, culminating in state-enforced whiteness through the policy of apartheid. This policy acted out the ideological underpinnings of whiteness in a literal and thorough way, thus deliberately bringing about a world that seemed to confirm that whites were, indeed, superior. State structures manipulated the economy, labor, the media, and the education system to produce a society that apparently evidenced the superiority of whites. Everywhere they looked, whites saw proof of the meniality of blackness, confirming the appropriateness of their social entitlement—they were better equipped to deal with leadership and management and to make education and capital work to the benefit of self and nation. The accumulation of assets seemingly accrued to them because of their inherent qualities; an arrangement that seemed as logical as it was natural. To a great extent, they were protect-

ed from deeper self-analysis through state editing of reality, especially
in the form of thoroughgoing media censorship. To some extent at least,
and in varying degrees, they colluded with one of the most rigorous
examples of collective perceptual selection in modern history, screening
out of awareness a great deal of what was going on around them.

Whiteness in South Africa has shared this characteristic selectivity
with its ideological family elsewhere. Whites, generally, do not have
insight into their whiteness. This results in a pervasive blindness to the
impact of racialization upon societies in general, to how lives are affected by race, and to how their own whiteness is premised upon others
being positioned as blacks with all that such a positioning entails.
Scholars agree that, until quite recently, whiteness has been invisible for
the majority of Euro-American whites (Dyer 1988, 1997; Frankenburg
1993; Martin et al. 1996; Morrison 1992; Nakayama and Krizek
1995).

Studies have been emerging, however, that indicate that whiteness
is beginning to be experienced differently, even in countries such as the
United States. Indeed, the fact that scholars there have begun to study
whiteness in the United States is an indication that it is coming into
focus for that society. Moreover, because many whites now perceive
that being white may in fact adversely affect their life's chances, they
are beginning to embrace the discourses of racialization, arguing that
they are now disadvantaged through "reversed racism." Where before
racialization was denied in order to protect privilege, racial discourses
are now needed to achieve that same purpose (see, for example,
Gallanger 1997).

The manner in which racialization has played itself out in South
Africa has shared some characteristics with this new "besieged" whiteness in the United States. Their racialization has always been highly
visible to whites themselves, something that had to be protected against
all odds. They always knew they were white and that it was the single
most important feature of their lives, affecting all their life chances
(Steyn 1996). The logic of racialization was intrinsic to the taken-for-
granted reality of white South Africa. People were socialized into what
was regarded as the appropriate social space for them, and material and
social resources were articulated accordingly. A culture of entitlement
was pervasive and entrenched; unequal opportunities were rationalized
rather than obfuscated. The lives of others formed an undifferentiated
backdrop to the mobility, range of choice, and comforts of privilege that
were "normal." Advantage extended to people of this sociopolitical
grouping whether or not they as individuals consented to it or even con-

sciously sought it. Yet, as a collective, whites made the myriad of daily choices that perpetuated their preferential status. The ballot vote was one choice among many other choices, which may have been less visible but were cumulative and far-reaching.

Since the democratic elections, however, South African society has been committed to bringing about equality of opportunity and equity in access to resources for all the groups in the country. The political system now works to deconstruct racial privilege; the societal pressure is against whiteness. Blatant discrimination is outlawed, but more significant, the mechanisms that silently and unobtrusively reproduce privilege along racial fault lines are frustrated.

Perhaps not surprising, whites do not generally experience this dynamic as the introduction of social justice. Where a social identity has been premised upon the subordination of the Other, the normalization of society is experienced as the confiscation of entitlement, rather than equalization. Deeply held assumptions of desert and deservingness are flouted. Much the same dynamic is present in patriarchal societies when the advancement of women is experienced by men as detraction from their manhood, rather than an equitable redistribution of opportunity. In such circumstances, the new dispensation is perceived as aggressive, hostile to an established sense of self and impeding legitimate expectations. The subjective distortion is evident in a comment a fourth-year engineering student recently wrote in his midyear examination: "Over the last decade, South Africa has seen a radical change in the political and economic environment. The governmental priorities have shifted to apparently more pressing areas, such as poverty eradication and housing development, from some of the more basic governmental tasks. One such task is road traffic safety."

In the rest of this chapter, I wish to analyze three main aspects of the subjective South African experience of relinquishing racial privilege: a sense of culture shock; loss of certainty and the concomitant existential questions this raises; and the feelings of vertigo that accompany ideological change.

Culture Shock

I realise that I lived a very sheltered and privileged life. I feel unable to cope with the radical changes that are taking place in SA. I feel guilty about that and try to make amends in my small circle of interaction with people of colour.

—Woman, Cape Town

It is often noted that the past policies of the country prevented South Africans from getting to know each other. This ignorance was, of course, unequal. Black South Africans, as the oppressed, had no option but to learn as much about the oppressor as they could in order to manage their environment. The policy of apartheid, however, can be seen as institutionalized intercultural defense (see Bennett 1993). White South Africans were able to live an extremely ethnocentric existence, largely unaware of the lives and ways of the Other. Where some such awareness did exist, whites maintained their cultural distance through defensive mechanisms such as denigration of African ways and assertion of the superiority of the white ways (see Bennett 1993). As one person put it: "I am only comfortable with blacks and coloureds who also like Shakespeare, Brahms, Van Gogh, privacy and punctuality."

The knowledge that whites did have of Africans in the past was largely "cultural knowledge"—misinformation and negative stereotypes that circulated in the society more or less unchallenged. Additionally, the unequal power of the master-servant relationship enabled this state of denial to persist despite quite extensive personal contact. In these interculturally undemanding circumstances, whites could experience themselves as benign, even generous, despite the fact that they were implicated in an oppressive system. Provided the psychological distance was maintained, the racist underpinnings of white identity may not have been mobilized into aggression and could remain mostly out of individual awareness.

This comforting state of ignorance is characteristic of privilege; it is also one of the first casualties when a position of social control is lost. The changes taking place since 1994 have placed whites in a situation in which difference is suddenly "in their face." The existence of other ways of making sense of issues, fundamentally challenging to the white perspective, is impossible to deny. Moreover, as black South Africa works through its internalized oppression and gains confidence, whites are increasingly confronted with African views on differences in language and cultural activities within the country, and with interpretations of history and political events that are generally sympathetic to African experience. Difference is being encountered more on its own terms, and the certainties of old constructions of self and reality are threatened. Clearly, this is a fundamental challenge to white world view and identity, and the experience amounts to profound culture shock. In the words of another Capetonian: "I have been exposed only to Western culture although I have dabbled in Eastern philosophies and religions. I know very little about black customs and culture."

Generally, when planned training takes place in the area of intercultural learning, a skilled facilitator will be careful to balance the level of challenge in terms of the process that learners are put through and the content of the material presented. According to Bennett (1994), if one applies the model of intercultural training to what is happening to whites in South Africa, one could argue that the previous dispensation presented a low challenge in terms of both process (the kinds of interaction required) and content (the amount and accuracy of what whites needed to know about the Other). In such circumstances, learners rest— they can be quite complacent and there is little incentive to change. This low-challenge situation was converted quite suddenly into circumstances where whites are confronted by high challenge in terms of both process and content. White South Africans now work with Others as equals, sometimes superiors, and different attitudes and behaviors are expected of them. Moreover, changes are occurring within many different domains of South African society, each of which requires citizens to make adjustments. This means that the process of adaptation is very stressful, especially as this is not a mere sojourn in a foreign environment—the foreignness pervades the life circumstances they are permanently steeped in, with resultant high levels of anxiety and fatigue.

The Intercultural Training Model referred to above separates content and process. In life, of course, the dichotomy between process and content is blurred. As whites live day-to-day in the democratizing society, the knowledge constructions that guided action quite comfortably in the old regime no longer match the emerging society. The colonial knowledge constructions of Africa and Africans, which were the stock in trade of white cultural knowledge of the Other, systematically reproduced disdain for, and fear of, the African continent and its people (Steyn 1999). To the extent that whites hold onto these views, they experience profound dissonance in their new circumstances. White South Africans have to revise their knowledge constructions of those who are now in power, as well as of themselves as the previous benefactors of the apartheid regime. "Interacting with black acquaintances has made me feel less important. Humbler," a man confesses. This revision of knowledge structures has to happen while whites already function interdependently with those very people of whom they are largely ignorant and fearful. Trust, and faith in one's future, are difficult when one has been so poorly skilled for the reality one is to encounter.

The Intercultural Training Model predicts that learners who find the learning curve too steep may leave either physically or psychologically, through withdrawal from the process. In South Africa, this flight is paralleled quite closely in the steady flow of white emigration from the country. Because of the supranational nature of white racialization, whites can emigrate to countries where white identity is more supported, where the parameters of white world view remain more intact.

Whichever course whites take to reduce the dissonance, they need greater congruence between themselves and the environment in which they live. It means coming to grips with feelings of loss and relinquishing old certainties. Certain existential questions seem to predominate in this process of reframing what it means to be white in the new South Africa.

The next sections discuss four of these questions: Where is home? Can I share control? What is my role? And how does this all reflect on me?

Where Is Home?

It feels strange to have a government which does not have the white people's prosperity at heart, but wants to change everything to the advantage of the other people.
—Man from the Northern Province

As the preceding analysis has demonstrated, the changes in the political dispensation of the country have changed the psychological and cultural space in which the inhabitants of the country live. For many whites, the changes have made them feel out of place. There is a loss of the familiar, of the certain, of well-known roles, of comfort zones. "Home" is not only a physical place, it is a location that feels culturally congruent and supportive of a "secure, safe, familiar, protected, and homogenous identity" (Martin and Mohanty 1987). This entails a psychological space that would also support collective knowledge constructions, even projection and repression if they clearly demarcate "us" from "them." "Home" has become unfamiliar, even alien, now that it is no longer protected white space—the group areas of the mind are now more difficult to maintain. Subjectively, this can be experienced as a form of displacement. As one man expressed it: "There is no room for us anymore in our own country."

There are, of course, different ways out of this dissonance. For some, the solution is to relocate physically, to where, whatever the challenges of adaptation may be, the dominant ethos nevertheless requires a less radical self-redefinition. They seek countries where the basic building blocks of "white," "Western," and "European" (often English-speaking) remain mostly intact. A friend who has subsequently emigrated to England, wrote: "I look to overseas to develop a reputation as a scientist and teacher. . . . The climate does not feel supportive here, and I think it will become less so."

For others, the solution lies in establishing a "home" within the country. The Afrikaner Volksfront, for example, firmly believes that the only way to satisfy the Afrikaner's identity needs is to provide a physical piece of land in which self-determination can be pursued. For yet others, it seems safest to open up the privileged space of whiteness somewhat, forming an alliance with coloreds and Indians who in effect become "whitened" in the process and help to buffer the zone of privilege.

Alternatively, white South Africans have to reframe their identity in such a way that it is more congruent with the new South Africa. This requires rejecting many of the tenets of the colonial narratives that informed white South Africa and taking a different stance toward Africa and Africans, toward oneself as part of Africa. It requires a willingness to be more experimental, trying on new roles and moving beyond the culturally tried and tested toward a more heterogeneous identity. It requires, in short, forging a more complex self that will feel more "at home" in a country that is redefining itself as African. One young man expresses this desire: "I realise I need to understand and identify different cultures of people I meet and marry it with my own. I certainly feel part of a richer culture now than ever before."

Can I Share Control?

> At a political level I am very happy, very pleased that SA has begun a process of change towards, I hope, normalcy! Interpersonally, I feel marginal, insecure and isolated.
>
> — A Capetonian

Closely linked with the loss of "home" is a sense of loss of autonomy. In the old order, dependence on the Other was kept out of sight. Those who were in power could believe that the way that they defined self and Other, political agendas, and social situations was reality. Economically, whites set the terms of production and organized labor practice. Certainly on the face of it, they determined their own circumstances.

The situation now is such that they have to take into account other perceptions — perceptions that have considerable power and may name their behavior, interpret their past, or set terms for their future. Other views may affect the parameters of their selfhood, and influence their economic prospects. In short, whites have to negotiate the way ahead in a more dialogic manner. The interdependence of whites and Africans in the new South Africa is visible, undeniable, and increasingly balanced in power. Subjectively, rather than being experienced as establishing mutuality, this loss of control can be experienced as oppression, as denial of the right to self-determination and of a reasonable claim to autonomy.

Moving beyond this subjective interpretation is particularly difficult in a context where one has been taught to fear deeply that which one now has to trust in order to enter a more dialogic relationship. Whites in South Africa have been taught to dismiss Africans' judgment and their ability to run affairs and to disregard their opinions and views. The dominant structure of feeling toward Africa and Africans has been a deep-seated Afro-pessimism. With such a mindset, entrusting one's future here is to be a helpless victim as the country descends into chaos and becomes increasingly "Third World," and as one's resources are sucked into the bottomless financial demands of Africa.

What Is My Role?

> Being white means that I am part of the culture that has developed SA socially and economically and has created an orderly way of life which appears to be what the blacks want—perhaps the presence of whites will help the attainment of blacks' goals without too much disruption.
>
> —Man from Gauteng

Until recently, the Eurocentric assumption has been that history making is the domain of the white male. White men took the important decisions that shaped policy and society, steering the course that events would follow. They were able, largely, to bring about their own desires, to mold their milieu in their own image. Since 1994, whites have moved off center stage and occupy a more supportive role, maintaining some capacity to influence the contours of things to come. For those who are accustomed to centrality, this relativization is experienced as being marginalized. The acute feelings of being sidelined and irrelevant are, of course, a function of how accustomed whites have been to power and influence, rather than an accurate account of the reaches of their peripherality. Whites occupy positions of power way beyond their proportional slice of the population, especially through their economic power.

Linked to this issue is the fact that the old order guaranteed the legitimacy of the role of whiteness in South African society. In the self-constructions on which white identity is based, legitimacy was inherent in Europe's role in relation to Others. As the bearer of the "essence" of progress, development, cultural achievement, and scientific advancement, Europe "naturally" had the task of bringing cultural improvement, good governance, and development to Africa, which lacked this essence and was trapped in backwardness (Blaut 1993). The economic advantage that gravitated to whites was the "natural" consequence of this role. To sustain this relationship, all parties needed to believe that Africans could not take charge successfully. At the heart of whiteness in South Africa, there is a secret investment in the backwardness of Africa and Africans. White South Africans believed that they were holding the country together, ensuring that it remained well governed and that commerce and industry would flourish.

The (relatively) peaceful revolution that the country underwent has placed people in government that do not accept this basis of white legitimacy. Africans have moved onto center stage and have taken control of the political processes. One of the tenets of the struggle philosophy was that the minority white government was illegitimate, not a government that represented the people's interests. This does not amount to a rejection of the role that white South Africans can play in building the country. Pragmatic common sense recognizes that harnessing the skills, knowledge, and resources concentrated in white hands is necessary for the stability of the country in the short term, and its growth and prosperity in the longer term. Moreover, the policy of the ruling party emphasizes the need for inclusivity, based on nonracialism.[3] Legitimacy in this context comes from being willing to participate in, and be part of, the project of building a fairer society, a society that believes in the intrinsic value of all its members, Africans and Westerners. The notion of an African renaissance,[4] which sees Africa as the center of its own regeneration after centuries of colonial exploitation, is an important ideological counter to the assumptions of the European Diffusion Model, and therefore to the reproduction of whiteness. The implication is that there is no essential reason why Africa should not generate the impetus and provide the talent for prosperity. It needs appropriately enabling circumstances, as opposed to the disabling dynamics of the past.

A crucial barometer in the development of white identity in South

Africa is the stance that whites will take to this notion of African renaissance. The resistance among those who wish to maintain the status quo is clear in this comment of a caller to a radio talk show on SAFM, *Talk at Will*: "Africa can't have a renaissance—the term refers to rebirth. In the context of Europe, there was an ancient civilization which was the inspiration for the reawakening. Africa doesn't have that. How can we talk about a rebirth in this context?"

How Does All This Reflect on Me?

> I was a puppet of circumstances—I did not milk the system because I was white.
>
> —Man from Stellenbosch

Those who have written about identity formed within conditions of structured privilege have commented on the "surplus morality" that is appropriated to the self (Memmi 1990). Through mechanisms such as blaming the victim, people with power can be thoroughly exploitative, and yet maintain their belief that they hold the moral high ground. In the old order, white self-constructions were often self-congratulatory: dignity, distinction, and status were integral to whiteness. Whiteness was a form of quality-assurance of worthiness.[5]

One of the most difficult aspects of living in the new South Africa for whites is that the moral reprehensibility of the white system that preceded the new government has been clearly demonstrated and is difficult to defend. There is very little to pin self-respect onto now that the previously voiceless are telling their stories. The Truth and Reconciliation Commission has brought to public consciousness the dark side of whiteness—the underbelly has been exposed. However they may try to escape the pain, whites have to deal with feelings of guilt for that which has been done in their name, a guilt that is inextricably tied up with being white in this society. The difficult part is to be honest about how seductive the benefits were. A woman expressed this openly in response to a question: "One has to fight the eternal sense of guilt of being part of something one didn't really believe in, but was passive to some extent in responding to."

Frankenberg (1993) found that power avoidance was a salient characteristic of white discourse in the United States, where whites use discourses of color blindness to evade acknowledging their implication in unequal power relations. White discourses in South Africa certainly reflect that evasion, but there is also a pervasive need to deny guilt. The desire to establish innocence is unmistakable. Many commentators have observed that an inquirer is hard-pressed to find anyone who supported apartheid in South Africa. Even the Truth and Reconciliation Commission allows a loophole. White South Africans can maintain that the apartheid government officials, police and military office bearers, as a small group of active perpetrators, are the ones who "did" apartheid. They themselves "didn't know" and therefore do not bear any culpability. Those who opposed the regime often claim considerably more credit than they are entitled to, as if white liberal opposition was the decisive factor in bringing about the fall of the old government.

In all cases, the impulse is to underplay personal involvement in, and profit from, the old system. To admit that one had been implicated would be tantamount to recognizing that some sort of reparation is in order, and this is antipathetic to preserving privilege (see Farred 1997). A respondent acknowledges this embroilment: "Being white means that one has to come to terms with the possibility that some form of expiation is required on one's part; and also the fact that one is no longer more privileged and may conceivably be less so in the future."

One of the many strategies employed by "white talk" [6] is to represent issues in equalizing terms, thereby underplaying the need for some sort of special adjustment on the part of whites. An often-heard lament at diversity workshops is: "We've all been damaged by apartheid." True as this is, it does not reflect the qualitative difference in the experience—while we may all have been damaged, we did not all suffer. Strategies such as the above indicate how discourses of privilege can be difficult to pin down. At one level the comment seems reconciliatory, yet it disguises that the hardest emotional work is still being left to those who were oppressed. In this case, the "me-too" appeal to having been damaged is exactly an appeal to be exonerated from the implications of deeper self-examination.

The third dimension of subjective experience of loss of privilege that this chapter analyzes can be called a sense of vertigo. The disorientation results from having placed faith in certain ideological underpinnings that provided a sense of reality and identity, and then being confronted with a changed reality that disconfirms this ideology.

Ideological Vertigo

In recent times it has become a battle to live a normal life.
—School pupil, Karoo

The function of ideology is to provide a "logic" for human society. It furnishes a script that lays out the appropriate positioning of groups relative to each other and presents an interpretation of where society is heading, and why. This chapter has emphasized that whiteness is built upon certain ideological underpinnings. The subjective experience of losing white privilege in South Africa is clearly a function both of the objective extent of the "fall," as well as of people's immersion in the ideology that propped up the old order. For those who are gripped by the ideology, the "fall" is traumatic, challenging the very foundation of their reality. Those whose faith in the ideology is less fundamentalist in tenor are able to process the change a great deal more comfortably and are more likely to have a realistic understanding of their new context.

As long as the ideological assumptions are in place, the underlying, unconscious logic that informs the white position will be that attempts to achieve greater equity in the society are assaults on their reasonable expectations for a "normal" life. While few would acknowledge it in such bald terms, the inequality of the old order, with its concomitant poverty and human indignity, though unfortunate, at least felt *logical*. The present situation therefore seems to be an inversion of common sense. A sixteen-year-old schoolgirl articulates this vertigo: "I feel that being white is now to be oppressed. The racism is inverted."

If the ideology is strongly enough rooted, "white talk" will write off contradictory circumstances as proof of the illogicality, impropriety, and illegitimacy of the new order, thus protecting a white world view. "The problem with them is that they have developed a culture of entitlement. They think they should get everything, whether they have worked for it or not." With these words, taken from an informal conversation, a middle-aged woman indicates how the deep-seated assumption of *white* entitlement is being violated. This assumption is "normal" and therefore she is not fully aware of it. In effect, her argument is that "their" claim to advancement is outrageous, exactly because she does not believe they are entitled to a different place in the new society. The loss of white privilege, on the other hand, is outrageous, precisely because whites have actually always been correctly placed. In other words, "they" want "our" place. Her comment reflects no insight into the structural advantage that fostered the culture of entitlement to which she subscribes, a license that ensured that superior employment would gravitate toward her people more or less regardless of individual merit and enabled assets to be passed on over generations, steadily accumulating wealth.

The above illustrates the sense of inversion experienced when the new reality does not match the old ideology; yet for those whose idiom is "white talk," the new society can provide evidence of the validity of the ideology. Reports about crime, violence, maladministration, and corruption seem to confirm what many whites feel they always knew about "them," drawing on colonial constructions of the nature of Africa and Africans. Insofar as such expectations are confirmed, the world at least retains some vestiges of logical coherence and psychological familiarity. Yet the only long-term prospect for coming to terms with the loss of privileged positioning is seeing the ideology for what it is, and being prepared to let it go.

Conclusion

The privileges of whiteness are constructed from a position of power. The issue for those who cling to the belief that privilege is their due becomes how to hold onto the privilege, once the power has started to sap away. We can expect that many white South Africans will attempt to reframe their roles in South African society in a way that superficially will meet the demands of the new South Africa, while leaving the privileges substantially intact. After all, the ideology of white privilege has proven to be protean in its ability to configure, and to reconfigure, under different and changing circumstances, while keeping its fundamental tenets in place. Yet it is still true that the circumstances in South Africa, where white power has been decentered, are some of the most promising in the contemporary world to deconstruct whiteness. Any intervention that aims to achieve this goal, however, needs to consider the subjective experience of the loss of privilege.

In current jargon, white people need to be helped to make a paradigm shift. This paradigm shift would entail moving from the ethnocentric positions of denial, defense, and minimization of difference that enable blindness, indifference, and lack of engagement to continue. The analysis presented in this chapter suggests that in South Africa, deconstructing whiteness can only take place if whites can be taken to the point where they take the processes of (de)racialization seriously. While to some extent the very nature of the changing society will probably advance such a process for many of its white citizens, the process will succeed best if it is consciously facilitated.

It would mean, first, that white South Africans must acknowledge the extent to which they have benefited from the old order. The Truth and Reconciliation Commission notwithstanding, few whites have actually admitted their own investment in the inequity of the past and shy from taking this significant step of leveling with themselves and their fellow citizens. Second, deconstructing whiteness in the South African context entails developing a critical understanding of the powerful colonial discourses that shaped the history of the country and the social identities of its peoples, giving sanction to deeply exploitative relationships. Whites need to develop a view of Africa and Africans that counters notions of cultural inequivalence and rejects any hidden agenda that perpetuates inequality. Finally, whites have to be encouraged to see it as their brief within the new South Africa to take the socioeconomic realities of others seriously, and to direct their energies away from protecting the privilege of some, to promoting development for all.

The need for strong political leadership and cultural role models among white South Africans has never been more critical. We must interrogate and resist not only the impulse to guard a turf of white oppositional space that encourages white South Africans to see themselves as victimized and besieged, but also the strategic maneuver to form alliances with other semiprivileged (light-skinned) groups.

It is a paradox of privilege that it can buy its own social and emotional retardation; the failure of humanity that characterized our past may be repeated at another level should white South Africans abdicate their share of responsibility toward reconstructing the society on an equitable footing. This time around, the same excuses of not having access to the means of understanding the issues will not hold water. Invitations to participate in eradicating poverty, to develop a spirit of community, and to join in the hoped-for renaissance of the country and region in ways that benefit all its citizens abound—implicitly and explicitly—in the young democracy. If they take up the offer held out by such new discourses to frame their sense of self into a more complex social identity that is grounded in, and committed to, Africa and its advancement, white South Africans can indeed construct a new social space for themselves, a space to which the benefits of deepening mutuality accrue.

Notes

1. The first use of the metaphor is attributed to Archbishop Desmond Tutu.

2. This is undoubtedly true for all social groupings in the country, and interesting revisionings of identity are taking place in, for example, the colored

community in the country. Many social commentators also point out the difficulty among the African community in discarding identities largely molded within a culture of dependency.

This chapter assumes that "race" is a social construction. To make for easier reading, however, the scare quotes that signal this for terms such as "white," "colored," and "black" will be omitted from here onward, trusting the reader's ear to recognize the tone.

3. Also nonsexism, but my analysis does not examine the gendered nature of whiteness in South Africa.

4. Thabo Mbeki, successor to President Nelson Mandela, is promoting the concept.

5. This is not to discount the discomfort experienced by whites who felt shamed by the apartheid system. Identity formation being as complex as it is, the two are not mutually exclusive.

6. The term I have coined (Steyn 1998b) to refer to the discourses present in white, middle-class South African society that attempt to preserve white privilege. The discourses are marked by cynicism and evidence a great deal of Afro-pessimism.

References

Allen, T. W. 1994. *The Invention of the White Race*. Vol. 1: *Racial Oppression and Social Control*. New York: Verso.

Bennett, J. 1994. "Content and Process: Balancing Challenge," in J. Bennett and M. Paige, eds., *Training Design for International Multicultural Programs*. Portland: Summer Institute for Intercultural Communication.

Bennett, M. J. 1993. "Towards Ethnorelativism: A Developmental Model of Intercultural Sensitivity," in R. M. Paige, ed., *Education for the Intercultural Experience*. Yarmouth, ME: Intercultural Press.

Bhabha, H. 1990. "Interrogating Identity: The Postcolonial Prerogative," in D. Goldberg, ed., *Anatomy of Racism*. Minneapolis: University of Minnesota Press, pp. 283–294.

———. 1994. "Remembering Fanon: Self, Psyche and the Colonial Condition," in P. Williams and L. Chrisman, eds., *Colonial Discourse and Post-Colonial Theory: A Reader*. New York: Columbia University Press, pp. 498–516.

Blaut, J. M. 1993. *The Colonizer's Model of the World: Geographical Diffusionism and Eurocentric History*. New York: The Guilford Press.

Brantlinger, P. 1985. "Victorians and Africans: The Genealogy of the Myth of the Dark Continent." *Critical Inquiry* 12: 166–203.

Delgado, R., ed. 1995. *Critical Race Theory: The Cutting Edge*. Philadelphia: Temple University Press.

Dyer, R. 1988. "White." *Screen* 29: 44–65.

———. 1997. *White*. London: Routledge.

Fanon, F. 1990 [1952]. "The Fact of Blackness," in D. Goldberg, ed., *Anatomy of Racism*. Minneapolis: University of Minnesota Press, pp. 108–126.

———. 1994 [1963]. "On National Culture," in P. Williams and L. Chrisman, eds., *Colonial Discourse and Post-Colonial Theory: A Reader.* New York: Columbia University Press, pp. 298–516.

Farred, G. 1997. "Bulletproof Settlers: The Politics of Offence in the New South Africa," in M. Hill, ed., *Whiteness: A Critical Reader.* New York: New York University Press, pp. 63–78.

Fishkin, S. F. 1995. "Interrogating 'Whiteness,' Complicating 'Blackness': Remapping American Culture." *American Quarterly* 47, no. 3: 428–466.

Frankenberg, R. 1993. *White Women, Race Matters: The Social Construction of Whiteness.* Minneapolis: University of Minnesota Press.

Gallanger, C. A. 1997. "White Racial Formation: Into the Twenty-First Century," in R. Delgado and J. Stefanic, eds., *Critical White Studies: Looking Behind the Mirror.* Philadelphia: Temple University Press, pp. 6–11.

Guillauman, C. 1995. *Racism, Sexism, Power, and Ideology.* New York: Routledge.

Hyde, C. 1995. "The Meanings of Whiteness." *Qualitative Sociology* 18, no. 1: 87–95.

JanMohammed, A. R. 1985. "The Economy of Manichean Allegory: The Function of Racial Difference in Colonialist Literature." *Critical Inquiry* 12: 59–87.

Lipsitz, G. 1995. "The Possessive Investment in Whiteness: Racialized Social Democracy and the 'White' Problem in American Studies." *American Quarterly* 47, no. 3: 369–387.

———. 1998. *The Possessive Investment in Whiteness: How White People Profit from Identity Politics.* Philadelphia: Temple University Press.

Martin, B., and C. T. Mohanty. 1987. "Feminist Politics: What's Home Got to Do with It?" in T. De Lauretis, ed., *Feminist Studies: Critical Studies.* Bloomington: Indiana University Press.

Martin, J. M., R. L. Krizek, T. N. Nakayama, and L. Bradford. 1996. "Exploring Whiteness: A Study of Self-Labels for White Americans." *Communication Quarterly* 44, no. 2: 125–144.

Marx, A. W. 1998. *Making Race and Nation: A Comparison of South Africa, the United States, and Brazil.* Cambridge: Cambridge University Press.

Maurice, E. 1980. "School Protests Started in 1890." *The Argus*, June 5.

Memmi, A. 1990 [1957]. *The Colonizer and the Colonized.* H. Greenfield, trans. London: Earthscan Publications.

Morrison, T. 1992. *Playing in the Dark: Whiteness and the Literary Imagination.* Cambridge, MA: Harvard University Press.

Nakayama, T. K., and R. L. Krizek. 1995. "Whiteness: A Strategic Rhetoric." *Quarterly Journal of Speech* 8, no. 3: 291–310.

Nederveen Pieterse, J. 1992. *White on Black: Images of Africa and Blacks in Western Popular Culture.* New Haven: Yale University Press.

Omi, M., and H. Winant. 1994. *Racial Formation in the United States: From the 1960s to the 1990s.* New York: Routledge.

Roediger, D. R. 1991. *The Wages of Whiteness: Race and the Making of the American Working Class.* New York: Verso.

———. 1994. *Toward the Abolition of Whiteness: Essays on Race, Politics and the American Working Class.* New York: Verso.

Said, E. W. 1979. *Orientalism*. New York: Vintage Press.
Stam, R., and E. Shohat. 1994. "Contested Histories: Eurocentrism, Multiculturalism, and the Media," in D. T. Goldberg, ed., *Multiculturalism: A Critical Reader*. Cambridge, MA: Blackwell Publishers, pp. 296–324.
Steyn, M. E. 1996. "Whiteness Just Isn't What It Used to Be: White Identity in the New South Africa." Master's thesis, Arizona State University.
———. 1998a. "Who Are You and What Have You Done with the Real Hottentots? The Legacy of Contested Colonial Narratives of Settlement in the New South Africa," in J. N. Martin, T. K. Nakayama, and L. A. Flores, eds., *Readings in Cultural Contexts*. Mountain View, CA: Mayfield, pp. 104–113.
———. 1998b. "Seeing Through Whiteness: An Ethnography of Privilege." Paper presented at the national conference of the South African Anthropological Association. Irene Park, Pretoria.
———. 1999. "Whiteness in Context: A Personal Narrative," in T. K. Nakayama and J. Martin, eds., *Whiteness: The Communication of Social Identity*. Thousand Oaks, CA: Sage, pp. 264–278.
Steyn, M. E., and K. B. Motshabi, eds. 1996. *Cultural Synergy in South Africa: Weaving Strands of Africa and Europe*. Randburg, South Africa: Knowledge Resources.
Thornton, R. 1996. "The Potentials of Boundaries in South Africa: Steps Towards a Theory of the Social Edge," in R. Werbner and T. Ranger, eds., *Postcolonial Identities in South Africa*. London: Zed Books, pp. 136–161.
Wander, P. C., J. N. Martin, and T. K. Nakayama. 1999. "Whiteness and Beyond: Sociohistorical Foundations of Whiteness and Contemporary Challenges," in T. K. Nakayama and J. N. Martin, eds., *Whiteness: The Communication of Social Identity*. Thousand Oaks, CA: Sage, pp. 13–26.
Wray, M., and A. Newitz, eds. 1997. *White Trash: Race and Class in America*. New York: Routledge.

5

Dance of Deception: A Reading of Race Relations in Brazil

Abdias do Nascimento and Elisa Larkin Nascimento

WHEN SOUTH AMERICA was still, to Europeans, a far-fetched hypothesis of adventurers and dreamers confirmed only by information coming out of Africa,[1] Spain and Portugal were already dividing up the continent. By the terms of the Tordesillas Treaty of 1494—a kind of early Berlin Conference in Iberian royal style—the Portuguese landed themselves the largest territory, virtually a subcontinent, comparable in area to the United States,[2] seven times the size of South Africa,[3] and dwarfing all the other nations of the region. It is a territory of fabulous natural wealth, beginning with the soil itself, which "when one plants, will grow anything,"[4] and a subsoil brimming with precious metals. Waterways, forests, and huge expanses of fertile land sweep the Amazon, the Pantanal, and numerous other diverse regions; abundant fauna await the fisherman's net and the sportsman's hunt. In modern terms, the country harbors the world's greatest biodiversity.

With such a material base to build upon and a current population of almost 166 million, it is hardly surprising that today Brazil is routinely cited high on the list of future world powers. It has a solid industrial base, a modernized agricultural capacity, and an expanding tertiary sector highly attractive to foreign investment. Powerful armed forces, satellite and space technology, nuclear power capacity, abundant hydro-electric resources, natural gas, and renewable fuel developed from sugar cane alcohol can be counted as only a few showcases of Brazil's enormous richness of resources. Yet they exist side by side with scenes of backwardness in which time seems to have halted ages ago, with human progress banned by the squalid poverty of "Barren Lives."[5]

Such contrasts cannot be understood without taking into account their racial dimension: the "barren lives" of Brazil are overwhelmingly nonwhite. While the roots of inequality have much in common with those in other developing countries, there are singularities that shape and influence their contours and the perspectives for policies designed to address them. In the case of racial inequality in Brazil, as compared with the United States and South Africa, the outstanding singularity is the absence of racial segregation by law and the accompanying national culture of "racial democracy" that has acted as a smoke screen to mask very stark racial inequities.

Inequality in Brazil: A General Picture

Wilmot James's description of South African economic development (Chapter 2) fits Brazil like a glove: its "economic progress in the twentieth century has been a compound of oppressive exploitation and rational-technical advance." Albeit commanding an advanced position in terms of economic development—ranked among the top ten economies in the world—Brazil compares unfavorably with its neighbors in terms of social development (Table 5.1). In 1995, its per capita gross internal product was significantly lower than Argentina's or Uruguay's but three times higher than Paraguay's. Yet, 43 percent of Brazilian households were poverty-stricken, a proportion higher than in Paraguay and more than four times greater than in Argentina and Uruguay (Cruz 1998: pp. 27–28). Brazil had the lowest literacy rate and by far the highest mortality rate among children under five years of age: fifty deaths per thousand, as opposed to about eighteen per thousand

Table 5.1 Comparative Data for Mercosur Countries

	Argentina	Brazil	Paraguay	Uruguay
Area (thousands of km)	2,737	8,457	397	175
Population	35,219,612	157,871,980	4,959,713	3,146,200
Gross Domestic Product Per Person	$5,120	$3,370	$1,148	$6,550
Domiciles in Poverty	10.0%[a]	43.0%	41.0%	7.0%
Literacy	96.2%	79.9%	91.2%	98.0%
Child Mortality Rate	25.3	50.2	29.0	24.4
Monthly Minimum Wage	$400.00	$108.00	$234.00	$88.00

Source: CEPAL 1995; Cruz 1998, pp. 28–29.
Notes: a. Urban only. GDP in constant 1990 U.S. dollars; deaths per thousand for children under 5; after the February 1999 currency crisis, the value of the minimum wage in Brazil dropped to less than that cited here for Uruguay—about US$75.00 by the end of 1999; Mercosur is a "common market" in Central and South America.

among African Americans in the United States (Asante and Mattson 1991: p. 166). The minimum wage was about four times lower than that of Argentina and less than half that of Paraguay. The value of the monthly minimum wage at this writing is equivalent to about US$75.00, more than ten times below what is defined as poverty in the United States.

Brazil in 1999 ranked after only Sierra Leone with the second most inequitable income distribution in the world;[6] income concentration consistently has increased over time (Tables 5.2, 5.3, and 5.4). Equally

Table 5.2   Distribution of National Income in Brazil, 1960–2000 (by percentages)

	1960	1970	1980	1990	2000
Poorest 50%	18%	15%	14%	12%	11%
Richest 20%	54	62	63	65	64
Inequality index	3	4.1	4.5	5.4	5.8

Source: IPEA/IBGE; Mantega 1998, 1999, projection for 2000.

Table 5.3   Inequality Index for Brazil, 1981–1995

Proportion of Income for	1981	1985	1988	1990	1993	1995
Poorest 10%	0.78	0.76	0.59	0.58	0.38	0.43
Poorest 20%	2.5	2.4	2.0	2.0	1.8	1.9
Poorest 30%	5.0	4.8	4.2	4.1	4.1	4.2
Poorest 40%	8.4	8.0	7.2	7.1	7.4	7.3
Poorest 50%	12.9	12.3	11.2	11.2	11.6	11.6
GINI coefficient	0.59	0.60	0.62	0.62	0.61	0.61

Source: Compiled by the Institute of Applied Economic Research (IPEA) with data from the 1996 National Survey of Domicile Samples (PNAD).

Table 5.4   Composition of Brazil's Gross Domestic Product, 1990–1996 (by percentages)

Year	1990	1991	1992	1993	1994	1995	1996
Capital	33	38	38	35	38	40	41
Labor	45	42	44	45	40	38	38

Sources: IBGE and *Folha de São Paulo;* Mantega 1998.

as important as the abject levels of poverty accentuating this inequality
are the extravagantly high levels of income held by the rich (Roque and
Corrêa 1998: p. 3).

Over time, the poor not only become poorer but are subjected to
ever more desperate living conditions. While an ostentatious minority
elite consumes luxury imports in urban shopping centers, physicians in
rural and poor, urban areas are writing prescriptions for rice, beans, and
milk to cure one of the diseases afflicting most children: hunger.

Racial Inequality in Brazil

Before dealing with the racial aspect of inequality, one must make clear
how racial groups are identified.[7] Official Brazilian census data use two
color categories for African descendants: *preto* (literally, "black") for
the dark-skinned and *pardo* (roughly, mulatto and mestizo) for others.
This distinction has proved so arbitrary and subjective as to be essentially useless, yet it leads those unfamiliar with the Brazilian demographic context to mistake the smaller *preto* group for black. It is now
accepted convention to identify the black population as the sum of the
preto and *pardo* categories, referred to as *negro, afro-brasileiro,* or
afro-descendente. In English, "black," "African Brazilian," and "people
of African descent" refer to this same sum of the two groups. The
"white" and *"pardo"* categories are notoriously inflated, and the *"preto"*
diminished, by the tendency of African-descended interviewees to classify themselves as white or mulatto (Mortara 1970). This fact is essential to our reading of the information presented below.

Racial hierarchy and segregation are etched indelibly in contrasting
landscapes of luxury and privation. African Brazilians in disproportionate numbers live in urban shantytowns called *favelas, mocambos,* or
palafitas. To visit Rio de Janeiro's Central Station[8] is to witness danger-
ously dilapidated trains taking hours to transport mostly black workers
from the huge metropolitan area called the Baixada Fluminense to their
jobs in the capital city, a scene that recalls black South Africans' com-
mute from segregated townships. The racial contrast between a public
school in the Baixada—or in poor suburbs or *favelas* almost anywhere
in Brazil—and a university in a rich area like Rio de Janeiro's Zona Sul
suggests the difference between a township school and a white university in South Africa. Although South Africans have black universities and
had them even under apartheid, African Brazilians have nothing comparable.

While the Baixada Fluminense has been ranked by the World Health Organization as the second most miserable poverty pocket in the world after Bombay, its situation is not exceptional in Brazil; similar scenarios are common throughout the country. For this reason, it provides a representative portrait of inequality.

Almost entirely black, the five Baixada municipalities[9] are also almost entirely sewerless; children play in the stench of open gutters that carry filth through mud-ridden, mosquito-infested streets. They are called "black gutters" (*valas negras*), a characteristically racist expression identifying African-Brazilian people with the untreated sewage to which they are exposed. Leprosy and epidemics of preventable diseases such as dengue remain largely untouched by public policy in these areas. Seventy percent of Baixada children are severely undernourished. The Baixada rivals South African townships not only in poverty but also in violence; more people are killed there by homicide than by automobile accident.

Extremely unbalanced development levels within this immense nation result in enormous regional differences. Perhaps the greatest gap of social inequality separates dwellers in urban areas from miserably poor rural populations of which African Brazilians are the majority (IBGE 1997: p. 46). If the Baixada Fluminense can be compared to South African townships, Brazil's Northeast and Northern regions could be likened to Bantustans. The undercounted Afro-Brazilian group (the sum of the *preto* and *pardo* categories), officially about 45 percent of the overall population, is concentrated at about 70 percent (Table 5.5) in these regions. Here, the practice of slavery generally goes unpunished, and semislavery is by no means uncommon. Assassinations of rural labor union officials and community leaders are routine matters of

Table 5.5 Population Percentage by Color or Race, 1996

	White	*Preta*	*Parda*	Asian	Native Brazilian Indian
Brazil	55.2%	6.0%	38.2%	0.4%	0.2%
Urban North[a]	28.5	3.7	67.2	0.4	0.2
Northeast	30.6	6.1	62.9	0.1	0.2
Southeast	65.4	7.4	26.5	0.6	0.1
South	85.9	3.1	10.5	0.4	0.1
Central-West	48.3	4.0	46.6	0.6	0.5

Source: PNAD 1996; excludes those who did not declare their color.

Note: a. "Urban North" excludes the rural area of Rondônia, Acre, Amazonas, Roraima, Pará, and Amapá States in the northern region.

impunity: about a thousand were actually murdered between 1964 and 1986. Countless other deaths went unrecorded (SBPC 1987).

The tiny Asian group appearing in Table 5.5 (less than 0.5 percent) represents the most recent in a series of immigration waves encouraged by the Brazilian government since the late nineteenth century. Active in agriculture, this mostly Japanese community is concentrated in prosperous rural areas of the Central-West as well as urban centers in the developed Southeast. In the poor Northeast, Asians amount to 0.1 percent of the population. Despite their very recent arrival in comparison with blacks, who have been in Brazil for five hundred years, Asians generally enjoy superior access to education, income, occupation, and housing. Edson Lopes Cardoso (1999) has noted the contrast between two major urban neighborhoods named Liberty: the Asian one in São Paulo, the capital city of São Paulo State (Southeast region), and the African-Brazilian Liberty of Salvador, the capital of Bahia State in the Northeast. In São Paulo, it seems natural that the streets of Liberty are hung with signs saying "wanted: Oriental office boy" or "Japanese clerk required." No one finds it strange that Liberty banks have Asian tellers or its stores have Asian managers. In Salvador's Liberty, bank tellers and store managers are generally white, while any stated preference for blacks in hiring, education, or access to services is indignantly condemned by Bahian society as racist.

Native Brazilian "Indians," original dwellers of this land, have been the victims of genocide in a myriad of forms since colonial times. As a result, they now make up a smaller part of the overall population than Asians, even in the Central-West region where they are most numerous. Living today in hopelessly squalid poverty, deprived of their land and tradition, their youth plagued with suicide in epidemic proportions, Native Brazilians continue their struggle for survival. Over history, they have been alternately despised and romanticized, becoming the symbol of this century's modernist movement among elite urban artists and intellectuals. Its slogan of cannibalism (*antropofagia*) is an appropriate image of how white Brazilian society and culture metaphorically "ate up" and digested what they defined as Native Indian and Afro-Brazilian traditions, producing what they defined as a new "syncretic" modern culture. This self-laudatory image was at once self-deluding. While modernists believed they were rejecting colonial European standards in favor of "more authentic" Native Brazilian and African ones, they in fact understood little if anything of Native Brazilian or African tradition and were merely mouthing slogans newly articulated but Western in essence.

What truly distinguishes Brazil from South Africa or the United States is not so much the nature of social injustice as the ideological dance of deception. Traditionally, analysts have been so enamored of the idea of harmony among races in Brazil as to largely ignore racial inequalities. When acknowledged, they are somewhat unnervingly attributed to what Brazilian intellectuals refer to as "the social question," as opposed to "the racial question." Inequalities of a racial nature are imputed to the historical legacy of slavery, with current or recent discrimination deemed insignificant to their composition. While the existence of "prejudice"—contrary to that of "discrimination"—is recognized, it is seen as merely an aesthetic problem exercising little, if any, influence on social reality.[10]

The power of such ideas has been so central in the articulation of the Brazilian national consciousness as to endow them with a status akin to taboo. Recently, however, the racial nature of inequality progressively has been demonstrated by social-science research,[11] to the extent that today Roque and Corrêa (1998) observe that "two factors of disparity cross over different levels of reproduction of social inequality and have deep roots in Brazilian culture: gender and race."

Gender and Race Disparities

Yet in Brazil the gender distinction cannot be adequately understood without considering race. In the income hierarchy, race is the first determining factor, then gender. White women retain a clearly privileged position in relation to black men, and Afro-Brazilian women are left at the very bottom of the scale for income and job prestige.

Income disparities among racial groups exist regionally. Table 5.7 shows that the North and Northeast, where African Brazilians are the large majority, have the lowest income and economic activity levels in

Table 5.6   Average Earnings by Gender and Race

White men	6.3
White women	3.6
Black men	2.9
Black women	1.7

Source: IBGE 1994.
Note: Expressed in multiples of the monthly minimum wage (the end of 1999, about US$75).

Table 5.7   Income and Inequality Rates by Region

	Average Monthly Income (R$)	Gini Index	Rate of Economic Activity
Brazil	290	0.590	59.1
Urban North[a]	236	0.569	54.9
Northeast	158	0.590	57.9
Southeast	366	0.569	58.1
South	325	0.567	64.6
Central-West	290	0.599	61.6

Sources: IBGE 1997; PNAD 1996.
Notes: Population 10 years of age or over, with or without income; R$ = Real, Brazilian currency. a. "Urban North" excludes the rural area of Rondônia, Acre, Amazonas, Roraima, Pará, and Amapá States in the northern region.

the country and the highest inequality rates (Gini coefficient).[12] Table 5.8, which shows average family income by region, confirms that the regions with majority Afro-Brazilian populations are by far the poorest.

There are also consistent and very significant differences among race or color groups within the regions. For example, in the richer states of the Southeast region, Rio de Janeiro and São Paulo, the incidence of miserable poverty is two to three times as high among blacks as whites (Table 5.9). In the Northeast, the proportion of blacks in miserable poverty is a third higher than that of whites; in the North/Central-West it is more than 60 percent higher.

Table 5.8   Average Family Income, 1996

	Multiples of Minimum Wage					
	2 or less	2 to 5	5 to 10	10 to 20	Over 20	No income
Brazil	22.9%	29.2%	21.0%	12.5%	8.4%	3.7%
Urban North[a]	23.1	31.4	20.7	12.0	6.4	5.1
Northeast	40.6	30.2	11.9	5.4	3.6	5.1
Southeast	14.1	27.4	25.4	16.6	11.4	2.9
South	17.8	30.5	24.9	13.9	8.7	2.6
Central-West	21.7	32.1	20.0	11.5	8.7	4.3

Source: PNAD 1996.
Notes: Expressed in multiples of the monthly minimum wage; excluding those who did not declare income. a. "Urban North" excludes the rural area of Rondônia, Acre, Amazonas, Roraima, Pará, and Amapá States in the northern region.

Table 5.9   Percentage in "Miserable Poverty" by Region and Color, 1998

State/Region	White	Preta[a]	Parda[a]
		Color	
Rio de Janeiro (Southeast)	6.0	12.7	13.8
São Paulo (Southeast)	4.0	12.3	8.7
South	15.2	23.8	27.9
Minas Gerais/Espírito Santo (Southeast)	19.4	37.7	35.1
Northeast	38.5	51.3	49.5
North/Central-West	14.0	26.9	23.2

Source: IBGE, PNAD 1988; special compilations, courtesy of Nelson do Valle Silva/ IUPERJ.
Notes: "Miserable poverty" includes per capita family income up to 1/4 minimum wage. a. *Preta* plus *parda* equals "black."

In Brazil, blacks generally earn less than half as much as whites (Silva 1998). White men earn almost four times as much as Afro-Brazilian women, who earn less than half the value of white women's average income.[13] About 26 percent of blacks, compared to 16 percent of whites, earn less than the minimum wage, while 1 percent of blacks as opposed to 4 percent of whites earn more than ten times the minimum wage. Educated African Brazilians earn less than whites with the same education, and in higher income brackets whites receive about 5.6 times more income than blacks. In all these situations, black men earn more than black women do, but white women earn more than black men do (PNAD 1987).

Table 5.10 shows that fully twice as many blacks (*pretos* plus *pardos*) as whites live in "miserable poverty," earning only up to one-fourth the value of Brazil's monthly minimum wage. The inverse relation prevails at higher income levels; the proportion of whites who enjoy higher incomes is three, four, or five times that of blacks. Only in the group receiving one-half to one minimum wage (earning US$32 to $75 a month) are differences of race or color less accentuated. About one-fourth of each group—whites, *pretos,* and *pardos*—appear in this category, a fact that speaks clearly of poverty levels in Brazil. At the next level up, among those earning US$76 to $152, the proportion of whites is twice as high as that of blacks, a gap that grows as income levels rise.

African-Brazilian women embody the feminization of poverty observed by the women's movement internationally over the last

Table 5.10   Per Capita Family Income by Color, 1988

	Color		
Per Capita Family Income	White	*Preta*[a]	*Parda*[a]
Up to 1/4 minimum wage	14.7%	30.2%	36.0%
1/4 to 1/2 m.w.	19.2	27.4	26.8
1/2 to 1 m.w.	24.2	24.9	20.7
1 to 2 m.w.	20.2	12.0	10.6
2 to 3 m.w.	8.2	2.7	2.9
3 to 5 m.w.	6.5	1.6	1.8
5 to 10 m.w.	4.5	0.8	0.9
10 to 20 m.w.	1.5	0.3	0.2
20 or more m.w.	0.3	0.1	0.0
Total	100%	100%	100%

Source: IBGE, PNAD 1988; special compilations by Nelson do Valle Silva/IUPERJ; courtesy of Nelson do Valle Silva/IUPERJ.

Notes: The minimum wage is approximately US$75 per month. a. *Preta* plus *parda* equals "black."

Table 5.11   Unemployment Rates by Gender and Race, 1996

	Total	Men	Women	White	Black[b]
Brazil	6.9%	5.7%	8.8%	6.6%	7.7%
Urban North [a]	7.7	6	10.2	6.8	8.2
Northeast	6.3	5.2	7.8	5.7	6.5
Southeast	7.7	6.2	9.8	7.4	8.7
South	5.4	4.5	6.6	5.1	8.1
Central-West	7.9	6.2	10.5	7.6	8.7

Source: PNAD 1996.

Notes: Percentage of population 10 years of age or over, with or without income. a. "Urban North" excludes the rural area of Rondônia, Acre, Amazonas, Roraima, Pará, and Amapá States in the northern region. b. *Preto* plus *pardo* equals "black."

decades. Eighty percent of employed black women are concentrated in manual occupations; more than half of these are domestic servants, and the rest are self-employed in domestic tasks (washing, ironing, cooking), among the lowest-paid in the economy. About one in four African-Brazilian female heads of households earns less than half the minimum wage (Castro 1991). These parameters have remained consistent or have worsened over time.[14] Unemployment statistics, indicating higher unemployment rates among blacks, suggest that African-Brazilian women account for more than their share of the extraordinarily high rates among women in general.

Education Disparities

Not only are black families disproportionately concentrated among the poor, but their per capita income levels are lower. Thus, more people in the family must work for equivalent household earnings. Children often leave school to "help the family" by cutting sugar cane, working harvests or mines, or selling candy at traffic signals. Illiteracy rates among African Brazilians are more than double those among whites, and the percentage of blacks with nine years of schooling or more is almost three times smaller than that of whites. According to one study, about two-thirds of African-Brazilian children obtain a basic education, whereas about 85 percent of white children do. Once through elementary school, a black child's chances of going on to secondary school are on the order of 40 percent, whereas a white child's are 57 percent. African Brazilians who graduate from high school have about half the chance of white students to go on to university (Sant'Anna and Paixão 1998: pp. 112–114.)

The following tables give a picture of education and literacy levels by region, gender, and color. Table 5.12 shows that illiteracy rates are by far the highest in the poor and mostly black Northeast, where enrollment rates are lowest; differences between men and women are more accentuated there. According to Table 5.13, differences in education levels are significantly greater between blacks and whites than between men and women in all the regions, a fact confirmed by Table 5.14. Here again, race is more significant than gender. Half as many white women as black women have only one year or less of schooling, while the difference between white men and black men is only slightly smaller. In

Table 5.12   Illiteracy and Enrollment Rates by Region and Gender, 1996

	Illiteracy Rates			Enrollment Rates		
	Total	Men	Women	Total	Men	Women
Brazil	14.7%	14.5%	14.8%	91.2%	90.6%	91.8%
Urban North[a]	11.6	11.2	11.9	92.1	92.1	92.2
Northeast	28.7	31.1	26.6	86.4	84.8	88.0
Southeast	8.7	7.5	9.9	94.1	93.9	94.3
South	8.9	7.8	9.9	93.6	94.1	93.0
Central-West	11.6	11.3	11.8	92.9	92.5	93.4

Source: PNAD 1996.
Notes: Percentage of persons 15 years of age or over. a. "Urban North" excludes the rural area of Rondônia, Acre, Amazonas, Roraima, Pará, and Amapá States in the northern region.

Table 5.13   Average Years of Schooling by Gender and Color, 1996

	Total	Men	Women	White	Black
Brazil	5.3	5.2	5.4	6.2	4.2
Urban North [a]	5.2	4.9	5.4	6.3	4.7
Northeast	3.9	3.6	4.2	4.8	3.5
Southeast	6.0	6.0	6.0	6.6	4.9
South	5.8	5.8	5.8	6.0	4.3
Central-West	5.5	5.2	5.5	6.3	4.7

Source: PNAD 1996.
Notes: Persons 10 years of age or over. a. "Urban North" excludes the rural area of Rondônia, Acre, Amazonas, Roraima, Pará, and Amapá States in the northern region.

Table 5.14   Adult Years of Schooling by Gender and Color, 1996

Years of Schooling	Men			Women		
	White	*Preto*[a]	*Pardo*[a]	White	*Preta*[a]	*Parda*[a]
No school/ less than 1 year	16.2%	24.0%	23.4%	11.2%	25.5%	21.0%
1 to 3 years	17.0	23.8	25.8	15.7	21.4	23.2
4 to 7 years	36.6	33.9	32.0	35.5	32.3	33.7
8 to 10 years	15.6	11.2	10.5	15.3	11.5	11.5
11 to 14 years	14.4	6.1	7.1	16.4	8.2	9.2
15 or more years	6.2	0.9	1.2	5.9	1.1	1.4
Total	100	100	100	100	100	100

Source: PNAD 1996; special compilation by Nelson do Valle Silva/IUPERJ; courtesy of Nelson do Valle Silva/IUPERJ.
Notes: Percentage of persons 20 years old or older. a. *Preto/preta* plus *pardo/parda* equals "black."

this category, as in all the others, the difference between white men and white women (about 30 percent) is significantly smaller than the black/white disparity, and the difference between black men and black women is even less accentuated. In the group with eleven to fourteen years of schooling, the proportion of black men and women is about half that of white men and women, respectively. Black women are slightly more present than black men in the higher-education categories, but this gap is negligible when compared with the difference between blacks and whites—a whopping six times more in the category for fifteen years of education or more.

Public education is notoriously inferior in quality to private schooling, which mostly white, privileged pupils attend. Brazil's military regime, which ruled from 1964 to 1985, was largely responsible for creating this situation. The effects of its education policies far outlasted the dictatorship, eroding or destroying the public school system and turning education over to the private, education-for-profit lobby. Quality public education, which did exist before the 1970s, was virtually erased. Today, the public system of primary and secondary education fails to prepare pupils for university, while gratuitous public university education is available almost exclusively to an elite able to pay expensive tuition at private primary and secondary schools.

Indeed, removing mention of the descendants of India and of "excellent" schooling (even at best, educational standards in Brazil are less than excellent), the following description of South Africa's education system (James and Lever, Chapter 2 of this volume: p. 44) could well have been written to describe Brazil's as a

> schooling system [that] struggles to enroll all eligible pupils, fails to retain the majority of them to secondary level, and offers them a quality of schooling that varies from excellent for a minority to abysmal for the majority. The rapid expansion of tertiary educational involvement by Africans has meant their enrollment in the less technical directions since most schools for African pupils fail to qualify them in mathematics and science. The technical and commercial elite remains predominantly white and Indian as a result.

Disparities in Mortality and Living Conditions

Life expectancy is shorter among blacks than whites, even taking into account differences in income and education levels. While regional differences in infant and child mortality rates are enormous, these rates are significantly higher among blacks in all regions. Perhaps most compelling are racial disparities in living conditions (sewage, garbage collection, treated water) shown in Tables 5.18 and 5.19. Again, they prevail over and above the stark inequalities among regions.[15]

Table 5.15 Life Expectancy at Birth by Race

	1940/50	1970/80
Whites	47.5	66.1
Nonwhites	40	59.4

Source: PNAD 1990, in Bento 1998, p. 61.

Table 5.16   Life Expectancy at Birth by Race, Income, and Education, 1996

	Income		Education	
	Lowest Levels	Highest Levels	1-4 Years	4 Years or More
Whites	59.5	70.4	66.2	72.3
Nonwhites	55.8	63.7	62.2	66.6

Source: PNAD 1996, in Bento 1998, p. 61.

Table 5.17   Child Mortality Rate by Gender and Color, 1996

	Infant Mortality		Child Mortality	
	Male	Female	Male	Female
Brazil	48.0	36.4	65.5	49.7
Urban North[a]	45.2	34.6	—	41.6
Northeast	71.7	60.8	105.7	33.5
Southeast	27.7	17.2	41.4	74.8
South	25.2	14.8	36.2	50.0
Central-West	29.5	19.3	46.1	35.1

	Infant Mortality		Child Mortality	
	White	Black	White	Black
Brazil	37.3	62.3	45.7	76.1
Urban North[a]	—	—	—	—
Northeast	68	96.3	82.8	102.1
Southeast	25.1	43.1	30.9	52.7
South	28.3	38.9	34.8	47.7
Central-West	27.8	42.0	31.1	51.4

Source: PNAD 1996.
Notes: Mortality for children under 5 is estimated from 1993; all rates per person for every 1,000. a. "Urban North" excludes the rural area of Rondônia, Acre, Amazonas, Roraima, Pará, and Amapá States in the northern region.

Disparities in Public Images

School curricula and literature generally depict a white Brazil, omitting or distorting the history and culture of Afro-Brazilians. In the same way,

Table 5.18   Sanitation by Race of Heads of Household, 1996

	Treated Water		Sewage Disposal	
	White	Black	White	Black
Brazil	81.0%	64.7%	73.6%	49.7%
Urban North[a]	63.0	54.8	56.5	41.6
Northeast	64.2	52.6	47.0	33.5
Southeast	89.1	52.6	86.8	74.8
South	77.0	52.6	69.2	50.0
Central-West	72.0	76.8	43.6	35.1

Source: PNAD 1996.
Notes: "Sewage disposal" includes either sewage collection system or septic tank; percentage of heads of households. a. "Urban North" excludes the rural area of Rondônia, Acre, Amazonas, Roraima, Pará, and Amapá States in the northern region.

Table 5.19   Housing Infrastructure by Color, 1996

	Color			
Housing Conditions	White	*Preta*[a]	*Parda*[a]	TOTAL
Domestic garbage collection	70.8%	53.1%	47.8%	61.0%
Piped water	84.2	61.6	56.1	72.1
Electricity	92.1	81.8	78.0	86.1
Rustic homes, one room or accommodation	3.2	11.9	11.6	7.0
Refrigerator	81.0	58.5	54.1	69.4
Television	82.9	64.1	59.4	72.8

Source: PNAD 1996; courtesy of Nelson do Valle Silva/IUPERJ.
Notes: Percentage of inhabitants. a. *Preta* plus *parda* equals "black."

the mass media present an image of Brazil that looks Scandinavian, whereas nearly half the population is of African descent even according to distorted, official statistics. When depicted, African Brazilians are generally stereotyped in subordinate positions. Publicity images with racist connotations have been denounced frequently in recent years.

Stereotype-based discrimination is very concrete in Afro-Brazilian life, especially in the form of police repression. Blacks notoriously are "suspect"; citizens as well as African diplomats, taken for "uppity" Negroes, whose fancy cars could only be stolen, have experienced arbitrary detention. Convictions are disproportionately high among indicted blacks, only one among countless forms of discrimination in the justice system (Oliveira et al. 1998). The homes of *favela* dwellers are routinely invaded by police who often use physical abuse against them. Deaths and injuries among innocent bystanders during police operations are common. Violence against children and adolescents, internationally recognized since the Candelária and Vigário Geral massacres, victimizes African Brazilians in 80 to 90 percent of the cases.

While hotly denied in everyday discussion, job and pay discrimination are well-documented realities (PNDH 1998; Nascimento 1997–1999).[16] Other types of daily discrimination affect blacks in Brazil as in any segregated society. One current form takes place in banks, where automatic metal-detector doors block out black customers in situations where whites routinely would be let in. Also, Afro-Brazilians face frequent unfounded accusations of shoplifting and exceptionally rigorous demands for identification and documentation when paying by check.[17]

Historical Roots of Inequality

Modern Brazil's beginnings lie in the same process that brought into being countries like the United States and South Africa: Europe's heady expansion out of the fifteenth century, Portuguese navigators in the lead, bound to wrench from the lands of indigenous peoples exclusive dominion over the wealth and women of the world.

Portuguese and Spanish colonialists sought less to build a home in a new land than to transfer wealth to Europe. Institutionalized rape of nonwhite women was a fact as basic to structuring these societies as white women's subjugation. From Brazil's beginnings, foreign debt and a production policy based on monoculture and mineral extraction for export set the tone of macroeconomic policies that consistently have bled the nation to this day.

Perhaps the difference that most marks the historical and contemporary presence of Africans in Brazil, compared with the United States, is that Africans and their descendants have constituted the majority of its population, as in the minority white settler regime of South Africa. All of South and Central America have majority populations of indigenous and/or African descent. This fact brings into focus the first agile step in the dance of deception, for the title "Latin" America betrays the imposition, often by violent means, of a European identity on non-Latin peoples. Its companion pirouette, the notion of "discovery" applied to a land of advanced civilizations inhabited over millennia, obscures the process of genocide unleashed against those peoples for centuries. From this process emerged an America that is "Latin" to the extent that its minority white elites have succeeded in repressing its peoples.

Importation of Africans to Spanish and Portuguese colonies began much earlier than in the United States. From 1502 to 1870, South and Central America imported 5.3 million enslaved Africans, with Brazil accounting for 3.6 million. In the same period, some 450,000 Africans were brought into the United States (Chiavenato 1980). Brazil's relative proximity to Africa meant prices so low that it was more profitable to buy a new African than to preserve a slave's health. Africans generally lasted about seven years, after which they were replaced, a procedure not economically sound in the United States. The southern United States' image of slave cabins contrasts sharply with colonial Brazil, where the *senzala* was similar to a landed slave ship, housing hundreds at a time.

Brazil was the last Christian country to abolish slavery in 1888. No measures were taken to integrate new African-descended citizens into the national economy or society. Many stayed on plantations as semi-slaves or moved from *senzalas* to urban hills, forming *favelas*. Some of these had earlier beginnings as Quilombos.[18] Santos (1994, 1996) cogently demonstrates how the nature of slavery's abolition is crucial to the interrelated factors causing and characterizing African Brazilians' exclusion from society.

During colonial and abolitionist periods, the non-Latin majority in South and Central America was generally on the order of three-fifths to two-thirds. In 1872 in Brazil, blacks numbered 6.1 million compared with 3.7 million whites. Abolition brought panic to the ruling elite, which hurried to set about constructing public policies aimed at rubbing out the "black stain" and "purifying the nation's racial stock."[19] The goal announced by the Brazilian delegate to the 1911 Universal Races Congress in London was to eliminate African descendants[20] by the year 2012 (Skidmore 1974: p. 66). The subjugation of women, both white and black, was of course key to this sort of policy planning.

These policies had two cornerstones: (1) massive state-subsidized European immigration under laws excluding undesirable races and (2) cultivation of the whitening ideal based on the subordination of women and the slogan "Marry White to Improve the Race." Here the politics of deception stand out in bold relief. Until very recently in academic research, European immigration was considered by respected analysts (e.g., Prado Jr. 1966) as necessary due to a "lack of qualified labor" to compete in Brazil's fledgling industrial economy. Social science, like society, simply obliterated from the employment equation the majority population of emancipated African Brazilians who, enslaved or free, not only had been responsible for highly skilled labor but also had been "qualified" to operate every technological change hitherto introduced in the economy. The fact is that jobs now went to "more desirable" Europeans whose subsidized arrival was intended to contribute to the "improvement" (the whitening) of Brazilian racial stock (Skidmore 1974).

The majority population of African descent embodied a potential threat to the minority elite's political power that was translated into the discourse of national unity. Combined with notions of pseudo-scientific racism, this discourse established Africanity or blackness as anti-Brazilian. While Brazil has always had Africans, they were transformed into foreigners by an almost exclusively European definition of "national identity."

Between 1890 and 1914, more than 1.5 million Europeans arrived in São Paulo alone, 64 percent with travel fare paid by the state government (Andrews 1991). Meanwhile, stigmatized not only as unqualified but also as dangerous and disorderly (Gomes 1995),[21] black men were virtually excluded from the new industrial labor market. African-Brazilian women went to work for a pittance—if for anything at all besides room and board—as cooks, nursemaids, washerwomen, and street vendors. Afro-Brazilian religious communities,[22] led mostly by black women, made survival and human development possible for Afro-Brazilian people despite police persecution.

Such is the historical backdrop of the severe income, employment, housing, and other disparities affecting African Brazilians today. While not generally characterized by legal mandates (albeit numerous laws did explicitly establish racist policies, including the inscription of eugenics into the 1934 Constitution), these inequalities clearly constitute a stark reality of de facto segregation.

Whitening, Demography, and Color Classifications

In Brazil, as in all of "Latin" America, the culture of whitening (*embranquecimento* or *blanqueamiento*) based on the subjugation of women leads the *mestiçagem/mestizaje* ballet in intricate toesteps around the conviction that Iberian elites created a cordial and harmonious form of race relations (Dzidzienyo 1971). Closely associated are two corollaries: (1) that slavery there was a more benevolent institution,[23] and (2) that the absence of legalized racial segregation and a constitutional provision of equality before the law were sufficient to evidence a nonracist society. Both notions have had enormous impact not only on the Brazilian popular conscience but also on the country's image abroad.[24]

The very existence of the mestizo population has been taken as a final guarantee against the existence of racial discrimination, in contrast to "truly racist" countries such as the United States and South Africa, where the dancers of the racial democracy ballet believe there is no race mixture.[25] Allegations that miscegenation was based on mutual consent for intermarriage or on cordial sexual relations among the races have been unmasked by African-descent writers, who show it as a function of subordinating black women since colonial times.[26]

The notion of harmonious relations in a benevolent slave system is not unlike the rosy portrayals of the antebellum South in U.S. literature and cinema classics. But the "Latin" flavor of *machismo* marks this ideology profoundly, as illustrated in the sweet picture of miscegenation painted, for example, by Pierre Verger (1977: p. 10). He describes how the white sons of plantation owners

> would roam the fields together with the black youngsters who served as their whipping boys but also as their playmates and schoolmates. They adopted African reactions and patterns of behavior. Later on, they would undergo their sexual initiation with the colored girls working in the big house or in the fields, thus infusing elements of sensual attraction and comprehension into their relations with what one has chosen to call persons of different races.

Sexual abuse against subordinated women is a matter of domination, whether in war (from the Roman legions and Atilla the Hun to Bosnia and Kosovo) or in the maintenance of rule by force in colonial or authoritarian regimes. Miscegenation as its fruit says little about comprehension or attraction among human beings, but speaks eloquently of violent control over women. The genius of the Brazilian ideology is to make this violence the meat of self-laudatory discourse in which the white elite purges itself of responsibility for its excesses of oppression.[27] Gilberto Freyre (1940, 1946) is its master. He graphically describes the horrors of torture committed against enslaved Africans, then concludes by leaving such pearls as this one shining against the backdrop of inequality in Brazil:

The crossbreeding so widely practiced here corrected the social distance which otherwise would have remained enormous between plantation mansion and slave quarters. What the large-landholding, slave-
owning monoculture produced in the way of aristocratization,
dividing Brazilian society into classes of masters and slaves, . . . was
in great part neutralized by miscegenation's social effects. Indian and
African women, at first, then mulatto women, the yallers, octoroons
and so on, becoming the white master's domestics, concubines and
even legitimate wives, played a powerful role in Brazil's social
democratization. (Freyre 1969: p. 34)

Such ideas are intricately combined with a social hierarchy of color that
has been defined by African-American intellectuals of the region as *pig-
mentocracy*,[28] in which lighter skin is identified with greater prestige
and economic status. Social reward is offered not only for "improving"
the race but also for rejecting African identity and assuming European
cultural values and criteria of personal beauty.

The social compulsion to whiteness is a common heritage of colo-
Central to this problem are the intricacies of discourse around the
mulatto woman. Her image as a paragon of beauty in the rosy portrayal
of nonracist society has been roundly denounced (Nascimento 1978;
Bennett 1995; Gilliam and Gilliam 1996; Gilliam 1998) as a smoke
screen and an excuse for sexual exploitation. The ultimate aesthetic
ideal in Brazil is really the blue-eyed blonde,[29] who, unlike the mulatto
woman, is not stereotyped as easy or loose. As one traditional saying
goes: "White ladies for marrying, black women to do the work, mulatto
women to fornicate" (Nascimento 1977: p. 46).

The social compulsion to whiteness is a common heritage of colonial regimes, and analysts like Frantz Fanon (1967) and Albert Memmi
(1965) have long since revealed its attendant psychological problems.
Rather than being seen as one of white supremacy's many faces or as a
legacy of colonialism, it is presented as proof positive of Latin
antiracism. The following example eloquently states the ruling elite's
effort to portray Brazil as a white country irrespective of its demographic reality:[30] "the predominance of the white contingent [of the Brazilian
population] is evident, since in Brazil even those of mixed race who
have a small or large amount of Negro or Indian blood, but without one
of these groups' physical traits, are considered white. Which demonstrates the absence of any discrimination of racial nature, in terms of the
person's ethnic origin" (Diegues Jr. 1977: p. 121).

In Brazilian social science, enormous energies are dedicated to this
last proposition: there is an essential difference between rejection of
African color and rejection of African origin. The hypodescendancy criterion[31] is considered racist, whereas "prejudice of mark," pigmentocra-

cy's color criterion, is taken as arbitrary and innocent, a purely aesthetic aversion to the darker phenotype (Nogueira 1955, 1959). Theorists dissociate African phenotype from African origin and conclude that Latinos evolved a "more benign" form of prejudice, nonracial in nature.[32]

The whitening ideology has posed a demographic quandary[33] by pressuring census interviewees to declare themselves in the lighter of three official color categories: *branco* ("white"), *preto* ("black"), or *pardo* ("mulatto"). Statisticians recognize the resulting distortion of population statistics, in which "the *preto* group loses a great deal, the *pardo* group gains much more than it loses, and the white group gains a lot and loses nothing" (Mortara 1970: p. 458).[34] While official statistics put the sum of *pretos* and *pardos* at 48 percent, estimates that take into account their distortion by the whitening ideal are closer to 70 or 80 percent. The category *pardo*, a catchall group used since 1940 to accommodate the extremely subjective classifications used by Brazilians, is widely recognized as awkward and artificial. Yet when interviewees spontaneously classified themselves, the result was citation of 136 different color categories, reflecting the effort of the lighter-skinned not to be classed in the same categories as those any darker in hue (Vieira 1995: p. 27).

Undoubtedly, hegemony belongs to *moreno*, a term that gives full rein to the subjective wanderings of Brazilian color consciousness. It can be used to describe very dark black people or very light mestizos, depending upon the point being made. Generally, the point is to get around saying "black" (*preto* or the more popular *escurinho*), even if the person in question can be placed in a range of color variations that most certainly indicate African origin.

This brings us to the real nature of the plethora of color designations: euphemism. The pejorative connotation of words such as "black" (*negro, preto, escuro*) make almost any of these expressions traditionally an insult; thus, considerable effort is made politely to avoid them. The generally pejorative notion of Africanity is carefully weeded out of Brazilian national identity except in very specific instances such as music, cuisine, religion, and sports. In these cases, it is defined largely by those who did not create it and then displayed as "proof" of racial harmony and tolerance of diversity.[35] Since African identity is still vaguely assessed as a threat to national unity, terms intimately associated with Africanity are avoided partly as a matter of citizenship loyalty.[36] Frequent protests are heard that someone is not black or of African origin, but Brazilian.

Voices and Viewpoints

A major consequence of de facto, as opposed to de jure, discrimination
is that those excluded lose their voice. Indeed, if racism is deemed not
to exist, with what legitimacy can its targets' voice be raised? White
spokesmen have assumed and been granted the legitimacy to speak for
blacks. Challenging this procedure traditionally is considered "reverse
racism."

The following illustrative exchange (*Cadernos Brasileiros* 1968:
pp. 70–72) took place between this senior author and Clarival do Prado
Valladares, a member of the white Bahian elite who in 1966 represented
Brazil at the First International Festival of Black Arts in Daka.[37] Here
he was acting as moderator of a 1968 panel on abolition:

> Nascimento (N): . . . in the Federal Council of Culture, of which the
> Moderator is one of the members, we do not see one Black representa-
> tive of Black culture.
>
> Valladares (V): But sir, you see in the Federal Council of Culture
> men very concerned with Negro Culture in Brazil, authors of defini-
> tive works.
>
> N: Perfect, but I think the Black people also have the right, them-
> selves, to advocate their own problems.
>
> V: The Negro in Brazil is not represented only by pigmentation:
> the Negro in Brazil is Brazil. . . . I believe that I have, more than the
> most pigmented of people, the consciousness of a Brazil with its
> Negro values; I have struggled for them and also dedicate myself to
> the biography of those values. . . . If the Federal Council of Culture
> does not have characteristically a Negro by epiderm, it has someone
> who is zealously vigilant of Negro culture.
>
> N: Perfect. I think that is formidable and I thank Your Excellency,
> but this precisely confirms the eternal . . . process of Brazilian pater-
> nalist racism.

That this issue does not belong to an obsolete, if recent, past was
graphically driven home in 1996, when the Ministry of Justice sponsored a groundbreaking event on affirmative action.[38] In the plenary
sessions, Brazilian "experts" on race relations, nearly all of them white,
joined African-American affirmative-action specialists from the United
States as panelists.[39] Some of the affirmative-action specialists (Gilliam
1998) found themselves uncomfortably sharing the podium with
authors publicly contested by African-Brazilian intellectuals and
activist in the antiracist movement. Ironically, these intellectuals and
activists formed the great majority of the audience. Prominent anthropologist Roberto da Matta addressed this audience, declaring that racial

democracy, even though it had not been fully realized, was "a generous idea. . . . After all, *each of us* have had, from childhood, at least one black friend whose affection we have cultivated throughout our lives." The audience might have asked, "Each of who?" Da Matta's statement was a crystal clear expression of the racial identity implicitly assumed by "Brazilian society's" spokesmen when considering questions of race, particularly when speaking from the lofty heights of academic authority.

As Ghanaian scholar Anani Dzidzienyo (1995: p. 355) has observed: "The success of [Afro-Brazilian] struggle ultimately hinges on the *legitimacy of a black perspective* in national public discourse" (emphasis added). The criteria used to organize this event made it clear that the white perspective still prevails.

Correcting the Record

Never has the Afro-Brazilian voice been silenced. The history of Africans' fight for freedom and against discrimination in Brazil is intense and extensive, covering the entire national territory and history,[40] albeit excluded from conventional versions still taught in the nation's schools. While this chapter is not the place to document this history,[41] a few remarks are in order to restore the balance in favor of the Afro-Brazilian voice.

Whatever the tendency to invoke the "social question" or the color criterion, race is paramount to African Brazilians; the effect of de facto or color discrimination on their living conditions is equivalent to that of de jure or racial discrimination.[42]

More important, as Dzidzienyo (1995: p. 345) notes: "race relations . . . can be understood only in the context of the power relations involved. Indeed, it is precisely the dimension of power and its unequal distribution that frames race relations throughout the Americas." Gains won by the Afro-Brazilian movement in the context of power relations are the heart of the next section, in which recent developments are considered.

New Perspectives

In looking at recent tendencies,[43] perhaps the black movement's most outstanding gain has been progressively legitimating its perspective, namely that the "racial question" is a national issue of citizenship demanding the articulation of specific public policy. Second, while still very far from proportionate, Afro-Brazilian participation in elected and appointed posts of power has increased. Third, racism is viewed increasingly as a question of human rights.

In contrast to the United States and South Africa, where explicit racial oppression gave legitimacy to black peoples' organized struggles, the racial-democracy ideology deprives the dominated population of its base for collective self-defense and self-uplifting. Brazil lacks a tradition of an integrated civil rights movement, a void exacerbated by two major periods of authoritarian rule (1937–1945 and 1964–1985). Mostly white, leftist political leaders fighting to overcome military regimes saw the race question as their last priority and as a threat to the unity of democratic forces.

In 1937, the Brazilian Black Front, a mass civil rights movement based largely in São Paulo (Quilombhoje 1998), was closed down along with all political parties, banned by the New State dictatorship in a wave of censorship and repression. In the 1960s, when antipoverty programs were being implemented in response to the U.S. civil rights movement, Brazil's military dictatorship[44] implemented policies to further concentrate wealth, exacerbating inequality by unleashing brutal repression against opposition forces. Congress was closed in 1968, leftist political leaders went into exile, and the race question was defined as a national security matter. Any public discussion of the race issue was prohibited by decree.

During the two major periods of reorganization of Brazilian democracy (1945–1950 and 1977–1985), Afro-Brazilian movements were active if largely solitary in their campaigns for policy measures to combat racism. As the New State dictatorship gave way to a constitutional assembly in 1945, black organizations unsuccessfully proposed inclusion of measures against racism in the new national charter (Nascimento and Larkin-Nascimento 1992, 1997). In the 1970s, Afro-Brazilian organizations proliferated across the country. Yet only very recently, in the 1980s and 1990s, have they found solid support among allies in other social movements.

The women's movement is one example. Lélia González (1986) and other African-Brazilian women have documented their experience in the 1970s with a middle-class feminist movement largely insensitive to the race question. In their view, feminism voiced the concerns of white women whose liberation depended largely on the availability of underpaid domestic labor, mostly by black women. The role of the feminist movement in creating political space in which to exercise the idea of diversity is undeniable. It is also a fact that many African-Brazilian women did political work first within the black movement, where their specific concerns led them to organize independently as black women. From this base, a new and richer encounter ensued between organized black women's groups and the feminist movement. In 1995, African-Brazilian women took visible part in the delegation to the United Nations Women's Conference in Beijing. Recently, councils on women's rights in local, state, and federal governments have been created as a result of women's mobilization, bringing gender-specific public policy into focus. Black women slowly are making dents in the overwhelmingly white council representation, but their presence is still far from proportionate to their percentage in the female population. Nevertheless, their concerns increasingly are coming to be recognized as legitimate specific needs, not only in the councils but by the women's movement as a whole.

With the rise of the Afro-Brazilian voice came self-definition. Color designations were generally replaced by terms that unite rather than divide, such as *afro-brasileiro*, *negro* ("black"), and *afrodescendente* ("African-descended"). The Afro-Brazilian movement and its allies set the standard of using the sum of the official categories *preto* and *pardo* to quantify the black population.[45] Whatever the lingering academic fascination with color categories, the fact is that we have named ourselves and moved on to more important work.

Foremost among recent phenomena is the rise of an Afro-Brazilian movement made up of nongovernmental organizations (NGOs) and community leaders actively engaged in labor unions, political parties, Christian churches, religious communities of African origin, cultural organizations, and so on. Raising the "racial question" in each area, often facing opposition and hostility, the black movement over time won allies and convinced consciences. Perhaps the most visible expression of this trend was the effective substitution of November 20, the anniversary of Zumbi's death in defending the Republic of Palmares, for May 13, the anniversary of slavery's abolition, as the national day of Afro-Brazilian commemoration.[46] The country has followed this lead since the 1980s; now the media, public and private schools, cultural institutions, and neighborhood organizations join in celebrating November 20 as National Black Consciousness Day, a change that demonstrates the power of the united Afro-Brazilian voice.

Perhaps the most important social movement of recent years is the Landless Workers' Movement (MST). Despite its billing as a recent phenomenon, the MST brings back to the fore an issue that mobilized Brazilians in the early 1960s during João Goulart's presidency.[47] Forty years later, land reform is still a need that has become much more than urgent. Afro-Brazilians generally will be among the first to gain from land reform, and the MST leadership has at least rhetorically recognized the need to combat racism, making public reference to Zumbi and the Palmares Republic as models and examples of grass-roots freedom struggles.

In addition to progressively discrediting the "racial democracy" myth, which nevertheless still carries great weight, the Afro-Brazilian movement has developed independent community action with important impact. One example is the University Admissions Preparation Courses for Blacks and Poor People, which exist in several states and municipalities. The goal is to increase access of young Afro-Brazilians and poor people to higher education. Some have succeeded in getting universities to open subsidized admissions for students from these courses.[48]

Afro-Brazilian participation in the halls of power—political parties, elected offices, and government agencies—has grown. In 1982, when the first direct elections were held as dusk fell over the military dictatorship, this senior author was the only African Brazilian sent to Congress with a mandate to represent this population.[49] Today, while by no means approaching what would be proportionate representation, the weight of the black voice has been increased. Countless administrative appointments as well as the election of two governors and one vice-governor,[50] an ever-increasing number of state and city legislators, three senators, and enough congressmen brought together in 1997 an incipient Afro-Brazilian Caucus.[51] Pressure brought by the black movement through its elected representatives influenced Brazil's South Africa policy in the 1980s and 1990s.[52]

In 1982, the idea of administrative policy geared toward attending to specific needs of the Afro-Brazilian population was generally taken as far-fetched and certainly racist. But with the black movement's growing and increasingly effective mobilization and political presence (Nascimento 1985), the idea began to evolve. Advisory bodies were created within government structures and agencies in an increasing number of state and city administrations.[53] On the federal level, the Ministry of Culture created an advisory group and then a Commission for the Centennial of Slavery's Abolition in 1988, out of which was born the Palmares Cultural Foundation.

In 1988, the Constitutional Congress approved several measures proposed by the Afro-Brazilian community through its black elected members. Among others, these provisions established racism as a crime without bail or statute of limitations (Article 5, Section 42); determined the demarcation of the lands of contemporary Quilombo communities (Article 68, Transitional Provisions); announced the pluricultural and multiethnic nature of the country, providing that the state would protect manifestations of Afro-Brazilian culture among others (Article 215, Paragraph 1); preserved as national patrimony the sites of former Quilombos and their documents (Article 216, Section 5); and mandated inclusion of "the contributions of different cultures and ethnicities to the formation of the Brazilian people" in history courses (Article 242, Section 1).

Since 1988, promulgation of Federal Law 7.716 defining the crime of racism, as well as a plethora of state and municipal laws, many in the area of education, have attested to the movement's growing strength (Silva Jr. 1998).

The assistance to Quilombo communities mentioned in the constitution (Article 68, Transitional Provisions) is a policy area that illustrates a certain symbiosis between Afro-Brazilian communities, the black movement, and government response. These communities, found throughout the country, suffer precarious living conditions and threats from surrounding landowners encroaching on their lands, ownership of which is often undocumented. Since the 1988 Constitution incorporated this demand of the black movement, a few have won legal title to their land and some form of assistance (CEN 1996: pp. 29–31; PR 1998: pp. 25–28).

In 1991, Governor Leonel Brizola of Rio de Janeiro State inaugurated the Extraordinary Secretariat for Defense and Promotion of Afro-Brazilian Populations (SEAFRO), the first and only top-level state government agency created to deal specifically with the articulation and implementation of public policy for the Afro-Brazilian community.[54] However, predictably, opposition arose in the state legislature under the allegation of reverse racism. Challenges to the constitutionality of the administrative law creating SEAFRO prevented its being made a permanent agency, and it was abolished by the succeeding administration.

This fact underlines the hallmark importance of the creation of Belo Horizonte's City Secretariat for Black Community Issues, inaugurated by Mayor Célio de Castro in December 1998.[55] It was approved by the city legislature as a permanent agency. Nevertheless, like SEAFRO it was abolished by the succeeding administration.

Not until the mid-1990s was affirmative action seriously consid-

ered. Its first expression in Brazil, a bill for compensatory action presented to the House of Deputies (Nascimento 1983–1986, vol. 1), was
not widely supported or taken to plenary vote. However, the notion of
affirmative action began to take hold, and the bill was reintroduced in
the Senate in 1997 (Nascimento 1997–1999, vol. 1).

In 1995, national and international celebration of the Zumbi's Third
Centennial consolidated the enlarged scope of Afro-Brazilian mobilization, demonstrated in the Zumbi dos Palmares March on Brasília
Against Racism, in Favor of Citizenship and Life. A Program for
Overcoming Racism and Racial Inequality was presented to the president by the march organization's national executive committee; it still
stands as a basic synthesis of the black community's demands (CEN
1996). Perhaps the highest expression of this moment was the inscription of Zumbi's name alongside that of independence hero Tiradentes in
the national shrine of Brasília's Pantheon of Freedom.[56]

By 1995, discussion and proposal of antidiscriminatory public policies was the order of the day (Munanga 1996). On the day of the Zumbi
march, responding to its demands, the federal government created an
Interministerial Working Group for Valorization of the Black
Population (GTI). Signing the decree creating the GTI (Silva Jr. 1998:
p. 76), the president made an unprecedented official statement (PR
1998) recognizing the existence of racial discrimination and the need
for concrete measures to combat it. The GTI's mandate is to study, formulate, propose, discuss, and articulate executive, legislative, and judicial antidiscriminatory public policy measures with the respective government agencies. It also is to stimulate private initiative policy,
"looking to the development and participation of the Black Population"
and "consolidating the Black Population's citizenship."[57]

Underfunded and understaffed, the GTI's prospects for producing
significant results are dubious at best. Nevertheless, it has drawn up
forty-six affirmative-action proposals now under government consideration (PR 1998: p. 62). One of its most important potential functions
will be to enlarge the range of government agencies involved in antidiscrimination policy measures. The Strategic Matters Secretariat held an
event on affirmative action, and the Army Ministry has been
approached for the reforestation of the site of Palmares, various needs
of the Quilombo communities, and demarcation of their lands (PR
1998: pp. 76–77).

Among the most outstanding developments in recent federal government policy is the creation within the Ministry of Justice of the
National Human Rights Program (PNDH). It works closely with the

GTI and includes in its proposals for governmental action a section on the black population made up of twenty-two short-, medium-, and long-term goals (PNDH 1998: p. 61). These proposals include support for "positive discrimination" and "compensatory policies" to combat racial inequality and to improve the Afro-Brazilian community's socioeconomic status. Indeed, the GTI sponsored a series of seminars on affirmative action, and the Ministry of Justice organized an international event as well.[58] Concrete policy results, however, are extremely limited in comparison with the apparently broad scope and dimension of this government apparatus and discourse.

That the need for affirmative action is being discussed in government circles is an enormous step forward. Unfortunately, the president himself has contributed to the general bias against affirmative action by identifying it with quotas and alleging that it "implies ignoring the evaluation of merit" (PR 1998: pp. 29–30). This notion is foremost in Brazilian society's resistance to antidiscrimination policy.

Major labor unions have fought this resistance by breaking the traditional leftist taboo that raising the racial discrimination issue would divide the working class. They have created internal agencies whose literature supports antidiscrimination policy (CUT/CNCDR 1997, 1998). The Inter-American Labor Union Institute for Racial Equality — INSPIR — was formed in 1999, expressing the broad reach of such initiatives (INSPIR/DIEESE 1999).

This development led workers' organizations in 1994 to bring a case before the International Labour Organization (ILO) for noncompliance with Convention No. 111 on Employment Discrimination, ratified by Brazil in 1965. Responding to the ILO citation, Brazil requested technical cooperation. In 1996, the Labor Ministry instituted its Working Group for the Elimination of Employment and Occupation Discrimination (GTEDEO),[59] a tripartite body created with ILO technical support for implementation of Brazil's commitments under ILO Convention No. 111. A multidisciplinary working group was created within the ministry to "incorporate the question of discrimination into routine actions and activities" (PNDH 1998). One of the major questions it has addressed is the promotion of equality through collective bargaining (MTb/OIT 1998). Whether the working group will institute concrete measures beyond consciousness raising is an open question.

Inclusion of measures to advance actions against racism in the National Human Rights Program not only characterizes racial inequality as a question of human rights but also characterizes nondiscrimination as a citizenship right.[60] In a clear expression of this trend, the Rio de Janeiro State administration, inaugurated in January 1999, created a Secretariat for Human Rights and Citizenship with a policy emphasis on racial inequality.

Strategies and Opportunities

In considering strategies and opportunities, we will divide the discussion into three parts. First, we will consider the substance of antidiscrimination policy in Brazil, then the general policy context into which it needs to be inserted. Finally, we will evaluate strategies favoring effective implementation of antidiscrimination policy.

Antidiscrimination Policy: Substance

Space limitations prevent detailing each public policy proposal, but certain areas of emphasis are objects of general consensus. The first is acquisition of skills (occupational, technical, and academic) and training for antidiscrimination work. In an increasingly technological economy, job and pay discrimination must be combated not only with target programs raising the pertinent issues in the workplace but also with training, specialization, and development of labor skills. Moreover, consolidation of recent gains and development of new proposals for antidiscrimination work will be possible only with the training and multiplication of capable community leaders. Programs of this nature are an important initiative.[61]

Intimately linked to this is the second priority: education. Inequality is less a question of initial access to school and more of the means to stay there. Thus, the fight against child labor is primary; it has been addressed in some areas[62] by state aid to families for each child kept in the classroom. Closely associated is the need to educate young people and adults to compensate for earlier lack of schooling and to reduce illiteracy. Education efforts must also include technical and occupational training as well as secondary and university-level education. Specific college preparation and admissions programs are needed, including but not limited to existing community efforts and cooperation between universities and NGOs. Public policy must address the need for Afro-Brazilian access to higher education, compensating losses resulting from recent restriction of tax benefits that made possible subsidized college admissions. Also crucial are the reformulation of curricula, an issue partly addressed by development of the new National

Curriculum Parameters (MEC 1998) and critical review of school books and children's literature, a project partially implemented by the Ministry of Education.

A third priority is communications media. The enormous impact of television and radio on individual and group identity development in modern society is well known. The racist tendencies of Brazilian telecommunications programming were graphically underscored in 1979, when Angola's state television corporation sought partnership with Brazil. The new African state was forced to decline the offer of one of Brazilian educational TV's most popular programs, based on a traditional children's literature classic,[63] because its racist stereotyping rendered it unfit for viewing by children in Africa. Most Brazilians take the stereotyping so much for granted that they hardly understood the problem. Pressure from the Afro-Brazilian movement has resulted in some, but not enough, reformulation by television networks.[64] The Palmares Cultural Foundation and the GTI established a partnership with the federal government's TVE, producing minidocumentaries, miniseries, and programs. The current federal administration has a stated policy to include in its publicity images all groups making up the Brazilian multiracial population. Further efforts must be made to promote the elimination of discrimination in the private telecommunications sector. The specter of censorship, the almost absolute power of one broadcasting monopoly, and the continued prevalence of the "racial democracy" myth (and its corollary aversion to the "politically correct") have fortified a general state of lethargy.

Specific health programs directed to the black population must take into account not only genetically linked diseases (sickle-cell anemia) but also those with higher incidence and more concentrated health impact on African Brazilians (mioma, hypertension, occupational diseases). Health issue campaigns (e.g., AIDS, leprosy) designed to reach the Afro-Brazilian public are needed, as well as sewage, sanitation, and preventive public health care in Afro-Brazilian communities. The current federal administration has taken small steps in the first two areas through seminars and training initiatives for health workers (PR 1998: pp. 62–71). However, the state of the public health system is deplorable, and monies raised by the special tax levied specifically to fund health care are being flagrantly diverted to other uses (ITM 1998; Roque and Corrêa 1998).

As for police violence, experience in São Paulo and in Rio de Janeiro during SEAFRO's existence included courses on discrimination and human rights in police-training programs, consciousness-raising campaigns, and creation of special police agencies. This is particularly sticky terrain since the police institution is replete with Brazilians of African descent who have internalized racist stereotypes and are less sensitive than hostile to the issues raised by Afro-Brazilian NGOs and human rights organizations (Silva 1994).

Finally, the economic base of the Afro-Brazilian community cannot continue to be composed of jobs alone. Except in the Southeast region (particularly São Paulo and, to a lesser extent, Rio de Janeiro), independent black-owned business is close to nonexistent; the need to stimulate and support the strengthening of Afro-Brazilian capacity to build a sustainable capital base is paramount. Cooperation among African-Brazilian and African-American or African business is a promising perspective.[65]

One problem crosscuts all these areas: the need for reliable data to formulate public policies and evaluate their impact. Inclusion of information on race or color in birth and death certificates and other vital records, hospital and other institutional records, employee records, official documents, and other records is a chief concern (CEN 1996; Munanga 1996; PNDH 1998).

Several forceful suggestions are being negotiated with the Brazilian Institute of Geography and Statistics (IBGE) as it gears up for the 2000 census (Sant'Anna 1998): that the census item "color" be associated with one on "origin"; that the *pardo* category be reviewed, and the term *negro* (black) used to complement classifications by color (*preta/negra*) and origin (*negra/africana*); that the racial/ethnic composition of the population be recorded in the whole population and not just in samples, as has been the case to date; and that census takers be trained to deal with the race/color question.

General Policy Perspectives

While recent advances are considerable, they are far from adequate to deal with the enormous dimensions of inequality in Brazil. In evaluating strategies, three main issues are central. First, the limitations of government action are vast, particularly at the federal level. Second, the effectiveness of partnership depends on how closely citizens'-watch groups and other NGOs critically evaluate the progress and effectiveness of government policy on all levels. Third, Brazilian society still strongly resists antidiscrimination programs and the very discussion of racism as an issue. More broadly, it also resists discussion and action on human rights itself, a proposition generally identified with the idea of pampering criminals.

Two dynamically related dimensions emerge: the need to strengthen the voice of NGOs to influence government action and the need to shift government priority in the direction of effective policies that eliminate inequality. Policy restructuring is needed on two fronts: (1) policies to combat hunger, poverty, income inequality, and inequalities in general living conditions (housing, health care, education, sanitation, running water), and (2) policies that deal directly with racial inequality (such as those discussed in the previous subsection).

The first group of policies would specifically benefit African Brazilians, by far the majority of the poor and needy. However, it has been amply demonstrated (ITM 1998; Roque and Corrêa 1998) that macroeconomic policies recently approved by the International Monetary Fund and pursued by the federal government are entirely inadequate for reaching this goal. Monetary stabilization based on maintenance of the highest interest rates in the world (around 50 percent), fiscal reform anchored in privatization of lucrative state enterprises and the general dismantling of the state, cuts in social spending and massive dismissal of civil servants, denationalization of the economy and concentration of capital, stimulation of imports against exports—all these policies result in stagnation, unemployment, and corrosion of national productive capacity. This occurs in a context of cuts in government-provided services, particularly the already underfunded and deteriorating public-health and education systems. Monies unavailable in the federal budget are improvised by imposing supposedly temporary levies such as the CPMF,[66] while official budget money is used to support failing banks.[67] Social security and pension benefits, whose real value has diminished, are now further taxed and restricted. The 1999 devaluation crisis only underscores the artificiality of this administration's much-applauded "success" in combating inflation; it was already clear in 1997–1998 that overall inequality indexes had increased since 1993 (Roque and Corrêa 1998) and that these policies favored transnational capital rather than Brazilian enterprise, economy, or employment (Salomão and Gonçalves 1998).

Macroeconomic strategies favoring growth are not enough to reverse this situation; policies supporting national production and export are needed. Land and agrarian reform are urgent, immediate needs, including restriction of impunity in rural violence. Implementation of minimum income programs is imperative. Since 1991, two bills proposing minimum-income programs were introduced in Congress; neither has reached a vote. Of eighty state and municipal programs proposed, four are in effect, only one on a permanent basis.[68] If minimum-income proposals meet resistance, hope is small indeed for complementary redistributive programs, the need for which is evident in the extremes of inequality exhibited by Brazil.

Continuation of the work of NGOs monitoring economic policies is crucial, particularly the initiatives taken in the context of the Social Development Watch program associated with the United Nations (ITM 1998).

Strategies for Implementation of Antidiscrimination Policy

As for the second group of policies, those dealing with racial inequalities, their positive effect will necessarily be limited in this overall context. Indeed, the National Human Rights Program (PNDH 1998: p. 45) virtually admits this fact by announcing that its work will emphasize civil rights in a context where social and economic rights are severely restricted by social inequality and probably will remain so.

Nevertheless, specific programs responding to the organized Afro-Brazilian community's demands and addressing public policy directed to racial inequality cannot be ignored. A symbiotic relationship has grown between the action of Afro-Brazilian militants and NGOs on the one hand and government policy on the other. The language and measures adopted by government agencies and in laws have been developed largely by the influence of movement NGOs, intellectuals, and activists directly participating in their formulation or indirectly contributing through actions and writings. However, their capacity to effectively monitor the concrete application of these measures is severely limited by lack of financial means, personnel, and infrastructure.

Thus, important strategies for the Afro-Brazilian movement will be: securing sufficient political weight to guarantee the continuity of the gains made in state policy, including the maintenance and development of government agencies and programs already created at municipal, state, and federal levels;[69] involving new government resources (infrastructure, personnel, agencies) in antidiscrimination programs; and implementing effective legislation. The greatest challenge will be overcoming societal resistance to human rights and affirmative-action policies.

Further empowerment of Afro-Brazilian organizations themselves must accompany these strategies, for the effectiveness of government agencies' work depends on critical and cooperative participation of labor unions, professional organizations, NGOs, and community groups. They in turn must use the agencies' existence and the material they produce to legitimate and advance the goals of local programs. Indeed, the most visible result of agencies' work to date has been production of useful material (e.g., PNDH 1998; PR 1998, MTb/OIT 1998; MEC 1998).

Among the most formidable obstacles to effective policy change is the lack of strong, well-organized political parties capable of translating the demands of social movements into executive and legislative action. Democracy in Brazil is greatly impaired by the continued power of corrupt local strongmen and entrenched elites.

The role of antidiscrimination law has been questioned (Dzidzienyo 1995) in a society where the existence of rhetorical but ineffective legal norms has never guaranteed racial equality. The laws inscribed in the new Brazilian social order have a definite role but not as a result of their effective enforcement. Rather, they constitute a resource and a weapon in the hands of organized civil society to help implement the victories it has won that result in formulation of state policy. Also, legislation reflects progress in and tools to continue the task of overcoming societal resistance to the need for antidiscrimination measures. The international context is particularly important in this respect: the already visible action taken to implement ILO Convention No. 111 can be seen as a model for new initiatives.

In the end, the role of community organizations undoubtedly will remain a strategic imperative. It will be, as it has been, the African-Brazilian people themselves who push governmental and nongovernmental institutions toward measures to build equality.

Perhaps in this respect, the "racial democracy" myth can be seen optimistically as a relative takeoff advantage. In societies where civil rights victories have changed institutional structures, the difficulties in denouncing and combating discrimination tend to become similar to those faced by the Afro-Brazilian movement to date. Denial of the racial nature of inequalities, appropriation by conservative forces of the discourse of equality, and allegations that antidiscrimination policy constitutes "reverse racism" led one of the present authors years ago to question whether post-Bakke[70] forms of discrimination in the United States were similar to Brazilian ones (Larkin-Nascimento 1980). Similarly, democratic South Africa is now facing the need for state policy to address de facto racial inequalities with the legal structures of apartheid no longer intact; the demands of those excluded are urgent indeed. These situations are familiar to Afro-Brazilian activists, who insist upon devising ways to gain ground nevertheless.

In Brazil, the "racial democracy" legacy renders as onerous as in the United States the burden of proof of discrimination required to justify or generate public policy, while condoning the nonaccountability of white society for past racism observed in the United States by our colleague Charles Hamilton (Chapter 7 of this volume: p. 212). Likewise, the cynical stigma he observes against the "politically correct" is prevalent here. These elements may be countered in South Africa by the vivid memory and international condemnation of apartheid, which leave less room for doubt as to the need for and basic fairness of affirmative-action policy. More important, however, is the political dimension: as the voting and party majority in South Africa, Africans are formulating and carrying out public policy. By its nature, this situation implies that limitations imposed by the political power equation are less constraining than in the United States or Brazil. Thus, while the Afro-Brazilian movement has made great gains, it is still true here, as in the United States, that "race relations are simply not a top priority on the national agenda" (Hamilton, Chapter 7: p. 213). To the extent that the African-Brazilian majority overcomes the effects of the "racial democracy" taboo, it will place its concerns increasingly on that agenda. But there is still, indeed, a long road to walk.

Directions

While the dance of deception still carries great weight in the social relations of everyday life, it seems certain that Brazil is moving toward a time when invocations of its multiracial nature will be reformulated in terms that reflect a legitimate Afro-Brazilian self-definition. Political action has resulted in victories including substantive changes in government policy, legislation, and academic evaluation. These actions further strengthen the Afro-Brazilian voice, which increasingly has commanded its own choreography in partnership with organized civil society. Undoubtedly, this development is changing the face of Brazilian society and its discourse. While eradication of inequality is still a remote possibility, recognition of the need to address its specific dimensions is a necessary step toward making viable the policies necessary to achieve that goal.

Conclusion

W.E.B. DuBois announced in 1903 that the twentieth would be the century of the color line. Indeed, these last hundred years have witnessed the worldwide efforts of Africans to end the sundry forms of domination that characterize racism, colonialism, and their legacies lately expressed in neoliberalism and globalization. Africans worldwide played a crucial role in the development of international human rights and of international law and solidarity. The rise and progress of these two tendencies has marked the world indelibly.

The new millennium will increasingly witness the rise of the Afro-Brazilian voice and that of African peoples in the Americas, Asia, and Africa. Their participation in human development will doubtlessly demonstrate the force and weight of their potential to overcome the obstacles of race discrimination.

Appendixes

Abbreviations

CAAS: Center of African-American Studies.

CEAP: Centro de Articulação das Populações Marginalizadas (Center for Articulation of Marginal Populations), Rio de Janeiro.

CEDEPLAR: Centro de Desenvolvimento e Planejamento Regional (Center for Regional Planning and Development), UFMG.

CEN: Comissão Executiva Nacional, Marcha Zumbi dos Palmares contra o Racismo, a Favor da Cidadania e da Vida (National Executive Committee, Zumbi dos Palmares March Against Racism, in Favor of Citizenship and Life).

CEPAL: Economic Commission on Latin America and the Caribbean.

CHRI: Comparative Human Relations Initiative, Southern Education Foundation.

CNCDR: Comissão Nacional Contra a Discriminação Racial (National Committee Against Racial Discrimination), CUT.

CNDH: Comissão Nacional de Direitos Humanos (National Human Rights Committee).

CUT: Central Única dos Trabalhadores (Unified Workers' Central).

DIEESE: Departamento Intersindical de Estatísticas e Estudos Sócio-Econômicos (Inter-Union Department of Statistics and Socio-Economic Studies).

EPPG: Escola de Políticas Públicas e Governo (Public Policy and Government School), UFRJ.

FASE: Fundação de Órgãos para Assistência Social e Educacional (Foundation for Social and Education Assistance Agencies).

FFCL/USP: Faculdade de Filosofia, Ciências e Letras (Faculty of Philosophy, Science and Letters), USP.

GTEDEO: Grupo de Trabalho para a Eliminação da Discriminação no Emprego e na Ocupação (Working Group for the Elimination of Employment and Occupation Discrimination), MTb.

GTI: Grupo de Trabalho Interministerial para Valorização da População Negra (Interministerial Working Group for Valuing the Black Population), Ministry of Justice.

IBGE: Instituto Brasileiro de Geografia e Estatística (Brazilian Institute of Geography and Statistics).

ILO: International Labour Organization.

INSPIR: Instituto Sindical Interamericano pela Igualdade Racial (Inter-American Labor Union Institute for Racial Equality).

IPEA: Instituto de Pesquisa Econômica Aplicada (Institute of Applied Economic Research).

IPEAFRO: Instituto de Pesquisas e Estudos Afro-Brasileiros (Afro-Brazilian Studies and Research Institute), Rio de Janeiro.

IPHAN: Instituto do Patrimônio Histórico e Artístico Nacional (National Artistic and Historical Patrimony Institute).

ITM: Instituto del Tercer Mundo (Third World Institute), Montevideo, Uruguay.

IUPERJ: Instituto Universitário de Pesquisas do Estado do Rio de Janeiro (University Research Institute of Rio de Janeiro).

MEC: Ministry of Education and Culture, now the Ministry of Education.

MINC: Ministry of Culture.

MNDH: Movimento Nacional de Direitoos Humanos (National Human Rights Movement).

MTb: Ministry of Labor.

OAB: Ordem dos Advogados do Brasil (Order of Attorneys of Brazil).

OIT: Organização International do Trabalho (International Labour Organization).

PNAD: Pesquisa National por Amostragem de Domicílios (National Survey by Domicile Sample).

PNDH: Programa Nacional de Direitos Humanos (National Human Rights Program).

PPV: Pesquisa de Padrão de Vida (Standard of Living Survey).

PR: Presidência da República (Presidency of the Republic).

SBPC: Sociedade Brasileira para o Progresso da Ciência (Brazilian Society for the Advancement of Science).

SEAFRO: Secretaria Extraordinária de Defesa e Promoção das Populações Afro-Brasileira (Extraordinary Secretariat for Defense and Promotion of Afro-Brazilian Populations), Rio de Janeiro State Government.

SEF: Southern Education Foundation.

TVE: Televisão Educativa (Educational Television), Federal Government.

UCLA: University of California at Los Angeles.

UFG: Universidade Federal de Goiás (Federal University of Goiás).

UFMG: Universidade Federal de Minas Gerais (Federal University of Minas Gerais).

UFRJ: Universidade Federal do Rio de Janeiro (Federal University of Rio de Janeiro).

UnB: Universidade de Brasília.

USP: Universidade de São Paulo (São Paulo University).

Tables

The following tables present additional data on racial inequalities in Brazil.

Table 5.20   Sanitation and Electricity Conditions, 1996

	Treated Water	Sewage System	Septic Tank	Garbage Collection	Electricity
Brazil	74.2%	40.3%	23.3%	87.4%	92.9%
Urban North[a]	59.7	8.9	39.7	64.7	96.8
Northeast	56.2	15.3	22.4	72.9	81.7
Southeast	86.5	69.0	13.9	92.9	97.8
South	77.0	14.0	52.6	95.6	96.8
Central-West	65.5	15.0	11.3	89.2	93.2

Source: PNAD 1996.
Notes: Percentage of domiciles with service. a. "Urban North" excludes the rural area of Rondônia, Acre, Amazonas, Roraima, Pará, and Amapá States in the northern region.

Table 5.21   "Miserable Poverty" by Color and Gender, 1988

Head of Family's Gender	Color		
	White	*Preta*[a]	*Parda*[a]
Male	14.6%	30.5%	36.2%
Female	15.4	28.9	34.9

Source: IBGE, PNAD 1988; special compilations, courtesy of Nelson do Valle Silva/IUPERJ.
Notes: Percentage of each group; see Table 5.9 for definition of "miserable poverty." a. *Preta* plus *parda* equals "black."

Table 5.22   "Miserable Poverty" by Color and Educational Level

Head of Family's Educational Level	Color		
	White	*Preta*[a]	*Parda*[a]
No schooling/less than 1 year	35.0%	45.9%	53.9%
1 and 2 years	25.5	34.5	42.3
3 and 4 years	13.3	21.4	26.4
5 and 8 years	8.1	13.5	16.2
9 years and more	1.4	2.9	5.3

Source: IBGE, PNAD 1988; special compilations, courtesy of Nelson do Valle Silva/IUPERJ.
Notes: Percentage of each group; see Table 5.9 for definition of "miserable poverty." a. *Preta* plus *parda* equals "black."

Table 5.23   "Miserable Poverty" by Color and Number of Dependents, 1988

Number of Dependents in Family	Color		
	White	*Preta*[a]	*Parda*[a]
0	4.2%	9.4%	10.2%
1	6.2	11.1	15.6
2	8.5	17.6	20.9
3	13.1	27.4	30.9
4	21.3	38.6	40.9
5	31.5	42.8	54.3
6	46.9	65.1	60.7
7 to 10	65.8	75.1	71.0
11 and more	88.0	95.2	84.2

Source: IBGE, PNAD 1988; special compilations, courtesy of Nelson do Valle Silva/IUPERJ.
Notes: Percentage of each group; see Table 5.9 for definition of "miserable poverty." a. *Preta* plus *parda* equals "black."

Table 5.24   "Miserable Poverty" by Color and Age of Head of Family, 1988

Age of Head of Family	Color		
	White	*Preta*[a]	*Parda*[a]
Up to 29	14.6%	31.0%	32.1%
30 to 39	15.6	34.2	39.1
40 to 49	14.9	30.5	39.0
50 to 59	12.5	24.6	29.3
60 or more	12.7	23.7	29.8

Source: IBGE, PNAD 1988; special compilations, courtesy of Nelson do Valle Silva/IUPERJ.
Notes: Percentage of each group; see Table 5.9 for definition of "miserable poverty." a. *Preta* plus *parda* equals "black."

Table 5.25   Percentage of Positive Responses to the Question: "Have You Ever Worked?" (by gender and color)

Age	Men			Women		
	White	*Preto*[a]	*Pardo*[a]	White	*Preta*[a]	*Parda*[a]
9	6.2%	12.3%	12.0%	0.0%	3.0%	2.5%
10	9.5	9.6	26.4	3.5	1.5	7.0
11	8.9	2.2	28.4	5.6	0.0	9.2
12	18.8	26.6	34.1	7.3	15.1	14.6
13	27.6	30.9	51.5	20.7	28.2	19.0
14	32.0	45.1	19.8	23.3	26.2	20.4
15	39.0	48.9	60.5	23.9	26.8	34.6
16	57.4	75.1	70.9	34.0	60.4	37.9

Source: IBGE/PPV 1996–1997; compiled by Nelson do Valle Silva/IUPERJ; courtesy of Nelson do Valle Silva/IUPERJ.
Note: a. *Preto/preta* plus *pardo/parda* equals "black."

Notes

1. Ivan Van Sertima (1976) provides a detailed, minutely researched presentation of this circumstance.
2. Excluding Alaska and Hawaii.
3. In square miles, Brazil's area is 3,286,470 as opposed to South Africa's 471,442.
4. Celebrated expression of Pero Vaz de Caminha, scribe of Brazil's "discoverer" Pedro Álvares Cabral, in the first letter written to the Portuguese court from Porto Seguro (in what is now Bahia State). Cabral landed there in 1500.
5. English-language title of Nelson Pereira dos Santos's classic film *Vidas Secas* on life in the poorest desertified areas of the Brazilian Northeast.
6. World Bank, *World Development Report, 1999–2000.*

7. We have always taken the stand that race is not a biological but a socially and culturally constructed reality, which makes it no less grounded in fact. What changes is the scientific location of the fact (social rather than biological).

8. The train and bus station serving the Rio de Janeiro metropolitan area made famous by the award-winning film *Central do Brasil*.

9. São João de Meriti, Duque de Caxias, Nova Iguaçu, Belford Roxo, Nilópolis. The data cited are taken from the report of the World Health Organization seminar held in São Paulo (1991).

10. Literature supporting this kind of analysis ranges from works such as Gilberto Freyre's sustaining the notions of "racial democracy" and "Lusotropicalism" (1940, 1946, 1963, 1959) or Donald Pierson's *Negroes in Brazil* (1967), to Oracy Nogueira's notion (1955, 1959) of "prejudice of mark" as opposed to that of "origin," which grounded the aesthetic prejudice theory. Other expressions of this line of thought, emerging from the political and ideological left, emphasized that indictment of racial discrimination would constitute a peril to the harmonious unity of the working class.

11. Fernandes 1964, 1972; Hasenbalg 1979; Oliveira, Porcaro, and Araújo 1981; Silva 1998–all contributors to Lovell's study (1991).

12. Possibly, the extremely high Gini coefficient in the Central-West region reflects the concentration there of the Native Brazilian Indian population.

13. Oliveira, Porcaro, and Araújo 1981; Gonzalez 1986; PNDH 1998; IBGE 1994. In São Paulo, the most highly developed city in the nation, white workers' average hourly wage according to the 1980 IBGE Census was equivalent to less than 48 U.S. cents; for blacks it was less than 25 cents.

14. Oliveira, Porcaro, and Araújo 1981; Gonzalez 1986; Lovell 1991; Silva 1998.

15. Health indicators are not generally available by race or color. Official data on medical visits to health care facilities (IBGE 1999) show that "in the North Region only one annual visit per inhabitant can be accounted for, [while] in the Southeast Region this average is 2.8 visits per inhabitant per year, bearing evidence that there are strong regional inequalities in the distribution." As for the availability of hospital beds, "The North Region (with 2.3 beds per 1,000 inhabitants) and the Northeast Region (with 3.1) are not as well served as the Southeast, South and Central West Regions, with over 4 beds per 1,000 inhabitants."

16. Countless incidents of job discrimination also are left undocumented by victims or witnesses who judge it more expedient not to confront the issue for fear of offending the discriminator and suffering some consequence, such as losing the inferior pay or position offered or being taken to the courts in a lawsuit for slander.

17. Having already presented the normal documents, Rio de Janeiro city councilwoman Jurema Batista's official city council identification recently was refused upon one of these extraordinary demands. The incidents cited are taken from a collection of newspaper clippings from 1997 and 1998 furnished by CEAP.

18. Maroon societies or communities founded by escaped and rebellious slaves or ex-slaves.

19. Such proposals go back to early colonial times and were subscribed by Latin abolitionists. Fray Alonso de Sandoval defended whitening as the solution to the "black stain" in his 1627 work, *El mundo de la esclavitud negra en América* (Bogotá: Empresa Nacional, 1956). José Antonio Saco, eminent nineteenth-century Cuban historian, exclaimed: "We have no choice but to whiten, to whiten, to whiten, and so to make ourselves respectable" (Larkin-Nascimento 1981: p. 130).

20. Both the "black race" and *métis* ("mixed-bloods") are cited textually in the delegate's statement.

21. Gomes (1995) studies the revelation of such stereotypes in anthropological and anthropometric technique implanted in Rio de Janeiro and Bahia police institutes in the 1930s.

22. *Terreiros* of Candomblé, Xangô, Macumba, and other African-derived religions as well as Catholic brotherhoods.

23. Pierson (1967: pp. 45,76) characterized slavery in Brazil as "ordinarily a mild form of servitude."

24. A classic expression of this conscience and its irony before historical fact is the following statement made by Brazilian diplomat José Sette Câmara (1974: p. 14) at a time when international authorities were reviewing abundant evidence of racist atrocities committed by the Portuguese in African colonies seeking independence: "Portuguese colonialism is different. The absence of racial discrimination, the ease of miscegenation, the disposition of the colonial Whites to stay, to grow and prosper with their new lands, exist in the Portuguese [African] colonies as they existed in Brazil. The Africans themselves recognize all these positive peculiarities of Portuguese colonization."

25. A fine example of this discourse comes from the ranks of Brazilian diplomacy. Ambassador Guilherme Figueiredo (1975) describes Brazil to the largely African audience of a seminar against apartheid as a multiracial country "free of racial problems," race mixture having "prevented the problems of racial discrimination" from existing. He contrasts Brazil's "anti-racist formation, its miscegenation" to the United States, whose 25 million blacks he judges to be "almost without mixture, almost always pure."

26. Nascimento 1977, 1978, 1980; Carneiro 1997; Sant'Anna 1998; Gilliam 1998. The objective of Iberian colonialism being to extract wealth rather than to settle a homeland, white women were not initially brought from Europe. African women became the permanent and compulsorily available sexual property of white masters, perhaps in greater numbers but exactly as they did in segregationist white settler regimes such as South Africa and the United States.

27. Such sleight of hand is found today in commonplace encounters with white Brazilians: "Me, racist? When I was a baby, I nursed at the breast of a black nanny."

28. Report of the 2nd Congress of Black Culture in the Americas (Panama 1982).

29. Beauty contests traditionally exclude black and mulatto women, hence the initiative of the Black Experimental Theater in the 1940s and 1950s to organize beauty contests among them (Nascimento 1997).

30. In 1966, the Ministry of Foreign Relations published an English-language introductory book titled *Brazil 1966*, in which it informed, under the

heading "Color: the majority of the Brazilian population is made up of Whites, the percentage of persons of mixed blood being minute."

31. The "one drop" rule: any amount of African blood classifies one as black.

32. Suggestion that the color criterion rejects non-European peoples and extols whiteness is deemed an implicitly imperialist kind of reverse racism favored by African Americans from the United States. See the exchanges among Fry 1995; Hanchard 1994b, 1996; and Gilliam 1998.

33. This is true not only in Brazil but also in other "Latin" countries (Larkin-Nascimento 1980).

34. In a survey (Hasenbalg and Silva 1993) where interviewers classed respondents according to the traditional census categories *brancos*, *pretos* and *pardos*, the respondents also classed themselves substituting the options *mulato* and *moreno* for *pardo*. Less than half of those identified as *pretos* so classed themselves; 18.3 percent declared themselves white, and 28.9 percent said they were mulattos.

35. While the living, dynamic weight of Afro-Brazilian cultural influence on the country is cited routinely to support racial democracy theories, Dzidzienyo (1995: p. 348) remarks: "Here lies a fascinating contradiction: between the incorporation into the legitimate national arena of erstwhile African-derived religious, cultural, and social traditions once considered societally or politically subversive because of their 'primitive' provenance, and the absence of a corresponding insertion of Afro-Latin Americans into areas and structures of power and privilege from which they have traditionally been excluded."

36. An interesting example is the controversy around the martial art of *capoeira*, which involves a whole school of thought, called *regionalista,* that rejects out of hand the idea of *capoeira*'s African origin, claiming it was developed wholly in Brazil. When asked why *capoeira* could not have an African origin, one *regionalista* stated to this junior author that "everything seems to come from outside, don't we have the right for at least one thing to be Brazilian?"

37. On the qualification of Brazil's representation at this festival, see Abdias do Nascimento, "Open Letter to the First World Festival of Negro Arts," *Présence Africaine* (English edition) 30 (1966): 58.

38. The International Seminar on Multiculturalism and Racism: The Role of Affirmative Action in Contemporary Democratic Societies (Brasilia, July 1996).

39. Credit should be given to Professor Hélio Santos, Dr. Carlos Moura, and others who made efforts, to some extent successful, to have African Brazilians included in the program.

40. Moura 1972; Freitas 1982, 1985; Lima 1981; Morel 1979; Nascimento and Larkin-Nascimento 1992, 1997.

41. See the essay "Reflections on the Afro-Brazilian Movement, 1928–1997," prepared by the present authors for the Comparative Human Relations Initiative (Nascimento and Larkin-Nascimento 1997).

42. This fact was driven home in a much-discussed incident in 1993, when Ana Flávia Peçanha de Azeredo was barred from the social elevator on racial

grounds (*Veja*, July 7, 1993). A light-skinned mulatto and daughter of Albuíno Azeredo, then governor of Espírito Santo State, she was barred as black— *negra*—and identified herself as black. Her social status made it clear that this was not a case of racially neutral "social" discrimination against the poor. This incident led to much academic discussion around the color criterion versus hypodescendancy in Brazil (Hanchard 1994b, 1996; Fry 1995).

43. For a more detailed account of this material, see Nascimento and Larkin-Nascimento 1997.

44. In 1964, President João Goulart was deposed in a U.S.-supported military coup that became viciously repressive, especially after the Institutional Act of 1968. In 1985, the Congress chose the first civilian president in indirect election, but democracy was not fully reestablished until direct presidential elections were held in 1989.

45. The need for statistical information was seen to outweigh in importance the distortion attributed to the whitening factor (inflation of the "white" group by evasion from the *pardo* category).

46. May 13 is now defined as a day of reflection on the false nature of abolition. Zumbi was the last elected leader (king) of the Republic of Palmares, a conglomeration of maroons—Quilombos—located in the Brazilian Northeast (today's state of Alagoas). With a peak population of about thirty thousand, enormous for the period (1595 to 1695), Palmares repeatedly fought off Portuguese, Dutch, and Brazilian colonial expeditionary forces sent to destroy it over the century during which it existed. Beyond its opposition to the institutions of slavery and colonial rule, Palmares is also a paradigm of the efforts of Africans collectively to reconstruct their lives in freedom in the Americas in organized economic, social, cultural, and political communities. See Price 1979; Moura 1972; Nascimento 1989.

47. During Goulart's administration, democratic and grass-roots social movements were very active, and land reform was one among several major social programs envisioned by the government in the effort to respond to these movements' demands.

48. In Rio de Janeiro, the Pontifical Catholic University and others offered some two hundred tuition grants.

49. These elections were for the federal Congress, state governors, and local and state legislatures. The indirect presidential election was held in 1985; Tancredo Neves, elected by the Congress, died days before his inauguration, and Vice President-elect José Sarney took office in his place. Nascimento's campaign in 1982 gave absolute priority to the representation of African people's interests: the fight against racism and racial discrimination and the articulation of positive measures benefiting Afro-Brazilians. His activity in Parliament (1983–1987) maintained these aims as priorities. As federal congressman, he presented bills of law proposing affirmative-action programs and making racial discrimination a crime with severe sanctions; he also proposed that Brazil end diplomatic and commercial relations with the apartheid regime in South Africa. He was active in the creation of the Ministry of Culture's Abolition Centennial Committee, whose work led, over the long run, to the creation of the Palmares Cultural Foundation. Before he took office, there had been members of the Brazilian Congress who could be classed as "African

Brazilian" but who did not recognize or identify themselves as such. Instead, they "passed" as whites and represented the interests of the elite or advocated the class struggle in general, denying the existence of racism and the need for antidiscrimination or affirmative action measures in Brazil. In contrast, among the very few African-Brazilian legislators who have taken office after Nascimento left the Chamber of Deputies in 1987, many did and do identify themselves as black and support measures to combat racism.

50. Governors Albuíno Azeredo of Espírito Santo and Alceu Collares of Rio Grande do Sul were elected by the PDT in 1990. Former Senator Benedita da Silva of Rio de Janeiro took office as vice governor in January 1999.

51. This caucus has met informally but has not yet developed concerted action on concrete issues.

52. Nascimento 1985; see also *Afrodiaspora* 2, 3, 4, and 5 (Rio de Janeiro: IPEAFRO, 1983–1986).

53. The first of these advisory bodies was the São Paulo State Council on Participation and Development of the Black Community, instituted in 1984 by Governor Franco Montoro.

54. Among its actions were the constitution of a Specialized Police Agency for Crimes of Racism, a public service for attending complaints of victims of racism, workshops and technical training in diversity sensitivity for military police, the Strength of Youth project of occupational training for adolescents, teacher-training programs in different regions of the state for affirmative educational policy with respect to African and Afro-Brazilian history and culture, and publication of material for use in such programs (Larkin-Nascimento 1993, 1994).

55. Secretary Diva Moreira and Adjunct Subsecretary Maria Mazzarella Rodrigues are both militants of black community movements, as are Abdias Nascimento and Vanda Maria de Souza Ferreira, who served as secretaries of Rio de Janeiro's SEAFRO.

56. Implementing Senator Benedita da Silva's Bill of Law 27/1995 to this effect (Silva 1997), Zumbi's name was inscribed on March 21, 1997. The Pantheon of Freedom is a museum located on the Capitol Square (Praça dos Três Poderes) where the executive, legislative, and judiciary branches are seated. The shrine, called the Gallery of National Heroes, contains a huge book sculpted in bronze, whose pages had been inscribed only with the name of Tiradentes himself.

57. Presidential decrees of November 20, 1995, and February 7, 1996 (Silva Jr. 1998: pp. 76–81). The decree makes specific mention of competency to act in the areas of research, study, and publication of statistics and other information; mobilization of new resources for programs and initiatives benefiting the black population and optimization of their use; and black presence in the communications media. The GTI is composed of eight black movement representatives working with members from nine federal ministries.

58. International Seminar on Multiculturalism and Racism: the Role of Affirmative Action in Contemporary Democratic Societies (Brasilia, July 1996).

59. Presidental decree of March 20, 1996 (Silva Jr. 1998: pp. 82–83).

60. "The Program will deal with *obstacles to full citizenship* that lead to systematic violation of rights" (PNDH 1998: p. 45, emphasis added).

61. The Palmares Cultural Foundation sponsored a pioneer course in Capacitation in Public Administration for the Afro-Brazilian Community (Brasília, November 1998).
62. For example, Brasília, the federal district.
63. Monteiro Lobato's *Sítio do Pica-Pau Amarelo*.
64. See the essays by Antônio Carlos Arruda da Silva and Sueli Carneiro in Munanga 1996: pp. 121 139.
65. I Fórum Empresarial das Afro-Américas: Brasil-EUA. Explorando Oportunidades num Mundo Globalizado. Coletivo de Empresários Afro-Brasileiros, Universidade do Estado da Bahia, Morehouse College. Mimeo, 1999.
66. Contribuição Provisória sobre Movimento Financeiro (CPMF) is a tax on financial transactions intended to fund the public health system.
67. In 1995–1997, the federal government rescued many banks whose outrageously high profit margins had been sustained by financial speculation in an inflationary economy.
68. Belo Horizonte, Campinas, and Vitória are cities with provisional programs benefiting families with children up to fourteen years of age, providing a monthly per capita income of R$40.00 (about US$20.00), with the proviso that the children stay in school. Brasília, the federal district, has a permanent program reaching about 25,000 families.
69. Brazilian politics are marked by a powerful tradition: incoming administrations tend to eradicate the work of their rivals leaving office, dismantling state agencies and policies created and starting over anew.
70. In the Bakke case (1976), a white medical student alleged reverse discrimination to strike down an affirmative-action university admissions policy and won in the U.S. Supreme Court. This case was a landmark, ushering in an era of discrediting and dismantling affirmative action based largely upon their characterization as "reverse racism."

References

Andrews, George Reid. 1991. *Blacks and Whites in São Paulo, Brazil, 1888–1988*. Madison: The University of Wisconsin Press.
Asante, Molefi K., and Mark T. Mattson. 1991. *The Historical and Cultural Atlas of African Americans*. New York: Macmillan.
Bennett, Eliana Guerreiro Ramos. 1995. "Gabriela, Cravo e Canela—Jorge Amado and the Myth of the Sexual Mulata in Brazilian Culture." Presentation, Ninth Annual Conference on the Novel in Spanish Language (University of Texas–Panamerican, Edinburgh, Texas, May 16).
Bento, Maria Aparecida Silva. 1998. *Cidadania em Preto e Branco*. São Paulo: Editora Ática.
Cadernos Brasileiros, *Oitenta Anos de Abolição*. 1968. Rio de Janeiro: Cadernos Brasileiros.
Câmara, José Sette. 1974. "O Fim do Colonialismo." *Tempo Brasileiro* 38/39 (special issue: *Brasil, Africa e Portugal*). Rio de Janeiro.
Cardoso, Edson Lopes. 1999. Presentation to seminar on Afro-Brazilian

Historical, Social, and Political Atlas (Rio de Janeiro, April 24–35, sponsored by FASE).

Cardoso, Fernando Henrique. 1962. *Capitalismo e Escravidão no Brasil Meridional.* São Paulo: Difusão Européia do Livro.

Carneiro, Sueli. 1997. "Raça, classe e identidade nacional." *Thoth: Pensamento dos Povos Africanos e Afrodescendentes* 2. Brasília: Senado Federal, Gabinete do Senador Abdias Nascimento.

Castro, Mary Garcia. 1991. "Mulheres chefes de família, racismo, códigos de idade e pobreza no Brasil (Bahia e São Paulo)," in Lovell 1991, pp. 121–160.

CEN. 1996. *Marcha Zumbi dos Palmares Contra o Racismo, a Favor da Cidadania e da Vida.* Brasilia: Cultura Grafica.

CEPAL. 1995. *Report on Differences in Equity: Latin America, the Caribbean and the Social Summit.*

Chiavenato, Júlio. 1980. *O Negro no Brasil: da Senozala à Guerra do Paraguai.* São Paulo: Editora Brasiliense.

Cruz, Anabel. 1998. "Mercosul: Iniqüidades na Integração," in ITM 1998.

CUT/CNCDR. 1998. *Pela Igualdade de Oportunidade para a População Negra no Mercado de Trabalho.* São Paulo: CUT.

———. 1997. *A CUT na Construção da Igualdade Racial.* São Paulo: CUT.

Diegues Jr., Manuel. 1977. *Africa in the Life and Culture of Brazil.* Brasília: Ministry of Foreign Relations.

Dzidzienyo, Anani. 1995. "Conclusions," in Minority Rights Group 1995, pp. 345–358.

———. 1971. *The Position of Blacks in Brazilian Society.* London: Minority Rights Group.

Fanon, Frantz. 1967. *Black Skin, White Masks.* New York: Grove Press.

Fernandes, Florestan. 1972. *O Negro no Mundo dos Brancos.* São Paulo: Difusão Européia do Livro.

———. 1964. *A Integração do Negro à Sociedade de Classes.* São Paulo: FFCL/USP.

Figueredo, Guilherme. 1975. "Apartheid, a Discriminação Racial e o Colonialismo na África Austral." Report to the Ministry of Foreign Relations by the Brazilian delegate to the International Seminar Against Apartheid, Racial Discrimination and Colonialism, Kitwe-Lusaka, Zambia, June-August 1967. *Tempo Brasileiro* 38/39 (special issue: *Brasil, Africa e Portugal*). Rio de Janeiro.

Freitas, Décio. 1985. *A Revolução dos Malês: Insurreições Escravas.* 2nd ed. Porto Alegre: Editora Movimento.

———. 1982. *Palmares, A Guerra dos Escravos.* 4th ed. Rio de Janeiro: Editora Graal.

Freyre, Gilberto. 1969. *Casa Grande e Senzala*, 14th ed. Rio de Janiero: José Olympio Editora.

———. 1963. *The Mansions and the Shanties: The Making of Modern Brazil.* New York: Alfred A. Knopf.

———. 1959. *New World in the Tropics: The Culture of Modern Brazil.* New York: Alfred A. Knopf.

————. 1946. *The Masters and the Slaves: A Study in the Development of Brazilian Civilization*, trans. by Samuel Putnam. New York: Alfred A. Knopf.

————. 1940. *O Mundo que o Português Criou*. Rio de Janeiro: Editora José Olympio.

Fry, Peter. 1996. "O que a Cinderela negra tem a dizer sobre a 'política racial' no Brasil." *Revista USP* 28: Dossiê Povo Negro—300 Anos (December 1995/ February 1996)

Gilliam, Angela. 1998. "Globalização, identidade e os ataques à igualdade nos Estados Unidos: esboço de uma perspectiva para o Brasil." *Revista Crítica de Ciências Sociais* 48 (June).

Gilliam, Angela, and Onik'a Gilliam. 1996. "Negociando a Subjectividade da Mulata no Brasil." *Estudos Feministas* 3, no. 2: 525–543.

Gomes, Olívia Maria da Cunha. 1995. "1933: um ano em que fizemos contatos." *Revista USP* 28, São Paulo (December-February): 142–163.

Gonzalez, Lélia. 1986. "Mulher Negra." *Afrodiáspora: Revista do Mundo Negro* 3: 6–7. Rio de Janeiro: IPEAFRO.

Hamilton, Charles V. 2001. "Not Yet *E Pluribus Unum*: Racism, America's Achilles' Heel," Chapter 7 in this volume.

Hanchard, Michael. 1994a. *Orpheus and Power: The Movimento Negro of Rio de Janeiro and São Paulo, Brasil 1945–1988*. Princeton: Princeton University Press.

————. 1994b. "Black Cinderella? Race and the Public Sphere in Brazil." *Public Culture* 7: 165–185.

————. 1996. "Americanos, Brasileiros e a Cor da Especificidade Humana: uma Resposta a Peter Fry." *Revista USP* 31.

Hasenbalg, Carlos. 1979. *Discriminação e Desigualdades Raciais no Brasil*. Rio de Janeiro: Editora Graal.

Hasenbalg, Carlos, and Nelson do Valle Silva. 1993. "Notas sobre a desigualdade racial e política no Brasil." *Estudos Afro-Asiáticos* 25 (December).

————. "O Preço da Cor: Diferenças raciais na distribuição da renda no Brasil." *Pesquisa e Planejamento* 10 (April): 21–44.

IBGE. 1999. "Minimum National Social Indicators Set." IBGE Internet site.

————. 1997. *Pesquisa Nacional por Amostra de Domicílios, 1996: Síntese de Indicadores*. Rio de Janeiro: IBGE.

————. 1994. *Mapa do Mercado de Trabalho*. Rio de Janeiro: IBGE.

INSPIR/DIEESE. 1999. *Map of the Black Population in the Labor Market*. São Paulo: INSPIR/DIEESE.

ITM. 1998. *Observatório da Cidadania* 2. Montevideo: ITM.

James, Wilmot, and Jeffrey Lever. 2001. "The Second Republic: Race, Inequality, and Democracy in South Africa," Chapter 2 in this volume.

Larkin-Nascimento, Elisa. 1994. *Sankofa: Resgate da Cultura Afro-Brasileira*. 2 vols. Rio de Janeiro: SEAFRO.

————, ed. 1993. *A África na Escola Brasileira*. 2nd ed. Rio de Janeiro: SEAFRO.

————. 1981. *Pan-Africanismo na América do Sul*. Petrópolis/Rio de Janeiro: Vozes/IPEAFRO.

———. 1980. *Pan-Africanism and South America*. Buffalo, NY: Afrodiaspora.
Lima, Lana Lage da Gama. 1981. *Rebeldia Negra e Abolicionismo*. Rio de Janeiro: Editora Achiamé.
Lovell, Peggy, ed. 1991. *Desigualdade Racial no Brasil Contemporâneo*. Belo Horizonte: CEDEPLAR/UFMG.
Mantega, G. 1998. "Brasil: Determinantes e Evolução Recente das Desigualdades no Brasil," in ITM 1998.
MEC. 1998. *Parâmetros Curriculares Nacionais*. 10 vols. Brasília: Ministry of Education.
Mehedeff, N. 1997. "Reformulação da Política de Qualificação Profissional." Contribuição ao I Seminário Nacional Observatório da Cidadania, Rio de Janeiro, July.
Memmi, Albert. 1965. *The Colonizer and the Colonized*. Boston: Beacon Press.
Minority Rights Group. 1995. *No Longer Invisible: Afro-Latin Americans Today*. London: Minority Rights Group.
Mitchell, Michael. 1984. "Race, Legitimacy and the State in Brazil." *Afrodiáspora: Revista do Mundo Negro* 2, no. 4. Rio de Janeiro: IPEAFRO.
Morel, Edmar. 1979. *A Revolta da Chibata*. 3rd ed. Rio de Janeiro: Editora Graal.
Morgan, Robin. 1999. "Human Here Inside of Me." Unpublished paper prepared for the Comparative Human Relations Initiative, Southern Education Foundation.
Mortara, Giorgio. 1970. "O desenvolvimento da população preta e parda no Brasil," in *Contribuições para o estudo da demografia no Brasil*. 2d ed. Rio de Janeiro: IBGE.
Moura, Clóvis. 1972. *Rebeliões da Senzala: Quilombos, Insurreições e Revoltas*. São Paulo: Editora Conquista.
MTb/OIT. 1998. *A Convenção no. 111 e a Promoção da Igualdade na Negociação Coletiva*. Brasília: MTb.
Munanga, Kabengele, ed. 1996. *Estratégias e Políticas de Combate à Discriminação Racial*. São Paulo: Editora da USP/ Estação Ciência.
Nascimento, Abdias, ed. 1997–1999. *Thoth: Pensamento dos Povos Afrodescendentes*. 6 vols. Brasília: Senado Federal, Gabinete do Senador Abdias Nascimento.
———. 1997. "Teatro Experimental do Negro." *Negro Brasileiro Negro, Revista do Patrimônio Histórico e Artístico Nacional* 25. Brasília: IPHAN/MEC.
———. 1989. *Mixture or Massacre in Brazil*. 2nd ed. Dover: The Majority Press.
———. 1983–1986. *Combate ao Racismo*. 6 vols. Brasília: Câmara dos Deputados.
———. 1985. *Povo Negro: A Sucessão e a Nova República*. Rio de Janeiro: IPEAFRO.
———. 1980. *O Quilombismo*. Petrópolis: Editora Vozes.
———. 1978. *O Genocídio do Negro Brasileiro*. Rio de Janeiro: Editora Paz e Terra.

———. 1977. *"Racial Democracy" in Brazil: Myth or Reality.* Ibadan: Sketch Publishers.

Nascimento, Abdias, and Elisa Larkin-Nascimento. 1998. "Comentário ao Artigo 4º," in *Direitos Humanos: Conquistas e Desafios*, ed. by CNDH/OAB. Brasília: Conselho Federal da OAB.

———. 1997. "Reflexões sobre o Movimento Negro, 1928–1997." *Thoth* 3: 69-102 (Brasília: Senado Federal).

———. 1992. *Africans in Brazil: A Pan-African Perspective.* Trenton: Africa World Press.

Nogueira, Oracy, 1995. "Preconceito de marca e preconceito racial de origem." *Anais do XXXI Congresso Internacional de Americanistas* 1. São Paulo: Editora Anhembi.

———. 1959. "Skin Color and Social Class," in Department of Cultural Affairs, Division of Science and Development (Social Science Monographs 7), *Plantation Systems of the New World*. Washington, DC: Pan-American Union.

Oliveira, David Dijaci de, Elen Cristina Geraldes, Ricardo Barbosa de Lima, and Sales Augusto dos Santos, eds. 1998. *A Cor do Medo*. Brasília: UnB, Editora UFG, MNDH.

Oliveira, Lucia Helena Garcia de, Rosa Maria Porcaro, and Tereza Cristina N. Araújo. 1981. *O Lugar do Negro na Força de Trabalho*. First reprint, 1985. Rio de Janeiro: IBGE.

Paes e Barros, R., and R. Mendonça. 1997. "Desigualdade no Brasil: Fatos, Determinantes e Políticas de Combate." Mimeo. Rio de Janeiro: IPEA.

Pierson, Donald. 1967. *Negroes in Brazil*. Carbondale and Edwardsville: Southern Illinois University Press.

PNAD. 1997. Pesquisa Nacional por Amostra de Domicílios. Rio de Janeiro: IBGE.

———. 1996. Pesquisa Nacional por Amostra de Domicílios. Rio de Janeiro: IBGE.

———. 1988. Pesquisa Nacional por Amostra de Domicílios. Rio de Janeiro: IBGE.

———. 1987. Pesquisa Nacional por Amostra de Domicílios. Rio de Janeiro: IBGE.

PNDH. 1998. *Brasil, Gênero e Raça*. Brasília: Minstério do Trabalho.

PPV. 1996–1997. *Pesquisa de Padrão de Vida*. Rio de Janeiro: IBGE.

PR. 1998. *Construindo a Democracia Racial*. Brasília: Presidência da República.

Prado Jr., Caio. 1966. *A Revolução Brasileira*. São Paulo: Editora Brasiliense.

Price, Richard, ed. 1979. *Maroon Societies. Rebel Slave Communities in the Americas.* 2nd ed. Baltimore and London: Johns Hopkins University Press.

Quilombhoje, ed. 1998. *Frente Negra Brasileira: Depoimentos*. Brasília: Minc.

Rodrigues, Nina. 1945. *Os Africanos no Brasil*. 3rd ed. São Paulo: Companhia Editora Nacional.

Roque, Atila, and Sonia Corrêa. 1998. "A Agenda do Ciclo Social no Brasil: Impasses e Desafios." *Observatório da Cidadania no Brasil*, Report no. 2 (Mimeo).

Salomão, Luis Alfredo, and Reinaldo Gonçalves. 1998. *A Desnacionalização da Economica Brasileira e a Política do Governo FHC*. Rio de Janeiro: EPPG/UFRJ/Fundação Alberto Pasqualini.

Sant'Anna, Wânia. 1998a. "Gênero, Raça e Identidade Nacional. Os Sugestivos Sentidos da Aclimatação aos Trópicos." *Proposta* 27, no. 76 (March-May). Rio de Janeiro: FASE.

―――. 1998b. "Decifra-me ou Eu te Devoro." Mimeo, for CEBRAP of São Paulo.

Sant'Anna, Wânia, and Marcelo Paixão. 1998. "Muito Além da Senzala: Ação Afirmativa no Brasil," in ITM 1998.

Santos, Hélio. 1996. "Uma Visão Sistêmica das Estratégias Aplicadas contra a Discriminação Racial," in Munanga 1996.

―――. 1994. "Uma Teoria para a Questão Racial do Negro Brasileiro: a Trilha do Círculo Vicioso." *São Paulo em Perspectiva* 8, no. 3 (July-September): 56–65.

SBPC. 1987. *Ciência Hoje* (supplement) 5, no. 28 (January-February).

Silva, Benedita da. 1997. *Projetos de Lei da Senadora Benedita da Silva*. Brasília: Senado Federal.

Silva, Jorge da. 1994. *Relações Raciais e Direitos Civis*. Rio de Janeiro: LUAM.

Silva Jr., Hédio. 1998. *Anti-Racismo: Coletânea de Leis Brasileiras (Federais, Estaduais, Municipais)*. São Paulo: Editora Oliveira Mendes.

Silva, Nelson do Valle. 2000. "Extensão e Natureza das Desigualdades Raciais no Brasil," in Antonio Sérgio Alfredo Guimarães and Lynn Huntley, eds., *Tirando a Máscara: Ensaios sobre o racismo no Brasil*. São Paulo: Paz e Terra.

Singer, Paul. 1995. *Um Mapa da Exclusão Social do Brasil*. São Paulo: Elisa.

Skidmore, Thomas E. 1974. *Black into White: Race and Nationality in Brazilian Thought*. New York: Oxford University Press.

Van Sertima, Ivan. 1976. *They Came Before Columbus: African Presence in Ancient America*. New York: Random House.

Vieira, Rosângela Maria. 1995. "Brazil," in Minority Rights Group 1995, pp. 19–46.

Verger, Pierre. 1977. "African Religion and the Valorization of the African Descendants in Brazil," in O. Oyelaran, ed., *Faculty Seminar Series,* vol. 2. Ife: University of Ile-Ife, African Languages and Literatures Department.

6

The Misadventures of
Nonracialism in Brazil

Antonio Sérgio Alfredo Guimarães

IN THE NINETEENTH century, racial theories sustained various national and nationalist ideologies[1] and were the basis not only of European nation-states' legitimacy but also of European colonialism in Africa. Later, especially in the 1920s and 1930s, racialism and the concept of race came to be widely used by nation-states with imperialist aspirations such as Nazi Germany. In great part because racialism and the concept of race generated such pernicious consequences, the reaction of enlightened forces, especially many scientists (biologists, anthropologists, and sociologists) was to peremptorily reject the concept of race.[2]

In Brazil, the building of nationality was, very early in this century, positively affected by the discrediting of the concept of race, which had always represented an enormous obstacle to the nation's builders, given the incongruence between, on the one hand, the importance of mulattos and mestizos in social life and, on the other, the malefic effects that racialist theories had attributed to hybridization (Skidmore 1974; Stephan 1991; Schwarcz 1993). With the appearance of Gilberto Freyre's *Mansions and Shanties* in 1933, the starting shot was sounded for a great change in the way science and Brazilian social and political thought would approach Africans and their descendants, hybrids or not. Freyre's work, which introduced the anthropological concept of culture into national erudite circles, and recognized African peoples' contributions to Brazilian civilization, was a landmark. It challenged the old racialist discourse of science (Rodrigues 1935) and, above all, the continued influence that the Italian school of legal medicine still exercised in national medical and judicial milieus.[3]

In a way, as expressed in the social sciences—which had Gilberto Freyre, Sérgio Buarque de Holanda (1936), and Caio Prado Junior

(1937) as their foremost exponents—in regionalist literature—Jorge Amado (1933, 1935), José Lins do Rego (1934, 1935) and others—and in the emerging cultural industry—erudite or folk culture—Brazilian modernity found a common national destiny in overcoming racialism and in valuing the cultural heritage of Brazilian blacks, mulattos, and *caboclos.**

It is not strange, then, that in Brazilian intellectual circles, the concept of race, in addition to expressing the ignorance of those who used it, came also to denote racism. "Race" came to mean only "determination," "will power," or "character" but almost never "subdivisions of the human species"; these came to be designated only by a person's color: *branca* ("white"), *parda* (roughly, "mulatto"), *preta* (roughly "dark black"), and so on. These colors came to be considered objective, concrete, unquestionable realities without moral or intellectual connotations. Such connotations were rejected as "prejudice."

It is very interesting to observe how this antiracialist ideal was absorbed into the Brazilian way of being. Indeed, the perception became a cliché that for Brazilians races do not exist and that what is important in terms of life opportunities is a person's social class (which more than economic position means a certain lifestyle guaranteed through education and cultural habits). The truth is that, given such broad and profound acceptance of such an ideal, the great question is to understand why antiracialism has come under attack in the last few years, undergoing systematic criticism from black movements and from some social scientists.

If we ask a Brazilian who adheres to this ideal why today one speaks of "race" in Brazil, perhaps he would not hesitate to blame this fact on U.S. influence.[4] Such a response would be in tune with what Brazilians have thought, at least since Gilberto Freyre: race is a foreign invention, itself a sign of racism, that does not exist for the Brazilian people. This response has a trait I would like to stress: denial of the existence of racism and racial discrimination in Brazil. In other words, the antiracialist ideal of rejecting the existence of "races" quickly fused with the policy of denying racism as a social practice. The idea is that in Brazil there exists only "prejudice," meaning mistaken individual perceptions, which tend to be corrected in the course of continuing social relations.[5]

---

* *Caboclos* refers to mixed-race persons of indigenous Brazilian and white ancestry.—*Translator's note*.

If, as Appiah reminds us (1992), racialism does not necessarily imply racism, then even more clearly antiracialism does not, in practice, signify antiracism.[6] Nor does denying the existence of races eliminate discriminatory treatment and the reproduction of social inequality among races. Let us explore these issues in Brazil.

The Transformation of
Antiracialism into an Oppressive Ideology

The reduction of the antiracist agenda to antiracialism was a world phenomenon. The conflation of antiracism with antiracialism, already reflected in the social sciences of Europe and the United States, was first brought to Brazil by Freyre, and then spread into sociological and anthropological practice by the first social scientists to exercise their office in the country.[7] The perfect synthesis between the intellectual consensus and Brazilian common conventional wisdom was recalled, in an ironic tone, by Arthur Ramos, in his Brazilian introduction to Pierson's book, dated 1942 (1971: p. 69): "But it is well to record that, using his objective methods of studying human relations, Pierson comes to the same conclusions that were accepted, let us say, traditionally." Pierson was asserting that social identification based on race did not define opportunities in life in Brazil, whether in economic terms, in terms of social honor, or in terms of power. This was a strong statement, given the evidence of blatant inequalities.[8]

To support such a strong thesis, social scientists constantly cited the use of "color" instead of "race," in local society. In their view, this use evidenced the absence of social groups to which one could refer with precision as "racial," meaning groups that use racial indentities in social and political life.

The emergent inquiries into race relations took two diverse paths. The first, of greater interest for social anthropology, was followed primarily by those who sought to understand "social races,"[9] meaning the different forms of racial classification employed in multiethnic societies. Thales de Azevedo (1996: p. 34), for example, asserted that "color" in Brazil is more than pigmentation: in addition to other physical features (hair texture, format of nose and lips), it also includes noncorporal markers such as dress, speech, mannerisms, and so on.[10]

Studies coordinated by Azevedo and Wagley contributed also to making the thesis stick, so much so that a process of whitening was in operation in Brazil, if not in biological terms, as the old school of racialist anthropology advocated, at least in social terms. In other words, there was a tendency among upwardly mobile blacks and mulattos to become socially white, since "color" meant more than merely pigmentation. Azevedo cites Guerreiro Ramos, who then played an outstanding role in the leadership of the black movement, as saying: "the Brazilian Black person can be whitened, to the extent that he raises his economic status and acquires the behavior styles of the ruling groups. Brazilian social screening operates more in terms of culture and of economic status than in terms of race" (Ramos 1946; quoted in Azevedo 1966: p. 35).[11]

Oracy Nogueira (1985), for his part, argued that in Brazil it was the color mark (physical appearance) that counted, in terms of social distinction, and not biological origin (race) as in the United States. Later, supported by these studies, Carl Degler (1991) formulated the famous thesis of the "mulatto escape hatch," according to which mulattos' and mestizos' social climbing resulted in their co-optation by a regime of social inequality, depriving blacks of a more prepared and educated political leadership.

In general, studies of classification systems promoted the idea that in Brazil there is no clear rule of racial affiliation. On the contrary, classification in Brazil, it was asserted, is based on a person's physical appearance. These studies greatly reinforced Pierson's conclusion about the nature of race relations in Brazil.[12]

The second path, more properly sociological, was paved by explicit or nonexplicit challenges to the class concept used by Pierson and later by Harris. In this view, class at once signified color, status, and economic position. Pierson's and Harris's views of social change in Brazil were also challenged. Florestan Fernandes (1955), analyzing the passage from the slave order to class society, came to the conclusion that this transition preserved to a great extent the hierarchical direction and the racial order of slave society. He asserted that blacks were integrated into class society in a subordinated manner, "color prejudice" being the expression of the Brazilian ruling classes' resistance against adapting to the new competitive order. Examining the same transition, Azevedo (1966), for his part, interpreted the situation of Brazilian blacks as corresponding to that of a *ständ*, meaning a prestige group, in which color and social origin restrict individuals' social mobility and life opportunities.

Present in both Fernandes's and Azevedo's work is the idea that Brazilian society is not exactly a class society in the Weberian sense, meaning a market society in which free individuals compete and associate with one another in search of life opportunities, power, and prestige, but a society still hierarchically ordered by *groups* based on family origin and color.

In sum, from the sociological and anthropological studies of the 1950s and 1960s, the following notions emerged: First, the idea was put forth that in Brazil there exist no races but rather colors, as if the *idea* of race did not underlie that of "color" and could not, at any moment, be used to replenish social identities. Second, a consensus was reached that in Brazil it was physical appearance and not origin that determined someone's color, as if there were some precise biological way to define races, and as if all forms of appearances were not themselves conventions. Third, the false impression was left that in Brazil no one could be the target of discrimination on the basis of race or color, since there were no unequivocal criteria of color classification. Fourth, the idea was cultivated that educated mulattos and lighter blacks would always be absorbed economically, integrated culturally and socially, and co-opted politically by the white establishment. Finally, the consensus was formed that the order of racial hierarchy, still visible in the country, was merely a leftover from the past era of black enslavement.

Recovering the Concept of Race

It was this set of beliefs, added to a militant antiracialism, that came to be known as "racial democracy." In the years of the military dictatorship, between 1968 and 1978, "racial democracy" became a dogma, a kind of Brazilian state ideology.

Thus, reduction of antiracism to antiracialism, and its utilization to deny the facts of discrimination and growing racial inequalities in the country, in the end became a racist ideology per se, a denial of the discriminatory order and concretely existing racial inequalities. It was precisely the obscurantist function of antiracialism in this country that came increasingly to irritate the black population, especially the portion that had never wanted to be whitened and was referred to in the chromatic terminology as *escurinhos* ("dark"), *morenos* ("dark brown"), *roxinhos* ("purple"), and by so many other terms that denote some disadvantage. This tension between an antiracist ideal, which correctly denied the biological existence of the races, and a national ideology that denied the existence of racism and of racial discrimination ended up becoming insufferable and unsustainable.

It is precisely from this point that the need arises to theorize "races" as social constructions, forms of identity based on an idea that is biologically erroneous but socially effective in building, maintaining, and reproducing differences and privileges. While the races do not exist in the strictly realist sense of science, they nevertheless exist in the social world and direct the actions of human beings.

Where do these "social races" come from? Sartre (1948), in "Black Orpheus," his famous introductory essay to the poetry of Négritude, suggests a dialectic in which black people's adherence to the idea of race is a kind of "antiracist racism." (I would call it "racialist antiracism"). Importantly, Sartre calls our attention to the fact that one cannot struggle against what does not exist. To put it another way, if blacks do not believe in the existence of races, they would also have to believe that they themselves do not fully exist as people, given that they are partially perceived and classified as a race by others.

Teleologies aside, Sartre's suggestion leads us to consider the political fact that identities are only in part chosen by their subjects, even though their subjects also, more or less entirely, take them on. In the last analysis, the question comes down to whether there is any chance of fighting racism when the idea that race continues to broadly differentiate and privilege people's opportunities in life is denied.

Indeed, in Brazil the theorization around "races," defined as ways of classifying and identifying that can produce communities, associations, or simply individual ways of acting and thinking, constitutes for sociology a useful tool. The concept is useful for revealing and understanding political behavior and institutions that, even inadvertently, lead to systematic discrimination and to inequality of opportunity and treatment among color groups.

The recent history of this concept in Brazilian sociology dates from the end of the 1970s, when Nelson do Valle Silva (1978) and Carlos Hasenbalg (1978) studied the phenomenon of growing social inequalities between whites and blacks in the country. They revisited the work of Bastide and Fernandes (1955), Azevedo (1955), Costa Pinto (1953), and others who, in the 1950s, studied class and color group relations in Brazil. Contradicting these authors, Silva and Hasenbalg asserted that such inequalities unequivocally have a racial component that cannot be wholly explained by differences in education, income, or class, nor diluted into shades of color. These studies of racial inequality proliferated, shedding new light on the situation of Brazilian blacks in terms of income, employment, residence, and education, and are now complemented by studies on inequality of treatment, that is, racial discrimination. It is precisely such inequality of opportunity and treatment with which the sociological concept of race is designed to deal.

Studies of racial inequality[13] demonstrate, first, that it is possible and correct to aggregate color data into two groups (white and non-white), for there are no substantive differences between the nonwhite groups (*pardos* and *pretos*[14] in particular) in terms of any important variable: income, education, residence, and so on. To the contrary, the great difference is between *pardos* and *pretos* and the white group. Second, even when the variables of status and of social class are exhausted in explicative models (income, schooling, birthplace, place of residence, etc.), a substantial unexplained residue persists, which can only be attributed to individuals' color or race.

These data prompt revisiting and contesting the theories made popular in the 1950s. Even though color differences may be important for an individual's chances to rise socially, taken as a whole, opportunities and color gradations do not correspond. From the structural point of view, the system is polarized. There is no mulatto "escape hatch." Hasenbalg's interpretation (1979) rejects the hope expressed by Fernandes (1965) that blacks can achieve a belated integration in class society. Hasenbalg asserts that the subordinated integration of blacks has created a situation of permanent disadvantage that prejudice and racial discrimination merely tend to reinforce. Hasenbalg and Silva (1992), however, seem increasingly discontent with the absence of microsocial studies that could reveal the mechanisms by which the system maintains its polarization despite the apparent fluidity of race relations.

Some work and research carried out by businesses and schools reveals that these mechanisms are reflected in normative standards and values strongly rooted in the national identity, which end up establishing blacks' place in the labor market and in society. Undoubtedly, among these mechanisms the main one is black people's differential access to and performance in the educational system, whose diplomas serve as the foundation for a rigid hierarchical structure legitimated by the notion of individual merit.

On the other hand, the still-pioneering studies of racial discrimination in the country[15] tend to emphasize the importance of an order based in part on prestige groups (*stånd*), which still guides interaction between whites and blacks, shaping the meaning and expectations of social action. The legitimacy of different forms of violence and discrimination for significant portions of the population ends up indeed limiting the exercise of full citizenship.

Racist practices almost always are disguised, for those who perpetuate them, by the conjunction between a sense of hierarchical differentiation on one hand and informality of social relations on the other, which
makes permissible different types of offensive verbal behavior and conduct that threaten individual rights. This is racism, sometimes without
intention, sometimes "in fun," but always with consequences for the
rights and opportunities of those victimized.

Comparing Racist Systems

In Brazil, as in the United States and South Africa, racism as an ideology was a transitory way of justifying the social order, first of slavery or
colonization and later of settlement, servitude, or sharecropping. In
other words, the economic and political subordination of blacks was
first justified by conquest and the sheer force of the masters and only
later by the notion of biological and/or cultural inferiority of the subjugated, this before being justified by poverty and individual and group
characteristics.

The United States was, however, among the three, the first country
to constitute itself as a state of law and justify inequality among individuals only by their immanent characteristics that emerge in situations
of free-market competition. This fact, along with the white population's
resistance against accepting ex-slaves' full equality of rights, facilitated
the acceptance of a racist doctrine to justify curtailing black people's
rights. The United States hosted for a time a juridical duality. In the
United States racism, as a legal system, could therefore easily be dismantled and reversed within the legal system itself, without need for
major transformation of the political system or reconstruction of nationality. When the ideology of racism ceased to be legitimate, it was
declared illegal, and racism as a system began to be attacked by corrective public policies.

In South Africa, the European conquerors and colonizers ended up
building a pluri-national state, isolating the native peoples and not recognizing their citizenship rights. At the same time, the South African
national state instituted conditions of subcitizenship to incorporate ethnic minorities (colored, Asians, and Indians) in an unequal way. Racism
was, then, raised to a state doctrine, completely regulating economic
and political life and social relations. The destruction of apartheid had
to mean, for this very reason, a process of rebuilding a truly national

state, where the nonracialist principle of human rights could, for the first time, be instituted.

In Brazil, racism developed in a different way, present in social practice—a racism of attitudes—but unrecognized by the legal system and denied by the nonracialist discourse of nationality. With independence, the liberal state of law established in 1822 simultaneously guaranteed the masters' and ruling classes' individual liberties and the continuation of slavery. After abolition in 1888, this duality of treatment before the law was extended to the system of "colonelship" or *colonato*[*] that replaced slavery. In other words, constitutionally granted individual rights and freedoms were not guaranteed in social practice. The practices of discrimination and unequal treatment are still the rule in social relations. On the other hand, the Brazilian elite had problems with wholly accepting racism as a doctrine and ended up rejecting it completely, making nonracialism and cultural and biological miscegenation national ideals to be widely promoted among all individuals in the nation state. Taking this into account, whites in Brazil were defined in the most inclusive manner possible, so as to include all mixed-bloods with close to European appearance and even, at the extreme, to include all those who enjoy the privileges of citizenship.

What are the social mechanisms and institutions that permit the functioning of racism as a legally unrecognized system in Brazil?

First, there was a change in the form of social legitimization of discourse on differences. The explanations of social inequalities earlier attributed to the races were replaced by explanations that used the concept of culture, thereby leaving intact the notion of white or European culture and civilization's superiority over black and African culture and civilization. The latter was described publicly as "uncultured" and "uncivilized."

Second, the notion of color officially replaced "race." Through the color continuum, the major part of the population with some African ancestry continued to be classified not as black but as white or mixed, for which a large gamut of names are used, mostly the color *morena*, a designation that was originally used for whites with dark hair and

---

[*] The phrase "system of colonelship or *colonato*" refers to local power relations in which individual landowners called "colonels"—a designation not of military rank but of de facto political and armed force—arbitrarily and officially or unofficially rule over the lives of those living on or near their lands.—*T.N.*

skin.[16] This way of racially classifying oneself keeps the negative stereotype of blacks intact but eliminates from this category most mixed-bloods who, for this very reason, continue to have their self-esteem assaulted by such stereotypes. Principally in the labor market, these racial stereotypes are mixed with class stereotypes to generate the employee selection criterion known as "good appearance" (Damasceno 1998; Sansone 1993), responsible for the reproduction of most racial inequalities in occupations and income.

Third, race relations are supported by a broad system of social hierarchy and inequality of treatment before the law that contaminates all social relations. If the informal segregation of blacks was the norm in Brazil until very recently,[17] it can be said without risk of error that unequal treatment of individuals before the law is currently common and informal practice in Brazil. The same phenomenon of negative stereotyping of black somatic traits supports the mechanism of "police suspicion," which makes blacks the preferred victims of police abuse and abuse by security guards in the streets, public transportation, department stores, banks, and supermarkets (Guimarães 1998).

Fourth, nonracialism, an integral part of the building of modern Brazilian nationality, was ingeniously and mistakenly equated with antiracism. So in Brazil, to deny the existence of races means to deny racism as a system. On the other hand, to recognize the idea of race and promote any antiracist action based on this idea, even if the author is black, is interpreted as racism. Indeed, many manifestations of discrimination based on color are peremptorily denied as having any racial motivation, since races do not exist, only colors, seen as objective, concrete characteristics, independent of the idea of race. Such manifestations are more easily recognized as having class motivation. In this way, the illegitimate character of segregation or discrimination is taken away. Class differences in Brazil, unlike in the United States, are considered legitimate grounds for inequality of treatment and opportunities among persons.

Fifth, the situation of poverty in which the greater part of the Brazilian population finds itself constitutes, in and of itself, a mechanism to make individuals feel inferior and leads to forms of personal dependence and subordination that, by themselves, would be sufficient to explain certain discriminatory behaviors. Since such behaviors can also be observed in relation to nonblacks, racism is disguised. The same argument can also be used to explain the class character of governmental and institutional acceptance and perpetuation of racial inequalities (Hasenbalg 1996; Heringer 1996).

After the abolition of slavery, Brazilian racism has almost always operated through mechanisms of impoverishment, i.e., cultural and economic destitution of blacks and mechanisms of verbal abuse based on class and color.[18] In general, Brazilian racism, when publicly expressed, is done so in discourse on the cultural inferiority of African peoples and the low cultural level of their traditions and descendants.

Roughly speaking, this racism went through two major phases: the first was open but informal racial discrimination, reinforced by class and gender discrimination, which generated a de facto segregation of private and public spaces (city squares and streets, social clubs, bars and restaurants, and so on).[19] In the current phase, with racial discrimination and segregation under fire, strict market mechanisms or psychological means perpetuate racial inequality.

Thus, the major problem for combating racism in Brazil is its invisibility. Racism is repeatedly denied and confused with forms of class discrimination. How, then, has the black movement historically been able to make racism a problem, or in other words, how has the black movement managed to begin to make racism visible in Brazil?

The Social Movement of Blacks in Brazil—Antiracism

The collective mobilization of Brazilian blacks, in this century, begins with the Black Front of the 1930s, active principally in São Paulo. Its main target was spatial and social segregation of blacks, which occurs systematically through informal and illegal, but commonplace, racial discrimination.

The nationalist ideology of integration and assimilation threaded through the Black Front left out of this mobilization the defense of African cultural heritage such as Candomblé and Umbanda,[*] seen as relics of primitivism, albeit cultivated by the white Brazilian elite, principally novelists and anthropologists.

The Black Experimental Theater, active mainly in Rio de Janeiro in the 1950s, broadened the antiracist agenda in Brazil. Its leaders struggled against the whitening ideal, white aesthetic values, and the devaluation of African cultural heritage. The movement's predominant ideology remains, however, nationalist and integrationist. The idea that we are

---

[*] Candomblé and Umbanda are religions of African origin practiced in Brazil.—*T.N.*

one nation and one people remains wedded to the denial of races as a physical reality and the search for a redefinition of Brazil in black-mestizo terms. Guerreiro Ramos,[*] especially, denies the existence of a black question in Brazil, preferring to speak of a popular question—blacks, in Brazil, are the Brazilian people—and of a pathology of Brazilian whites, who think themselves European and white, when they are neither one nor the other (Ramos 1957).

Only in the 1980s, following the period of military dictatorship when the integrationist idea of "racial democracy" became an official ideology and black institutions were banished, did the black movement begin more and more to assume a racialist[20] and multicultural discourse. The two previous targets—the struggle against segregation and racial discrimination and the fight to recover black self-esteem—are now reinterpreted to value African heritage and detach it from adaptations and syncretism with Brazilian national culture. Moreover, now another battleground arises, this one against racial inequalities. In other words, beyond individually committed acts of racial discrimination, the fight is now against the unjust structure of distribution of wealth, prestige, and power between whites and blacks. Battles on this turf, now unconnected to any mono-cultural and universalistic system of ideals—such as socialism—have led to the demand for corrective, compensatory, or affirmative policies directed toward the black population.

At this point, two observations are necessary. First, despite the occurrence of an ideological change in black mobilization, the agenda of this mobilization is ideologically neutral, meaning it can coexist with the most varied spectrum of ideological tendencies in the black movement. This agenda could be summed up as an antiracist fight on three fronts: (1) recovering black self-esteem through modification of aesthetic values, reappropriation of cultural values, recovery of black people's role in national history, revival of racial and cultural pride, and so on; (2) fighting against racial discrimination by universalizing the guarantee of individual rights and freedoms to include blacks, mestizos, and the poor; and (3) counteracting racial inequalities through public policies that could establish, in the long- and medium-term time frame, more balance in wealth, social prestige, and power between whites and blacks.

The second observation refers to the enormous difficulties encountered by antiracist institutions of collective black mobilization. These

---

[*] Afro-Brazilian sociologist.—*T.N.*

difficulties have received two types of diagnosis: either the black movement is a middle-class movement, far removed from the people's interests (which are more directed to material survival)[21] or the black movement is the prisoner of an ideological misunderstanding (Hanchard 1994). I do not believe that either of these diagnoses is correct per se, in the sense of exclusively explaining the relative failure of black mobilization. What do I see as the main difficulty for collective mobilization of blacks in Brazil? Let me explain.

Among the tools used to legitimize the subordination of a people, ethnic group, race, or social class are: (1) military power demonstrated by conquerors; (2) racial, color, or ethnic charisma (the biological or cultural justification); and (3) individuals' socioeconomic and cultural achievement (poverty and subordination as "proof" of inferiority). On the other hand, familiar forms of resistance to subordination always involve: (1) family solidarity; (2) ethnic solidarity; (3) racial solidarity; and (4) class solidarity. All of these are much more efficient when capable of forming alliances around one or more of these forms of solidarity. All of them presuppose some kind of charismatic mobilization leading to the creation of social identities.

Clearly, in Brazil class mobilization has been the most successful form of mass mobilization precisely because certain privileges of treatment before the law and inequalities of life opportunity are more visibly and verbally linked to class distinctions.[22] It is not surprising, then, that a considerable part of the black population feels more attracted to leftist political parties than to black institutions.[23] Moreover, color charisma, broadly utilized in Brazil to monopolize life opportunities, operates on a largely individual basis, making even the development of family solidarity move toward more strongly supporting lighter-skinned family members (as commonly occurs with the male gender) than family members as a whole. In this way, racial solidarity is much more difficult to mobilize in Brazil than in South Africa or the United States. Similarly, not only is ethnic solidarity in Brazil restricted to certain areas of immigration, but also it is not broadly correlated to race, as in South Africa.

One can see, then, from what I have just said, that racial charisma cannot be utilized by the Brazilian black movement just for collective mobilization, i.e., that the building of black identity in Brazil does not work principally for political mobilization, as it does in the United States. The utilization of racial charisma in Brazil has been much more effective in reinforcing black self-esteem, in other words, more effective at the level of fighting the internalization of racist values than in politically confronting the system of racism. Racial identity in Brazil has been formed and will continue to be formed by bypassing family and community solidarity. This is why Brazilian blacks find their potential allies based on class or on the plane of the more basic struggle for the inalienable rights of human beings.

Where material and cultural privileges associated with race, color, and class exist, the first step to an effective democratization consists precisely in naming the bases of these privileges. Far from having a balkanizing effect on nationality, as those who fear racialism believe, or a revolutionary political effect, as those who fear nonracialism believe, the mobilization of race charisma has, in Brazil, a much more circumspect effect. While bypassing family and community solidarity, it makes possible the change from individual experiences of insubordination to acts of collective resistance.

The fact is, however, that generalized complaints exist, from the left and from the right, about the political isolation of the black movement and its limited capacity for mass mobilization and representation of its interests.

Those who point out that the black movement does not recruit more adherents because, to black people, its discourse sounds like the language of losers or opportunists are correct.[24] In other words, according to popular thought, when one does not have the strength to change a situation, it is better to remain silent than to expose oneself to demoralization by way of impotent complaint.[25] This situation, however, is changing. On the one hand, the movement has increasingly appropriated the liberal discourse of universal rights, equality of opportunities, and equality of treatment, opening up an important battlefront in the area of rights and the implementation of an egalitarian legal order. On the other hand, the human rights movement, SOS Racism services,[26] Carnival communities that mobilize black charisma, and even the Pentecostal movement (Burdick 1999) have broadened the masses' experience with egalitarian treatment in public spaces and increased their respective audiences' feelings of self-esteem, which makes indictment of discrimination and racial abuse more acceptable.

It seems to me that it is on another front, the battlefront against racial inequalities, that the antiracist movement confronts the greatest difficulties in Brazil. This is for two reasons: first, because Brazilian society does not recognize racism, whether by attitude or system, as being responsible for racial inequalities in the country; and second, and consequently, because racial inequalities themselves are seen as social class inequalities that affect Brazilian society as a whole and are brought on by abstract entities such as imperialism, economic underdevelopment, poverty, and so on. Thus, whether to face discrimination and social stigmatization or to try to reverse racial inequalities, the black movement confronts a strongly established consensus, a consensus created and reproduced by two above-mentioned features: color gradations, which make all Brazilians, even those closest to their black ancestry, active participants in the system that stigmatizes darker people; and the generalized practice of treatment inequality, or if one prefers, of a kind of clientelism.[27]

Political Conservatism and the Reaction against Black Racialism

On the political plane, three social movements are most visible in Brazil today: the landless workers, organized by the Landless People's Movement (Movimento dos Sem Terra—MST); the human rights movement, which involves various institutions and organizations of civil society; and the black movement that fights against racial discrimination and inequalities and is led almost entirely by black nongovernmental organizations.

Of these movements, the MST is undoubtedly the one most able to disrupt the Brazilian social order. This is true for several reasons. It uses violent methods of confrontation, such as the invasion of rural properties; it is linked to opposition political parties; and it has not found any institutional form of accommodation with governmental powers (although a Land Reform Ministry has been created almost exclusively with the aim of counteracting and engaging in dialogue with the MST).

The human rights movement took shape in the 1960s, when the fight against the military dictatorship and for the reestablishment of the state of law was still in progress. It obtained full recognition from the Fernando Henrique Cardoso administration, which created a Human Rights Secretariat and adopted a governmental National Human Rights Plan. Recently, the main activity of this secretariat has been to work with state police forces to discipline police and restrain abuses in dealing with the population in general, and with criminals in particular. But it also has taken action against race discrimination and other kinds of human rights violations. Although the movement in favor of respect for human rights has the support of a significant portion of the population, argued against it is a considerable body of public opinion that defends traditionally brutal methods of dealing with urban criminality and advocates, among other items, the freedom to bear arms and the death penalty.

The fight against racial discrimination and inequalities also has encountered resistance from Brazilian public opinion. The struggle against racism in Brazil, as we saw previously, took a direction contrary to the shaping, from the 1930s on, of the national imagination and scientific consensus. The Unified Black Movement and other black organizations made demystifying the "racial democracy" creed a priority in their struggle, denying the cordial nature of race relations and asserting that in Brazil racism is engrained in social relations. Moreover, the movement reinforced its policy of building a racial identity by referring to all people (not only to *pretos*[*]) with any African ancestry as *negros* ("blacks").

This change by itself would already explain a great deal of the public reaction against the black movement. On one hand, anthropologists such as Roberto DaMatta and Peter Fry warned that racial democracy is not merely a "false ideology" but in fact a founding myth of Brazilian nationality,[28] in addition to being unassailable as an ideal. Fry (1994: p. 126) goes further, arguing that as an ideology, racial democracy, far from acting as a cover for racist attitudes or becoming itself racist, counters the ideology that allows race discrimination to operate in Brazil. At the same time, the more the black movement indicted Gilberto Freyre for transmitting a rosy picture of the country's race relations, the stronger became some intellectuals' rejection of the attempt to demonize Freyre.

The tension between the black movement and the Brazilian academy is also great when racial identity is at issue. By defining *negros* as all African descendants and identifying these as the sum of the census categories *preto* and *pardo*, the movement committed two scientific heresies: first, it adopted as a criterion of identity not self-identification, as modern anthropology prefers, but biological lineage; second, it ignored the fact that, in great part in Brazil, the population that defines itself as *parda* has not African but Native Brazilian Indian origin. The pretense of identifying someone as "black" by their lineage, ignoring the way people classify themselves or trace their origins, also made room for two accusations: that the black movement tries to impose U.S. racial categories on Brazil and that it professes to believe in biological races (racialism).

---

[*] Very dark-skinned black people, as in the official Brazilian census category.—*T.N.*

To the extent that the black movement gained more political promi-
nence, especially when it began to promote the idea of public policies
directed at the black population, thus threatening consolidated interests
and privileges, the discomfort in the academy tended easily to turn into
political conservatism. Intellectual reactions like those of Fry (1994) or
Harris et al. (1993) ended up giving way to gratuitous accusations of
"reverse racism," "intellectuals at the service of Yankee imperialism,"
"cultural subordination," and so on.[29]

Even though it has the support of prominent intellectual allies, the
truth is that the black movement still has great need of "white"[30] intellectuals to overcome the resistance of the academic establishment,
which still to a great extent shuts African Brazilians out of its higher
echelons. The best example of this fact is the considerably negative
reaction of professors at the country's best universities to any effort to
concede to black people, and even to the poor, privileged access to public universities.* Seeing itself as an élite that came into being through
intellectual merit, the Brazilian university community does not accept,
in any form, the idea of using any criterion of entrance other than the
vestibular† exam.[31]

Also in relation to the establishment, it is helpful to recall that of
late the great advances in the struggle against racism in Brazil are taking place on legal-political ground and not only ideological ground. It is
a fact that the 1988 Constitution, by introducing "collective rights" and
"diffuse rights" into the country, recognized as subjects of law the
broad segment of Brazilian society organized as nongovernmental
organizations. But it is also a fact that the same constitution instituted
the Public Ministry†† as guardian of these new rights. Thus, on the one
hand, the 1988 Constitution's provision making racial prejudice and

---

* Public universities, which offer the best quality higher education in Brazil,
are accessible almost exclusively to upper-class students who have had access
to private (paid) primary and secondary education. Ironically, these public universities are gratuitous, while middle- and lower-middle-class students at private universities pay very high tuition fees when measured against their income
standards.—*T.N.*
† The *vestibular* is a standardized test, similar to the SAT in the United States,
which traditionally has been used as the sole criterion for admission to
Brazilian universities. In this admissions process, no other evaluation is made
of a candidate's merits or achievements.—*T.N.*
†† The Public Ministry is a branch of the judiciary dedicated essentially to
overseeing the enforcement of rights and duties by public authorities. It
includes, among others, prosecutors, the equivalent of district attorneys, government agency attorneys, and public defenders.—*T.N.*

discrimination criminal offenses opened the way in some places, such as São Paulo, for the creation of "SOS Racism" programs and specialized police stations; in other places, such as Salvador, it prompted the creation within the Public Ministry of special departments or sections to combat racial crimes. By the same token, the new constitutional order made way for the articulation of compensatory policies defending the social rights of marginalized populations that guarantee the fulfillment of commitments contained in international agreements signed by Brazil. It was, therefore, foreseeable that a large number of black intellectuals should concentrate their energies on legal action, which made the importance of lawyers, prosecutors, district attorneys, and state agency attorneys increase within the black movement, as well as that of activists in the SOS Racism programs.

Clearly, as the importance of legal action increases for blacks, the need also arises for more and better technical and ideological preparation to influence public opinion in general, and that of judges and appellate court justices in particular, about the need for action on racial discrimination. This is true because judicial decisions have rapid repercussions in the press, be they arrests for the crime of racism or measures taken on public civil actions in defense of diffuse rights. From the intellectual point of view, the reactions encountered by black lawyers and prosecutors in the judiciary and in the courts from judges, justices, and appellate court magistrates, as well as journalists' reactions in the same context, are still very primitive.

Indeed, as we emphasized above, there is a great gap between sociological thinking, generated and transmitted in the faculties of philosophy and social sciences, and the thinking transmitted in schools of law or journalism. A result of this fact is that Brazilian magistrates and attorneys, having belatedly rejected the racist ideas of Lombroso and Rodrigues, still remain attached to the intellectual consensus led by Freyre in the 1930s and 1940s. In other words, for a decisive part of the Brazilian elites, the only alternative to the scientific racism prevailing at the end of the twentieth century remains as yet the ideology of racial democracy. The black movement, then, needs to make clear the differences between its racialism and the previous racialism, and in order to do this it must also listen to what its critics are really saying.

The defense of racial identity as a right of self-identification and the rejection of biological "races" as oppressive social constructions are both just. So, too, is the criticism of the mystifying function of Brazilian racial democracy[32] or the critique of the hierarchical society still in effect in Brazil (DaMatta 1985; Adorno 1995; Guimarães 1998), or the demonstration that social inequalities among whites and blacks have, in Brazil, an undeniable racial base (Hasenbalg 1978; N. Silva 1978; Lovell 1989; Telles 1992). All these points need to be integrated in order to prevent just and healthy criticisms of racialism from recharging a politically conservative and racially cynical elite. The old consensus on racial democracy, to which in the 1930s and 1940s blacks and whites, right and left, liberals and socialists all adhered, seems to be definitively shattered.

The Limits of Black Racialism

The modern Brazilian black movement, as we have seen, was created in the 1930s and re-created in the 1970s as a program to fight race discrimination and to integrate blacks into class society. At first, it struggled to build the racial democracy that later acquired a farcical veneer. It first denied races and preached color as an "accident" and later demanded racial dignity and pride as a way to oppose oppression.

Lately, the black movement has accumulated victories in the fight against discrimination. In 1988, the country's constitution declared racism a crime without statute of limitations or recourse to bail; in 1989, a statute was passed to regulate the punishment of such crimes; and in the following years, in 1990 and 1997, other laws improved on its provisions. SOS Racism services were created to support the victims of discrimination; specialized police stations were instituted to give more protection to the black population; and black politicians were elected by activists concentrated in the political parties' secretariats to combat racism, mainly those of the center-left and labor parties. In addition, the politics of racial identity bore visible fruits in various parts of the country, and cultural groups asserting black and Afro-Brazilian identity flourished, such as *Bailes Black*, *Blocos Afro*,[*] rap groups, Funk Dance events, and so on. Racial identification itself has changed shape, at least in certain social sectors, and it is common today for media personalities who would have defined themselves as *morenos*[†] or even as whites to identify themselves and be accepted as black.

---

[*] *Bailes Black* are popular dances attended mostly by black youth, where soul and other African-American music is played. *Blocos Afro* are Afro-Brazilian music and dance groups that play and perform, particularly in the Carnival context, the most well known being Olodum of Salvador, Bahia.—*T.N.*
[†] Roughly, *moreno* means brunette or dark-complexioned, but not black or mulatto.—*T.N.*

The struggle against discrimination is now beginning to be waged with another, much broader struggle: the struggle against racial inequalities and for development of more encompassing public policies that compensate for the political, social, and economic exclusion of the black population.

But despite the immense progress and the enormous efforts made in terms of identity politics, the truth is that among potential blacks (the *pardos* and *pretos* of the census whom some activists call *negros*), who compose 40 percent of the Brazilian population according to data from a sample survey (Table 6.1), only a minority has converted to the movement's racial appeal. Also according to these data (Table 6.2), only 7

Table 6.1   Induced Responses to the Question "What Color Are You?"

Color	Frequency	Percentage
White	2,522	49.6
Preto	606	11.9
Pardo	1,454	28.6
Asiatic	141	2.8
Native Brazilian Indian	326	6.4
Other	32	0.6
Total	5,081	100.0

Source: Unpublished data, DataFolha Research Institute, 1995.

Table 6.2   Spontaneous Responses to the Question "What Color Are You?"

Color	Frequency	Percentage
White	1,946	38.3
Moreno	1,769	34.8
Light *Moreno*	375	7.4
Pardo	302	5.9
Preto	221	4.3
Negro	135	2.7
Light	84	1.7
Mulatto	39	0.8
Escuro	34	0.7
Asiatic	28	0.6
Dark *Moreno*	29	0.6
Other	72	1.4
Doesn't know	47	0.9
Total	5,081	100.0

Source: Unpublished data, DataFolha Research Institute, 1995.

percent of the Brazilian population identifies itself as *negra* ("black") or *preta* ("dark black"), while 43 percent prefer to identify themselves as *morenos* and the rest as whites (38 percent), *pardos* (6 percent) or another color.

Thus, while the struggle against discrimination forced explicit recognition of the racial category that inspired discrimination, leading, moreover, to a broad definition of black as the category subjected to prejudice, the struggle for affirmative action for blacks will likely benefit the 7 percent of the population that self-identifies themselves as *pretos* or *negros*. How will the movement react to this evidence? How will white society react?

In political terms, the consequences are great: if the black movement gives up the racialism of racial descent (made on the basis of physical traits or biological lineage) in exchange for a racialism of chosen identities, it may be tempted, in time, to abandon majority politics in favor of minority politics.[33] Brazilian black racialism has two incomparable virtues: the correlation between blacks, broadly defined, and poverty is so great that to say the poor are poor because they are black, and not because the country is poor, is an excellent strategy for placing responsibility on the country's elites, which to this day hide their more petty interests behind theories such as racial democracy or economic underdevelopment. This black strategy combines well with leftist revolutionary aspirations and with the new mobilization in favor of human rights and respect for citizenship. On the other hand, minority politics in a society where the majority suffer poverty and social and political exclusion run the risk of losing legitimacy.

This dilemma explains, perhaps, why black leadership has, wisely indeed, often been content to accommodate its demands for affirmative policies to broader formulas such as "blacks and the poor." This is because it is well known that, whether by the criterion of racial self-identification or by that of third-party attribution,[34] the black population is much smaller than many might hope.

Conclusion: Toward an Integrated Antiracist Agenda

For analytical purposes, one can think of an antiracist agenda in three dimensions: state, nation, and individuals.

At the state level, the main concern should be the search for guarantees of individual rights and freedoms, independent of any identity or charismatic affiliation—gender, race, religion, ethnicity, color, class.

Declaration of this principle, including nonracialism, is already part of the constitutional charters of the three countries; the question, then, is to obtain legal and practical guarantees for its enforcement, especially in Brazil and South Africa.

The principle of state nonracialism, however, does not mean that special legislation—with precise timetables and targets—cannot be designed to attack prevailing and enduring forms of privilege building in the three societies.[35] In the United States, the mobilization of racial charisma is so effective that it makes whites, independently of class, benefit from racial oppression. In Brazil, color charisma meshed together with class, placing poor whites in a situation closer to blacks and mestizos than middle-class whites. In South Africa, racial charisma is also associated with ethnic charisma. These different constellations of oppression make it necessary to diversify corrective public policies or affirmative action: in Brazil, to deal with poor populations of different colors; in South Africa, to take account of African ethnic groups. Moreover, in Brazil and in South Africa, there is a preliminary condition: to guarantee respect for human rights of all citizens and equal treatment of all before the law.

On the level of nationhood, it seems to me that the great challenge of the twenty-first century will be the rebuilding of nationalities on pluri-cultural and pluri-ethnic grounds. The nation-state's ideals of assimilation and integration must be replaced by integration at the state level (of law and rights) and by a policy of valuing the different ethnicities and cultural heritages of the social groups that today make up the population of any country. Contrary to the nineteenth-century equation (one nation-state = one race = one culture) we will have: one state = various cultural heritages = various races = various ethnicities. Not that a unified civic culture cannot be developed, but such a culture cannot mean denial of the diverse cultural traditions and heritages that form a nation.[36] In the same way, nonracialism at this level makes no sense. If the mobilization of racial charisma exists, the best way to fight it is to grant opportunities for stigmas to be transformed into positive qualities. The fight against racism assumes the guarantee of individual liberties and treatment equality (on the state level) as well as the positive nature of group identities (on the individual level), but is neutral on the level of nationality.

At the level of individuals and their group identities, antiracism should look to racial stigmas—those of color, race, and class—in Brazil. This means interfering in governments' educational policies but also creating strong black institutions that can sustain the black populations' self-esteem through the fight against racial and color discrimination and through the revaluing and reinterpretation of black cultural heritages.

Notes

1. The equation "one language = one people = one race = one nation" often served as the basis for demanding a state's creation. See Benedict Anderson 1992.

2. In other words, there are no subdivisions of the human species that can be unequivocally identified by genetics and to which distinct physical, psychological, moral, and intellectual qualities can be ascribed. The moral and intellectual differences among human groups (reasonably stable populations in a given territory) may be scientifically explained, then, only by cultural differences. The concepts of "population" in biology and of "ethnicity" in social sciences should, therefore, substitute the concept of "race," thenceforth transformed into an expression, *tout court*, of scientific backwardness or racism.

3. The racialist theories of Nina Rodrigues and of Cesare Lombroso enjoyed a certain prestige up until the middle of the last century in the country's law schools, where modern sociology was slow to penetrate. The modernity brought by Freyre, on the contrary, was rapidly assimilated by the Bahian school of social anthropology, which always laid claim to the intellectual heritage of Nina Rodrigues, such as Querino 1938; Ramos 1937, 1956; Carneiro 1948; Azevedo 1955; and Lima 1971.

4. Ironically, a Brazilianist, Charles Wagley, was one of the first to attribute to foreign influences the racism already observable in large Brazilian cities in the 1950s. "Observers, both Brazilians and foreigners, have the impression that at the same time the West introduces into Brazil its industrial techniques and processes, it also introduces its racist attitudes and theories" (Wagley 1952: p. 165).

5. On the other hand, when the notion of "racial prejudice" is conceived in a strong way—as virulent—it is said that, in Brazil, there exists only discrimination, and not prejudice. A good example of this posture is found in the introduction to the second Brazilian edition of Pierson's book (1971).

6. What I designate by the term "racism" always carries three dimensions: a conception of biological races (racialism); a moral attitude treating members of different races in different ways; a structural position of social inequality among the races, originating in this treatment.

7. In this way, we owe to Donald Pierson (1942), then a Ph.D. candidate in Chicago under the advisement of Robert Park, the sociological articulation of the thesis that Brazil is a "multiracial class society." By this, Pierson meant above all that there were no barriers to social interaction and mobility among Brazilians of different ethnic-racial origins that could be attributed to "race" in itself, the existing barriers being better understood as consequences of the eco-

nomic and cultural order. He took as evidence of his thesis the social interaction among whites, mulattos, and blacks in Bahia and the fact that one finds
blacks and mulattos in all social circles in Salvador.

8. Such inequalities inspired the following comment from Robert Park
(in Pierson 1971: p. 84), who had visited Salvador two years before Pierson
began his fieldwork in that city:

> In any case, for the foreigner who visits one of the hills where rich
> people live in Bahia, it is a somewhat bizarre experience to hear, com-
> ing from among the palm trees of the neighboring valleys where the
> poor live, the insistent ruffle of African drums. So narrow are the spa-
> tial distances that separate the Europe located in the hills from the
> Africa located in the valleys, that it is hard to perceive the breadth of
> the social distances that separate them.

9. Charles Wagley and Marvin Harris (1958: p. xv) coined the expression: "In this study, when we deal with 'race,' we are speaking of 'social race,'
of the way members of a society classify themselves and each other according
to physical characteristics, and not of biological concepts of race." See also
Harris and Kottak 1963 and Wagley 1965.

10. In the words of Azevedo (1996: p. 34): "Apparently these terms [*branco, preto, mulato, pardo, moreno, caboclo*] describe certain physical types; in
reality, their meaning is socially conditioned, albeit basically related to racial
traits, especially skin color, hair, and facial shape." See also Azevedo 1966.

11. Indeed, in the first French-language edition, published in 1953,
Azevedo cites the first phrase of Ramos's sentence but without identifying it,
which he does only in the Brazilian edition of 1955, when he gives the complete reference of Ramos's interview. I am citing it from the second Brazilian
edition of 1996.

12. As Harris states (1964: p. 61):

> A Brazilian is never merely a "white person" or a "colored person"; he
> is a rich and well-educated white person or a poor and unschooled col-
> ored person. The product of this qualification by education and by
> financial resources determines the adoption of subordinate or superior
> attitudes between specific individuals, in face to face relations. . . .
> There are no racial groups against which discrimination occurs. There
> are, in contrast, class groups. Color is one of the criteria of class iden-
> tity; but it is not the only criterion.

13. Among these studies: Bairros 1988; Castro and Guimarães 1993;
Lovell 1989; Porcaro 1988; Telles 1992.

14. Roughly, *pardos* means mulattos and *pretos* means very dark-skinned
black people. These are official Brazilian census categories. (Translator's note.)

15. See Adorno 1995; Ribeiro 1995; J. Silva 1998; and Guimarães
1998.

16. Today, only between 5 percent (census) and 10 percent (sample sur-

veys) of the Brazilian population calls itself black. Burdick (1998) correctly calls attention to the fact that the percentage of blacks that so define themselves in Brazil is large in spite of the way it is reported by sociologists. In my case, the "only" in the above phrase means merely that a large number of persons who would be classified as blacks by lighter others do not classify themselves that way but as *pardos* (mulattos).

17. Frances Widdance Twine (1998) detects, through interviews, that in a small town in the Rio de Janeiro countryside the practice of segregation of blacks lasted practically until the 1987 Constituent Assembly debates that criminalized racism.

18. "Charisma" is used in this text in the sociological sense it was given by Nobert Elias (1998: p. 106) as "a successful claim of a group to superior graces and virtues, by way of eternal gift, in comparison with other groups, branding these effectively with qualities described collectively as inferior and as eternal attributes."

19. Such segregation is well documented by anthropological and sociological literature, which, however, in some cases preferred in its interpretations to observe that some influential blacks overcame such segregation. Pierson 1942; Azevedo 1955; Twine 1998.

20. Racialist in the sense of evoking the charisma of the black race and making one of its goals the formation of a black racial identity.

21. See, in this tradition, among others, Pinto 1953 and Andrews 1998.

22. Studies on workers' mobilizations in Brazil also point to moral values, such as dignity, being more important than material interests for the success of these campaigns. See, in this respect, Abramo 1990.

23. This fact is recorded by Andrews 1998.

24. See Andrews 1998; Twine 1998; and Burdick 1998.

25. See Twine 1998.

26. See Carneiro 1998.

27. "Personalization" is a term that refers us more immediately to the more sociological, not only legal, aspects of treatment inequality. See DaMatta (1990: 58–87).

28. Myth, for the anthropologists, is more than "false ideology." It means the symbolic expression of the set of ideas that organize the social life of a certain community.

29. A good example of poorly informed conservatism are the passages of Bourdieu and Wacquant (1998) with reference to Brazil.

30. In the case of Brazilian intellectuals, the majority of them light-skinned mestizos, the situation is even more complex, given that the black movement, contradicting its own criteria, tends to treat them as "white."

31. This restriction is being slowly countered. The new Educational Policy and Fundamentals Law made entrance to higher education more flexible, and the National Secondary Education Exam (ENEM), already in use, makes possible an effective mechanism of alternative evaluation of academic merit, already partially accepted by some universities.

32. See Nascimento's "Dance of Deception," Chapter 5 in this volume.

33. The same is true for a very restricted attribution that includes, for example, only *pretos*.

34. Even the black movement refuses to use the term "black" to refer to middle-class African descendants, who define themselves as whites.

35. "I define privilege in terms of unjust advantage, a preferential situation, or systematic primacy in the search for social values (whether money, power, position, education or anything else)" (Blauner 1972: p. 22).

36. See Appiah 1992.

References

Abramo, Lais. 1990. "O Resgate da Dignidade." Master's thesis, University of São Paulo, FFLCH.

Adorno, Sérgio. 1995. "Discriminação racial e justiça criminal em São Paulo." *Novos Estudos Cebrap*, no. 43 (November).

Amado, Jorge. 1933. *Cacau*. Rio de Janeiro: Ariel.

———. 1935. *Jubiabá*. Rio de Janeiro: José Olympio.

Anderson, Benedict. 1992. *Imagined Communities*. London: Verso.

Andrews, George Reid. 2000. "Forms of Black Political Response in Brazil," in the Comparative Human Relations Initiative, ed., *Beyond Racism: Embracing an Interdependent Future, Color Collage*. Atlanta: Southern Education Foundation, pp. 96–103.

Appiah, Kwame Anthony. 1992. *In My Father's House: Africa in the Philosophy of Culture*. New York: Oxford University Press.

Azevedo, Thales de. 1966. "Classes sociais e grupos de prestígio," in *Cultura e situação racial no Brasil*. Rio de Janiero: Ed. Civilização Brasileira. pp. 30–43 (originally published in 1956 by Arquivos da Universidade Federal da Bahia, Faculdade de Filosofia, Salvador, no. 5. Republished by Ensaios de Antropologia Social, Salvador: Progresso, 1959).

———. 1996 [1955]. *As elites de cor, um estudo de ascensão social*. São Paulo: Cia. Editora Nacional. New edition: Salvador: Edufba.

Bairros, L. 1988. "Pecados no paraíso racial: o negro na força de trabalho na Bahia, 1950–1980," in João Reis, ed., *Escravidão e invenção da liberdade*. São Paulo: Brasiliense, pp. 289–323.

Barreto, Elba S. de Sá, and Dagmar Zibas. 1996. *Brazilian Issues on Education, Gender and Race*. São Paulo: Fundação Carlos Chagas.

Bastide, R., and F. Fernandes. 1955. *Relações Raciais entre Negros e Brancos em São Paulo*. São Paulo: Anhembi.

Blauner, Robert. 1972. *Racial Oppression in America*. New York: Harper & Row.

Bourdieu, Pierre, and Loïc Wacquant. 1999. "On the Cunning of Imperialist Reason." *Theory, Culture and Society* 16, no. 1: 41–58.

Burdick, John. 1998. "The Lost Constituency of Brazil's Black Movements." *Latin American Perspective* 25, no. 98.

———. 1999. "What Is the Color of the Holy Spirit? Black Ethnic Identity and Pentecostalism in Brazil." *Latin American Research Review* 34, no. 2.

Carneiro, Edison. 1948. "Candomblés da Bahia, Salvador." Secretaria da Educação e Saúde.

Carneiro, Sueli. 2000. "Estratégias legais para promover a justiça social," in

Antonio Sérgio Alfredo Guimarães and Lynn Huntley, eds., *Tirando a Máscara: Ensaios sobre o racismo no Brasil*. São Paulo: Paz e Terra.

Castro, Nadya, and S. A. Guimarães. 1993. "Desigualdades raciais no mercado e nos locais de trabalho." *Estudos Afro-Asiáticos*, no. 24: 23–60.

Damasceno, Caetana Maria. 2000. "'Em casa de enforcado não se fala em corda': Notas sobre a construção social da 'boa' aparência no Brasil," in Antonio Sérgio Alfredo Guimarães and Lynn Huntley, eds., *Tirando a Máscara: Ensaios sobre o racismo no Brasil*. São Paulo: Paz e Terra.

DaMatta, Roberto. 1985. *A Casa e a Rua*. São Paulo: Brasiliense.

———. 1990. "Digressão: a fábula das três raças, ou o problema do racismo à brasileira," in *Relativizando, uma introdução à antropologia social*. Rio de Janeiro: Rocco, pp. 58–87.

DataFolha Research Institute, Pequisa. 1995. "300 Anos de Zumbi." Unpublished data.

Degler, Carl N. 1991 [1971]. *Neither Black nor White*. Madison: University of Wisconsin Press.

Elias, Nobert. 1998. "Group Charisma and Group Disgrace," in Johan Goudsblom and Stephen Mennell, eds., *The Nobert Elias Reader*. Oxford: Blackwell Publishers.

Fernandes, Florestan. 1955. "Cor e estrutura social em mudança," in R. Bastide and F. Fernandes, eds., *Relações Raciais entre Negros e Brancos em São Paulo*. São Paulo: UNESCO/ANHEMBI.

———. 1965. *A Integração do Negro na Sociedade de Classes*. São Paulo: Cia. Editora Nacional.

Freyre, Gilberto. 1946. *The Masters and the Slaves*. Trans. Samuel Putnam. New York: Knopf.

Fry, Peter. 1994. "O que a Cinderela Negra tem a dizer sobre a 'política racial' no Brasil." *Revista da USP*, no. 28.

Guimarães, Antonio S. A. 1998. *Preconceito e discriminação—queixas de ofensas e tratamento desigual dos negros no Brasil*. Salvador: Novos Toques.

Hanchard, Michael. 1994. *Orpheus and Power: The Movimento Negro of Rio de Janeiro and São Paulo, Brazil, 1945–1988*. Princeton: Princeton University Press.

Harris, Marvin. 1964. *Patterns of Race in the Americas*. New York: Walker and Company.

Harris, Marvin et al. 1993. "Who Are the Whites? Imposed Census Categories and the Racial Demography of Brazil." *Social Forces* 72, no. 2 (University of North Carolina Press) (December): 451–462.

Harris, Marvin, and Conrad Kottak. 1963. "The Structural Significance of Brazilian Categories." *Sociologia* 25, no. 3: 203–208.

Hasenbalg, Carlos. 1978. "Race Relations in Post-Abolition Brazil: The Smooth Preservation of Racial Inequalities." Ph.D. dissertation, University of California, Berkeley.

———. 1996. "Entre o mito e os fatos: racismo e relações raciais no Brasil," in Marcos C. Maio and Ricardo V. Santos, eds., *Raça, Ciência e Sociedade*. Rio de Janeiro: Edicion Fiocruz/Centro Cultural Banco do Brasil.

Hasenbalg, Carlos, and Nelson do Valle Silva. 1992. *Relações raciais no Brasil*. Rio de Janeiro: Rio Fundo Editora.

Heringer, Rosana. 1996. "Introduction to Analysis of Racism and Antiracism in Brazil," in Benjamin Bowser, ed., *Racism and Antiracism in World Perspective*. Newbury Park/London/New Delhi: Sage Publications, Sage Series on Race and Ethnic Relations, no. 13, pp. 203–207.

Holanda, Sérgio B. 1936. *Raízes do Brasil*. Rio de Janeiro: José Olympio.

Lima, Vivaldo da Costa. 1971. *A Família-de-Santo nos Candomblés Jeje-Nagôs da Bahia*. Salvador: Mestrado em Ciências Sociais.

Lovell, Peggy. 1989. "Income and Racial Inequality in Brazil." Ph.D. dissertation, University of Florida, Gainesville.

Munanga, Kabengele. 1999. *Rediscutindo a Mestiçagem no Brasil*. Rio de Janeiro: Editora Vozes.

Nogueira, Oracy. 1985 [1954]. "Preconceito Racial de Marca e Preconceito Racial de Origem—Sugestão de um Quadro de Referência para a Interpretação do Material sobre Relações Raciais no Brasil," in *Tanto Preto Quanto Branco: Estudos de Relações Raciais*. São Paulo: T. A. Queiroz.

Pierson, Donald. 1971 [1942]. *Brancos e Pretos na Bahia (Estudo de Contacto Racial)*. São Paulo: Editora Nacional [*Negroes in Brazil: A Study of Race Contact in Bahia*. Chicago: University of Chicago Press].

Pinto, Luis Aguiar Costa. 1998 [1953]. *O Negro no Rio de Janeiro, Relações de raças numa sociedade em mudança*. Rio de Janeiro: Companhia Editora Nacional.

Porcaro, R. M. 1988. "Desigualdade racial e segmentação do mercado de trabalho." *Estudos Afro Asiáticos*, no. 15: 171–207.

Prado Junior, Caio. 1965 [1937]. *A Formação do Brasil Contemporâneo*. Colônia: Editora Brasiliense.

Querino, Manoel. 1938. *Costumes Africanos no Brasil*. Rio de Janeiro: Civilização Brasileira.

Ramos, Alberto Guerreiro. 1946. *Entrevista ao Diário Trabalhista*. Rio de Janeiro: 24.III.

———. 1957. *Introdução Crítica à Sociologia Brasileira*. Rio de Janeiro: Andes.

Ramos, Arthur. 1937. *As Culturas Negras no Novo Mundo*. Rio de Janeiro: Casa do Estudante do Brasil.

———. 1956. *O Negro na Civilização Brasileira*. Rio de Janeiro: Casa do Estudante do Brasil.

Rego, José Lins do. 1934. *Menino de Engenho*. Rio de Janeiro: José Olympio.

———. 1935. *Moleque Ricardo*. Rio de Janeiro: José Olympio.

Ribeiro, Carlos A. Costa. 1995. *Cor e criminalidade: Estudo e análise da Justiça no Rio de Janeiro (1900-1930)*. Rio de Janeiro: UFRJ.

Rodrigues, Raymundo Nina. 1935. *Os Africanos no Brasil*. 2nd ed. São Paulo: Cia. Editora Nacional.

Sansone, Livio. 1993. "Pai preto, filho negro. Trabalho, cor e diferenças de geração." *Estudos Afro-Asiáticos*, no. 25: 73–98.

Sartre, Jean-Paul. 1948. "Orphée Noir," in Léopold Sedar Senghor, ed., *Anthologie de la nouvelle poésie nègre et malgache*. Paris: PUF.

Schwarcz, Lília M. 1993. *O Espetáculo das Raças*. São Paulo: Cia. das Letras.

Silva, Jorge da. 1998. *Violência e racismo no Rio de Janeiro*. Niterói: EDUFF.

Silva, Nelson do Valle. 1978. "White-Nonwhite Income Differentials: Brazil 1960." Ph.D. dissertation, University of Michigan, Ann Arbor.

Skidmore, T. E. 1974. *Black into White: Race and Nationality in Brazilian Thought*. New York: Oxford University Press.

Stepan, Nancy. 1991. *The Hour of Eugenics: Race, Gender and Nation in Latin America*. Ithaca: Cornell University Press.

Telles, Edward. 1992. "Residential Segregation by Skin Color in Brazil." *American Sociological Review*, no. 57 (April): 186–197.

Twine, France Winddance. 1998. *Racism in a Racial Democracy: The Maintenance of White Supremacy in Brazil*. New Brunswick, NJ: Rutgers University Press.

Wagley, Charles. 1965. "On the Concept of Social Races in the Americas," in D. B. Heath and R. N. Adams, eds., *Contemporary Cultures and Societies in Latin America*. New York: Random House.

———, ed. 1952. *Race and Class in Rural Brasil*. Paris: UNESCO.

Wagley, Charles, and Marvin Harris. 1958. *Minorities in the New World*. New York: Columbia University Press.

7

Not Yet "E Pluribus Unum": Racism, America's Achilles Heel

Charles V. Hamilton

"E PLURIBUS UNUM"—"out of many, one." Americans are proud of this motto. It signifies an aspiration, an ideal of a united society committed to a common set of principles and goals. Americans imprint this motto on their currency and display it on public buildings. It represents the noble sentiments of the Preamble to the Constitution of the United States: to establish justice, insure domestic tranquillity, provide for the common defense, promote the general welfare, secure the blessings of liberty. Indeed, American pride in this motto is as much a part of the essence of "Americanism" as the pledge of allegiance to the flag, which enunciates "One nation, under God, with liberty and justice for all." Americans have a propensity for the grand declaration, the articulation of high societal purposes, even as they constantly recognize that such pronouncements reflect predilections, not necessarily realities.

Certainly this disjunction between pronouncement and reality has been manifested throughout American history in the glaring failure to fully incorporate peoples of African descent under the banner of "E Pluribus Unum." Slavery, human peonage, *legal* racial segregation, and de facto discrimination have served to undermine achievement of the "unum." "Racism" has been and remains America's Achilles' heel, its vulnerable spot in its profession of a society dedicated to the protection and prosperity of all.

But the motto persists. To some it is a reminder of what the society at least formally strives to achieve, even if it falls painfully and embarrassingly short much of the time. It is an expression of the best instincts and intents of the society as a whole. To others it is a kind of weapon to point up the hypocrisy, weakness, and venality of a society whose entire history is fraught with calculated and intended contradictions of the motto.

In any case, one can expect to be reminded of the motto at every turn. It greeted waves of immigrants from Europe in the nineteenth century and served as a guide for subsequent upward mobility for many of those from that continent who came seeking religious freedom and, above all, opportunity to acquire property and a decent livelihood. The deal was, for many, readily acceptable—namely, subscribe to certain precepts of "Americanism": self-reliance, loyalty to their new country, respect for individual rights and private property. To many immigrants, this was a bargain worth entering, and, without question, to many it was a contract reasonably fulfilled. One political scientist described the experience as follows:

> For the immigrants, becoming an American could mean accepting and identifying with American social, economic, and political values and institutions—whose appeal had, of course, been a principal reason for their immigration in the first place. In effect, a bargain was struck: ethnic groups retained so long as they wished their ethnic identity, but they converted to American political values, ideals, and symbols. Adherence to the latter was the test of how "American" one was, and it was perfectly compatible with the maintenance of ethnic culture and traditions. The primordial or organic ties remained in large part ethnic; the political or ideological ties were American. (Huntington 1981: p. 27)

To say the bargain was struck does not, by any means, suggest that there was no breach of the agreement. Ethnic historical experience in the United States is replete with accounts of overt segregation and discrimination. Employment signs at factory gates in the nineteenth century advised: "No Irish Need Apply." Resorts and recreational facilities advertised: "No dogs or Jews Allowed." "Gentiles Only" signs were common in rental and employment ads. In some instances, these anti-ethnic acts simply went unchallenged and were tacitly accepted, until a burgeoning civil rights movement for protection of African Americans was launched. In other instances, the ethnic groups formed their own socioeconomic, communal associations that helped them negotiate the worst practices of a prejudicial society. In addition, one historian noted: "However prejudiced white Anglo-Saxons were in practice, they were ashamed to endorse nativism [antiforeign, anti-Catholic, anti-Semitic, anti-Negro] in principle. Equally important, an expanding economy in an under-populated country required a steady influx of new hands.

Immigration alleviated the labor shortage, and economic need overpowered moral and aesthetic repugnance" (Schlesinger Jr. 1991: p. 9).

All of this, obviously, was a delicate, subtle process. No one assumed that national identities would disappear immediately, but such identities should not be a hindrance to success through individual enterprise and capitalist competition. The delicacy was magnified by the fact that African descendants in this new land of opportunity were at the same time experiencing precisely different circumstances. They and their forebears came *as* property, not *seeking* property. They were not expected to be self-reliant. Rather, dependency was a requirement of their residence. The open, competitive market—either their accumulation of assets or their ability to market their skills in fair competition—never applied to them.

Needless to say, immigrants from Asian countries were closer to African descendants than European in terms of their legal and economic conditions. What remained distinctive about the African Americans, of course, was the mode of entry. They came as property and had to spend centuries establishing their sheer humanity as a matter of law before they could begin to function as citizens.

Little wonder that a society with such a fractured, differential history of group relations and experiences would have a serious problem dealing with such a lofty motto as "E Pluribus Unum." Various groups view that phrase from their own experiential vantage point. To some it is a reasonable reflection of reality, not quite complete, but in time will likely become so. To others, it is a source of understandable cynicism and frustration, especially when counseled by the more privileged—white and black—to behave with patience, perseverance, and forgiveness.

One lesson learned is that America's Achilles' heel is not so easily dispatched.

What's to Be Done and How:
The Necessity for Coalitions

Discussions and actions on race, racism, and race relations continue in the United States as the country moves into the twenty-first century. "The problem of the color line," aptly described by W.E.B. Du Bois in 1903, appears to be no less intense now as it was when he wrote those words over ninety years ago (Du Bois 1961). Americans of all races and ethnic identities continue to grapple with seemingly interminable problems, albeit different now in many significant ways—politically, socially, and economically. Even as debates persist over how to identify racial groups (or, indeed, whether race per se is a relevant category or simply a "socially constructed" one with no scientific justification), the causes of racial disparities and the remedies to be pursued in overcoming those inequalities, the country has seen a plethora of conferences, studies, reports, and calls for constructive action. All this is taking place even as there is evidence (cited later) that most Americans do not see race relations as a top priority. A familiar mantra accompanying these activities asserts that on the one hand progress has been made, but on the other hand there is more to be done.

It is precisely what constitutes this future action ("what's to be done") that bedevils and dominates the current status of race, racism, and race relations in the United States. No one denies the more than three hundred years of legally sanctioned slavery, segregation, and discrimination of blacks. A crucial debate, however, is how important that legacy is or should be. No one denies that blacks in the United States were deliberately subordinated and denied opportunities to advance. The people who perpetrated these acts were openly explicit and unapologetic in their intent. A critical debate now centers around at least two current themes. First, since there are no longer constitutional and legal restrictions requiring or permitting such restrictions, why is there a continuing need to give protection to the former "victims"? Second, the current discussions include far more groups than occupied attention until only a few decades ago. What about nonblack groups (e.g., immigrants from places other than Africa); women, who were also denied constitutional and legal rights; homosexuals; senior citizens; and the physically handicapped?

Thus, the current situation in the United States has seen the growing arena of groups, in addition to African Americans, who have come forth to claim their status as legitimate beneficiaries of a civil rights movement started essentially in the name and interest of blacks. In a sense, this movement unleashed a host of frustrations and indignities experienced by other groups in the society. As logical as this development might seem, it has not been without its opponents.[1] And, important to understanding how the future is likely to unfold, this new dimension of expanded claimants significantly affects the development and success of political movements attempting to combat continued racial discrimination. In other words, there is little prospect in the near future of successful efforts to deal with race without corresponding efforts to deal with sexism and socioeconomic inequalities that cross racial and ethnic boundaries. A recent survey published by the Southern Regional Council concluded: "Americans are more supportive of public policies designed to offer help based on economic status than those targeted at racial minorities. The class versus race edge prevails regarding government spending priorities, affirmative action programs, and general policies to improve socioeconomic conditions" (Southern Regional Council 1998: p. 15).

This latter point has been a bone of contention for some time. Earlier, some observers fervently argued (even in the worst years of legal oppression) that the main problem was "not race but class." Put simply, race was a camouflage, a disguise to hide an intent to wage a carefully crafted "class war" against all of the poor. Thus, if the white poor could see blacks as their enemy, they would divert their focus away from the real cause of their own lowly plight, namely the white affluent. This argument persists today, but its progressive proponents are currently more sophisticated in conceding the independent role of racism in this complex situation, notwithstanding the passage of laws prohibiting overt discrimination. At least, the current analyses—from across the political spectrum—tend to recognize that race *and* socioeconomic status are simultaneously important factors in dealing with existing economic disparities in the society.

The urge to subordinate race to class was also motivated (even if ever so subtly) by the notion that if race/racism was given a prominent position, the matter would likely *not* be sufficiently treated. Antagonistic racial feelings (historically intertwined with sexual relations) were so deeply embedded that many people simply felt such issues were beyond the bounds of rational public discourse. Racial fears were not what "polite" company talked about, at least not openly, as Gunnar Myrdal observed in his study of this country's "dilemma." These were matters best left unprobed for fear of uncovering a hard core of animosity, fear, almost "innate" abhorrence of "the Other," the different, and especially the "dark heathen," and the desire "to be with one's own kin and kind." Better then to avoid (if not to deny) the issue by clothing it in other forms such as economic conditions and the need for education. This way, society could more comfortably (and that is exactly the appropriate word) deal with policies aimed at helping all people afflicted with common problems (unemployment, poor health, bad education, etc.). These were acquired, not ascriptive problems. They did not require people to focus on things that seemed immutable (such as physical racial features). They also permitted another more comfortable mindset—namely, a focus on individual effort. If one applied oneself, worked hard, played by society's rules, and did not dwell on racial discrimination based on a group's identity, but strove to improve one's own talents in a competitive society, the American system of egalitarianism and individual merit would reward such behavior—in time.[2] Wasn't this, after all, one of the important lessons of other identifiable groups (especially the European immigrants) coming to this country and faced with dire conditions of discrimination? Was it not the lesson inspired by Jews, Asians (especially the "model minorities"), Irish, Italians, and many others? They relied on tightly knit communal associations, complained little or not at all about overt discriminatory practices (in some cases adopting such practices to their own self-help endeavors), and slowly lifted themselves as individuals *and* as members of a group.

Whether this was a way to avoid (or deny) the centrality of the black/white conundrum, this attitude very likely was a powerful one in influencing (in fact, politicizing) how Americans thought about racism and race relations—and equally as likely, still do. They extrapolated out—not from the idealistic words of the Declaration of Independence or Constitution—but from their own historical and current experiences. They were assimilating into the American way of receiving those different from themselves. And to a large extent, if this approach worked for them, then why not for others? To be sure, virtually everyone mouthed "E Pluribus Unum," but they also winked. The "unum" really meant only under certain, quietly understood circumstances. How was the process orchestrated? The answer: by not raising too loudly the obvious dominance of one element, while the various "many" took whatever opportunities they could get to improve their lot. This was America's pragmatic way of coming to terms with its internal contradictions— with its Achilles' heel.

Precisely because of this persistent proclivity to dodge issues of racism and prejudice, no useful discussion should proceed without recognizing the need to address *how* issues are framed and organizations mobilized to confront the multiple problems of racial, economic, and gender inequities still plaguing society. In other words, "what's to be done" will be determined by a serious consideration of how to articulate the "solutions."

This current reality will be complicated by the different historical experiences of the various groups and, particularly important, the differential political power of the groups. The latter point speaks to the crucial matter of forming political alliances so necessary for building effective strategies in policymaking circles. Needless to say, the finite resources available in attempts to ameliorate unequal conditions aggravate this problem.[3] Under any configuration of political-economic power, African Americans are a clear minority and as a group are likely to remain so. Unlike South Africa or even Brazil, sheer numbers cannot be a particularly encouraging factor in the African-American calculus of what is to be done. Thus, they must seek to form coalitions with others who have similar interests and needs or who have a need to seek support from the group at any given time for their own special interests. This will be difficult for a variety of reasons. Except under the most unusual circumstances will those who have more give up willingly even a portion of what they have to those who have much less. Moral, philosophical arguments in the face of entrenched self-interests are valuable but should not be taken as inevitably controlling.

The rest of this chapter attempts to respond to these complex, difficult, and perennial matters.

What Has Been Done and Why:
Pressure at Home and International Vulnerability

What have been the primary historical developments that have shaped the current reality? This question obviously focuses attention on the accelerating struggle against racism over the last half century. It is impossible to overlook or underestimate the rising protest movements—in the courts, legislatures, and executive branches—that raised the society's consciousness of and receptivity to the demand of justice and opportunity. These efforts were tedious, halting, at times violent, and in many important instances successful. They successfully ended de jure segregation, greatly extended voting rights to places (especially in the South) correctly described as "closed societies," and opened up several arenas of socioeconomic activity previously off-limits—in the public and private sectors. The stories of these developments have been told often and well. To be sure, accounts disagree on the relative weight given to various forms of protest action. Hardly surprising. Some accounts lean heavily toward the efficacy of the constitutional/legal challenges pursued through the courts, noting the significance of redefining and overturning long-held constitutional precedents (such as the "separate but equal" doctrine allowing legal segregation).

This period represented perhaps the greatest display of liberal coalition politics in modern American history. The civil rights movement activated not only black Americans but liberal religious, labor, youth (especially on college campuses), and multiracial civic organizations as well. Many conducted protest campaigns in their own local communities, raised funds for support of voter registration drives and other anti-segregation efforts, joined important lobbying in Congress, and were a viable presence in tense areas of conflict. Organized labor was an important source for support funds and providing numbers for protest marches and other activities. Many local unions in the North were especially helpful, but some were also part of the problem. Many local craft unions practiced racial discrimination well into the 1960s in apprenticeship programs and in various other ways. This caused a constant battle between civil rights leaders and national labor leaders. The latter were officially on record in support of civil rights but maintained that they could not (and would not attempt to) expel locals who pursued discriminatory practices and openly excluded blacks. This punishment was a test of commitment called for by civil rights leaders, but without success. The coalition of labor and civil rights forces was a crucial one, but one constantly characterized by friction between "friendly allies."

civil rights groups always supported the basic aims and policies of organized labor—the right to organize and bargain collectively, union shops, minimum wage, improved working conditions, and broader benefits—and they clearly recognized the value of the labor movement, politically and economically. At the same time, several very important union affiliates were unapologetically segregated. (This was truer of the craft unions than of the industrial unions.) Roy Wilkins of the National Association for the Advancement of Colored People (NAACP) summed up the reality:

> It must be understood that all organized bodies have their primary and secondary purposes. The primary purpose of the NAACP is to combat discrimination against Negroes. The primary purpose of labor organizations is to protect the wages, hours, and working conditions of its members. Civil rights activity for them is desirable but must be secondary. Inevitably these differences in emphasis will produce tensions in greater or less degree. (Hamilton and Hamilton 1997: p. 109)

And so they did, but no one misunderstood that organized labor and civil rights forces were essentially in the same liberal/progressive camp. Their main common constituencies came from the working classes, black and white.

Another major force was the religious community. The black churches had always been important in organizing and leading protests as far back as the struggle for the abolition of slavery. The church was a central (in many instances the only) meeting place for civil rights groups, and black ministers were natural leaders to turn to. If a large part of the civil rights struggle was the moral argument supporting universal human rights and dignity, one could expect religious institutions to be key participants in making that case. Especially important were prominent white leaders—Christians and Jews—who joined nationally and locally. All the religious activity symbolized the prospect of interracial harmony, nonviolent protest, and the ultimate possibility of achieving what was frequently called "the beloved community" (Lewis and D'Orso 1998: pp. 13, 73–75, 82–87, 475). This religious imprimatur gave the struggle not only a strong moral stance but also a kind of "softer," more forgiving, more reconciling, less antagonistic edge than could be found in a sheer politico-economic power struggle. It spoke of loving one's enemy, not of permanent anger. It served to remind the larger society of the basic humanness of the goals sought. Not that these arguments were always readily or universally accepted or believed by racist opponents, who often had their own religious interpretations justifying separation of the races.

In the final analysis, the religious/moral component of the civil rights struggle in the United States, at its peak in the 1960s, was a crucial factor on the national and international scene.

Some observers note the critical role played by mass protest movements, which provided not only the issues but the drama that brought into sharper focus the injustices frequently talked about in quasi-private, polite forums or courtrooms. This view is quick to emphasize the importance of mass media in communicating these dramas.

In 1963, President John F. Kennedy was candidly, if cryptically, admitting as much in commenting on the effects of the violent reactions of the Birmingham, Alabama, police to the peaceful civil rights demonstrations in that city. After the commissioner of safety, Eugene "Bull" Connor, ordered dogs and fire hoses turned loose on marching protesters, media pictures were on front pages and television screens throughout the world. In a meeting a few weeks later at the White House with civil rights leaders, Kennedy commented that opinion of Connor should not be too harsh because, in his own way, he had done a lot for civil rights that spring. The moral outrage that erupted nationwide provided a more receptive atmosphere for the president to submit a stronger civil rights bill to Congress (which later passed as the Civil Rights Law of 1964). A vast national and international audience was getting, really for the first time, constant living-room exposure to the depths of feelings, frustrations, and aspirations of thousands (who very likely represented millions more) who were no longer prepared to suffer the indignities of American apartheid quietly.

These were definitely dynamic events, accompanied by stimulating oratory calling on the country to live up to its high ideals of freedom, justice, and opportunity. All these phenomena helped politicize and mobilize a major national constituency for changing the old order. Even the "long hot summers" of urban rioting in the 1960s served to highlight the growing frustrations, notwithstanding the possibility, as some commentators asserted, that many of the rioters were likely as motivated by criminal opportunities for looting and personal gain as they were by the chance to make a political statement. Strongly condemned as lawless, the riots certainly found voices of understanding among policymakers and opinion leaders who, while calling for an end to the rioting, knew that something more than promises had to be delivered. Indeed, laws were passed—good ones. Changes did occur—important ones. Study commissions were appointed (nationally and locally) and, invariably, acknowledged that "more needs to be done" to redress legitimate grievances.

The early to mid-1960s was a period of enormous socioeconomic political change in the country. Major civil rights laws and social policies were enacted. In a sense, this period was more liberal and progressive than the New Deal of the 1930s. The 1960s not only dealt with economic issues; it provided the legislative framework for dismantling legal apartheid and extending political rights that the New Deal left intact. The Civil Rights Act of 1964 and the Voting Rights Act of 1965 were seminal pieces of legislation for this country.

In addition, in the wake of the trauma from the assassination of President Kennedy, President Lyndon B. Johnson announced a new thrust at reducing poverty in the country. This War on Poverty (Economic Opportunity Act of 1964) was accompanied by a prolific output of liberal legislation. In the 89th Congress—1965 to 1967—181 bills of the 200 Johnson requested were passed. There were major new health care provisions attached to Social Security (Medicare) and for the poor (Medicaid), aid to elementary and secondary education with provisions for additional grant money to poorer school districts, work-study grants for college students, model-cities funds for community development projects, rent supplements for needy tenants, aid to urban mass transit systems, support for the arts and humanities, and environmental-protection laws.

The Johnson administration labeled this bevy of liberal public policy activity as policies in pursuit of "the Great Society." And, indeed, for a brief time there was enthusiastic and spirited activity in desolated, isolated communities—North and South. The most public attention focused on the "community action" programs of the War on Poverty. The law promised to have "the maximum feasible participation" of persons in the communities to be served; that is, participation in decision-making on how the incoming federal funds would be spent. Several problems quickly developed, which were not entirely unpredictable. First, political control of the local organizations planning and implementing the programs (budget making, hiring personnel, designing programs) would be an issue in many places. These local battles were not always racial but were also power struggles between groups and individuals eager to reap the spoils of the incoming federal largess. Second, the programs mostly emphasized providing social services to the poor, whereas some policymakers wanted a War on Poverty that put far more emphasis on creating real public-sector jobs for people in the poor communities. This issue was connected to a third problem: money. The national budget for the endeavor was annual, subject to approval each year, which made long-term planning and attracting first-rate officials precarious at best. And, of course, complaints were made that too little money was appropriated for the task, given the enormous socioeconomic problems throughout the country.[4]

However, a number of successful individual programs resulted from this burst of liberal activity. Head Start, early education programs for poor preschoolers, proved to be very beneficial overall. Health programs for poor mothers and infants helped many young people get a healthy start in life. School lunch programs fed many children who came to school hungry through no fault of their own. Job Corps programs for the young gave work experience. These successes were easily overlooked or undermined, however, by the more glaring internecine fights and charges of fraud and corruption. And as in most ambitious undertakings, there were just enough proven cases of fraud and ineptness to arm conservatives who never agreed with the basic philosophy of governmental assistance in the first place.

Whatever the faults and weaknesses of particular antipoverty programs, those programs acknowledged that society was committed to helping provide opportunity to the less fortunate. On both fronts—civil rights and social welfare—the Great Society, if only for a brief time, made more than salutary efforts to doing something tangible in the struggle to achieve "E Pluribus Unum."

It was also a time, unfortunately, when the country was becoming

increasingly involved in the Vietnam War, competing not only for federal budget funds but for attention from social activists who had been
helpful in the antisegregation movement. As the country seemed to be,
if ever so painfully, coming to grips with its racial anxieties at home, it
was beginning to unravel over a questionable venture in Southeast Asia
that would prove as demoralizing and confrontational at home as any
phenomenon since the Civil War.

These developments culminated in the 1960s, and that heightened
period of social-protest movements has not reappeared since. In fact, a
perceptible backlash began in the late 1960s. Many people concluded
that reforms had gone too far, too fast. Now that laws were on the books
clearly prohibiting segregation and discrimination, individuals now
needed to spend less time protesting and more time preparing themselves to take advantage of the opportunities these laws opened up. The
past was behind us; those horrible days were over. No longer would
society have to contend with decisions (public or private) made on the
basis of racial identity. If before, people were treated as members of
subordinated groups, this would and should now give way to treatment
of people on the basis of individual merit—*all* people.

Therefore, in the midst of the dynamic decade of the 1960s, when
some civil rights proponents suggested what *they* meant by "more needs
to be done," their ideas met a wall of resistance that persists three
decades later in debates over affirmative action. Looking at the history
of segregation and continuing racism, Whitney M. Young Jr. of the
National Urban League proposed in 1963 a limited period of five years
for paying special attention to those subject to past American apartheid.
He envisioned an effort in the United States similar to the post–World
War II Marshall Plan to help rebuild war-torn Europe. Thus, he called
for a "Domestic Marshall Plan." He argued that this was fair and sound
policy. Otherwise, how else could the nation overcome centuries of
deliberate and successful policies of deprivation and denial? To him,
this was a stark reality (Young 1964). It was as real as the need to deal
with the consequences of weakened European countries. He emphasized the need for "better housing [and] more jobs," stating:

> If we embark upon a five-year program to end slum conditions, for
> example, people would see visible signs of change after the first year,
> and they would believe that the nation really means to end slums and
> they know that they too will have decent housing in a measurable and
> short period of time. Only such a timetable will convince the ghetto
> population that conditions are changing and riots can only retard
> advances. (Young 1967)

Young and the National Urban League were not then (or now) perceived as one of the more "militant" or "radical" protest groups. Far from it. The organization had an established reputation of working with corporate and government authorities on a cooperative, almost conciliatory basis. Coming from such a "respectable" source, the Domestic Marshall Plan idea could not be labeled as the "extremist" position of an "irresponsible" source. In the summer of 1967, following riots in Newark, Detroit, and several other urban areas, *Time* magazine carried a picture of Young on its cover. Many commentators noted the helpless, almost irrelevant role of most established civil rights leaders like Young. A caption over Young's picture virtually conceded this conclusion. It quoted Young as saying: "You got to give us some victories" (*Time* 1967).

It was an agonizing plea of recognition that black leaders who were attempting to serve as a bridge between the impoverished and the establishment were in an unenviable position. They were unable to respond to the needs of the poor without the cooperation of the establishment who had resources to legitimate their leadership roles.

Notwithstanding the pleas and the precariousness of some black leadership, the response to Young's Marshall Plan was quick and predictable. Neither was its rejection only from racial bigots, but also from some people otherwise sympathetic to the civil rights cause. A white civil rights supporter strongly disagreed with Young in language familiar in today's affirmative-action debates: "Compensation for Negroes is a subtle but pernicious form of racism. It requires that men be dealt with by society on the basis of race and color rather than on the basis of their humanity. It would therefore as a public policy legalize, deepen, and perpetuate the abominable racial cleavage that has ostracized and crippled the American Negro" (Haselden 1963: p. 43).

Neither did this person think it was fair to penalize those whites for the sins of their forefathers: "It leaves the descendants of the exploiters a guilt they cannot cancel and with the descendants of the exploited a debt they cannot collect . . . Slavery corrupts ambition and self-reliance; so too does patronizing social status" (Haselden 1963: p. 43).

While recognizing the importance of social movements, one should also consider two other critical phenomena in thinking about developments that have shaped the current reality: (1) the World War II fight against Nazism and fascism and (2) the Cold War struggle between communism and American democratic capitalism. Causal connections in such analyses should be made cautiously, but it is reasonable to assume that these events provided an international context that facilitated the argument and activism against American apartheid and racism.

As to the first—the fight against Nazism and fascism—the United States entered the war against dictatorial regimes that were avowedly at variance with any semblance of respect for democratic ideals. Germany was blatantly anti-Semitic and racist. It made no attempt to hide its views on these issues.

At the same time, civil rights advocates lost no opportunity in pointing out the irony of the United States proclaiming a doctrine of Four Freedoms and denouncing dictatorships while maintaining a rigidly segregated society on its own soil. There could be no escape from the embarrassing contradictions. African-American newspapers kept up a steady attack on segregated U.S. military units, lynchings, and all other vestiges of American racism. The banner of the "Double V" (victory abroad and victory at home) was raised in every possible circumstance—editorials, speeches, war bond rallies, letters to public officials, cartoons (depicting Adolf Hitler and segregationist Senator Theodore Bilbo of Mississippi as two of a kind). civil rights protesters against discrimination in hiring at defense plants marched in picket lines with placards that read: "Hitler Must Run This Plant—They Don't Employ Negroes." In one instance, the FBI sought advice from the Department of Justice regarding letters from black soldiers printed in *The People's Voice,* a New York City black newspaper owned and edited by the Reverend Adam Clayton Powell Jr. The soldiers complained bitterly of racist treatment overseas. The FBI under J. Edgar Hoover wanted to know if publication of such letters constituted seditious acts. Many civil rights activists were not deterred, however, in their criticisms. Reporting to a meeting of the NAACP in 1944, Executive Secretary Walter White told of his visits to military installations overseas:

> I wish it were possible for me to tell you truthfully that the alchemy of war and fighting to destroy Nazism had transformed the racial behavior in the armed services overseas. I cannot do so. We have merely transplanted to other lands the American pattern, both good and bad . . . Basically, the root of all our difficulties overseas is in insistence on racial segregation.
>
> As long as our government insists on segregation in an army and navy allegedly fighting for democracy, the chasm between the races will be perpetuated and broadened with resultant bitterness on both sides. (White 1974: pp. 482–483)

America's official responses were, at best, tortured and uncomfortable. Understandably so. Racial bigotry in Nazi Germany or segregated

America could not be defended in a society that put great stock in distinguishing itself from its enemy on the grounds of freedom, justice, and respect for the integrity of individuals. At the least, the war heightened the dilemma of the American creed, and it was not surprising that black military personnel returned from the war even more determined to pursue the second "V."

The onset of the Cold War presented yet another international context for the struggle against racism. The United States and the Soviet Union became locked in an ideological struggle for the next forty-five years. In the United States, communism replaced Nazism/fascism as the premier enemy. Newly independent nations, especially in Asia and Africa, became targets of persuasion to adopt one ideological regime or the other. (This competition had strategic as well as moral, philosophical consequences.) But as long as the United States presented the democratic/capitalist face with a disfiguring racist blot, it could hardly go into that struggle fully armed. There remained too many imperfections to legitimate its claim of moral *and* socioeconomic superiority. A nation that trumpeted the desirability of a free-market society but maintained closed labor and housing markets based on race was vulnerable to charges of hypocrisy at the least. Again, few American officials could honestly deny this, and some did not try. In 1946, as the Cold War battle lines were becoming increasingly apparent, then Acting Secretary of State Dean Acheson stated:

> The existence of discrimination against minority groups in this country has an adverse effect upon our relations with other countries. We are reminded over and over by some foreign newspapers and spokesmen that our treatment of various minorities leaves much to be desired. While sometimes these pronouncements are exaggerated and unjustified, they all too frequently point with accuracy to some form of discrimination because of race, creed, color, or national origin. Frequently, we find it next to impossible to formulate a satisfactory answer to our critics in other countries; the gap between the things we stand for in principle and the facts of a particular situation may be too wide to be bridged. An atmosphere of suspicion and resentment in a country over the way a minority is being treated in the United States is a formidable obstacle to the development of mutual understanding and trust between the two countries. We will have better international relations when these reasons for suspicion and resentment have been removed. (Acheson 1947: p. 146)

Such statements from important sources are matters of record. Precisely how influential they were in any given instance is difficult to establish. But it is reasonable to assume that the ideological fight against communism was compromised in some ways by existing racism in the United States. This was so even during the McCarthy period of the 1950s when some civil rights advocates took great pains to convince others that they had no affinity for communism. The real targets of the struggle were the minds of people of other countries who were potential military allies (with strategic bases) or political allies or friendly economic markets. Several incidents occurred involving African diplomats traveling from the United Nations in New York to Washington, D.C. They often were openly discriminated against by segregationist owners of public accommodations. Such confrontations always brought anguished apologies from American officials, but the embarrassing experiences (for the Africans and the Americans) were not overlooked in the ideological atmosphere of the Cold War. Whatever its relative advantage vis-à-vis the Soviet Union in terms of military power and economic growth, the United States was more than mildly compromised by its own internal racial problems. Such moral discomfort could hardly be mitigated by the argument, frequently made in this country, that communist countries were surely no better in extending freedom to their own citizens. The point was to be different from—and better than—the communists in significant, substantive ways, not to be *less* racist and *less* oppressive.

These historical developments had a cumulative effect on the character and nature of the civil rights struggle. In the earlier years, many important campaigns had quite definitive, universally shared benefits. Victories over de jure segregation in most places saw "colored" and "white" signs come down immediately or at least instantly ignored. Victories in court over the discriminatory practices of local voter registrars, in some instances but not all, resulted in literally thousands of black citizens lining up to register and to vote. Segregated interstate travel changed virtually overnight. These were visible, tangible pieces of evidence that "progress" was being made. And importantly, *all*—who ate in public restaurants, rode local buses, were of voting age—could immediately change their daily habits of living. (There were variations, of course, but earlier victories often were defining moments in the lives of millions of people.)

Later, after the seminal decade of the 1960s, victories often were more elusive and individually experienced. Achieving certain goals, especially in the economic sphere, resulted in improvements but did not immediately impact the lives of masses of people. This is especially evident when examining socioeconomic indicators of change. Ending employment discrimination, desegregating colleges and universities, achieving real open-housing laws—all are absolutely important. But all blacks, for a variety of reasons, have not experienced the benefits and certainly not to the same degree. Those who cannot afford homes in new neighborhoods or pass the entrance tests to schools of higher learning or possess the job skills to take advantage of new employment opportunities—these blacks (and there are many) seemingly have little over which to rejoice. Victories—yes; universally and immediately shared—no.

Unfortunately, this inevitable consequence, given the different levels of economic and educational achievements of blacks under legal segregation, spawned a mistaken notion that the successes of the earlier civil rights struggle benefited only a middle-class black cadre—not the masses. Legal segregation and discrimination held down all blacks in one form or another, irrespective of economic status. Once those legal barriers were lowered, one would expect a more-than-qualified segment to compete successfully on the open market sooner than many others. Thus, instead of contributing to a growing class schism in the black community, the civil rights movement has successfully exposed what was always known—that many blacks could and would compete in the larger society if given the chance. According to another mistaken notion, major civil rights organizations failed to address this situation in their earlier struggles. Knowledge of the history of major organizations' efforts to deal with the economic problems of lower-class blacks as well as the civil rights issues would dispel this inaccurate conclusion (Hamilton and Hamilton 1997). The challenge, then, was to continue the struggle to broaden the base of those capable of competing. In a sense, this task would be much more difficult than overcoming segregation laws on the books. It would certainly mean less than universal rejoicing at the achievement of every "breakthrough."

Encouraging Trends and Disturbing Developments

This section highlights three general areas of concern: some socioeconomic data, developments on the civil rights front, and the ascendance of an ideologically conservative mood in responding to issues of race, racism, and race relations.

Any assessment of "progress" or changes in the complicated arena of American race relations is a mixture of good and bad news. Regarding socioeconomic indicators—looking specifically at key health data, housing conditions, employment, education, and family income—

hard numbers over recent decades give a good sense of what has happened when comparing whites, blacks, and frequently Hispanics. In most instances, the data show steady progress in absolute terms for blacks. Yet there remains in some cases a major gap between blacks and whites that suggests much must be done in moving toward "E Pluribus Unum."

Life expectancy for black females since 1970 has increased by six years and by four years for black males. Note the persistent gap with their white counterparts.

Table 7.1   Life Expectancy at Birth by Race and Gender (number of years)

Birth year	White Male	White Female	Black Male	Black Female
1970	68.0	75.6	60.0	68.3
1994	73.2	79.6	64.9	74.1
2000 (projected)	74.2	80.1	64.6	74.7
2005 (projected)	74.7	81.0	64.5	75.0

Source: U.S Bureau of the Census 1997, *Statistical Abstract of the United States*, p. 88.

Infant mortality has decreased but is still more than double for blacks than whites.

Table 7.2   Infant Mortality

Birth year	White	Black and Other	Black
1980	10.9	20.2	22.2
1985	9.2	16.8	19.0
1990	7.6	15.5	18.0
1994	6.6	13.5	15.8

Source: U.S. Bureau of the Census 1997, *Statistical Abstract of the United States*, p. 22.
Note: Per 1,000 live births.

Reported AIDS cases have increased considerably for blacks, more than doubling from 1981 to 1996. The same is true for Hispanics. In spite of the much smaller population size, blacks have a higher absolute number of reported AIDS cases than whites.

Employment data by occupation over a recent thirteen-year period show increasing numbers for females, blacks, and Hispanics in most job

Table 7.3   Reported AIDS Cases, 1981–1996

1981–1996	1990	1992	1993	1994	1995	1996
			Non-Hispanic White			
268,746	22,302	22,446	47,597	32,808	29,500	26,324
			Non-Hispanic Black			
203,025	13,205	16,052	38,025	30,972	29,195	28,764
			Hispanic			
84,443	5,672	6,766	15,443	12,577	11,569	10,865

Source: U.S. Bureau of the Census 1997, *Statistical Abstract of the United States,* p. 142.
Note: Persons of Hispanic origin may be of any race.

Table 7.4   Conditions of Housing Units, 1995 (in thousands by householder characteristic)

	All Occupants		Black		Hispanic	
	Owner	Renter	Owner	Renter	Owner	Renter
Total units	63,544	34,150	5,137	6,637	3,245	4,512
2 or more living rooms or recreation rooms	26,179	2,762	1,659	355	925	197
Signs of rats in last 3 months	2,219	1,489	230	555	193	463
Holes in floors	503	571	106	177	71	125
Exposed wiring	873	887	88	240	80	175
Rooms without electric outlet	891	925	130	269	44	147
Open cracks or holes	1,943	2,584	356	750	168	426

Source: U.S. Bureau of the Census 1997, *Statistical Abstract of the United States,* p. 728.

categories. There are no exceptionally large gains, but the trend lines move upward (except for blacks in the farming category) (see Table 7.5).

Educational attainment data over three-plus decades show substantial improvements, but a big gap persists by race and gender (Table 7.6).

Clearly, there is a positive correlation between education and earnings, but where level of education is constant, whites earn more than blacks or Hispanics. Interestingly, as for females, race/ethnicity shows little difference in earnings. This is decidedly not the case with males, where white males at all levels outearn black and Hispanic males (Table 7.7).

ment, and voluntary implementation of fair employment practices by private industries and public agencies.

Crime, the criminal justice system, and the racial breakdown of victims and inmates are all disturbing parts of any project examining racism in the United States. There can never be any semblance of "E Pluribus Unum" as long as criminal statistics and the law enforcement system reflect any bias based on race. Blacks, as the data show, are clearly in a distressed situation.

A government report in 1998 concluded: "Blacks represented 43 percent of arrests, 54 percent of convictions, and 59 percent of prison admissions for violent crimes in 1994, indicating that arrested blacks are more likely to be convicted, and convicted blacks are more likely to be imprisoned, compared with whites (Council of Economic Advisors 1998: p. 51).

The homicide rate for black males (per 100,000) was 65.1 in 1994. The numbers in Table 7.10 are ominous, to say the least.

The death penalty is a volatile issue in American society, infused with moral arguments (pro and con) and racial overtones. Some opponents who do not raise the immorality point (i.e., it is morally wrong for the government to take a person's life as punishment) argue that blacks

Table 7.10   Homicide Rate by Race and Gender, 1970–1994

Year	Total	White		Black	
		Male	Female	Male	Female
1970	8.3	6.8	2.1	67.6	13.3
1980	10.7	10.9	3.2	66.6	13.5
1981	10.3	10.4	3.1	64.8	12.7
1982	9.6	9.6	3.1	59.1	12.0
1983	8.6	8.6	2.8	51.4	11.3
1984	8.4	8.3	2.9	48.7	11.2
1985	8.3	8.2	2.9	48.4	11.0
1986	9.0	8.6	3.0	55.0	12.1
1987	8.7	7.9	3.0	53.3	12.6
1988	9.0	7.9	2.9	58.0	13.2
1989	9.2	8.2	2.8	61.1	12.9
1990	10.0	9.0	2.8	69.2	13.5
1991	10.5	9.3	3.0	72.0	14.2
1992	10.0	9.1	2.8	67.5	13.1
1993	10.1	8.6	3.0	69.7	13.6
1994	9.6	8.5	2.6	65.1	12.4

Source: U.S. Bureau of the Census 1997, Statistical Abstract of the United States, p. 204.
Note: Victim rates per 100,000 resident population in specified group.

have been disproportionately subject to death by state execution because of a racist law enforcement system. This argument pervades discussions of the discriminatory nature of the criminal justice system. It points to evidence of "racial profiling" whereby law enforcement officers operating on stereotypical prejudices tend to stop, search, and arrest blacks (for suspicion of creating a crime or resembling the profile of wanted criminals) more so than whites. Denied as a prevalent practice for some time, more recently state and local authorities are candidly admitting that such behavior is more prevalent among law enforcement officials than previously thought.

Recent trends in the struggle against racial discrimination are characterized by increased pronouncements from virtually all quarters condemning such practices, but growing difficulties in the evidence needed to prove that such practices still exist. It takes rather concrete evidence or outright admission to finally convince authorities of a serious problem. To be sure, there is no socially acceptable defense today of blatant racism or discriminatory acts. But when civil rights advocates attempt to establish the existence of discrimination and seek remedies to alleviate such practice, they are met with increasingly high standards of proof of actual harm experienced by identifiable individuals. At the same time, there is a clear trend away from according legitimacy to the lingering effects (legacy) of past discrimination. To establish such a connection, more than a historical account of the past frequently is necessary. In fact, it is very likely that such accounts will be met with unapologetic concession accompanied by an admonition that the legacy of a racist past is *not* relevant for future action.

No clearer illustration of this is found than in the words of former U.S. senator Alan Simpson (R–Wyo). The occasion was a Senate confirmation hearing in 1987 on Judge Robert H. Bork. President Ronald Reagan had nominated Bork for appointment as associate justice of the U.S. Supreme Court. Bork's judicial and scholarly record did not please civil rights advocates, who strongly testified against his confirmation. One witness, Professor John Hope Franklin,[5] gave a concise history of racial segregation and discrimination laws since World War II (including his own experiences in being forced to use segregated trains traveling interstate). He noted how Bork had been on the opposite side of legal struggles against a de jure segregated system. Such a past record, according to Franklin and many others, should disqualify Bork from a seat on the highest court of the land. But Simpson, a Bork supporter, was not convinced. While complimenting Professor Franklin on his "eloquent" presentation ("You make the Constitution live for your students. There's no question about that. I'm certain of that."), he made it clear that he did not see the relevance of that historical lesson to the task at hand. He stated:

> The issue is that was a different time. Indeed, it was. So that's the way it is. And the extraordinary poignancy of your remarks, and the story about going back to the Negro coach, those things happened. . . . If we are going to feel guilt about what we did in this country in 1964, we'll never get anywhere in this country. . . . How long are we going to pick old scabs in this country? It stalls us from progress. Those things happened. They were repugnant. They were repulsive. We've made tremendous strides. (*Nomination of Robert H. Bork* 1987: p. 736)

This clearly reflects the thinking of more than a small segment of the society on how it intends *not* to hold itself accountable for past racism. (This sentiment is reminiscent of the argument made in the 1960s against Whitney Young's Domestic Marshall Plan discussed earlier.)

The trend today is to treat the use of race as an allowable policy concern only after "strict scrutiny" reveals there is no other way to remedy the complaint, and *if* it can be shown there is a compelling state interest to be served by using racial classification. Neither should one assume that arguments pushing for "diversity"—in the workplace, in schools, in neighborhood housing—will necessarily be accepted as meeting the "compelling state interest" test.

There is also a trend toward permitting states to exercise more power, especially regarding "social programs," and removing the federal government as much as possible from responsibility. The importance of this trend lies in the fact that civil rights forces have historically relied on national government, not the states, in the battle for racial justice and economic opportunity. "States' Rights" have traditionally meant that some states (especially earlier in the South) would be less receptive to calls for racial justice. With pressing economic issues facing African Americans, there is little cause for optimism from many other states and regions in dealing not only with race but with social-welfare issues.

The current trend toward "devolution" of more power and responsibility to state/local levels would suggest that blacks will have a more difficult time convincing their nonurban state legislatures to respond to their needs of justice and opportunity. In competition with each other for resources, states inevitably seek to attract industries of economic growth. Therefore, they want to provide as low a tax base as possible, which means less state expenditures for health, welfare, and even education for the state poor and needy. States are concerned about giving tax rebates and other infrastructural incentives, and these matters take priority in the long run. Some states are more affluent than others and will deal with these problems more easily. However, the nature of interstate competitiveness does not augur well for how the least among state citizens will have a reasonable advantage in their bid for state resources. In this regard, the devolution trend is an ominous one.

A third element, flowing from the second, is a decided conservative mood. (Less national government involvement is part of this trend.) More reliance on market forces and private self-help efforts are also aspects of this trend. An important dimension is a much more visible, if not discernibly larger, cadre of black conservative voices challenging the preeminence of traditional civil rights advocates. These voices have always been around, but they are more voluble today and are accorded more public attention. They take positions against affirmative action and favor privatized solutions (for example, school vouchers and even privatizing Social Security), fewer government programs for alleviating poverty, and unfettered market-economy measures.

Like their white counterparts, black conservatives are not a monolithic voice, but they take positions that directly challenge the views of traditional civil rights advocates on both antidiscrimination remedies and efforts to provide economic opportunity. While black conservatives by no means voice the majority sentiment in black communities—as consistently demonstrated by voting behavior and opinion polls—their views nonetheless provide a strong counter to the traditional ideological stance of civil rights advocates.[6] Such voices operate to legitimize a *white* majority conservative mood. Although they hardly represent more than 10 percent of black voters nationally, they still keep conservative hope alive that more blacks will hear and heed their arguments and join them.

Again, their main utility lies not in a broad base among the black masses but in the credence they give white conservatives. Now, the latter can have less fear of being branded racist if black conservatives have agreed with them. This imputation of legitimacy extends to race issues and to economic policy. But it is the latter area that is especially significant to the ideological conservatives. The race issue (affirmative action, mainly) is not *as* important as the fundamental principles of a maximum market economy unburdened by government regulation. Race relations, as will be noted later, is simply not a top priority on the national agenda, voluminous public pronouncements notwithstanding. But control and direction of the economy is and always will be the central concern. To have prominent African Americans (members of a minority group with obvious economic disadvantages) articulating strong antistatist, procapitalist views reaffirms the conservative stance—among whites who after all are in the majority.

The very vocabulary of popular political discourse is further evidence of a conservative mood. One of the most insidious terms to slip into social relations dialogue is "politically correct." If one demonstrates by word or deed sensitivity to racial, ethnic, gender, or physical identities and disabilities, one is being "politically correct." Frequently, this has the pejorative implication of overreacting or responding to a "fad," done only to curry favor from a special group. The sensitivity is seen as pandering, much as a politician does for voter support. Why such demonstrated sensitivity is labeled "politically" correct—instead of being perceived as acting responsibly civil in a multiracial, ethnic, plural society—is seldom, if ever, questioned.

Yet we know that language, words, and images are important in mass societies. This is particularly true in political democracies where appeals to voters must be made. Political office seekers today virtually eschew the "L" word—liberal—and have no hesitancy in labeling themselves as some form of "conservative": fiscal conservative, compassionate conservative, pragmatic conservative, fiscal conservative/social moderate, and so on. Since the Ronald Reagan years of the 1980s, the ideological pendulum has moved, if not to the far right, to a more moderate/centrist/conservative position. Such perceptions are frequently documented not only in opinion surveys but in careful analyses of voting records of congressional members by various national interest groups and the ratings those groups, liberal and conservative, give the legislators for home-district consumption. Of course, they take as their reference base the peak years of civil rights and socioeconomic activism of the 1960s. Then, especially under President Johnson, the country experienced its last days of political liberalism—the Great Society. (In actual terms, as noted earlier, it was a rather short period from 1963 to 1968, with the decline beginning in 1967.) Those years are gone, and even President Clinton proclaimed "the end of big government" in his 1995 State of the Union address.

Thus the conservative mood today essentially means little likelihood for consideration of a "full employment" bill, universal health care for all, or serious federal resources for strapped local school districts. Where public-sector budgets show a surplus, conservatives opt to cut taxes rather than increase expenditures for the needy. Any serious conversation about the future struggle against current racism and its legacy in the United States, along with expanding economic opportunity, must be conducted in the context of a society that basically prefers its national government to be less, not more, active in socioeconomic matters. And if these topics are raised when the private-sector economy is performing well for a vast number of ordinary working-class people, one will find how quickly the conversation can become muted.

Opportunities and Strategies

In such an environment, one would be justified in having little optimism about great leaps forward in the near term. And yet, the United States is a fortunate country. Even though it has not achieved the "E Pluribus Unum" to which it aspires, the country in 1999 enjoyed a decidedly more optimistic mood among black Americans than one might expect. This suggests that blacks might well be more realistic about the present and future on racial matters than even some whites. (This point will be covered in the concluding section.) Except in rare episodic moments, the American system seldom responds other than in slow, prodding, incremental ways. In a sense, the 1960s spoiled many liberals by leading them to feel that decade would become the rule (in terms of the pace and direction of race and race relations, at least) rather than the exception. Another incontrovertible fact is that certain absolutely crucial things *did* happen and societal attitudes underwent fundamental changes. Most politicians can no longer engage in the kind of race-baiting politics that supported American apartheid in an earlier time. In 1999, Senate Majority Leader Trent Lott (R–Miss) was put in the awkward position of having to explain his association with the Council of Conservative Citizens. The national organization is an outgrowth of the old prosegregation White Citizens Council formed in the 1950s to resist school desegregation. Now, at least, prominent politicians must seek to distance themselves from such associations and are forced to give tortured explanations denying agreement with many of the groups' more outspoken racist views.[7] Likewise, corporations can no longer *openly* defy laws on equal employment practices. Real estate agents must now be most clever and inventive in practicing racial discrimination in the housing sales and rental markets. Without question, many are up to the task, but now at least the efforts have to be made on penalty of legal repercussions.

What Are Some Opportunities?

According to a scientific study conducted by the Southern Regional Council (SRC) in 1996, a majority of Americans are, in fact, receptive to certain efforts to reduce racial inequality. But they are also concerned about the costs of government programs to achieve this goal. The report was candid in pointing out that racial inequality was not an issue uppermost in the minds of most white Americans (Southern Regional Council 1998). It found significant white support for such measures as more resources for education, strong enforcement of antidiscrimination laws, and even affirmative action where "quotas" or "preferential treatment" were not part of the equation. Part of the problem, the report concluded, was confusion over the meaning of "affirmative action." And if more time was spent educating the public in this regard, positive results might be forthcoming. Likewise, there was genuine hope that liberal forces could be mobilized around an enlightened race relations agenda.

Importantly, the SRC report concluded: "Americans are more supportive of public policies designed to offer help based on economic status than those targeted at racial minorities. This class versus race edge prevails regarding government spending priorities, affirmative action programs, and general policies to improve socio-economic conditions" (Southern Regional Council 1998: p. 15).

This report is essentially encouraging, but there are important cautionary observations. First, the fact that "class" has an edge over "race" as an approach is not a revelation to long-struggling civil rights groups (Hamilton and Hamilton 1997). Those groups have always understood the political problems of raising the race issue in American policymaking. Thus, going back to the New Deal, they supported "universal" social programs fully aware that many blacks would not benefit from those programs on a nondiscriminatory basis, but they compromised and did not raise this race issue in many instances. They adopted a social-welfare agenda that clearly recognized the social *and* political wisdom of such a strategy. Therefore, they supported "full employment" even though they knew this did not mean "fair employment." They supported universal health care for all, even though they knew that health care would be allocated on a discriminatory and segregated basis.

The same was true with public-housing legislation and educational resources, such as teacher salaries. Fighting *these* realities meant a continued, vigilant civil rights agenda. That is, the struggle to obtain "fair" (nondiscriminatory) employment should not be abandoned; it simply was not politically wise to link it to the effort to obtain "full" employment. Thus, a "dual agenda" strategy had to be pursued, and over the years this very fact of race, racism, and race relations in the United States has characterized the civil rights struggle. Very often, civil rights groups were advised *not* to raise the race issue out of fear of losing broader support for class issues. At times, they followed this advice and strategy but at a cost. Importantly, the civil rights forces tried repeatedly to seek allies among the white liberal forces. They were sometimes successful but often were rebuffed precisely because of the preference of class over race.

Only the brief, liberal burst of activism in the 1960s saw a breakthrough that provided the opportunity for important gains on both agendas simultaneously. In other words, the SRC finding of preference for class over race in the 1990s is an old story known all too well to civil rights groups faced with hard political realities. And as the report honestly records, these realities are no less important now than they were decades ago. The opportunity today, however, lies in the fact that there are antidiscrimination laws in place. Now, a decision does not have to be made between advocating one agenda at the political expense of the other. There can be a political campaign for "universal" social policies, which, if enacted, cannot legally discriminate. And there can be simultaneously vigorous efforts to overcome de facto discrimination. Theoretically, the two struggles ought not be in conflict, but there is an additional political caveat here that will be explained in the concluding section.

The data in the SRC report (and it is not the only encouraging one) have to be understood in another important political context. Aggregate national survey results can (and do) show encouraging possibilities for liberal policymaking. But the decisionmaking institutions in the United States are far more complex entities. Congress, for instance, is composed of 435 separate House of Representative districts and 100 Senate seats (two per state). Legislators listen as often as not to *their* distinct and locally based constituents, who, in fact, elect them to national office and to whom they are beholden for tenure. Built-in checks and balances in the governmental process complicate policymaking even more. No one political institution (the House of Representatives, the Senate, or the presidency) can act without the concurrence of the others or only on certain occasions with a "super," two-thirds majority vote.

This system of internal checks and balances was put in place at the drafting of the U.S. Constitution in 1787. The purpose was to limit the likelihood of a tyrannical majority. In addition, intricate rules of policymaking give considerable power to entrenched, resourceful interest groups. A process of bargaining, negotiating, and compromise is the rule. Survey data cannot capture all the intricacies involved in moving an issue from general agreement to final outcome. What happens in the final stage when vested interests (that might well not represent a national majority view) craft a final piece of legislation may not look anything like survey results in a national poll—which understandably cannot probe and reflect all the vital interests sitting at the table determining what the legislation ultimately will be.

This is a frustrating aspect of American politics in a federalist, pluralist system, but it is the constitutional way Americans define and pursue their version of political democracy. National survey respondents are not at the bargaining table. Less visible but more powerful, numerically smaller interests are. But this conclusion does not counsel giving up on efforts to build broad opinion support. It is simply an admonition that American democratic politics involves much more in pluralist policymaking than meets the eye—or gets reflected in an opinion survey.

Another recent phenomenon demonstrating changing times and the conundrum of race and democratic politics involved the reelection of a black Democratic congressman from a predominantly white district in Georgia. (This also illustrates some of the substantive policy accommodations that have to be made to be "successful" in the electoral arena.) U.S. Representative Sanford D. Bishop Jr. previously represented a predominantly black constituency until congressional district lines were redrawn. Now he represents Georgia's 2nd Congressional District in southwest Georgia. The population is 60 percent white, 39 percent black, and 1 percent other. Per capita income is $12,602 for whites and $5,529 for blacks. Twelve percent of whites and 43 percent of blacks live below the poverty line. Seventy-one percent of white adults over twenty-five years of age have a high school degree compared with 44 percent of blacks. In this setting, some were apprehensive that whites would not vote for this NAACP veteran of the civil rights movement who was an admirer of Dr. Martin Luther King Jr. *But they did.* Bishop beat his white Republican opponent by 57 percent to 43 percent in 1998.

To some observers, this proved that whites in a southern state with a long history of segregation and discrimination could set aside race and vote on other bases. It was proof that congressional districts need not be drawn to favor blacks. White support validated the legal and political arguments that it was not necessary to create minority/majority districts to get blacks elected to Congress. White voters could rise above racial prejudice after all. As one citizen stated: "Sanford actually represents people without regard to race, and when he does that people forget his race" (*New York Times* 1998: p. A1). But there is more to the story. Bishop was doing what American politicians are at times required to do to get elected. He changed his views to appeal to the majority in his district. One reporter wrote:

> Mr. Bishop has earned the fealty of white constituents through his aggressive advocacy for federal farm programs, balanced budgets, welfare reform, school prayer and gun ownership. To suit his district, he has switched positions on issues like the assault weapons ban, which he first supported and later opposed. He advertises himself as a conservative and reinforced that claim by becoming the only black member of the right leaning Democratic caucus known as the Blue Dogs. (p. A12)

In the racial head count in Congress, official records accurately show a black congressman occupying the seat from Georgia's 2nd Congressional District. It remains to be seen, given the economic disparities between whites and blacks in his district, whether the latter will benefit in any significant way from his holding office. In the final analysis, the representative's concrete stand on policy issues will tell whether the "color blind" political action of his white supporters translates into economic benefits for masses of his black constituents as well as whites. In this instance, being "color blind" for one group of voters could result in negative economic consequences for another group. No one will ever have to mention race overtly to explain this result. They simply will be politicians in a democratic society doing the will of a majority of constituents.

Are There Promising Strategies?

There are hardly any eureka-type revelations here. There is no hidden silver bullet that, if only discovered, would end racism with neat dispatch. America has been at this process and these issues for quite some time. But times do change. It is difficult to foresee the importance of a new international dimension intruding to facilitate positive change, as was seen with World War II and the Cold War. Neither is a "crisis" (a widespread economic depression or a burst of mass 1960s-style protests) likely to serve as a catalyst for moving the lack of popular concern or low priority of race to a much higher position on the public agenda. Certainly not in the near term.

The more effective strategies will likely include (as unsatisfying and relatively unrewarding as these might seem) more of the same tedious efforts at coalition building, taking advantage of the egalitarian ethos (as opposed to an earlier permissive race-baiting atmosphere). In the legal realm, the civil rights movement has developed its longest and most substantively adept leadership strategies, which remain promising. They lie not so much in constitutional or statutory interpretation but in the realm of acceptable proof of existing discrimination. Given the covert, subtle nature of much discrimination, this means careful gathering of evidence leading to hard-to-refute allegations.

One approach is described as "auditing research."[8] Teams of job applicants or housing seekers are sent to answer ads: a black team and a white team. The white team follows the black team. Results have shown clear instances where the minorities have been denied at much higher rates than whites. These experiments have been criticized on methodological and ethical grounds, but their results have been quite useful in exposing the racism lying comfortably beneath the surface in American society. Perfecting these strategies for use in law enforcement should be a major priority. Once discrimination is established, the penalties (revocation of licenses, stiff fines, publication of abuses) should be as stringent as possible to match the rhetoric of public indignation at continued discrimination. Weak punishment will be of little, if any, value and might well aggravate the problem because it would provide a relatively painless, permissive way to continue old behavior. Another approach could involve a carefully constructed argument to demonstrate the ingenious nature of the "color-blind" stance. Here, instances such as Georgia's 2nd Congressional District could serve to pierce the defense that race is not involved in otherwise seemingly acceptable political behavior. This is very difficult, since racial discrimination and not poor economic condition per se is constitutionally prohibited. But if a relationship can be established between race, economic condition, and representative conduct, the "strict scrutiny" test might be met. There are no certainties here, but social scientists, economists, and lawyers ought to explore this territory. There is more to the vagaries of this subject than the simplistic, misleading sobriquet for justice called "color blindness." Considerable evidence will turn up regarding "auditing research" and the race/economic areas. The point is to persuade decisionmakers (legislators and jurists) of the probative value of this evidence.

Conclusion: "E Pluribus Justitia"

At the beginning of the preceding section, reference was made to encouraging signs of an optimistic mood among blacks in the United States. Given the constant public exposure of conditions and incidents with racist implications — racially motivated crimes, educational achievement gaps, episodic flare-ups in the criminal justice system, and blatant discriminatory acts by corporate and public officials — a recent survey by the major think tank devoted to African-American interests, the Joint Center for Political and Economic Studies, should be of interest to policymakers.

Table 7.11 shows blacks and whites still differed significantly on the single most important problem facing the country in 1998. The most troubling topics: crime, violence, and drugs among 21.7 percent of blacks (compared with 10.3 percent of whites) versus the moral crisis for 20.6 percent of whites (compared with 10.2 percent of blacks). While a big gap exists between the races on "race relations," this problem ranks low on the list of concerns for both groups. Unfortunately, the survey gives no information specifying the meaning of "race relations," as was done with some other broad categorical topics.

Table 7.11   Responses to "What Do You Think Is the Single Most Important Problem Facing the Country Today?" (1998)

Topic	Population		
	Black %	White %	General %
Crime, violence, drugs	21.7	10.3	11.7
Employment (jobs, good-paying jobs, poverty, homelessness)	17.3	5.8	7.6
Education	15.7	17.2	15.8
Moral crisis (morals, family values, Clinton scandal)	10.2	20.6	19.4
Economy	8.4	9.8	11.6
Health care	7.6	6.3	5.5
World affairs (foreign policy, terrorism, world economy, lack of leadership)	5.2	16.9	16.0
Race relations	3.8	0.8	0.8
None/don't know	10.4	11.3	11.9
Numbers surveyed	850	709	850 [a]

Source: Joint Center for Political and Economic Studies, *Public Opinion 1998: Political Attitudes,* by David Bositis, October 1998, p. 244.
Note: a. Includes 94 blacks.

In Table 7.12, the survey noted that for the first time in a Joint
Center survey, blacks responded more favorably than the general population when asked whether they are financially better or worse off than
a year ago. It is interesting that younger blacks (18 to 25; 26 to 35)
show very high "better" response percentages over "same." Only
among those 51 to 64 years old is there a smaller percentage of "better"
to "same." Note also the responses by income category. Only the lowest
(less than $15,000) and the $75,000–$90,000 category register higher
for "same" over "better." Given the importance of education, the educational cohorts in this table should be monitored carefully. In fact, in
light of the relative economic boom in the country, these data suggest
that blacks in sixteen demographic categories perceive themselves
doing "better" than the previous year and doing the "same" in seven
categories. Whereas, for the general population, the numbers are five
("better") and eighteen ("same").

Such results, then, should lead one not to be too surprised about the
result revealed in Table 7.13. A majority of blacks (51 percent) feel the
country is going in the right direction. But only 43.3 percent of the general population share this view. The demographic categories for blacks
indicate a general consensus on this view, with only six categories registering a negative feeling: 18 to 25 years, 36 to 50 years, secular conservatives *by the widest margin*, with incomes less than $15,000 or
$75,000–$90,000 by substantial margin, and more than $90,000. Thus,
the poorest and the most affluent blacks are inclined to view the country
as going in the wrong direction.

On balance, one should be encouraged by these opinion data, even
though survey experts point out that such results are at best snapshots at
a particular moment and can be countermanded by new, negative
events. While they indicate wide racial differences in some instances,
they do not augur dire omens against continued progress and consequential optimism. In fact, the opposite could be gleaned from the data.
Namely, with persistent diligent pursuit of both the civil rights agenda
and the social-welfare/economic agenda, more positive results could be
forthcoming in a reasonable time. One must always add here the
absolute importance of a continuing healthy, growing economy.

Little has been said in this chapter about the impact of immigration
on the topic of racism in America. But this is a development that must
be recognized and *used*.

Immigration of non-European groups, particularly Hispanic and
Asian, will continue at great rates. This will obviously have consequences for the indigenous American population. It always has. But

Table 7.12 Responses to: "Would You Say That You Are Financially Better Off, Worse Off, or About the Same Now as You Were a Year Ago?"

	Black Population					General Population			
	Better %	Same %	Worse %	D/K %	(N)	Better %	Same %	Worse %	(N)
Total	51.0	38.0	9.2	1.8	850	36.5	47.1	16.5	850
White	—	—	—	—	—	31.5	50.9	17.6	709
Men	49.0	37.3	13.7	—	400	37.4	42.0	20.6	412
Women	52.7	38.7	5.2	3.4	450	35.6	50.8	12.6	438
18–25 years	46.9	29.5	19.3	4.3	127	43.8	30.3	25.8	89
26–35	65.3	27.3	6.8	0.5	168	49.4	45.2	5.4	166
36–50	47.4	40.8	11.8	—	257	38.5	41.2	20.3	301
51–64	36.6	55.0	4.3	4.1	175	31.3	47.0	21.7	166
65+	77.7	21.0	1.3	—	88	16.4	75.9	7.8	116
Northeast	57.1	31.9	6.9	4.1	153	40.1	49.4	10.5	172
Midwest	43.5	46.5	9.5	0.6	156	33.2	48.8	18.0	205
South	50.8	37.1	10.3	1.8	452	36.5	49.0	14.5	296
West	54.3	38.8	6.9	—	88	36.7	39.5	23.7	177
Liberal	55.0	36.0	6.9	2.2	333	42.8	36.7	20.5	229
Moderate	46.6	44.7	10.7	—	354	41.6	47.5	11.0	255
Secular Conservative	7.6	58.0	34.4	—	24	34.8	41.7	23.5	132
Christian Conservative	70.3	27.8	2.0	—	115	22.4	65.8	11.7	196
Less than HS	43.1	47.1	9.8	—	97	23.5	52.9	23.5	51
HS Graduate	54.5	31.8	10.8	2.9	277	36.0	40.4	23.7	228
Some College/Tech	53.3	41.8	5.0	—	184	34.7	54.4	10.9	239
College Degree +	49.2	40.5	7.5	2.8	259	38.7	46.7	14.6	315
Less than $15,000	16.9	59.9	23.2	—	75	17.8	35.6	46.7	45
$15–35,000	51.9	48.1	—	—	129	36.3	53.5	10.2	157

Source: U.S. Bureau of the Census, *Statistical Abstract of the United States.*

Table 7.13   Responses to "Do You Feel Things in the Country Are Generally Going in the Right Direction, or Do You Feel Things Have Pretty Seriously Gotten Off on the Wrong Track?"

	Black Population				General Population			
	Right Direction %	Wrong Track %	D/K %	(N)	Right Direction %	Wrong Track %	D/K %	(N)
Total	51.0	42.3	6.7	850	46.0	46.1	7.9	850
White	—	—	—	—	43.3	48.5	8.2	709
Men	51.3	44.2	4.6	400	51.9	42.5	5.6	412
Women	50.7	40.7	8.6	450	40.4	49.5	10.0	438
18–25 years	43.3	54.4	2.3	127	44.9	43.8	11.2	89
26–35	51.3	44.4	4.3	168	42.2	48.2	9.6	166
36–50	44.5	46.0	9.5	257	50.5	44.9	4.7	301
51–64	57.2	30.0	12.8	175	41.6	49.4	9.0	166
65+	77.5	22.5	—	88	49.1	43.1	7.8	116
Northeast	47.5	41.5	11.1	153	50.0	42.4	6.4	172
Midwest	50.1	40.4	9.5	156	51.2	45.4	6.3	205
South	51.5	43.7	4.8	452	48.3	50.0	6.8	296
West	55.8	40.1	4.1	88	43.2	44.1	13.0	177
Liberal	50.3	37.4	12.3	333	52.8	31.9	15.3	229
Moderate	54.5	43.2	2.3	354	43.1	50.2	6.7	255
Secular Conservative	19.3	80.7	—	24	61.4	37.1	1.5	132
Christian Conservative	52.5	47.5	—	115	37.2	56.1	6.6	196
Less than HS	81.8	18.2	—	97	39.2	43.1	17.6	51
HS Graduate	46.7	44.1	9.2	277	36.4	57.0	6.6	228
Some College/Tech	45.4	42.4	12.2	184	53.1	40.6	6.3	239
College Degree +	48.7	47.8	3.5	259	48.3	45.4	6.3	315
Less than $15,000	45.6	54.4	—	75	24.4	66.7	8.9	45
$15–35,000	56.5	30.8	12.6	129	45.2	52.2	2.5	157

Source: U.S. Bureau of the Census, *Statistical Abstract of the United States.*

now and in the future, these new immigrants will be vibrant competitors in the economic market. Unlike an earlier time, they cannot be subjugated, discriminated against, or legally exploited. They will further challenge the goal of "E Pluribus Unum," and they ought to be allies for any coalitions aimed at vigorous enforcement of antidiscrimination laws. All groups must be protected. These newer immigrants will less likely be persuaded to shed their cultural habits and "assimilate," if only because the old "melting pot" thesis has, fortunately, been discredited. The "unum" envisioned is not necessarily one ultimate, homogeneous cultural canvas but a situation where many groups can live respectfully not as "one" but in "justice." More vibrant, truly competitive immigrant groups could contribute to the development of a more cosmopolitan society.

So much of America's coming to grips with its Achilles' heel is factored through the prism of anguish, fear, and guilt regarding the country's history of slavery and sanction of segregation, its treatment of indigenous peoples who were already here, and its earlier racist/exclusionist immigration laws. Newer, added groups arriving on different terms should help the country transform itself into a truly international beacon—truly unprecedented in modern history—where many different peoples can live and prosper without the undemocratic and racist rules of an earlier time. Of course, as racial, ethnic, and gender barriers fall, the country will face a totally new situation: for the first time in its history, all the citizens will have a chance to compete in a truly open and fair economic market. If increased immigration can speed this process, it will serve a historic purpose.

Finally, whatever the signs are of a hopeful, optimistic mood among blacks, a willingness by whites to accept some class-based remedies, and indeed encouraging socioeconomic trends, one should not be sanguine that these phenomena will be self-fulfilling. A truly open and fair economic market will not emerge without conscious *public* initiatives not only to permit people to participate but to prepare them to do so. In this regard, the data on "Disturbing Developments" reported earlier should be given careful attention. The country is not yet at "E Pluribus Unum."

Thus, one of the most important and difficult tasks is to stem the pendulum swing toward "less government" by continuing to make the argument for national responsibility. Whatever else is known about the story of America's engagement of these issues, this country has only progressed when the national community (especially through the lead of the national government) has been actively involved. This does not mean to the exclusion of state/local entities or the private sector. But the best vehicle for orchestrating and representing a collective will to deal with collective problems is a national democratic system. This is not an easy proposition to push at a time when there is less inclination to spend sufficient resources on new programs. It is certainly a difficult posture to take at a time of economic boom, and there is a mood to give more leeway (and less regulatory restrictions) to the private sector. Likewise, if the Joint Center survey data hold up, opponents of more-activist government can point to the generally optimistic feelings of African Americans about the future. But these feelings should reflect a mood to build on, not to rest on. There are needy groups in the society that still suffer from racial and economic obstacles.

It has ever been the case that those who need public protection the most are those who have the least private resources to protect themselves and provide for their families. Whether on the civil rights front (struggle against racism) or on the social-policy front (universal social programs), the country has not reached the stage where *all* its citizens are free to compete in the open market on anything resembling an equitable playing field.

Making this case and pursuing it vigorously remains the challenge.

Notes

1. See Glazer 1997. "There were significant differences in the ways European immigrant groups assimilated. But there are orders of magnitude in difference. The differences between the rate of assimilation of Irish and Germans, or Italians and Jews become quite small when we contrast them with the differences over time between white European immigrants of any group and American blacks. These differences create different perspectives, on our historic past, on our present, on the shape of our culture" (p. 155). And, ". . . we also cannot ignore the remarkable and unique degree of separation between blacks and others. The caste characteristic still holds, and one evidence of it is either black or not—partial degrees of blackness, despite the reality of a very mixed genetic inheritance, will not be recognized, not by our Census, not by our society. We do not recognize partial or loose affiliation with the group, or none at all, for blacks, as we do for all other ethnic and racial groups" (p. 158).

2. One is tempted here to draw attention to the Brazilian preference, as described by the Nascimentos in Chapter 5 of this volume, that is, the preference, by some, to refer to "the social question" as opposed to "the racial question." Likewise, Wilmot James, Chapter 2 in this volume, discusses the "reality" and "near-term inevitability" of racial consciousness in the South African context. There appears to be in that country a recognition of this stage of devel-

opment, even if it is attacked as a "re-racialization" of South Africa. (The American equivalent response is "reverse discrimination.")

3. This is a problem clearly common to all three countries in this project. But, in the United States, it is certainly one of political will to allocate existing sufficient resources, not so much whether the economy can afford the cost.

4. In 1966, a huge consortium of civil rights, liberal, labor, religious, and a variety of civic-minded individuals signed what was called "The Freedom Budget for All Americans." Calling for $185 billion over a ten-year period, the economic plan represented the most idealistic *and sincere* thinking of the liberal community at that time about what was needed to achieve the "unum" the country had been espousing for centuries. It emphasized a full-employment economy, universal health care, full educational opportunity programs, and much more. Many people observed that one important aspect of the plan was that it was "for all," not only for black Americans. (In a sense, this grandiose proposal parallels The Freedom Charter issued by the African National Congress in South Africa several years earlier, at least in terms of hopes and aspirations.) Needless to say, the Freedom Budget received a polite but negative reception in the corridors of power in Washington, D.C. It was never really taken seriously.

5. Professor Franklin in 1997 was selected by President Bill Clinton to chair the President's Initiative on Race. Clinton's charge stated: "Today, I ask the American people to join me in a great national effort to perfect the promise of America for this new time as we seek to build our more perfect union. . . . That is the unfinished work of our time, to lift the burden of race and redeem the promise of America." *New York Times*, June 14, 1997.

6. See *Journal of Blacks in Higher Education* 1998, and Conti and Stetson 1993, for a full review.

7. Kifner 1999. The senator initially stated that he had "no firsthand knowledge" of the organization's views, although he had addressed the group and met with the members. The senator's uncle called him an "honorary member." Predictably, Senator Lott issued a statement saying: "I have made my condemnation of the white supremacist and racist view of this group, or any group, clear. Any use of my name to publicize their view is not only unauthorized— it's wrong."

8. See details in Fix and Struyk 1993; Cross 1990; Heckman and Siegelman 1993; Bendick 1994: pp. 25–48.

References

Acheson, Dean. 1947. "Letter from Dean Acheson to the Fair Employment Practice Committee, May 8, 1946," in *To Secure These Rights*, *The Report of the President's Committee on Civil Rights*. New York: Simon & Schuster.

Bendick, Marc. 1994. "Measuring Employment Discrimination Through Controlled Experiments." *The Review of Black Political Economy* (Summer).

Bositis, David. 1998. *Public Opinion 1998: Political Attitudes*. Washington, DC: Joint Center for Political and Economic Studies (October).

Conti, Joseph G., and Brad Stetson. 1993.*Challenging the Civil Rights Establishment: Profiles of a New Black Vanguard.* Westport, CT: Praeger.

Council of Economic Advisers. 1998. *Changing America: Indicators of Social and Economic Well-Being, by Race and Hispanic Origin.* President's Initiative on Race (September).

Cross, H. 1990. *Employer Hiring Practices: Different Treatment of Hispanic and Anglo Job Seekers.* Washington, DC: The Urban Institute.

DuBois, W.E.B. 1961 [1903]. *The Souls of Black Folk: Essays and Sketches.* New York: Fawcett Publications Inc.

Fix, Michael, and Raymond Struyk, eds. 1993. *Clear and Convincing Evidence.* Washington, DC: The Urban Institute.

Glazer, Nathan. 1997. *We Are All Multiculturalists Now.* Cambridge, MA: Harvard University Press.

Hamilton, Dona Cooper, and Charles V. Hamilton. 1997. *The Dual Agenda.* New York: Columbia University Press.

Haselden, Kyle. 1963. "Should There Be Compensation for Negroes? No," *New York Times Magazine* (October 8).

Heckman, James, and Peter Siegelman. 1993. "The Urban Institute Audit Studies: Their Methods and Findings," in Fix and Struyk, eds., 1993.

Hoover, J. Edgar. 1943. In "Adam Clayton Powell, Jr. Memo" to the Assistant Attorney General. Washington, DC: Files of the Federal Bureau of Investigation (July 1).

Huntington, Samuel P. 1981. *American Politics, The Promise of Disharmony.* Cambridge, MA.: The Belknap Press of Harvard University Press.

Journal of Blacks in Higher Education. 1998. "A Collection of Views of Black Conservatives on Affirmative Action," in no. 20 (Summer).

Kifner, John. 1999. "Lott, and Shadow of a Pro-White Group," *New York Times* (January 14).

Lewis, John, with Michael D'Orso. 1998. *Walking with the Wind.* New York: Simon & Schuster.

Mydral, Gunnar. 1944. *An American Dilemma.* New York: Harper and Bros.

New York Times. 1999. "Racial Profiling in New Jersey" (April 22).

———. 1998 (December 30).

———. 1997 (June 14).

Nomination of Robert H. Bork to Be Associate Justice of the Supreme Court of the United States. 1987. In *Hearings Before the Committee on the Judiciary, United States Senate.* 1st Session, 100th Congress. Washington, DC: U.S. Government Printing Office (September 23).

Sack, Kevin. 1998. "In the Rural White South, Seeds of a Biracial Politics," *New York Times* (December 30).

Schlesinger Jr., Arthur M. 1991. *The Disuniting of America: Reflections on a Multicultural Society.* Knoxville, TN: Whittle Books.

Southern Regional Council. 1998. *Seeking an America as Good as Its Promise: Remedies for Racial Inequality, The Public's Views.* Atlanta, GA: Southern Regional Council.

Time. 1967 (August 11).

U.S. Bureau of the Census. 1997. *Statistical Abstract of the United States; The National Data Book.* Washington, DC: U.S. Government Printing Office.

White, Walter. 1974. "White Supremacy and World War II," in Herbert A. Aptheker, ed., *A Documentary History of the Negro People*. In *United States, 1933–1945*. Secaucus, NJ: The Citadel Press.

Young Jr., Whitney M. 1964. *To Be Equal*. New York: McGraw-Hill.

———. 1967. "Testimony of Whitney Young Prepared for the National Advisory Commission on Civil Disorders." In LBJ Papers, Lyndon Baines Johnson Library (Executive SP/JL, box 48, October) Austin, University of Texas.

8

The Women's Movement in the United States: Confronting Racism and Sexism

Leslie R. Wolfe

At the risk of seeming ridiculous, let me say that the true revolutionary is guided by great feelings of love.

—Che Guevara

Preface: A Personal Note

This chapter presents some verbal snapshots of the U.S. women's movement in the context of gender and race relations. This has been central to my work and life since 1972—when I first went to work at the National Welfare Rights Organization and then to the U.S. Commission on Civil Rights; and today it is in full flower in the work of the Center for Women Policy Studies.

In all of these years, I have shared with many other feminists the mission to speak out about racism-plus-sexism as having a unique quality of oppression for women of color. We have talked about the importance of "doing our homework" about other sisters' origins, cultures, and histories. We have encouraged white feminists to be outspoken against racism and not to leave that task solely to women of color. We have insisted on our responsibility to root out the vestiges of racism in ourselves, in our organizations, and in our feminist theory and policy priorities. And we have talked to women of color as well about multiethnic visions of feminism and the importance of doing the hard work to break down racial, ethnic, and cultural barriers both to sisterhood and to the institutional change that will foreshadow an egalitarian future.

Setting the Stage: Defining Our Central Premises

In a very significant corner of the women's movement, we have struggled for many years to build a feminism that confronts both sexism and racism, that is truly a multiracial and egalitarian partnership. For white women, this means understanding their skin privilege in the context of gender oppression—and then rejecting it outspokenly. Together, white women and women of color can bridge the great divide of racial dominance that has been our shared but silent legacy throughout our histories in the United States.

Seven central premises shape this chapter; they also should guide our continuing conversations and strategies to confront racism and sexism simultaneously.

The first premise characterizes both our diversity and connectedness in a single image: we who believe in freedom are in the same boat. Some of us—by virtue of our race, class, gender, sexual orientation, marital status, immigration status, or language—are in first-class cabins, and some of us are in the cargo hold. We are not the captain. The boat is stratified by race, class, and gender; it is often brutal and it is governed by patriarchal assumptions. If we remain isolated in our separate cabins and cargo holds, we cannot transform this society, this boat. We need to open our doors wide to each other.

But to do so, we must recognize that there is always a gender dimension to race relations; this is premise number two. Applying a gender lens to all of our work helps us see race relations more clearly and understand the inextricable links between racism and sexism, white supremacy and male supremacy, as they play out in increasingly complex and destructive ways.

Third, we who believe in freedom must place at the center of our analysis and activism an understanding of the combined impact of racism-plus-sexism on women of color—who have bravely faced these dual systems of dominance that still shape our society. An understanding of this particular reality enriches our understanding of both racism and sexism and thus of the realities faced by both men of color and white women. As African-American feminist Anna Julia Cooper said in a speech to an audience of women in 1892:

> We take our stand on the solidarity of humanity, the oneness of life, and the unnaturalness and injustice of all special favoritism, whether of sex, race, country or condition. . . . The colored woman feels that woman's cause is one and universal; and that . . . not till race, color,

sex, and condition are seen as accidents, and not the substance of life; not till the universal title of humanity to life, liberty, and the pursuit of happiness is conceded to be inalienable to all; not till then is woman's lesson taught and woman's cause won   not the white woman's nor the black woman's, not the red woman's but the cause of every man and of every woman who has writhed silently under a mighty wrong. Woman's wrongs are thus indissolubly linked with all undefended woe, and the acquirement of her "rights" will mean the final triumph of all right over might, the supremacy of the moral forces of reason, and justice, and love in the government of the nations of earth. (Cited in hooks 1981)

Since the days of Anna Julia Cooper and her colleagues, the women's movement in the United States has been in struggle against both racism and sexism.[2] As a fourth premise, it is essential that we understand this truth about the women's movement—that it is more than what some have called "the white women's movement" or "mainstream women's organizations." Feminism in the United States is wonderfully diverse and embedded in communities throughout the country. It is a kaleidoscope of many faces and many voices; that most have not been heard or seen by the "mainstream" does not deny their existence or their strength.

The women's movement *is* these many and diverse scholars, activists, and organizations—many of which are led by women of color who carry on the brave tradition of African-American feminists of the nineteenth and early twentieth centuries—Anna Julia Cooper, Maria Stewart, Sojourner Truth, and countless other foremothers. And the women's movement is also their white feminist sisters who share this mission and struggle and who have said to both white women and men of color that ending one oppression is not enough.

So, when we talk about the women's movement in the 1990s, "inclusiveness" is an inappropriate term and strategy because it implies that the "real" movement is a white and middle-class one; to persist in using the term "inclusiveness" is to persist in the errors of the past by making invisible the feminist organizing and thinking of feminists of color (Wolfe and Tucker 1995).

As Beverly Guy-Sheftall notes, "The history of American feminism has been primarily a narrative about the heroic deeds of white women" (Guy-Sheftall 1995: p. xiii). The act of reclaiming the submerged history of African-American feminism should also ensure that the leadership of women-of-color feminists today is not submerged by the assumption that they must be "included" in other groups.

The women's movement is unique in its persistent engagement in discourse—often appropriately angry—about racism and classism in our movement. Indeed, this remains a central issue for the women's movement as we struggle with the ways in which racism and classism intersect with sexism to oppress all women. For all our failures, the women's movement is a model of the struggle to address these interrelated oppressions based in assumptions of dominance, grounded in fear and hatred of differentness. More than any other progressive movement, the women's movement has struggled with these issues in every realm.

We have not always been successful by any means, but we have engaged in this transformational debate since the nineteenth century. We have made enormous progress in knitting a seamless web of analysis and activism that confronts biases of sex, race, class, and sexual orientation. Sadly, these struggles have been and remain virtually invisible to most people through the media.

And by "we," I do mean feminists, because feminism demands both personal *and* institutional change—by women and men of all backgrounds and by the institutions that govern our lives. But many women are not feminists, many white women remain tied to their white skin privilege, and many otherwise progressive and egalitarian men remain tied to patriarchal assumptions.

The fifth premise points to the future: we have different histories in the United States, but our futures are entwined. As Chicana scholar Aida Hurtado reminds us: "white men use different forms of enforcing oppression of white women and of women of color. As a consequence, these groups of women have different political responses and skills, and at times these differences cause the two groups to clash" (Hurtado 1989: p. 843).

And while African-American women have historically been enslaved and brutalized by white men, white women have, as Patricia Hill Collins reminds us, "been offered a share of white male power but only if they agree to be subordinate" (Collins 1990: p. 189). Collins speaks of slavery days with both rage and generosity. She suggests that perhaps white women would have saved black women from some of the horrors of slavery if they had had the power to do so, or perhaps white women were simply grateful they had escaped the brutal realities of slavery by virtue of their race.

Without a doubt, this conversation about the persistence of that legacy remains an essential one for the women's movement. Otherwise, white women will not examine its impact on them and will not seek to end skin privilege with the necessary passion, but rather will seek to gain equality with those white men who rule our world. And then, the unexamined life of white skin privilege will continue to infect our movement.

But this is changing, in large measure because the movement is so wonderfully diverse and diffuse, encompassing women's groups organized everywhere. This is the strength of the women's movement. In fact, since the late 1970s, the unreported "news" of the women's movement has been the building of women-of-color organizations with avowedly feminist agendas and feminist discourse and the flourishing of black feminist theory and multiethnic women's studies.

Today, what some have called "mainstream" and others have called "white" women's organizations acknowledge that talking about "women" and "people of color" as separate categories fails to capture reality as it renders women of color invisible. While these organizations continue their worthy struggle for self-transformation, most do not yet reflect the diversity in their boards and senior staffs that their public pronouncements on issues would anticipate.

However, in this post-Beijing era, women worldwide speak in one voice: women's rights are human rights. The continuing development of antiracist feminist ideology and organizing by African-American, Latina, Asian-American, white, and Native American feminists is a promise that the women's movement in the United States will win its struggle for racial and ethnic solidarity and build a common agenda for our shared struggle against both sexist and racist social, political, economic, and personal structures.

Origins of Multiethnic Feminism

The nineteenth-century women's movement emerged into an era of industrial development and the restructuring of work and family lives, the growth of social reform movements and intellectual ferment that emphasized individual freedom and—quite literally—the "rights of man" (Hole and Levine 1971; Wolfe and Tucker 1995). But the first half of the nineteenth century also was a time in the United States when Native Americans were being forcibly driven from their ancestral lands by Anglo "settlers" living out an ideology of Manifest Destiny to conquer the continent for European Americans. It was a time when the descendants of Africans who had been kidnapped from their ancestral lands still were legally enslaved as chattel throughout the South, forbidden by law and custom to be educated, to marry, and to maintain their own families (Wolfe and Tucker 1995). These were the brutal realities that shaped the lives of African-American women and Native American women and that most of their white sisters could not imagine or comprehend—or experience as central concerns in their own lives.

And so, while the movement for the abolition of slavery, launched in the 1830s, was the birthplace of the women's rights movement for both white and African-American women, they followed parallel but often segregated paths. Though undervalued by their white sisters, as Paula Giddings reminds us, "all Black women abolitionists (and most of the leading Black male abolitionists) were feminists" (Giddings 1984: p. 55).

But, like their white male abolitionist counterparts, virtually no white abolitionist/feminist women—save Sarah and Angelina Grimke— understood the potential power of a coalition between white and black women. Thus, though the early white feminists recognized the impact of sexist oppression on women's lives (see the 1848 Seneca Falls Declaration of Sentiments [Women's Rights Convention 1969]), it was left to the African-American feminists to bring it all together (see hooks 1981; Collins 1990; Guy-Sheftall 1995).

That the early white feminists could not and did not transcend race and class is disappointing—even infuriating—to us as we look back, but it is hardly surprising given the race relations and patriarchal assumptions of their time. So too, black women's suspicion of white women's motives, and black men's belief—expressed even by early feminist Frederick Douglass—that suffrage for black men must precede suffrage for women, black and white, is hardly surprising. But one hundred years later, such thinking is inexcusable and counterproductive.

Sojourner Truth spoke for many African-American feminists of the day when she expressed the fear that if black men won the vote and not black women, they would dominate black women as white men dominated white women. In 1867, during the debate over whether women should step aside in favor of black male suffrage, she said:

> There is a great stir about colored men getting their rights, but not a word about colored women; and if colored men get their rights and not colored women theirs, you see the colored men will be masters over the women, and it will be just as bad as it was before. So I am for keeping the thing going [the struggle for women's suffrage] while things are stirring; because if we wait till it is still, it will take a great while to get it going again. (Guy-Sheftall 1995: p. 37)

Indeed, African-American feminists throughout the nineteenth century argued that the struggle must be simultaneously focused on the liberation of blacks—both men and women—and white women.

But most progressive white men, feminist white women, and black men struggling for race equality could not hear this truth. And very few black women were welcomed as leaders in either the earlier interracial abolitionist societies or in the emerging feminist movement. These painful issues of race and class bias persist in liberation movements to our own day.

When suffrage became the women's movement's top priority after the Civil War—when their struggle to win the franchise and equal protection of the law for women failed—feminism suffered. Facing ever more powerful and vicious opposition during the next half century, white suffragists became more willing to accommodate racist and conservative views, to gain "respectability" for woman suffrage among the white men who had the power to grant or withhold it. These single-minded white suffragists, then, often expressed racist and nativist views—suggesting that white men would more safely give the vote to their own sisters and wives than to immigrant and dark-skinned men.

Tragically, these and other white suffragists' tactics—including the strategy of expediency to avoid alienating southern white members of the national suffrage association—further divided women by race. And later, the huge suffrage march of 1913 was segregated. Black women's groups—including Mary Church Terrell and the Delta Sigma Theta sorority women of Howard University and Ida Wells-Barnett and the Alpha Suffrage Club—were told they must "bring up the rear" (Giddings 1984).

But African-American women organized their own campaign for suffrage to ensure their own future equality, and by the 1900s, black suffrage clubs were active in every part of the country (Giddings 1984). When woman's suffrage was finally won on August 26, 1920,[3] when the 19th Amendment joined the Constitution, the earlier vision of feminism as a movement to end women's subjugation had faded and dwindled, not to be revived in full force until the late 1960s and early 1970s.

Separately, therefore, white and African-American women built strong organizations that survived to support the revived women's movement decades later[4] but also perpetuated and solidified the bitterness and distrust of the latter years of the suffrage struggle. This was the shared but silent legacy of white and African-American women at the dawn of the new era of activism for social change in the 1960s and 1970s.

funded programs to attack sex bias and discrimination—also brought issues of combined race and sex bias to the fore despite the loss of the constitutional guarantee of the Equal Rights Amendment.

However, feminist initiatives that would reach more deeply into the social and economic bases of women's lower status and confront the combined impact of racism and sexism on women more directly—addressing women's poverty, for instance—have been far less successful.

Hence, our sixth premise points to future struggles by first acknowledging that our success inevitably engendered an antifeminist and racist backlash that linked "respectable" conservative groups with old-time hate groups and newer militia and other hate groups. And since the Reagan administration, the far right's agenda has increasingly shaped federal policy—with its overt hostility to women's rights, to affirmative action, to gay and lesbian rights, and to welfare rights and programs to alleviate poverty.

This is connected to what I have been calling, since the early 1980s, the "You've Come a Long Way, Baby" backlash, which—portrayed throughout the mass media (see Faludi 1991) and now in the voices of more sophisticated antifeminist women's groups such as the Independent Women's Forum—suggests that the women's movement is both dangerous *and* dead, that in this "post-feminist" and "post–civil rights" era we have achieved equality for those women and men of color who are capable of having it, that civil rights and feminist leaders are over the hill and out of touch, that feminism has caused women's problems and made women victims, that affirmative action is preferential treatment of the unqualified, and that welfare programs keep African Americans in poverty that is tantamount to slavery.

The second phase of the "You've Come a Long Way Baby" backlash tries to speak to upper-income working women who are pushing through the glass ceiling and thus threatening the status quo that keeps white men at the very top. This backlash thus suggests that women's career success is meaningless and dangerous both to themselves and their families; it seeks to restore the cult of domesticity, popular in the Victorian era and the 1950s (see Faludi 1991), suggesting that white, upper-income women are dropping out of the work force, having finally come to their senses and realized that true joy and fulfillment is to be had only in the kitchen and the nursery.

But the underlying theme of this subtle backlash, and of many progressive workplace programs, is that working women must solve the problems of "balancing work and family" themselves, thus submerging feminist demands for the real transformation of workplace cultures to accommodate our traditional, feminist family values and to consider the needs of the vast majority of working women who do not have the option to opt out.

Facing Our Dilemma

In the 1990s, the progressive agenda still is hampered by our either/or thinking, which shapes our work and thought in too many ways. We still speak of "women" and "people of color"—assuming that "all the women are white, all the blacks are men, but some of us are brave" (Hull, Scott, and Smith 1982).

It remains a powerful dilemma that in the progressive community, with a few exceptions, organizations remain focused on race or gender, rarely both. It is left to organizations led by women of color and their allies to make these links and demand that their colleagues in both the women's movement and the civil rights movement respond to the self-defined needs and strategies of women of color.

Hence the dilemma of what my sister-colleague Jennifer Tucker calls "sexist multicultural education." Hence the dilemma of our recent struggles to save affirmative action because it "helps" white women more than "minorities"—read "men of color" but rarely "women of color."

Hence, the willingness of many liberal proponents of welfare reform to ignore its assault on poor women in the guise of helping their "innocent" children—thus effectively punishing poor women, particularly African-American and Latina women, for their poverty and devaluing their motherhood. Indeed, the recent discourse on poverty is a classic "blame the victim" strategy that suggests that welfare is bankrupting the nation, that poor women are the villains rather than the victims of economic dislocations and discrimination, and that punitive welfare reform proposals to force women from welfare to working poor status—but still in poverty—will help the nation's economic recovery.

Hence the dilemma of the reproductive-rights agenda. After *Roe v. Wade*, women of color, active supporters of the right to choose abortion,[6] built strategies for expanding the definition of reproductive rights to address issues of forced sterilization of low-income women of color and lack of access to reproductive health care, including prenatal care and "choice" regarding contraception and pregnancy as well, and to link women's reproductive rights to an expanded agenda for social and economic rights focused on low-income women and women of color.

Yet some white feminists persisted in speaking of reproductive rights solely to mean abortion rights, thus denigrating the larger agenda of women of color (Davis 1991). The UN conferences in Cairo and Beijing, however, have made the reproductive rights and health agenda formulated by women of color the hallmark of their principles.

Hence the dilemma that both academic and independent women-focused think tanks and research centers conduct policy-relevant research on issues affecting women—but are rarely led by women of color in partnership with white women; nor is it the top priority of their agendas to focus explicitly on confronting racism and sexism simultaneously. And hence the similar dilemma that virtually none of the major progressive think tanks or research institutes that study urban affairs, civil rights, or poverty focus explicitly on the inextricable link between race and sex bias, with women of color at the *center* of their analyses, their agendas, or their leadership.

Women's organizing at the local and state levels points toward the forms of feminism that continue to flourish. Many women's groups in communities of color lead the way, combining advocacy for systemic change with provision of services to meet women's emergency needs and to respond to crises in women's lives that exemplify women's oppression—rape, woman abuse and domestic violence, poverty and welfare, AIDS, access to health care, denials of reproductive rights, sexual harassment and workplace discrimination, for example (Wolfe and Tucker 1995).

Transformation of Consciousness

Perhaps the most powerful success of feminism has been in its transformation of public consciousness and rewriting of the public discourse on women's equality and the changing roles of women and men in the workplace, the family, and in public life. This national consciousness raising has changed our world and brought half a revolution to fruition.

The aspirations and experiences of countless women—and men—have been transformed; girls and their parents and teachers do not scoff quite so often at the notion of women in the Senate, in sports, and in the space program. And women of color are visible in all of these.

Public opinion polls consistently reveal that most adults support women's rights. By 1989, 85 percent of African-American women and

64 percent of white women expressed support of "a strong women's movement to push for changes that benefit women" (*New York Times* 1989).

The death of feminism has been reported in the media virtually since the birth of the women's movement, perhaps as wishful thinking. But today, the movement is stronger and more diverse; a powerful mass movement of women is growing throughout the country, led in large measure by low-income women, by women of color, and by younger women who are shaping our "feminist futures" (see Findlen 1995).

Feminist Futures

For the women's movement in the United States, the Beijing Platform for Action[7] does for the twenty-first century what the Seneca Falls Declaration did for the nineteenth and the Houston International Women's Year conference did for the late twentieth.

In the post-Beijing era, the women's movement in the United States more than ever before sees itself as part of global women's movements and is moving to make its centerpiece the confrontation with all forms of oppression based on a system of dominance — sex, race/ethnicity, class, sexual orientation, national origin, language, marital status, disability, and age. We are building our kaleidoscopic vision of women's many perspectives and experiences — women of color and white women, low-income women and middle/upper-income women, immigrant women of many generations, younger and older women, women with disabilities, straight, lesbian, and bisexual women.

Indeed, the participants in the Center for Women Policy Studies' Think Tank on the Future of the Women's Movement in 1993 were unanimous in understanding that solutions to the problems that women will confront — as both their poverty and their vulnerability to male violence continue to increase — require structural and societal changes that only a mass multiracial, multiethnic, and multicultural feminist movement of women can bring. Finally, as feminists define issues and build strategies, we will confront the politics of difference and respond to the various challenges of language that our ethnocentricity and monolingualism impose upon non-English-speaking and immigrant women in the United States.

As we learn new ways to value our diversity, we must also create new images. For many years, I have used the image of the kaleidoscope because, unlike the traditional images of mosaics and tapestries and quilts—which suggest something fixed, static, and inflexible—the kaleidoscope is a collection of exquisite and unique pieces that are in constant movement. Each functions as an important, equal part of the larger whole, always moving around a central point, always touching, and changing place—and no one can exist or function without the others; change is the nature of the kaleidoscope. And the kaleidoscope that is the women's movement is enlarging, as more and more women enter to address their shared personal struggles to overcome institutionalized sex, race, and class bias and discrimination in their own lives and communities (Wolfe and Tucker 1995).

In many ways, the Beijing Platform guides our forward movement to the twenty-first century. Despite our progress in changing law and policy during the past twenty-five years, multiethnic feminist visions do not yet shape society nor do all women partake of its benefits equally. While the "glass ceiling" is a real barrier for many working women who are climbing ladders into "the white male club" at the top, for example, the vast majority of working women in the United States are trapped on the "sticky floor" at the bottom of the economic ladder.

Yet when others count our successes as a movement, they point to the increased numbers of women who have entered formerly male-dominated professions, who have climbed the corporate ladder, who have become college professors and presidents, who have become visible in the media, who have become successful business owners, and who have been elected to public office. In short, despite feminist ideology to the contrary, we find our success measured by the number of women who make it close to the top in a rigidly hierarchical structure.

While issues of violence, economic justice, and opportunity have long been hallmarks of the feminist agenda, in the future the movement must measure its success by how well it changes the lives of women who have been relegated to the bottom, whether by race or poverty or language or disability or sexual orientation—or by a combination of these factors—our sisters who are the most oppressed, despised, and disadvantaged (Wolfe and Tucker 1995).

As we honor women at the top, we also hold them accountable to women who are less privileged; we expect them to make common cause with the women who answer their phones, clean their homes and offices, make their clothes, and serve their lunch. We expect women elected officials to use their positions to transform the public debate on every aspect of domestic and foreign policy to move the needs of women and girls of all ethnic and class backgrounds, both straight and gay, "from margin to center."

Just as the early feminists defined women's needs in the context of specific forms of discrimination, so in the post-Beijing era, the powerful message that "women's rights are human rights" provides the context and the theory to shape both women's movements and human rights and race-relations movements worldwide. Finally, therefore, the women's movement in the United States will continue to expand its ability to think and act globally for women, if we are to confront the worst offenses of sexism and racism, classism and heterosexism — including AIDS, the lack of reproductive freedom, and the persistence of violence against women. The U.S. women's movement must address these crises in our own country even as we make common cause with sister organizations and movements globally.

All of our governments and cultures devalue women, accept our second-class status, allow the violation of our human rights, and seek to control our lives. These are the patriarchal values that women's movements must confront. It is the challenge of our feminist future.

Thus, our final premise is a call to action. As women and men committed to this vision in our own countries and communities, we have more to do together. And for this, we must create safe spaces to continue coming together to share our truths in an atmosphere of reconciliation and solidarity. We must transcend ourselves to build this egalitarian future. Perhaps we should be guided by Che Guevara's words: "The true revolutionary is guided by great feelings of love" (Guevara 2000: p. 158). And by Ella Baker's: "We who believe in freedom cannot rest until it comes" (Baker/SNCC Conference 2000).

Notes

1. Also see Wolfe and Tucker 1995.

2. See the monumental and exquisite book, *Words of Fire*, in which Beverly Guy-Sheftall (1995) has restored to a new generation much of our previously lost African-American feminist thought—from the 1830s to the present day. Activism in the early 1990s includes the 1994 conference of African-American feminists held at the Massachusetts Institute of Technology, the 1991 declaration of African American Women in Defense of Ourselves, and the agenda of the African American Women and the Law conference and its resulting National Network.

3. Women in Puerto Rico did not gain the right to vote until 1932; Isabel Andreu de Aguilar, who wrote the first memorandum to the Puerto Rican legislature demanding women's suffrage, was one of many leaders in this struggle (Miranda 1986).

4. Women's organizations also existed among all of the Asian immigrant

groups; Latina and Native American women organized within their communities as well, but they had very little interaction with Anglo-American women.

5. These statutes enacted during the 1970s included:

- Title IX of the Education Amendments of 1972, prohibiting sex discrimination in federally funded education programs;
- the Equal Credit Opportunity Act of 1974, prohibiting sex discrimination in the granting of consumer credit;
- the Women's Educational Equity Act of 1974, providing federal funds for the creation of teacher training, curriculum reform, and other programs to eliminate sex bias in education, from preschool through graduate and professional school;
- the 1972 amendment to Title VII of the Civil Rights Act of 1964 that expanded its coverage to employees in educational institutions;
- the 1978 amendments to the Fair Housing Act, to prohibit sex discrimination in mortgage lending;
- the Rape Prevention and Control Act of 1975, the first to recognize rape as a federal policy issue and to establish a program of federally funded research on rape;
- the Comprehensive Health Manpower Training Act and the Nurse Training Act, which prohibited sex discrimination in nursing and medical schools and other federally assisted health training programs;
- the 1972 expansion of the mandate of the U.S. Commission on Civil Rights, to address sex as well as race bias and discrimination in its research, legal analyses, public hearings, and reports;
- the Pregnancy Discrimination Act of 1978, which overturned a Supreme Court ruling that discrimination against "pregnant persons" did not constitute sex discrimination as it applied equally to all pregnant persons, regardless of sex.

6. Organizations such as MANA (Mexican American Women's National Association), for example, had adopted a prochoice position early in its history.

7. In the United States, virtually every local, state, and national women's organization has been conducting some sort of "bringing Beijing home" activity since the UN Conference in 1995. The Center for Women Policy Studies and the Women's Environment and Development Organization, for example, created a U.S.-relevant version of the platform—the Contract with Women of the USA—as an organizing tool for women's groups and for women state legislators nationwide.

References

Alexander, M. J. 1996. *The Third Wave: Feminist Perspectives on Racism.* Brooklyn: Kitchen Table, Women of Color Press.

Anderson, A., and S. Verble eds. 1982. *Words of Today's American Indian Women: Ohoyo Makachi.* Wichita Falls, TX: Ohoyo Inc.

Andolsen, B. H. 1986. *"Daughters of Jefferson, Daughters of Bootblacks": Racism and American Feminism.* Macon, GA: Mercer University Press.

Asian Women United of California. 1989. *Making Waves: An Anthology of Writings by and About Asian American Women.* Boston: Beacon Press.

Awkward, M. 1995. *Negotiating Difference: Race, Gender, and the Politics of Positionality.* Chicago: University of Chicago Press.

Baker, Ella/SNCC Conference. 2000. "'We Who Believe in Freedom Cannot Rest': Ella J. Baker ('Miss Baker') and the Birth of the Student Non-Violent Coordinating Committee." African American Cultural Center, North Carolina State University. http://www.ncsu.edu/ncsu/chass/mds/ellahome.html

Bannerji, H. 1995. *Thinking Through: Essays on Feminism, Marxism, and Anti-Racism.* Toronto: Women's Press.

Basu, A., ed. 1995. *The Challenge of Local Feminisms: Women's Movements in Global Perspective.* Boulder, CO: Westview Press.

Bell, L. A., and D. Blumenfeld, eds. 1995. *Overcoming Racism and Sexism.* Lanham, MD: Rowman and Littlefield.

Berry, M. F. 1986. *Why ERA Failed: Politics, Women's Rights, and the Amending Process of the Constitution.* Bloomington: Indiana University Press.

Bird, C., et al. 1979. *What Women Want: From the Official Report to the President, the Congress and the People of the United States.* New York: Simon & Schuster.

Brenner, J. 1993. "The Best of Times, the Worst of Times: US Feminism Today." *New Left Review* (July-August): 101–159.

Bunch, C. 1987. *Passionate Politics: Feminist Theory in Action.* New York: St. Martin's Press.

Cade, T., ed. 1970. *The Black Woman: An Anthology.* New York: Signet.

Caraway, N. 1991. *Segregated Sisterhood: Racism and the Politics of American Feminism.* Knoxville: University of Tennessee Press.

Cleage, P. 1994. *Deals with the Devil, and Other Reasons to Riot.* New York: Ballantine.

Cobble, D. S. 1994. "Recapturing Working Class Feminism: Union Women in the Postwar Era," in J. Meyerowitz, ed., *Not June Cleaver: Women in the Postwar U.S., 1945–1960.* Philadelphia: Temple University Press.

Collins, P. H. 1990. *Black Feminist Thought: Knowledge, Consciousness, and the Politics of Empowerment.* Boston: Unwin Hyman.

Cyrus, V., ed. 1997. *Experiencing Race, Class, and Gender in the United States.* 2nd ed. Mountain View, CA: Mayfield.

Davis, A. 1983. *Women, Race, and Class.* New York: Vintage.

———. 1985. *Violence Against Women and the Ongoing Challenge to Racism.* Latham, NY: Kitchen Table Press.

———. 1989. *Women, Culture and Politics.* New York: Random House.

Davis, F. 1991. *Moving the Mountain: The Women's Movement in America Since 1960.* New York: Simon & Schuster.

Donaldson, L. E. 1992. *Decolonizing Feminisms: Race, Gender and Empire Building.* Chapel Hill: University of North Carolina Press.

Dworkin, A. 1978. *Right Wing Women.* New York: G. P. Putnam.

Echols, A. 1989. *Daring to Be BAD: Radical Feminism in America 1967–1975.* Minneapolis: University of Minnesota Press.

Eisenstein, Z. R. 1994. *The Color of Gender: Reimaging Democracy*. Berkeley: University of California Press.

Faludi, S. 1991. *BACKLASH: The Undeclared War Against American Women*. New York: Crown.

Findlen, B., ed. 1995. *Listen Up: Voices from the Next Feminist Generation*. Seattle: Seal Press.

Flexner, E. 1975. *Century of Struggle: The Woman's Rights Movement in the United States*. Cambridge, MA: Harvard University Press.

Frankenberg, R. 1993. *White Women, Race Matters: The Social Construction of Whiteness*. Minneapolis: University of Minnesota Press.

Freeman, J. 1975. *The Politics of Women's Liberation: A Case Study of an Emerging Social Movement and Its Relation to the Policy Process*. New York: David McKay Company Inc.

———. 1994. *WOMEN: A Feminist Perspective*. 5th ed. Mountain View, CA: Mayfield.

Gelb, J., and M. L. Palley. 1987. *Women and Public Policies*. Princeton: Princeton University Press.

Giddings, P. 1984. *When and Where I Enter: The Impact of Black Women on Race and Sex in America*. New York: William Morrow.

Gilmore, G. E. 1996. *Gender and Jim Crow: Women and the Politics of White Supremacy in North Carolina, 1896–1920*. Chapel Hill: University of North Carolina Press.

Golden, M., S. R. Shreve, eds. 1995. *Skin Deep: Black Women and White Women Write About Race*. New York: Nan A. Talese.

Goldstein, L. F. 1988. *The Constitutional Rights of Women: Cases in Law and Social Change*. Madison: University of Wisconsin Press.

Gordon, V. V. 1987. *Black Women, Feminism, and Black Liberation: Which Way?* Chicago: Third World Press.

Green, R. 1992. *Women in American Indian Society*. New York: Chelsea House Publishers.

Griffith, E. 1984. *In Her Own Right: The Life of Elizabeth Cady Stanton*. New York and Oxford: Oxford University Press.

Grimke, S. 1970 [1838]. *Letters on the Equality of the Sexes and the Condition of Woman*. New York: Source Book Press [Boston: Isaac Knapp].

Guevara, C. 2000. *Che Guevara Speaks*. New York: Pathfinder.

Guillaumin, C. 1995. *Racism, Sexism, Power, and Ideology*. London and New York: Routledge.

Guy-Sheftall, B., ed. 1995. *Words of Fire: An Anthology of African-American Feminist Thought*. New York: The New Press.

Gwin, M. C. 1985. *Black and White Women of the Old South: The Peculiar Sisterhood in American Literature*. Knoxville: University of Tennessee Press.

Hall, K. F. 1995. *Things of Darkness: Economies of Race and Gender in Early Modern England*. Ithaca, NY: Cornell University Press.

Hole, J., and E. Levine. 1971. *Rebirth of Feminism*. New York: Quadrangle Books Inc.

hooks, bell. 1981. *Ain't I a Woman: Black Women and Feminism*. Boston: South End Press.

———. 1984. *Feminist Theory: From Margin to Center*. Boston: South End Press.

———. 1989. *Talking Back: Thinking Feminist, Thinking Black*. Toronto: Between the Lines.

———. 1990. *Yearning: Race, Gender, and Cultural Politics*. Toronto: Between the Lines.

———. 1995. *Killing Rage: Ending Racism*. New York: H. Holt and Co.

Hudson-Weems, C. 1994. *Africana Womanism: Reclaiming Ourselves*. Troy, MI: Bedford.

Hull, G., P. B. Scott, and B. Smith. 1982. *All the Women Are White, All the Blacks Are Men, But Some of Us Are Brave: Black Women's Studies*. Old Westbury, NY: The Feminist Press.

Hurtado, A. 1989. "Relating to Privilege: Seduction and Rejection in the Subordination of White Women and Women of Color." *Signs* 14, no. 4: 833–855.

Jaimes, M. A., and T. Halsey. 1992. "American Indian Women: At the Center of Indigenous Resistance in Contemporary North America," in M. A. Jaimes, ed., *The State of Native America*. Boston: South End Press.

James, J. 1996. *Resisting State Violence: Radicalism, Gender, and Race in U.S. Culture*. Minneapolis: University of Minnesota Press.

Koedt, A., E. Levine, and A. Rapone, eds. 1973. *Radical Feminism*. New York: Quadrangle Books Inc.

Ladner, J. 1972. *Tomorrow's Tomorrow: The Black Woman*. Garden City, NY: Doubleday.

Lerner, G., ed. 1972. *Black Women in White America: A Documentary History*. New York: Vintage.

Lorde, A. 1984. *Sister Outsider: Essays and Speeches*. Trumansburg, NY: Crossing Press.

Mansbridge, J. 1986. *Why We Lost the ERA*. Chicago: University of Chicago Press.

McIntosh, P. 1992. "White Privilege and Male Privilege," in J. Andrzejewski, ed., *Human Relations: The Study of Oppression and Human Rights*. Needham Heights, MA: Ginn.

Miranda, L. R. 1986. *Hispanic Women in the United States: A Puerto Rican Woman's Perspective*. Washington, DC: Miranda Associates.

New York Times. 1989. August 20.

Noble, J. 1978. *Beautiful, Also, Are the Souls of My Black Sisters: A History of the Black Woman in America*. Englewood Cliffs, NJ: Prentice-Hall Inc.

Petchesky, R. 1984. *Abortion and Woman's Choice: The State, Sexuality, and Reproductive Freedom*. Boston: Northeastern University Press.

President's Commission on the Status of Women. 1963. *American Women: Report of the President's Commission on the Status of Women*. Washington, DC: U.S. Government Printing Office.

Redstockings, eds. 1978. *Feminist Revolution*. New York: Random House.

Riggs, M. 1994. *Awake, Arise, and Act: A Womanist Call for Black Liberation*. Cleveland: Pilgrim Press.

Rothenberg, P. S., ed. 1995. *Race, Class, and Gender in the United States: An Integrated Study*. New York: St. Martin's Press.

Shah, S. 1994. "Presenting the Blue Goddess: Toward a National Pan-Asian Feminist Agenda," in K. Aguilar-San Juan, ed., *The State of Asian America*. Boston: South End Press.

Shult, L., S. Searing, and E. Lester-Massman, eds. 1991. *Women, Race, and Ethnicity: A Bibliography*. Madison: University of Wisconsin System/ Women's Studies Librarian.

Tobach, E., and B. Rosoff, eds. 1994. *Challenging Racism and Sexism: Alternatives to Genetic Explanations*. New York: Feminist Press at the City University of New York.

Wallace, M. 1978. *Black Macho and the Myth of the Superwoman*. New York: The Dial Press.

Wandersee, W. D. 1988. *On the Move: American Women in the 1970s*. Boston: G. K. Hall.

Ware, C. 1970. *Womanpower: The Movement for Women's Liberation*. New York: Tower.

Wilson, M., and K. Russell. 1996. *Divided Sisters: Bridging the Gap Between Black Women and White Women*. New York: Anchor Books.

Wing, A. K., ed. 1996. *Critical Race Feminism: A Reader*. New York: New York University Press.

Witt, S. H. 1981. "Past Positives and Present Problems," in Ohoyo Resource Center. eds., *Words of Today's American Indian Women: Ohoyo Makachi*. Wichita Falls, TX: Ohoyo Inc.

Wolfe, L. R. 1981. "Indian Women and Feminism," in A. Anderson and S. Verble, eds., *Words of Today's American Indian Women: Ohoyo Makachi*. Wichita Falls, TX: Ohoyo Inc.

Wolfe, L. R., and J. Tucker. 1995. "Feminism Lives: Building a Multicultural Women's Movement in the United States," in A. Basu, ed., *The Challenge of Local Feminisms: Women's Movements in Global Perspective*. Boulder, CO: Westview Press.

Women's Rights Convention. 1969. *Women's Rights Conventions, Seneca Falls & Rochester, 1848*. New York: Arno.

Zack, N., ed. 1996. *Race/Sex: Their Sameness, Differences and Interplay*. New York: Routledge.

9

The Social Construction of Racial Privilege in the United States: An Asset Perspective

Melvin L. Oliver

DISCOURSE ABOUT THE causes of racial inequality in the United States is highly fractured and disjointed. Many people believe that there are no longer any encumbrances related to race that constrain and limit the achievement of economic and social status for racial minorities in contemporary U.S. society (Schuman, Steeh, and Bobo 1985). Others contend that people of color face innumerable obstacles that white people never have to think about or face in their pursuit of the "good life" (McIntosh 2001). Can both of these perspectives be true? This chapter attempts to go beyond these highly polarized viewpoints and to create a more nuanced view of how we can understand the continuation of racial privilege in the absence of systematic rules of racial inequality.

I want to develop the notion that even with the scaffolding of racial discrimination dismantled, the past has trapped us in a legacy of racial inequality and privilege that is a powerful constraint or limit on our sense of possibilities for economic and social equality. At different levels and in different contexts, white racial privilege economically or socially continues to be reproduced. Using the United States and black/white racial inequality as a case study, I want to propose a way to look at how that racial privilege has been socially constructed and, in so doing, provide a framework for moving past these inequalities.

Moving Beyond the Polarities of Race and Class

The desperate economic and social situation of many African Americans is without question. As William Julius Wilson has convincingly shown in his works, "the most disadvantaged segments of the

251

black urban community" have come to make up the majority of "that heterogeneous grouping of families and individuals who are outside of the American occupational system" and who are euphemistically called the "underclass" (Wilson 1978: p. 8; also see Wilson 1987 and 1996). With little or no access to jobs, trapped in poor areas with bad schools and little social and economic opportunity, members of the underclass resort to crime, drugs, and other forms of self-defeating behaviors to make a living and eke some degree of meaning out of their impoverished existence. While these facts are not in dispute, what is in dispute is our understanding of the source of such resounding levels of racial inequality. What factors were responsible for their creation and what are the sources of their continuation? It is on this topic that sociologists and other social scientists have, for the most part, polarized their thinking by focusing exclusively on factors of either race or class (Willie 1979).

The operative analysis in the United States is that class has replaced race as the key to understanding black disadvantage. The argument for class, most eloquently and influentially stated by William Julius Wilson in his 1978 book, *The Declining Significance of Race*, suggests that the racial barriers of the past are less important than present-day social-class attributes in determining the economic life chances of black Americans. Education, in particular, is the key attribute in whether blacks will achieve economic success relative to white Americans. Discrimination and racism, while still actively practiced in many spheres, have marginally less effect on black Americans' economic attainment than whether or not blacks have the skills and education necessary to fit in a fluid economy. In this view, race assumes importance only as the lingering product of an oppressive past. As Wilson observes, this time in his 1987 book, *The Truly Disadvantaged*, racism and its most harmful injuries occurred in the past, and they are today experienced mainly by those on the bottom of the economic ladder as "the accumulation of the disadvantages . . . passed from generation to generation" (p. 120). With the structure of racial inequality dismantled legally, the economic status of blacks is purely a result of their class experiences, particularly their educational backgrounds. Proof of this is often cited with the existence of a black middle class, which is held up as evidence that race is no longer important.

The case for race suggests that race has had a unique cultural meaning in American society wherein blacks have been oppressed in such a way as to perpetuate their inferiority and second-class citizenship. Race in this context has a socially constructed meaning that is acted on by whites to purposefully limit and constrain the black population. The foundation of this social construction is the ideology of racism. Racism is a belief in the inherent inferiority of one race in relation to another. Racism both justifies and dictates the actions and institutional decisions that adversely affect the target group. Racism is thus at the core of the impoverished situation that the African-American underclass faces. Racism in schooling, housing, and employment limits the ability of blacks to achieve through education, have the options to live where they want and where opportunities are most plentiful, and to work in occupations and industries that provide livable wages and mobility ladders (Kozol 1993; Zubrinsky and Bobo 1996; Darity and Mason 1998; Johnson and Oliver 1992). Most important, the effects of racism are felt equally by lower-class blacks and middle-class blacks, although under different circumstances (Franklin 1991). Blacks in occupations that seem immune from racism are still limited in their ability to achieve at the same levels as their white colleagues by a more complex, yet equally debilitating racism (Feagin and Sikes 1994; Cose 1993).

Both of these perspectives have produced illuminating insights and compelling evidence. However, each also has major failings. The emphasis on racism creates problems of evidence. Especially in the contemporary period, as Wilson (1978) points out in *The Declining Significance of Race*, it is difficult to trace the enduring existence of racial inequality to an articulated ideology of racism. The trail of historical evidence proudly left in previous periods is made less evident by heightened racial sensitivity to legal sanctions and racial civility in language. Thus those who still emphasize race in the modern era speak of covert racism and use as evidence racial disparities in income, jobs, and housing. In fact, however, impersonal structural forces whose racial motivation cannot be ascertained are often the cause of the black disadvantage that observers identify. Likewise, class perspectives usually wash away any reference to race. Moreover, the class-based analysis that blacks united with low-income white workers and other disadvantaged groups would be the most likely source of collective opposition to the current socioeconomic arrangement, has given way to continued estrangement between these groups. The materialist perspective that policy should address broad class groups as opposed to specific racial groups leaves the unique historical legacy of race untouched.

Obviously, a complete understanding of racial inequality must include elements of both race and class. Race is a necessary element in understanding the sources of racial inequality and its continuation; class is important in understanding its changing character in response to larger economic and sociopolitical changes. Both are necessary in helping us understand the role of social policy in either exacerbating or lessening inequality. I argue that a focus on "assets" and an assets approach can help us bring together both race and class in ways that are enlightening in terms of better understanding the sources and continuation of racial inequality, as well as in ways that are beneficial in helping us to think about how to address the current maladies of increasing racial inequality.

An Assets Perspective on Material Inequality

The emphasis on using the polar concepts of race and class to understand contemporary black/white inequality in the United States rests in part on a focus on explaining one type of inequality—income inequality. Income is the standard way to study and evaluate family well-being and progress in social justice and equality in the United States. When analysts use income, they believe they are capturing the most important material asset available to families. In many cases, they believe they are in fact measuring the totality of material resources that are of consequence to the social and economic standing of the average family. In fact, however, they are missing an important element of an individual's or family's material resources: financial assets or wealth.[1]

Although related, income and wealth have different meanings. Wealth is the total extent, at a given moment, of an individual's accumulated assets and access to resources, and it refers to the net value of assets (e.g., ownership of stocks, money in the bank, real estate, business ownership, etc.), less debt held at one time. Wealth is anything of economic value bought, sold, stocked for future disposition, or invested to bring an economic return. Income refers to a flow of dollars (salaries, wages, and payments periodically received as returns from an occupation, investment, or government transfer, etc.) over a set period, typically one year. Income is associated with the consumption of goods and services and standard of living, while assets are associated with savings, investment, and asset accumulation. Assets provide for their owner a command over future resources. They can be used to strategize about an individual or family's life chances.

The key point here is that wealth is what people use to create and take advantage of mobility opportunities. Income, in contrast, is what people use for day-to-day necessities. Wealth, especially substantial wealth, often brings income, power, and independence. Significant wealth relieves individuals from dependence on others for an income, freeing them from the authority structures associated with occupational differentiation that constitutes an important aspect of privilege in the United States and elsewhere. Command over resources inevitably anchors a conception of life chances. While resources theoretically imply both income and wealth, the reality for most families is that income supplies the necessities of life, while wealth represents a kind of "surplus" resource available for improving life chances, providing opportunities, securing prestige, passing status along to one's family, and influencing the political process.

The sine qua non character of wealth that makes it an appropriate lens into understanding the nature of racial privilege is its intergenerational character. It allows us to connect the past and the present together in ways that income and other economic indicators do not allow. Since assets are passed down from generation to generation, they contain in them the sociological "DNA" that connects policies, practices, and dimensions of the past to contemporary realities. Let us turn to an empirical example that gives us a new insight into the current ways in which race and class are played out in contemporary racial inequality.

Race, Class, and Wealth Inequality

Most observers measure the character of racial justice in the United States through the lens of income. Once each year the U.S. Census Bureau takes a thermometer reading of how well we are doing in terms of economic justice, with its publication of the latest results of the Current Population Survey's comparison of black/white income inequality. The measure is a simple ratio. It provides how much the average black family makes for every dollar that the average white family possesses. For over twenty years now, this figure has percolated around the 58–62 percent level. That is, for every $1.00 the average white family makes, the average black family makes 58 cents to 62 cents depending on the year and the nature of the business cycle. When the figure is close to 62 cents on the dollar, progress is celebrated; when it is closer to 58 cents on the dollar, the lack of progress is condemned.

A focus on wealth changes the picture of racial inequality and our notion of progress. Using the U.S. Bureau's 1987 Survey of Income and Program Participation, one of the few large-scale social surveys that contain significant data on the wealth of average Americans, a different picture emerges. As Figure 9.1 shows, the ratio of black to white income is 62 percent of median white family income. However, the

Figure 9.1 Black/White Ratios on Income and Wealth

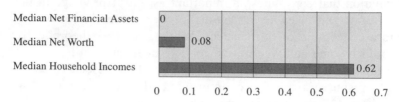

Median Net Financial Assets   0

Median Net Worth   0.08

Median Household Incomes   0.62

0   0.1   0.2   0.3   0.4   0.5   0.6   0.7

Source: All data are from electronic files of the U.S. Bureau of the Census, Survey of Income and Program Participation 1987, Wave 4.

wealth disparities are drastically different. It is quite a gestalt change when we move from income to wealth.

The ratio of black to white net worth (the value of all assets minus any debts) shows that blacks have a median net worth of 8 cents for every $1 of net worth that whites have. For net financial assets (excludes equity in homes and cars from the net worth calculation, leaving only cash assets) the figures are even less. As you see, there is no ratio for that because over 62 percent of all black households in the United States have less than zero or negative net financial assets. This is a common lament; we owe more than we have. What does this mean? Well, imagine that a family was to lose an income stream and they were forced to support themselves on savings and other assets. If that were to happen, nearly eight out of ten African-American families would not be able to survive on poverty-level consumption with their level of net financial assets for three months. Comparable figures for whites are one-half those of African Americans. Thinking about the social welfare of children, these figures are even more significant. Nine out of ten black children live in asset-deficient households that would not be able to support them for three months if an income stream were to disappear (Oliver and Shapiro 1995: pp. 88–89). A class analysis of this inequality would quickly point out that these differences have to do more with class than race. The prudent analyst would first test these disparities by controlling for class elements. What one would find if the class analysis is correct is that the racial difference would either disappear or be substantially reduced. Figure 9.2 provides this kind of test by examining black/white ratios of income and wealth for middle-class blacks and whites. The class argument is that they should show little racial difference, that is, the ratio should approach 100 percent because all the differences are really captured in class background.

Figure 9.2   Black/White Ratios on Income and Wealth for Different Definitions of "Middle Class"

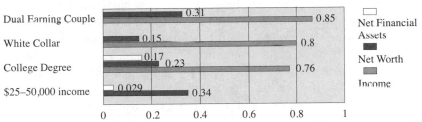

Source: All data are from electronic files of the U.S. Bureau of the Census, Survey of Income and Program Participation 1987, Wave 4.

Since class is a slippery concept, I have used different measures of class that capture a variation of what is considered to be important elements of class by contemporary thinkers. First, we have examined class as defined by income, looking at only those with "middle incomes" for the time period (annual incomes between $25,000 and $50,000 per year). Second, we have examined class as measured by education, including only those in the analysis who have earned a bachelor's degree or higher. Third, we have examined class as measured by occupational position, including all households with a worker in a white-collar occupation. Finally, we have examined class as measured behaviorally, by including all two-parent households where both parents have full-time jobs in the labor market.

Figure 9.2 presents the results of looking at these elements of class for income and wealth inequality. Three things are clear. First, only for income does the class analysis come close to being supported by the data. Dual-earning couples come closest to parity at about 85 cents on the dollar, while those with a college degree only go up to 76 cents on the dollar. Second, for net worth, being middle-income, college-educated, white-collar, or in a dual-earning couple does relatively little for the acquisition of wealth. Middle-income earners generate the most net worth, at about 35 cents for every dollar that their white counterparts have, to a low of 15 cents on the dollar for white-collar jobholders. Third, when the issue is net financial assets, the results continue to be rooted clearly in race, not class. For net financial assets you cannot even generate ratios because over half of the black middle class have zero or negative net financial assets.

This data clearly show that race and class have different effects depending on whether you are focusing on income or wealth. Race is the important determinant of wealth, while for income, class has more salience. By shifting our gaze from income to wealth, we have uncovered an important contemporary example of where race is dominant. But this finding has greater importance theoretically and in terms of public policy because of the intergenerational character of wealth. Since wealth captures not only contemporary resources but also material assets that have historic origins, assets capture inequality that is the product of the past because it is passed down in part from generation to generation.

The Social Construction of Racial Privilege

A focus on wealth or assets allows us to deconstruct the origins and maintenance of racial privilege. It helps us uncover the footprints of the past that weigh heavily on the present. Economists often emphasize that wealth is a consequence of a combination of factors: inheritance, rates of savings, and income. I do not so much disagree with this calculus, as I am concerned that economists have not properly appreciated the social context in which the processes in question take place. I want to suggest another perspective that posits that it is the social structure of investment opportunity, a process that has been racially constructed to provide privilege and opportunity for whites in general, and the middle and higher classes in particular, that is responsible for driving these differences. Blacks and whites have faced an opportunity to create wealth that has been structured by the intersection of class and race. Economists rightly note that blacks' lack of desirable human capital attributes places them at a disadvantage in the wealth accumulation process. However, those human capital deficiencies can be traced, in part, to barriers that denied blacks access to quality education, job-training opportunities, and other work-related factors. In order to deconstruct this process you must investigate public policies and private actions that determine how people have been able to make asset accumulation a part of their lives.

Three concepts help organize a whole set of findings that give us an opportunity to look at how this kind of disparity is socially constructed. First, the notion of the racialization of state policy, that is, how state policy has actually created opportunities—differential opportunities for blacks and whites to be part of asset accumulation. Second, the notion of an economic detour that is quite peculiar to African Americans as an ethnic group in America. Where all ethnic groups have come to the United States and seen entrepreneurship and business opportunities as an economic possibility, African Americans have taken an economic detour. It is not that African Americans have not been involved in business and entrepreneurship but that their level and extent of involvement has been so much less when compared to other ethnic groups. Finally, there is a synthetic notion—the sedimentation of inequality—that pulls all this together in a way that integrates the intergenerational consequences of having low net worth over a long historical period of time. Below I explain these notions in greater detail, along with a sociohistorical analysis that illuminates the way racial inequality in wealth has been socially constructed (Oliver and Shapiro 1995: pp. 33–52).

The Racialization of State Policy

The context of one's opportunity to acquire land, build community, and generate wealth has been structured particularly by state policy. In the United States, slavery itself was the result of state policy that gave blacks severely limited economic rights. Slaves were by law not able to own property or to accumulate assets. In contrast, no matter how poor whites were, they had the right—that is if they were males—if not the ability, to buy land, enter into contracts, own businesses, and develop wealth assets that could build equity for themselves and their families. Thus slavery is the touchstone of racialized state policy that lays the foundation for differential opportunities for blacks and whites to accumulate assets. Other policies soon reinforced this racial divide.

One instrumental set of policies in this regard related to the various homestead laws that opened up the East and Southeast during colonial times and the West during the nineteenth century. These vast giveaways of land from public to private interests created vastly different opportunities for black and white settlers. As one commentator notes, these land grants "allowed three-fourths of America's colonial families to own their own farms" (Anderson 1994: p. 123). In contrast, blacks were promised "forty acres and a mule" and instead received virtually no material assets from legal emancipation (Lanza 1990; Du Bois 1935). Even after emancipation, black homesteaders in such places as California found their claims were not legally enforceable (Beasley 1919). Thus, the most massive asset accumulation policy ever put in place, the transfer of public lands to private hands, was largely unavailable to African Americans.

The next set of policies that racialized benefits for blacks and whites came out of the massive reforms associated with the New Deal. Chief among them was the cornerstone of that revolution, the old-age insurance program of the Social Security Act of 1935. This beacon of enlightened social policy excluded most African Americans and Latinos by exempting agricultural and domestic workers from coverage, as well as other marginalized low-wage workers (Mink 1990). Because minority wages were so low, minority workers fell disproportionately below the threshold of coverage in comparison to whites. They were twice as likely not to be covered by Social Security insurance than whites because of their lack of earnings (Quadango 1994: pp. 20–24, 161). Moreover, several other sets of New Deal policies had even more devastating effects on the ability of blacks to secure wealth. These included the institution of the Federal Housing Authority (FHA); the Supplementary Social Security Act, which laid the foundation for the basic program for mothers raising their children alone, Aid to Families with Dependent Children (AFDC); and the United States Tax Code.

The development of low-interest, long-term mortgages backed by the federal government marked the appearance of a crucial opportunity for the average American family to generate a wealth stake. The purchase of a home has now become the primary mechanism for generating wealth (Eller and Fraser 1995). However, the FHA's conscious decision to channel loans away from the central city and to the suburbs has had a powerful effect on the creation of segregated housing in post–World War II America.[2] Borrowing the standards of private-sector mortgage providers, the government instituted a "formal and uniform system of appraisal" that systematically denied loans to communities that were in the midst of racial transition, all black, or "undesirable" (Jackson 1985: p. 196). The FHA even went so far as to provide a "model" restrictive covenant to white home buyers so they could insure that their neighborhoods would remain racially exclusive and in demand. The FHA's success was remarkable: housing starts jumped from 332,000 in 1936 to 619,000 in 1941. The incentive for home ownership increased to the point where it became, in many cases, cheaper to buy a home than to rent one (p. 206).

However, African Americans were not able to take advantage of these homeownership opportunities. Locked out of arguably the greatest mass-based opportunity for wealth accumulation in American history, African Americans who desired and were able to afford home ownership found themselves consigned to central-city communities where their investments were affected by the self-fulfilling prophecies of the FHA appraisers: cut off from sources of new investment, their homes and communities deteriorated and lost value in comparison to those homes and communities that FHA appraisers deemed "desirable." One infamous housing development of the period—Levittown—provides a classic illustration of the way blacks missed out on this asset-accumulating opportunity. Levittown was built on a mass scale, and housing there was eminently affordable, but thanks to FHA financing, as late as 1960 "not a single one of Long Island Levittown's 82,000 residents were black" (Jackson 1985: p. 241).

The public welfare system that provides benefits to single women and their children has had a peculiarly negative impact on the opportunity for blacks to accumulate assets. The relatively small sums that have been transferred to these families have been accompanied by restrictions on their ability to accumulate assets. An "asset test" has been the norm for eligibility for AFDC. As a consequence, women enter welfare on the economic edge. What little savings that remain are usually drawn down to meet routine emergencies and shortfalls. The result is that AFDC has become for many women, especially African-American women, a state-sponsored policy to encourage and maintain asset poverty (Sherranden 1991: p. 64).

A substantial portion of state expenditures takes the form of tax benefits or "fiscal welfare" (Howard 1998). These benefits are hidden in the tax code as taxes individuals do not have to pay because the government has decided to encourage certain types of activity and behavior and not others. Tax advantages may come in the form of different rates on certain types of income, tax deferral, or deductions, exclusions, and credits. Many are asset-based; if you own certain assets, you receive a tax break. In turn, these tax breaks directly help people accumulate financial and real assets. They benefit not only the wealthy but also the broad middle class of homeowners and pension holders as well. More important, since blacks have fewer assets to begin with, the effect of the tax code's "fiscal welfare" is to limit the flow of tax relief to blacks and to redirect it to those who already have assets. The seemingly race-neutral tax code thus generates a racial effect that deepens rather than equalizes the economic gulf between blacks and whites (Bartlett and Steele 1992; Moran and Whitford 1996).

Two examples illustrate how racialized policy functions in the current tax code: lower tax rates on capital gains and the deduction for home mortgages and real estate taxes. Each of these taxes produces a differential flow to blacks and whites because blacks have fewer and different types of assets than whites with similar income. However, for more than nine of every ten tax filers (93 percent) no capital gains taxes

Company, by 1949 over three hundred African-American firms dotted the business section of Durham, dubbed "Hayti." What is remarkable about Durham is that this economic vitality lasted so long (p. 180). In other places, the record is not so successful.

Several examples illustrate that when black businesses thrived by either excelling in the contours of the economic detour or by breaking through the detour and into white markets, the response was violent and obliterating. Two such examples were Wilmington, North Carolina, and Tulsa, Oklahoma. In each case, black entrepreneurs had built up significant retail centers that rivaled white business counterparts and in some cases were so attractive to the white market that they competed for white market share. In Wilmington, "there was grumbling among the white professional classes" because "black entrepreneurs, located conspicuously downtown, deprived white businessmen of legitimate sources of income to which they thought they were entitled" (Prather 1984: p. 179). In Tulsa, the Greenwood district encompassed forty-one grocers and meat markets, thirty restaurants, fifteen physicians, five hotels, two theaters, and two newspapers (Butler 1991: pp. 206–221). Both of these thriving communities' economic engines were destroyed by white violence precipitated by baseless accusations concerning the sexual assault of a white woman. The results were the same. In Wilmington, black entrepreneurs were driven out and "immediately after the massacres, white businesses moved in and filled the economic gap left by the flight of the blacks" (Prather 1984: p. 183). In Tulsa, eighteen thousand homes and businesses were left in cinders, ending "the efforts of entrepreneurs . . . of the Greenwood business district" (Butler 1991: p. 209). While these events have recessed from the public imagination, and in some cases the public record, they form a collective narrative with similar incidents from all over the United States that reinforces African Americans' antipathy and ambivalence around self-employment and entrepreneurship. The lack of important assets and indigenous community economic development has thus played a crucial role in limiting the wealth-accumulating ability of African Americans.

The Sedimentation of Racial Inequality

The third concept, the "sedimentation of racial inequality," is synthetic in nature. The notion is that in central ways the cumulative effects of the past have seemingly cemented blacks to the bottom of society's economic hierarchy. A history of low wages, poor schooling, and segregation affected not one generation of blacks but practically all African

Americans well into the twentieth century (Lieberson 1980). The best indicator of this is wealth. Wealth is one indicator of material disparity that captures the historical legacy of low wages, personal and organization discrimination, and institutionalized racism. The low level of wealth accumulation evidenced by current generations of African Americans best represents the economic status of blacks in the American social structure. In contrast, whites in general, but well-off whites in particular, had far greater structured opportunities to amass assets and use their secure financial status to pass their wealth and its benefits from generation to generation. What is often not acknowledged is that the same social system that fosters the accumulation of private wealth for many whites denies it to blacks, thus forging an intimate connection between white wealth accumulation and black poverty. Just as blacks have had "cumulative disadvantages," many whites have had "cumulative advantages." Since wealth builds over a lifetime and is then passed along to kin, it is an essential indicator of black economic well-being.

This analysis has tried to draw attention to how past racial inequality in policy and practices socially structures racial privileges in the form of vastly different wealth resources for black and white families, even among those with roughly equal accomplishments. The social injustice is not just an artifact of how the past structured inequality: contemporary institutional discrimination contributes to structuring and maintaining the racial wealth gap. One key area is housing. The next section examines perhaps the most important institutional sphere in which this inequality is passed along.

Contemporary Social Constructions of Racial Privilege: The Case of Housing

Home ownership is without a doubt the single most important means of accumulating assets for the typical American family. Home equity constitutes the largest share of net worth, as it accounts for about 44 percent of total measured net worth (Eller and Fraser 1995). Federal housing taxation and transportation policies have traditionally reinforced racial residential segregation (Massey and Denton 1994). This continuing segregation has an enduring significance on blacks' quest for asset accumulation, but continuing institutional and policy discrimination also intensifies it. First, access to credit is important because whom banks deem to be creditworthy delineates a crucial moment of institutional racial bias in the process of securing home ownership that will have lasting consequences. The second area of potential discrimination concerns the interest rates attached to loans for those approved for buying homes. Third, as is well known, housing values ascended steeply during the 1970s and 1980s, far outstripping inflation and creating a large pool of assets for those already owning homes. Did all homeowners share equally in the appreciation of housing values, or is housing inflation color-coded?

The home ownership rate for blacks is about 20 percentage points behind whites. As the previous analysis alluded to, this difference is not merely the result of income or class differences. It is rather a product of the historical legacy of residential segregation, redlining, FHA/Veteran's Administration policy, and discrimination in real estate and lending markets (Yinger 1995; Massey and Denton 1994). How does this historical legacy and contemporary state of affairs contribute to the racial gap in wealth resources?

In order to purchase a home, families first must qualify for a home mortgage. Several Federal Reserve Board studies based on the outcome of all loan applications, the release of which is mandated by federal legislation, demonstrate that blacks are rejected for home loans 60 percent more often than equally qualified white families (Oliver and Shapiro 1995; Ladd 1998). Equally qualified here also means creditworthiness. Thus, no matter how egregious past discrimination may have been in this sector, grave levels of racial discrimination are still alive in the financial mortgage markets.

The second stage examines mortgage rates for those fortunate enough to buy homes. On average, African Americans pay about .33 percent higher mortgage interest rates than white families. Melvin Oliver and Thomas Shapiro's *Black Wealth/White Wealth* (1995) showed that the mortgage rate difference is not due to where the home is located, purchase price, or when the home was bought. A third of a percentage point may not sound like much. Consider that the median home purchase price is about $120,000 with, say, a $12,000 down payment, leaving a mortgage of $108,000. On a typical thirty-year loan this amounts to "only" a $25-per-month difference. However, over the loan period a typical African-American homebuyer will pay $9,000 more in interest to financial institutions than the average white one. Bankers insist they do not discriminate by charging different rates for black and white customers. Instead, it is far more typical for whites to bring greater assets to the table, use them to lower the amount of the loan or to pay "points" on the loan, and consequently receive a lower interest rate on their mortgage. Indeed, an extraordinary proportion of young, first-time homebuyers receive financial assistance from their parents. Both white and black young couples use this familial transfer to help with the down payment and/or to pay points.

This process reveals a key to understanding how past inequality is linked to the present and how present inequalities will project into the next generation. Essentially, past injustice provides a disadvantage for blacks and an advantage for many whites in how home purchases are financed. And because similar home mortgages cost African-American families $9,000 more, blacks pay more to finance their homes and end up with less home equity in the future.

The third stage brings home equity into the analysis. The 1994 Survey of Income and Program Participation data on home equity show that buying homes seems to increase the wealth assets for all able to afford them. However, the valuing of homes and home equity is color-coded. (This analysis includes only those currently still paying off home mortgages and thus provides a very conservative estimate of the dynamics.) The mean value of the typical home owned by white families increases $28,605 more than the rise in value of the same home owned by blacks. *Black Wealth/White Wealth*, again, found that region, length of ownership, purchase price, when the home was purchased, and so on, did not explain racial differential in home equity. This $28,000 difference is a compelling index of bias in housing markets that costs blacks dearly.

The explanation lies in how the dynamics of residential segregation impact housing markets. It is a contemporary illustration of the economic detour that blacks confront. A white family attempting to sell its house in a relatively homogeneous white community is limited only by market forces, that is, economic affordability. A similar African-American family attempting to sell its home in a community that is more than 20 percent nonwhite faces normal market limits as well as racial dynamics. The pool of potential buyers is no longer 100 percent of the affordable market: for all practical purposes, most of the potential white buyers are not interested in such neighborhoods (Yinger 1995; Massey and Denton 1994). The potential buyers are now mainly other blacks and possibly other minorities who can afford the home. The economic detour notion shows how the marketplace for whites is the entire society while the marketplace for blacks is severely restricted. In turn, this helps explain why housing values do not rise nearly as quickly or as high in African-American communities or in those more than 20 percent nonwhite.

Taken together, these forms of contemporary bias cost the current generation of blacks about $82 billion dollars. If these biases continue unabated, they will cost the next generation of black homeowners $93 billion. On the basis of this logic, one could take the $93-billion figure as the minimal target of public and private initiatives needed to help create housing assets in the black community (Oliver and Shapiro 1995: p. 151).

Thus, white racial privilege is being socially constructed even in a context of federal antidiscrimination law through the everyday workings of housing policy, mortgage lending, and individual and institutional biases. Connected to the social constructions of the past, it is clear that both race and class are continuing sources of racial privilege.

Conclusion and Implications

By focusing on assets or wealth, we were able to demonstrate that race is central to the social construction of privilege. While class and race are clearly important, it would be a mistake to focus exclusively on class when thinking about the substantive and policy challenges that we face in achieving a more just society. The contemporary inclination to put the past behind us and to focus purely on the present underplays the deep, historically rooted economic cleavages between the races. The interaction of race and class in the social structuring of the wealth-accumulation process is clear. Historical practices, racist in their essence, have produced class hierarchies that, on the contemporary scene, reproduce wealth inequalities. As important, contemporary racial disadvantages deprive those in the black community from building on their wealth assets at the same pace as similarly situated white Americans. The shadow of race falls most darkly, however, on the black underclass, whose members find themselves at the bottom of the economic hierarchy. Their inability to accumulate assets is thus grounded primarily in their low-class background. The wealth deficit of the black middle class, by contrast, is affected more by the racial character of certain policies deriving in part from the fears and anxieties that whites harbor regarding lower-class blacks than by the actual class background of middle-class blacks. As Raymond Franklin suggests in his *Shadows of Race and Class* (1991: p. xxvi): "the overcrowding of blacks in the lower class . . . casts a shadow on middle-class members of the black population that have credentials but are excluded and discriminated against on racial grounds."

Given the mutually reinforcing and historically accumulated race and class barriers that blacks encounter in attempting to achieve a measure of economic security, it seems clear that the focus on job opportunity is not sufficient to the task of eradicating racial disadvantage in the United States. Equal opportunity, even in the best of circumstances, does not lead to equality. This is a double-edged statement. First, equal-opportunity policies and programs, when given a chance, do succeed in lowering some of the more blatant barriers to black advancement. But given the historically sedimented nature of racial wealth disparities, a focus on equal opportunity will yield only partial results. Blacks will make some gains but so will whites, with initial inequalities persisting at another level. The question becomes: How do we link the opportunity structure to policies that promote asset formation and begin to close the wealth gap?

We can achieve racial justice through the social construction of policies that promote asset building on a more democratic and equal basis rather than the social construction of inequality that has been the hallmark of the last three hundred years. First, we must directly address the historically generated as well as current institutional disadvantages that limit the ability of blacks, as a group, to accumulate wealth resources. Second, we must resolutely promote asset accumulation among those at the bottom of the social structure who have been locked out of the wealth accumulation process, be they black or white. Third, we must take aim at the massive concentration of wealth that is held by the richest Americans. Without redistributing America's wealth, we will not succeed at creating a more just society (Wolff 1996). Even as this agenda is advanced, policies that safeguard equal opportunity must be defended. In short, we must make racial justice a national priority.

This has implications for any national situation in which racial oppression has been a key historical and contemporary reality, such as in Brazil and South Africa. National policy must recognize that current patterns of racial inequality will not magically be addressed by focusing exclusively on "economic growth," "natural market forces," or "equal opportunity" to address historically sedimented patterns of racial disadvantage. By moving the focus from income inequality to asset inequality, the need becomes apparent that policy needs to be constructed that is directed at both racial and class disadvantage. Only in this way will there be the opportunity to break the cycle of inequality that taps the potential of all citizens to develop social and economically secure lives.

Notes

1. This section borrows heavily from the ideas of Oliver and Shapiro 1989, 1990, 1995; and Sherraden 1991.
2. See Feagin and Parker 1990; Lipsitz 1998; Squires 1994; Jackson 1985.

References

Anderson, Claud. 1994. *Black Labor, White Wealth: The Search for Power and Economic Justice*. Edgewood, MD: Duncan and Duncan.

Baron, Harold M. 1971. "The Demand for Black Labor: Historical Notes on the Political Economy of Racism." *Radical America* 5, no. 2: 1–46.

Bartlett, Donald L., and James B. Steele. 1992. *America: Who Really Pays the Taxes?* New York: Touchstone.

Beasley, Delilah. 1919. *Negro Trail Blazers of California*. Los Angeles: Times Mirror Print and Binding House.

Blauner, Bob. 1972. *Racial Oppression in America*. New York: Harper.

Bloch, Herman David. 1969. *The Circle of Discrimination: An Economic and Social Study of the Black Man in New York*. New York: New York University Press.

Bonacich, Edna. 1976. "Advanced Capitalism and Black-White Relations in the United States: A Split Labor Market Interpretation." *American Sociological Review* 37: 547–559.

Butler, John Sibley. 1991. *Entrepreneurship and Self-Help Among Black Americans: A Reconsideration of Race and Economics*. Albany: State University of New York Press.

Cose, Ellis. 1993. *The Rage of the Privileged Class*. New York: Modern Reader Paperback.

Darity, William A. Jr., and Patrick L. Mason. 1998. "Evidence on Discrimination in Employment: Codes of Color, Codes of Gender." *Journal of Economic Perspectives* 12, no. 2 (Spring): 63–90.

Du Bois, W.E.B. 1935. *Black Reconstruction in America*. New York: Harcourt and Brace.

Eller, T. J., and Wallace Fraser. 1995. "Asset Ownership of Households: 1993," in *U.S. Bureau of the Census. Current Population Reports, P70-47*. Washington, DC: U.S. Government Printing Office.

Feagin, Joe R., and Robert Parker. 1990. *Building American Cities: The Urban Real Estate Game*. Englewood Cliffs, NJ: Prentice Hall.

Feagin, Joe R., and Melvin P. Sikes. 1994. *Living with Racism: The Black Middle-Class Experience*. Boston: Beacon Press.

Foner, Eric. 1988. *Reconstruction: America's Unfinished Revolution*. New York: Harper.

Franklin, Raymond S. 1991. *Shadows of Race and Class*. Minneapolis: University of Minnesota Press.

Howard, Christopher. 1998. *The Hidden Welfare State: Tax Expenditures and Social Policy in the United States*. Princeton: Princeton University Press.

Jackman, Mary, and Robert Jackman. 1980. "Racial Inequalities in Home Ownership." *Social Forces* 58: 1221–1233.

Jackson, Kenneth T. 1985. *Crabgrass Frontier: The Suburbanization of the United States.* New York: Oxford University Press.

Jaynes, Gerald, and Robin Williams, eds. 1989. *A Common Destiny: Blacks and American Society.* Washington, DC: National Academy Press.

Johnson, James H. Jr., and Melvin L. Oliver. 1992. "Structural Changes in the U.S. Economy and Black Male Joblessness: A Reassessment," in George Peterson and Wayne Vroman, eds., *Urban Labor Markets and Job Opportunity.* Washington, DC: Urban Institute Press, pp. 113–147.

Kozol, Jonathan. 1993. *Savage Inequalities.* New York: Random House.

Ladd, Helen F. 1998. "Evidence on Discrimination in Mortgage Lending." *Journal of Economic Perspectives* 12, no. 2 (Spring): 41–62.

Lanza, Michael L. 1990. *Agrarianism and Reconstruction Politics: The Southern Homestead Act.* Baton Rouge: Louisiana State University Press.

Leiberson, Stanley. 1980. *A Piece of the Pie.* Berkeley: University of California Press.

Light, Ivan. 1972. *Ethnic Enterprise in America.* Berkeley: University of California Press.

———. 1980. "Asian Enterprise in America: Chinese, Japanese, and Koreans in Small Business," in Scott Cummings, ed., *Self-Help in America: Patterns of Minority Business Development.* New York: Kennikat Press, pp. 33–57.

Lipsitz, George. 1998. *The Possessive Investment in Whiteness: How White People Profit from Identity Politics.* Philadelphia: Temple University Press.

Massey, Douglas S., and Nancy A. Denton. 1994. *American Apartheid: Segregation and the Making of the Underclass.* Cambridge: Harvard University Press.

McIntosh, Peggy. 2001. "White Privilege and Male Privilege: A Personal Account of Coming to See Correspondences Through Work in Women's Studies," in Margaret L. Andersen and Patricia Hill Collins, eds., *Race, Class, and Gender: An Anthology.* Belmont, CA: Wadsworth.

Mink, Gwendolyn. 1990. "The Lady and the Tramp: Gender, Race, and the Origins of the American Welfare State," in Linda Gordon, ed., *Women, the State, and Welfare.* Madison: University of Wisconsin Press, pp. 92–122.

Moran, Beverly I., and William Whitford. 1996. "A Black Critique of the Internal Revenue Code." *Wisconsin Law Review* 751.

Oliver, Melvin L., and Thomas M. Shapiro. 1989. "Race and Wealth." *Review of Black Political Economy* 17: 5–25.

———. 1990. "Wealth of a Nation: At Least One-Third of Households Are Asset Poor." *American Journal of Economics and Sociology* 49: 129–151.

———. 1995. *Black Wealth/White Wealth: A New Perspective on Racial Inequality.* New York and London: Routledge.

Ong, Paul, and Eugene Grigsby. 1988. "Race and Life Cycle Effects on Home Ownership in Los Angeles, 1970 to 1980." *Urban Affairs Quarterly* 23: 601–615.

Oubre, Claude. 1978. *Forty Acres and a Mule: The Freedman's Bureau and Black Land Ownership.* Baton Rouge: Louisiana State University Press.

Prather, H. Leon. 1984. *We Have Taken a City.* Rutherford, NJ: Fairleigh Dickinson University Press.

Quadagno, Jill. 1994. *The Color of Welfare.* New York: Oxford University Press.

Schuman, Howard, Charlotte Steeh, and Lawrence Bobo. 1985. *Racial Attitudes in America: Trends and Interpretation.* Cambridge, MA: Harvard University Press.

Sherraden, Michael. 1991. *Assets and the Poor: A New American Welfare Policy.* New York: Sharpe.

Squires, Gregory D. 1994. *Capital and Communities in Black and White.* Albany: State University of New York.

Stuart, Merah S. 1940. *An Economic Detour: A History of Insurance in the Lives of American Negroes.* New York: Wendell Malliett.

U.S. Bureau of the Census. 1987. Survey of Income and Program Participation, Wave 4 (electronic data).

Willie, Charles V., ed. 1979. *The Class-Caste Controversy.* Bayside, NY: General Hill.

Wilson, William Julius. 1978. *The Declining Significance of Race.* Chicago: University of Chicago Press.

———. 1987. *The Truly Disadvantaged.* Chicago: University of Chicago Press.

———. 1996. *When Work Disappears.* New York: Knopf.

Wolff, Edward N. 1996. *TOP HEAVY. A Study of Increasing Inequality of Wealth in America.* Updated and expanded edition. New York: Free Press.

Woodward, C. Van. 1955. *The Strange Career of Jim Crow.* New York: Oxford University Press.

Yinger, John. 1995. *Closed Doors, Opportunities Lost: The Continuing Costs of Housing Discrimination.* New York: Russell Sage Foundation.

Zubrinsky, Camille, and Lawrence Bobo. 1996. "Prismatic Metropolis: Race and Residential Segregation in the City of the Angels." *Social Science Research* 25: 335–374.

PART 2

COMPARATIVE ISSUES

IN THIS SECTION, the contributors explore key issues with salience in each venue. In "Race, Human Capital Inequality, and Income Distribution," authors Lesley O'Connell and Nancy Birdsall make a compelling case for investment in education as a key means by which to reduce racial inequality and equip people of African descent with skills needed to take advantage of opening economic, social, and political opportunities for advancement. Without investment in education at all levels, especially in basic education in South Africa and Brazil, these nations will be hobbled in the highly competitive technology and information-driven era into which the world is moving.

Francis Wilson, in "Globalization: A View from the South," demonstrates the need for enhanced efforts to broaden educational opportunity and skills development by documenting how the globalizing world economy is impacting the fortunes of South Africa. That nation's history of underinvestment in black African education has weakened South Africa's place in world markets, and the efforts of government to redress inequality are increasingly affected by global economic trends, multinational businesses, and multilateral institutions. Although framed in a South African context, this chapter contains broad lessons and implications for Brazil, other developing nations, and the United States as well.

Jonas Zoninsein's piece considers the economic consequences of racial discrimination on the national economies of Brazil, South Africa, and the United States. "GDP Increases from Ending Long-Term Discrimination Against Blacks" examines foregone productivity due to discrimination and the implications for national efforts to meet development goals. In effect, he marshals data to make the business case for inclusion and diversity.

john a. powell considers remedies for discrimination by analyzing and critiquing the way in which affirmative-action policies have been conceptualized and articulated in the United States in "Transformative Action: A Strategy for Ending Racial Hierarchy and Achieving True Democracy." While defending the need for targeted efforts to help blacks overcome the disadvantages and injury suffered due to discrimination, powell considers ways of redirecting societal attention away from the victim of discrimination to the composition of institutions and structural arrangements that disadvantage blacks, often without conscious intent by their leaders to do so.

These days, much is written about civil-society institutions and the need for these institutions to counterbalance the power of government and provide a place for experimentation and community building by the people whom government is there to serve. Emmett Carson, in "The Seven Deadly Myths of the U.S. Nonprofit Sector: Implications for Promoting Social Justice Worldwide," examines the track record of such institutions in relation to diversity and social justice and the assumptions that undergird the operations of this sector.

Gay McDougall, in "Racial Discrimination as a Violation of International Law: International Standards and Mechanisms," shares perspectives on the emergent international standards and structures developed to combat racism and discrimination and promote adherence to human-rights values. While still largely aspirational, these values are now implicated in trade relations and international affairs among nations. Human-rights standards and mechanisms are increasingly looked to by victims of discrimination as needed complements to domestic efforts to combat racism.

These chapters, read together, give a sense of how a constellation of transnational developments, trends, and practices are increasingly interacting with efforts in Brazil, South Africa, and the United States to reduce racial discrimination and inequality. They touch on issues with implications for all who would reduce unfairness due to race and point the way toward new strategies, venues, and institutions that must be engaged.

—The Editors

10

Race, Human Capital Inequality, and Income Distribution

Lesley O'Connell and Nancy Birdsall

EDUCATION IS THE people's asset. It can be the great leveler, but it also can be disequalizing depending on its distribution and the returns rewarded to it by the market. This chapter examines the interplay among race, education, and income inequality in South Africa, Brazil, and the United States. South Africa's and Brazil's low education attainment compared to other middle-income countries reflects their highly unequal distribution of education, with high education for a few combined with limited attainment for the great majority. In both countries, race is a central factor, with nonwhites doing systematically worse than whites in education and in income. Compared to Brazil and South Africa, the United States, with four times greater per capita income, has high average levels and a relatively equal distribution of education. But differences in education by race are also notable in the United States.

We know from economic analyses that a higher average level and a more equal distribution of education contribute to a more equal distribution of income, as well as enhancing overall economic growth. Thus all three countries could benefit from policies to increase and better distribute educational opportunities—both in terms of more equitable societies and higher sustainable rates of economic growth.

In South Africa, the main challenge is to implement new postapartheid programs that will reach the previously underserved African population. In Brazil, closing education gaps requires deepening the efforts of the last five years to spend more on good-quality primary and secondary education that will benefit the poor. Because many Afro-Brazilians are poor and vice versa, policies that improve educational opportunities for the poor will reduce systematic differences in education by race as well. In the United States, where the secondary-school completion rate of African Americans is nearly identical to the rate for whites, differences in university attendance are the most visible source of continuing wage and income differentials. The less visible differences in the quality of preuniversity education in the United States, with schools in the poor inner cities spending less per child than schools in the wealthier suburbs, contribute to lower university attendance and to lower wages and incomes for African Americans.

In South Africa and Brazil, education levels of the poor and of blacks are still strikingly low compared to the average in each society; advances in education for these groups have the potential to redress larger and broader differences in income, jobs, and thus well-being between racial and income groups. In the United States, there is still room for narrowing differences in education and income between African Americans and white Americans, but doing so requires considering not only education policies (especially improving the quality of secondary schooling and financial access to university training) but dealing more effectively with such broader issues as discrimination in housing (with its effect on access to good-quality schooling) and in the labor market.

We begin with a theoretical consideration of why education is important to the discussion of inequality and economic growth, and then turn to an analysis of the state of education in South Africa, Brazil, and the United States.

Why Education Matters:
Economic Theory and Empirical Evidence[1]

Education is an asset, a form of capital, the accumulation and distribution of which increases an economy's growth potential and affects income distribution. In this section, we summarize the economic theory and empirical evidence underlying economists' views of education as an asset.

More Education Contributes to Growth

In neoclassical growth models, human capital accumulation is as critical to the growth process as physical capital—growth is stimulated by increasing savings and investment in education, a critical input to human capital. The more recent endogenous growth models attribute an even stronger role to human capital. Sustainable growth in these models is a result not only of the additional human capital that more education represents but of positive externalities generated by education in the form of new ideas and technologies and their quicker invention and adaptation. New ideas and technologies are critical to high sustained growth and in turn rely on high levels of human capital.

It is obvious that the educational attainment of populations is closely associated with income levels across countries. But the association does not necessarily indicate causality: educational attainment could be the result as much as the cause of income growth and high income levels—in economic terms, a luxury consumer good that is increasingly demanded as income rises. To pin down causality, studies of the determinants of growth in developing countries in the last decade or so have relied on assessment of how the level of education, e.g., enrollment rates, at the beginning of a period has affected income growth in subsequent years. These types of studies find a strong and positive effect of educational attainment on growth rates (Barro 1991; Barro and Sala-I-Martin 1995; Levine and Renelt 1992). Barro (1991: appendix, table 1, column 1) shows that the contribution of education is among the most robust findings of the growth regressions, proving to be relatively insensitive to changes in either specification or sample composition. Recent findings confirm human capital's contribution to growth but highlight the importance of the policy environment. López, Thomas, and Wang (1998) find that education's contribution to growth is augmented in open and competitive markets, while economic policies that suppress market policies reduce the effect of education.[2]

The findings of these empirical analyses are consistent with human-capital theory in stressing that education augments cognitive and other skills, which in turn augment the productivity of labor (T. W. Schultz 1961; Becker 1960), as well as with microeconomic evidence that better-educated workers earn higher incomes and, for women in particular, are more effective in household production of children's good health and schooling (T. P. Schultz 1988; Strauss and Thomas 1995).

Birdsall, Ross, and Sabot (1995) use the Barro results to assess the magnitude of the contribution of education to rates of economic growth. They report, on the basis of simple simulations, that increases in a country's primary- and secondary-school enrollment rates of half a standard deviation above the means of those variables would translate into nearly a 1.5 percentage point increase in the annual per capita growth rate (e.g., at the 1960 means, an increase in primary enrollment from 75 to 90 percent, and in secondary enrollment from 22 to 34 percent). The cumulative effect of this annual difference in growth rates over twenty-

five years is large. The simulation indicates that a country with primary-
and secondary-school enrollments half a standard deviation above the
average in 1960 would have had, by 1990, a GDP per capita 40 percent
higher than a country with 1960 enrollments half a standard deviation
below the average.

More Equally Distributed Education Contributes to Growth

Cross-country analysis of Birdsall and Londoño (1997: appendix, table
2) upholds the finding that education accumulation, along with capital
accumulation, is good for growth.[3] Their analysis also suggests that the
distribution of education affects growth, controlling for the level of
education. Birdsall and Londoño report that the degree of inequality in
the distribution of education has a strong and robust negative effect on
growth (table 1, columns 2 and 3). The variable measuring the distribution of education is highly robust;[4] its negative effect operates independently not only of the education-level variable but also of the positive effect of trade openness and the negative effect of natural-resource
endowment.

Moreover, the distribution of education appears to explain much of
the widely reported effect of inequality of income on growth (Birdsall,
Ross, and Sabot 1995; Alesina and Rodrik 1994; Persson and Tabellini
1994). When asset distribution variables (of land and education) are
included, the negative effect of income inequality per se on growth
loses statistical significance (Birdsall and Londoño 1997: table 1,
columns 2 and 3 versus column 1). Thus, the constraint to growth posed
by *income* inequality apparently reflects differences in a fundamental
element of economic structure, namely the access of different groups to
productive assets, including land and education.

Education, the Great Leveler

The correlation between asset accumulation and income concentration
is not surprising. Analysis across countries shows that an unequal distribution of assets, especially of education, affects income growth of the
poor disproportionately. Table 1 in Birdsall and Londoño (1997:
columns 4 to 6) shows the results of estimating the effects of the initial
distributions of education and land on the growth in income of the poor
across time periods. Income growth of the poor is affected positively by
overall growth (an elasticity well above one; column 1) and by capital
accumulation (columns 2 and 3). Income growth of the poor is negatively affected, however, by the uneven distribution of land and of edu-

cation. The negative effects on income growth of the poor are twice those of their effects on average income growth (column 2).

Contrasting the divergent performance of Latin America and East Asia illustrates the links among the distribution of education, income inequality, and growth. In Latin America, only a relatively small proportion of the total population has completed secondary or higher education. These relatively few skilled workers earn a substantial wage premium due to their limited supply. Thus a poor distribution of education contributes to differentials in the returns to different levels of education, magnifying the effect of education gaps on income inequality. Londoño and Székely (1997: appendix, figure 1) estimate that the low level of education of Latin American workers and the enormous inequality in educational assets account for the largest portion of the region's excessive inequality, larger than other contributing factors—lower physical capital accumulation, the relative abundance of natural resources, and high concentration of land. The Gini coefficient for Latin America is high, about 0.50 for the region as a whole.[5] (Brazil's very high Gini coefficient increases the regional average.) That is approximately fifteen points above the average for the rest of the world (and on par with that of South Africa, which is the second highest in the world). The Latin American experience stands in marked contrast to that of East Asia, where education gains ensured a large supply of skilled workers, eroding any substantial premium they might have earned above the wages of the unskilled (Birdsall, Ross, and Sabot 1995: appendix, figure 2). Driven by the increasing productivity of the initially poor, East Asian countries, which began the postwar period with relatively low asset inequality, were able to grow at high and sustained rates over more than three decades. In contrast, most countries of Latin America, with greater inequality of assets and presumably fewer opportunities for the poor, grew less.

We now examine education levels and distribution in South Africa, Brazil, and the United States. How do the facts in these countries fit with these average effects of education throughout the world? How will economic changes affect the links among education, future income growth, and future income inequality, especially across different racial groups?

Education and Inequality Across Countries

A comparison of South Africa, Brazil, and the United States draws upon rich points of similarity and differences. To begin, each country's population is ethnically diverse, a result of their colonial history, but they

vary by majority-minority breakdown and by the degree of racial intermarriage in the society. South Africa's sizable majority (77 percent) is
African, with the minorities being whites (11 percent), coloreds (9 percent), and Indians (3 percent).[6] Brazil's largest population group is
white, constituting 55 percent, closely trailed by the second largest
group, *pardo*, defined as of mixed race or color (mulatto or mestizo),
representing 38 percent of the population. Afro-Brazilians represent 6
percent. In the United States the large majority is white, comprising 73
percent of the population. African Americans represent a sizable minority (12 percent), as do Hispanics (11 percent).[7] The Asian-Pacific community represents 3.6 percent of the population, while the remaining 0.7
percent are Native American (The White House 1999).

South Africa and Brazil rank among high middle-income
countries.[8] But with respective income Gini coefficients of .58 and .60,
they are among the most unequal countries in the world.[9] They also
have exceedingly poor distribution of land, with Gini coefficients
exceeding .70 and an unequal distribution of education (Table 10.1). As
a result, despite these countries' income levels, much of the population
in South Africa and Brazil suffers low standards of living, including relatively low education attainment. The United States is a much richer
country, with over eight times the per capita GNP of South Africa and
six times that of Brazil. Compared to Brazil and South Africa, its
income is more equally distributed. It has by far one of the most equal

Table 10.1   Comparative Analysis of the Three Countries

Country	1997 GNP per capita (US$) (a)	Projected Total Pop. in 2000 (millions) (b)	Secondary enrollment (mid-1990s, net %) (c)	Income Gini (latest) (d)	Land Gini (latest) (e)	Education Gini[a] (latest) (f)
Brazil	4,790	170	19	.601	.852	.461
South Africa	3,210	40	63	.584	.701	.473
United States	29,080	278	90	.401	.754	.172

Sources: By column: (a) 1999 World Development Indicators; (b) UN population division
1998 revision; (c) 1999 UNESCO *Statistical Yearbook*; (d) 1999 World Development
Indicators and Deininger and Squire High Quality data set; (e) Deininger and Squire, personal
correspondence; (f) authors' calculations using Barro and Lee (1993) data set, population 25
years and older.

Notes: a. Using this summary measure of inequality, South Africa in 1990 has a less equal
distribution of education than Brazil. However, analysis of 1995 data surveying different population groups indicates that Brazil's distribution of schooling is more unequal.

distributions of education in the world and has achieved a high level of overall schooling, with virtually universal primary and secondary enrollment. Nonetheless, there are pockets of poverty, and only in the last two years has what was, since 1973, an increasing trend of income inequality been reversed.

Finally, the countries differ in their history of interracial relations, influencing the nature of inequality in each country. Distinguished among multiethnic countries for its degree of intermarriage and assimilation, Brazil is often cited as a racial democracy. As a result, distinguishing between race and class inequality in Brazil is difficult. Although most literature focuses on class-based inequities, inequities clearly fall along ethnic lines: not only are the Afro-Brazilian and *pardo* populations more likely to be poor, but they consistently have lower education attainment than the white population within the same income category. Still, there are many poor that are not Afro-Brazilians, and the white population in lower-income categories tends to have worse educational outcomes than the higher-income Afro-Brazilian and *pardo* populations.[10] The discussion of Brazil in this chapter focuses on the poor distribution of human capital across economic classes, noting when possible the disparate education opportunities and outcomes across ethnic groups. Because of the high correlation of poverty and race in Brazil, much of the analysis explaining high dropout rates among the poor can be extrapolated to help explain relatively poor education attainment by Afro-Brazilians. We also highlight the differential access to good-quality education across regions, which reflects the geographic concentration of poverty and race in Brazil.[11]

In stark contrast, South Africa lived under apartheid for fifty years. With a legacy of legal racial segregation, South Africa's inequalities clearly fall along racial lines.[12] Inequality is also high within racial groups; for example, African households have a Gini coefficient of .54, a number nearly as high as the overall Gini. Recent studies have found that within-group inequality is at least as important as between-group inequality in explaining South Africa's overall inequality (Leibbrandt, Woolard, and Woolard 1996). Not surprisingly, poverty is also highly concentrated by race: 61 percent of Africans and 38 percent of coloreds are poor, compared to 5 percent of Indians and 1 percent of whites (UNDP-SA 1998).

The United States falls somewhere in between South Africa and Brazil on this continuum. Like South Africa, the United States has struggled with the dismantling of legal racial segregation and in the last four decades has implemented various policies and programs to reduce racial discrimination. As in Brazil, the challenge in the United States is to deal with more-subtle barriers to equal opportunity among population groups. The extent to which these policies should be based on race is an ongoing debate.

South Africa[13]

Under apartheid, an unequal distribution of resources between white and nonwhite education systems, as well as between primary and secondary schooling, the latter of which mainly benefited white students, combined with explicit rationing of education opportunities by race to create unequal access to and quality of education in South Africa overall, and especially along racial lines. As a result, South Africa has low education quality and attainment and a poor distribution of human capital compared to other middle-income countries, although both attainment and distribution have improved over the last few decades (Table 10.2). South Africa's high illiteracy rate (18 percent) reflects the country's history of limited education, especially for Africans.

Access to education in South Africa has increased significantly for all population groups. Using 1995 Household Survey data, Lam (1999) tracks advances in education across five-year birth cohorts. He reports that the mean years of schooling received by the younger nonwhite cohort (born in 1971–1975), 9.3 years, is almost threefold the attainment of the oldest cohort (born in 1926–1930), 3.4 years. School attainment also increased for the white birth cohorts but less dramatically (from 10.6 to 11.8 years) (Table 10.3). Measured by a consistently decreasing standard deviation and coefficient of variation of years of schooling, the distribution of education, within population subgroups as well as for the population as a whole, improved over time.[14]

But advances in schooling have been uneven across groups, including within the nonwhite population, which has a higher coefficient of variation—and hence more uneven distribution of schooling—than the white population. Since 1980, Africans' average education increased the most, but from a lower base. As a result, they continue to have the lowest attainment, averaging five years of schooling (Table 10.4).

Moll (1996) reports the expansion in Africans' access to primary education since 1960; in twenty years enrollment almost tripled from 1.5 to 4.1 million. Net enrollment rates increased from 59 percent to 88 percent during the same period. Although enrollment of African secondary-school students also increased, their net enrollment rates remained a paltry 28 percent. Increased access to primary education among

Table 10.2   Education Achievements Across Countries

	1997 GNP per capita (a)	Average years of schooling (b)		Distribution of human capital[a] (c)		Secondary Enrollment (net) (d)	Illiteracy % (e)	Education Expense (% of GNP) (f)	Higher Education Expense (% of total) (g)
		1960	1990	1960	1990	mid-1990s	1995	1996	mid-1990s
South Africa	3,210	4.1	4.8	1.102	.887	58	16.7	7.8	14
Brazil	4,790	2.9	3.6	1.160	.967	19	16.8	5.1	26
United States	29,080	8.7	12.0	0.486	.318	90	—	5.4	25[b]
Middle-Income Countries									
Argentina	8,950	5.0	7.8	0.730	.567	—	3.6	3.5	20
Chile	4,820	5.0	6.0	0.771	.708	58	5.1	3.4	16
Mexico	3,700	2.4	5.9	1.209	.776	51	10.5	4.9	17
Malaysia	4,530	2.3	5.6	1.474	.806	—	15.5	5.2	20
Philippines	1,200	3.8	6.7	1.038	.672	59	5.9	3.2	18
Thailand	2,740	3.5	5.2	1.081	.896	—	5.8	4.1	16
Korea	10,550	3.2	9.3	1.288	.475	97	3.1	3.7	8[b]
Poland	3,590	6.7	10.0	0.612	.380	85	0.3	7.5	11[b]
Turkey	3,130	2.07	3.35	1.362	1.112	51	18.0	2.2	35

Sources: By column: (a) The World Bank 1999; (b) and (c) Barro and Lee 1993; (d)–(g) UNESCO 1999.

Notes: a. measured by the coefficient of variation (see endnote 3); b. includes capital expenditures.

Table 10.3   South Africa: Schooling Attainment and Distribution Across Population Groups by 5-Year Age Cohorts, 1995 (October Household Survey)

	Mean			Standard Deviation			Coefficient of Variation		
Age group	Nonwhite	White	Total	Nonwhite	White	Total	Nonwhite	White	Total
				South Africa					
20–24	9.30	11.78	9.49	3.07	1.38	3.05	0.33	0.12	0.32
25–29	8.71	12.08	9.05	3.61	1.43	3.60	0.41	0.12	0.40
30–34	7.97	11.95	8.50	3.88	1.61	3.90	0.49	0.14	0.46
35–39	7.41	12.00	8.14	3.89	1.70	4.00	0.52	0.14	0.49
40–44	6.55	11.84	7.46	4.02	1.80	4.23	0.61	0.15	0.57
45–49	5.98	11.58	7.00	4.03	1.74	4.30	0.67	0.15	0.61
50–54	5.25	11.49	6.40	4.01	1.66	4.41	0.76	0.14	0.69
55–59	4.53	11.15	5.77	4.00	1.77	4.51	0.88	0.16	0.78
60–64	4.11	10.91	5.45	3.91	2.01	4.51	0.95	0.18	0.83
65–69	3.4	10.64	4.98	3.71	2.11	4.55	1.09	0.20	0.91
Total	7.22	11.63	7.85	4.14	1.76	4.18	0.57	0.15	0.53

Source: Lam and Duryea 1999.

Africans is reflected in the shrinking though still significant percentage
of adult Africans with no schooling. That number was cut in half from
30 percent in 1970 to 14 percent in 1991, with equivalent gains in the
proportion with some primary schooling, which increased from 24 to 38
percent (Tables 10.5 and 10.6). The percentage of the population with

Table 10.4   Evolution of Years of Schooling Across Population Groups

Year	Total	Africans	Coloreds	Indians	Whites
1980	5.43	3.63	5.72	6.98	10.96
1991	6.86	5.53	6.94	8.78	11.67
% increase	26	52	21	26	6

Source: South Africa in Brief.
Note: Population 25 years and older.

Table 10.5   Evolution of African Enrollment from 1960 to 1980

	Africans				Total population	
	Primary	Net enrollment (%)	Secondary	Net enrollment (%)	Primary Net enrollment (%)	Secondary Net enrollment (%)
1960	1.5 million	59	.048 million	3	82	27
1970	2.6 million	76	.122 million	6	—	—
1980	4.1 million	88	1 million	28	—	—

Source: Moll 1996.

Table 10.6   Educational Expansion in South Africa: Distribution of the Labor Force in 13 South African Cities Across Levels of Education, 1970–1991

Year	Group	Educational attainment[a] (%)			
		None	Primary	Secondary	Higher
1970	All	17	20	58	5.4
	African only	30	24	46	.2
1980	All	13	29	49	8.8
	African only	22	43	33	1.3
1991	All	10	26	55	9
	African only	14	38	47	1

Source: Moll 1996.
Note: a. Included in this category if attained any year of schooling in that level.

no schooling remains high; the October 1995 Household Survey indicated that 17 percent of the African adult population had received no schooling.[15]

Despite their advancement in primary education, Africans have faced limited opportunity to continue on to secondary education. Historically, racial quotas limited Africans' access to secondary and higher education, and restrained the advancement of coloreds and Indians into higher education. Statistics show that in 1990, in a country in which Africans have about six times the population of whites, there were seven times as many white secondary-school students as Africans and twelve times as many white university students (Mboya and Mwamwenda 1994). As a result of the poor education outcomes among Africans and rationing, whites are concentrated in the higher education levels. Over one-third of white males have completed higher education, compared to about 2 percent of African men (Schultz and Mwabu 1998). Accordingly, African levels of education fall far short of that reached by other population groups in South Africa, especially whites, which average twelve years of schooling (Table 10.4).

And gains in enrollment were made at the expense of quality. Strong primary and improved secondary enrollment (116 and 84 percent, gross) belie a problem of poor attendance, high repetition, and low pass rates, especially among Africans and coloreds. Disproportionately low spending on African schools, which had a larger and expanding number of students, led to marked disparities in the quality of education provided to the four major racial groups under the apartheid policy of separate educational systems.

While the ratio of per-child government spending on schooling for whites versus Africans improved over the 1980s, in 1994 it was still about 5:1 (Moll 1996). With strained resources and a growing school-age population, schools attended by African students suffer from overcrowded classrooms: the teacher-pupil ratio among African schools is at least 1:41 (cited as much as 1:80) compared to 1:16 among whites. In addition, students in African schools lack adequate materials, equipment, and facilities. In 1993, only 11 and 39 percent of African children lived in communities where the primary school had a library and the secondary school had a science laboratory, respectively, compared to almost 100 percent for Asian and white children (Case and Deaton 1999). The quality of teaching and teacher training also varies significantly among population groups. One study indicated that only 4 percent of African teachers have university education compared to 97 percent of white teachers. Moreover, already-limited learning conditions in

African schools were exacerbated by the effect of strikes, riots, and other disruptions associated with the political acts in opposition to apartheid (Mboya and Mwamwenda 1994). With the postapartheid government beginning in 1994, Africans now have legal access to higher-quality schools once designated solely for whites, as well as schools once solely for coloreds, and African enrollment in those schools is increasing. But because white schools once covered only 10 percent of the total population, integration of those schools is obviously not a solution in itself.

Poor quality indicators coincide with poor education outcomes. Africans have the highest illiteracy rate, 23.4 percent, compared to 8.9 percent among coloreds, 4.5 percent among Indians, and 0.5 percent among whites.[16] Although they improve with age, Africans' literacy and numeracy test scores are almost half those of whites of equivalent ages (Table 10.7). Africans also have the lowest pass rate on matriculation exams, at 49 percent compared to 97 percent among white candidates (Table 10.8). High repetition among African primary schools is also a problem, reaching 20 to 46 percent in some areas. Although education achievement has improved among younger cohorts, disparities remain; in 1994, 23 percent of Africans aged fifteen to nineteen had not passed standard 4 grades (MWPD-SA 1998).

Differences in education attainment and quality contribute to dramatic wage differentials across population groups. African men and women receive wages that are 17 and 21 percent, respectively, that of their white counterparts. Colored men and women earn slightly higher wages at 26 and 32 percent, and Indian men and women earn wages rela-

Table 10.7   Literacy and Numeracy Test Scores Across Population Groups, 1993

Age	Literacy scores		Numeracy scores	
	Africans	Whites	Africans	Whites
13 years	2.64	5.32	1.77	4.89
14 years	2.87	4.57	2.02	3.86
15 years	2.92	5.76	2.25	4.15
16 years	3.35	6.00	2.44	5.21
17 years	3.14	5.81	2.22	5.38
18 years	3.46	5.88	2.59	5.65
No. in sample, 13–18 years	756	108	756	108

Sources: Based on test results of a subsample of individuals from the *South African Living Standards*, Statistics South Africa 1993; Case and Deaton 1999.

Table 10.8   Education Outcomes Across Racial Groups (in percentages)

	African	Colored	Indian	White
1979				
Candidates	19	10	7	64
Passes	73	89	95	—
Matriculation				
Exemptions	28	32	31	49
1986				
Candidates	52	9	6	33
Passes	52	68	87	93
Matriculation				
Exemptions	13	15	33	44
1994				
Candidates	79	5	3	13
Passes	49	87	93	97
Matriculation				
Exemptions	13	22	51	42

Source: Based on James 1998, citing South Africa Survey, 1996/1997.

tively closer to those of white men and women, earning 46 and 52 percent of their wages (Table 10.9). Wage differentials across races decrease but remain substantial even after controlling for years of education, type of advanced diploma, and other factors, reflecting some degree of race discrimination in the labor market. But Schultz and Mwabu (1998) find that almost half of the large differences in wages between racial groups are explained by differences in education attainment. This calculation does not control for the differences in education quality discussed above, which if incorporated would undoubtedly increase the effect of educational differences on wage differentials, while reducing the unexplained portion that measures, in part, discrimination. Schultz and Mwabu also found that urban and rural wage gaps interplayed with residential segregation under apartheid to further drive race-wage differentials as nonwhites had restricted labor mobility and were unable to move to higher-wage areas. Africans' greater rural residential location accounted for as much as 12 percent of their lower wages.

Skewed private returns to education conspire with an uneven distribution of schooling and drive race-wage differentials by race. Moll (1996) reports unusually low and declining returns to primary schooling among all ethnic groups, but especially among Africans in the period 1960 to 1990, and reports consistently strong returns to secondary education. Differences in quality of education at the two levels (with primary education marked by higher teacher-student ratios and lower per-

Table 10.9   Differences in Education Attainment and Private Returns Across Groups, 1993

Group	(Years) Education Attainment	Private returns to level of education (%)		
		Primary	Secondary	Higher
Africans				
Male	7	8.4	15.8	29.4
Female	7	6.2	24.9	39.6
Colored				
Male	8.6	1.4	18.7	18.6
Female	8.2	2.3	19.9	30.7
Indians				
Male	10.6	—	21.4	21.4
Female	9.3	—	12.6	30.4
Whites				
Male	11.8	—	8.4	15.1
Female	10.4	—	5.2	13.9

Source: Schultz and Mwabu 1998.
Note: Percent of the population 16 to 64 years. The zero or negative returns to primary education for whites and Indians resulting from this regression are explained by the very few observations in the sample under this category, given practically universal completion of primary school among these two groups.

student expenditures) and a relative scarcity of secondary-school graduates are supply-side factors contributing to the skewed returns. Schultz and Mwabu (1998) find that returns to schooling increase for most groups at higher levels of schooling but with exceptionally large wage gains for higher education among nonwhite men and women, substantially larger returns than received by comparably educated whites (Table 10.9). These findings imply that workers with higher levels of education are relatively scarce, especially among the nonwhite population, and receive premiums compared to the poorly educated majority. Lam (1999) reports similar findings and contrasts returns to education in Brazil (see the section on Brazil below).

Low returns to primary education probably also reflect a sagging labor market for the relatively unskilled. Unemployment rates, broadly defined, are as high as 30 percent, indicating a lack of dynamism in the formal economy. The informal economy is a growing source of low-quality employment, providing work to about 1.7 million people (MWPD-SA 1998). Consistent with the poor distribution of human capital across races, Africans suffer a disproportionately high unemployment rate, at 42 percent (using an expanded definition), almost eight times that of the white labor force (5 percent) (Table 10.10). They also make up 86 percent of the informal sector (UNDP-SA 1998). Within the formal sector, Africans hold the least-skilled, least-remunerated jobs, with scant opportunities for training and upward mobility (Table 10.11). A large proportion of the nonwhite population (25 percent) also reports zero earnings, an important factor to South Africa's high earnings inequality (Lam 1999).

In short, although education attainment and distribution have improved in South Africa, poor education is still a major barrier to non-whites' economic advancement. The quality of primary education is particularly poor in schools formerly designated for Africans. Improving all primary schools and increasing access to secondary and higher education for Africans and coloreds are major challenges in South Africa that can yield major benefits in raising economic growth while reducing the country's historic burden of high inequality of wages and income by race.

We now turn our attention to human capital accumulation in Brazil.

Table 10.10   South African Unemployment Rates Across Population Groups (in percentages), 1995

	Africans	Coloreds	Indians	Whites
Total	42.5	20.9	12.2	4.6
Male	34.1	18.3	11.1	4.2
Female	52.4	24.1	14	5.1

Source: South Africa Statistics 1995, October Household Survey.

Table 10.11   Occupational Structure by Race Distribution (in percentages), 1995

Occupation	Africans	Coloreds	Indians	Whites
Senior management	2.9	2.0	10.7	14.6
Professional	2.0	1.7	6.7	8.4
Technical	9.6	6.6	11.9	18.5
Clerical	7.8	10.8	20.9	22.5
Services	11.2	11.6	13.3	10.6
Crafts	10.2	14.3	16.0	15.0
Operators	14.0	12.3	12.7	3.8
Low-skilled	40.1	38.8	6	1.6

Source: James 1998, citing October Household Survey, 1995.

Brazil

Brazil's low education attainment is directly related to its weak distribution, with healthy increases in the years of schooling for a few while the poor majority experience limited advancement in education.[17] With practically universal primary enrollment since 1965, the main deficit continues to be low secondary enrollment, especially among the poor, and especially among the poor Afro-Brazilian and *pardo* population. Over the last thirty years, enrollment rates have increased, but at a slow pace and at the expense of quality. While recent attention to education has probably improved indicators,[18] in 1990 the adult population on average had attained less than four years of schooling, well below that achieved by countries of similar per capita GNP (Table 10.2).

As in South Africa, there have been important gains in education in Brazil. Lam (1999) traces advances in education of both the white and nonwhite population by examining increased schooling across five-year birth cohorts. Citing 1995 Household Survey data, he reports that the average years of schooling of the youngest nonwhite age cohort (born in 1971–1975) was 5.65 years, almost four times the average attainment of the oldest nonwhite cohort, 1.48 years. Similar increases in education are seen among the white population. While education attainment is low for both the white and nonwhite population in Brazil, the gap between the two is lower than in South Africa. Increases in schooling for both the white and nonwhite population correspond with improved distribution of education over time, as seen in a continuous decline in the coefficient of variation of years of schooling (Table 10.12). The increase, peak, and then decline in the standard deviation probably reflect an early worsening of the distribution with the initial expansion of education in Brazil, measured by an increasing mean.[19]

Despite progress, Brazil has significantly lower education attainment relative to other middle-income countries. Comparison of 1995 education data for South Africa and Brazil (Tables 10.3 and 10.12) highlights Brazil's worse level and distribution of schooling (Lam 1999). The youngest Brazilian cohort has received on average 6.65 years of schooling compared to 9.49 years by the South African counterpart. The better-educated Brazilian white population has received almost two fewer years of schooling than the least-educated nonwhite South African population. Brazil also has a more uneven distribution of education, with a coefficient of variation of years of schooling of .56 compared to .32 in South Africa. See "Comparison of Schooling" below

Table 10.12   Brazil: Schooling Attainment and Distribution Across Population Groups by 5-Year Age Cohorts, 1995 (PNAD Household Survey)

	Mean			Standard Deviation			Coefficient of Variation		
Age group	Nonwhite	White	Total	Nonwhite	White	Total	Nonwhite	White	Total
20–24	5.65	7.51	6.65	3.56	3.62	3.71	0.63	0.48	0.56
25–29	5.48	7.55	6.61	3.92	4.00	4.10	0.72	0.53	0.62
30–34	5.23	7.46	6.50	4.02	4.25	4.30	0.77	0.57	0.66
35–39	4.84	7.23	6.21	4.06	4.40	4.42	0.84	0.61	0.71
40–44	4.31	6.73	5.71	4.02	4.58	4.52	0.93	0.68	0.79
45–49	3.45	6.03	4.97	3.84	4.65	4.52	1.11	0.77	0.91
50–54	2.91	5.22	4.28	3.57	4.48	4.29	1.23	0.86	1.00
55–59	2.40	4.46	3.61	3.22	4.17	3.94	1.34	0.94	1.09
60–64	2.00	4.04	3.24	2.97	3.99	3.75	1.48	0.99	1.16
65–69	1.48	3.73	2.87	2.53	3.92	3.62	1.71	1.05	1.26
Total	4.43	6.54	5.64	3.96	4.39	4.34	0.89	0.67	0.77

Source: Lam 1999.

for a more detailed comparison of education and the effect on earnings inequality in Brazil and South Africa.

Brazil's poor showing in education reflects the concentration of education achievement among the rich. Almost all children begin school, but the poor drop out early and in large numbers (Figure 10.1). In the early 1990s, although 92 percent of the poor in Brazil completed grade one, only 16 percent continued to complete primary school. As a result, though Brazil's per capita income is fourteen times higher than Kenya's, its poor children were attaining a median of just four years of education, almost half that attained by poor children in Kenya. (The only East African country with lower attainment of the poor is Uganda [Filmer and Pritchett 1999].) Still, compared to other Latin American countries, Brazil has the highest gap in education attainment between income groups.[20] Among twenty-one-year-olds, average years of schooling is ten for the richest 10 percent of households and four for the poorest 30 percent, creating a six-year education "wealth gap." The gap for children in rich versus poor households is smaller among fifteen-year-olds—prior to the ages when the rich are more likely to complete secondary school and go on to university. In a sign of progress, the gap for fifteen-year-olds declined between the 1980s and 1990s (Berhman, Birdsall, and Székely 1998).

Based on student flow analysis, Klein (1997) explores differences in enrollment rates across income brackets, ethnic groups, and geo-

Figure 10.1   Brazilian Education Attainment Across Income Groups

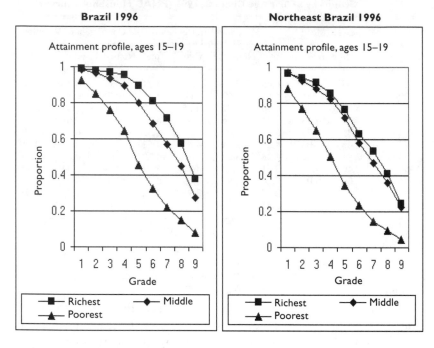

Source: Filmer and Pritchett 1999.

graphic regions. While enrollment in first grade is near universal, access for the poorest quartile drops dramatically after the first years of primary, with only 44 percent continuing to grade five and only 6 percent enrolling in grade eleven. In contrast, the majority of students in the upper-income quartile continue through the entire education cycle, with over 60 percent attending the eleventh grade (Table 10.13).

Accompanying Brazil's poor income-based distribution of human capital is evidence of disparities in education attainment across ethnic groups. Klein (1997) reports lower enrollment rates among the Afro-Brazilian/*pardo* population compared to the white population within each income quartile, yielding overall lower levels of schooling.[21] In 1996, whites registered two full years of education higher than that attained by the Afro-Brazilian and *pardo* population (Table 10.14). Within the nonwhite Brazilian population, education attainment varies significantly: *pardo*, 4.7 years; Afro-Brazilian, 4.2 years; Asian, 9.5 years; and indigenous, 3.2 years (Lam 1999).

Table 10.13   Enrollment Rates Across Income Quartiles by Grade, 1995

			Grades (enrollment by proportion of eligible population)								
Quartile 1	1	2	3	4	5	6	7	8	9	10	11
Total	.939	.822	.720	.603	.444	.327	.252	.188	.116	.081	.060
White	.967	.890	.803	.688	.526	.407	.319	.250	.166	.110	.076
Afro-Braz./											
Pardo	.927	.788	.685	.563	.406	.298	.231	.168	.100	.072	.052
Quartile 2	1	2	3	4	5	6	7	8	9	10	11
Total	.965	.901	.839	.752	.611	.477	.388	.312	.210	.176	.141
White	.980	.938	.900	.837	.714	.561	.445	.353	.243	.200	.167
Afro-Braz./											
Pardo	.954	.875	.799	.709	.559	.435	.350	.280	.186	.153	.124
Quartile 3	1	2	3	4	5	6	7	8	9	10	11
Total	.983	.952	.914	.857	.761	.643	.571	.505	.368	.330	.284
White	.988	.973	.950	.909	.822	.706	.608	.545	.411	.360	.311
Afro-Braz./											
Pardo	.978	.927	.880	.809	.699	.588	.519	.461	.351	.311	.265
Quartile 4	1	2	3	4	5	6	7	8	9	10	11
Total	.993	.981	.962	.933	.881	.826	.795	.760	.672	.647	.607
White	.994	.987	.975	.953	.920	.863	.825	.797	.700	.677	.639
Afro-Braz./											
Pardo	.990	.968	.929	.884	.801	.747	.694	.645	.568	.534	.503

Source: Klein 1997.

Table 10.14   Years of Schooling by Sex and Population Groups (over 10 years of age)

	Total (average)	Male	Female	White	Afro-Brazilian and *Pardo*[a]
Brazil	5.3	5.2	5.4	6.2	4.2
Urban North[b]	5.2	4.9	5.4	6.3	4.7
Northeast	3.9	3.6	4.2	4.8	3.5
Southeast	6.0	6.0	6.0	6.6	4.9
South	5.8	5.8	5.8	6.0	4.3
Central West	5.5	5.2	5.5	6.3	4.7

Source: IBGE/Pesquisa Nacional por Amostra de Domicilios 1996.
Notes: a. *Pardo* indicates mixed race or color (mulatto, mestizo). b. Excludes data for the rural area of the states of Rondônia, Acre, Amazones, Roraima, Pará, and Amapá.

Although whites continue to receive more schooling than other population groups, the gap has closed considerably. In 1960, whites were six times as likely as Afro-Brazilians to have completed nine years of schooling or more. Over subsequent decades, education levels rose substantially, yielding absolute gains in education for all. Afro-

Brazilian workers continued to receive less education, especially at the higher levels of schooling, but the portion with no education declined significantly, falling from 43 percent of women and 26 percent of men in 1960 to 17 percent each in 1980 (Table 10.15) (Lovell 1994). Similarly, literacy among the nonwhite population in Brazil increased substantially (Table 10.16).

Disparities in education across regions reflect the geographic concentration of race and poverty in Brazil.[22] Most of the Afro-Brazilian and *pardo* population live in the North and Northeast, which have much

Table 10.15 Evolution of Education Attainment Across Population Groups in Brazil

	1960		1980	
Years of Schooling	Whites	Afro-Brazilian	Whites	Afro-Brazilian
		(percentages)		
Women				
0	14	43	5	17
1 to 4	51	50	30	42
5 to 8	17	4	18	19
9+	18	3	47	22
Men				
0	10	26	7	17
1 to 4	66	67	41	51
5 to 8	13	5	21	20
9+	11	2	31	12

Source: Lovell 1994.
Note: Workers aged 18 to 64 years.

Table 10.16 Levels of Education [a] and Literacy [b] Across Population Groups in Brazil

		Whites	*Pardos*[c]	Afro-Brazilians
Literacy	1950	59.3	31.1	26.7
	1987	87.7	71.0	70.5
Secondary Schooling	1950	4.9	0.5	0.2
	1987	13.9	8.0	5.3
University Schooling	1950	1.2	0	0
	1987	9.2	2.0	1.0

Source: Andrews 1993.
Notes: a. Of the population 25 years and older; completed levels of schooling. b. Of the population 5 years and older. c. *Pardo* indicates mixed race or color (mulatto, mestizo).

lower education attainment, income levels, and overall standards of living. The white population is concentrated in the far more wealthy urban and industrial Southeast. Illiteracy in the Northeast, at 29 percent, is over three times higher than in the Southeast and is twice the national average. A comparison of the years of schooling of the labor force is equally revealing: in 1996, almost half of the labor force in the Southeast had eight or more years of schooling, while in the Northeast, 53 percent of the labor force had no more than three years of schooling (Table 10.17). A regional comparison of enrollment rates in Brazil show similar patterns (Table 10.18).

Unlike apartheid in South Africa, in which an unequal distribution of human capital was explicitly created along racial lines as a matter of policy, human capital inequalities in Brazil have been produced by the interplay of less visible forces.

Table 10.17   Attainment Gaps by Region in Brazil (by percentage of population)

| Group | Illiteracy Rate | Years of Schooling of the Labor Force (population aged 10 years and over) | | | |
		3 or less	4 to 7	8 to 10	11 or more
Brazil	14.7%	31.3%	32%	14.5%	22.0%
Urban North[a]	11.6	30.0	29.3	17	23.2
Northeast	28.7	52.7	23.1	8.9	15.2
Southeast	8.7	21.3	34.3	17.5	26.8
South	8.9	22.3	40.9	15.4	21.0
Central West	11.6	29.1	33.6	14.8	22.1

Source: IBGE/Pesquisa Nacional por Amostra de Domicilios 1996.
Note: a. Excludes data for the rural area of the states of Rondônia, Acre, Amazones, Roraima, Pará, and Amapá.

Table 10.18   Enrollment Rates Across Regions by Grade, 1995

| Region | Grades (enrollment by proportion of eligible population) | | | | | | | | | | |
	1	2	3	4	5	6	7	8	9	10	11
Brazil	.969	.910	.859	.790	.681	.582	.509	.443	.347	.303	.270
North	.977	.939	.880	.813	.721	.634	.553	.487	.383	.331	.303
Northeast	.931	.818	.729	.645	.533	.447	.380	.327	.257	.239	.219
Southeast	.989	.966	.933	.886	.794	.689	.603	.522	.410	.359	.317
South	.991	.967	.939	.883	.776	.652	.560	.484	.373	.331	.280
Central west	.986	.951	.903	.838	.723	.601	.508	.442	.345	.322	.289

Source: Klein 1997.

To begin, Brazil's high income inequality has both resulted from and perpetuated an unequal distribution of human capital. High income inequality has meant that more households are liquidity-constrained, unable to borrow and without the resources necessary to keep their children in school.[23] In 1989, Brazil and Malaysia had similar levels of per capita income. But due to Brazil's highly unequal income distribution, the poorest quintile in Brazil had only about one-half the absolute income level of the poorest quintile in Malaysia (Table 10.19). Given an income elasticity of demand for secondary education of 0.50 (a conservative figure), if the distribution of income had been as equal in Brazil as in Malaysia, secondary enrollments among poor Brazilian children would have been more than 40 percent higher (Birdsall, Bruns, and Sabot 1996). There is some evidence that, among the poor, the income elasticity of demand for basic schooling exceeds 1.0, in which case secondary-school enrollments among poor Brazilian children would have been more than 80 percent higher. One quantitative study of the effect of income inequality on schooling suggests that, of the 27 percentage point secondary-school enrollment rate gap between Brazil and Korea in the 1970s, more than 20 percentage points can be attributed to Brazil's greater income inequality and resultant lower enrollment of poor children (Williamson 1993).[24]

Income inequality and the depth of poverty in Brazil have made it difficult to expand secondary education. Table 10.13 traces the steep drop-off in enrollment by the poor compared to the richer quartiles. Despite almost universal access to primary education, the poor repeat more and drop out more than the rich. (In the first grade, repetition among the poorest quartile [55.7 percent] is over twice that of the wealthiest [21.4 percent] [Klein 1997].) As a result, a student from the bottom income quartile has small probability of completing primary

Table 10.19   Absolute Income Share of Lowest Quintile

	GNP per capita (US$, PPP adjusted)	Income share of bottom 20% of households (%)	Per capita income of bottom 20% of households (US $)
Malaysia, 1989	4,674	4.6	1,075
Brazil, 1989	4,271	2.4	513

Source: Birdsall, Bruns, and Sabot 1996 cite Summers and Heston 1995 for GNP, Deininger and Squire 1996 for income share data.

education (15 percent) and an even smaller likelihood of finishing secondary (4 percent). Given these odds, it is not surprising that, of the population fifteen to thirty-one years of age, the poorest 30 percent account for less than one-fourth of those with five to eight years of education and less than 10 percent of those with more than eight years of schooling (Herran and Rodriguez 1999, citing analysis of the 1996 PNAD). The failure of the poor to complete primary schooling limits opportunities to expand access to secondary education. This is also the case in rural areas where there is a significant decline in rural enrollment between primary and lower-secondary levels.[25] Despite high primary enrollment, secondary enrollment continues to be low in Brazil, with especially low enrollment in the Northeast (Table 10.20).

In addition to the lack of resources thwarting their educational progress, the poor face weak incentives to continue their schooling, given the low quality of public education. The problem in Brazil, like other Latin American countries, is not primarily one of low public expenditures on education (though economic turnarounds and continued growth in the school-age population have strained the available per capita resources, especially in the 1980s). Brazil's public expenditures on education are about 5.1 percent of GNP, above the average of 3.9 percent for all developing regions (UNESCO 1999). Rather, the problem has been ineffective public school systems—on which the poor

Table 10.20   Regional Comparison of Enrollment and Expected Completion Rates

Region	Average number of grades completed	Primary enrollment (net)	Students expected to complete 8th grade	Upper secondary enrollment (net)	Students expected to complete 11th grade
Brazil	6.0	95%	50%	31%	26%
Northeast	4.4	90%	35%	14%	20%
Southeast	6.6	97%	65%	43%	35%

	Bahia Flow Simulation (1997)		São Paulo Flow Simulation (1997)	
	% completing cycle	Years required	% completing cycle	Years required
Grades 1–4	78%	6.2	94%	4.3
Grades 5–8	54%	11.5	71%	8.7
Grades 9–11	41%	15.2	51%	12.0

Source: Klein model with 1995–1996 system efficiency rates, cited in Herran and Rodriguez 1999.

The United States

The United States has one of the highest education attainments in the world, with virtually universal primary and secondary enrollment and strong enrollment in higher education. Since 1960, postsecondary enrollment increased from 32 to 81 percent. Similarly, college completion rates increased sharply during the 1960s and early 1970s, rose more slowly between the mid-1970s and early 1990s, and picked up again in the mid-1990s. The average years of schooling of the adult population rose from 8.7 years in 1960 to 12 years in 1990 (Table 10.2). With the increasing demand for college graduates and the increase in schooling attainment in the United States, high school completion, once a ticket for income mobility, has lost much of its value. Expanding access to higher education to African Americans, who have comparatively low enrollment rates, especially among males, is a policy challenge.

Increasing access to education has been one of the key strategies to redress racial inequities in the United States. The 1954 landmark decision *Brown v. Board of Education of Topeka, Kansas*, which declared that separate educational facilities were inherently unequal, catalyzed a series of decisions dismantling racial segregation. This decision completed the reversal of the 1896 decision *Plessy v. Ferguson* in which the Supreme Court legitimized the Jim Crow laws that codified racial segregation in the South. Further progress was made with the impetus of the 1964 Civil Rights Law and subsequent federal employment legislation. Education programs have also been fertile ground for affirmative-action initiatives.

As a result, over the last four decades, and especially since the 1970s, African Americans have made significant progress in gaining access to education and raising educational achievement. More are attending primary and secondary school, graduating from high school, and attending college and graduate and professional schools. For example, in 1940, only 7 percent of African Americans twenty-five years and older had completed high school. By 1980, that proportion had increased to 51 percent, and by 1997 it further increased to 63 percent. In 1995, African Americans' high school completion rate nearly equaled that of white Americans (Table 10.25). Since the early 1970s, African Americans' dropout rates have fallen and test scores have risen. Dropout rates fell by one-third from 21 percent in 1972 to 14 percent in 1993 (U.S. Department of Education 1995). Over the last two decades, African-American test scores improved faster than white Americans in reading, math, and science, narrowing the achievement gap (Garibaldi

Table 10.25   U.S. Education Advancement Across Population Groups

Year	African Americans	White Americans	Overall
	High School Completion Rates (percentages of 18- to 24-year-olds)		
1975	64.8	83.0	80.8
1995	76.9	81.9	80.8
	High School Completion Rates (percentages of 25- to 29-year-olds)		
1975	71.0	84.4	—
1995	86.5	87.4	—

Source: Garibaldi 1997.

1997). Furthermore, college-bound African Americans made substantial gains in college entry achievement tests relative to white Americans. From 1976 to 1993, the achievement gap fell by almost one-fourth. Plus, the percentage of African Americans enrolled in college immediately after high school increased in the late 1980s after having fallen in the early 1980s (U.S. Department of Education 1995).

Despite these advances, disparities across population groups remain. African Americans' repetition and dropout rates (18.1 percent and 13.7 percent, respectively) are almost twice that of white Americans (10.5 percent and 7.7 percent) (U.S. Department of Education 1995). White Americans continue to outperform African Americans in achievement tests. White Americans scored higher than their African-American peers in mathematics, reading, and writing, averaging 25, 30, and 22 points higher in each age group. In science, between 1969 and 1996, African-American students on average scored 47 points lower than white Americans (Garibaldi 1997). African Americans also score the lowest on college entrance achievement tests compared to other population groups (Tables 10.26 and 10.27).

These lower achievement scores reflect, in part, disparities in the quality of education available to African Americans. In the United States, states and local school districts provide the majority of funding for public primary and secondary education (over 90 percent of public funding). Differences in the quality of education reflect economic differences across communities. The correlation between low education achievement and poor urban schools does not bode well for minority students, who are the main group in high-poverty urban schools. According to a report by the Department of Education, 69 percent of

Table 10.26   Education Achievement by African Americans and White Americans Across Age Groups, Average Proficiency Scores

	White Americans			African Americans		
	Age 9	Age 13	Age 17	Age 9	Age 13	Age 17
Reading						
1971	214	261	291	170	222	239
1980	221	264	293	189	233	243
1992	218	266	297	184	238	261
Mathematics						
1973	225	274	310	190	228	270
1982	224	274	304	195	240	272
1992	235	279	312	208	250	286
Science						
1973	231	259	304	177	205	250
1982	229	257	293	187	217	235
1992	239	267	304	200	224	256

Source: U.S. Department of Education, NCES 1995.

Table 10.27   College Achievement Test Scores, by Racial/Ethnic Group

Asian-American Students	White American Students	National Average	Hispanic-American Students	African-American Students
		1997 Average SAT Scores		
1056	1052	1016	934	857
		1997 Average ACT Scores		
21.7	21.7	21	19	17.1

Source: Garibaldi 1997.

students who attend high-poverty urban public schools are minorities (U.S. Department of Education 1996). The out-migration of white Americans to suburban areas has contributed to an economic segregation of schools. In 1972, 63.6 percent of African-American students attended schools with less than half white enrollment. In 1997, that percentage increased to 67.1 percent (Garibaldi 1997).

In addition, the college enrollment gap is increasing between African and white Americans. Over a twenty-year period, the college-going rate of African-American high school graduates increased by less than 2 percent, while the overall average increased by 6 percent (Table

10.28). Moreover, after two decades, twenty-five- to twenty-nine-year-old African Americans continue to be half as likely as their white counterparts to have completed four years of college (U.S Department of Education 1995). In 1997, one-third of white Americans had completed a four-year college degree, compared with only 14 percent of African Americans (Council of Economic Advisers [CEA] 1998). A contributing factor to African Americans' lower completion rates may be that they are more likely to attend a community college. In 1994, whites were twice as likely to enroll in a four-year college as a two-year college, while African Americans were only one and half times as likely. Students who begin their higher education at a two year college are less likely to receive their bachelor's degree compared to their counterparts who begin at a four-year college (U.S. Department of Education 1997).

College enrollment and attainment is particularly low among African-American males. Increases in African-American college enrollment figures mainly reflect increases in female enrollment. The gap in the number of bachelor's degrees received by African-American women compared to men almost tripled between 1976 and 1994 (Table 10.29).

Table 10.28 College-Going Rates of High School Graduates (by percentages)

Year	African Americans	Overall
1975	32.8	36.2
1995	34.4	42.0

Source: Garibaldi 1997.

Table 10.29 College Attendance and Completion Among African Americans by Gender

Year	Males	%	Females	%	Total	Female/Male
College Enrollments of African Americans						
1995	556,000	38	918,000	62	1,474,000	1.65:1
Baccalaureate Degrees Awarded to African Americans by Gender						
1976	25,026	43	33,489	57	58,515	1.34:1
1994	30,648	37	52,928	63	83,576	1.73.1
Increase	22%		58%			

Source: Garibaldi 1997.

The growing college enrollment gap between African and white Americans is of concern given the higher payoff awarded to college education. In the United States, as the level of schooling has increased and as production has become more skill-intensive, employers have required higher degrees of education as a sign of competence. As a result, the premium to college education has doubled with the simultaneous doubling of the high school dropout penalty (Table 10.30). These premiums to higher education hold across population groups. Earnings among twenty-five- to thirty-four-year-old African Americans (particularly women) show a good payoff for investment in education. In 1992, African-American males who have completed high school earned 35 percent more than their counterparts with nine to eleven years of schooling, while those with a bachelor's degree earned 83 percent more. The relative payoff to African-American females completing high school is similar to males, but the payoff to graduating from college is significantly higher: African-American females completing college earn 113 percent more than their counterparts with nine to eleven years of schooling (U.S. Department of Education 1995).

A policy challenge in the United States is to translate African Americans' increased high school completion to increased college attendance. The anomaly in the United States is that an increasing number of African-American males are graduating from high school but not

Table 10.30 Percentage Differences in Average Weekly Wages of Men with Indicated Education and Wages of High School Graduates

	Less than 10 years out of school		1–40 years out of school	
Years	White Americans	African Americans	White Americans	African Americans
High School Dropout				
1967–1971	−17.9	−20.3	−17.4	−20.1
1993–1997	−30.3	−24.8	−32.8	−28.2
1–3 Years of College				
1967–1971	19.4	22.0	17.8	13.9
1993–1997	35.4	52.7	23.6	30.4
College Graduates				
1967–1971	41.0	49.2	44.2	39.2
1993–1997	95.7	96.4	84.0	93.4

Source: Welch 1999.

continuing on to college, even though college offers higher returns. The concern is that they are investing in a level of schooling with lower and declining returns (Figure 10.2 and Table 10.31). Table 10.31 illustrates the evolution of private returns to education of African-American males, showing the dramatic increase in premiums to college graduates and in penalties to high school dropouts.[30]

Differences in education attainment and quality contribute to wage inequality and disparate labor market outcomes in the United States. Median wages of African Americans are substantially lower than those

Figure 10.2   Comparison of African-American Males' Private Returns to Education

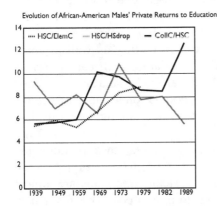 

Source: Based on data from Carnoy 1995.

Table 10.31   Evolution of Private Returns to Education Among Males (by percentages)

Category	1939	1949	1959	1969	1973	1979	1982	1987
Whites								
HSC/ElemC	9.1	7.5	6.4	6.4	5.7	6.2		
HSC/Hsdrop	9.6	6.7	4.6	6.2	7.4	7.9	9.1	7.8
CollC/HSC	10.9	9.1	10.4	10.8	8.6	9.5	9.8	11
African Americans								
HSC/ElemC	5.5	6	5.4	6.7	8.4	8.9		
HSC/Hsdrop	9.4	7	8.2	6.5	10.8	7.8	8	5.6
CollC/HSC	5.7	5.8	6.1	10.2	9.8	8.6	8.5	12.7

Source: Carnoy 1995.

of white Americans (around 25 percent lower). In the period between the early 1960s and the mid-1970s, African-American men's wages rose, relative to white American men, but then declined for at least ten years. The evidence over the last decade is mixed, with some studies showing continued deterioration or little change in relative pay for African-American men and others showing improvement. African-American women reached near parity in the mid-1970s with white American women's wages, but their relative pay has fallen since. In addition to lower wages, African Americans face higher unemployment rates compared to white Americans. Over the last twenty years, unemployment (measured as "without a job but actively seeking work") among African Americans has been over 10 percent with a recent dip to below 9 percent, over twice the national average. Part of these differentials in wages and unemployment are explained by disparities in education, though differentials persist within levels of schooling as well, probably reflecting differences in education quality as well as some degree of discrimination.[31] Participation rates among African-American males are lower than that of white American males and have declined more rapidly. In the United States, across population groups, the decline in male labor-force participation is concentrated among men with less education (CEA 1998).

With comparatively higher unemployment rates, lower participation rates, and lower median wages, it is not surprising that African Americans have a higher poverty rate. African Americans are almost three times as likely as white Americans to live in poverty (26 versus 8 percent).[32] The median income of white American families is nearly twice that of African-American families. In a sign of encouragement, since the early 1990s African-American family income has risen and poverty rates have fallen, reaching an all-time low in 1996 (CEA 1998).[33]

Despite persistent gaps in education and disparate labor market outcomes, there is evidence that expanded access to education among African Americans has provided a vehicle for economic mobility. Welch (1999) argues that, although widening returns to education have contributed to wage inequality, the differentials have instilled healthy incentives for investing in education and facilitated economic mobility of previously disadvantaged groups. This observation holds true for African Americans. Although their median wages continue to be lower than white Americans, Welch observes that African Americans' position in wage distribution improved considerably over the last thirty years. In the period 1967–1997, the proportion of African-American men earning in the lowest quartile of the wage distribution of whites fell from 58.4 percent to 42.6 percent. It is as though one in four of the lower-paid workers moved to the higher wage ranges.[34] A similar, but more extreme, story can be told of African-American women, whose representation in the lowest quartile of the wage distribution fell from 85.1 percent to 41.2 percent. It is as if over half of the lower-wage women moved into higher wage categories. While white American men continued to earn higher wages in the period 1967–1997, the representation of African-American men in the upper quartile of the wage distribution increased by 70 percent. That of African-American women increased by tenfold (1,000 percent) (Welch 1999).

Evidence of education's contribution to economic mobility underscores the need to address systemic imbalances across population groups in access to quality education, in means of financing higher education, in labor market returns, and in demand for education. Differences in quality of education and underrepresentation in courses that improve chances to pursue higher education may hinder African Americans in their college application. Given their higher probability to live in poverty, financial obstacles also present a challenge. In the United States the children of the rich have always been more likely to go on to college. In 1995, 83 percent of high school graduates from the wealthiest families (the top 20 percent of all households) enrolled in college, compared with 34 percent from the poorest (the bottom 20 percent) (Birdsall 1998a). Attention must also be given to the demand for college education, especially among African-American males. The percentage of young African-American males (20 percent) who are neither in school nor working is twice that of young white American men (9 percent). A pattern of earnings differentials within levels of schooling, reflecting a history of discrimination, may have discouraged demand. For example, in 1992, twenty-five- to thirty-four-year-old white American college graduates earned 23 percent more in 1992 than African-American college graduates of the same age (U.S. Department of Education 1995). Since 1979, the relative pay of college-educated African-American males fell by more than 10 percentage points (CEA 1998).[35] In some cases, an "opposition culture" downplaying scholastic success as disaffiliating with the African-American community may explain some part of the performance gap in education.[36]

There is evidence that wage inequality in the United States reflects education-based wage differentials that have instilled healthy incentives for investment in education and facilitated economic mobility across population groups. However, if high wages appear to be based on endowment, such as wealth or race, or systemic imbalances in access to education (through different qualities of schooling, unequal access to the means of financing higher education, or distorted returns to schooling from discrimination) hinder economic mobility, wage inequality may instill perverse incentives. Workers may get discouraged and opt out of the market instead of pursuing strategies for upward mobility, such as investing in education. To some degree, this phenomenon may be in play in some of the industrialized countries, where inactivity explains a growing portion of nonemployment, especially among the less skilled workers (Green 1996). Murphy and Topel (1997) observe that in the United States the largest increases in nonemployment among less skilled workers is explained by inactivity, not unemployment.

Reflections

Education is the people's asset. Among assets that generate income across the world, it is the most equally distributed—and based on the postwar trend in most countries, it has become even more broadly distributed. Education is an investment that contributes to growth and, like other assets (land and physical capital), its distribution affects the distribution of income. In the economic lives of people, opportunities matter. And in economies where a substantial portion of the population has little or no human capital (a critical productive asset), only a part of the population can exploit the growth process, thereby inhibiting average growth and increasing income inequality.

These findings square with our larger intuition of structural shifts in the global marketplace. As the industrial age yields to the information age, the key asset for generating income is no longer capital in the traditional sense, but human capital. Reflecting this transition, income inequality has become more closely related to wage and salary inequality than to inequality of land or capital assets.[37] And wage inequality in most market-driven economies is closely tied to the increasing gap between the earnings of the educated and less educated. As one of us has suggested elsewhere, the issue of distributive justice that Marx outlined is likely to be drawn in the future on the fault line not between capitalists and workers, but between the more and less educated of the world (Birdsall 1998a).

Given the increasing importance of human capital in the present and future marketplace, it is encouraging that the levels and distribution of education have improved for all population groups in each of the countries studied. Schooling levels have especially improved for non-white populations, but these advances were made from a lower base; hence disparities in education performance persist across population groups in South Africa, Brazil, and the United States. The uneven distribution of education in each country is correlated with higher poverty for the nonwhite population. Reducing the disparities in education across population groups in each of the countries studied in this chapter is key to reducing income differences.

In South Africa, an explicit policy under apartheid to ration education resources and opportunities by race produced a poor distribution of human capital; Africans and coloreds have substantially lower education attainment and apparently much poorer quality of education, indicated by the virtually zero return to primary education, for blacks (in contrast to the very high returns to those few blacks who complete secondary education or better). As South Africa progresses in opening its market and reintegrating with the world economy, improving the distribution of assets, especially education, is key to reducing current high income differences both between and within races.[38] This requires not only the dismantling of institutional barriers but also consideration of remedial policies to ensure equal opportunity in education (such as access to credit and means of financing education) to avoid economic segregation. The challenge in South Africa lies in improving the low quality of primary education, especially for Africans, and expanding access to secondary and higher education.

Brazil has an even lower education attainment and more uneven distribution of education than South Africa. In addition to unequal access to quality education across income groups, there is evidence of disparities across ethnic groups as well. In Brazil, poverty and economic policies have conspired to produce low and unequal human-capital accumulation, with high dropout rates among the poor, especially the nonwhite poor, and a concentration of higher education among the wealthy. Like South Africa, Brazil faces the dual challenge of expanding access to secondary education, while improving the quality of primary schooling. Policies need to address the differential access to quality education across regions, which reflects the geographic concentration of poverty and race in Brazil. Steps to improve education for Brazil's poor, including improving the quality of primary schooling, facilitating financing for education, and avoiding implicit subsidies to capital that discourage job creation, should improve the distribution of human capital across population groups. Given the strong effect of parents' education on the household demand for schooling in Brazil, such interventions are necessary to break the intergenerational cycle of low education and low income. Otherwise, a growing demand for skilled labor and increasing wage dispersion could exacerbate Brazil's already high income inequality as it further integrates in the world economy.

Unlike South Africa and Brazil, the United States has one of the highest levels of schooling and most equal distributions of education in the world. Nonetheless, differences in education attainment and quality persist across population groups. A main policy challenge in the United States is to convert significant advances in African Americans' high school completion rates to greater college attendance, especially among African-American males, given the increasing premium awarded to higher education. There is evidence that increasing wage inequality in the United States, resulting from widening returns to education, may facilitate economic mobility by providing healthy incentives for investment in education. However, for education to be the great leveler, systemic imbalances in access to quality education, in the means to finance higher schooling, as well as the effects of discrimination, must be addressed.

Although South Africa is furthest behind on the continuum of race relations, in some ways it is at a distinct advantage. With the postapartheid national mandate for reform, it has a window of opportunity to dismantle institutional barriers while laying the foundation for more equal opportunities across the board. Brazil and the United States lack such a catalyst and therefore must build consensus for reform policies to remedy less visible barriers to opportunities for their nonwhite populations.

Notes

1. This section relies heavily on Birdsall 1998b.
2. Failure to control for policy and for the distribution of education (see below) has in other cross-country studies led to less robust findings on the effect of education on growth.
3. Birdsall and Londoño (1997), appendix, table 2, shows the results of estimating a traditional growth equation across countries, using the best recently available data on the distribution of income (Deininger and Squire 1996). For these estimates, those countries were selected with Lorenz curves available for two periods of time separated by at least five years, with income estimates per capita in international purchasing power prices, and with information on physical capital investment, the education of the labor force (which were used to construct the measure of human-capital distribution), land distribution, and trade indicators.

4. In these regressions, the standard deviation of years of education of adults aged twenty-five years and older is used as the measure of the distribution of education. The level of education is entered as a separate variable. Another measure of the distribution of education, the coefficient of variation of the years of schooling, is mean-adjusted, controlling for the effect of an increasing level of schooling on dispersion. For both the standard deviation and the coefficient of variation, a higher value indicates a higher level of inequality.

5. The Gini coefficient is another measure of inequality, the value of which ranges from zero to one, with higher values signifying a less equal distribution.

6. Statistics based on 1998 midyear estimates published by the South African Statistics Center.

7. Hispanic is not of course a racial category. The census of 2000 in the United States permitted respondents to identify their race separately from the option of identifying themselves as Hispanic.

8. According to the World Bank's income classifications.

9. In South Africa, the poorest 40 percent of households receive only 11 percent of total income, while the richest 10 percent receive over 40 percent.

10. While there is little debate that Afro-Brazilians are more likely to be found in the lower socioeconomic order, there are different schools of thought on these disparities. The class-over-race school contends that racial distinctions do not inhibit social mobility in and of themselves in Brazil, but that human-capital inequality rooted in income disparities prevents social advancement — access to education and opportunities would thus ensure social mobility, uninhibited by racial prejudice. The race-over-class school posits that these social inequalities are rooted in racial discrimination that must be eradicated if there is to be social mobility among Afro-Brazilians (Lovell 1994).

11. Since the days of slavery, most Afro-Brazilians have lived in the rural Northeast, which has much lower education attainment, income levels, and overall standards of living. The white population is concentrated in the far more wealthy urban and industrial Southeast.

12. One study estimates that the poor distribution of income between racial groups accounts for 37 percent of total income inequality.

13. When reviewing South African statistics, it should be kept in mind that there are no generally accepted set of reliable population and socioeconomic data for the entire country. Although eleven population censuses were conducted since 1904, their coverage was limited because some of the former homelands were not included. Furthermore, the methodology used in the enumeration of populations residing in informal settlements around major cities was flawed. The quality of data gathered varied by racial groups and provinces (MWPD-SA 1998).

14. See endnote 3.

15. Defined as the population aged twenty years and older.

16. 1991 Human Development Index for the Republic of South Africa. Figures may be revised due to the 1996 Census.

17. This section relies heavily on Birdsall 1998b.

18. During the administration of Fernando Henrique Cardoso, elected president in 1994, federal spending on education increased substantially, with

substantial priority to primary schooling; enrollment data indicate this effort has improved access and quality for poor children.

19. See endnote 3.

20. Based on household surveys data for fifteen countries of Latin America, cleaned and compiled at the Inter-American Development Bank (IDB), using consistent measures of income, education and other variables, as reported in IDB 1998; see also Behrman, Birdsall, and Székely 1998.

21. Nonetheless, income also matters. In each income quartile, beginning with the fourth to sixth grade, the white population has lower enrollment rates than the Afro-Brazilian/*pardo* population of the higher-income quartile (Table 10.13).

22. Differences in education opportunity reflect differences in resources and spending across the country. The rich states in Brazil have spent as much as six times more on education than the poorer states. In an effort to redress this imbalance, the Fondo de Desenvolvimento do Ensino Fundamental guarantees a minimum level of expenditure in grades one through eight across the country, redistributing resources in favor of poorer states and municipalities.

23. Flug, Spilimbergo, and Wachtenheim (1998) show that financial depth explains much of the differences in secondary schooling across countries.

24. Innovative programs have been designed in the 1990s to address the poor's limited education attainment using demand-side financing. The *bolsa escola* program guarantees a minimum wage to low-income families keeping their children in school, as long as they attend regularly. Intended to fight child labor by countering the opportunity cost of going to school, the program has led to a significant reduction in both school repetition and dropouts (the latter of which dropped from 10 to 0.4 percent). Another program encourages school enrollment by depositing a scholarship to a beneficiary family's savings account if the child successfully completes the year and is promoted to the next grade. Partial withdrawals of the amounts are allowed once the child completes the fifth grade, the eighth grade, and then secondary schooling (Vawda 1997).

25. While 25.9 percent of total primary enrollment is rural, only 5.2 and 1.1 percent of lower- and upper-secondary enrollment, respectively, are rural (Herran and Rodriguez 1999).

26. Lam and Duryea (1999) report large effects of parental education on child schooling attainment at low levels of schooling. An increase in either the mother's or father's schooling from zero to four years is associated with about a 2.5-year increase in the grade attainment of fourteen-year-old children. When controlling for race, region, age at marriage, and husband's income, the effect is 1.0 years for mothers and .7 years for fathers. Lam and Duryea (1999) estimated the effect of single years of schooling of both wife and husband of 5,792 couples with a fourteen-year-old child at the time of the 1984 Pesquisa Nacional por Amostragem de Domicílios (National Survey by Domicile Sample; PNAD).

27. Lam (1999) analyzes 1995 Household Survey data for each country. Both surveys are nationally representative (South Africa: 1995 October Household Survey, 32,000 households; Brazil: 1995 Pesquisa Nacionalidade Amostra de Domicílios [PNAD], 85,000 households) and were conducted by the respective country's statistics bureau (Statistics South Africa and IBGE).

28. Mean monthly earnings normalized relative to nonwhites with zero schooling.

29. In contrast, trading school distributions or returns to schooling between the two countries would produce almost no effect on the earnings inequality of each. Lam (1999) explains that, due to the convex relationship between schooling and earnings, South Africa's lower schooling inequality and higher mean attainment combine to produce similar earnings inequality as Brazil's higher schooling inequality and lower mean attainment.

30. The increase in returns to higher levels of education has been associated with an increasing level of schooling in the United States. As schooling has expanded, the rates of return to lower levels of schooling have declined relative to higher levels. The changing rate of returns to different levels of schooling over time has significant implication for income inequality. Those population groups who have obtained more than the average investment in education have experienced increased earnings over time relative to those who have obtained less than the average. In contrast, lesser-educated groups have experienced lower earnings not only because of their lower schooling but also because the payoff to lower levels of schooling have declined relative to higher levels as the overall level of schooling has expanded (Carnoy 1995).

31. In a human-capital model, two candidates of different races, with the same years of schooling and the same years of education should, absent other factors, receive the same remuneration. In this model, the residual (the unexplained portion of the income difference) in part captures the effect of discrimination (at the most establishing a ceiling for its potential effects), as well as the interplay of other factors. Using the residual, Carnoy (1995) measures the "discrimination rate" after equalizing schooling, experience, region of work, marital status, foreign birth, and industry of work to that of white American, full-time-employed adult males. He found that the discrimination rate fell between 1939 and 1982, but rose in the 1980s. For African Americans it represented about 16 percent of white American male income. (See Birdsall and Sabot 1991 for theories of discrimination.)

32. In 1998, per capita income among whites ($22,952) was almost double that of African Americans ($12,957) (U.S. Department of Commerce [USDC] 1999, citing the March 1999 Current Population Survey).

33. The 1998 poverty rate for African Americans is the lowest since 1959, the earliest year for which poverty statistics are available (USDC 1999).

34. It is striking that the African-American males who moved to higher wage quartiles did not just bubble up to the next range but were evenly distributed through the higher quartiles of the wage distribution.

35. Cooper and Cohn (1997) report that African-American males receive the lowest private rate of return to higher education compared to other groups, but that the private return is still more significant than for other levels of schooling. They calculate internal rates of return to college for African-American males of 12.1, compared to 19.3 for females and 14.2 for white American males and females.

36. Ogbu (1994) examines the gap in school performance and the persistence of inequality between African Americans and white Americans in spite of changes in opportunity since the 1960s. He challenges the shift of attention

from race-based to class-based discrimination, arguing that most advances of African Americans have been due to nonmarket forces, i.e., legislation, executive orders, civil suits, etc., and that there are lingering racially discriminating institutions in the United States. He contends that social mobility mainly benefited the middle-class and college-educated African American, and asserts that African Americans historically have not been adequately rewarded for their education achievement and may not have the same optimism for economic mobility associated with scholastic achievement. He attributes, in part, the performance gap in education to community forces and an "opposition culture" that has downplayed scholastic success as disaffiliating from the African-American community.

37. See, for example, Barros, Duryea, and Székely 1998.

38. With expanding opportunities for Africans, skill differentials already have widened while racial differentials have narrowed. The Gini coefficient of earnings of urban African men increased from .25 in 1980 to .38 in 1993, while the ratio of mean earnings of white men to African men fell from 6:1 in 1980 to 4:2 in 1993 (Schultz and Mwabu 1998).

References

Alesina, A., and D. Rodrik. 1994. "Distributive Politics and Economic Growth: A Critical Survey of the Recent Literature." *The Quarterly Journal of Economics (U.S.)* 109 (May): 465–490.

Andrews, G. R. 1993. "Desigualdade Racial en Brasil y en Estados Unidos: Un Estudio Estadístico Comparado." *Desarrollo Económico* 33 (July-September): 130.

Barro, R. J. 1991. "Economic Growth in a Cross Section of Countries." *The Quarterly Journal of Economics (U.S.)* 106 (May): 407–443.

Barro, R. J., and J. Lee. 1993. "International Comparisons of Educational Attainment." Paper presented at conference "How Do National Policies Affect Long-Run Growth?" World Bank, Washington, D.C., February.

Barro, R. J., and X. Sala-I-Martin. 1995. *Economic Growth.* New York: McGraw-Hill.

Barros, R., S. Duryea, and M. Székely. 1999. "What's Behind Latin American Inequality?" Mimeo. Office of the Chief Economist, Inter-American Development Bank.

Becker, G. 1960. "An Economic Analysis of Fertility," in National Bureau of Economic Research, *Demographic and Economic Change in Developed Countries.* Princeton: Princeton University Press.

Becker, G., and H. G. Lewis. 1973. "On the Interaction Between the Quantity and Quality of Children." *Journal of Political Economy* 81, no. 2: S2799–S2808.

Behrman, J., N. Birdsall, and M. Székely. 1998. "Intergenerational Mobility in Latin America: Deeper Markets and Better Schools Make a Difference," in N. Birdsall and C. Graham, eds., *New Markets, New Opportunities, Economic and Social Mobility in a Changing World.* Washington, DC: Brookings Institution and Carnegie Endowment for International Peace.

Birdsall, N. 1998a. "Life Is Unfair: Inequality in the World." *Foreign Policy* (Summer).

―――. 1998b. "Education: The People's Asset." Paper prepared for the conference "Asset Distribution, Poverty and Economic Growth," Brasilia, Brazil, July 14–17; <http://www.worldbank.org/landpolicy/brazil/papers. htm>.

Birdsall, N., B. Bruns, and R. Sabot. 1996. "Education in Brazil: Playing a Bad Hand Badly," in Nancy Birdsall and Richard Sabot, eds., *Opportunity Foregone: Education in Brazil.* Washington, DC: Johns Hopkins Press for the Inter-American Development Bank.

Birdsall, N., and J. L. Londoño. 1997. "Asset Inequality Does Matter: Lessons from Latin America." *American Economic Review* 87, no. 2 (May).

Birdsall, N., D. Ross, and R. Sabot. 1995. "Inequality and Growth Reconsidered." *World Bank Economic Review* 9, no. 3 (September).

Birdsall, N., and R. Sabot, eds. 1991. *Unfair Advantage: Labor Market Discrimination in Developing Countries.* Washington, DC: World Bank.

Brazilian Institute for Geography and Statistics (IGBE). 1996. Pesquisa Nacionalidade Amostra de Domicílios (PNAD).

Carnoy, M. 1995. "Race Earnings Differentials," in M. Conroy, ed., *International Encyclopedia of Economics of Education.* 2nd ed. Oxford and New York: Pergamon.

Case, Anne, and Angus Deaton. 1999. "School Inputs and Educational Outcomes in South Africa." *The Quarterly Journal of Economics* 114, no. 3.

Cooper, S. T., and E. Cohn. 1997. "Internal Rates of Return to College Education in the United States by Sex and Race." *Journal of Education Finance* 23 (Summer).

Council of Economic Advisers (CEA). 1998. *Changing America: Indicators of Social and Economic Well-Being by Race and Hispanic Origin.* The President's Initiative on Race. Washington, DC: CEA.

Deininger, K., and L. Squire. 1996. "A New Data Base for Income Distribution in the World." *World Bank Economic Review* 10, no. 3 (September).

Filmer, D., and L. Pritchett. 1999. "The Effect of Household Wealth on Educational Attainment: Evidence from 35 Countries." *Population and Development Review* (March).

Flug, K., A. Spilimbergo, and E. Wachtenheim. 1998. "Investment in Education: Do Economic Volatility and Credit Constraints Matter?" *Journal of Development Economics* 55 (April).

Garibaldi, A. M. 1997. "Four Decades of Progress . . . and Decline: An Assessment of African-American Educational Attainment." *Journal of Negro Education* 66, no. 2.

Green, A. E. 1996. "Exclusion, Unemployment, and Non-employment." *Regional Studies* 31, no. 5.

Herran, Carlos, and Alberto Rodriguez. 1999. *Secondary Education in Brazil: Time to Move Forward.* Draft report. The World Bank and The Inter-American Development Bank, September.

Inter-American Development Bank (IDB). 1998. "Facing Up to Inequality in Latin America," in *Economic and Social Progress in Latin America.* Baltimore: Johns Hopkins University Press.

James, W. 1998. "A Profile of Racial Inequality in South Africa." Institute for Democracy in South Africa. Mimeo.

Klein, Ruben. 1997. "Indicadores Educacionais para Subpopulações Caracterizadas pela Cor." *Revista Ensaio, Avaliação e Políticas Públicas em Educação, Rio de Janeiro* 5, no. 17 (October-December): 495–514.

Lam, D. 1999. "Generating Extreme Inequality: Schooling, Earnings, and Intergenerational Transmission of Human Capital in South Africa and Brazil." Research Report No. 99-439. Population Studies Center, Institute for Social Research, University of Michigan.

Lam, D., and D. Levison. 1992. "Declining Inequality in Schooling in Brazil and Its Effects on Inequality in Earnings." *Journal of Development Economics* 37.

Lam, D., and S. Duryea. 1999. "Effects of Schooling Fertility, Labor Supply and Investments in Children." *The Journal of Human Resources* 34, no. 1 (Winter) (University of Wisconsin Press).

Leibbrandt, M. V., C. D. Woolard, and I. D. Woolard. 1996. "The Contribution of Income Components to Income Inequality in South Africa: A Decomposable Gini Analysis." Washington, DC: World Bank.

Levine, R., and D. Renelt. 1992. "A Sensitivity Analysis of Cross-Country Growth Regressions." *American Economic Review* 82, no. 2 (September).

Londoño, J. L., and M. Székely. 1997. "Distributional Surprises After a Decade of Reforms: Latin America in the Nineties," in R. Hausman and E. Lora, eds., *Latin America After a Decade of Reforms: What Comes Next?* Washington, DC: Inter-American Development Bank.

López, R., V. Thomas, and Y. Wang. 1998. "Addressing the Education Puzzle: The Distribution of Education and Economic Reforms." Policy Research Working Paper 2031. Economic Development Institute, Office of the Macroeconomic Management and Policy Division. Washington, DC: World Bank.

Lovell, P. 1994. "Race, Gender, and Development in Brazil." *Latin American Research Review* 29, no. 3.

Mboya, M. M., and T. S. Mwamwenda. 1994. "Quality Education in Black Schools of South Africa." *International Journal of Educational Development* 14, no. 4.

Ministry for Welfare and Population Development, South Africa (MWPD-SA). 1998. *White Paper on Population Policy*. Approved by the Portfolio Committee for Welfare and Population Development, March. <http://www.polity.org.za/govdocs/white_papers/popwp.html>.

Moll, P. 1996. "The Collapse of Primary Schooling Returns in South Africa 1960–1990." *Oxford Bulletin of Economics and Statistics* 58: 185–209.

Murphy, K. M., and R. Topel. 1997. "Unemployment and Non-employment." *American Economic Review: Papers and Proceedings* 87, no. 2 (May): 295–300.

Nangulu-Ayuku, A. 1998. "The New South Africa: Education for Reconstruction in the Post–Cold War Era." *Scandinavian Journal of Development Alternatives* 17: 99–104.

Ogbu, J. 1994. "Racial Stratification and Education in the United States: Why Inequality Persists." *Teachers College Record* 96, no. 2 (Winter).

Park, Y., D. Ross, and R. Sabot. 1995. "Educational Expansion and the Inequality of Pay in Brazil and Korea." Center for Development Economics. Williamstown, MA: Williams College.

Persson, T., and G. Tabellini. 1994. "Is Inequality Harmful for Growth?" *American Economic Review* 84, no. 3.

Psacharopoulos, G. 1994. "Returns to Investment in Education: A Global Update." *World Development* 22, no. 9: 1325–1343.

Schultz, T. P. 1988. "Education Investment and Returns," in H. B. Chenery and T. N. Srinivasan, eds., *Handbook of Development Economics*. Amsterdam: North Holland Press.

Schultz, T. P., and G. Mwabu. 1998. "Wage Premia for Education and Location, by Gender and Race in South Africa." Economic Growth Center, Yale University.

Schultz, T. W. 1961. "Investment in Human Capital." *The American Economic Review* 51, no.1 (March).

Statistics South Africa. 1995. October Household Survey. Pretoria, South Africa.

———. 1993. *South African Living Standards*. Pretoria, South Africa.

Strauss, J., and D. Thomas. 1995. "Health, Nutrition, and Economic Development." Labor and Population Program Working Paper Series, 92-23. Santa Monica, CA: Rand Corporation.

Summers, R., and A. Heston. 1995. "The Penn World Tables, Mark 5.6." University of Pennsylvania, Department of Economics, Philadelphia, PA.

United Nations Development Programme (UNDP). 1997. *Human Development Report*. New York: Oxford University Press.

United Nations Development Programme–South Africa (UNDP-SA). 1998. "Poverty and Inequality in South Africa, Summary Report." Prepared for the Office of the Executive Deputy President and the Inter-Ministerial Committee for Poverty and Inequality, May; <http://www.undp.org.za/docs/pubs/poverty.html>.

United Nations Educational, Scientific, and Cultural Organization (UNESCO). Various years. *Statistical Yearbook*. Lanham, MD, and New York: Bernan Press and UNESCO Publishing.

U.S. Department of Commerce (USDC). 1999. "Household Income at Record High; Poverty Declines in 1998, Census Bureau Report." U.S. Department of Commerce News, September 30; <http://www.census.gov/press-release/www/1999/cb99-188.html>.

U.S. Department of Education (USDE), National Center for Education Statistics (NCES). 1997. *Minorities in Higher Education*. Series on the Condition of Education 1996, no. 9. Washington, DC: U.S. Department of Education, Office of Educational Research and Improvement.

———, NCES. 1995. *The Educational Progress of Black Students*. Series on the Condition of Education 1994, no. 2. Washington, DC: U.S. Department of Education, Office of Educational Research and Improvement.

———, NCES. 1996. *Urban Schools: The Challenge of Location and Poverty*. Washington, DC: U.S. Department of Education, Office of Educational Research and Improvement.

Vawda, Ayesha. 1997. "Brazil: Stipends to Increase School Enrollment and

Decrease Child Labor—A Case for Demand Side Financing." The World Bank Group; <http://wbln0018.worldbank.org/hdned>.

Welch, F. 1999. "In Defense of Inequality." Richard T. Ely Lecture, New York City.

White House. 1999. "The Face of America." The President's Initiative on Race; <http://www.whitehouse.gov/initiatives/oneamerica/face.html>.

Williamson, Jeffrey G. et al. 1993. *Human Resources in Development Along the Asia-Pacific Rim*. Singapore and New York: Oxford University Press.

World Bank. Various years. *World Development Indicators*. New York: Oxford University Press.

11

Globalization:
A View from the South

Francis Wilson

In this globalized world, no single country can live or work on its
own. We are all tied together in a common destiny.
> —Nelson Mandela, Cape Town, September 1999

The meaning of globalization has been described in many different
ways. But the defining moment of global consciousness may well have
been on that first journey around the moon just before Christmas 1968
when "for the first time humanity saw its home from afar, a tiny, lovely
and fragile 'blue marble' hanging in the blackness of space"[1] in those
extraordinary images beamed back to an awestruck world glued to its
television sets. The vastness of space, the fragility of the "space-ship
earth"[2] on which we dwell, and the reality of our common destiny all
became embedded at the back of our minds in a way that changed us
forever. Not that it made the world any less fractious, nor less prone to
split into warring camps. But something changed at that time. An
awareness of the sea around us;[3] of the ozone layer above;[4] of our
growing interdependence, including our capacity to destroy life on the
planet. With increasing awareness of mutual dependence came also a
greater sense of insecurity.

It is against this background that we can perhaps best examine the
phenomenon of globalization, which at the beginning of the twenty-first
century seems to be the idea that "proffers a popular narrative for a new
epoch in world affairs" (McGrew 1998: p. 7). While its precise meaning remains ambiguous, with all the dangers of "a suitcase word,"[5] it
nevertheless captures a real sense of the spirit of the times. For this reason it is worth pausing to unpack its meaning with some care before

going on to consider its implications from the perspective of southern Africa.

Definitions

According to the International Monetary Fund, to take the word from one horse's mouth, "Globalization refers to the growing economic inter-dependence of countries world-wide through the increasing volume and variety of cross-border transactions in goods and services, and of inter-national capital flows, and also through the more rapid and widespread diffusion of technology" (quoted in R. Solomon 1999: p. 165). This admirably clear and straightforward definition contains much of what is generally understood by the word. But not everything. For as Anthony McGrew (1998) has shown, we are conceptualizing a moving target. He identifies three different interpretations of globalization: three positions held by those whom he labels "hyper-globalists," "sceptics," and "trans-formationalists." For the first group, the process is leading to a "border-less" world: "The hyper-globalist account identifies the rise of the glob-al economy, the emergence of institutions of global governance, and the global diffusion and hybridization of cultures, with a radically new world order; one which prefigures the demise of the nation state" (p. 11).

For the "sceptics," however, a distinction has to be made between a process of internationalization (through growing linkages between national economies) and that of globalization with ever weakening national boundaries. The skeptics do not believe that the latter process is an inevitable consequence of the former. Moreover, they tend to the view that contemporary levels of interdependence (in terms of trade, investment, and labor flows) are by no means unprecedented when compared with the late nineteenth century.

While international economic conditions may constrain what gov-ernments can do, governments are by no means immobilized. Furthermore, internationalization has differential impacts; its social and political consequences vary considerably between states, depending upon their relative power, as well as between policy sectors. Thus, "the internationalisation of capital may not merely restrict policy choices, but expand them as well" (McGrew 1998: pp. 13–14).

Third, there are the "transformationalists" who "argue that contem-porary patterns of globalization are unprecedented; that they are pro-ducing new patterns of inclusion and exclusion in the global political economy; and that governments are having to adapt to a world in which there is no longer a clear distinction between the foreign and domestic, internal and external affairs" (p. 14). At the core of the transformationalists' case is a conviction that contemporary globalization is reconstituting or "re-engineering" the power functions and authority of national governments (p. 15).

We shall not continue to summarize the remainder of McGrew's incisive essay, but use these three perspectives together with his conclusion as the basis for our own analysis, which sees globalization as "a multi-dimensional . . . historical process which involves something more than simply flows and connections between nation-states and across national territorial boundaries" (pp. 19, 21).

Historical Perspectives

Just as there are many dimensions to the process of globalization, so too are there many starting points. For some it has been going on since the dawn of time as human beings, growing in consciousness, interacted in recurring patterns of exploration, cooperation, and conflict. For others it began most clearly with the European voyages of the fifteenth and sixteenth centuries as men set sail to seek riches beyond the edges of the world they then knew. For yet others, globalization began with the impact of the colonialism that followed the early travelers. For many in Africa, the story begins with the appalling predations of the European slave traders, particularly down the western coast (Tandon 1999: p. 19). And so on, right down to the present time when there is debate as to whether globalization really began with the fall of the Berlin Wall in 1989, the explosion of the World Wide Web in the early 1990s, or the establishment of the World Trade Organization in 1995.

For the purposes of this chapter we will focus on the present period within the context of global industrial expansion since the end of the Napoleonic Wars in 1815. This period of nearly two centuries is one in which the twin themes—of technology-driven change combined with ongoing pressures (and resistance) to reduce political barriers to trade—run like unbroken threads.

The industrial revolution was driven by technical innovation. The effective harnessing of steam by James Watt and his colleagues to drive the emerging wheels of industry (Ashton 1948: chap. 3); the invention of new technology for spinning and weaving; the development of railways and of steamships; all these and more revolutionized the production and marketing of textiles and iron. Costs fell sharply; demand both at home and abroad increased dramatically and British trade leaped ahead. Exports tripled in the first half of the nineteenth century while imports rose nearly fivefold (Ellsworth and Leith 1975: p. 197).

But there were severe restrictions on trade. Agriculture was protected and food prices were high, but the farm lobby backed by landed gentry with the implicit support of their laborers fought ferociously against all pressures to reduce food tariffs. However, in the aftermath of the Irish famine, the Corn Laws were finally repealed in 1846, and for the next two generations, until 1914, Britain remained open to imports without restriction. In 1815, the country was still largely self-sufficient in food; by 1900, nearly 60 percent of wheat and flour consumed in the country was imported (Ellsworth and Leith 1975: p. 197). It was paid for by manufacturers in the growing cities. Britain was becoming the workshop of the world, and in the process the population—driven from the land by new methods of production, which required fewer workers to grow more food, and pulled to the factories by their insatiable demand for labor to produce for the world market—moved to the towns and cities of industrial Britain on the rapidly expanding railway network. Between 1801 and 1871, the urban population rose from 31 percent to 61 percent of the total. The social consequences of this process were appalling as documented by a whole range of writers from Dickens to Engels, but gradually a political movement grew that widened the franchise and enacted laws not only to curb the wilder abuses in mines and in factories but that also taxed some of the wealth to pay for workmen's compensation, unemployment insurance, old age pensions and other goals of the labor movement.

On the continent the impact of the new technology and the consequences of the need to trade were no less dramatic. In Germany, for example, the century began with some 300 independent territories, each with its own customs and currency system. By 1880 (Ellsworth and Leith 1975: pp. 195, 203), virtually all the local tariffs, dues, and tolls that impeded commerce had been swept away. There too, as in the rest of Europe and in North America, industrialization and urbanization were accompanied by political movements that within each country fought to establish a countervailing power strong enough to tame the raw energy unleashed by the entrepreneurs.

At international level many restrictions on foreign trade were systematically dismantled in the heady years of expansion after the abolition of the Corn Laws. But this process was not without resistance, and powerful arguments were raised, both in Europe and the United States, in favor of a return to protection (Kenwood and Lougheed 1983: p. 80). In the United States, for example, the threat of cheaper imports (including agricultural products from Canada) was met by rising opposition that culminated in the passage in 1890 of the McKinley Act, which raised the average level of tariffs to 50 percent. Apart from one brief respite in 1913, it was to be more than fifty years before the United States at the end of World War II began seriously to remove the shutters of protection.

It was at the Bretton Woods Conference of 1944, when the foundations of the International Monetary Fund (IMF) and the International Bank for Reconstruction and Development (the World Bank) were laid, that the powerful industrial countries, renouncing autarky, began the long, slow, negotiated journey to an open world of trade.

It is necessary to acknowledge this history for several reasons. First is the recognition that for many countries (including the United States) there can be circumstances where for significant groups, representing even a majority of the population, protection is in their interests. Indeed, as John Gray has remarked, "The foundations of American prosperity were laid behind the walls of high tariffs" (Gray 1998: p. 104). For individual countries, the costs and benefits of tariffs change over time. The ambiguities remain. The second reason is that it reminds us of the singular importance of political activity, undertaken as people sought, country by country, to humanize a process that swept them off the land like a tidal wave. It reminds us further of the hard-won discovery that the values of the market must themselves be subject to higher values. The slave trade, itself an early manifestation of globalization, was banned and slavery itself finally abolished after a prolonged campaign. Similarly, Lord Shaftesbury and the early trade unionists fought long and hard against the use of child labor in British coal mines, even though many industrialists argued that such prohibitions would surely harm poor families who would be further deprived without the income brought home by their children (Wilson 1998).

The consequences of inventions and technological change were inexorable. Falling costs of production through mechanization, falling costs of transport through the harnessing of steam power to trains and ships, and falling costs (in terms of time) of the transmission of information through the invention first of the telegraph and subsequently the radio all led to a massive expansion in the movement of goods, capital investment, and people both within and between countries. The century from Britain's reduction of basic food tariffs in 1846 to the new beginning signified in the decisions taken at the Bretton Woods conference in

1944 was a century in which the world found itself, despite many set-backs, increasingly, if uneasily, urbanized and bound together.

Global Dimensions of Trade

With that historical background, we turn now to an examination (no less brief) of some of the more significant aspects of globalization during the latter half of the twentieth century. While the developments of the last decade seemed to intensify the process considerably, it is helpful to see the more recent events in a slightly longer time frame.

Recognition that the postwar world would require special structures to prevent a reversion to the trade barriers and financial-exchange controls that shackled the world economy in the 1930s led forty-four countries to meet [6] in July 1944 to hammer out articles of agreement for two new organizations: the International Monetary Fund and the International Bank for Reconstruction and Development, more commonly known as the World Bank (Kenwood and Lougheed 1983: pp. 249 ff). A third new body, the International Trade Organization (ITO), was also proposed, but its establishment proved to be an altogether more arduous and difficult task. As a first step, in 1946, twenty-three countries decided to negotiate to reduce and bind customs tariffs (World Trade Organization 1999). The first round of negotiations in Geneva during the next year led to some 45,000 tariff concessions affecting 20 percent of world trade and to mutual acceptance of some of the trade rules of the draft ITO Charter. This was the General Agreement on Tariffs and Trade (GATT), which entered into force in January 1948 and formed the basis for trade negotiations over the subsequent half-century. For although the charter for establishing the ITO was agreed to in March 1948, strong opposition was expressed, particularly in the U.S. Congress. In 1950, the United States government effectively killed the ITO when it announced that it would not seek congressional ratification of the Havana Charter.

Meanwhile, multilateral negotiations to reduce tariffs further continued under the auspices of GATT, which played an effective if ad hoc role as umbrella "international organization" without any solid legal foundation.

But for the next four decades round after round of trade negotiations, involving steadily increasing numbers of countries dealing with a widening range of difficult trade issues, were held in terms of GATT. The means were creating the end. Finally, the Uruguay round led, by fits and starts, through seven and a half years of difficult negotiations that more than once seemed to run into a brick wall, to a revised General Agreement of Tariffs and Trade and to the commitment, signed at Marrakesh in April 1994, to establish a new international body: the World Trade Organization (WTO), which opened its office doors in January 1995.

Many issues remained unresolved—notably, from the perspective of the developing world, the inordinately high levels of protection of agriculture in most of the rich industrial countries. Nevertheless it is possible to look back over the half-century from the end of World War II to the establishment of the WTO and to see that the long, difficult process of negotiation achieved a great deal in terms of facilitating the growth of world trade. In the thirty years after 1950, for example, the increase in the volume of international trade exceeded the increase in the volume of production almost every year (Kenwood and Lougheed 1983: p. 299). Indeed, "the momentum of trade liberalisation helped ensure that trade growth consistently out-paced production growth throughout the GATT era" (World Trade Organization 1999). Volumes of goods and services traded across international borders grew from 25 percent of world GDP in 1970 to 45 percent in 1990 (World Bank 1995: p. 51). And this thrust has continued. "Trade in goods and services," reported the World Bank in 1999, "has grown twice as fast as global GDP in the 1990s, and the share attributable to developing countries has climbed from 23 to 29 percent" (World Bank 1999: table 1, pp. 230–231).

However, although the expansion of world trade induced by the reduction of tariffs and the establishment of a more solid negotiated framework was clearly one of the factors leading to rapid economic growth in so many countries since World War II, it is also clear that not everybody benefited. Development has been very uneven.

New Technology

Another dimension of the process of globalization since World War II has been the dramatic reduction, driven by new technology, in the costs of transport and communication. Table 11.1 shows the figures.

While the costs of flying and telephoning fell sharply, with revenue per passenger mile falling by two-thirds between 1950 and 1980, and transatlantic calls from New York to London dropping by a factor of fifteen in the thirty years from 1960 to 1990, it is in the field of computers and the development of the World Wide Web that the changes have been

Table 11.1   Declining Cost of Transport and Communications (1960 = 100)

Year	Sea Freight		Air Transport		Telephone		Computers
	$/ton	index	$/mile	index	$/3 min	index	
1930	60	222	0.68	283	245	533	—
1950	34	126	0.30	125	53	115	—
1960	27	100	0.24	100	46	100	100
1970	27	100	0.16	67	32	70	16
1980	24	89	0.10	42	5	11	3
1990	29	107	0.11	46	3	7	1

Source: UNDP *Human Development Report 1999*, p. 30.

as revolutionary as they have been unexpected. Few people recognized its significance when the microcomputer was first introduced in 1971. Indeed, even as late as 1979, a professor of computer science at the Massachusetts Institute of Technology, attacking Daniel Bell's belief that developments in computer technology would lead to an "information society," asked rhetorically: "Will the home computer be as pervasive as today's television sets? The answer must certainly be no" (Weizenbaum 1980: p. 553). Yet even a professor at MIT might be forgiven for not foreseeing the near future when Bill Gates himself almost missed the bend in the road ten years later when the information revolution sped off, via the World Wide Web, into cyberspace. It is the acceleration of change that is perhaps the biggest change of all: "Five years ago," reported the *Scientific American* in October 1999, "less than 1 percent of U.S. households were on-line; now one-third of them are, representing 50 million people. In contrast it took radio 38 years, telephone 36 years, television 13 years and cable TV 10 years to achieve similar levels of penetration" (quoted in Bane and Bradley 1999: p. 92). And all this before the introduction of high-speed broadband.

Capital Flows

One immediate consequence of the new computer technology and the information revolution that followed it has been a massive increase in the flow of capital between countries (R. Solomon 1999: pp. 108–116). At first, during the 1980s, the increase was confined to flows between industrialized, developed countries. Thus gross capital flows from fourteen industrial countries (mostly to each other) rose from an average of some $65 billion a year in the latter half of the 1970s to approximately $460 billion in 1989 (p. 109). This surge in the 1980s was followed by a second wave of capital in the 1990s, this time largely to developing countries. Table 11.2 shows what happened.

By 1996 nearly three-quarters of the flow (including remittances) went to twelve countries, of which China, Mexico, Brazil, and Malaysia were the most important. Sub-Saharan Africa received less than 5 percent of the total, but this "was up from near zero in 1990" (R. Solomon 1999: p. 114). These flows were immensely important as became visibly, albeit negatively, apparent with the Mexican crisis of 1994–1995 and, more ominously, with the sharp fall of various East Asian currencies, starting with the *baht*,[7] in 1997.[8] But it is also worth noting that "for industrial countries as a whole, the $250 billion of portfolio investments in developing countries in 1994 accounted for less than 0.5 percent of total portfolio holdings"(p. 116). It is precisely in this "paradox of the importance of the insignificant" that there lies one of the greatest problems of globalization from the perspective of developing countries. A loss or gain of a fraction of 1 percent in the value of total holdings matters but is not the end of the world for portfolio managers, members of the industrial world's electronic herd so vividly described by Thomas Friedman.[9] But those short-term speculative funds can cause immense damage to much smaller, more fragile economies if either they pour in or, more seriously, pour out without being carefully managed from the perspective of the same fragile economies. And in the 1990s there were many countries in Africa, Asia, and Latin America, to say nothing of the emerging economies of Eastern Europe, that found themselves sailing in small boats on very choppy financial seas over which they had little control.[10]

Table 11.2 Net Private Capital Flows to Developing Countries, 1989–1996 (US$ billions)

1989	1990	1991	1992	1993	1994	1995	1996
36	44	57	91	157	161	184	244
index 100	122	158	253	436	447	511	678

Source: Robert Solomon, *The Revolution in International Finance Since 1980*, p. 114.

Note: For the index, 1989 at $36 billion is taken as 100. Thus $44 billion (=122) for 1990 shows a 22% increase, etc.

Environmental Perspectives

Part and parcel of the globalization of the latter half of the twentieth century has been a growing concern about the link between economic growth, industrialization, and the expansion of international trade on the one hand and the possibility of irreversible environmental damage to the planet on the other. This concern has found expression within the World Trade Organization itself in a report on trade and the environment published in October 1999 in preparation for the Third Ministerial Conference meeting in Seattle.[11] While the report is fairly upbeat about the problem, arguing (without being too simplistic about the environmental consequences, both good and bad, of economic growth) that it is soluble, it is interesting and encouraging to note how much emphasis it places on the importance of political accountability and good governance and on the role of civil society in pressuring governments to adopt appropriate policies at both national and international levels. Where the report, perhaps inevitably, is less forthright is in its failure to spell out how the imbalance in power relations between the governments of rich industrial countries and those of developing countries itself affects the framework of the debate. Nevertheless, compared with thirty years ago, there has been considerable increase in international debate and activity by both governmental and nongovernmental organizations, for most seem aware that "climate change, loss of biodiversity and illegal dumping of toxic waste pose a growing threat to global welfare."[12] Significant though these developments have been, there are powerful voices, particularly within civil society, arguing that the overall response to the environmental challenges presented by the current patterns and trends of world production and consumption, spurred on by globalization, is hopelessly inadequate.

Culture

From the dangers of environmental damage implicit in current patterns of economic growth, we move to consider another no less pervasive dimension of the process: the cultural consequences. This aspect of globalization is no less controversial than the debate about the environment and possibly more so, as the values of culture are so much more difficult to define. But consider the following facts.

World trade in goods with a cultural content (from printed matter to television equipment) almost tripled between 1980 and 1991. "For the

United States the largest single export industry is not aircraft, computers or automobiles—it is entertainment, in films and television programmes. Hollywood films grossed more than $30 billion world-wide in 1997, and in 1998 a single movie, *Titanic*, grossed more than $1.8 billion" (United Nations Development Programme [UNDP] 1999: p. 33). As the UNDP goes on to report, "The vehicles for this trade in cultural goods are the new technologies. Satellite communications technology from the mid-1980s gave rise to a powerful new medium with a global reach and to such global media network as CNN. The number of television sets per 1,000 people almost doubled between 1980 and 1995, from 121 to 235. . . . But the global market for cultural products is becoming concentrated, driving out small local industries. At the core of the entertainment industry—film, music and television—there is a growing dominance of US products, and many countries are seeing their local industries wither" (p. 33).

Nor is this cultural dominance confined to films, music, and television. The expanding fast food empires of McDonalds or Kentucky Fried Chicken are part of the same process. "Today, for better or for worse," observes Thomas Friedman (1999), "globalization is a means for spreading the fantasy of America round the world" (p. 235). But the concern, outside the United States, runs deeper than that. "The Western world," write the authors of *Globalization and Its Discontents*, "spreads materialism and consumerism as the paramount values" (Burbach, Nunez, and Kagarlitsky 1997: p. 23). It is the rise of these values as an integral part of the process of globalization and their long-term consequences for society at all levels that disturbs so many perceptive observers.

Growth of the Information Society

The technological developments driving globalization are also the forces leading to the growth of the information society. "Today," writes Lester Thurow (1996), "knowledge and skills stand alone as the only source of comparative advantage. They have become the key ingredient in the late twentieth century's location of economic activity" (p. 68). In identifying the fundamental features of the new economy that has emerged during the last half of the twentieth century, Manuel Castells (1993) points to the facts that "sources of productivity—and therefore of economic growth in real terms—are increasingly dependent upon the application of science and technology, as well as upon the quality of information and management, in the processes of production, consumption, distribution and trade" (p. 15).

From this, Castells identifies the second fundamental feature of the new economy as being "the shift, in advanced capitalist societies, from material production to information-processing activities" (p. 17). Thus, citing Marc Porat, he goes on to show that the real transformation of the economic structure of advanced societies is the emergence of the "information economy," "wherein an ever-growing role is played by the manipulation of symbols in the organization of production and in the enhancement of productivity" (p. 17). It is striking to note that by 1990 in the four industrial countries of France, (West) Germany, the United Kingdom, and the United States, anything between 40 percent and 47 percent of the employed population were "engaged in information-processing activities, whether in the production of goods or in the provision of services, and the proportion continues to rise over time" (p. 17). This is Alvin Toffler's Third Wave (1980).

After considering other fundamental features of the new economy, including the transformation of the organization of production and the extent to which it all takes place at a global level, Castells (1993) makes the simple but profound observation that the current revolution in information technologies "has created the material infrastructure needed for the formation of a global economy, in a movement similar to that which lay behind the construction of the railways and the formation of national markets during the nineteenth century" (pp. 19–20).

This has led to what Castells calls the "informational economy" (p. 20), which in turn has caused a fundamental shift at both national and global levels in the relative demand for skilled (well educated) and unskilled (less educated) labor. It is this that lies at the root of the widening inequality currently observed in many different contexts.

Widening Inequality

Correlation does not imply causation. Nevertheless, the widening inequality that has taken place both within and between countries since the 1970s is widely perceived to have been caused at least in part by the accelerated globalization that has taken place since then. Within the United States, for example, between 1967 and 1997 the average (inflation-adjusted) income, measured in thousands of dollars, of the richest 5 percent of households rose 71 percent from $126 to $215; average income of the top 20 percent (which includes the above 5 percent) rose

56 percent from \$79 to \$123, while the average income of the bottom 20 percent of households rose only 29 percent off a very low base from \$7 to \$9. In terms of the gap, measured as a ratio, between the richest and poorest 20 percent, it widened from 10.3:1 to 13.7:1 (Doyle 1999: p. 20).

There are many interlocking causes of this widening gap, including, it is argued, the new technology (particularly computers) as well as the decline of trade unions, whose greater strength in Europe seems to account, at least in part, for the somewhat slower increase in inequality. Nevertheless, both in Europe and the United States the globalization of trade is seen by many as a significant factor depressing wages and threatening the jobs of the less skilled (Doyle 1999: p. 20). But not everybody agrees. In a careful study of the impact of globalization on labor markets in the United States, Europe, and Japan, the authors conclude that "the overall role played by trade with developing countries seems to have been relatively small in all Trilateral countries" (Thygensen, Kosai, and Lawrence 1996: p. 104). But they do not deny the observed growing inequalities within these countries. To redress these, they argue, the most efficient course of action (in the long run) "is to upgrade the skills of the workforce, hence gradually shifting the relative supply of skilled and less-skilled" (p. 106).

More striking, however, than the growing inequality within many industrialized countries is the widening chasm between rich and poor countries across the globe. An analysis of long-term trends in world income distribution (between countries) "shows that the distance between the richest and the poorest country was about 3:1 in 1820, 11:1 in 1913, 35:1 in 1950, 44:1 in 1973 and 72:1 in 1992" (UNDP 1999: p. 38). In 1998, according to the World Bank, GNP per capita in Switzerland was US\$40,080 while in the Democratic Republic of Congo (formerly Zaire) it was US\$110. Measured more realistically at purchasing-power parity, the figures for richest (Luxembourg) and poorest (Tanzania) countries on the World Bank tables were US\$37,420 and US\$490, respectively, implying a gap of 76:1. For the three countries on which this book is focused, the gap between the United States on the one hand and Brazil and South Africa on the other is significant, but the changes over the past twenty years are more complex, as Table 11.3 shows.

Converting all GNP/capita figures into dollars at current exchange rates shows a clearly widening gap, dramatic in the case of the United States and South Africa. But converting the figures at purchasing-power parity, i.e., in terms of what they could actually buy, we find that the

Table 11.3   **Gap Between Average Incomes in United States, Brazil, and South Africa, 1979–1998**

Country	GNP/capita 1979 U.S.$	GNP/capita 1979 U.S. Ratio	GNP/capita 1998 U.S.$	GNP/capita 1998 U.S. Ratio	GNP/capita 1998 [@PPP] U.S.$	GNP/capita 1998 [@PPP] U.S. Ratio
United States	10,630	1.0:1	29,340	1.0:1	29,340	1.0:1
Brazil	1,780	6.0:1	4,570	6.4:1	6,160	4.8:1
South Africa	1,720	6.2:1	2,880	10.2:1	6,990	4.2:1

Source: World Bank 1981 and 1999.

gap in 1998, while still of the order of four or five to one, is not as wide as might have been expected. Unfortunately, comparative figures in terms of purchasing-power parity are not available for earlier years, and thus it is difficult to be certain about trends. Nevertheless, the broad picture of a widening gap across the full width of the global spectrum between rich and poor countries is surely valid.

But for South Africa, as for Brazil, the real problem lies in the depth of inequality within the country and the fact that the pressures of globalization seem to be exacerbating it. The questions that face countries in the Southern Hemisphere, particularly, is under what conditions might the process of globalization have the effect of reducing rather than increasing the levels of poverty and inequality? Is it possible to achieve such conditions? In seeking to answer these questions, we turn to consideration of the impact of globalization as seen from the South African point of view.

View from South Africa

South Africa, of course, has been caught up in the process of globalization and industrialization for almost as long as Europe or the United States. Indeed, the establishment of Cape Town in 1652 as a refueling station for the Dutch East India Company needing to stock up on provisions on its way to the Far East, the importation of slaves into the Cape for the next two centuries, the consequences of their emancipation by the colonial government in 1834–1838, were all part of a process that bound South Africa increasingly to the world economy. In the context of this chapter it is not irrelevant to note that a large proportion of the slaves imported to the Cape at the beginning of the nineteenth century came from Portuguese slave traders sailing their ships (as late as 1818) from northern Mozambique to Brazil via Cape Town.[13]

After the abolition of slavery, the next major shift occurred with the discovery of minerals in the latter part of the nineteeth century and the subsequent investment, by the industrializing world of Europe and America, in deep-level mining and in the railways necessary to extend the transport links from the sea to the interior.

This is not the place for a detailed assessment of South Africa's history seen from the perspective of globalization. But it is important to note in passing that South Africa's peculiar pattern of industrialization was profoundly shaped by the political forces of the time. The development of the oscillating migrant labor system, which remains at the heart of the gold-mining industry to this day, was not inevitable, but its emergence had a profound and devastating impact on the shape of society in South Africa for the next century. Its consequences, not least in providing the underlying structural backbone to apartheid and in generating rural poverty, were profound.[14] These are the shadow sides of an economy that, precisely because of its long and close links to the global economy in terms of investment, migration, and trade, finds itself entering the twenty-first century as the most powerful economy on the African continent (Wilson 1995). Herein lies the paradox of globalization: that the forces that drive it contain the potential for both good and evil. The real challenge, particularly for less powerful countries, lies in finding ways to harness them as beneficially as possible.

In the very month of South Africa's first democratic election (April 1994), the Marrakesh Agreement was signed, marking the end of the Uruguay round of the GATT and setting the stage of the establishment of the WTO in January 1995. The new government was pitched head-first into the swirling waters of the new globalization. How to respond?

Apart from the need to ensure a continuation of the extraordinarily smooth political transition, the major challenges facing the Mandela government were essentially economic: how to generate rapid economic growth in an economy that had run down; how to redress as quickly as possible the widespread poverty, unemployment, and deep inequality; how to overcome the inheritance of racially skewed distributions in ownership of (and access to) all forms of assets, not the least being human capital. These problems are delineated in more detail elsewhere in this book,[15] and so we pause only briefly to note two fundamental points, each illustrated by a small table. The first relates to unemployment, the other to human capital and the legacy of racism in the information age.

Democratic South Africa inherited an economy in which unemployment averaged 30 percent. But this average masked a society with major fault lines. Table 11.4 shows the general picture.

Unemployment is far higher for black South Africans than for whites, for rural people, for women, and among the young. More detailed analysis reveals that for black (African) youngsters in 1993 the rate of unemployment was of the order of two-thirds (65 percent), while for elderly whites in the decade before retirement it was only 2 percent.

This underlying division within South African society both reflects and is reflected in the inheritance in terms of human capital.

While 90 percent of whites came into the new South Africa with at least standard 6 (i.e., eight years of schooling), more than half (54 percent) of blacks did not. And while three-fifths of whites had completed school, only one-tenth of blacks had done so. Small wonder then that in 1995, when nearly one-quarter (23 percent) of whites were in professional or senior management positions, only one in twenty (4.9 percent) of black Africans were. At the bottom end of the economic pyramid, 40

Table 11.4　Unemployment in South Africa, 1993 (by major dividing lines)

Race	Black	White
	39%	5%
Geography	Rural	Urban
	40%	22–26%
Gender	Women	Men
	35%	26%
Age	16–24	55–64
	53%	15%

Source: *South Africans Rich and Poor: Baseline Household Statistics* 1994, pp. 141 ff.
Note: These figures include those wishing to work but too discouraged to look for it.

Table 11.5　Human Capital in South Africa, 1993 (percentage)

Age	Completed	Black [African]	White	All
14 and older	Standard 6 or more	46	90	55
16 and older	Standard 8 or more	27	83	38
18 and older	Standard 10 or more	11	61	20

Source: *South Africans Rich and Poor: Baseline Household Statistics* 1994.
Note: Standard 1 starts after two years of schooling. Thus standard 6 implies completion of eight years of schooling, etc.

percent of black South Africans were in elementary occupations when the proportion of whites in similar positions was only 1.6 percent.

It is in this context that one can begin to assess the policies pursued by the South African government in the years after 1994 and to consider further possible strategies for the years ahead.

Strategic Response

The new government packaged its responses in essentially two ways: the Reconstruction and Development Programme (RDP) introduced in 1994; and a policy of Growth, Employment, and Redistribution (GEAR) introduced in 1996. There has been considerable controversy as to whether GEAR effectively undercut the RDP or whether, as its architects insisted, it was designed specifically to create the conditions for the RDP to be most effective. For our purposes it is sufficient to note that both are concerned with poverty and unemployment but that GEAR is more focused on the macroeconomic challenges of globalization. In particular, and perhaps most controversially, it is in terms of GEAR that the government has formulated its policy with regard to macroeconomic discipline and to trade liberalization. But these are not the only two policies to be considered. There are, it is suggested, at least seven clusters of policies that must be developed in any overall strategic response to the new global economic realities. This is not the place to discuss them in detail, but it is perhaps helpful to note them briefly for the purpose of stimulating further debate.

Macroeconomic Policy

It is ironic to reflect that during the 1970s and 1980s one of the major concerns of democratic policymakers was on the dangers of "macroeconomic populism." Would it be possible, wondered even the most sympathetic of observers,[16] for a new democratic government in South Africa to avoid the pressures to spend ever more public money on overcoming the legacy of poverty and inequality. But the lessons from Brazil and elsewhere were taken to heart, and the new democratic officers, under the strong advice of the IMF pilots, have sailed the South African ship of state firmly away from the dangers of inflation. Indeed, there are many who would argue that in assessing the trade-off between less inflation and more employment, the monetary policies of the new South Africa have, if anything, been too restrictive.[17] However, few

would disagree with the observation that the globalization of the 1990s
has made careful macroeconomic management by all countries more
essential than it has ever been. And, as those defending the tight monetary policies point out, South Africa stood up remarkably well to the
battering that emerging economies took in the wake of the collapse of
various East Asian currencies, led by the Thai *baht* in 1997.[18]

Trade Liberalization

South Africa's new government's rise to power coincided, as we have
seen, almost to the day with the signing of the Marrakesh agreement of
GATT in 1994. The main effect of the change of government seems to
have been to ensure that South Africa's new tariff program, which took
effect with the establishment of the World Trade Organization, was
carefully discussed not only with industrialists but also with labor
unions and with a technical group of the Southern Africa Customs
Union.[19] The net result is that the country, which for many years pursued a policy of import substitution behind high tariff walls, has moved
rapidly since 1995 to simplify a complex tariff regime and to lower the
overall level of protection. This has not been unopposed, and in
September 1999, thousands of members of the South African Clothing
Textile Workers Union marched in Cape Town to protest further import
tariff reductions, which they believed would lead to further job losses in
an already bleeding sector (*Sunday Independent* 1999). But government
seems determined to push tariff reduction—at times even faster than the
pace required by the WTO—as part of a process of forcing all sectors of
the economy to become globally competitive as rapidly as possible. The
complex debate as to the wisdom of this policy, particularly with regard
to the timing of tariff reductions, lies well beyond the scope of this
chapter. For our purposes it is sufficient to note that South Africa's
democratic government clearly believes that it has no option but to follow the path that, one way or the other, all members of the World Trade
Organization are being pressed to tread.

Battling for a Level Playing Field

It is precisely in differences between theory and practice that some of
the greatest difficulties lie. Consider agriculture. The United States,
with the passage of the Freedom to Farm bill in 1996, has begun the
gradual but painful process of weaning farmers from government subsidies. But already, huge difficulties are apparent. It is estimated that by

1999 net income for grain farmers was 30 percent lower than it had been when the legislation was passed. The number of farmers leaving the land in the Midwest is estimated to have quadrupled (Hage 1999). And all this despite massive government "emergency" support for farmers in 1998 and 1999 (*Economist* 1999). For other countries of the Organization for Economic Cooperation and Development (OECD) the politics of agricultural protection is even more difficult. In Japan, for example, an overriding policy of full employment has led to a wide range of interventions, particularly in agricultural production and in the retail trade in order to protect jobs. (Luttwak 1999: pp. 116–126.) For the Japanese, as for the Europeans, lowering the barriers to imports of all agricultural products from the rest of the world is exceedingly painful. Yet that is the logic of globalization. Indeed, from the perspective of the South, it is a fundamental precondition for any kind of justice in the global economy.[20] Thus the Cairns Group of fifteen major agriculture-exporting countries, which includes both South Africa and Brazil, is pushing all members of the World Trade Organization hard for agreement on a mandate "for real liberalisation of trade in all agrifood products." This means, said a spokesperson for the group, "providing substantial improvements in market access, the elimination of trade distorting agricultural subsidies, and fairer trading rules."[21] And, one might add, avoidance of the misuse of "eco-labeling" as a way of raising nontariff barriers to entry. But in the face of strong resistance from powerful economies, such improvements are by no means guaranteed, particularly in practice.

Another dimension of trade negotiations that, from the South African perspective, are particularly difficult, relate to those with the European Union in the context of South Africa's membership of the Southern African Development Conference. Balancing the interests of Zambia and Zimbabwe against those of South Africa, where powerful trading blocs are in no mood to take prisoners in their negotiations, is not easy.

Job Creation Through Export Growth

Autarky is not an option, and South Africa, like the rest of the world, has to find its markets where it can. This is not the place for a detailed analysis of the country's trade and production policies.[22] We shall do no more than note five areas where South African thinking, more advanced in some sectors than in others, is seeking to use the opportunities of the new globalization to increase wealth and to create more jobs.

Competitive manufacturing. One model of what is possible is to be seen in the response of the South African automotive industry as it has shifted from its earlier program of import substitution to one of export promotion in the face of tariff reduction.[23] One particularly interesting development is to be seen in the growing ties with the German automotive industry, all of whose major producers have plants in South Africa. This is the only country in the world, outside of Germany, where this is the case, and it enabled South Africa in 1998 to export R3.9 billion (US$650 million) of components to Germany as well as to increase vehicle exports to Europe, Latin America, and the Indian Ocean rim (Black 1999: p. 29).

Services via the World Wide Web. South Africa has the infrastructure and the know-how to do far more than it has yet managed by way of using the Internet to create service jobs. The potential for developing a comparative advantage in a wide range of services—from typing telephone directories, to processing used airline tickets, to the maintenance and creation of software as has happened in India, for example— exists.[24] It remains to be imaginatively exploited.

Tourism. It hardly needs to be pointed out that South Africa has the global connections, the local infrastructure, the scenery, the political and cultural frisson, to become one of the major tourist destinations of the world. It also has the crown jewels, in the form of easy access to the "Big Five" game animals roaming its parks.[25] But can South Africa tame the crime that so discourages tourists? And if the crime is brought under control, can the country find a way of encouraging mass tourism that does not become destructive of precious aspects of the wider society?

Minerals: from extraction to benefaction. South Africa was caught up in the acceleration of globalization in the late nineteenth century essentially as an exporter of raw materials. One hundred years later these mineral exports remain significant but not sufficient to power a full-employment economy in the twenty-first century. But there is no reason why the forces behind the current acceleration of globalization cannot be used to ensure far greater benefaction or value added to these minerals in their country of origin. The future demand for gold will come not from the world's central bankers wishing to bury it in their vaults but from their wives, daughters, and sons wishing to wear it as jewelry.

Intensive small-scale agriculture. Alvin Toffler tells the story of the villagers in a remote part of China who use the Internet to market their garlic to a chain of restaurants in Europe.[26] South Africa has the potential, already well exploited by Chile, for example, to use its climate and its seasons for a massive expansion of its agricultural production. The dangers of falling prices through overproduction have to be watched very carefully in this sector, but market-niche opportunities abound, as a recent exporter of strawberry plants to Turkey has discovered.[27]

Education and Training

Elsewhere in this book[28] the human-capital legacy of apartheid and of South Africa's long history of racist colonialism is spelled out in some detail. It is here that the fundamental problem of globalization as it has taken place in the 1990s is most apparent. For the world is moving into an information economy in a context where the major legacy of racism within countries and of colonialism between them is that those who were exploited and marginalized in the past are least prepared to benefit from it, while the children and grandchildren of those who benefited in the past are more likely to have the education and the skills necessary to do well. It is in this context that Michael Lind's warning about the United States strikes a particularly ominous warning for all three countries, not the least of which is South Africa: "The chief danger confronting the twenty-first-century United States is not Balkanization but what might be called Brazilianization . . . [by which] I mean not the separation of cultures by race, but the separation of races by class" (quoted in Gray 1998: p. 117).

It is here that the greatest challenge lies: How, in economists' jargon, to overcome the racial distribution of human capital (in the form of education and training) embedded within national and international populations?[29] There seems to be no alternative to a long march through the transformation of the educational and training systems of each country. For South Africa, quite apart from the immense difficulties of getting the educational system (particularly primary and secondary schools) functioning adequately, there is the problem of finding ways of training large numbers of people to be able to manage institutions, schools, universities, and even small businesses so that they work. This lack of capacity is currently one of the most disabling weaknesses in the South African economy: perhaps the worst legacy of apartheid and one of the most urgent problems to be solved if the future is to be genuinely nonracial, just, and peaceful. It is in this context that countries like South Africa, desperately short of skilled persons, would want to argue the case for ensuring that OECD countries that import professionals (e.g., doctors) trained at great public expense in the South should pay back some of those costs by means of a levy.

Regional Perspectives

We can do no more here than to draw attention to the fact that, as noted above, South Africa is part of a wider regional economy to which it has been bound for a century and more by an unusual network of oscillating migration plus the usual ties of transport, investment, and trade. The implications of these links and the geographic bias in the pattern of capital accumulation that has resulted lie well beyond the scope of this chapter. But no consideration of appropriate policies in the face of globalization can ignore these aspects. Nor is it possible to ignore the fact that South Africa is caught, with the rest of the region, in a whirlwind whose outcome is likely to be even more devastating than most people yet understand. The onslaught of AIDS in Botswana, Malawi, and Zimbabwe, to name only three countries of the Southern African Development Council, has reduced the previously rising life expectancies by several years (UNDP 1999). South Africa has begun to feel the first gusts of the gale whose final impact seems likely, for a range of complex reasons, to be even more devastating. The only hope at this stage is international action, backed by the financial and medical resources of the OECD countries, to search for better drugs and to disseminate, in an affordable way, those that already exist.

Strengthening Global Rule of Law and Protocol

The AIDS crisis in Africa may require a degree of global solidarity that the world finds difficult. Yet all the forces of globalization point to the fact that we can no longer live in a laissez-faire environment where the rule of law is primarily conceived of within the boundaries of the nation-state. As John Gray concludes at the end of his analysis of global capitalism:

> A regime of global governance is needed in which world markets are managed so as to promote the cohesion of societies and the integrity of states. Only a framework of global regulation—of currencies, capital movements, trade and environmental conservation—can enable the creativity of the world economy to be harnessed in the service of human needs. (1998: p. 199)

As the industrial revolution spread from country to country during the nineteenth and twentieth centuries, the harsh effects of urbanization and industrialization were gradually tempered by the rise within each nation-state of trade unions, socialist movements, and other countervailing powers to reduce the levels of inequality through taxation and the funding of pensions, unemployment insurance, universal education, and so forth. The challenge of the twenty-first century will be to find appropriate ways of governing a democratic world whose economies are growing ever more interdependent but where the unevenness of globalization includes widening inequality between rich and poor and a process of fragmentation that divides "communities, nations and regions into those that are integrated and those that are excluded" (UNDP 1999: p. 36).

Good signs of the possibility of some form of global governance emerging include the fact that central bankers, recognizing their mutual vulnerability, are in regular close communication with each other (R. Solomon 1999; E. H. Solomon 1997: p. 213). Another sign is the quest for international uniformity in maritime law (Hare 1999). Other, more solid indications include the Montreal Protocol signed in 1989 to tackle the problem of the hole in the ozone layer (Benedick 1998). Indeed, the environmental movement, despite its despair at not making the impact on governments and multinational corporations that it would wish, is surely one of the most hopeful signs of the effectiveness of civil society in increasing global awareness and a sense of global responsibility.[30] Less hopeful signs include the extent of U.S. isolationism manifested in its refusal to sign so many painstakingly crafted international treaties including, more recently, those banning nuclear testing and the use of land mines. These refusals point also to the dangers, as perceived from the South, of the extent to which globalization can become a new form of imperialism, particularly when driven by the huge multinational corporations whose own budgets rival those of many industrial countries (UNDP 1999: p. 32). Another aspect of devising appropriate structures to regulate if not govern a democratic world is the need to find ways of redistributing resources beyond the boundaries of the nation-state. How can individual countries of powerful trading blocs move beyond the politics of aid to the politics of global solidarity? How is it possible to strengthen the rules of law and protocol at the global level in a way that takes into account the interests and views of all? Are those who live in countries that believe so strongly in democracy willing to extend the principle beyond the boundaries of the nation-state? These are tough questions, but they will not go away by being ignored. It is these to which the world will have to find answers in the twenty-first century if the process of globalization is not to tear the world apart in ways that we cannot now foresee.

Conclusion

Globalization, like urbanization that is driven by many of the same forces, is an inexorable process that cannot be wished away. But the way in which it manifests itself is not inevitable. Just as the novelists and reformers of the nineteenth and twentieth centuries have fought to humanize the process of urbanization that almost everywhere was brutal in its impact, so too the struggle of the twenty-first century will be to humanize the process of globalization, now rapidly accelerating under the impact of the new information technologies. The worst aspects of globalization, including widening inequalities and the extent to which people, countries, and regions can be marginalized, are not inevitable, but the ideology of the minimal state combined with the almost total absence of consciousness of the need for global government in some form makes it unlikely that countervailing pressures will be mounted without a long, uphill battle. Meanwhile, there remains the fact that the legacy of the racism embedded in a century and more of the industrial-ization of South Africa, as well as that of Brazil and the United States, will not easily be dissolved. The challenge of the century that lies ahead is how to harness the powerful forces of globalization for the sake of a common humanity rather than humanity allowing itself to exist for the sake of the current materialist values of globalization, which left to itself will simply divide the rich from the poor, the elite from the mar-ginalized, and the successful economies from the disintegrating states.[31]

Seen like this, the task seems almost too daunting to contemplate. But one insight that South Africans do have from their particular van-tage point is the realization, albeit grudging at times, that the view of the future from 2001 is infinitely better than it was in 1989. One unam-biguous good for which the process of globalization in recent years can take some of the credit has been the sweeping away of the legalized racism of apartheid. From a South African perspective, the first stage in the long march to a just society happened far sooner than anybody in the 1970s or 1980s believed was possible. The second stage will also be long and likewise require much perseverance, sacrifice, and vision. But why should it not also succeed?

Notes

1. For further details, see NASA's web site: <http:// www.nasa.gov>.

2. See Kenneth Boulding's seminal essay, "The Economics of the Coming Spaceship Earth" (1970).

3. It was in the introduction to the second edition of *The Sea Around Us* that Rachel Carson (author also of *The Silent Spring*) drew specific attention to the dangers of dumping radioactive nuclear waste into the ocean.

4. See fuller discussion in Benedick 1998.

5. The ambiguities of the meaning of "development" were first brought to this writer's attention by French-speaking colleagues with their scathing indictment of *un mot valise,* into which one packs whatever meaning one chooses for the occasion.

6. At Bretton Woods in New Hampshire.

7. Thailand's currency.

8. For details of these various crises and their link with international capital flows, see R. Solomon (1999: pp. 119 ff).

9. Friedman (1999: pp. 93 ff). It is worth noting that the instability of the electronic herd, its tendency to bolt, is likely to increase as a result of the "democratization of the market," whereby the number of individual U.S. investors buying and selling shares directly online has nearly trebled, from 3.7 million to 9.7 million in two years, 1997–1999. The assets being managed in these online brokerage accounts are expected to grow more than sevenfold from \$415 billion in 1999 to \$3 trillion in 2003. I am grateful to Steve Suitts for drawing my attention to this information from the report of the U.S. Securities and Exchange Commission to be found at <http://www.sec.gov/studies/cybex-sum.htm> .

10. See Portes and Vines (1997: p. 12) for proposals to deal, inter alia, with the volatility of capital flows and the lack of accepted mechanisms for a financially distressed country to work things out in an orderly manner.

11. World Trade Organization Secretariat 1999. The highest decisionmaking body of the World Trade Organization, the Council of Ministers of the member countries, met first in Singapore, 1996, then in Geneva in 1998. The third meeting opened in Seattle, November 30, 1999.

12. Group for Environmental Monitoring, Trade and Sustainable Development (1998: p. 1). See also OECD 1998.

13. Reidy 1997. I am grateful to Nigel Worden for drawing my attention to this work.

14. See Wilson and Ramphele (1989: pp. 190 ff) for further discussion.

15. See especially James and Lever, Chapter 2; O'Connell and Birdsall, Chapter 10.

16. See, for example, Elliot 1984.

17. See Thurow (1996: chapter 9) for a discussion of the inflation versus unemployment trade-off in the context of globalization. See also R. Solomon (1999: pp. 142 ff).

18. For a discussion of the East Asian crisis and the role of private capital flows, see R. Solomon (1999: pp. 129 ff).

19. For a careful analysis of the impact of the policy, see Tsikata 1999.

20. See Finn 1996, especially chapter 6, for a careful and perceptive analysis of the issues.

21. Speaking at the Commonwealth heads of government meeting in Durban. *Business Day*, November 12, 1999.

22. For an excellent critique, see Nattrass 1998.

23. For a detailed analysis, see Black 1999.

24. See, for example, "Indian Business: Spice Up Your Services," in the *Economist,* January 10-16, 1998.

25. Buffalo, elephant, leopard, lion, and rhinoceros.

26. On a visit to South Africa, October 1999.

27. I am grateful to Mrs. Wawa Damane for this information.

28. See above, as well as James and Lever, Chapter 2, and O'Connell and Birdsall, Chapter 10, of this volume.

29. See, in particular, Lam 1999.

30. See, for example, Ray (1995: chapter 15).

31. See, for example, Korten 1990.

References

Ashton T. S. 1948. *The Industrial Revolution 1760–1830*. London: Home University Library.

Bane, P. William, and Stephen P. Bradley. 1999. "The Light at the End of the Pipe." *Scientific American* (October).

Benedick, Richard E. 1998. *Ozone Diplomacy: New Directions in Safeguarding the Planet*. 2nd ed. Cambridge MA: Harvard University Press.

Black, Anthony. 1999. "The South African Automotive Industry in a Globalizing World." Unpublished paper. University of Cape Town (September).

Boulding, Kenneth. 1970 [1966]. "The Economics of the Coming Spaceship Earth." Republished in *Beyond Economics: Essays on Society, Religion and Ethics*. Ann Arbor: University of Michigan.

Burbach, Roger, Orlando Nunez, and Boris Kagarlitsky. 1997. *Globalization and Its Discontents: The Rise of Post-modern Socialisms*. London: Pluto Press.

Business Day. 1999 (November 12).

Carson, Rachel. 1961. *The Sea Around Us*. Oxford: Oxford University Press.

———. 1962. *The Silent Spring*. London: Hamilton.

Castells, Manuel. 1993. "The Informational Economy and the New International Division of Labour," in M. Carnoy et al., eds., *The New Global Economy in the Information Age*. University Park: Pennsylvania State University Press.

Doyle, Rodger. 1999. "Income Inequality in the U.S." *Scientific American* (June).

Economist. 1998. "Indian Business: Spice Up Your Services" (January 10-16).

———. 1999. "The Battle in Seattle" (November 27-December 3).

Elliot, Charles. 1984. "The Economics of Transition: Some Notes on the

Supply Side," Carnegie Conference Paper, no. 137. Cape Town: Self-published.

Ellsworth, P. T., and J. Clark Leith. 1975. *The International Economy*. 5th ed. New York: Macmillan.

Finn, Daniel. 1996. *Just Trading: On the Ethics and Economics of International Trade*. Nashville: Abingdon Press.

Friedman, Thomas L. 1999. *The Lexus and the Olive Tree*. New York: Farrar, Strauss and Giroux.

Gray, John. 1998. *False Dawn: The Delusions of Global Capitalism*. New York: The New Press.

Group for Environmental Monitoring, Trade and Sustainable Development. 1998. *A Guide for the Perplexed*. Johannesburg: Self-published.

Hage, Dave. 1999. "Bitter Harvest." *The Nation* (October 11).

Hare, John. 1999. "Of Black Books, White Horses and Sacred Cows: The Quest for International Uniformity in Maritime Law." Unpublished address to the British Maritime Law Association, London (November 11).

Kenwood, A. G., and A. L. Lougheed. 1983. *The Growth of the International Economy 1820–1980*. London: George Allen and Unwin.

Korten, David C. 1990. *Getting to the 21st Century*. West Hartford, CT: Kumarian Press.

Lam, David. 1999. "Generating Extreme Inequality: Schooling, Earnings, and Intergenerational Transmission of Human Capital in South Africa and Brazil." Research Report no. 99-439, Population Studies Center, University of Michigan (August).

Luttwak, Edward. 1999. *Turbo-Capitalism: Winners and Losers in the Global Economy*. New York: HarperCollins.

McGrew, Anthony. 1998. *Understanding Globalization: The Nation-State, Democracy and Economic Policies in the New Epoch*. Stockholm: Swedish Ministry for Foreign Affairs.

National Aeronautics and Space Administration (NASA). 1999. Web site: <http://www.nasa.gov> (November).

Nattrass, Nicoli. 1998. "Globalisation, Employment and Labour Market Institutions in South Africa," Working Paper 14. Potchefstroom: South African Network for Economic Research (November).

Organization for Economic Cooperation and Development (OECD). 1998. *Globalisation and the Environment: Perspectives from OECD and Dynamic Non-member Economies*. Paris: OECD.

Portes, Richard, and David Vines. 1997. *Coping with International Capital Flows*. London: Commonwealth Secretariat.

Project for Statistics on Living Standards and Development. 1994. *South Africans Rich and Poor: Baseline Household Statistics*. Cape Town: SAL-DRU.

Ray, James L. 1995. *Global Politics*. 6th ed. Boston: Houghton Mifflin.

Reidy, M. C. 1997. "The Admission of Slaves and 'Prize Slaves' into the Cape Colony, 1797–1818." Master's thesis, University of Cape Town.

Security and Exchange Commission. 1999. At <http://www.sec.gov/studies/cybexsum.htm> (December).

Solomon, E. H. 1997. *Virtual Money: Understanding the Power and Risks of*

Money's High-Speed Journey into Electronic Space. Oxford: Oxford University Press.

Solomon, Robert. 1999. Quoting IMF's "World Economic Outlook" (May 1997) in *Money on the Move: The Revolution in International Finance Since 1980.* Princeton: Princeton University Press.

South Africans Rich and Poor: Baseline Household Statistics—SALDRU. 1994. Cape Town: SALDRU.

Sunday Independent. 1999 (September 12).

Tandon, Yash. 1999. "Globalization and Africa's Options." *Journal of Development Economics for Southern Africa* 1, nos. 4 and 5 (April).

Thurow, Lester. 1996. *The Future of Capitalism.* London: Nicholas Brealey Publishing.

Thygesen, Niels, Yutaka Kosai, and Robert Z. Lawrence. 1996. *Globalization and Trilateral Labor Markets: Evidence and Implications.* New York, Paris, and Tokyo: Trilateral Commission.

Toffler, Alvin. 1980. *The Third Wave.* London: William Collins.

Tsikata, Yvonne M. 1999. "Liberalization and Trade Performance in South Africa." Informal discussion paper. Washington, DC: World Bank.

United Nations Development Programme (UNDP). 1999. *Human Development Report 1999.* New York: Oxford University Press.

Weizenbaum, Joe. 1980. "Once More, The Computer Revolution," in Tom Forester, ed., *The Microelectronics Revolution.* Oxford: Basil Blackwell.

Wilson, F. 1995. "South Africa: The Problems in a Deeply Divided Society," in A. K. Bagchi, ed., *Democracy and Development.* London: Macmillan.

———. 1998. "Sustainability, Full Employment and Globalization: Contradictions or Complements?" in Julio de Santa Ana, ed., *Sustainability and Globalization.* Geneva: WCC Publications.

Wilson F., and M. Ramphele. 1989. *Uprooting Poverty: The South African Challenge.* New York: W. W. Norton.

World Bank. 1995. *Workers in an Integrating World: World Development Report 1995.* New York: Oxford University Press.

———. 1999. *Entering the 21st Century: World Development Report 1999/2000.* New York: Oxford University Press, table 1, pp. 230–231.

———. 1981. *World Development Report 1981.* New York: Oxford University Press, table 1, p. 135.

World Trade Organization (WTO). 1999. "Roots: From Havana to Marrakesh." <http://www.wto.org/> (November 13).

World Trade Organization Secretariat. 1999. *Trade and Environment Report.* Geneva: WTO.

12

GDP Increases from Ending Long-Term Discrimination Against Blacks

Jonas Zoninsein

THIS CHAPTER ARGUES that discrimination against blacks and the resulting racial inequality generate an economic cost that is paid by the entire
society in Brazil, South Africa, and the United States. High rates of
unemployment, gaps in the accumulation of human capital, and concentrated poverty among blacks translate into lower than optimal levels of
resource utilization, aggregate production and income, and the creation
of wealth for these nations.

Since its inception, capitalism has reproduced socioeconomic
inequality between whites and blacks. This morally unacceptable outcome is continuously replicated in our nations in spite of many collective
action and reform efforts oriented to eliminate discrimination against
blacks. The autonomous existence of racial discrimination as a social
practice, independent from and previous to modern capitalism, as well as
racial discrimination's positive feedback with capitalist relations in production and distribution, explain its long-term presence and persistence.
"Genocide, slavery, disenfranchisement, violence, poverty, segregation,
and ghettoization are the backdrops for contemporary discrimination"
(Albeida, Drago, and Shulman 1997). This downside of the civilizatory
process is much older than capitalism. But it is also its contemporary.

This chapter stresses that the proper conceptualization of racial discrimination is a crucial requirement for its measurement both as a
national and a global phenomena, and for the formulation of effective
policies and programs oriented to dismantle this perverse mechanism
that works against the quality of life of the majority populations of
Brazil and South Africa, and in the United States as well. Neoclassical
economics and political economy constitute two available paradigms
that guide the conceptualization of racial discrimination and inequality

as an economic phenomena. The first section of this chapter evaluates how these theories can contribute to explain the system-wide mechanisms of long-term discrimination against blacks and of racial inequality. This section also describes how long-term discrimination against blacks leads to a less than optimal rate of growth of aggregate production and income in a market economy.

The long-term and global nature of racial discrimination are then demonstrated. The significant potential gains in GDP due to ending long-term discrimination against blacks in Brazil, South Africa, and the United States show the pervasive nature of the phenomena. These gains also demonstrate that the public-policy programs implemented so far to eliminate racial discrimination and inequality in these economies are incomplete. The next section tentatively proposes a posthegemonic approach to challenge racism and racial discrimination at the local, national, and global levels. The final section summarizes the argument of the chapter and suggests directions for political initiatives and future networking.

Explaining Long-Term
Racial Discrimination in Capitalism

This section compares the neoclassical notion of labor market discrimination with the political-economy concept of system-wide discrimination. It argues that discrimination against blacks simultaneously occurs in many markets and institutions of modern society and that a measurement of its economic costs must consider the overall impact of long-term discrimination. The strength of the political-economy approach results from its emphasis on a dynamic model of competitive markets and on the interactions among the multiple instances in which oppression and discrimination against blacks take place. The following summary of the neoclassical and political-economy models relies on my synthesis of the classical theory of competition and persistent wage differentials developed by Botwinick (1993) and the political-economy model of racial and gender discrimination proposed by Albeida, Drago, and Shulman (1997).

Discrimination in Labor Markets
According to Neoclassical Economics

The neoclassical or mainstream model of competition argues that discrimination in labor markets is not long-lasting; discrimination in labor markets can take the form of lower wages for blacks relative to that of whites with the same skill levels and performing similar productive tasks under similar working conditions; job segregation of blacks into lower-paying jobs; and higher unemployment and underemployment rates for blacks relative to whites. Widespread persistent discrimination is ultimately explained by the lack of competition among employers and employees, and/or incomplete and imperfect information in labor markets.

The "taste" or "preference for discrimination" by employers generates higher costs because it restricts competition. These higher costs are directly paid for by the discriminating agents and translate into higher prices for labor power. For neoclassicals, this type of discrimination in the labor markets is efficient in allocative terms since it expresses the use of scarce resources according to the preferences of economic agents. Subsequently, this chapter demonstrates that long-term discrimination is suboptimal from a dynamic point of view. Society as a whole pays for the costs of unemployment and underemployment of resources and slower formation of human capital over multiple production periods by accepting reduced production, income, and national wealth.

Neoclassical economists assume that competition coupled with the diversity of tastes and preferences eliminates labor market discrimination. Competition among employers should increase production and profits due to the expanding presence of employers without a preference for discrimination who are willing to hire from a larger pool of applicants. Labor market discrimination may also occur when employers judge an individual candidate's abilities based on incomplete or imperfect knowledge of his or her potential performance characteristics. For example, employers may believe that blacks will perform poorly in the job due to weaker education, problems in their homes or their community, or social isolation. When the cost of obtaining additional information about an individual candidate and the profile of a certain group is high, employers may discriminate "statistically" against a particular individual. Statistical discrimination is inefficient in allocative terms since hiring of candidates is conducted on the basis of incomplete and imperfect information. In addition, because testing may present positive externalities, it is undersupplied by the market.

Again, neoclassical theory predicts that competition would eliminate statistical discrimination in labor markets. Competitive employers would have an incentive to introduce better and cheaper tests and assessments of the qualifications and the potential performance of individual candidates and specific groups. Innovations in tests and assessments can enable employers to expand profits when the gains in profits resulting from identifying and hiring highly productive individuals would outweigh the additional costs involved in designing and implementing innovative tests and assessments.

Since competition is supposed to eliminate labor market discrimination against blacks, neoclassical economists add two arguments when confronted with the evidence of persistent discrimination. First, labor market discrimination is disappearing, but the market may be slow in producing its effects due to ad hoc institutional rigidities, including lack of government action in promoting the free operation of markets. Alternatively, consumers in product markets where employees are highly visible may maintain discrimination against blacks and be willing to pay the additional costs required as a result of their prejudice.

Orthodox microeconomics measure labor market discrimination by identifying actual income differences among racial and ethnic groups and using statistical analysis to break the differences down into those categories that can be explained by employers' discrimination and those that are explained by productivity-linked characteristics, such as formal education, experience, type of occupation, geographical location of the markets, and residence of the employees, among others. The residual left after these additional variables are taken into account is used as a measure of the racial discrimination in the labor markets.[1]

Toward a Political Economy of Long-Term Discrimination

The neoclassical notion of labor market discrimination is incomplete and misleading. It does not explain how free competition in itself produces income differentials among equally qualified workers who labor under similar conditions. This myopia is due to the perception of economic agents as simply price takers, thereby abstracting many crucial elements of real-world competition. It treats competition and markets unilaterally as a process leading to an equilibrium in prices and quantities, and to the homogenization of the technical conditions of production and the profit rates within and between industries. The continuous revolution in the technical conditions of production, the re-creation of technological rents in different industries and firms, the evolution of the skills required by constantly redesigned labor processes, the changes in distribution of property rights, and access to finance, among other structural economic variables, are omitted from the study of free competition. As a corollary, neoclassicals fail to explain the nonending interaction of disequilibrium and equilibrium tendencies that produce permanent hierarchies in the technical methods of production and productivity of the labor force, in the level of skills of the labor force, and in the rates of profit within individual industries and across the economy as a whole.

The political-economy approach to competitive markets, by contrast, takes this permanent heterogeneity in the technical and economic conditions of production as the basis for understanding the factors and circumstances that produce substantive intra- and interindustry wage differentials among workers with similar skills and the constant generation of jobs with substandard working conditions and below-average wage rates. In addition, the political-economy perspective treats involuntary unemployment and underemployment as permanent elements of an economy that requires restraint over demands for higher wages and strict discipline in the labor process. Third, its method takes into account the impact of the uneven (and sometimes racially discriminatory) efforts to organize workers to raise the wage rate against the downward pressures from managers and unemployed workers and to improve working conditions.

The political economy of competitive wages, prices, and profit-rates determination also recognizes that increases in the productivity of labor within individual industries and in the economy as a whole do provide relevant limits to increases in the level of wages since the profitability of capital must be protected, but they do not automatically determine the level of wages. As a matter of fact, increases in the productivity of labor can occur simultaneously with declining real wages, as illustrated by the experience of the U.S. economy since the 1970s.

These components of the political-economy approach constitute the analytical framework for explaining the discriminatory pattern of a disproportionate number of blacks to low-paying jobs and to the pool of the unemployed and underemployed individuals, their lower wages and salaries relative to whites with similar skills, and their less developed skills relative to whites. Racial discrimination interacts with the process of economic growth through a variety of channels and effects.

The accumulation effects of racial discrimination occur when employers and managers discriminate or induce discrimination against blacks by employees to reduce collective action by labor in a common struggle over wages. The wages of both blacks and whites would thus fall and the expected profits would increase. Productivity effects may result from employers' use of race to divide labor and reinforce managerial control over the organization and intensity of the labor process. Productivity effects also occur when discrimination influences negatively the skills of blacks. Distributional effects among diverse racial groups may take place when racial discrimination improves the chances of the nondiscriminated employees to earn higher wages, be promoted, enhance job security, benefit from tighter networks, reinforce job segregation, and accumulate human capital faster. Distributional effects affect the composition of aggregate demand and the direction of technical change.

The net impact of these effects on the profitability of capital and the rate of economic growth will depend on the interplay of all these forces under the specific historical conditions in each country, including the particular phases of the business cycle. In general, however, it is reasonable to argue that there might be a path to economic growth where elimination of discrimination against blacks reinforces a positive cycle of income redistribution and lower levels of unemployment. Elimination of racial discrimination could generate (via increased trade union strength, increased cooperation in the labor process, and enhanced accumulation of human capital) a sustained increase in the wage rate, aggregate demand, production, and profits.

Contrary to neoclassical economics, the political-economy approach incorporates into the analysis of racial discrimination those factors that influence the levels of employment, the skills and productivity of the labor force, particularly those of blacks. Some examples of the components of a system-wide feedback mechanism leading to lower skills and higher levels of unemployment among blacks are: the legal systems of racial segregation; the unequal distribution of property rights over capital assets among the races; the uneven strength of civil society; labor market discrimination by employers; geographical, residential, educational, and occupational segregation; and the unequal effectiveness of government programs, particularly in the areas of public safety, human security, and education.

The full construction of a political-economy model of discrimination against blacks, however, requires a detailed discussion of the historical forces that have reproduced their own particular forms of racial discrimination in different nations, markets, and institutions. Some patterns can illuminate in broad terms this discussion. Poverty, social isolation, and the decay of civil and economic society among blacks probably reinforce gaps in the differential accumulation of skills. Anecdotal and incomplete information on these differential skills facilitate the formation of stereotypes regarding blacks and supports white discrimination against blacks, thereby contributing to maintaining blacks in poverty. Geographical, residential, and educational segregation facilitate job segregation and the slower development of skills, lead to the lower productivity of blacks relative to whites, and income inequality, thus reinforcing racial discrimination in the financial and real estate markets as well. Demand discrimination in the labor market may discourage blacks (particularly teenagers) from investing in education. Their less developed skills and inevitable higher-than-average unemployment rates then reinforce prejudices and discrimination by employers.

One crucial aspect in these interactions is the impact of system-wide racial discrimination on the accumulation of human capital by blacks. Wealthy countries and communities not only have access to a larger and more technologically advanced stock of physical capital, but through investment of time and money in education and training, they can generate a larger and more effective stock of human capital. Human capital refers to the labor force that is sufficiently skilled to operate sophisticated machinery; that can contribute to the implementation of new methods of economic activity; and that can enhance the positive impact of teams and organizations in the production and delivery of goods and services. By investing in education and training, households and employees not only raise the market value of the labor power that they can supply in the future, but they have a positive impact on productivity and the rate of growth of the economy.[2]

A more specific dimension emphasized by the political-economy approach to racial discrimination is the influence of average human capital and the socialization mechanisms of a community on the effectiveness of the investment of households and individuals in education and training. Elimination of overt discrimination against blacks in the labor market and affirmative-action programs contribute to reducing overall income inequality among whites and blacks and increase the social and geographic mobility of the most advantaged black individuals. However, this process of upward mobility among some blacks together with the relocation of economic activity can leave behind a large and impoverished black community. In such a geographically segregated and socially isolated community, civil society, economic society, and local government would experience a decline in their joint ability to deliver the incentives and instruments to promote further investment by households and individuals in human capital.

The trend of the segmentation of black communities is aggravated when the computer and communications revolution and the growing international mobility of capital—as currently observed in the economies of Brazil, South Africa, and the United States—eliminate high wages in the manufacturing sector and expand employment for less skilled employees through outsourcing operations and in the tertiary and informal sectors of economic activity. Under these circumstances, past discrimination and income inequality may indefinitely affect future generations of blacks.

Methods to measure long-term discrimination must be able to capture the multifactor processes as well as their impact on aggregate employment, production, and income as described above. The next section presents a methodology for the international and comparative study of discrimination against blacks, one that quantifies the system-wide impact of long-term racial discrimination and the resulting loss of optimality in economic performance.

A Preliminary Measure of
Long-Term Discrimination Against Blacks

This section presents estimates of the economic gains that society as a whole would accrue by terminating long-term discrimination against blacks and the cycle of racial inequality in Brazil, South Africa, and the United States. The concepts and methodology adopted to estimate the gains in gross domestic product (GDP) that would follow when income inequality between blacks and whites is eliminated are based on the original work of Andrew Brimmer (1966, 1995). Brimmer calculated the gains for the economy of the United States as a whole, which originated from two sources: (1) the gains in aggregate production and income arising from the fuller use of the existing education, skills, and experience of the black population; and (2) the gains in aggregate production and income due to developing the potential education, skills, and experience of the black population to levels similar to that of whites. The joint outcome of the two effects translates into the potential gains that would accrue to GDP if inequality in earnings due to labor market discrimination and the human-capital gap of blacks relative to whites were eliminated.

The materialization of these potential gains can only occur over various generations as the legacy of past and current discrimination against blacks is overcome and both the labor force and capital assets are restructured, leading to significant productive, geographic, and occupational changes in the economy. The prerequisites and accompanying conditions for the materialization of the potential gains from overcoming long-term racial discrimination raise timely questions about the appropriate economic strategy, which will be enunciated in the next section of this chapter. The relevance of Brimmer's work lies in its demonstration of the gains for society as a whole (not just for the blacks) if the loss of optimality of the market economy resulting from racial discrimination and income inequality were consistently avoided in the future.

Brimmer's first step was to estimate the gain to the economy that would occur if the educational achievement of American blacks was fully used. The U.S. Census Bureau's *Current Population Reports on Money Income of Households, Families, and Persons in the United States* provided Brimmer with the primary data to initially answer the following question: What would be the gain in GDP if blacks with a given level of education had the same average earnings as whites in the jobs that blacks actually hold? For each age-sex-education group reported by the U.S. Census Bureau, the mean earnings of blacks were multiplied by the number of persons in each category and the results totaled to produce the amount of money income received by blacks in a given year. This money level was called the "Base Case." Next, for each of the same age-sex-education categories, the mean earnings of blacks was changed to equal the mean earnings of whites and the multiplication and summation operations used in the Base Case were repeated. The resulting percentage increases in earnings were called the "Adjusted Case I: Full Use of Present Education."

Brimmer's second step consisted of estimating the gain in income that would result if the educational levels of blacks would improve to the point where they equaled the levels achieved by whites, and if blacks had the same mean earnings as whites at the same level of education. The percentage increases in earnings resulting from these calculations relative to the Adjusted Case I were called the "Adjusted Case II: Full Use of Improved Education." Table 12.1 presents the Adjusted Cases I and II for 1992 as well as the "Adjusted Case III: Total Gain from Full Use of Present and Improved Education," which results from adding the first two percentage increases in earnings of blacks. (Brimmer presents estimates for 1967, 1973, 1979, and 1992.)

As a third step, Brimmer used the percentage increases in earnings to estimate total gains in GDP. These gains in GDP consisted of increments in both labor and capital incomes. Initially, the wage and salary components of GDP were raised by the percentage increases in earnings reported in Adjusted Cases I, II, and III. In addition, Brimmer also introduced an ad hoc procedure of raising the entrepreneurial component of GDP by one-half the percentage increase in wage and salary income for Adjusted Cases I, II, and III. This entrepreneurial component was not included in the estimates presented below.

Table 12.1   **Gains in GDP from Eliminating Income Inequality Between Blacks and Whites (%) in Brazil, South Africa, and the United States**

	Brazil (1990)	South Africa (1993)	United States (1992)
Gains in earnings from full use of the educational achievements of blacks:			
Adjusted Case I: Full use of present education			2.70
Adjusted Case II: Full use of improved education			2.04
Adjusted Case III: Total gains from full use of present and improved education	24.94	183.70	4.74
Gains in GDP derived from an increase in the component of wages and salaries	9.04	96.60	2.80

*Sources :*Brazil, Fundação Instituto Brasileiro de Geografia e Estatística. *Pesquisa Nacional por Amostra de Domicílios - PNAD* de 1990 (Rio de Janeiro: FIBGE, 1991); Fundação Getúlio Vargas. "As Contas Nacionais de 1980–1981." *Conjuntura Econômica* 47, no. 1 (January 1993). South Africa, *South Africa Rich and Poor: Baseline Household Statistics—SALDRU* (Cape Town: SALDRU, 1994); International Monetary Fund, *South Africa—Selected Economic Issues* (Washington, DC: IMF, July 1996 and September 1997). United States, Andrew F. Brimmer. "The Economic Cost of Discrimination Against Black Americans," in Margaret Simmons, ed., *Economic Perspectives on Affirmative Action* (Washington, DC: Joint Center for Political and Economic Studies, 1995).

The methodology adopted for estimating the gains in GDP for Brazil and South Africa followed the steps adopted by Brimmer to the extent permitted by the available data. Some relevant adjustments were introduced to take into account the more aggregated nature of the primary data available in Brazilian and South African statistical sources on the incomes of different racial groups. In both the Brazilian and South African cases, the available information about the income differentials of distinct races did not consider specific age and education groups.

For Brazil, the Base and Adjusted Case III data were calculated on the basis of the average monthly labor income of employed individuals published by the Pesquisa Nacional por Amostra de Domicílios (PNAD) de 1990 (1990 National Survey of Household Statistics). Table 12.2 presents the original data used to generate the results presented in Table 12.1. The Base Case was obtained by calculating the actual income of each racial group described in the 1990 statistics. The Adjusted Case III was obtained in the following way: for each sex, the mean income of blacks and mulattos was changed to equal the mean income of whites and the results summed to produce the amount of total labor income to be generated if income inequality was eliminated. The final step was to use the percentage increase in income from labor to estimate gains in GDP. The wage and salary component of GDP was raised by the percentage increase in income reported in the Adjusted Case III.

For South Africa, the Base and Adjusted Case III were calculated by using the income distribution data from the 1994 report *South Africans Rich and Poor: Baseline Household Statistics*, published by SALDRU. Table 12.3 shows the original data used to generate the results presented in Table 12.1. The Base Case was obtained by calcu lating the actual household income of each racial group observed in 1993, taking into account the differences between male- and female-headed households. All sources of household income were included (regular wage, casual labor, self-employment, agriculture, remittances, rent, other), since the SALDRU report does not present individual income differentials for each type of income and according to the sex of

Table 12.2   Brazil: Average Monthly Labor Income of Employed Individuals by Race and Sex, 1990

	Income		Population	
	Cruzeiros (1990)	%	Millions	%
Total	24,956		144.06	100.0
Male	29,388		70.73	
Female	16,924		73.33	
White	32,212		79.67	55.3
Male	38,254	100.0	38.64	
Female	21,507	100.0	41.03	
Black	13,295		7.06	4.9
Male	15,578	40.7	3.49	
Female	9,682	45.0	3.57	
Mulatto	15,308		56.62	39.3
Male	17,817	46.6	28.31	
Female	10,498	48.8	28.31	

Source: Fundação Instituto Brasileiro de Geografia e Estatística, *Pesquisa Nacional por Amostra de Domicílios—PNAD de 1990* (Rio de Janeiro: FIBGE, 1991).

Table 12.3   South Africa: Average Monthly Household Income by Race and Sex of the Head of Household, 1994

	Number of Households	Income Rand(1994)	Income %
Total	8,240,000	2,089	
Male-headed	6,122,000	2,417	
Female-headed	2,117,000	1,142	
White	1,417,100	6,394	
Male-headed	1,209,500	6,930	100
Female-headed	207,600	3,269	100
African	5,990,000	1,005	
Male-headed	4,252,000	1,075	15.5
Female-headed	1,737,900	833	25.5
Colored	617,100	2,057	
Male-headed	476,300	2,199	31.7
Female-headed	140,800	1,576	48.2
Indian	215,800	4,009	
Male-headed	184,200	4,320	
Female-headed	31,600	2,199	

Source: *South Africans Rich and Poor: Baseline Household Statistics—SALDRU* (Cape Town: SALDRU, 1994).

the individual. The Adjusted Case III was obtained by applying to the income of African and colored households a procedure similar to the one used for the Brazilian estimate. The final step used the percentage increase in total household incomes to estimate gains in GDP. To maintain uniformity in the procedures, the wage and salary component of GDP was raised by the percentage increases in income reported in the Adjusted Case III.

The resulting gains in GDP are summarized in Table 12.1. The cost of racial inequality for society as a whole is visible in the three countries. The economies of Brazil, South Africa, and the United States would expand by 9.04, 96.60, and 2.80 percent, respectively, as a result of potentially ending long-term racial discrimination against blacks.

The 96.6 percent estimate for South Africa fully illustrates the loss of optimality in a market economy due to long-term racial discrimination. There, since the oppressive system of apartheid was eliminated only recently, income differentials between whites and blacks are significantly larger than in either Brazil and the United States. Blacks (Africans and coloreds) constitute 85 percent of the population, compared to 44 percent in Brazil and 12 percent in the United States. If blacks had the same average earnings and productivity as whites, the South African economy would practically double in size. The current GDP per capita of US$3,200 would increase to a level close to that of US$6,000. In the case of the United States, not only is the income gap between blacks and whites significantly less than that of South Africa and Brazil, but blacks represent a significantly smaller proportion of the total population. As a consequence, the potential effect of ending long-term discrimination against blacks in the United States is comparatively smaller.

This macroeconomic view indicates the critical relevance of adopting a specific strategy oriented toward promoting the end of long-term racial discrimination as an instrument for improving overall economic performance in Brazil, South Africa, and the United States. The acceleration of human-capital accumulation by blacks, lower levels of unemployment, and the end of labor market discrimination against blacks would generate a positive impact on the productivity of labor, and aggregate production and income. In case this strategy were simultaneously adopted in these three countries (and others where racial discrimination exists), its synergistic effects on global economic performance would produce even larger effects than those presented in this chapter, due to the additional opportunities created for international trade and investment.

Affirmative Action and Beyond: A Five-Part Model of Social Agency

The analyses presented in the previous sections indicate that the policies oriented to eliminate long-term discrimination against blacks in Brazil, South Africa, and the United States ought to supersede affirmative action. Affirmative action must be linked to and supplemented by multiple and simultaneous public-policy efforts oriented to: (1) accelerating the accumulation of human capital, and (2) promoting lower levels of unemployment and underemployment among blacks and the less skilled population in general.[3]

These linkages can be explored with reference to the recent proposal from President Clinton's Advisory Board for the Initiative on Race to hire 35,000 new teachers to work at low-income-area schools in the United States. This proposal addresses simultaneously the failures and decay of primary and secondary education in the poorer neighborhoods and the need to supplement affirmative action with programs oriented to increasing university recruitment and retention of black students. Although this specific proposal moves public policy in the right direction, its success will depend on how this government initiative is articulated with other levels that decisively impact upon education.

Critics of affirmative action emphasize the need for universities to open their doors to disadvantaged individuals without resorting to what they call "preferential treatment" based on race and/or gender. For many of these critics, increases in the effectiveness of primary and secondary education through privatization and supply competition would smoothly expand opportunities for the economically and educationally disadvantaged without lowering university admission standards.

This policy approach, however, assumes that education failure and decay are mainly problems of excessive bureaucracy and faculty and staff complacency. Critics of affirmative action simplify matters to mobilize the support of families with diverse backgrounds who, together with black families, are most directly suffering the impact of the computer revolution, downsizing, industrial capital relocation, and real wage decline. The forces behind supply of K–12 education, nevertheless, are significantly more complex. They include the multiple factors present in the process of socialization and emotional transformation by which children develop into adults and productive citizens. As a consequence, the reform of the primary and secondary school systems must rely on a model of agency broader than the newest offspring of laissez-faire economics, so-called school choice.

I suggest the following five-part model of social agency to accelerate the accumulation of human capital among blacks and other disadvantaged social groups who have experienced the negative impact of long-term discrimination.[4] This five-part model differentiates among the state, civil society, economic society, political society, and markets. Civil society is that sphere of social interaction composed of a variety of uncoerced associations and relational networks formed for the sake of family, faith, interest, and ideology. Political and economic society are mediating institutions through which civil society articulates with political/administrative and market processes. Political society includes political parties, organizations, and public institutions such as parliaments and congresses. Economic society is composed of the organizations of production and distribution, as well as institutions of collective bargaining, unions, and trade associations.

Policies and programs oriented toward moving societies beyond racial discrimination must address in practice all these levels of agency. Anyone willing to develop an all-encompassing approach to promote primary and secondary education reform in inner cities and impoverished neighborhoods will immediately perceive the usefulness of this five-part model. The joint and interactive role of families, PTAs, community and religious organizations, local political and business leaderships, as well as existing school administrations and faculty will crucially determine the effectiveness and rapidity with which these additional 35,000 teachers can perform their work.

The success in moving public policy beyond affirmative action will also depend on the scope and direction of the country's general economic policy. Economic conditions such as the availability of jobs and accessibility of living standards above poverty levels not only constitute minimum general conditions for parents' involvement in the education of their children, community work, and citizenship enhancement, but also contribute to dilute the circumstances that feed into racial prejudice and discrimination in the labor market. Simultaneous with the interactive efforts mentioned in the previous paragraphs, previous sections of this chapter demonstrate that successful economic policies targeted to reduce long-term racial discrimination must decrease unemployment levels and increase the rate of creation of higher-paying jobs.

In the United States, the rate of unemployment has been falling continuously since mid-1992 (in June 1998 it was at 4.3 percent, a twenty-eight-year low). The rate of inflation also has declined between 1991 until the end of 1995 and has stabilized at very low levels since the end of 1995. GDP growth, employment growth, and labor force growth were all significantly higher since the end of 1995 than was expected. These levels contradict the view held by the majority of mainstream economists (and maintained, despite hard evidence to the contrary) that any attempt to push up GDP growth would be inflationary and destabilizing.

This suggests that there is room for adopting sensible growth-oriented policies by both promoting increases in labor force productivity (in part by raising public investment in infrastructure, K–12 education, job training, and civilian research and development) and allowing a gradual decline in unemployment rates with a flexible monetary policy.

Furthermore, the inflation costs of unemployment even lower than the current level could be small, tolerable, and easily reversed if prudence were one of the components of an expansionary policy.

Additionally, the design of economic policy should take into account the challenge posed by the increasing global mobility of capital for the sustainability of high and stable rates of economic growth and job creation. The last few decades show that the simple presence of capital controls in developing countries such as Brazil and South Africa does not preclude the possibility that unsound domestic policies may provoke excessive inflationary pressures, capital flight, balance-of-payment crises, and economic stagnation. The financial constraints to full employment and income redistribution apply, independent of financial globalization. In order to sustain the momentum of economic expansion, a prudent economic policy pursuing economic growth, the redistributive goals associated with full employment, and the social and redistributive programs of the welfare state must make sure that they do not create a wage-price spiral, a public debt spiral, or an unsound financial system.

However, for countries pursuing well-designed economic transformation programs associated with higher value-added production and the generation of rents from high technology, capital controls and a dose of domestic financial repression may provide the additional room and lagtime necessary for the maturation of new investment projects. Well-designed economic development plans create indigenously the noninflationary resources for redistributive and human-capital programs. When the investment projects are wisely selected, the increases in economic activity, profits, tax revenues, and exports can generate the amount and the composition of saving required to replenish the revolving fund (domestic and external) originally used to finance such investments. The financial crises of the 1980s and 1990s in developing as well as developed countries suggest that the constraints on developmental and redistributive economic programs are tighter in conditions of financial opening and globalization.

Economic growth cum macroeconomic stability in developing countries requires, therefore, that subsidies for capital formation, public investment in education and training, and transfers of technology must be paid for by noninflationary fiscal resources. Supporters of financial opening and liberalization naively recommend the complementary expansion of domestic saving based on a poor understanding of the sources of financial development. Contrary to their views, increases in foreign finance only complement domestic sources of finance when an autonomous national strategy of both economic growth and investment funding is simultaneously put in place, as suggested by the late development experiences of Germany, Japan, and the East Asian "tigers."

Summary and Conclusion

The political economy of racial discrimination discussed above argues that labor market discrimination against blacks, their higher-than-average levels of unemployment and underemployment, and their gap in the accumulation of human capital relative to the labor force as a whole, all influence aggregate production, income, and national economic growth. The estimates of the macroeconomic effect of racial discrimination provide empirical support for this theoretical proposition and suggest the significant negative impact of long-term discrimination against blacks on production and income in Brazil, South Africa, and the United States.

The challenge of the twenty-first century is to move society, in practice, beyond racism and long-term discrimination against blacks. The global nature of this project has been imposed by the black diaspora in the last five centuries and the continuing losses of wealth accumulation due to discrimination against blacks on three continents and in a multitude of cultures. The architecture by which social agency must design and complement the details of this project for the twenty-first century ought to take into account its global nature. This architecture includes global civil society's internal linkages—its linkages with states on various levels, including international organizations as well as with the national and international corporations, labor, and business associations. It describes the organizational targets for developing the networks required by blacks and their allies to establish the hegemony of a global coalition that will move beyond racism in practice and eliminate racial inequality in its various dimensions, including the economy.

The success of integrating national policies and initiatives against racial discrimination—required to confront racism as a historical phenomenon—will be in large measure a product of the effective deployment of global civil-society potentialities. These potentialities refer to the synergistic interactions within and among associational activities (civil societies) from different countries where racial discrimination is a relevant presence, among associational activities operating on different

levels (local, national, global), and among associational activities operating in different areas of concern (women's rights, civil rights, minorities' rights, human rights, labor rights, indigenous rights, etc.).

The politics of civil society also interact with the politics of economic and political society and can become an important component in
the formulation of public policy. A new arena where the politics of civil
society can be redeployed is macroeconomic policymaking. Creating an
international financial regime supportive of autonomous national implementation of economic policies and reduced international mobility for
financial capital can contribute to a progressive path toward full
employment, the end of discrimination against blacks, and a more equitable income distribution. Similarly, a vibrant civil society could
become a factor in the success of government initiatives to expand
funding and the supply of education.

Notes

1. Darity and Mason (1998) review the most recent empirical literature on
labor market discrimination in the United States and conclude that the available
data supports the hypothesis of racial discrimination. The limited evidence suggesting that racial discrimination is currently negligible in U.S. employment
practices is not robust. Darity and Mason also indicate that the strong evidence
of persistent labor market discrimination calls into question the neoclassical
theoretical apparatus. The political economy of racial discrimination presented
in the next section explores the implications of blending (along the lines suggested by Darity and Mason) the theory of classical competition with a theory
of racial discrimination that emphasizes matters of opportunity, power,
exploitation, and social and political control.

2. For a demonstration of the positive impact of the propensity for investing in human capital over the rate of economic growth, see Ray 1998. Lundberg
and Startz (1993) present a detailed analysis about the presence of negative
externalities in the process of human-capital accumulation by blacks.

3. Public policy toward discrimination against blacks in Brazil, South
Africa, and the United States must take into account different historical circumstances. Contrary to South Africa and the United States, in Brazil formal and
legal mechanisms of racial segregation were never implemented with the end of
slavery. As a result of this circumstance, as well as both the conservative and
progressive elites' success in promoting the ideology of racial democracy, there
has been little public support for affirmative-action programs. In South Africa,
the potential negative impact of white human-capital flight on the sustainability
of the democratic transition has imposed moderation in the application of affirmative-action policies. In both countries, the main public challenge is now the
design of an economic growth strategy oriented to promote higher rates of economic growth cum income redistribution for all disadvantaged groups. Blacks

constitute a very large proportion of the population in general, and resources for investment and social programs are extremely scarce. In the United States, the continuous income erosion from all the lower-earning groups in society, coupled with the implementation of three decades of affirmative action, seems to have exhausted the country's ability to further promote racial equality, unless policy efforts oriented to reducing inequality in society as a whole are adopted.

4. This five-part model was proposed by Cohen and Arato (1992). In the dichotomous model adopted by classical political economy, civil society conflates all other levels of social agency except the state. In Adam Smith, for example, civil society is the sphere of agency where the freedom of contract is the inner engine of accumulation. For Marx, civil society is also the sphere where the inner engine of accumulation resides, but this engine is based on the exploitation of the labor force by capital. For Cohen and Arato, however, civil society is the sphere of free socialization and progressive citizenship and must be differentiated from economic society, political society, the market, and last but not least, the state.

References

Albelda, Randy, Robert Drago, and Steven Shulman. 1997. *Unlevel Playing Fields: Understanding Wage Inequality and Discrimination.* New York: The McGraw-Hill Companies Inc.

Botwinick, Howard. 1993. *Persistent Inequalities: Wage Disparity Under Capitalist Competition.* Princeton: Princeton University Press.

Brimmer, Andrew F. 1966. "The Negro in the National Economy," in John P. Davis, ed., *The American Negro Reference Book.* Englewood Cliffs, NJ: Prentice-Hall

———. 1995. "The Economic Cost of Discrimination Against Black Americans," in Margaret Simmons, ed., *Economic Perspectives on Affirmative Action.* Washington, DC: Joint Center for Political and Economic Studies.

Cohen, Jean L., and Andrew Arato. 1992. *Civil Society and Political Theory.* Cambridge, MA: MIT Press.

Darity Jr., William A., and Patrick L. Mason. 1998. "Evidence on Discrimination in Employment: Codes of Color, Codes of Gender." *Journal of Economic Perspectives* 12, no. 2: 63–90.

Fundação Getúlio Vargas. 1993. "As Contas Nacionais de 1980–1981." *Conjuntura Econômica* 47, no. l (January).

Fundação Instituto Brasileiro de Geografia e Estatística. 1991. *Pesquisa Nacional por Amostra de Domicílios—PNAD de 1990.* Rio de Janeiro: FIBGE.

International Monetary Fund. 1996 and 1997. *South Africa—Selected Economic Issues.* Washington, DC: IMF, July and September.

Lundberg, Shelly, and Richard Startz. 1993. "On the Persistence of Racial Inequality." Unpublished paper.

Project for Statistics on Living Standards and Development (SALDRU). 1994.

by the color of their skin but by the content of their character" (Faircloth 1995). King, like so many civil rights advocates in the United States and antiapartheid activists in South Africa, saw the deracialization of discourse and decision as the path to racial justice and democracy. More recently, neoconservatives and others in the United States have co-opted this language, perverting its meaning and undermining its underlying spirit. Such people typically couch their stance as "color-blindness."

According to this view, school admission, job hiring and promotion, contracting, and so forth should be determined solely according to an individual's "objective merit." Race, the argument goes, should not be a factor—even in an effort to compensate for or otherwise address the disadvantage experienced by members of certain racial or ethnic groups at the hands of racism—because to do so would be to engage in reverse racism. This notion of "color-blindness" is sometimes equated with the U.S. Supreme Court's use of the strict scrutiny form of judicial review under the Equal Protection Clause of the 14th Amendment (Gotanda 1996). However, it is also utilized more broadly as a moral imperative for a race-neutral, valid, and positive racial social vision in which individuals' thoughts and efforts are not judged by the color of their skin. Not surprisingly, this claim to neutrality and validity is false. As one scholar argues, "Race color-blindness when applied to the complexities of civil society—to actual decisionmaking in such areas as contracting, employment, and admissions—is not race-neutral. Instead, it is a disguised form of racial privileging" (Gotanda 1996: p. 1139).[3]

Unfortunately, this racial privileging has recently begun to shed its disguise in the United States as individual,[4] institutional,[5] and governmental[6] opposition to affirmative action increases. Meanwhile, the nation faces constant, daily, practical reminders that race is as crucial a factor as ever in shaping life chances and experiences (Winant 1994). Perhaps it is this denial of persistent racial injustices that prompted President Clinton in June 1997 to propose a year-long national "conversation" about race (*New York Times* 1995). Attention to the present experiences in South Africa might further this conversation. ·

As did the post–civil rights United States, postapartheid South Africa is pushing for the elimination of race from official discourse. The overarching vision is often referred to as "nonracialism." Unlike the ideology of "color-blindness," however, "nonracialism" includes a strategy to eliminate persistent racial inequalities. As the 1996 constitution states, "[The] Republic of South Africa is one sovereign democratic state founded on . . . non-racialism and non-sexism" (South African

Constitution 1996). The South African Bill of Rights also states that "everyone is equal before the law and has the right to equal protections and benefit of the law." More explicitly, the constitution outlaws only "unfair" discrimination and permits "legislative and other measures designed to protect or advance persons, or categories of persons disadvantaged by unfair discrimination."[7] Indeed, President Nelson Mandela promised that affirmative action would be introduced to redress the imbalances created by apartheid (Sonn 1993). This is still in keeping with "nonracialism," however, in that Mandela warned against abuse and nepotism: "Nor are we saying that just as a white skin was a passport to privilege in the past, so a black skin should be the basis of privilege in the future. . . . Affirmative action must be rooted in principles of justice and equity" (p. 9).

This push can be distinguished, then, from the disingenuous efforts and rhetoric of neoconservatives and neosegregationists in the United States in that the South Africans calling for "nonracialism" are generally those sincerely committed to racial justice (much like King and his contemporaries in the United States).[8] At the same time, however, the term itself may lead to confusion on the part of many South Africans, underplaying their experience of racial tension (Cose 1997) and perhaps numbing them to the racial injustices that continue to require remedy. As one South African scholar puts it:

> Granted there are no legal political distinctions on the basis of race, but there is a contradiction in it. On one hand [political leaders] say they make no distinction because of race. On the other, they say there is this legacy of racial discrimination you need to reverse. . . . Race matters a great deal and I think it will continue to matter. . . . [To the extent that the official policy of "nonracialism"] makes organizations and individuals feel they don't have to do anything else, it's a problem. (Cose 1997: p. 218)

The manner in which race is discussed in Brazil can offer cautionary insight to both the United States and South Africa. In a sense, Brazil began its postslavery period where South Africa and the United States find themselves today (albeit with different emphases, as discussed above), that is, with a race-neutral approach usually referred to as "supraracialism." According to this view, race and racism were not and should not be factors in public life. Whereas South Africa and the United States instituted segregationist and explicitly racially discriminatory policies immediately following the abolition of slavery, Brazil initially ignored issues of race and ethnicity in its drive to become a "racial democracy."[9] For the past two decades as well, the government has promoted a singular national identity that transcends racial categories. As President Fernando Henrique Cardoso claimed in his 1995 inaugural speech, "We Brazilians are a people with great cultural homogeneity" (Reichmann 1995: p. 35). Even if identification with African roots is promoted as part of the national identity, it is done so without reference to specific ancestry or other observable characteristics (Reichmann 1995).

Indeed, widespread belief exists in the country that racism is not a problem. Public discourse about it is novel and tentative, and access to statistics limited. If racial discrimination is acknowledged at all, it is dismissed as proof of African Brazilians' inability to compete economically or attributed to individual rather than institutional acts of bigotry. Even social activists in Brazil focus on inequitable class structure as the underlying cause of racial disparities (Reichmann 1995).

As in the United States, this denial of race has masked the real racial inequalities that exist. Lack of truly enforceable antidiscrimination legislation in Brazil[10] (Andrews 1992) has contributed to the privileging of whites and the subjugation of everyone else.[11] Inequality in the workplace, schools, public health system, and politics (Reichmann 1995) has worsened so much since the 1950s that whereas the United States was then the more racially unequal, it is now Brazil (Andrews 1992). In fact, as one scholar notes, "racial democracy" is "a myth that play[s] the authoritarian role of denying racial difference and suppressing racial mobilization" (Winant 1994: p. 159). Only recently has a black movement been painfully building to challenge this situation.

Brazil's denial of race provides a lesson for both the United States, which wishes to be "color-blind," and South Africa, which hopes to become "nonracial," which is that ignoring race can lead not to "supraracialism" but to "*super*racialism." In neither the United States nor Brazil has the racial dimension of stratification and social inequalities been transformed (Winant 1994), although such a transformation was initiated in the civil rights era in the United States and may be gaining momentum in Brazil. South Africa, on the other hand, has just begun its transformative efforts, the results of which the world anxiously awaits.

Admittedly there are cultural, political, and economic factors particular to each of the three countries to be discussed below that prevent a simple comparison; however, certain lessons can be gleaned from the experiences of each country regarding racial patterns and public and private policy. This chapter will try to weave together the racial realities in the United States, South Africa, and Brazil as informed by the particular historical and social forces that have arisen in each country. In so doing, I hope to help answer the question: Are race-conscious policies appropriate as we head into the twenty-first century, and if so, can they be transformative?

The first section will analyze the meaning of race in each country, showing race to be a fluid, socially constructed, and culturally contingent concept. I will also discuss the importance of race in the context of the racialization of poverty and the persistence of white privilege. It should thus become evident that race-neutral policies are insufficient to achieve racial justice, let alone meaningful democracy. Next, I will consider traditional components and objectives of race-conscious policies, as exemplified by affirmative action. The following section will critically evaluate the effectiveness of race-conscious programs in each country with respect to the traditional justifications of affirmative action. Finally, the discussion will draw upon the insights and observations discussed previously and craft an alternative vision that is more effective both in achieving the traditional objectives of race-conscious programs and in securing true racial democracy. The strategy envisioned is not merely affirmative; it is also transformative.

The Meaning and Significance of Race

The title of the conference that spawned the chapters in this book, "Beyond Racism: Brazil, South Africa, and the United States in the Twenty-First Century," might lead some to conclude that we need not and should not continue to talk about race and racial discrimination.[12] The reality, however, is that race still shapes not only how we order our respective societies but also who and how we are individually and collectively. Simply ignoring this fact does not diminish the power of race and the pervasiveness of racial subordination. It would be wonderful to be "beyond racism," but we cannot reach that point until we fully acknowledge the nature and role of race and racism in our past and present worlds. We must have a better understanding of the crucial issue implicated—the persistence of racial hierarchy—before we can begin to think more effectively and creatively about how to eliminate and thus truly move beyond racism.

The Fluidity Yet Potency of Race as a Social Construct

The fluid but potent nature of race may seem paradoxical, even nonsense to some. Much of this confusion or skepticism flows from the

general—throughout its history, to be identified as African American—
or of another community of color—means to be thought of as having
experienced racial discrimination in the past and to be likely targets of
it in the future. Moreover, although the U.S. Supreme Court has been
reluctant to recognize it,[24] private discrimination has been as or more
prevalent and debilitating in the United States.[25] Likewise, racial discrimination and subordination have plagued South Africa and Brazil for
centuries (Robinson 1995). Michael Sandel and other late-modernist
thinkers have observed astutely that such experience plays a crucial role
in creating and shaping the self and individual and shared identities.[26]
Thus, in a concrete as well as metaphysical sense, the experience of
being categorized as a member of a subordinated group and discriminated against by the government and private institutions and individuals
has profound effects on one's sense of self and place in the world,
whether we are talking of the United States, South Africa, or Brazil
(Crenshaw 1988). Furthermore, the experience of being favored, even if
unacknowledged or unrecognized, constructs and can change what it
means to be white in each of these countries.[27] While black identity is
closely associated with exclusion and subordination, white identity is
clearly associated with the privilege of normalcy and inclusion.
Therefore, these historical dynamics, experienced individually and
communally by the racially subordinated or the racially privileged are
an important component of a better understanding of racial identity and
what race means in the three nations.[28]

The second vital element of a proper understanding of race is what
Gotanda calls "culture-race," which has three aspects: culture, community, and consciousness. As related to blacks in the United States he
claims that

> culture-race uses black to refer to African-American culture, commu-
> nity, and consciousness. Culture refers to broadly shared beliefs and
> social practices; community refers to both the physical and spiritual
> senses of the term; and African-American consciousness refers to
> Black Nationalist and other traditions of self-awareness and to action
> based on that self-awareness. (Gotanda 1991: p. 4)

Although Gotanda explains this concept in terms of the United States, it
can also be applied to South Africa and Brazil. Members of socially and
politically defined racial categories in all three countries certainly share
beliefs and modes of interacting with each other and the larger world.
Moreover, because of the racially discriminatory and segregationist
housing practices in South Africa and Brazil, which resemble housing

practices in the United States, community plays an undisputed physical as well as spiritual role in the understanding of race.[29] Finally, the PAC movement in South Africa and the Afro-Brazilian movement emerging now in Brazil exemplify the self-awareness and action that parallel the black nationalism in the United States (Sundiata 1987). All three of these aspects—culture, community, and consciousness—implicate and are implicated by a sense of identity, both individual and collective.

Because this conception of race is more fluid and contextualized than the rigid biological or essentialized conception, it recognizes the social, political, and economic content of racial categories. Embracing this understanding of race, then, makes possible the full exposure of the nature and persistence of racial hierarchy. Once exposed, it becomes feasible to determine how to dismantle it most effectively—and then to do just that.[30] This call to action will be explored further below. But first we must set out the elements and consequences of racial hierarchy in the United States, South Africa, and Brazil.

The Stability and Oppressiveness of Unaddressed Racial Hierarchy

As alluded to above, unchallenged racial hierarchy, because of its stability, institutionalizes, even legitimates, racial inequality.[31] In this context, there are two interrelated aspects to the solidification of racial inequality and the persistence of racial hierarchy. First, racial hierarchy means and depends upon the savage impoverishment of the racial Other through their systematic exclusion from opportunity structures, that is, good schools, adequate employment, sufficient health care and diet, financial capital, avenues for meaningful participation in public and political life, decent housing, and critical mentor and information sources. Second, racial hierarchy hinges upon the unjustified enrichment of whites and thus the preservation of white privilege. The racialization of poverty and maintenance of white privilege are two sides of the same coin; one cannot exist without the other.[32] As Trina Grillo has so insightfully observed, "You cannot get rid of subordination without eliminating the privilege as well" (Grillo 1995: pp. 18–19).

The Racialization of Poverty

The racialization of poverty basically means that the racial Others—that is, the nonwhites—in the United States, South Africa, and Brazil are disproportionately poor and often have little meaningful opportunity to improve their situation. In the area of earnings, the median net worth of nonwhite families in the United States is ten times less than that of white families (Urban Coalition 1995). Moreover, nonwhites are unemployed at shockingly high levels or, if they are fortunate enough to have a job, are underemployed or limited to the least-desirable jobs with the lowest wages. For example, in the United States, nearly 60 percent of all cleaners and servants are nonwhite (*Statistical Abstract of the United States* 1992). In addition, most migrant farm workers in the United States, often exposed to subhuman conditions, are primarily nonwhites.

Similarly, in South Africa, nearly 50 percent of nonwhites are unemployed, almost ten times the rate of whites (Ford 1996). Moreover, a disproportionate number of nonwhites who have had the chance to work, especially under apartheid, have little option but to work in the highly hazardous mineral mines with little in the way of monetary or other compensation (Krattenmaker 1993; Cell 1982; Cose 1997). Regardless of occupation, black South African households earn nearly 6.2 times less than white households (Cose 1997).

Even worse, in Brazil, racial inequality has increased since the 1950s and has now eclipsed that of the United States. This is mainly due to lack of migration from economically depressed regions, disproportionate distribution of wealth, and inaction on the federal level to combat racial discrimination (Andrews 1992). As a result, the average income for nonwhites is half that of whites (Silva 1985; Luft 1995). In fact, whites earn 57 to 73 percent more than blacks in the same occupation. Because of discriminatory hiring practices in nonmanual occupations, only 2.7 percent of economically active blacks hold management positions, while over 55 percent hold positions in manual labor. Moreover, blacks with a college education have earned less than whites with a junior-high education (Reichmann 1995).[33]

In all three countries, nonwhites are also confined to the most economically devastated and crime-infested neighborhoods, as exemplified by urban cores of the United States, such as South-Central Los Angeles and the South Bronx of New York City; South African townships, such as Sharpesville; and slums, such as Jacarezinho, in and around Brazilian cities such as Rio de Janeiro. It is not surprising, then, that in South Africa, for example, great proportions of the nonwhites lack basic sanitation provisions (Ford 1996) and that in Brazil, for example, they are more likely to be arrested and convicted, die earlier, and lose their young (Reichmann 1995).

Furthermore, nonwhites in all three countries receive an inadequate education that almost inevitably dooms them to a vicious cycle of deprivation and despair. Although not the most extreme, the predicament for nonwhite students in the United States has become deeply troubling. Achievement scores have fallen and dropout rates have risen around the country for nonwhites, especially in racially and socioeconomically segregated schools.[34] This sad situation resembles what is also happening in South Africa, where as much as 80 percent of nonwhites cannot read beyond the fifth grade (Ford 1996; Krattenmaker 1993). Likewise in Brazil, just over 2 percent of nonwhites had completed more than twelve years of education in 1987, in schools that a 1980s national study found were of the worst quality available. In fact, nearly 40 percent of nonwhites have four years or less of schooling with an illiteracy rate twice that of whites (Reichmann 1995). In higher education, whereas blacks make up 45 percent of the general population, only 1 percent of the student body attend the country's largest public university (Moffett 1996). Informal social mechanisms in Brazil—like the media's portrayal of blacks in subordinate and criminal roles—also work to exclude them from equal opportunities.[35]

In short, nonwhite adults live in extreme, concentrated poverty in disproportionate numbers, and many of their children, because of the lack of opportunities and hope, are destined for a similar fate—that is, so long as racial hierarchy remains intact.

The Persistence of White Privilege

The other side of nonwhite poverty and subjugation is white privilege. The two operate in tandem, reflecting and perpetuating the provision of economic, political, and social benefits to whites and the withholding of them to nonwhites. As will become clear in the next subsection, however, white privilege means much more than the racially discriminatory distribution of resources and access to institutions; it implicates the very core of who we are individually and collectively. White privilege and racial hierarchy are not just descriptive, they are constitutive. For now, however, the analysis will focus on the descriptive facet of white privilege in all three countries.

The United States provides, perhaps, the easiest starting point because so much work has been and is being done on the issue of white privilege in that country. For much of its history, in order to belong, to be fully accepted, and to have the accompanying access in the United States, one has had to be construed as white. It was state policy, then, to police the resulting color line (Winant 1994). For example, the

Naturalization Act of 1790, passed only a few months after the ratification of the Constitution, stated that only "free white persons" were eligible for citizenship and the concomitant benefits. Every naturalization act from 1790 until 1952 included similar language restricting citizenship to whites (Lopez 1996). In fact, the United States jurisprudence has long treated "whiteness" as a property right from which benefits are accrued: "in any mixed community, the reputation of belonging to the dominant race, in this instance the white race, is property, in the same sense that a right of action, or of inheritance, is property."[36] Peggy McIntosh has spoken metaphorically to describe white privilege as "'an invisible knapsack' of provisions, maps, guides, codebooks, passports, visas, compasses, and blank checks."[37]

White privilege has also taken the form of public and private policies beneficial to whites and detrimental to nonwhites. For instance, the federal government has provided substantial assistance regarding home mortgage financing since the 1930s.[38] Federal agencies, however, have directed almost all loans and resources toward whites and white neighborhoods that remained so (as they do even today) through redlining (Johnson 1995; Massey and Denton 1993; Oliver, Chapter 9 of this volume; Schill and Wachter 1995). The New York City metropolitan area provides a graphic example. Around the 1940s, per capita lending in mostly white Long Island was sixty times greater than that in the primarily nonwhite Bronx (Massey and Denton 1993). Although Congress eventually outlawed explicitly governmental discrimination of this sort (42 U.S.C. 1994), private lending institutions continue to favor whites when considering loan applications, whether it be for loans for starting up a business or purchasing a home (Galster 1993; Bates 1989). Even individuals, although supportive of the principle of equal opportunity, are far less likely to give up their white privilege when it comes to supporting federal enforcement of antidiscrimination laws (Reichmann 1995).[39]

In addition to superior access to capital, white privilege has meant the outrageous governmental subsidization of the exclusive, affluent, and mostly white suburbs that supposedly typify the "American Dream." As of 1994, the federal government spent $123 billion on highway construction and billions more for infrastructure expansion and maintenance to serve these white suburbs (Judd and Swanstrom 1994). In addition, state governments have delegated their zoning power to local governments; many of the white suburban governments have abused this power by enacting exclusionary zoning ordinances. These ordinances operate to preclude the construction of affordable housing and to artificially inflate property values in the white suburbs by confining low- and moderate-income housing to the urban cores (Roisman and Tegler 1990). As a result of these practices, 89 percent of whites in the United States' suburbs live in communities with less than 1 percent African Americans.

A glance at several other indicators confirms what we should already know: whites are better positioned in the United States because of white privilege. For example, the net worth of whites is $43,143 more than that of nonwhites (Oliver and Shapiro 1995). In addition, a much greater proportion of whites own homes than nonwhites (Leigh 1993). Whites also live, in disproportionate numbers, in the suburbs that have better access to the nation's opportunity structures.[40]

White privilege has also plagued South Africa. Once in power in the 1920s, the Afrikaners passed affirmative-action legislation for whites, securing against the loss of jobs to cheaper black labor. As one South African university rector notes, "The plain nepotism based on Afrikaner chauvinism, which represents the most extreme form of affirmative action, was strongly propagated" (Sonn 1993: p. 7). For example, the Apprenticeship Act of 1944 gave control of entry into trades to white unions. By 1952, whites made up the work force of 80 percent of South African railways and harbors and 68 percent of the post office. Worse yet, by 1978, 90 percent of the key public-sector positions were filled by whites (Sonn 1993). Finally, with regard to land ownership, only whites were given that right. The accumulation of wealth, therefore, was racialized (Cose 1997). In other words, prior to the dismantling of apartheid, the state explicitly created and viciously upheld white privilege:

> The only people with any semblance of rights in South Africa are those defined as "white" . . . these South Africans actually have something more akin to privilege than rights because many of the draconian measures of the state are theoretically and practically color blind. All others in South Africa, regardless of the differential status ascribed to them by legislation, do not have civil rights.[41]

In postapartheid South Africa, whites make up just 13 percent of the population, yet they earn 60 percent of the nation's total income (Cose 1997), hold 80 percent of the professional and 93 percent of management positions in the private sector, and own 90 percent of privately controlled lands (Ford 1996). In fact, of forty-one nations examined in

the World Bank's *World Development Report,* none had a greater
income inequality than South Africa. Brazil had the second-greatest gap
(Cose 1997).

It is not difficult, then, to document white privilege in Brazil as
well. For example, the fruits of economic growth flow disproportionately to the top 20 percent of Brazilian society (Andrews 1992). The
Brazilian communities consisting of million-dollar beach-front condo-
miniums are almost entirely white, while the poorest region of the
country, the Northeast, is overwhelmingly black (Robinson 1995). In
addition, almost all public figures, prominent business people, successful politicians, and the others who wield power in Brazil are white
(Sundiata 1987). Furthermore, the faces seen on television and in
magazine advertisements are almost exclusively white.[42] This means
that whites not only obtain most news reporting, acting, and modeling
jobs but also receive the more intangible benefit of being seen as better, as the ideal to which all Brazilians should aspire (Frayssinet
1996).

The Nonneutrality of "Race-Neutrality"

Given the persistent problem of racism and conflict over race, some
well-intentioned activists and many policymakers in the United States
and South Africa want to begin to exclude all considerations of race
from the process of making and evaluating policy. As discussed above,
the United States refers to this approach as "color-blindness" and South
Africa as "nonracialism." In Brazil, the debate is at a different point;
many want to continue the official exclusion of race or "supraracialism," seeing no need to insert race into the equation. For the sake of
clarity, "race-neutrality" will be used in the remainder of this chapter to
refer to all three of these concepts. Whatever one calls it, however, this
general approach to understanding race is mistaken, if not insincere and
manipulative.

"Race-neutrality" allows and, in fact, requires the preservation of
the racial status quo (Young 1990). The status quo is neither neutral nor
just, because in each country it embodies extreme social, political, and
economic stratification along racial lines: in short, racial hierarchy.
Even defenders of classical liberalism, such as John Rawls, recognize
that when the overarching structures and institutions are unjust and are
allowed to remain intact, it is impossible to secure a just or democratic
society (Rawls 1971). "Race-neutrality" in the United States, South

Africa, and Brazil, then, cannot be the path to racial justice and meaningful democracy because it accommodates and enables, rather than dismantles, racial hierarchy.

Racial hierarchy, so long as it remains intact, leads to two major difficulties. First, as discussed in the preceding subsection, it subordinates the racial Other, nonwhites, by severely limiting access to critical resources, institutions, and opportunities. At the same time, it privileges the racial norm, whites, by creating and legitimating a myriad of policies, practices, and institutions that slant, in subtle and conspicuous ways, the playing field in their favor. Second, racial hierarchy, unchallenged, shapes who we are individually and collectively, thereby legitimating and reproducing itself even as the years pass and the contexts change (Mahoney 1995; Calmore 1995; Goldberg 1993; Bell 1992). A brief consideration of the constitutive ramifications of racial hierarchy will illustrate this tragic reality.

In the United States, South Africa, and Brazil the existence of racial hierarchy has led to overt and covert racial discrimination and racial segregation or even exclusion in housing, employment, education, and public accommodations. This segregation and exclusion have devastating consequences for individual and collective formation and development. They increase racial misunderstanding and mistrust, fostering a collective obliviousness among whites to the plight of nonwhites and resentment and despair among nonwhites (Goldberg 1993). As one South African policymaker, Bonganjalo Goba, notes, "In South Africa, we have underplayed ethnic identities because we are moving to be a nonracial democracy." The reality is that ethnic rivalries and racial alienation will persist "as long as the economy is perceived to be in the hands of whites, there will be tension in this country."[43]

Not only does this misunderstanding and mistrust create racial conflict, it also distorts the process of individual and societal constitution. Because whites and nonwhites live, experience, and interact (to the extent necessary or possible) in a world shaped by racial hierarchy, identities and realities take on certain assumptions, expectations, and norms along racial lines. As explained earlier, race remains important to one's understanding of the self and the possibilities for the world; race means not only lived histories but also culture, community, and consciousness—our individual and shared experiences and realities (Gotanda 1991). Therefore, racial inequality—both privilege and subordination—color these constitutive experiences and realities and play a large role in shaping who we are and who we are becoming. The United States, for example,

> is experiencing a totally unprecedented racial situation in which there
> is a large-scale uncertainty about the meaning of race and the proper
> orientation of state racial policies. On the one hand, race continues to
> structure everyday life, social practices of all types, and the person-
> al—indeed even the unconscious—dimensions of everyone's identity.
> On the other hand, the susceptibility of race to further state interven-
> tion or political action—beyond that deriving from the moderate egal-
> itarianism of the civil rights movement—is denied, not only on the
> racial right, but also among many on the left and in various nationalist
> currents. (Winant 1994: pp. 163–164)

That the role of racial hierarchy in this constitutive process is largely
invisible gives it that much more distortive power and legitimacy
(Frankenberg 1994).

Unchallenged, this hierarchy and its constitutive impact will continue in the United States, South Africa, and Brazil. Because the opportunity structure continues to be racialized to the benefit of whites in each
country, racial isolation and subjugation mean exclusion from the
avenues for meaningful advancement (Cummins 1996). In light of this
racial isolation, in combination with the racial misunderstanding discussed above, the neglect of nonwhite and the privileging of white communities become natural, even inevitable (Goldberg 1993). The social,
economic, and institutional difficulties that flow from the isolation of
nonwhites in poverty-stricken communities with little opportunity or
hope become an ex post facto justification for the past subordination of
nonwhites and the privilege of whites.[44] Many whites, and even some
nonwhites, begin to interpret the outgrowths of racial isolation to be
proof of the laziness, irresponsibility, and criminality of nonwhites and
thus the meritorious nature of whites' position of privilege.[45] In the
same way, the social and economic inequality and accompanying problems provide an "objective" rationale for the white power structure to
subordinate and privilege in the future.[46] It should be readily apparent,
then, that the problem of racism cannot just be willed away.

Brazil is the closest of the three nations to having tried just that. It
has not yet benefited from a wave of state action at the federal level to
combat racial discrimination, as in the United States' case. Nor has it
officially acknowledged in its constitution that remedying past inequality is necessary to achieve true equality, as in South Africa's case, and
that the cost of leaving racism structurally unaddressed is high. Instead
it has resisted redistributive policies and denounced them as reverse discrimination, all in the name of "supraracialism" and "racial democracy." Such denial has been acknowledged by some Brazilians as oppressive:

As long as whites don't accept that racism exists, its impossible for blacks to come out competing for jobs. They'll say, "No, you're a candidate as an individual person, not as a black." So it's harder. Now you have to admit first that racism exists. Even the directors of the unions don't want to admit it and they say, "No, forget about that, we have to stay united, work together." So I think its complicated, blacks claiming a percentage. (Reichmann 1995: p. 39)

As will be discussed below, Brazil is changing. Race is becoming politicized and activists are making some headway. Yet, their denial of race should cause the United States to pause in its regressive movement toward dismantling its affirmative-action programs and abandoning its belief that the federal government can do anything at all to remedy racial hierarchy. Brazil's experience should also lead South Africa to resist weakening its forward-moving attempt to dismantle the massive remnants of apartheid. Activists and policymakers in all three nations should take deliberate and effective steps to address the racial inequality that undermines social justice and meaningful democracy. Toward this end, an examination of race-conscious policies should prove helpful.

Race-Conscious Policies in Brazil, South Africa, and the United States

Because affirmative action remains the most widely known of race-conscious policies and because it has important social, political, and economic implications in the United States, South Africa, and Brazil, it will provide a good basis for analyzing the desirability and potential of race-conscious policies in general. Although not entirely comparable to one another, a comparison of the affirmative-action programs of the three countries follows. Before evaluating the experiences of each country, however, we must be clear about what we mean by affirmative action and how it has been justified.

The Main Goals of Affirmative Action

A 1993 *Report to the President*, prepared as the Clinton administration reevaluated affirmative action in the United States, offers a concise statement of the first aim of affirmative action: "The primary justification for the use of race-conscious measures is to eradicate discrimination, root and branch."[47] The elimination of discrimination has been seen as the way to ensure equality of opportunity regardless of one's race. To this end, affirmative action seeks to provide benefits to persons specifically based upon their membership in a specified group (Ford 1996). The second rationale for affirmative action is closely related to the first and is backward-looking in nature. This justification flows from the recognition of deliberate and pervasive discrimination in the past and the need to compensate people of color for the resulting harm and deprivation (Skidmore 1996; Wiseman 1993). This is especially true in South Africa, where the entire economy barred 75 percent of the population from participation. This second rationale, then, sees affirmative action as a means to achieving racial reconciliation (Ford 1996). The third objective of affirmative action is also closely related to the first but is forward-looking in nature. This rationale holds that for our democracies to succeed, diversity must be embraced and promoted (Skidmore 1996; *Affirmative Action Review* 1993). Put another way, proponents of affirmative action consider it to be a way to ensure a truly inclusive process of selection and promotion and, ultimately, a more democratic society (Wiseman 1993).[48]

The Typical Components of Affirmative Action

Before examining the form affirmative action takes or might take in the United States, South Africa, and Brazil, it is important to note the different methods of race-conscious practices generally covered under the umbrella of affirmative action, as suggested by Oppenheimer (1996). They include: (1) quotas, or the use of minimum or maximum participation levels in selection of minority group members; (2) preferences, or the use of race as a selection factor; (3) self-studies, or the examination of past and present selection decisions to determine if discrimination has been a factor; (4) outreach and counseling, or efforts to diversify the pool of applicants by reaching out to minorities; and (5) antidiscrimination, or the affirmative commitment to prevent or avoid discrimination through policies, training, and complaint resolution. All but the first of these methods is common in the United States, the nation with the longest-standing affirmative-action policies of the three countries, that is if we do not count the de facto affirmative-action programs for whites in all three countries that have created and preserved white privilege and nonwhite subordination. The United States, therefore, offers a good starting point.

Although affirmative action in the United States can be traced back to the Reconstruction amendments to the U.S. Constitution,[49] in its modern-day form it dates to the Civil Rights Act of 1964[50] and presidential executive orders from the same period.[51] Under the mandate of the Civil Rights Act, companies with more than fifteen employees are required to submit yearly reports on workplace diversity to the Equal Employment Opportunity Commission and otherwise to take concrete steps, such as more-inclusive recruiting processes and workplace training programs, to prevent discrimination and ensure equal opportunity for all.[52]

Subsequent affirmative-action programs have varied since their inception depending on the context; nonetheless, several basic features can be identified. First, affirmative-action programs are legitimate only if fashioned to remedy past discrimination.[53] Without evidence of this discrimination any preferential action is impermissible (Oppenheimer 1996).[54] Second, while affirmative-action programs may expand the pool of eligible candidates in order to promote racial diversity, they must not include quotas, set-asides, or other rigid numerical requirements.[55] These programs also must be narrowly drawn and applied as flexibly as possible so as to be minimally disruptive and not unduly burdensome to whites.[56] Finally, affirmative action must be limited in duration and periodically reviewed to determine if it is still necessary in a particular context.[57] If these requirements are met, race-conscious plans have received Supreme Court approval (Oppenheimer 1996). Most recently, however, affirmative-action programs that strive for diversity in higher education have been called into question,[58] although the federal administration continues to stand behind such measures when appropriately fashioned.[59] Nonetheless, the national mood seems more hostile to affirmative action than ever (Ford 1996).

South Africa, by contrast, enjoys relatively broad support for its recent foray into affirmative action, which it defines as "laws, programmes or activities, designed to redress past imbalances and to ameliorate the conditions of individuals and groups who have been disadvantaged on the grounds of race, colour, gender, or disability."[60] As indicated in the first section of this chapter, measures designed to advance persons disadvantaged by unfair discrimination are explicitly constitutional, even if they are discriminatory, as long as they are "fair" (Ford 1996). Indeed, many African National Congress government officials believe that the survival of the nation depends on such measures. This is largely so because "South Africa's vast legacy of racial disadvantage is characterized by much more dramatic socio-economic inequality than exists between racial groups in the United States" (Ford 1996: p. 1957). Consequently, affirmative-action policies usually consist of aggressive efforts to hire and promote nonwhites in the public and private sectors. It is perhaps this aggressiveness that renders the policies controversial among non-Africans, despite their legality and broad official support (Ford 1996).

Although just beginning to take shape, the components of affirmative action in South Africa are both familiar and not so familiar. Perhaps drawing on the experience in the United States, South African programs thus far have no formal quotas, yet other components would seem quite controversial there. In the public sector, for example, while the government is reluctant to fire whites in order to remedy their overrepresentation, it does not hesitate to utilize virtually "nonwhites-only" hiring policies.[61] As one South African scholar and businessman observes:

> The transformation of the public service is . . . the most important condition for black advancement . . . Transformation is also necessary in order to change the image of certain government departments that have become symbols of oppression and humiliation to blacks . . . Unless competent blacks with good political credentials are appointed to key positions in these departments it is going to be very difficult to turn them into the symbols of nation-building that they should be. It therefore follows that black advancement in the public service must not only come gradually from the bottom, but that there must also be appointments to strategic positions at senior levels. (Wiseman 1993: p. 17)

In the private sector, aggressive affirmative-action measures have also begun, but voluntarily, partly because of economic incentives and partly because of the government's ability to otherwise compel such action. In fact, although no law yet requires set-asides or preferences, an office in the Labour Ministry has been created to monitor progress (Ford 1996). Some businessmen call for even more radical action:

> What is really required very urgently from the private sector is an act of statesmanship—something that rivals what Mr. N. Mandela and Mr. F. W. de Klerk are struggling to achieve at the political level—a new beginning that clearly demonstrates the commitment of business to justice and equity. An example of an action that would have the desired impact is the initiation of a credible *programme directed at increasing black ownership and control of selected major companies within an agreed time span of say three to five years.* (Wiseman 1993: p. 18, emphasis added)

To prepare for this equitable representation in and ownership of South African corporations, vigorous training must be provided. In the meantime, as one South African scholar argues, less qualified blacks should be hired:

> There is nothing wrong with selecting a black candidate with less qualifications if it is in the best interest of the organization or of the firm or of the country. The charge is that this is tokenism only holds on two scores: (a) if the intention is to keep the organization white with a sprinkling of black faces, or (b) if the blacks are forced to comply with racist practices and are denied the opportunity to grow and even change the environment. Breaking down racial discriminatory practices must not be followed by a system of benign benevolence which continues to breed dependency and inferiority. (Cose 1997: p. 218)

In addition to public- and private-sector affirmative-action measures, the government also affects equitable changes through its Reconstruction and Development Program. At the heart of President Mandela's vision, this program employs public works and economic development projects to improve the nation's vast and impoverished African townships (Ford 1996). The Truth and Reconciliation Commission attempts to remedy racial inequalities from a different perspective, through a national dialogue about and reconciliation of the nation's past. Under apartheid, agents of the state inflicted pain and death on those who sought change. The commission, chaired by Archbishop Desmond Tutu, grants amnesty to those who confess, fashions a record of evils perpetuated, and makes amends to affected families (Cose 1997).

In Brazil, affirmative action is not as well developed. The main reason for this is a lack of concerted effort at the federal level. Although the Brazilian Ministry of Justice, with the help of Helio Santos, is currently drafting an affirmative-action policy, no such official program exists as yet. Despite the fact that racial discrimination has increased since the 1960s and 1970s and that Brazil has alternated places with the United States as the more racially unequal of the two, activists have made little headway. Elites resist redistributive policies and hold on to the "supraracial" denial of race in their pursuits of a racial democracy (Andrews 1992). Nonetheless, led by a core of Brazilian lawyers, trade unionists, and black-movement members, activists have been able to politicize race and break down these techniques to deny racial inequalities more than in the past. The state-patrolled racial line is becoming more nuanced (Winant 1994) as activists begin to establish departments to represent them and progressive leaders begin to face the issues (Reichmann 1995). As one federal deputy admits: "We must concretize the issue with specific proposals, to break through the official farce that in Brazil there is no racism, but also to try 'positive discrimination' — places in the universities, quotas . . . I believe it's a necessary stage; it shouldn't be permanent but it is necessary."[62]

The private sector has also attempted to affect change. Increasing numbers of private actors, especially multinational corporations (oddly enough), have instituted diversity policies that include some of the features of affirmative-action programs in South Africa and the United States. In fact, voluntary corporate diversity programs have emerged in several forms, the most significant of which are internship and scholarship programs and hiring policies that explicitly make racial diversity a goal (Moffet 1996). In a different type of effort, a conference of unionists met in 1994 to strategize over the role of labor in combating racism and advocating antidiscrimination social policies.[63]

A Comparative Evaluation of Affirmative Action

We now attempt to selectively evaluate the effects of the above-described affirmative-action measures. This assessment focuses somewhat on the United States, particularly in the areas of employment and higher education, simply because South Africa has only recently begun to institute such measures and Brazil is still in the process of formulating them. Nonetheless, this section will try to incorporate findings and insights from the South African and Brazilian experiences as well.

Affirmative Action and the Elimination of Racial Discrimination

Affirmative action has been effective at reducing—but not eliminating—racial discrimination with respect to hiring, promotion, and wages in the United States (Darity 1995; Leonard 1984a, 1984b, 1985, 1990). Nearly all empirical studies have found that employers respond to the presence of affirmative-action requirements by hiring more people of color and paying them more (Montgomery 1996). For example, before the Civil Rights Act of 1964, the median earning of a black male worker was only 60 percent of that of a white male worker. By 1993, however, the gap had narrowed so that the median earning of a black male worker was about 75 percent of that of a white male worker (*Affirmative Action Review* 1993). Nonetheless, racial discrimination remains a major factor in the United States (Montgomery 1996). For example, adjustments for racial differences in education and work experience can only explain about 50 percent of wage gap between black men and white men and 33 percent of the gap between black women and white men (*Affirmative Action Review* 1993).

In South Africa, Nelson Mandela's government prompted ambitious affirmative-action goals.[64] Although it is too early to say conclusively, the preliminary results suggest that affirmative action is effective at reducing employment discrimination. For example, between October 1994 and April 1995, the number of blacks employed in the civil service rose by about 5,800 (Ford 1996). The most dramatic increases have occurred in security services, through the use of such shake-up strategies as black appointments to commissionerships in the police force and integration of armed forces.[65] Likewise in the private sector, some sources have reported that between 59 and 94 percent of South African companies have undertaken some variety of affirmative-action program, although others have responded less diligently. On a more hopeful note, however, the Black Management Forum was striving for 70 percent black corporate supervisors, 40 percent middle managers, and 30 percent senior managers by the year 2000 (Ford 1996).

As for Brazil's attempt to eliminate racial discrimination, little progress has been documented. The lack of federal action mentioned above, compounded with an economic crisis in the 1980s, a continued concentration of blacks in economically stale areas, and the resistance of half the population provides activists with formidable barriers to real improvement (Andrews 1992). As one observer notes:

> Victories are partial . . . as African Brazilian organizations and their colleagues in unions and parties are frequently attacked for uncritically adopting foreign ideology and promoting policies that don't reflect the "Brazilian reality." In part, those attacks draw upon a nationalist defense of the status quo, but they also reflect a more profound critique of the dominant model of universal individual rights and remedies —a model often loosely associated with U.S.-style affirmative action. (Reichmann 1995: p. 39)

Affirmative Action and Racial Compensation and Reconciliation

Although the quantitative analysis indicates that affirmative action has benefited people of color (as the above example illustrates as well), the impact of such programs has not sufficiently compensated for past discrimination because they have not produced a significant redistribution of resources and power (Montgomery 1996). In fact, it is a myth that affirmative-action programs have meant the imposition of reverse racism on whites. The net result is that affirmative action has had little significant impact for either people of color or whites in the United States (Montgomery 1996). As for South Africa, compensation and reconciliation are integral parts of their nascent affirmative-action policies,[66] although it is too premature to evaluate their impact. But as one South African leader claims:

> We are inheriting not only attitudes as in the United States, we are inheriting a national ideology [and] structure that were in place for years and years. . . . We talk of a rainbow nation because we have to create an image for the world . . . because we have been shameful . . . but to heal people and to heal nations is not easy. The healing process has to take place in the world from generation to generation.[67]

Unfortunately this healing process appears lacking in Brazil. The small-scale, informal diversity policies of some of the Brazilian institutions only highlight the nation's overall need to address issues of compensation and reconciliation.

Affirmative Action and Racial Inclusiveness and Diversity

A comparison between the United States and South Africa on the one hand and Brazil on the other offers a good illustration of the value of affirmative action in promoting racial inclusiveness and diversity. For example, in the United States, the number of blacks in the professions doubled between 1960 and 1972. In addition, the number of black engineers tripled and the number of blacks in Congress and state legislatures doubled between roughly the same period (Sowell 1981). Similarly, South Africa has experienced a significant increase in black representation in both public- and private-sector employment. By contrast, Brazil, because of its lack of affirmative-action policies, has had little success attaining greater diversity and inclusivity. African Brazilians have amassed little political clout, holding less than 5 percent of all nationally elected congressional posts, and few leadership positions among the twenty-six political parties and hundreds of trade unions (Reichmann 1995). The manifesto of one black Brazilian movement consequently declared: "Of twenty-four governors, hardly two are black. We don't have blacks as Ministers of State. Of the 548 federal deputies and senators, the number of blacks is less than 10. . . . We don't have generals, admirals or black brigadiers. . . . We don't have one black diplomat" (Sundiata 1987: pp. 70–71). Although some Brazilian institutions, mostly in the private sector, have implemented diversity programs more recently, little data exists as to their impact.

Likewise, a comparative observation can be made in the area of higher education, this time between the United States and Brazil. For some time now since the civil rights era, the U.S. Supreme Court has supported the use of racial considerations in university admissions programs.[68] Acting on the finding that "the interest of diversity is compelling,"[69] institutions of higher learning in the United States have taken various approaches to increase minority enrollment. When one such approach was successfully challenged in the state of Texas,[70] black enrollment plummeted. For example, at the University of Texas Law School in 1996, thirty-one of sixty-five admitted blacks enrolled, but in preparation for fall 1997, only eleven blacks had been admitted and none had yet enrolled at the time of this writing.[71] The comparison with Brazil lies in the fact that in 1993 a call was made for special admission quotas for black students in the new Rio de Janeiro State University at Campos (Reichmann 1995). This call was ignored. Perhaps Brazil, as well as South Africa, could learn from the recent regressive experience in the United States. Without affirmative action, efforts at achieving racial inclusivenes and diversity fail.

An Alternative Vision: Transformative Action

It is time . . . for those of us committed to racial . . . equity to advance a more fundamental critique of existing [affirmative-action] conventions. It is time to discuss how conventional . . . criteria do not function fairly, democratically, or even meritocratically for many . . . who are not members of racial . . . minorities. To reclaim the moral high ground, we must broaden and expand the terms of engagement . . . we can move from an incrementalist strategy of inclusion for a few to a transformative vision of reform for the many. (Sturm and Guinier 1996: p. 956)

All things considered, a conventional conception of affirmative action has been only moderately successful at achieving its objectives in the United States, especially in light of the fact that productivity has not been adversely affected by its implementation (Holzer and Neumark 1996; Leonard 1990; Montgomery 1996). In addition, affirmative action appears to be on the road to a degree of success in South Africa. Nonetheless, affirmative action has its limitations.[72] The crucial drawback of affirmative action in any of the three countries is that it is only affirmative; it does not address the overarching structural forces that shape the environment in which affirmative action is crafted and implemented. Therefore, the racial hierarchy remains in force, privileging whites and subordinating nonwhites in often subtle ways that distort, if not significantly impede, the processes of change that affirmative action could represent. A more effective alternative for securing racial justice and meaningful democracy, then, must go a step further. This strategy must be both affirmative and transformative. Transformative in this context means exposing, directly challenging, and dismantling the racial hierarchy that legitimates and perpetuates the favoritism of whites and the subjugation of nonwhites.

Transformative Action Distinguished from Affirmative Action

To differentiate between transformative and affirmative action does not mean to engage in simple wordplay. Admittedly, an implicit goal of affirmative action is to change substantially institutional and economic arrangements and therefore transform. Nonetheless, the nature of affirmative action, its components and policy aims, confine it to the parameters set forth by and within the current system of white privilege.[73] Speaking metaphorically, affirmative action seeks to change the size of the pieces of pie distributed without questioning what goes into the pie and challenging who controls the preparation and distribution of the pie. To put it more concretely, affirmative action, even in its most aggressive form, tries to address nonwhite subordination without focusing on white privilege. Indeed, it often further entrenches white privilege. The current claim of innocent whites and reverse discrimination operates to both obscure black subordination and assume normalcy of white privilege. So long as white privilege remains intact, antisubordination efforts can only go so far.[74] As a consequence, racial hierarchy not only remains but also takes on a pernicious sense of legitimacy, inevitability, and permanency.[75] Winant (1994), in describing the current predicament faced by Brazil and the United States, indirectly articulates the shortcomings of affirmative action:

> In neither country has the racial dimension of stratification and social inequality been seriously transformed. Rather, the more overt manifestations of racism have receded, as white supremacy in the United States and the blanket denial of racism in Brazil have been weakened, *without any fundamental reorganization of the racialized social structures of the two societies.* (p. 164, emphasis in original)

Notwithstanding the Mandela administration's heroic efforts, the same can be said of South Africa. Many of the most powerful decision-making posts in the government and the private sector continue to be held by whites, many of whom held these same positions of power during the apartheid era (Marcuse 1995). Thus, the way issues are talked about, understood, and addressed, let alone identified, remains shaped by assumptions and realities that flow from white privilege and racial hierarchy. It does not appear remarkable that all U.S. presidents and vice-presidents, chief justices, Senate and House majority leaders, and well over 90 percent of CEOs are white males. This is explained, if it is addressed at all, as the natural distribution of the market based on merit and individualism. Without question, the reality of persisting white privilege undermines the transformative potential of progressive policy initiatives such as affirmative action in all three countries.

Transformative action, by contrast, must expose and address both racial subordination and privilege and therefore dismantle racial hierarchy. What this means specifically will be explored in the next subsection. For now, suffice it to say that a transformative approach must address the most important levels and aspects of economic and social life in each country in a fundamental manner.[76] "Transformation" describes not just the goals of racial justice and substantive democracy, it also describes the means or process for working toward those ends. This strategy, then, must focus not simply on eliminating discrimination or effecting a more racially just distribution of resources (as embodied by a more racially equitable wage structure, for example) but also on striving to ensure that everyone participates in redefining and reshaping our respective democracies, which in turn helps to reform ourselves individually and collectively. Consequently, this transformation must be institutional, communal, and personal, as well as experiential and attitudinal.

The Possible Features of a Transformative-Action Policy

Among its possible features, a transformative-action policy must embody and promote a contextualized conception of race in place of the essentialized version that has legitimated or otherwise facilitated the persistence of racial hierarchy. In so doing, such a strategy must make apparent the social, economic, and political forces that have contributed to the current position of nonwhites and whites. An important implication is that racial inequality will no longer be seen as due to the individual intellectual failings of some and merit or skill of others. Under this strategy, personal weaknesses and strengths will certainly be acknowledged, but more important, structural forces will be identified and addressed. In this context, critics of affirmative action within the United States, South Africa, and Brazil will, for example, no longer be able to dismiss glibly the academic difficulties of nonwhite children as due to a lack of values or motivation of the racial Other. A transformative-action policy must also spark the dialogue and action that will reveal the role of, for example, inadequate resources and staffing of predominantly nonwhite elementary schools in diminishing educational achievement and subsequent social and economic advancement.

A second feature of a transformative-action policy must be a comprehensive integration strategy. Integration, under this approach, *does not mean assimilation* in any sense of the word.[77] If we are to eliminate discrimination and establish true democracy, that which is inclusive and participatory, we must look beyond simply hiring or university admission policies and practices. We must act on all fronts; we must "rethink the whole."[78] To use the elementary-school example again, if such institutions with large nonwhite populations continue to struggle with the inferior resources that flow from nonwhite subordination and white privilege operating in tandem, these children will not be in a position to take advantage of affirmative-action hiring or university admission practices. These children will have been forced out of the competition, so to speak, a long time before they could get to the point of benefiting from such policies (Ford 1996; Cummins 1996). The issue of residential location provides another example of the importance of a comprehensive strategy. Nonwhite children in the United States, South Africa, and Brazil continue to be confined, in disproportionate numbers, in neighborhoods devastated by poverty, crime, despair, and the lack of access to any form of opportunity,[79] while white children in these three countries continue to be situated in neighborhoods where most of the needed survival and economic resources are provided. Such spatial segregation, isolation, and stigmatization occurring in the three nations is as powerful as it is subtle in continuing the oppression codified by apartheid and Jim Crow many years ago (Cummins 1996; Marcuse 1995). Is it any wonder, then, that so many nonwhite children, compared to their white peers, struggle?

A comprehensive integration element, that is, the integration of the workplace, schools, neighborhoods, civic organizations, and other public spaces, will effectively address this sad predicament in two ways. First, meaningful integration will enhance nonwhites' access to the opportunity structure, thereby adjusting whites' access to an equitable level. This means that there will be a racially just distribution of resources and power and all members of each society will have similar life chances and choices. Second, integration of the workplace, schools, neighborhoods, and other public spaces will mean greater interaction and dialogue between and among the races, the constitutive force of which should not be underestimated. The interaction and dialogue that results from such integration is the key to mutual respect and understanding that, in turn, provide the bedrock of meaningful democracy (Evans and Boyte 1986; powell 1996; DuBois 1971; Dewey 1916).

Lastly, a transformative-action policy must strive to "water the roots, not the branches" (Ford 1996). Realizing that lasting improvements for nonwhites are not solely achieved through "resource transfers to individuals based upon ascribed identity characteristics," transformative action must utilize broader efforts "to provide meaningful access, earlier in life, to the institutions and mechanisms by which society cultivates the human capital that makes individuals attractive for admission, employment, or promotion on their own" (Ford 1996: pp. 2014–2015). Indeed, the ground in which these roots are tended might need to be altered through the development of transformed institutions and mechanisms of opportunity. Of course, it will be necessary to ensure that non-white individuals have opportunities to succeed within these transformed structures as well.

It is impossible to say precisely how a transformative-action policy would look in each country. Even if put in place, it would undoubtedly change as we and our respective contexts and realities change. The basic approach for all three nations, however, might include the following strategies:

- The focus on ending white privilege and the prevalent ideology of "whiteness";
- The enactment and vigorous enforcement of rigorous antidiscrimination and racially inclusionary laws that provide punitive consequences and incentives for recalcitrance and compliance, respectively, regarding housing, education, employment, public health and safety, financial capital, and so forth;
- The creation and ongoing monitoring and adjustment of racial diversity goals with respect to all important aspects of economic and social life;
- The creation and expansion of forums and other public spaces where people of different racial identities can talk and engage

each other and themselves and where racial-diversity programming can be developed and conducted;
- The redistribution of cultural, social, political, and economic resources, including the capacity to define values, norms, standards, and practices.

If this sounds all-encompassing, that is because it is. Nothing short of this will exorcise the demons of racism that still haunt and affect us in profound ways.

Conclusion

Racism, sadly, remains a powerful reality in the United States, South Africa, and Brazil. The only way we can overcome it is if we dismantle racial hierarchy. To do this, we must not essentialize race, and we must individually and collectively recognize that racial stratification of all three countries is not natural or inevitable. We must consider the ways persistent racial inequality flows from institutional (both public and private) and individual policies and practices that create, legitimate, and perpetuate the savage subordination of nonwhites and the unconscionable privileging of whites. Affirmative action, although somewhat successful, focuses only on trying to mitigate the subordination of nonwhites. Even though the scope of affirmative action is more limited than that of transformative action, paradoxically it has more difficulty vindicating its objectives. The reason for this is simple. Affirmative action does not try to alter substantially the ongoing and dramatic imbalance in the distribution of power and resources in favor of whites. In other words, without also addressing white privilege, it is mathematically impossible for affirmative action even to compensate fully nonwhites for the effects of past discrimination, let alone to forge a more inclusive, participatory democracy in Brazil, South Africa, or the United States.

Transformative action, in contrast, will simultaneously target racial subordination and privilege, producing more racial and substantive equity and equality. By dismantling racial hierarchy, such a strategy changes who we are communally and personally in a fundamental fashion. This paves the way for better mutual and self-understanding and the true elimination of racial discrimination. Under these, and only these, circumstances will we be able to create and maintain meaningful democracy in the United States, South Africa, Brazil, and the rest of the world.

Notes

1. In this chapter, "race" is defined broadly to include ethnicity and nationhood (as pertaining to indigenous populations).

2. To be "raced" signifies that racialization is a sociohistorical process by which racial categories are created. Before one can possess a racial identity there must be this process of "racing" in which the attributes that differentiate racial classifications are designated and given meaning. A top-down process, "racing" enables the more powerful group to deny the racial Other of its self-definition. "Racing," when viewed as a verb, is a mechanism for implementing and justifying domination and subjugation. To be "raced," then, is to be defined and shaped by racist oppression (powell 1997).

3. Gotanda further distinguished between a "sensitive" version of race color-blindness in which a decisionmaker is sensitive to race but attempts to discount it, and a "strong" version in which all race-related characteristics are discounted and all validity is denied to racial experience (Gotanda 1991).

4. See, for example, Biskupic 1997, a 1997 Washington Post-ABC News survey in which only 17 percent of white Americans polled think African Americans and other minorities should receive preference in college admissions to make up for past inequalities.

5. In California the California Civil Rights Initiative, Cal. Const. Art. 1, s 31 (a), dubbed Proposition 209, was adopted by the voters by a margin of 54 to 46 percent to eliminate public race- and gender-based affirmative-action programs. The Ninth Circuit Court of Appeals held that the initiative did not violate the equal protection clause and was not preempted by Title VII. *Coalition for Economic Equity v. Wilson*, 110 F. 3d 1431, 1437, 1448 (1997).

6. See, for example, *Hopwood v. Texas*, 78 F. 3d 932, 945 (5th Cir. 1996), cert. denied, 116 S. Ct. 2581 (1996) (use of race as a factor in preferential admission policy of University of Texas law school violates Equal Protection Clause of 14th Amendment).

7. See, for example, Sonn 1993, where it is argued that less qualified blacks should be hired and trained. "Other measures" include equitable ownership in corporations, and so on.

8. Some South African scholars are concerned, however, that nonracism is being used to protect racial exclusion, largely on the basis of "merit." See, for example, Sachs (1992): "Suddenly the biggest racists became the most ardent non-racists . . . people who have been discriminating all their lives discover the virtues of non-discrimination . . . and now there is nothing to stop anyone from achieving their just due on basis of merit alone. . . . To give special preference would, they assert, be as bad as denying them opportunities in the past" (p. 119).

9. In fact, even prior to abolition Brazil imported the largest number of slaves and officially encouraged cohabitation (Reichmann 1995).

10. The 1951 antidiscrimination statute, the Afonso Arinos Law, has been criticized for lack of enforcement mechanisms.

11. See generally, Sundiata 1987.

12. In this article, "racial discrimination" is also defined broadly to include discrimination based on ethnicity and nationhood.

13. See generally, Harris 1993; Gotanda 1991; Peller 1990. For a discussion of the importance of experience and context in informing perspectives and analysis, see also Abram 1996; Kuhn 1962.

14. See generally, Harris 1993; Gotanda 1991; Crenshaw 1988; Lawrence 1987.

15. See generally, Jordan 1968; Stanton 1960.

16. See generally, Gould 1981; Stocking 1968.

17. See generally, Hernstein and Murray 1994.

18. See, for example, *Saint Francis College v. Al-Khazraji*, 481 U.S. 604, 613 (1987): "The Court of Appeals was thus quite right in holding that § 1981 'at a minimum,' reaches discrimination against an individual 'because he or she is genetically part of an ethnically and physiognomically distinctive sub-grouping of homo sapiens.'" See also *Fullilove v. Klutznik*, 448 U.S. 448, 524 (1980) (Stewart, J., dissenting): "The color of a person's skin . . . [is an] immutable [fact]."

19. See, for example, Anderson 1988; Gerard 1990.

20. Vera 1996; Orten 1988. Compare the Brazilian understanding of racial composition to the one-drop rule in the United States, which made all gradations of racial difference insignificant. Winant 1994.

21. See generally, Silva and Halsenbalg 1992.

22. Robinson 1995. It is important to note that Brazil has made the distinction between blacks or *pretos* who are of predominantly African ancestry, and browns or *pardos,* who are of mixed racial ancestry, but that, nonetheless, the color line is drawn today between white and nonwhite (Andrews 1992).

23. As we have now understood that the racial categories of "black," "white," and the rest—"brown," "yellow," "nonwhite," "mestizo," etc.—are actually nonspecific constructs whose meanings change across countries, continents, regions, and even cities, such words will no longer be held in "scare quotes," and the reader is advised to appreciate their implicit ironies.

24. See generally, *Adarand Constructors, Inc. v. Peña*, 515 U.S. 200 (1995); *City of Richmond v. J. A. Croson Co.*, 488 U.S. 469 (1989); *Washington v. Davis*, 426 U.S. 229 (1976).

25. Such discrimination has constructed and now maintains a segregated United States, isolating people of color from meaningful opportunities and the chance to participate fully in economic and public life. For a discussion illustrating discrimination pervasive in the lending market see, e.g., Galster 1993; Long and Caudill 1992; Bates 1989. For an analysis of discrimination in the housing market see, e.g., Downs 1994; Massey and Denton 1993; Galster 1992.

26. See, for example, Sandel 1982.

27. For a discussion of this dynamic in the United States, in particular, see Harris 1993. For a discussion of how experience shapes identity and self, see Sandel 1982.

28. For an analysis of the United States experience, which also speaks to

the situation in Brazil and South Africa, see generally, Williams 1990; Bell 1987; Said 1978.

29. See generally, Mahoney 1995, where it is argued that segregation reflects and reinforces socially created concepts of "blackness" and "whiteness"; see also, Massey and Denton 1993, where it is argued that individual and collective use of space is race making. For example, "because of feedback between individual and collective behavior, neighborhood stability is characterized as a series of thresholds, beyond which various well-perpetuating processes of decay take hold." As this decay persists, whites move out and segregated neighborhoods of concentrated poverty grow into what the authors describe as a "ghetto."

> Given the lack of opportunity, pervasive poverty, and increasing hopelessness of life in the ghetto, a social-psychological dynamic is set in motion to produce a culture of segregation. Under the structural conditions of segregation, it is difficult for ghetto dwellers to build self-esteem by satisfying the values and ideals of the larger society or to acquire prestige through social accepted paths. . . . As new generations are born into conditions of increasing deprivation and deepening isolation . . . the culture of segregation becomes autonomous and independent. (Massey and Denton 1993: p. 184)

30. See generally, Young 1990.

31. See generally, Goldberg 1993.

32. Fontaine described the connection between the racialization of poverty and white privilege when discussing Brazil: "Even low class whites have benefited from the working of racial discrimination. . . . This explains why the bulk of the abandoned children of Brazil are black . . . why the overwhelming majority of the men and women in prison are black; and why in order to make ends meet millions of . . . black families have to take their children from school and send them to work . . . in one of the most systematic systems of child labor in modern times" (Sundiata 1987: p. 68).

The Kerner Commission, established by President Johnson to study the causes of civil unrest in the 1960s also recognized the interrelationship between racial subordination and white privilege: "What white Americans have never fully understood—but what the Negro can never forget—is that white society is deeply implicated in the ghetto. White institutions created it, white institutions maintain it, and white society condones it" (United States National Advisory Committee on Civil Disorders 1965).

33. This statistic was based on blacks that had received a college degree by 1976.

34. See, for example, Orfield 1993; Massey and Denton 1993; Wilson 1987.

35. Reichmann 1995. In a study of children's drawings in poor schools, it was found that children already project racial stereotypes by the age of seven or eight. Drawings portrayed black figures doing manual labor with unhappy faces and raggedy clothing, while white figures were portrayed as working in offices or standing by big cars, with happy faces and nice clothing.

36. *Plessy v. Ferguson*, 163 U.S. 537, 549 (1896). For an excellent discussion of this issue, see Harris 1993: "Property is a legal construct by which selected private interests are protected and upheld . . . . When the law recognizes, either explicitly or implicitly, the settled expectations of whites built on the privileges and benefits produced by white supremacy, it acknowledges and reinforces a property interest in whiteness that reproduces Black subordination" (pp. 1730–1731).

37. McIntosh (1988: p. 2).

38. See, for example, Schill and Wachter 1995.

39. According to one survey, 97 percent of whites support antidiscrimination in principle while only 38 percent support federal enforcement of employment discrimination laws (Oppenheimer 1996).

40. See, for example, Bureau of the Census 1990. For a comprehensive discussion of the ongoing significance of housing or place to life-chances and choices, see Cummins 1996.

41. Lowe (1989: p. 91); see also Marx (1996) discussing governmental enforcement of white privilege despite the accompanying inefficiencies and costs of racialized governmental regulation.

42. Frayssinet 1996. For a discussion of this phenomenon in Latin America in general, see Vera 1996.

43. Cose (1997: p. 218). Bonganjalo Goba is the head of South Africa's Institution for Multi-Party Democracy.

44. Cose 1997; see also generally, Mahoney 1988; Johnson 1995; Calmore 1995.

45. See, for example, Calmore 1995. See also, *U.S. v. Bakke*, 438 U.S. 265, 327 (1978)(plurality), where Justices Brennan, White, Marshall, and Blackmun stated that "claims that law must be 'color-blind' or that the datum of race is no longer relevant to public policy must be seen as aspiration rather than as description of reality. This is not to denigrate aspiration; for reality rebukes us that race has too often been used by those who would stigmatize and oppress minorities. Yet we cannot . . . let color blindness become myopia which masks the reality that many 'created equal' have been treated within our lifetimes as inferior both by the law and by their fellow citizens" (p. 327).

46. See, for example, Goldberg 1993; Bell 1992.

47. *Affirmative Action Review: Report to the President* (1993: p. 1.2.2); Wiseman 1993.

48. For a recent summary of the justification for affirmative action, see generally, Bermann 1996.

49. The 13th, 14th, and 15th Amendments, U.S. Const. Amend. XIII, XIV, XV.

50. Civil Rights Act of 1964, Pub.L. No., 88-352, 78 Stat. 241, 241-49, 252-66 (codified as amended at 42 U.S.C. ss 2000a-2000f [1994]).

51. Lauer 1996. The two orders were: Exec. Order No. 10,925, 3 C.F.R. 448 (1959-1963), issued by President Kennedy, which encouraged and coined the term "affirmative action"; and Exec. Order No. 11,246, 3 C.F.R. 339 (1964-1965), proscribing discrimination and compelling certain government contractors to make race a factor in selection through hiring goals.

52. See, for example, Simms 1995.

53. This was determined by the U.S. Supreme Court as applicable to state affirmative-action programs in *City of Richmond v. J. A. Croson Co.*, 488 U.S. 469, 498 (1989); and most recently to federal programs in *Adarand Constructors, Inc. v. Peña*, 515 U.S. 200, 2117 (1995).

54. The degree of evidence required varies depending on whether the entity is private or public.

55. In fact, the U.S. Supreme Court has held that, as a constitutional matter, affirmative action normally must have these attributes. See generally, *Adarand Constructors, Inc. v. Peña*, 515 U.S. 200 (1995); *Regents of the Univ. of Cal. v. Bakke*, 438 U.S. 265 (1978). But see *United States v. Paradise*, 480 U.S. 149 (1987) (upholding a 50 percent promotions quota for African Americans in a state law enforcement body in order to remedy the present effects of past discrimination).

56. See, for example, *Paradise*, 480 U.S. at 182-83; *Wygant v. Jackson Bd. of Educ.*, 476 U.S. 267, 280-81 (1985) (quoting *Fullilove v. Kluznick*, 448 U.S. 448, 484 [1980]): "When effectuating a limited and properly tailored remedy to cure the effects of prior discrimination, such a 'sharing of the burden' by innocent parties is not impermissible" (pp. 280–281).

57. *Local 28 of the Sheet Metal Workers' Int'l Ass'n v. EEOC*, 478 U.S. 421 (1986). See also generally, Baida 1994.

58. See, for example, *Hopwood v. Texas*, 78 F. 3d 932, 945 (5th Cir. 1996), cert. denied, 116 S. Ct. 2581 (1996) (use of race as factor in preferential admission policy of University of Texas law school violates Equal Protection Clause of 14th Amendment). Similar lawsuits in Washington and Florida are pending. See also the California Civil Rights Initiative, Cal. Const. Art. 1, s 31 (a), dubbed Proposition 209. Although the constitutionality of this amendment is not completely resolved, *Coalition for Economic Equity v. Wilson*, 110 F. 3d 1431, 1437, 1448 (1997), the California Board of Regents voted to drop race as a factor in admissions in 1995. Similar constitutional amendments barring affirmative action are being proposed in Florida, Colorado, Ohio, and Washington (Applebome 1997).

59. *Hopwood v. Texas*, 1996. The United States Department of Education, Office of Civil Rights, interprets Hopwood as applicable only to the "separate track" admissions policy utilized at the time of the suit. In fact, according to the department, Texas is under a clear legal obligation to root out past and present discriminatory practices; i.e., affirmative action is still appropriate for universities to employ.

60. *Hopwood v. Texas*, 1996, citing Republic of South Africa Ministry of Public Service and Administration 1995.

61. Ford 1996. This is the case with South African Airways, the national park service, and the state rail company, Transnet.

62. Reichmann (1995: p. 37). This quote was part of an interview granted by PT Federal Deputy Jose Genoino in December, 1992.

63. Reichmann 1995. The conference, which met in November, was entitled the Inter-American Trade Union Conference for Racial Equality and was convened by Vicente da Silva, president of the Unified Workers Central (Central Unica de Trabalhadores or CUT) and the São Paulo-based Center for the Study of Labor Relations and Inequality (CERT). Participants included rep-

resentatives of all three of Brazil's labor confederations, African-American delegates from the AFL-CIO, representatives of the A. Philip Randolph Foundation, and U.S. trade unionists.

64. Ford (1996: p. 1973):

> The state-owned national telephone company, Telkom, for example discovered in late 1993 that it had only one black manager among its 58,000 employees—and promptly adopted "an aggressive affirmative action plan to recruit, train, and promote many more." By August 1995, this plan had produced a further 82 black managers. By the end of 1998, Telkom aims to have blacks in 20 percent of its executive positions, 35 percent of its middle-management jobs, 45 percent of its supervisory jobs, and 70 percent of its other positions. For its part, the South African Broadcasting Corporation (SABC) set out to achieve a fifty-fifty racial balance by the end of 1997.

65. Ford 1996. The changes in the South African Police (SAP) have gone more smoothly than the integration of the various armed guerrilla fighters, etc., into the South African National Defense Force (SANDF).

66. See earlier discussion of the Truth and Reconciliation Commission.

67. Cose (1997: p. 220). The speaker here is Brigalia Bam of the South African Council of Churches.

68. See *Bakke*, 438 U.S. 265, 311-12, 314 (1978)(plurality).

69. Ibid., pp. 311–312, 314.

70. See *Hopwood v. Texas*, 78 F. 3d 932, 945 (5th Cir. 1996), cert. denied, 116 S. Ct. 2581 (1996).

71. Thomas 1997. Similar dramatic drops have occurred in California as a result of the regents' decision to curtail preferential admissions. See, e.g., "University Addresses Drop in Minority Enrollment," where the drop at Boalt Hall Law School on the Berkeley campus was 81 percent for blacks and 50 percent for Hispanics. In fact, at the time of the Hopwood challenge, only one black student of 280 that applied would have had a number high enough to put her in the category for those presumptively admitted. Moreover, of all minority candidates applying to all law schools in the nation, only 289 blacks scored high enough to place them in the law school's discretionary zone (Lauer 1996).

72. Montgomery 1996. For a discussion specifically addressing the limitations of affirmative action in the context of the severe neglect of human capital, see Ford 1996.

73. West (1992: p. 63): "The political power of big business in big government circumscribes the redistributive measures."

74. See, for example, Grillo 1995.

75. See, for example, Goldberg 1993; Crenshaw 1988.

76. For a discussion of a transformative approach in the context of regional housing and planning strategies, see Cummins 1996.

77. See, for example, powell 1996; Foner 1995; DuBois 1971; Dewey 1916.

78. Sturm and Guinier (1996: p. 958). As these two scholars put it:

We argue that affirmative action is an opportunity to take from the margin to rethink the whole. Affirmative active is not about exceptions to the norm: it is about the norm itself. Affirmative action, and the experience of those who have been previously excluded, provide a window on a much larger set of questions. These are the same questions that companies and educational institutions must face to meet the demands of an economy in transition: Can we define and predict ability to perform based on one-size-fits-all tests and criteria? How do we go about identifying the type of worker/student who will perform successfully under changing economic conditions? Is sameness fairness? Or must we reconsider the notion that in a complicated world there are simple and single solutions? How do we rethink the process and content of selection to better accommodate the demands of the twenty-first-century workplace?

One such "holistic" paradigm has been suggested by them in the area of recruitment, selection, and promotion. The goals would be: (1) to locate and develop workers who could do the job; (2) to attain genuine inclusion of underrepresented groups; and (3) to promote a collaborative opportunity structure that brings fresh perspectives to doing a better job.

79. See, for example, Cummins 1996. See also Cummins 1998. A new cause of action is proposed in the area of antidiscrimination litigation entitled "disproportionate" impact theory, which would provide a remedy for "*either* racial subordination *or* racial privilege." When utilized, this cause of action would enable the plaintiff to establish a rebuttable presumption of white privilege.

References

Abram, David. 1996. *The Spell of the Sensuousness: Perception and Language in a More-Than-Human World*. New York: Pantheon Books.

Affirmative Action Review: Report to the President. 1993. <http://www.whitehouse.gov/WH/EOP/OP/html/aa/aa-index.html> p. 1.2.2.

Anderson, Dave. 1988. "Greek Loses an Out Bet," *New York Times*, January 17.

Andrews, George Reid. 1992. "Racial Inequality in Brazil and the United States: A Statistical Comparison." *Journal of Social History* 26 (Winter): 229–263.

Applebome, Peter. 1997. "Texas Is Told to Keep Affirmative Action in Universities or Risk Losing Federal Aid," *New York Times,* March 26.

Baida, Andrew. 1994. "Not All Minority Scholarships Are Created Equal, Part II: How to Develop a Record That Passes Constitutional Scrutiny." *Journal of College and University Law* 21: 307.

Bates, Timothy. 1989. "Small Business Viability in the Urban Ghetto." *Journal of Regional Science* 29: 625.

Bell, Derrick. 1987. *And We Are Not Saved: The Elusive Quest for Racial Justice*. New York: Basic Books.

—––—. 1992. *Race, Racism, and American Law*. Boston: Little, Brown and Co.

Bermann, Barbara. 1996. *In Defense of Affirmative Action*. New York: Basic Books.

Biskupic, Joan. 1997. "Call to Renew Preferences Faces Resistance: Courts, Many White Voters Skeptical of Affirmative Action at Colleges," *Washington Post*, June 16, p. A8.

Bureau of the Census. 1990. U.S. Department of Commerce, Series P-60, no. 175. *Poverty in the United States: 1990 Current Population Reports*, p. 77.

Calmore, John. 1995. "Racialized Space and the Culture of Segregation: 'Hewing a Stone of Hope from a Mountain of Despair.'" *University of Pennsylvania Law Review* 143: p. 1233.

Cell, John. 1982. *The Highest State of White Supremacy: The Origins of Segregation in South Africa and the American South*. New York: Cambridge University Press.

Cose, Ellis. 1997. *Color Blind: Seeing Beyond Race in a Race-Obsessed World*. New York: HarperCollins.

Crenshaw, Kimberlé. 1988. "Race, Reform, and Retrenchment: Transformation and Legitimation in Antidiscrimination Law." *Harvard Law Review* 101: 1331.

Cummins, Justin. 1996. "Recasting Fair Share: Toward Effective Housing Law and Principled Social Policy." *Law and Inequality* 14: 339.

—––—. 1998. "Refashioning the Disparate Treatment and Disparate Impact Doctrines in Theory and in Practice." *Howard Law Journal* 41: 455.

Darity, William Jr., ed. 1995. *Economics and Discrimination*, vol. II. Brookfield, VT: Edward Elgar Publishing.

Dewey, John. 1916. *Democracy and Education 101*. New York: The Macmillan Co.

Downs, Anthony. 1994. *New Visions for Metropolitan America*. Washington, DC: The Brookings Institution; Cambridge, MA: Lincoln Institute of Land Policy.

DuBois, W.E.B. 1971. "Afterthought: The Problem of Humanity—The 'Voice of Voices'—The Fusion of Cultures—Not the 'Integration' of Colors," in Andrew G. Paschel, ed., *A W.E.B. DuBois Reader*. New York: Macmillan

Evans, Sara, and Harry Boyte. 1986. *Free Spaces: The Sources of Democratic Change in America*. New York: Harper & Row.

Fairclough, Adam. 1995. *Martin Luther King, Jr.* Reprint. Athens: University of Georgia Press.

Foner, Eric. 1995. "The Great Divide." *The Nation* 261: 487.

Ford, Christopher. 1996. "Challenges and Dilemmas of Racial and Ethnic Identity in American and Post-Apartheid South African Affirmative Action." *University of California at Los Angeles Law Review* 43: 1953, 1973.

Frankenberg, Ruth. 1994. "Whiteness and Americaness: Examining Constructions of Race, Culture, and Nation in White Women's Life Narratives," in Steven Gregory and Roger Sanjek, eds., *Race 63*. New Brunswick, NJ: Rutgers University Press.

Frayssinet, Fabiana. 1996. "Brazil: Slaves of Discrimination," International Press Service, July 15.

Galster, George. 1992. "Research on Discrimination in Housing and Mortgage Markets: Assessment and Future Direction."*Housing Policy Debate* 3: 639, 659.

———. 1993. "Polarization, Place, and Race." *North Carolina Law Review* 71: 1421, 1444.

Gerard, Jeremy. 1990. "CBS Gives Rooney a 3-Month Suspension for Remarks," *New York Times*, February 9.

Goldberg, David. 1993. *Racist Culture: Philosophy and the Politics of Meaning.* Cambridge, MA: Blackwell.

Gotanda, Neil. 1991. "A Critique of 'Our Constitution Is Color-Blind '" *Stanford Law Review* 44: 1.

———. 1996. "Failure of the Color-Blind Vision: Race, Ethnicity, and the California Civil Rights Initiative." *Hastings Constitutional Law Quarterly* 23: 1135, 1138.

Gould, Stephen Jay. 1981. *The Mismeasure of Man.* New York: W. W. Norton.

Grillo, Trina. 1995. "Anti-Essentialism and Intersectionality: Tools to Dismantle the Master's House." *Berkeley Women's Law Journal* 10: 16, 18–19.

Harris, Cheryl. 1993. "Whiteness as Property." *Harvard Law Review* 106: 1709.

Hernstein, Richard, and Charles Murray. 1994. *The Bell Curve: Intelligence and Class Structure in American Life.* New York: Free Press.

Holzer, Harry, and David Neumark. 1996. "Are Affirmative Action Hires Less Qualified? Evidence from Employer–Employee Data on New Hires." Madison: University of Wisconsin, Institute for Research on Poverty (discussion papers).

Johnson, Alex Jr. 1995. "How Race and Poverty Intersect to Prevent Integration: Destabilizing Race as a Vehicle to Integrate Neighborhoods." *University of Pennsylvania Law Review* 143: 1595, 1611–1612.

Jordan, Withrop. 1968. *White Over Black: American Attitudes Toward the Negro, 1550–1812.* Chapel Hill: University of North Carolina Press.

Judd, Dennis, and Todd Swanstrom. 1994. *City Politics: Private Power and Public Policy.* New York: Harper Collins College. pp. 180–181, 207–209, 392.

Kerner Commission. 1965. *Report of the National Advisory Committee on Civil Disorders.* Washington, DC: U.S. Government Printing Office.

Krattenmaker, Thomas. 1993. "Race Relations Law in a Reformed South Africa." *Harvard BlackLetter Journal* 10: 117, 120–121.

Kuhn, Thomas. 1962. *The Structure of Scientific Revolutions.* Chicago: University of Chicago Press.

Lauer, Robert A. 1996. "*Hopwood v. Texas*: A Victory for 'Equality' That Denies Reality." *St. Mary's Law Journal* 28: 109.

Lawrence, Charles III. 1987. "The Id, the Ego, and Equal Protection: Reckoning with Unconscious Racism." *Stanford Law Review* 39: 317.

Leigh, Wilhemina. 1993. "Home Ownership and Access to Credit." December 3. Unpublished manuscript on file with the Institute on Race and Poverty, University of Minnesota Law School, p. 11.

Leonard, Jonathan. 1984a. "Anti-Discrimination or Reverse Discrimination: The Impact of Changing Demographics, Title VII and Affirmative Action on Productivity." *Journal of Human Resources* 19, no. 2: 145.

———. 1984b. "The Impact of Affirmative Action on Employment." *Journal of Labor Economics* 2, no. 4: 439.

———. 1985. "What Promises Are Worth: The Impact of Affirmative Action Goals." *Journal of Human Resources* 20, no. 1: 3.

———. 1990. "The Impact of Affirmative Action Regulation and Equal Employment Law on Black Employment." *Journal of Economic Perspectives* 4: 47.

Long, James, and Steven Caudill. 1992. "Racial Differences in Homeownership and Housing Wealth, 1970–1986." *Economic Inquiry* 30: 83, 99.

Lopez, Ian Haney. 1996. *White By Law: The Legal Construction of Race*. New York: New York University Press.

Lowe, Gary. 1989. "South African Nationalism and the U.S. Civil Rights Movement: A Response to Orten." *Social Work* 34: 91.

Luft, Kerry. 1995. "Elevator Proposal Would Take Equality to the Top in Brazil," *Chicago Tribune,* September 1.

Mahoney, Martha. 1995. "Segregation, Whiteness, and Transformation." *University of Pennsylvania Law Review* 143: 1659.

Marcuse, Peter. 1995. "Transitions in South Africa: To What?" *Monthly Review* 47 no. 6: 38, n. 4.

Marx, Anthony. 1996. "Race-Making and the Nation-State." *World Politics* 48: 180, 182.

Massey, Douglas, and Nancy Denton. 1993. *American Apartheid: Segregation and the Making of the Underclass*. Cambridge, MA: Harvard University Press.

McIntosh, Peggy. 1988. "White Privilege and Male Privilege: A Personal Account of Coming to See Correspondences Through Work," in *Women's Studies* 2 (Wellesley College Center for Research on Women, Working Paper no. 189): 2.

Moffett, Matt. 1996. "Seeking Equality: A Racial 'Democracy' Begins Painful Debate on Affirmative Action," *Wall Street Journal,* August 6.

Montgomery, Edward. 1996. "A Look at Affirmative Action and Reparations in the United States." *International Policy Review* 6: 41, 43.

New York Times. 1995. "Opening a Conversation on Race," June 16.

Oliver, Melvin, and Thomas Shapiro. 1995. *Black Wealth/White Wealth: A New Perspective on Racial Inequality*. New York: Routledge.

Oppenheimer, David Benjamin. 1996. "Understanding Affirmative Action." *Hastings Constitutional Law Quarterly* 23: 921, 948.

Orfield, Gary. 1993. *Council of Urban Boards of Education, The Growth of Segregation in American Schools: Changing Patterns of Separation and Poverty Since 1968*. Alexandria, VA: National School Boards Association.

Orten, James. 1988. "Similarities and Differences in the U.S. and South African Civil Rights Struggles." *Social Work* 33: 299, 301.

Peller, Gary. 1990. "Race Consciousness." *Duke Law Journal* 1990: 758.

powell, john a. 1996. "Living and Learning: Linking Housing and Education." *Minnesota Law Review* 80: 749.

———. 1997. "The 'Racing' of American Society: Race Functioning as a Verb Before Signifying as a Noun." *Law and Inequality: A Journal of Theory and Practice* 15 (Winter): 99–125.

Rawls, John. 1999 [1971]. *A Theory of Justice*. Cambridge, MA: Belknap Press of Harvard University Press.

Reichmann, Rebecca. 1995. "Brazil's Denial of Race." *North American Congress on Latin America: Report of the Americas* 28 (May-June).

Republic of South Africa. Ministry of Public Service and Administration. 1995. White Paper on the Transformation of the Public Services (final draft).

Robinson, Eugene. 1995. "Over the Brazilian Rainbow: In This Multi-Hued Society, the Color Line Is a State of Mind," *Washington Post,* December 10.

Roisman, Florence, and Philip Tegler. 1990. "Improving and Expanding Housing Opportunities for Poor People of Color: Recent Developments in Federal and State Courts." *Clearinghouse Review* 24: 312, 343.

Sachs, Albie. 1992. *Affirmative Action and Black Advancement in Business.* Cape Town: South African Constitution Study Centre.

Said, Edward. 1978. *Orientalism*. New York: Pantheon Books.

Sandel, Michael. 1982. *Liberalism and the Limits of Justice*. New York: Cambridge University Press.

Schill, Michael, and Susan Wachter. 1995. "The Spatial Bias of Federal Housing Law and Policy: Concentrated Poverty in Urban America." *University of Pennsylvania Law Review* 143: 1285–1308.

Silva, Nelson do Valle. 1985. "Updating the Cost of Not Being White, in Brazil," in Pierre-Michel Fontaine, ed., *Race, Class, and Power in Brazil*. Los Angeles: Center for Afro-American Studies, University of California Press.

Silva, Nelson do Valle, and Carlos Halsenbalg. 1992. *Race Relations in Contemporary Brazil*. Rio de Janiero: Rio Fundo Editora.

Simms, Margaret, ed. 1995. *Economic Perspectives on Affirmative Action*. Washington, DC: Joint Center for Political and Economic Studies.

Skidmore, Thomas. 1996. "Affirmative Action in Brazil? Reflections of a Brazilianist." Unpublished manuscript prepared for the Conference on Affirmative Action sponsored by the Ministry of Justice, Brasilia, July 3–5.

Sonn, A. Franklin. 1993. "Afrikaner Nationalism and Black Advancement as Two Sides of the Same Coin," in Charl Adams, ed., *Affirmative Action in a Democratic South Africa*. Kenwyn: Juta.

South African Constitution. 1996. Ch. I, s 1(b).

Sowell, Thomas. 1981. *Ethnic America*. New York: Basic Book.

Stanton, William. 1960. *The Leopard's Spots: Scientific Attitudes Toward Race in America, 1815–59*. Chicago: University of Chicago Press.

Statistical Abstract of the United States. 1992. No. 654 (Full-Time Wage and Salary Workers by Selected Characteristics: 1983 to 1991). Washington, DC: Commerce Dept., Bureau of the Census, Economics and Statistics Administration, Data User Services Division.

Stocking, George Jr. 1968. *Race, Culture, and Evolution*. New York: Free Press.

Sturm, Susan, and Lani Guinier. 1996. "The Future of Affirmative Action: Reclaiming the Innovative Ideal." *California Law Review* 84: 953, 956.

Sundiata, I. K. 1987. "Late Twentieth Century Patterns of Race Relations in Brazil and the United States." *Phylon* 48: 65.

Thomas, Kate. 1997. "More 'Hopwood' Fallout: Minority Enrollment Down at Two Public Law Schools: Further Drops Expected." *The National Law Journal,* June 9.

United States Code Annotated. Title 42, The Public Health and Welfare. Chapter 45—Fair Housing. 42 U.S.C. §§ 3601-3631 (1994).

"University Addresses Drop in Minority Enrollment," *New York Times,* May 23, 1997, pp. A-11, C-3.

Urban Coalition. 1995. *The "Wealth Gap" Widens.* Census Analysis Update. St. Paul, MN: Urban Coalition.

Vera, Hernán. 1996. "The Vanishing Majority: The Local Globalization of Racism in Latin America." *International Policy Review Journal* 6.

West, Cornel. 1993. *Race Matters.* Boston: Beacon Press.

Williams, Patricia. 1990. *The Alchemy of Race and Rights.* Cambridge, MA: Harvard University Press

Wilson, William Julius. 1987. *The Truly Disadvantaged: The Inner City, the Underclass, and Public Policy.* Chicago: University of Chicago Press.

Winant, Howard. 1994. *Racial Conditions: Politics, Theory, Comparisons.* Minneapolis: University of Minnesota Press.

Wiseman, Nkuhlu. 1993. "Affirmative Action for South Africa in Transition: From Theory to Practice," in Charl Adams, ed., *Affirmative Action in a Democratic South Africa.* Kenwyn: Juta.

Young, Iris Marion. 1990. *Justice and the Politics of Difference.* Princeton: Princeton University Press.

14

The Seven Deadly Myths of the U.S. Nonprofit Sector: Implications for Promoting Social Justice Worldwide

Emmett D. Carson

THERE IS AN old saying that when the truth contradicts the myth, print the myth. Over 150 years ago, while visiting a young America, Alexis de Tocqueville noted that one of the things that distinguished America was its reliance on voluntary associations.

> Americans of all ages, all conditions, and all dispositions constantly form associations. They have not only commercial and manufacturing companies, in which all take part, but associations of a thousand other kinds, religions, moral, serious, futile, general or restricted, enormous or diminutive. The Americans make associations to give entertainments, to found seminaries, to build inns, to construct churches, to diffuse books, to send missionaries, the antipodes; in this manner they found hospitals, prisons, and schools. If it is proposed to inculcate some truth or foster some feeling by the encouragement of a great example, they form a society. (Tocqueville 1996: vol. 2, p. 106)

On the basis of this observation, an entire set of myths was formed about the American nonprofit sector that continues to form the basis of what many think about this sector today. The central beliefs are: (1) that the nonprofit sector is more efficient and innovative than government, and (2) that it is more concerned with the social welfare of people than the private sector because its actions are not motivated by profit or personal gain. While the nonprofit sector remains distinctive from the government and business sectors in its capacity to provide citizens with opportunities to engage in voluntary action to promote public benefit, other widely held beliefs about the American nonprofit sector are increasingly open to debate.

In the last decade, several international organizations and programs have been established with the goal of advancing and promoting the nonprofit sector worldwide.[1] While these organizations have made enormous efforts to recruit and involve people from around the world, the initial leadership and early funding have come largely from the United States. As these organizations have begun to develop bylaws, position statements, and marketing literature, the myths that are imbedded in beliefs about the U.S. nonprofit sector are being advanced inadvertently in countries throughout the world. As a result, countries that rely on the guidance of these organizations in developing their nonprofit sector may produce very different outcomes than expected.

This problem is compounded when one considers three worldwide developments—the demise of communism, national budget constraints, and concern over socioeconomic justice—that have created an unprecedented interest in understanding the role of the nonprofit sector within a democratic society. With the demise of communism as a viable alternative to the free-market system, new democracies in South America, Africa, and Eastern Europe must define the appropriate roles and mix of responsibilities for the government, business, and nonprofit sectors. There is no ideal mix, but rather choices that must be made based on each country's historical, cultural, and legal traditions. To the extent that these countries rely on a model of the nonprofit sector that incorporates significant aspects of the U.S. nonprofit sector, they are unlikely to get the anticipated outcomes due to a lack of understanding about the myths surrounding the U.S. nonprofit sector. Established democracies worldwide are facing severe budget constraints in providing services to assist the poor. This has created renewed interest in exploring the extent to which the nonprofit sector can replace or substantially augment programs and services to the poor that have been traditionally provided by government. Lastly, the nonprofit sector's role in promoting social and economic justice is of considerable interest in countries that, like the United States, enacted laws and engaged in social practices that legalized and socialized discrimination against people of African descent in nearly every facet of their existence.

While some of the myths about the U.S. nonprofit sector have been acknowledged and are openly discussed, there are significant limitations in the structure and operation of the sector as it relates to issues of racial and gender equality. The primary purpose of this chapter is to examine the myths related to the U.S. nonprofit sector and their implications for lessening racism and advancing social justice. In the United

States and abroad, it is hoped that such an exploration will help to bring much needed attention to the inherent and subtle biases that exist within the U.S. nonprofit sector as it relates to race and wealth. The next section provides a basic description of the nonprofit sector and how it operates. The subsequent sections examine seven myths about the U.S. nonprofit sector that have hidden implications for those concerned about using nonprofits to promote social-justice issues. The myths are: the myth of the U.S. origin of volunteerism and philanthropy; the myth of pure virtue; the myth of independent thought through financial independence; the myth of altruistic giving; the myth of volunteer-operated organizations; the myth of racial and gender equality; and the future myth of a societal safety valve.

There are at least two issues that should be noted before going forward. This chapter focuses largely on the U.S. nonprofit sector; however, where possible, examples are drawn from Brazil and South Africa. These countries were selected because they are the focus of the Southern Education Foundation's Comparative Human Relations Initiative for which this essay was commissioned. While Brazil, South Africa, and the United States each have vibrant nonprofit sectors, there has been only scant research on the nonprofit sectors of Brazil and South Africa compared to significant, ongoing research on the U.S. sector. Efforts to compare the number and activities of nonprofit-sector organizations in different countries are hampered by the different definitions and classifications of nonprofit organizations that exist within each country. In South Africa, the postapartheid government is currently in the process of rewriting many of its laws, including those governing the nonprofit sector. The former apartheid government had imposed major legal restrictions on the ability of antiapartheid groups to organize and to raise funds through charitable contributions. Among the many issues under consideration in South Africa is whether contributions to nonprofit organizations should result in a tax deduction for the donor.

Second, this chapter should not be interpreted as suggesting that it is inappropriate for American nonprofit leaders to encourage the development of the nonprofit sector in other countries or share their experiences. It does suggest that some of these individuals and institutions should be less rigid in their conceptualization of the appropriate relationship between the government, business, and nonprofit sectors and that public leaders be more critical in assessing the strengths and shortcomings of the U.S. nonprofit model.

What Is the Nonprofit/Nongovernmental Sector?

It is commonly accepted that every national economy can be divided into three sectors: government, business, and nonprofit. The government sector taxes citizens to provide goods and services. The business sector sells goods and services to consumers to make a profit. The nonprofit sector receives donations of time from volunteers and contributions of money from donors to provide services and engage in advocacy. The first indication of the inherent complexity of the nonprofit sector is that it is described in terms of what it is not rather than what it is (Lohmann 1989: pp. 367–383). In the United States, where reliance on the free-market system is paramount, the word *nonprofit* is used, whereas in countries where the government has typically provided most services, the word *nongovernmental* is more likely to be used. Other terms that are also used to describe this sector are: *voluntary sector, associations, civil society, independent sector, social sector,* and *third sector*.

At least part of the difficulty in establishing an appropriate name is that the nonprofit sector encompasses a wide array of organizations that serve causes, community, and individuals. This chapter will use the words *nonprofit* and *nongovernmental* interchangeably to include both grant-making and grant-seeking institutions. In the United States, there are over 38,000 grant-making foundations and over 1 million formal grant-seeking organizations, of which over 489,000 are categorized as 501(c)(3) "not for profit" organizations according to the U.S. tax code (Foundation Center 1996: p. 1). In Brazil, it is estimated that there are over 169,260 nonprofit civil associations and 11,076 foundations (Guimarães 1997). Unfortunately, there are no reliable statistics about the South African nonprofit sector at this time.

The role of the nonprofit sector is to provide the space or latitude within the law that allows for citizen participation (other than voting) in activities and causes that citizens believe receive insufficient attention or financial support by either the government or business sectors. It is the place within a democratic society that allows people to organize out of common interest for a cause or to provide services by contributing money and volunteering time. By serving as a vehicle for public discourse on competing ideas, the nonprofit sector provides a pressure release valve that sustains the core democratic system. Tocqueville observed:

> In America the citizens who form the minority associate in order, first, to show their numerical strength and so to diminish the moral power

of the majority; and, secondly, to stimulate competition and thus to discover those arguments that are most fitted to act upon the majority; for they always entertain hopes of drawing over the majority to their own side, and then controlling the supreme power in its name. (Tocqueville 1996: vol. 2, p. 196)

In the U.S. context, large-scale fundamental societal change that occurs through the nonprofit sector is often slow and difficult because a broad consensus must be developed among a multitude of competing voices. The accomplishments that are often attributed to the U.S. nonprofit system—for example, the civil rights movement and the women's suffrage movement—cannot be viewed independently of the freedoms guaranteed in the U.S. Bill of Rights. In particular, freedom of speech, freedom of religion, and right of assembly provided a national environment where nonprofit organizations could flourish. Stated differently, these freedoms allow citizens to believe whatever they want and to voice their opinions virtually anywhere they want to.

In addition to these individual freedoms, a free press has an important relationship in assisting nonprofit organizations to recruit financial contributors, volunteers, and members. As Tocqueville observed, uncensored communication increases the awareness of various ideas and enables citizens to more readily identify causes that they are willing to join by volunteering their time or making financial contributions (Tocqueville 1996: vol. 2, p. 112). A similar observation was reached in a scholarly paper on philanthropy in Brazil about "the importance of the media for the mobilization of public opinion and the development of philanthropy" (Guimarães 1997: p. 19). Without the range of individual freedoms guaranteed in the U.S. Constitution, the U.S. nonprofit system would likely operate very differently. Moreover, in another democracy with different cultural traditions, the same laws would likely generate different results. With this framework as background, the subsequent sections examine the major myths imbedded in discussions about the U.S. nonprofit sector and their implications for promoting socioeconomic justice within the nonprofit sector as well as throughout the country as a whole.

The Myth of the U.S.
Origin of Volunteerism and Philanthropy

There is a widespread misperception that the United States is singularly responsible for the spread of voluntarism. Peter Drucker, a noted international management specialist, made the following statement during a major address: "The tremendous growth of the volunteer in the West began in the U.S., where we have the oldest tradition; this movement is now rapidly coming up in Western Europe" (Sasakawa Peace Foundation 1994: p. 11).

Clearly, the idea of volunteering to help one's fellow neighbors did not begin in America. All of the world's great religions encourage its adherents to engage in charity and to help the less fortunate. Moreover, a growing body of research has begun to document that nearly every culture, over time, has had a unique history and tradition of giving (Joseph 1989). As a nation of immigrants, many of these giving and volunteer traditions are evident in the activities of each cultural group in the United States.

What is different about the U.S. nonprofit sector is the extent to which it is relied upon to promote ideas and provide services instead of government and business. The country's belief in this system is so strong that even groups that were initially denied legal status under U.S. law at the founding of the country (all who were not white male property owners) were able to use the nonprofit system to voice grievances and seek redress. With regard to African Americans, while the matter of slavery ultimately was not resolved through use of the nonprofit sector (notwithstanding the efforts of the abolitionist movement and the Underground Railroad) as discussed in myth seven, the nonprofit sector did provide the intellectual and ideological space for the women's suffrage movement, the civil rights movement, as well as the space for the ongoing discussions about gay and lesbian rights and a woman's right to an abortion. It should be noted that the women's suffrage movement gained the support of white men, in part, by suggesting that the votes of white women, influenced by their husbands and "racial" solidarity, would help to negate the impact of the African-American voter.

In addition to providing space for competing ideas, the nonprofit sector allowed African Americans, following the end of slavery, to provide essential services for themselves when these services were legally denied to them by nonprofit organizations and public agencies that assisted white Americans. As a result, African-American philanthropy and volunteering, which was allowed within limits, accounted for the creation of the first African-American churches, schools, banks, insurance companies, and a wide array of multipurpose mutual-aid associations. These institutions represented an essential survival mechanism for communities who could not rely on either the existing morality or legal structure for direct assistance.

As social protest activities for equal rights were successful in changing the laws from "separate but equal" to mandating increasing degrees of equality, the character of the nonprofit sector also has changed. A key observation is that a nation's laws are an important determinant in shaping nonprofit activity as it blends with specific cultural and historic traditions. While the United States did not invent volunteerism and philanthropy, it has relied on this mechanism to allow for competing voices and to provide services more so than other countries. As a result, African Americans and other groups have been able to use the nonprofit sector to bring their grievances and aspirations to the attention of the entire community.

The Myth of Pure Virtue

There is an inherent view in much that is written about the nonprofit sector that all actions that are undertaken within this sector are universally good. Lester Salamon has referred to this as the myth of pure virtue. He states:

> The nonprofit sector has grown and gained prominence in recent years fundamentally as a trustworthy and flexible vehicle for elemental human yearnings for self-expression, self-help, participation, responsiveness, and mutual aid. With roots often in religious and moral teachings, the sector has acquired a saintly self-perception and persona. The upshot has been a certain romanticism about its inherent purity, about its distinctive virtues, and about its ability to produce significant change in people's lives. (1995: p. 262)

A more accurate understanding of the nonprofit sector is that it is a vehicle that does not distinguish between the ethical merit or right or wrong qualities of ideas. What is considered to be a positive societal outcome by one group may significantly curtail the rights of another. The nonprofit sector equally supports racist and nonracist positions. Foundations and the grant-seeking organizations that they support can be found on every side of any societal issue. While the nonprofit sector is a powerful tool for social change within every democratic society, it is a tool that can be used to advance or curtail social justice. There are foundations and grant-seeking nonprofit organizations that support and oppose equal rights for women; equal rights for various racial groups, gays, and lesbians; a woman's right to abortion; and environmental protection and preservation, as well as other issues (People for the

American Way 1996). It is only in hindsight that a society declares which position was morally correct for its time.

An example of how U.S. philanthropy has mirrored the larger societal beliefs can be seen in foundation support of African American education (Carson 1996: pp. 2137–2141). Following slavery, few believed that African Americans could learn anything more than menial tasks. As a result, foundations focused on providing African Americans with vocational skills. By 1930, the "separate but equal" doctrine of the country, coupled with an emerging view within the African American community of a "talented tenth," led foundations to support liberal-arts education over vocational training at historically black colleges and universities. By the 1960s, the understanding that "separate is unequal" led foundations to support efforts to diversify predominantly white colleges and universities. Foundations and grant-seeking institutions, more often than not, reflect and act in accordance with the prevailing societal views.

The Myth of Independent
Thought Through Financial Independence

The belief that the nonprofit sector promotes independent thought stems from the belief that its operations are financially independent from government and business, thus providing an unbiased voice on social issues, which has been a powerful argument in support of the nonprofit sector in the United States and abroad. The idea of citizens believing in a cause so strongly as to voluntarily make contributions of time and money to support those efforts is often cited as a key feature of the American nonprofit sector.

We have something enormously special in the United States' third or independent sector that is often perceived more clearly by people from other countries than by Americans themselves. Many foreign visitors come to Independent Sector in Washington, D.C., each year to learn more about U.S. voluntary practices. These are not necessarily people who are unhappy with their political structures, but they are keenly aware that very real aspects of freedom and influence are missing when there isn't a third or buffer sector. At best, they find it restrictive and at worst oppressive when there is only the one governmental system for education, culture, or religion and when there is not a tradition of independent service and criticism (O'Connell and O'Connell 1988: p. 26).

The reality is that the nonprofit sector is far from being financially independent of government or business. In examining the sources of revenue for U.S. nonprofit organizations, one study found that nonprofit organizations are highly dependent on government contracts and fees for services to carry out significant portions of their work. It was estimated that nonprofits receive 31 percent of their income from government, 51 percent from fees for service, and 18 percent from private contributions (donations), the smallest share (Salamon 1992: p. 26). In addition, the U.S. government provides a financial incentive in the form of tax deductions to people who contribute to nonprofit organizations. While the relative importance of this provision is the subject of considerable debate, few argue that the tax deductibility of charitable contributions is a powerful incentive for individuals to contribute to charitable organizations. (This subject is more fully discussed in the next section on the myth of altruistic giving.) The U.S. government also has supported charitable organizations by providing them with service contracts to provide specific programs and services.

The same is true in Brazil, where nonprofit organizations that are designated as "public interest and associations" receive a variety of special advantages. These advantages include exemption from employer contributions to social security, eligibility to receive donations from federal and state agencies, charitable-deduction status, and eligibility to receive revenue from state lotteries, as well as other benefits. After complaints that some organizations were unfairly excluded from obtaining the special designation, the 1935 law was revised in 1990 to clarify that "eligibility is dependent on the organizations' ability to provide services without regard to race, creed, color or political conviction of actual or potential clients, and with a profit motive" (Londim 1993: p. 16). The view of an independent-thinking nonprofit sector is certainly not the perception of the nonprofit sector in some other countries where there are close ties between government and nonprofit organizations. In South Africa, for example, Nelson Mandela's African National Congress drew heavily from antiapartheid nongovernmental organizations for leadership positions throughout the new government.

There is growing overlap in the activities of the business, government, and nonprofit sectors. For example, governments are contracting with nonprofit organizations to provide assistance to the poor. To the extent the government is biased in awarding contracts to nonprofit organizations, those that are most critical of government policy or those who advocate on behalf of a discriminated-against constituency may find themselves less able to obtain government contracts and, as a result, secure their financial future. In Brazil, the Public Enterprise of the State of Rio de Janeiro works closely with nongovernmental organizations to provide sewage facilities, water ducts, and garbage collection. Over 150,000 people were reached in one project involving the Water and Sewer Company of Rio (Fisher 1992: p. 82). As federal and local governments continue their efforts to reduce costs by eliminating support for social programs, nonprofit organizations are creating profit-making enterprises to subsidize the charitable activity of the nonprofit organization (View 1995; Smith and Lipsky 1993).

While such efforts may make nonprofit organizations less dependent on government, it may also make them less responsive to the needs and interests of their primary constituents. As nonprofits manage profit-making enterprises, there is some concern that the business imperative to make a profit may undermine the social conviction of the nonprofit organization. For example, in an effort to satisfy the profit motive, will a nonprofit choose to sell an inferior product, restrain its social message, or pay its workers less than an adequate living wage in order to maintain its profit margin?

These are important questions, the implications of which are only now beginning to be fully appreciated. What is clear is that U.S. nonprofit organizations are heavily dependent on the favorable U.S. tax policies as well as revenues from government service contracts and revenues from profit-making ventures. This reliance may account for why considerable attention is given to generating financial resources, including tax incentives and self-generated income, in various manifestos that have been issued by several of the international organizations committed to promoting philanthropy worldwide. These issues are discussed in greater detail in the next section.

The Myth of Altruistic Giving

One of the most important and inspiring aspects of the nonprofit sector is the belief that citizens spontaneously and without added inducement make charitable contributions to support the causes that they believe in. The reality is that government tax incentives and the existence of enabling legal environments are often critical components for encouraging people to give. As discussed earlier, what has not been adequately appreciated is how the U.S. legal system, with its freedom of religion (believe anything), freedom of speech (say anything), and right of assembly (gather together anywhere), provided an enabling environment for the proliferation of nonprofit groups in the United States.

Unfortunately, when promoting the virtues of the nonprofit sector abroad, well-meaning advocates often forget that the enabling environment for the sector within a particular country is a key consideration that develops from each culture's charitable traditions and the country's unique history and politics. While the more astute proponents of encouraging the development of the nonprofit sector recognize the importance of an enabling environment, they often seek to promote an environment that in many respects appears very similar to that of the United States.

For example, in a widely circulated position statement, "Toward a Vital Voluntary Sector II: The Challenge of Permanence—An Action Statement," published by the International Fellows in Philanthropy Program of Johns Hopkins University, the signatories affirm their belief that deliberate action is needed to "ensure the survival of a vibrant nonprofit sector in countries around the world over the long run" (Institute for Policy Studies 1995: p. 1). While the signatories go on to acknowledge the existence and legitimacy of the multiplicity of differing relationships between the government, business, and nonprofit sectors in countries throughout the world, they nonetheless identify five areas that they deem to be most important: improving public awareness and support, generating financial resources, training and organizational capacity-building, sector service and support organizations, and research. The U.S. influence is imbedded throughout the document and is perhaps most prevalent in the section on generating financial resources. The signatories believe:

> Government must provide: i. a legal basis for legitimizing nonprofits, including legal recognition of nonprofit organizations in all their various forms; ii. tax incentives for nonprofits, including favorable treatment of the income of nonprofits and tax deductibility of gifts made to nonprofits by individual and corporate donors; and iii. subsidies for the work of nonprofits that is in the public interest. These subsidies may take various forms, including direct grants; purchase of service contract; in-kind assistance; set asides of tax revenue, lottery proceeds, and privatization income. (Institute for Policy Studies 1995: p. 3)

A similar, although less detailed recommendation has been adopted by the group CIVICUS. Specifically, CIVICUS calls for a "more supportive political, legal and fiscal environment that enables the freedom and autonomy of association," and "increased and stronger partnerships among corporate, government and civil society institutions" (CIVICUS 1995: p. 2).

There is little difference between the recommendations above and the current treatment of nonprofit organizations within the U.S. tax code. There are many countries in which nonprofits are not formally recognized and contributors do not receive tax deductions. There is no inherent reason that the nonprofit sector must be supported through tax incentives to be effective. In fact, there are some studies that suggest people would continue to give at nearly the same level without the need for a tax deduction (Clotfelter 1985).

The issue of whether individual contributors receive a tax deduction is important because the wealthier the person, the more valuable is the ability to avoid a tax. Put another way, poor people have less money to give and thus do not receive the same level of economic benefit from a tax deduction as a wealthier person. Tax systems that provide incentives (deductions) for people to contribute to the nonprofit sector may find that the issues and concerns of wealthier people—for example, arts and culture organizations—are more likely to be supported and financed. These same issues are evident in how charitable giving can be used to substantially reduce estate taxes. Wealthier people can leave some or all of their estate to the charitable organizations of their choice to provide support for the organizations' activities and reduce their overall tax liability. Obviously, poor people are less likely to utilize these tax provisions to support the charitable causes of most interest to them.

If, and there is no evidence that this is true, the wealthy are less likely to support social justice issues or income-redistribution issues (perhaps due to how some may have accumulated their wealth), nonprofit organizations focusing on social-justice issues may find it more difficult to raise the necessary financial support from wealthy contributors. This is likely to be true even when donors can receive a tax deduction. However, it is important to note that being well financed does not guarantee the broad-based public support necessary to implement a particular reform. Closely related to the myth of altruistic giving is the myth of volunteer-operated organizations.

The Myth of Volunteer-Operated Organizations

The image that is often presented of the U.S. nonprofit sector abroad is that most if not all nonprofit organizations rely heavily on volunteers to carry out their activities. While it is true that nonprofit organizations are more likely to rely on volunteers for some part of their operations (especially board governance) than either government or business, it is not accurate to suggest that most of the work of nonprofit organizations is accomplished with volunteers. In 1994, U.S. nonprofit organizations employed 9.7 million full- and part-time employees and 5.5 million full-time equivalent volunteers, which accounts for 62 percent of all volunteer employment in the U.S. economy (Hodgkinson and Weitzman 1996: pp. 28–29).

The image of the nonprofit sector as primarily dependent on volunteers is important to examine for several reasons. While volunteers play an important role in allowing nonprofit organizations to carry out their activities, large-scale, volunteer-operated nonprofit organizations are rare. Many nonprofit organizations are multimillion-dollar institutions that provide services to individuals throughout the country and require employees at all levels who have the necessary skills to ensure that quality services are provided and that financial contributions are prudently invested and accurately accounted for. This level of professionalism on a full-time basis cannot be reasonably expected of a volunteer or from a poorly paid work force. The view of a volunteer-driven nonprofit sector has contributed, in part, to why executive compensation of nonprofit leaders in the United States continues to be the subject of intense media interest. The belief in volunteers is so pervasive that there are those who believe that nonprofit professionals who request reasonable compensation, life insurance, medical benefits, and retirement plans are somehow less committed and motivated about their work.

When promoting the virtues of the nonprofit sector abroad, the image of nonprofit organizations that is often promulgated is that these institutions can be effectively managed and operated by volunteers. Lester Salamon makes the following observation:

> The belief [exists] that true nonprofit organizations rely chiefly, or even exclusively, on private voluntary action and private philanthropic support. This myth is particularly pervasive in American thinking about the nonprofit sector, but since the American nonprofit sector is widely perceived as one of the largest and most highly developed, it has affected thinking more broadly as well. (Salamon 1995: p. 263)

As stated, it is true that volunteers play a critical role in the governance of nonprofit institutions. Unfortunately, there is widespread anecdotal evidence that racial and ethnic groups are significantly underrepresented on the governing boards of foundations and grant-seeking nonprofits. While there are no reliable statistical data about the racial composition of the governing boards of grant-seeking nonprofit organizations, there are reliable data on the governance of foundations. The Council on Foundations has found that white males represent 64 percent of all foundation governing boards, compared to 27 percent for white women and 3 percent for both African-American men and women. The remaining 3 percent is divided among other ethnic groups (Council on Foundations 1996: p. 73). These data are significant because to the extent that the governing boards of nonprofit organizations are not racially diverse, those institutions are less likely to identify and be responsive to the needs of different groups, notwithstanding statements of nondiscrimination. The Ford Foundation was unique in pushing this issue to the forefront by requiring every nonprofit organization requesting a grant to identify the racial and gender composition of the organization's board and staff in evaluating whether to award a grant (Ford Foundation 1985: pp. ix–xvii). It is interesting to note that several organizations have been created in the United States with the purpose of recruiting and placing underrepresented groups on nonprofit governing boards.

   To the extent that hiring discrimination on the basis of race and gender occurs in the nonprofit sector, specific racial groups and women may find themselves less likely to be hired. Those that are hired may receive less total compensation compared to their colleagues in similar positions. This issue is examined more fully in the next section.

The Myth of Racial and Gender Equality

One of the most persistent beliefs about the nonprofit sector is that it is inclusive of all races and cultures and that issues of racism and sexism, where they exist, are isolated incidents that are not representative of the nonprofit sector as a whole. The reality, as noted earlier, is that the nonprofit sector reflects the spectrum between the most enlightened and most limited view of an issue at a given moment in history. Many of the oldest and most prestigious nonprofit organizations can look at their past histories and find that their organizations have not always equally provided services or advocated on behalf of minority communities or women. For example, in the United States, it is ironic that while the nonprofit sector can rightfully claim to have provided women opportunities for participation and leadership that were at one time denied to them in government and the private sector, it is seldom acknowledged that, reflective of the times, both then and now, women are paid less for their skills and talents than men.

The fact that the nonprofit sector can rightfully claim to have provided the necessary space for some of its members to challenge the status quo has obscured discussion of the nonprofit sector's collective behavior with regard to issues of diversity and inclusion in its hiring and employment practices. The most recent research on diversity within the nonprofit sector has raised troubling questions that refute commonly held beliefs about the nonprofit sector's commitment to a diverse and inclusive volunteer and paid work force. Notwithstanding the reliance of smaller nonprofit organizations on individual contributions and the growing percentage of racial minorities in the overall population, the U.S.-based Independent Sector has repeatedly found that people of color are simply not asked as frequently as white Americans to volunteer (Hodgkinson and Weitzman 1992: p. 210). Moreover, when asked, these same groups are far more likely to agree to volunteer. In short, these findings suggest that the strategy for increasing both giving and volunteering is for nonprofit organizations to simply ask specific racial and ethnic groups for their financial and volunteer support. What accounts for the apparent unwillingness of nonprofit organizations to ask people of color to volunteer? What does it say about the willingness of nonprofit organizations to be inclusive of different racial/ethnic groups?

Data from the U.S. Census compiled by the Nonprofit Academic Centers Council raises even more disturbing questions. The study, "Nonprofit Management and Leadership: The Status of People of Color," documents that in percentage terms, various racial and ethnic groups are underrepresented in the nonprofit sector across occupations as compared to the government and private sectors. Specifically, people of color account for 24 percent of the government sector, 21 percent of the private sector, and 17 percent of the nonprofit sector (Rogers and Smith n.d.). Other research has found that African Americans and other nonwhite ethnic groups working in foundations are underrepresented, academically more accomplished, and underpaid, compared to their European American colleagues (Burbridge 1995; Carson 1994).

At least part of the explanation for these findings may be that unlike government, which mandated and implemented affirmative-action plans, and the private sector that has begun to respond to equal employment legislation and consumer demand, small individual contributions coupled with a sizable volunteer work force may not encourage diversity in the nonprofit sector as rapidly as in other sectors. While the population growth of African, Hispanic, and Asian Americans is beginning to create new market pressures on nonprofit organizations to be more responsive to specific ethnic groups, the concern here is that the nonprofit sector's uncritical acceptance of its presumed achievements in this area (the myth of pure virtue) may be preventing a candid assessment of what the nonprofit sector has accomplished and what tasks remain.

Altogether, the available research data raise considerable questions about the predominant image of the nonprofit sector as inclusive and providing equal opportunities for people of color. What are the implications of the fact that people of color are disproportionately not asked to volunteer in nonprofit organizations that may, in some instances, purport to represent their interests? Given that volunteering is believed to lead to increased giving, why aren't these groups being asked? Why are people of color underrepresented as paid employees in the nonprofit sector? It is likely that discriminatory hiring practices account for some part of these findings. These issues suggest that those who would work through nonprofit organizations must be alert to internal organizational issues of racial and gender discrimination as they seek to address these and other social-justice issues in the larger society.

The Future Myth of a Societal Safety Valve

The nonprofit sector is not only an essential component in the U.S. safety net to provide services to the disadvantaged, but its advocacy role is essential for providing space for the expression of unpopular issues that would otherwise be ignored by the "majority wins" rules of our political system. This "majority wins" system can often lead to resentment and withdrawal by those who are not part of the winning majority. This feature strengthens rather than weakens the underlying political system. Tocqueville observed:

> They [governments] bear a natural goodwill to civil associations, on the contrary, because they readily discover that instead of directing the minds of the community to public affairs these institutions serve to divert them from such reflections, and that, by engaging them more and more in the pursuit of objects which cannot be attained without public tranquillity, they deter them from revolutions. (Tocqueville 1996: vol. 2, p. 118)

With one significant exception, the United States is widely recognized as having maintained an exceptionally stable democracy. This stability is due, in part, to the nonprofit sector that provides a constructive vehicle to promote change for citizens who disagree with the status quo. Again, the enabling environment in the United States is an essential underlying reason for this success. The one exception to the otherwise stable democracy in the United States was the Civil War. The issue of race and slavery was so divisive that the pressure release valve of the nonprofit sector was unable to contain it.

There are disturbing signs that the issue of race is once again building pressure on the U.S. democratic system that cannot be constructively diffused by the nonprofit sector. The current pressure is coming from a small segment of white Americans who have formed armed militia groups for the explicit purpose of overthrowing the U.S. government. While this may, at first, seem preposterous, these groups have: military training; amassed large stockpiles of guns, ammunition, and explosives; and carried out several attacks against government targets. It is somewhat surprising that some whites have chosen violence over peaceful change through the nonprofit sector. Considering that historical injustices that have been endured by African Americans and Native Americans in some areas continue to this day, one might have predicted that some of their members would have been more likely to take up arms. Rather than organizing to work within the system to promote change, neo-Nazi and militia groups have withdrawn from the democratic system. Unless efforts are made to successfully draw these individuals back into using the voting process and the nonprofit system to peacefully promote their views, the current violence is likely to continue to escalate. Such actions would make the future myth of the nonprofit sector as a societal safety valve an unfortunate reality.

Conclusion

Around the world, advocates for social justice are searching for new tools to combat the historic and ongoing problems of racism and discrimination. This search has become more important with the global dominance of democracy and the free-market system, as well as the need to address national budget constraints. The U.S. nonprofit system is often viewed as a successful model that has empowered dispossessed people to successfully harness and direct their own financial and volunteer resources (as well as those of supporters) to promote socioeconomic equality within the legal system. The nonprofit sector is also viewed as a way to stimulate citizen participation and provide services in lieu of, or in conjunction with, government. This chapter has examined the seven deadly myths of the nonprofit sector and their hidden implications for social-justice advocates. The myths are deadly because in addition to being misleading, they have hidden implications for social-justice advocates that may exacerbate rather than ameliorate the socioeconomic divisions that are their primary concern. This is especially relevant to advocates working abroad who may be less familiar with the opportunities and limitations presented by the U.S. nonprofit system.

The nonprofit sector can be a powerful tool for citizen self-expression and empowerment. However, it is clear that the U.S. nonprofit sector has hidden race and class considerations that should be explicitly recognized by those who would promote or use the nonprofit sector as a mechanism to address racism and socioeconomic inequality in the United States or abroad. There are enormous individual and institutional resources (financial and volunteer) that are directed through the nonprofit sector of different countries. Further analysis would appear warranted in examining how best to utilize the nonprofit sector to effectively address social-justice issues in light of the myths discussed in this chapter and the cultural and legal environment in each country. Without such forethought, advocates of using the nonprofit sector to address social-justice issues may unknowingly import some of the inequities and internal contradictions of the U.S. nonprofit sector.

Note

1. These organizations include: CIVICUS, a world alliance for citizen participation; the International Society for Third Sector Research; the Johns Hopkins University International Fellows in Philanthropy Program and Comparative Nonprofit Sector Project; and Indiana University Center on Philanthropy's Eastern European Initiative, among others.

References

Burbridge, Lynn. 1995. *Status of African Americans in Grantmaking Institutions.* Indiana University Center on Philanthropy. Indianapolis: Indiana University Press.

Carson, Emmett D. 1994. "Diversity and Equity Among Foundation Grantmakers." *NonProfit Management and Leadership* 4, no. 3 (Spring).

———. 1996. "Philanthropy and Foundations," in Jack Salzman et al., eds., *Encyclopedia of African-American Culture and History,* vol.1. New York: Macmillan.

CIVICUS: World Alliance for Citizen Participation. 1995. Self-published Annual Report.

Clotfelter, Charles T. 1985. *Federal Tax Policy and Charitable Giving.* Chicago: University of Chicago Press.

Council on Foundations. 1996. *Foundation Management Report.* 8th ed. Washington, DC: Council on Foundations.

Fisher, Julie. 1992. "Local Governments and the Independent Sector in the Third World," in Kathleen D. McCarthy et al., eds., *The Nonprofit Sector in the Global Community.* San Francisco: Jossey-Bass Inc.

Ford Foundation. 1985. "President's Review." New York: Self-published Annual Report.

Foundation Center. 1996. *Foundation Giving.* New York: Foundation Center.

Guimarães, Renato de Paiva. 1997. *Philanthropy as Social Investment: Trends and Perspectives on Philanthropy in Brazil.* New York: Center for the Study of Philanthropy, City University of New York, Working Paper No. 1 (Spring).

Hodgkinson, Virginia Ann, and Murray S. Weitzman. 1992. *Giving and Volunteering in the United States.* Washington, DC: Independent Sector.

———. 1996. *Nonprofit Almanac 1996–1997.* San Francisco: Jossey-Bass Publishers.

Institute for Policy Studies. 1995. *Toward a Vital Voluntary Sector II: The Challenge of Permanence—An Action Statement.* International Fellows in Philanthropy Program. Baltimore: Johns Hopkins University (June).

Joseph, James A. 1989. *The Charitable Impulse.* New York: The Foundation Center.

Lohmann, Roger A. 1989. "And Lettuce Is Nonanimal: Toward a Positive Economics of Voluntary Action." *Nonprofit and Voluntary Sector Quarterly* 18, no. 4 (Winter).

Londim, Leilah. 1993. "Defining the Nonprofit Sector: Brazil," in Lester M. Salamon and Helmut K. Anheir, eds., Working Papers of the Johns Hopkins Comparative Nonprofit Sector Project, no. 9. Baltimore: Institute for Policy Studies, Johns Hopkins University.

O'Connell, Brian, and Ann Brown O'Connell. 1988. *Volunteers in Action.* New York: The Foundation Center.

People for the American Way. 1996. *Buying a Movement: Right-Wing Foundations and American Politics.* Washington, DC: People for the American Way.

Rogers, Pier, and John Palmer Smith. N.d. "Nonprofit Management and Leadership: The Status of People of Color." Unpublished paper in author's possession.

Salamon, Lester M. 1992. *America's Nonprofit Sector: A Primer.* New York: The Foundation Center.

———. 1995. *Partners in Public Service: Government–Nonprofit Relations in the Modern Welfare State.* Baltimore: Johns Hopkins University Press.

Sasakawa Peace Foundation. 1994. *Crossover Between the Nonprofit and Business Sectors.* Tokyo, Japan: Self-published Symposium Report.

Smith, Steven, and Michael Lipsky. 1993. *Nonprofits for Hire: The Welfare*

State in the Age of Contracting. Cambridge, MA: Harvard University Press.

Tocqueville, Alexis de. 1996 [1835–1839]. *Democracy in America.* New York: Alfred A. Knopf Inc.

View, Jeniece. 1995. *A Means to an End—The Role of Nonprofit/Government Contracting in Sustaining the Social Contract.* Washington, DC: The Union Institute.

15

Racial Discrimination as a Violation of International Law: International Standards and Mechanisms

Gay McDougall

THE UNITED STATES, Brazil, and South Africa share in common the current realities and historical legacies of racism. All three are deeply divided societies in which racist policies have determined economic, political, and social privilege. Significant struggles have been waged within each of these countries to challenge the varied forms of racial discrimination that scar these societies. Only South Africa, in the fight against apartheid, has engaged successfully the international community in that campaign.

This chapter will describe the norms and institutional mechanisms that have been developed within the United Nations and other multilateral organizations that could be utilized by those involved in the war against racism in Brazil and the United States. The chapter also addresses how the new government of South Africa could use its new status in these international institutions to advance such efforts. At the end of the discussion, a case study develops, as an example, the contours of an international campaign to address the killings of street children in Brazil.

Emergence of the Modern International Regime to Combat Racism

Both direct and indirect instances of racial discrimination constitute clear violations of international law. In fact, in many respects principles of equality and nondiscrimination represent the most profound

435

norms that find expression today in the modern international human rights regime, a regime that grew up in the aftermath of World War II and in the midst of collapsing colonial regimes. Although racial discrimination was a broadly recognized offense of customary international law prior to the establishment of the United Nations, the world's revulsion and guilt over the state-sanctioned racism and genocide that flourished under the Nazi regime was a driving force behind the creation of both the United Nations and its human rights mechanisms. Beginning with the adoption of the UN Charter in 1945[1] and followed by the adoption in 1948 of both the Convention on the Prevention and Punishment of the Crime of Genocide[2] and the Universal Declaration of Human Rights,[3] particularly strong principles of nondiscrimination have steadily taken root within the UN's modern human rights lexicon.

More recently, the centrality of these principles was reiterated in the strongest of terms at an important forum on human rights in Vienna, Austria, in 1993. The Vienna World Conference on Human Rights created an opportunity for the international community to review the evolution that has occurred since the adoption of the Universal Declaration of Human Rights in 1948 in both the conceptualization and protection of human rights norms. State representatives at the Vienna conference adopted, by a consensus of 171 states, the Vienna Declaration and Programme of Action, which states in no uncertain terms that "respect for human rights and for fundamental freedoms without distinction of any kind is a fundamental rule of international human rights law. The speedy and comprehensive elimination of all forms of racism and racial discrimination, xenophobia and related intolerance is a priority task for the international community."[4] Once again, however, this statement, in addition to building on the principles enshrined in the UN Charter and the Universal Declaration of Human Rights, merely reaffirmed what had already emerged as a peremptory norm of customary international law.[5]

A group of international human rights treaties from the 1960s have perhaps contributed most substantially to the evolving international jurisprudence that has developed to confront the blight of racial discrimination. The UN General Assembly adopted three of the most important of these multilateral human rights treaties in the mid-1960s. In December 1965, the UN General Assembly adopted the International Convention on the Elimination of All Forms of Racial Discrimination (CERD), which advances an important definition of racial discrimination and which places on states parties* an obligation "to ensure that all public authorities and public institutions, national and local, shall act in conformity with this obligation."[6] A year later, in December 1966, the General Assembly adopted the International Covenant on Civil and Political Rights (ICCPR)[7] and the International Covenant on Economic, Social, and Cultural Rights (the Economic and Social Covenant),[8] both of which contain strong antidiscrimination clauses. Finally, a number of years later, the General Assembly adopted the Convention on the Elimination of All Forms of Discrimination Against Women, a treaty that contains important nondiscrimination clauses focusing on the eradication of gender-based discrimination, provisions which, when read with the CERD and with other human rights treaties, are particularly useful in addressing the intersection of discrimination based on both gender and race.[9]

In addition to these treaty-based efforts to eradicate racial discrimination, the United Nations' Economic and Social Council (ECOSOC) has also devoted significant resources to studying and countering the ongoing occurrence of racial discrimination throughout the world. In 1948, the Economic and Social Council requested that the UN Educational, Scientific, and Cultural Organization (UNESCO) develop a program to disseminate scientific facts that would counter commonly held racial prejudices (Banton 1996). This effort culminated in UNESCO's 1978 Declaration on Race and Racial Prejudice, which stated in the strongest of terms that "all human beings belong to a single species . . . all individuals and groups have the right to be different . . . any theory which involves the claim that racial or ethnic groups are inherently superior . . . has no scientific foundation and is contrary to the moral and ethical principles of humanity . . . any form of racial discrimination practiced by a State constitutes a violation of international law" (Banton 1996: pp. 24–25).

------

* This is an accepted, if awkward, term of art used in international law. It means the "states" or governments that are "party" to a treaty or another international legal instrument. Both words in the term carry the same singular or plural endings in treaties and legal documents (e.g., "state party" and "states parties"). Since a government may be party to a treaty by having signed it, but not a party to one of its protocols or implementing instruments, the term avoids having to say "states that are party to" or "governments that have signed" any particular document.

In 1947, the Economic and Social Council also authorized the creation of the Sub-Commission on the Prevention of Discrimination and the Protection of Minorities, the only subsidiary body of the Commission on Human Rights, to study these issues and, more important, to recommend innovative solutions to persistent patterns of racial discrimination (Banton 1996). In addition to a number of authoritative studies on both the causes and the social effects of racial discrimination, the subcommission has also proposed important protection schemes to promote the nondiscrimination principles that form the core of the modern human rights movement, including initial drafts of the CERD and the proposal to create a Committee on the Elimination of Racial Discrimination to oversee the implementation of the CERD.[10]

Many of these initial UN efforts to combat racism, particularly within the world's emerging postcolonial states, quickly led to more expansive undertakings on a number of fronts. Other important developments have included: two international conferences focusing on methods to combat racial discrimination, the designation by the UN General Assembly of three succeeding "Decades for Action to Combat Racism and Racial Discrimination," and, perhaps most important, a sustained international campaign against the racist practices of the former apartheid government in South Africa.[11]

Based on these various developments in the postwar period, the contours of an international regime to combat racial discrimination has emerged, and the United Nations remains the primary international actor tasked with enforcing this well-established human right to nondiscrimination. In general, over the past five decades the United Nations has also developed four broad enforcement mechanisms:

1. The international committees that oversee compliance with the human rights treaties, such as CERD and the ICCPR, scrutinize on a regular basis the laws, policies, and practices of states that are party to the treaty;
2. The UN Commission on Human Rights exerts "diplomatic pressure" through consultations with offending governments, appointing experts to undertake fact-finding missions to the country, and generating public exposure of violations and censure through adopting resolutions that disparage government practices;
3. In egregious situations, as with the apartheid policies of the former South African regime, the General Assembly and the Security Council may authorize sanctions or other enforcement actions; and

4. The UN Center for Human Rights implements an extensive program of "advisory services," offering offending governments
technical advice and prodding to ensure that they take appropriate steps to institute reforms.[12]

With the emergence of democratic governance in southern Africa,
the United Nations' human rights mechanisms have increasingly turned
their attention to more subtle, and in some ways more complex, forms
of racism. A recent resolution adopted in April 1997 by the UN
Commission on Human Rights, for example, notes that the commission
is

> deeply concerned that, despite continuing efforts, contemporary forms
> of racism, racial discrimination, [and more generally] any form of dis-
> crimination, *inter alia* against Blacks, Arabs, Muslims, xenophobia,
> negrophobia, anti-Semitism and related intolerance continue to persist
> and even grow in magnitude, incessantly adopting new forms, includ-
> ing new tendencies to establish policies based on racial, religious, eth-
> nic, cultural and national superiority or exclusivity. (UN Commission
> on Human Rights 1997)

Treaty-Based Enforcement
Mechanisms Within the United Nations

International Convention on the
Elimination of All Forms of Racial Discrimination (CERD)

The Convention on the Elimination of All Forms of Racial Discrimination was one of the first multilateral human rights treaties to be adopted
by the UN General Assembly following the adoption of the Genocide
Convention in 1948. The convention represents the single most important attempt on the part of the international community both to define
and to combat racial discrimination through a binding enforcement
regime. The United States and Brazil have both ratified the convention.
South Africa has signed the convention but has not yet taken the necessary steps to ratify it. Nonetheless, in light of South Africa's democratic
transition, and taking into account the fact that the CERD actually contains a clause in Article 3 specifically condemning apartheid, the South
African government should be expected to ratify the convention in the
near future.

The convention was adopted by the General Assembly in 1965 in
the midst of contentious Cold War debates over colonialism and neo-
colonial legacies in much of the developing world (Banton 1996). The

CERD defines racial discrimination in Article 1 as "any distinction, exclusion, restriction or preference based on race, colour, descent, or national or ethnic origin which has the purpose or effect of nullifying or impairing the recognition, enjoyment or exercise, on an equal footing, of human rights and fundamental freedoms in the political, economic, social, cultural or any other field of public life" (CERD 1969). The CERD, moreover, requires that all states parties address both direct and indirect discrimination in public life, including discrimination with respect to economic and cultural rights, along with traditionally recognized civil and political rights.

In addressing state obligations under the CERD, the convention focuses on the state's multiple responsibilities with respect to eliminating racial discrimination: A state party to the CERD "undertakes to engage in no act or practice of racial discrimination against persons, groups of persons or institutions" or to sponsor, defend, or support racial discrimination of any persons or organizations (CERD 1969). The first obligation, therefore, is a negative duty with respect to governmental actions. The state must refrain from engaging in or supporting any form of racial discrimination itself. This is an obligation that must be respected by all government officials at the federal, state, and local levels. In meeting this obligation, states are required to review, amend, rescind, or nullify laws, regulations, or policies that have the effect of creating or perpetuating racial discrimination.

Moreover, under the CERD a state has an affirmative duty that extends beyond a simple obligation to police the actions of governmental actors. A state party must also "bring to an end, by all appropriate means, including legislation as required by circumstances, racial discrimination by any persons, group or organization"; "encourage . . . multiracial organizations and movements"; and "take special and concrete measures to ensure the adequate development and protection of certain racial groups."[13]

States parties have an obligation to address acts of discrimination by nonstate actors in addition to acts of discrimination by agents of the state. That obligation is limited in scope, however, by the CERD's overarching definition of racial discrimination, which is contained in Article 1 of the convention. Within the meaning of the CERD, racial discrimination is defined in Article 1 as discrimination occurring within "public life,"[14] which, while it clearly reaches beyond merely the public sector, may not reach traditionally private interactions by nongovernmental actors. Several commentators have concluded, however, that the CERD essentially reaches as far as preexisting U.S. law in regulating the conduct of nonstate actors in traditional spheres of private life.[15] It is also important to note that the CERD specifically provides in Article 5 that a state's obligation to eliminate all discrimination in public life extends to the elimination of discrimination with respect to civil, cultural, economic, political, and social rights, including the rights to property, association, housing, education and training, equal participation in cultural activities, and rights of access to places of services intended for use by the public.

With regard to its substantive provisions, the CERD definition of racial discrimination is arguably broader than preexisting U.S. law in three important respects. First, the CERD carves out from the definition of racial discrimination the possibility of extensive affirmative-action programs that "ensure to such groups or individuals equal enjoyment or exercise of human rights and fundamental freedoms" (CERD 1969). Additionally, Article 2(2) authorizes states to, "when the circumstances so warrant, take, in the social, cultural and other fields, special and concrete measures to ensure the adequate development and protection of certain racial groups." Under recent U.S. Supreme Court decisions, the scope of lawful affirmative-action programs in the United States is much narrower than those that would be consistent with Articles 1(4) and 2(2) of the CERD.[16]

Second, obligations under the CERD require states parties to "take effective measures to review governmental, national, and local policies, and to amend, rescind, or nullify any laws and regulations that have the *effect* of creating or perpetuating racial discrimination wherever it exists."[17] A number of legal commentators have noted that this provision may reach beyond current constitutional protections under the 14th Amendment,[18] because the 14th Amendment has been held to require a showing of discriminatory intent in addition to discriminatory impact.[19] This divergence of the international standard for a finding of discrimination from the standard under U.S. law may be particularly significant with respect to racial inequities that are associated with the application of the death penalty in the United States.[20] It is worth noting, however, that in its ratification, the United States did not direct any language specifically to this aspect of the definition of discrimination, although U.S. cases have limited the availability of defenses based on discriminatory impact in various criminal contexts.[21]

Finally, the CERD takes a firm stand on the importance of criminalizing both racist speech and individual participation in organizations that espouse racist speech. Article 4 of the CERD provides that states parties shall criminalize the dissemination of all ideas based on racial superiority or hatred. In addition, states parties must prohibit all organizations that "promote and incite racial discrimination, and shall recognize participation in such organizations or activities an offence punishable by law." The Committee on the Elimination of Racial Discrimination, moreover, has reiterated in one of its general recommendations on the CERD that when the CERD was adopted, Article 4 was seen as "central to the struggle against racial discrimination" and that Article 4 specifically requires states parties to criminalize, among other things, the "dissemination of ideas based on racial superiority or hatred."[22] Needless to say, this position is squarely at odds with current interpretations of the 1st Amendment to the U.S. Constitution.[23]

Unfortunately, in ratifying the CERD, the U.S. Senate has sought to eviscerate the domestic legal significance of these distinctions. When the Senate ratified the convention, they qualified the ratification by attaching a package of "reservations, understandings and declarations" (RUDs) that limited the significance of the convention in U.S. law. The reservations addressed: freedom of speech, in light of 1st Amendment concerns; private conduct, to ensure that the CERD would not reach any further than preexisting legislation in addressing discrimination by nongovernmental actors in traditionally private spheres; and the CERD's dispute-resolution mechanisms, limiting the ability of states parties to appeal to the International Court of Justice (ICJ) under Article 22 in any dispute to which the United States is a party.

Perhaps the most troubling element in the package of RUDs that was submitted to the U.S. Senate by the Clinton administration, however, was a declaration stating that the substantive provisions of the CERD are "non-self-executing" and do not, therefore, provide independently enforceable, private causes of action that would allow petitioners access to U.S. courts to challenge violations of the convention (International Human Rights Law Group 1994). Legislation would have to be passed to implement the treaty provisions in U.S. law. This provision, while denying the citizens of the United States access to important domestic remedies for violations of the convention, does not in any way diminish the international legal obligations of the U.S. government under the convention (International Human Rights Law Group 1994). It does, however, expose the United States to justifiable claims of hypocrisy at the international level, as the U.S. government regularly encourages rogue states to sign major international human rights treaties, including the CERD, but refuses to extend the protections enshrined in these texts directly to U.S. citizens. Brazil did not attach RUDs to its ratification of the CERD.

The CERD's expansive notion of both the permissibility and the value of affirmative-action programs, particularly in light of a state party's obligations under the convention to address all forms of direct and indirect discrimination, offers a unique framework from which to approach the current realities and historical legacies of racist policies and practices in the United States, South Africa, and Brazil.

Enforcement of the CERD. As with most of the modern human rights treaties, the CERD creates an expert body, the Committee on the Elimination of Racial Discrimination, that is responsible for supervising the enforcement of the convention (CERD 1969). One of the committee's most important functions is to review initial and periodic reports that are required of all states parties to the convention detailing efforts to bring state laws and practices into conformity with the convention. In addition, the committee may also consider complaints lodged by one state party against another and receive and act upon petitions filed by individuals or groups alleging violations of the convention, when the state has accepted this jurisdiction under Article 14.

In general, when considering individual petitions, the committee does not issue judgments, as the committee has no means of enforcing any of the views that it may adopt in a case. Instead, the committee issues opinions, recommending potential settlements. All such exchanges are conducted on paper only—the committee does not hear oral testimony in individual cases—and there are no provisions for financial assistance to provide local groups with access to this procedure (O'Flaherty 1996). Moreover, exchanges remain confidential until the committee adopts an official opinion in a case. These final opinions, including a summary of all information received by the committee, are published in its annual report.

As of January 1996, the Committee on the Elimination of Racial Discrimination had adopted opinions in four cases against the Netherlands, France, and Norway. Another communication was declared inadmissible, and two cases were awaiting further action (O'Flaherty 1996). At present, however, there is no systematic procedure in place to allow the committee to track its recommendations to states parties in individual cases (O'Flaherty 1996), making it difficult to determine whether the committee has had any significant influence over states parties through this process. Moreover, although the Committee on the Elimination of Racial Discrimination may consider individual petitions claiming violations of the convention if the state party concerned has accepted this jurisdiction, few states have actually accepted this mechanism under Article 14 of the convention.[24] For the purpose of this discussion, it is unfortunate to note that neither the United States nor Brazil has recognized the authority of the committee to accept individual complaints under Article 14, and South Africa has not yet ratified the convention.

One attractive provision within the CERD is that unlike other human rights treaties, such as the Civil and Political Covenant and the Torture Convention, states parties to the CERD need not file a separate declaration recognizing the competence of the treaty body to consider interstate complaints. To date, however, no state party to the CERD has ever brought a complaint against another state party under Article 11.[25] This highlights the general reluctance of states to denounce the practices of other states, a reluctance that springs, presumably, out of a fear that such a denunciation would subject the denouncing state to similar scrutiny.

Despite these various limitations to the treaty's application, since 1993 the Committee on the Elimination of Racial Discrimination has developed a useful new procedure for examining situations where grave violations of the CERD are alleged to be taking place or where significant potential exists for grave violations in the immediate future. To date, the procedure has been invoked in eleven cases.[26] When the committee places a country in this early warning procedure, it will schedule public or private discussions on the situation and state representatives may be asked to appear. In most of the cases, the primary outcome of this process has been a request to a state party for an immediate report (O'Flaherty 1996). Nonetheless, the committee has also brought certain situations to the attention of the High Commissioner for Human Rights or the Secretary General. In the extreme cases of Bosnia and Herzegovina and Burundi, in 1995 the Committee on the Elimination of Racial Discrimination also brought both cases to the attention of the General Assembly and the Security Council (O'Flaherty 1996). Once a state is placed in the early warning procedure, it remains there indefinitely and may be considered repeatedly at meetings of the committee. Although NGOs have not yet done so, they may request that the committee place a country in this early warning procedure (O'Flaherty 1996).

The Committee on the Elimination of Racial Discrimination has also developed a procedure that allows the committee to consider country situations within states parties that are seriously delinquent in filing reports.[27] The committee will take the last report submitted as the basis for the committee's reconsideration under this procedure (O'Flaherty

1996).

In general terms, despite its slow and politicized start,[28] the committee has gained momentum, particularly in light of these new early warning procedures and the committee's decision that it should begin to scrutinize, *sua sponte,* conditions in those states parties with seriously overdue reports.

With the end of the Cold War, the committee is now at something of a crossroads. It must continue to assert its independence, but at the same time, the committee must also convince states parties to allow individual petitions under Article 14. Theo van Boven, a member of the CERD Committee, argues that the "centerpiece of international action to combat racism and racial discrimination should continue to be the International Convention on the Elimination of All Forms of Racial Discrimination as applied by the Committee on the Elimination of Racial Discrimination (CERD)" (Boven 1994: p. 30). This is clearly true, although states parties must first recognize the competence of the Committee on the Elimination of Racial Discrimination to receive individual petitions under Article 14 of the CERD, if the CERD is ever to become the single focal point in the international struggle to eliminate racial discrimination worldwide.

International Covenant on Civil and Political Rights (ICCPR)

The International Covenant on Civil and Political Rights contains two influential nondiscrimination clauses: Article 2(1), which prohibits discrimination in relation to any of the substantive rights enumerated in the ICCPR, and Article 26, which establishes an important independent right to equality. Article 26 states that "all persons are equal before the law and are entitled without any discrimination to the equal protection of the law. In this respect, the law shall prohibit any discrimination and guarantee to all persons equal and effective protection against discrimination on any ground such as race, colour, sex, language, religion, political or other opinion, national or social origin, property, birth or other status" (ICCPR 1966). The United States and Brazil have both ratified the ICCPR. As with the CERD, however, South Africa has signed the ICCPR but has not yet taken the necessary steps to ratify it.

By 1996, of 132 states parties to the ICCPR only 89 had accepted the First Optional Protocol, which recognizes the authority of the Human Rights Committee to consider individual petitions. Unfortu-

examining information concerning gross violations of human rights and fundamental freedoms on both a regional and a country-specific basis.[31] In addition, the commission may adopt resolutions denouncing human rights conditions in specific countries and may appoint country-specific special rapporteurs, individuals who are then charged with monitoring in detail human rights conditions in a given country or region. In exercising their mandates, country-specific special rapporteurs may conduct on-site investigations before reporting back to the annual meeting of the Commission on Human Rights.

The commission may also appoint special rapporteurs to monitor human rights from broader thematic perspectives. This has proven in recent years to be one of the most effective mechanisms developed by the commission both to enforce and to expand human rights standards. In particular, the special rapporteur on Contemporary Forms of Racism, Racial Discrimination, Xenophobia, and Related Intolerance has sought, through annual reports and country visits, to address modern instances of racism. Following on-site investigations to individual countries, thematic rapporteurs report back to the commission on specific findings. In presenting their findings, the commission's thematic rapporteurs will generally offer to use their "good offices" to push for reforms in the target country or, at a minimum, to establish a dialogue with individual states.

Surprisingly, many governments are often willing to go to rather remarkable lengths to avoid condemnation by the commission or by one of the commission's special rapporteurs. As such, the commission offers an important framework within which local activists may draw attention to persistent instances of racial discrimination and racist policies. Unfortunately, activists must recognize, at the same time, that the commission consists of official government representatives of UN member states. The commission is, therefore, a thoroughly political body, a forum where political wills are tested and strained each year through alliances and intense negotiations over which countries should be singled out that year for condemnation. China, for example, has deftly wielded its significant political clout for years to avoid any specific condemnation of its egregious human rights practices.

The special rapporteur on Contemporary Forms of Racism, Racial Discrimination, Xenophobia and Related Intolerance, Maurice Glélé-Ahanhanzo, visited the United States in October 1994 (Glélé-Ahanhanzo 1995) and Brazil in June 1995, and his reports on both countries highlight modern instances of racism and the failings of the political and the legal systems in those two countries to adequately address those problems (Glélé-Ahanhanzo 1996). The special rapporteur's final report on the United States concluded that "as he comes to the end of his investigation, the Special Rapporteur believes he can say that racism and racial discrimination persist in American society, even if not as a result of a deliberate policy on the part of the United States Government" (Glélé-Ahanhanzo 1995: para. III). The special rapporteur's report on Brazil similarly concluded that in Brazil, "it has to be acknowledged that what is generally considered to be a mere economic and social discrimination is *exclusion* based on race, colour, descent or ethnic or national origin, aimed at Indians, Blacks and people of mixed parentage" (Glélé-Ahanhanzo 1996: para. 32).

Unfortunately the special rapporteur's report on racism in the United States also demonstrates in painfully clear terms that the United Nations' human rights protection efforts remain constrained by suboptimal performance and significant deficiencies in financial support. Due to an inadequate budget and similarly inadequate research support, the special rapporteur's final report on the United States contained a significant number of legal and factual misconceptions and some disturbing generalizations, thereby presenting an opportunity for the U.S. government to issue a scathing critique of the special rapporteur's final conclusions.[32] Unfortunately, the U.S. response may have been justified with respect to the special rapporteur's general methodology, even if the underlying message of his report was largely correct, including the rapporteur's main conclusion that "racism and racial discrimination persist in American society" (Glélé-Ahanhanzo 1995), a basic conclusion that the U.S. government could not refute.[33]

Under another procedure, the "1503 procedure," the Commission on Human Rights is authorized to evaluate on a confidential basis specific petitions from individuals or nongovernmental organizations alleging the existence of "a consistent pattern of gross and reliably attested violations of human rights" (ECOSOC Res. 1503, 1970). Unfortunately this process is extremely time-consuming, as petitions must be considered by at least four separate UN bodies and all petitions remain confidential throughout the lengthy process.[34] The target governments are informed of the communications—although the identity of petitioners may be withheld—and given an opportunity to respond. The process often takes years to complete. With the exception of a few high-profile cases brought by large NGOs, it is clear that this process has not been terribly effective.

UN High Commissioner for Human Rights

Following the World Conference on Human Rights in Vienna in June 1993, the UN General Assembly created the post of UN High Commissioner for Human Rights in December 1993.[35] The high commissioner's mandate, which has undergone a significant period of clarification and evolution, calls on the commissioner to deploy human rights monitors and other experts to the field to document and report on human rights related violations;[36] to assist in human rights education in individual countries, including human rights training for the police or military; to assist in the reform of national legislation and in the drafting of national constitutions; to focus the attention of the United Nations' human rights machinery on particularly egregious human rights violations; and to offer the United Nations' good offices and mediation efforts in resolving human rights conflicts throughout the world.

Despite some initial difficulties in establishing a meaningful role for the high commissioner, over the long term the commissioner may prove especially useful in pressing the General Assembly and the Security Council to take specific enforcement actions to calm rapidly developing human rights crises in volatile regions. Above all, a strengthened position for the High Commissioner for Human Rights may ensure that situations involving grave human rights violations, including modern instances of systematic racial discrimination and genocide, are not allowed to rage out of control for months on end while the Security Council or the member states debate whether to act to quell the crisis, as was the case with respect to the genocide in Rwanda in 1994.[37]

Regional Human-Rights Systems

In addition to the UN mechanisms, there are three regional human rights mechanisms that also play a crucial role both in enforcing universal human rights standards and in setting new standards with respect to emerging international norms. As the Vienna Declaration and Programme of Action from the 1993 World Conference on Human Rights recognizes, the three regional systems in Africa, the Americas, and Europe "play a fundamental role in promoting and protecting human rights" (World Conference on Human Rights 1993). Ideally, these regional systems "should reinforce international human rights standards, as contained in international human rights instruments, and their protection" (World Conference on Human Rights 1993). The regional systems, therefore, should both complement and, as has been the case with the European system, push the human rights bodies within the United Nations to develop more expansive interpretations of basic human rights protections.

The three systems are based primarily on regional human rights treaties, although the Inter-American system was created under the Charter of the Organization of American States (OAS) rather than under the American Convention on Human Rights, and, as such, the Inter-American Commission has developed a more expansive interpretation of its own competence within the Americas. Both the African and European systems, in contrast, draw their respective mandates directly from the human rights treaties under which they were created. In comparing the three systems, at present the European system is clearly the most dynamic and the most successful in enforcing its binding decisions.[38]

The African System

The African Commission on Human and Peoples' Rights was established through the African Charter on Human and Peoples' Rights, which was adopted by the Assembly of the Heads of State of the Organization of African Unity in 1981. The commission has the authority under Articles 47 and 55 of the African Charter to consider interstate communications or complaints as well as NGO and individual complaints. To date, however, the African Commission has not yet received an interstate complaint under Article 47 (Ankumah 1996). Under Article 55, the African Commission may also consider individual complaints. Nonetheless, as with other treaty bodies, the African Commission does not have the authority to bind states parties through its decisions in individual cases. Moreover, under Articles 58 and 59 of the African Charter, opinions issued by the African Commission are subject to the approval of the Assembly of Heads of State and Government, a political body within the OAU. This subordination to a political body has seriously undermined the utility of the individual complaint mechanism (Ankumah 1996). Nonetheless, the African Commission has considered a number of individual communications — most filed by NGOs on behalf of individual victims. As of 1994, the African Commission had considered or was currently considering sixty-two communications, although at the same time the African

Commission reported that it had only one case in which a file had been "closed" (Ankumah 1996). South Africa adhered to the African Charter as of July 9, 1996.

Inter-American Commission

The Inter-American Commission on Human Rights was created under the OAS Charter and has competence, provided certain formal and substantive requirements are met, to consider petitions alleging human rights violations from or on behalf of individual victims. The commission will rely on the American Convention on Human Rights in adopting decisions, unless the state concerned is not a party to the American Convention, such as the United States, in which case the commission will issue its decisions based on the American Declaration of the Rights and Duties of Man (Shelton 1992). There have been numerous cases and decisions within the Inter-American system, but the commission has no authority to ensure that a state complies with its decisions. If a party has accepted the jurisdiction of the Inter-American Court, however, the commission may then refer a case to the court for a binding judgment and a consideration of damages. Brazil has ratified the American Convention, although Brazil has not accepted the jurisdiction of the Inter-American Court under Article 62 of the convention. The United States has signed but has not yet ratified the American Convention on Human Rights.

International Mechanisms and
the Role of Nongovernmental Organizations

Nongovernmental organizations (NGOs) play a critical role in the general treaty-based human rights machinery within the United Nations. Without assistance and prompting from NGOs, the United Nations' mechanisms would quickly deteriorate. NGOs with consultative status, and any local or affiliated NGOs that may piggyback on this consultative status, may intervene directly in many UN proceedings; file complaints; lobby member states to take action on a given issue; participate in the public debates during the sessions of the Commission on Human Rights; and submit factual or advocacy statements to the United Nations for circulation. NGOs may also interact with the international treaty bodies and submit "shadow reports" that critique and expand upon official government reports to the expert treaty bodies that monitor compliance with the International Covenant on Economic, Social and Cultural Rights; the ICCPR; the CERD; the Convention on the Elimination of All Forms of Discrimination Against Women; the Convention Against Torture and Other Cruel, Inhuman or Degrading Treatment; and the Convention on the Rights of the Child.

Conclusion

The international mechanisms described in this chapter can all be used with varying degrees of effectiveness to address racist policies and practices in Brazil and the United States. By the latter stages of the long struggle to end apartheid, every human rights mechanism within the United Nations had turned its attention to South Africa's racist policies. In many respects, the case of apartheid was unique — opposition to apartheid developed a degree of global consensus that totally isolated that regime by the end of the 1980s. That made enforcement actions by the United Nations a simpler proposition. Nevertheless, there are still important lessons that can be drawn from that experience.

One important lesson from the campaign against apartheid is that the international pressure was only effective as a complement to a vibrant struggle that was being waged from within the country. The international antiapartheid campaign was informed at every stage by the struggle that was taking place inside South Africa. Fortunately, as pressure for social change grew both internally and externally, the two movements began to nurture one another, adding synergy and momentum that served to animate both the internal and the external struggles. This symbiotic relationship was also fed by the activities of large international NGOs, many of which provided a necessary platform that facilitated the efforts of South African activists to interact with the United Nations' human rights machinery.

To date, the major emphasis within the institution of the United Nations to combat racism has been the international effort to end apartheid. In many important respects, the situations of racism that remain today on the international agenda for elimination present even greater challenges. The UN Commission on Human Rights has recently noted that "manifestations of contemporary forms of racism, racial discrimination, xenophobia and related intolerance bode ill for the international community. . . . racist propaganda and incitement to racial hatred are spreading and . . . racism is taking increasingly violent forms" (Shelton 1992: p. 122).

There have clearly been significant strides taken over the last five decades in developing mechanisms at the international level to combat racial discrimination, even though those mechanisms are still imperfect. Many of the shortcomings are related to the United Nations' permanent financial crisis, the sprawling nature of the UN bureaucracy, and the general lack of coordination on human rights issues. In many cases, however, the most significant limitation on UN action is related to the lack of political will that often exists on the part of UN member states.

Nonetheless, the UN mechanisms that have been established to combat racism and other human rights abuses are worthy of attention and offer activists worldwide a useful arena for linking domestic advocacy with international attention through a multifaceted human rights campaign. In addition, by simply participating in these UN efforts to expose and prevent racial discrimination, domestic rights groups add considerable momentum and expertise to these mechanisms. Such a commitment to improving UN mechanisms, moreover, is all the more crucial if domestic rights organizations hope to rely increasingly on international standards and mechanisms to animate domestic struggles over persistent patterns of racial discrimination, as such local advocacy efforts will depend in large part on both the credibility of the international bodies that are charged with addressing these violations and the quality of the evolving international standards themselves.

Appendix: Case Study

The following case study contains a draft plan outlining the international mechanisms that could be used to address ongoing instances of violence against street children in Brazil. This annex is intended merely as an example of the sort of advocacy strategy that local NGOs in the United States, South Africa, or Brazil might consider when designing similar international advocacy strategies around individual issues.

Violence Against Street Children in Brazil

Fact Pattern: The Commission on Human Rights' special rapporteur on Contemporary Forms of Racism, Racial Discrimination, Xenophobia and Related Intolerance, Maurice Glélé-Ahanhanzo, visited Brazil in June 1995. In his report to the Commission on Human Rights on his mission to Brazil, he noted that:

Violence against children is one of the most serious problems Brazil has to face. It mainly affects street children of Black and mixed parentage. . . . In the State of Rio de Janeiro in 1993, "Judge Siro Darlan, responsible for juvenile delinquents in Rio de Janeiro, registered 1,152 violent deaths of minors, 60 percent of which occurred in the town of Rio alone. The majority of the victims were Coloured male children." It is no easy matter to identify who is actually responsible for these murders, although members of the military or civilian police are suspected of belonging to death squads which are responsible for most of them. The investigation into the massacre at the Church of Candelaria, in Rio de Janeiro, in July 1993 revealed the involvement of police officers in child murder. (Glélé-Ahanhanzo 1996: § 56, quoting in part a survey by the International Federation for Human Rights)

Fact Pattern of Actual Case Before the Inter-American Commission on Human Rights: On or before December 28, 1991, Edson Damiao Calixto, a fourteen-year-old minor who lived in the slums on the outskirts of Recife, was beaten, shot several times, and abandoned by police who accused him of robbery in the vicinity. Edson survived, although he remains paralyzed from the injuries he received. In October 1993, three military police officers were accused of the crime. On February 22, 1994, an NGO organization (CEJIL) denounced the events before the Commission on Human Rights, requesting that Brazil be condemned for violating Edson's rights to physical integrity, protection from arbitrary detention, and due process. The commission opened the case on May 20, 1994. Although Brazil informed the commission in November 1994 that it had initiated legal proceedings in the military and civil tribunals, the prosecution did not progress. In November 1995, the commission requested additional information on the case from the petitioners. On January 18, 1996, CEJIL presented its observations regarding Brazil's response and documentation in support of the original denunciation.

Advocacy Strategy

CERD: File a shadow report with the Committee on the Elimination of Racial Discrimination. The next report from Brazil was due on January 4, 1998, although states are notoriously slow in filing mandatory reports with the committee.

At the outset, in appealing to the committee in a shadow report in 1998, groups should emphasize three points taken from the committee's final observations of Brazil's last periodic report. In its consideration in 1996 of Brazil's last report, the committee noted that:

The Statistical and qualitative information on the demographic composition of Brazil's population and on the enjoyment of political, economic, social and cultural rights provided in the State party's report
clearly show that the indigenous, black and mestizo communities suffer from deep structural inequalities and that the measures taken by
the Government effectively to combat those disparities are still insufficient. (CERD 1996)

The committee also noted, with significant concern, that in its last
report, Brazil submitted "little specific information on the implementation of the Convention in practice. In this connection, the Committee
takes note of the delegation's statement that the State party is ready to
continue the dialogue in the near future and to provide it with fuller
information on the measures taken to give effect to the Convention"
(CERD 1996: para. 2).

Finally, the committee recommended that the government of Brazil
"put more vigorously into practice its determination to defend the fundamental rights of indigenous peoples, blacks, mestizos and members
of other vulnerable groups, who are regularly the victims of serious
intimidation and violence, sometimes leading to their death" (CERD
1996: para. 19).

In addition to a factual report on the murder of street children, the
shadow report should also note that even if the attacks are being carried
out by paramilitary forces that are not under the direct control of the
Brazilian government, Brazil has an affirmative obligation under the
CERD to "bring to an end, by all appropriate means . . . racial discrimination by any persons, group or organization" (Center for Human
Rights 1988: p. 59). At the same time, it should be noted that there is
often a far more direct governmental involvement in these incidents, as
Human Rights Watch and other groups have concluded that the killings
are regularly conducted by on-duty police or by death squads comprising off-duty policemen (Human Rights Watch 1994).

In submitting a shadow report, an NGO, or a group of NGOs,
should prepare a *list of specific questions*—referring, whenever possible, back to Brazil's specific obligations under the CERD—and request
that the Committee on the Elimination of Racial Discrimination pose
the questions directly to the Brazilian government when Brazil presents
its next report to the committee.

Brazilian NGOs should *request a meeting* with members of the
Committee on the Elimination of Racial Discrimination before they
consider Brazil's next periodic report.

NGOs must develop and launch a *major press initiative* around the shadow report.

Brazilian groups should *make contact with other major international human rights groups* to seek their participation in an overall advocacy campaign around the shadow report.

Although it will be difficult working with South African NGOs, groups in Brazil should try to pressure the South African government to file an *interstate complaint* against Brazil under Article 11 of the CERD. (No interstate complaint has ever been filed with the committee, although it is at least theoretically possible, and South Africa is perhaps one of the few countries with sufficient moral credibility to pursue such a complaint. Before this can happen, however, South Africa will have to ratify the CERD—South Africa has signed but not yet ratified the convention.)

In both the shadow report and the press campaign accompanying the shadow report, *pressure Brazil to accept individual complaints* under Article 14 of the convention.

In both the shadow report and the press campaign accompanying the shadow report, press for a Third World Conference to Combat Racism, to be cosponsored by CERD and the subcommission, in which racism in Brazil could be addressed.

Link to other UN bodies. Brazilian NGOs should send a similar shadow report to the Committee on the Rights of the Child. Brazil's initial report to the Committee on the Rights of the Child was due in October 1992. As of 1996, Brazil had not yet presented a report.

Work with South African NGOs and major human rights NGOs to have them pressure the South African delegation to the Commission on Human Rights to introduce a *resolution at the commission* condemning the situation in Brazil and calling for the appointment of a *special rapporteur* to investigate human rights violations, including instances of racism, in Brazil. NGOs will also need to target support from friendly governments and from the European Union. The resolution could also ask for a second, follow-up visit by the special rapporteur on Contemporary Forms of Racism, Racial Discrimination, Xenophobia and Related Intolerance, or a joint mission to Brazil, in conjunction with a new special rapporteur on Brazil.

Third World Conference to Combat Racism: lobby for a conference to mark the end of the Third Decade and include Brazil on the agenda. The conference could be cosponsored by CERD and the subcommission.

1503 Procedure: NGOs may submit to the LTN Center for Human Rights a communication alleging a situation that appears "to reveal a consistent pattern of gross and reliably attested violations of human rights." The center sends the communication to the government concerned for comment and then sends a summary of both the communication and any government reply to a working group of the Sub-Commission on Prevention of Discrimination and Protection of Minorities for a private review. (The subcommission may request the full communication and response.) After review, the working group will decide whether to report the case to the full subcommission, which will then vote, in a closed session, on whether to transmit the communication to the Commission on Human Rights. Following discussion in a closed session at the commission, the commission will announce which countries it is reviewing under the 1503 Procedure, but the commission will not reveal the actions taken by the commission or the nature of the actual communication.

Respond to the report of the special rapporteur on Contemporary Forms of Racism, Racial Discrimination, Xenophobia and Related Intolerance, Maurice Glélé-Ahanhanzo, noting areas in which he did not present sufficient evidence and detailing any significant concerns that he may have omitted in his final report on Brazil. Request a follow-up visit, and then work with the special rapporteur to organize a productive set of follow-up meetings.

Consider a shadow report to the Human Rights Committee. At the same time, an advocacy campaign should also seek to pressure Brazil to accept individual and interstate complaints under the ICCPR.

Activism Within the Inter-American Commission[39]

File a complaint with the Inter-American Commission—contact other groups to see if similar complaints have been filed already. (CEJIL has filed a complaint against Brazil for the attempted homicide of a minor.)

Coordinate with human rights groups based in Washington, D.C., to ensure proper follow-up with the commission on the case.

Develop a media plan with respect to the communication.

Request a meeting with the members of the commission to discuss the case.

Notes

1. Charter of the United Nations, signed at San Francisco on June 26, 1945. Article 1, for example, proclaims that one of the primary purposes behind

the UN Charter, and the creation of United Nations system in general, is "to achieve international cooperation in . . . promoting and encouraging respect for human rights and fundamental freedoms for all without distinction as to race, sex, language, or religion." At the time of publication, many United Nations documents are found on-line through "Search Options" of the UN High Commissioner for Human Rights web site: <http://www.unchr.ch>.

2. Convention on the Prevention and Punishment of the Crime of Genocide, opened for signature December 9, 1948, 78 U.N.T.S. 277 (adopted by the UN General Assembly in New York on December 9, 1948, entered into force on January 12, 1951 [hereinafter referred to as the Genocide Convention]). Under the convention, the term *genocide* is defined in Article 2:

In the Convention, genocide means any of the following acts com mitted with intent to destroy, in whole or in part, a national, ethnical, racial or religious group, as such:
a. Killing members of the group;
b. Causing serious bodily or mental harm to members of the group;
c. Deliberately inflicting on the group conditions of life calculated to bring about its physical destruction in whole or in part;
d. Imposing measures intended to prevent births within the group;
e. Forcibly transferring children of the group to another group.

3. Universal Declaration of Human Rights, adopted December 10, 1948, U.N. GA Res. 217 (III 1948) (forty-eight states voted in favor of the Universal Declaration, no state opposed the Declaration, and eight states, including South Africa, abstained [hereinafter referred to as the Universal Declaration]). Following the adoption of the Charter of the United Nations, the Universal Declaration was adopted by the General Assembly to rectify the notable absence from the Charter of a clear enumeration of core human rights and fundamental freedoms. See Lillich 1991.

A growing consensus suggests that all or nearly all of the protections enumerated in the Universal Declaration have attained the status of customary international law. See, e.g., McDougal, Lasswell, and Chen 1980; Buergenthal and Maier 1990; Lillich 1991.

For the purposes of this chapter, it is important to note that the Universal Declaration clearly states in Article 2 that "everyone is entitled to all the rights and freedoms set forth in this Declaration, without discrimination of any kind, such as race, colour, sex, language, religion, political or other opinion, national or social origin, property, birth or other status." An important, independent right to equality is found in Article 7, which states that "all are equal before the law and are entitled without any discrimination to equal protection of the law. All are entitled to equal protection against any discrimination in violation of this Declaration and against any incitement to such discrimination."

4. World Conference on Human Rights (1993: para. 15, p. 33).

An earlier international conference on human rights, which was held in Tehran in 1968, similarly proclaimed in its final document that:

The peoples of the world must be made fully aware of the evils of racial discrimination and must join in combating them. The implementation of this principle of non-discrimination, embodied in the Charter of the United Nations, the Universal Declaration of Human Rights, and other international instruments in the field of human rights, constitutes a most urgent task of mankind, at the international as well as at the national level. (Center for Human Rights 1988: p. 44, quoting para. 8 of the "Proclamation of Tehran")

5. Violations of peremptory norms of general international law, *jus cogens,* constitute violations of international law, regardless of whether the state committing the offense, such as South Africa during much of its apartheid history, has consistently refused to recognize the right in question. In short, these are international principles from which no derogation is ever possible. The Restatement (Third) of the Foreign Relations Law of the United States recognizes that systematic racial discrimination constitutes a violation of peremptory norms of customary international law. (See Henkin 1982: p. 655.) The International Court of Justice has stated, most notably in the South West Africa (Namibia) advisory opinion against South Africa, that under the UN Charter member states have pledged to

observe and respect, in a territory having an international status, human rights and fundamental freedoms for all without distinction as to race. To establish instead, and to enforce, distinctions, exclusions, restrictions and limitations exclusively based on grounds of race, colour, descent or national or ethnic origin which constitute a denial of fundamental human rights is a flagrant violation of the purpose and principles of the Charter. (Legal Consequences for States of the Continued Presence of South Africa in Namibia [South West Africa], 1971 I.C.J. 16, 57 at § 131)

The court's reference to the term "in a territory having an international status" has been the subject of some debate, although as one observer has noted, this "cannot be interpreted to mean that, in the view of the court, to establish and to enforce distinctions, exclusions, restrictions and limitations exclusively based on grounds of race, color, descent or national or ethnic origin which constitute a denial of fundamental human rights is *not* a flagrant violation of the purposes and principles of the Charter, if committed elsewhere than in an international territory" (Schwelb 1972: pp. 348–349). See also the Barcelona Traction, Light & Power Co., Ltd. Case, in which the International Court of Justice has also noted that discrimination on the grounds of race violates customary international law (1970 I.C.J. 3, 32).

6. International Convention on the Elimination of All Forms of Racial Discrimination, opened for signature December 16, 1966, 660 U.N.T.S. 195 (adopted by the UN General Assembly in New York on December 21, 1965, entered into force on January 4, 1969 [hereinafter referred to as the CERD]). The CERD defines racial discrimination as "any distinction, exclusion, restriction or preference based on race, colour, descent, or national or ethnic origin which has the purpose or effect of nullifying or impairing the recognition, enjoyment or exercise, on an equal footing, of human rights and fundamental

freedoms in the political, economic, social, cultural or any other field of public life" (Center for Human Rights 1988: p. 58; Part I, Article I, Section 1 of CERD).

7. International Covenant on Civil and Political Rights, opened for signature December 16, 1966, 999 U.N.T.S. 171 (adopted by the UN General Assembly in New York on December 16, 1966, entered into force on March 23, 1976 [hereinafter referred to as ICCPR]). The ICCPR contains two influential nondiscrimination clauses: Article 2(1), which prohibits discrimination in relation to any of the substantive rights enumerated in the ICCPR, and Article 26, which establishes an important independent right to equality. Article 26 states that

> all persons are equal before the law and are entitled without any discrimination to the equal protection of the law. In this respect, the law shall prohibit any discrimination and guarantee to all persons equal and effective protection against discrimination on any ground such as race, colour, sex, language, religion, political or other opinion, national or social origin, property, birth or other status.

For a discussion of the application of these two nondiscrimination provisions, and related provisions in several regional human rights instruments, see Nowak 1993.

8. International Covenant on Economic, Social and Cultural Rights, opened for signature December 16, 1966, 993 U.N.T.S. 3 (hereinafter referred to as Economic and Social Covenant). Article 2(3) states that "the States Parties undertake to guarantee that the rights enunciated in the present Covenant will be exercised without discrimination of any kind as to race, colour, sex, language, religion, political or other opinion, national or social origin, property, birth or other status."

9. Convention on the Elimination of All Forms of Discrimination Against Women, opened for signature March 1, 1980, 1249 U.N.T.S. 14 (adopted by the UN General Assembly in New York on December 18, 1979, entered into force on September 3, 1981 [hereinafter referred to as CEDAW]). In particular, Article 2 demands that states parties "refrain from engaging in any act or practice of discrimination against women and to ensure through competent national tribunals and other public institutions the effective protection of women against any act of discrimination."

10. For a discussion of several of the initial subcommission drafts of the CERD, see Banton 1996.

11. For a summary of these various UN initiatives, see United Nations Action in the Field of Human Rights, U.N. Doc ST/HR/2/Rev.4, at 152-168 (1994); Banton 1996.

12. The Vienna World Conference on Human Rights stressed the need to strengthen "advisory services and technical assistance activities by the Centre for Human Rights. The Centre should make available to States upon request assistance on specific human rights issues, including the preparation of reports under human rights treaties as well as for the implementation of coherent and comprehensive plans of action for the promotion and protection of human rights" (World Conference on Human Rights 1993: § 68).

13. CERD at Article 2(1)(d) and (e) and Article 2. See also Article 4 (a) and (b) infra, which require that certain acts—including the dissemination of ideas based on racial superiority—be "declared an offense, punishable by law," and that membership in groups promoting such ideas must be prohibited.

14. CERD at Article 1. While there is some debate over the term "public life," several notable commentators interpret "public life" as meaning the opposite of private life, rather than referring in some way to governmental actions. See, e.g., Meron 1985.

15. See International Human Rights Law Group 1994 (noting that "the Convention appears to recognize, as does U.S. law, that limited areas of private activity are beyond the reach of nondiscrimination obligations. . . . It seems reasonable to interpret the term 'public life' as being consistent with the lines the U.S. law has drawn between activities that are and are not subject to those obligations").

Unfortunately, the Committee on the Elimination of All Forms of Racial Discrimination has not helped to clarify this confusing issue. The committee has never issued an authoritative interpretation of the term "public life" within the meaning of Article 1, and the work of the committee itself has not significantly clarified the areas of private life that the committee deems to be beyond the reach of the convention. See International Human Rights Law Group 1994.

16. See *City of Richmond v. J. A. Croson Co.*, 488 U.S. 469 (1989) (applying strict scrutiny to minority business set-aside programs in the city of Richmond); *Adarand Constructors, Inc. v. Pena*, 115 S.Ct. 2097 (1995) (mandating strict scrutiny of all federal, state, and local minority set-aside programs); *Shaw v. Reno*, 113 S.Ct. 2816 (1993) (holding that strict scrutiny must be applied in evaluating the constitutionality of a race-conscious North Carolina voting district drawn under the guidelines of the Voting Rights Act); *Miller v. Johnson* (finding a congressional district in Georgia unconstitutional and holding that strict scrutiny review is triggered whenever race is a predominant factor in drawing legislative districts).

17. CERD at Article 2(1)(c) (emphasis added); see also Banton (1996: pp. 65–66), noting that by adding the words "in effect," the convention seeks a broad definition of racial discrimination, "declaring that an action performed with a laudable intention could still be unlawful if it had a discriminatory effect. . . . To comply with the Convention a state has to enact laws prohibiting both actions with a discriminatory purpose (direct discrimination) and actions with a discriminatory effect (indirect discrimination)."

18. The Committee on the Elimination of Racial Discrimination, moreover, has stated in one of its eighteen general recommendations to states parties on the interpretation of the CERD, that "in seeking to determine whether an action has an effect contrary to the Convention, it will look to see whether an action has an unjustifiable *disparate impact* upon a group distinguished by race, colour, descent, or national or ethnic origin" (Compilation of General Comments and General Recommendations Adopted by Human Rights Treaty Bodies, U.N. Doc. HRI/GEN/ I /Rev. 1, at 68 [1994] [emphasis added]); see also Banton 1996 (quoting general recommendation XIV, as adopted by the committee in 1993); International Human Rights Law Group (1994: supra note 45, p. 60); Lawyers Committee for Human Rights (1996: p. 63)), *In the*

National Interest (1996 Quadrennial Report on Human Rights and U.S. Foreign Policy) (noting situations in which civil rights laws in the United States fail to meet international standards).

19. *Washington v. Davis*, 426 U.S. 229 (1976) (finding no constitutional support for the position that "a law, neutral on its face and serving ends otherwise within the power of government to pursue, is invalid under the Equal Protection Clause simply because it may effect a greater proportion of one race than another. Disproportionate impact is not irrelevant, but it is not the sole touchstone of an invidious racial discrimination forbidden by the Constitution.").

20. See International Commission of Jurists (1996: pp. 58–60), *Administration of the Death Penalty in the United States*. Similarly, although U.S. drug laws are facially neutral, evidence indicates that they have had discriminatory impact vis-à-vis African Americans generally and women of color in particular. The disparate impact of crack-cocaine sentencing has been particularly egregious. See, "Summary of Concerns About Race Discrimination in the U.S. Criminal Justice System," annex to letter submitted to Secretary of State Warren Christopher jointly by Human Rights Watch, International Human Rights Law Group, and the NAACP Legal Defense and Education Fund (October 27, 1996), citing Mauer and Huling 1995; U.S. Bureau of Justice Statistics 1995.

21. See, e.g., *McCleskey v. Kemp*, 481 U.S. 279 (1986) (holding that a defendant who raised an equal protection challenge to the administration of the death penalty in the United States based on statistical evidence alone must prove the existence of purposeful discrimination in order to ground an equal protection claim under the Constitution).

22. General Recommendation XV (42) on Article 4 of the CERD, "Compilation of General Comments and General Recommendations Adopted by Human Rights Treaty Bodies," U.N. Doc. HRI/GEN/1/Rev. 1, at §§ 1, 3 (p. 68).

23. See, e.g., *R.A.V. v. City of St. Paul*, 112 S.Ct. 2538, 2541 (striking down an ordinance that prohibited bias-motivated hate speech, including speech based on doctrines of racial superiority); see also International Human Rights Law Group (1994: supra note 45, pp. 48–53) (discussing constitutionally permissible limitations to 1st Amendment protections of both freedom of speech and freedom of assembly).

24. As of 1996, of the 150 states parties to the CERD, only 22 had made a declaration under Article 14 accepting the jurisdiction of the committee to receive complaints. See O'Flaherty 1996.

25. United Nations Center for Human Rights, The Committee on the Elimination of Racial Discrimination (Fact Sheet 12), at 7, GE. 91-15363-May 1991-11,070 (1991).

26. The countries include: Papua New Guinea, Rwanda, Burundi, Israel, Mexico, the former Yugoslav Republic of Macedonia, the Russian Federation, Algeria, Bosnia and Herzegovina, Croatia, and the Federal Republic of Yugoslavia (Serbia and Montenegro). See O'Flaherty 1996.

27. O'Flaherty 1996. The first report of a state party comes due one year after the convention enters into force, and reports are then due every four years

thereafter. The CERD itself states that reports are due every two years, but a number of states found this two-year reporting cycle to be overly burdensome and the committee agreed in 1988 that comprehensive reports should come due every four years instead, with brief reports to the committee during the interim period. For a discussion of this revision in the reporting process, see Banton 1996.

28. The Committee on the Elimination of Racial Discrimination, particularly in the early years, "considered with care the observations made about its work in the General Assembly debate, and sought guidance from the delegates while maintaining its own independence. . . . Sometimes its links with the General Assembly seemed too close, because some members of the Committee occasionally served in their national delegations to the Assembly and spoke on behalf of their governments when CERD's annual report was debated" (Banton 1996: p. 120). Although the Committee on the Elimination of Racial Discrimination has proven to be more independent in recent years, its sensitivity to criticism within the General Assembly has clearly tempered its work.

29. Iraq, the Federal Republic of Yugoslavia (twice), Peru, Bosnia and Herzegovina, Croatia, Angola, Burundi, Haiti, and Rwanda. See O'Flaherty 1996.

30. As of December 31, 1996, CERD had been ratified by 148 countries and the ICCPR had been ratified by 137 countries.

31. ECOSOC resolution 1235(XLII), adopted in 1967.

32. See United States of America 1995.

33. The U.S. response to the special rapporteur's report explains that "few would dispute that racism and racial discrimination do in fact continue to exist in various forms and at many levels of American society" (United States of America 1995).

34. A communication alleging a consistent pattern of gross human rights violations should be lodged first with the UN Center for Human Rights in Geneva. The petition will then be forwarded to the government concerned for comment and to a working group of the Sub-Commission on Prevention of Discrimination and Protection of Minorities, the only subcommission of the Commission on Human Rights. If the subcommission's working group, after evaluating the communication and any response from the government concerned, considers that the communication does in fact reveal a consistent pattern of gross human rights violations, the working group will then forward the communication to the full subcommission for comment. The subcommission, in a closed session, decides which communications should be forwarded to the Commission on Human Rights. The communication is then referred to a working group of the Commission on Human Rights, which makes recommendations to the full Commission on Human Rights. The commission will then vote in closed session on whether any actions should be taken. The commission may choose from a wide range of actions, including the authorization of a specific investigation or the establishment of an ongoing process to review the situation. At the end of the commission's session, a public announcement is made indicating which countries have been considered under this procedure, although the exact nature of the complaint is not revealed. The communication itself remains confidential throughout this tedious process, unless the commission ultimately

requests the Economic and Social Council to authorize the release of the specific allegations, which is, unfortunately, an exceptionally rare occurrence. For additional information, see Rodley 1992.

35. General Assembly Resolution 48/141, December 20, 1993. The General Assembly resolution lists the high commissioner's specific responsibilities as: promoting the effective enjoyment by all of civil, cultural, political and social rights, including the right to development; providing advisory services, technical and financial assistance in the field of human rights to states that request such assistance; coordinating United Nations education programs in the field of human rights; seeking to remove obstacles and impediments to the full realization of human rights worldwide; engaging in dialogue with governments to secure respect for human rights; enhancing international cooperation and coordination to promote and protect human rights; and to rationalize, adapt, strengthen, and streamline the UN's human rights machinery.

36. As of June 1997, the High Commissioner for Human Rights had established field presences in Abkhazia/Georgia, Burundi, Cambodia, Colombia, Gaza, Malawi, Mongolia, the Democratic Republic of the Congo (formerly Zaire), Rwanda, and the former Yugoslavia (Croatia, Bosnia and Herzegovina, and the Federal Republic of Yugoslavia).

37. For a discussion of the inaction of the United Nations in the face of the Rwanda crisis, see Human Rights Watch 1996.

38. Due to the limited scope of this discussion, the European system is not discussed in any significant detail in this chapter. For a detailed analysis of the European system and its case law, see generally, Gomien, Harris, and Zwaak 1996.

39. Note that there is no access to the Inter-American Court, as Brazil did not accept the jurisdiction of the court in ratifying the American Convention.

References

(Dutch) Advisory Committee on Human Rights and Foreign Policy, *The Role of the Sub-Commission on Prevention of Discrimination and the Protection of Minorities,* Advisory Report No. 20, pp. 2–6 (a publication of the Dutch Government).

Ankumah, Evelyn A. 1996. *The African Commission on Human and Peoples' Rights: Practices and Procedures*. Boston: Martinus Nijhoff Publishers.

Banton, Michael. 1996. *International Action Against Racial Discrimination*. Oxford: Clarendon Press.

Boven, Theo van. 1994. "Racism, Racial Discrimination, Xenophobia and Ethnic Violence," in Manfred Nowak, ed., *World Conference on Human Rights*. Geneva: Center for Human Rights.

Buergenthal, Thomas, and Harold G. Maier. 1989. *Public International Law in a Nutshell*. St. Paul, MN: West Publishing.

Bulletin: Prisoners in 1994. 1995. The U.S. Bureau of Justice Statistics, August.

Center for Human Rights. 1988. *Human Rights: A Compilation of International Instruments.* New York: United Nations.

Committee on the Elimination of Discrimination (CERD). 1996. UN Doc. CERD/C304/Add. 11. September 27.

ECOSOC Res. 1503 (XLVIII). 1970. UN Doc.

Glélé-Ahanhanzo, Maurice. 1995. "Special Rapporteur on Contemporary Forms of Racism, Racial Discrimination, Xenophobia, and Related Intolerance on His Mission to the United States of America from 9 to 22 October 1994 to the Commission on Human Rights," UN Doc. E/CN.4/1995/78/Add. 1.

―――. 1996. "Special Rapporteur on Contemporary Forms of Racism, Racial Discrimination, Xenophobia, and Related Intolerance on His Mission to Brazil, from 6 to 17 June 1995," Submitted Pursuant to Commission on Human Rights Resolutions 1993/20 and 1995/12, UN Doc. E/CN.4/1996/72, Add. 1.

Gomien, Donna, David Harris, and Leo Zwaak. 1996. *Law and Practice of the European Convention on Human Rights and the European Social Charter.* Strasbourg: Council of Europe Publishing.

Henkin, Louis. 1982. "Restatement of the Foreign Relations Law of the United States (Revised): Tentative Draft No. 3." *American Journal of International Law* 76, no. 3 (July): 653–657.

Human Rights Committee. 1994. Comm. no. 178.

―――. 1995. *Annual Report of the United Nations Human Rights Committee, 1995.* UN Doc. A/50/40.

Human Rights Watch. 1996. *Shattered Lives: Sexual Violence During the Rwandan Genocide and Its Aftermath.* New York: Human Rights Watch.

―――. 1994. *Final Justice.* New York: Human Rights Watch.

International Convention on the Elimination of All Forms of Racial Discrimination (CERD). 1969. Opened for signature December 16, 1966, 660 U.N.T.S. 195. Adopted by the UN General Assembly in New York on December 21, 1965, entered into force on January 4, 1969.

International Covenant on Civil and Political Rights (ICCPR). 1966. Opened for signature December 16, 1966, 999 U.N.T.S. 171. Adopted by the UN General Assembly on December 16, 1966, entered into force on March 23, 1976.

International Human Rights Law Group. 1994. *U.S. Ratification of the International Convention on the Elimination of All Forms of Racial Discrimination.* Washington, DC: International Human Rights Law Group.

Lillich, Richard B. 1991. *International Human Rights.* 2nd ed. Boston: Little, Brown.

Mauer, Mark, and Tracy Huling. 1995. *Young Black Americans and the Criminal Justice System: Five Years Later.* Washington, DC: The Sentencing Project.

McDougal, Myres Smith, Harold D. Lasswell, and Lung-chu Chen. 1980. *Human Rights and World Public Order.* New Haven, CT: Yale University Press.

Meron, Theodor. 1985. "The Meaning and Reach of the International Convention on the Elimination of All Forms of Racial Discrimination." *American Journal of International Law* 79, no. 2 (April): 283–318.

Nowak, Manfred. 1993. *U.N. Covenant on Civil and Political Rights.* Arlington, VA: N. P. Engel.

O'Flaherty, Michael. 1996. *Human Rights and the U.N.* London: Sweet and Maxwell.

Rodley, Nigel. 1992. "United Nations Non-Treaty Procedures for Dealing with Human Rights Violations," in Hurst Hannum, ed., *Guide to International Human Rights Practice*, 2nd ed. Philadelphia: University of Pennsylvania Press.

Schwelb, Egon. 1972. "The International Court of Justice and the Human Rights Clauses of the Charter." *American Journal of International Law* 66, no. 2 (April): 337–351.

Shelton, Dinah L. 1992. "The Inter-American Human Rights System," in Hurst Hannum, ed., *Guide to International Human Rights Practice*, 2nd ed. Philadelphia: University of Pennsylvania Press.

UN Commission on Human Rights. 1997. "Measures to Combat Contemporary Forms of Racism, Racial Discrimination, Xenophobia and Related Intolerance, Commission on Human Rights." Res. 1997/73.

United States of America. 1995. *Response to the Report of Maurice Glélé Ahanhanzo, Special Rapporteur on Contemporary Forms of Racism, Racial Discrimination, Xenophobia, and Related Intolerance, dated Jan. 16, 1995.* On file with author.

World Conference on Human Rights. 1993. "The Vienna Declaration and Programme of Action, United Nations Department of Public Information Reprint." DPI/1394-39399-August 1993-20M, at § 37 (p. 33).

PART 3

PROSPECTS

THE CHAPTERS IN this section sample current public discourse on race and inequality in Brazil, South Africa, and the United States. Comparatively speaking, these conversations are not only of interest in and of themselves but also for what they reveal about the stage of historical development in each country. South Africa, the youngest democracy of the three, still reflects the strong socialist sentiments evident in the struggle against apartheid and the governing alliance that today includes the African National Congress (ANC), the South African Communist Party (SACP), and the Congress of South African Trade Unions (COSATU).

Compared to the United States, the South African voices are also bravely experimental, perhaps naïvely so, revealing of South Africa's moment of optimism where, having achieved victory, so much seems possible. The same sense of the possible must have pervaded U.S. society at the time of its independence. Brazilians are increasingly emboldened by the interest of the world in their racial experience and by the growing recognition that their "great racial democracy" is a great deal less than the rhetoric of myth suggests.

South Africans and Brazilians are also preoccupied with the building of the institutions of democracy and justice. Having had these institutions for a very long time, Americans seek to defend the access African Americans and other minorities only recently achieved against the assault from the conservative right. In South Africa and Brazil, it is about building institutions and access for black people and women; in the United States, about defending access recently obtained. In South Africa and Brazil, democracy itself is at stake; in the United States, the civil rights of minorities.

The challenge in all three countries is to find democratic means to create and enhance opportunities for poor people and, as is the focus of this book, the unusually high concentration of poor people who are of African descent. The United States chose affirmative action and a host of other antidiscrimination and antipoverty measures in pursuit of this goal. South Africa, with domestic modifications in response to domestic conditions, has also followed this route. Brazil is beginning to examine such strategies as well. Much of the debate in this section is about the successes and failures of such measures in creating opportunities and a revisiting of the perennial question: Where do we go from here?

—The Editors

16

Prospects for a Nonracial Future in South Africa

Neville Alexander

SA remains a racially fractured society. Racial epithets and racist ideology may be suppressed in a show of political correctness, but race consciousness lurks beneath the surface, impeding the birth of a common patriotism and threatening, once again, to divide the nascent nation.

Mandela's dream of forging a united, non-racial nation across the chasms inherited from 45 years of National Party rule remains largely unfulfilled as he prepares to step down as president of the ANC in December. Even he—having made reconciliation a central theme of his presidency—has failed to attract support from the harmonious blend of colours captured in the phrase "rainbow nation."

—Patrick Lawrence (1997: p. 32)

The sickening recurrence of what are euphemistically labeled "racial incidents" in the new South Africa is an indication of the fact that much work and much agonizing await all those of us who cherish the notion of a "non-racial South Africa," which drove our struggle against the institutionalized racism of apartheid. In spite of these occurrences, it remains the case that most of the leadership of the country is committed, at least rhetorically, to the building of a nonracial democracy, a "rainbow nation" in which both unity and diversity will obtain. It is relevant, therefore, to ask the question: Under what conditions is the realization of such a new historical community possible?

Our optimism is based on historical, economic, and contemporary political considerations. It is a fundamental fact of our history that South Africa's diverse population has developed as an ensemble of interdependent individuals and groups such that it would be impossible in the foreseeable future for so-called white or black South Africans on their own to maintain, let alone improve, the country at its present level of economic development. This central fact has important implications in terms of both social and individual psychology. South Africans, regardless of color, language, religion, or gender, are necessarily disposed toward finding solutions that will sustain the coherence of the state and society.

Let us begin by considering one of the main historical factors that have shaped the consciousness of all the people of South Africa. It is a peculiar feature of South African history that different groups of people originating in many different parts of the world were integrated into the political economy of the country at different times and for different reasons, but in each case in order to carry out specific functions in the prevailing labor processes. Thus, to give an example, the core elements of the European ancestors of the present white Afrikaans-speaking population came to South Africa as merchants or as soldiers, servants of the mercantile Dutch East India Company. As colonial conquerors or, later, as settlers, they were destined to serve in administrative, commercial, and security capacities. Most of the forebears of people now labeled "Indian" were brought from India after 1860 as indentured laborers in order to work the sugar plantations of Natal. Most of those now labeled "black," or sometimes "African," after conquest, were integrated into the colonial capitalist economy as labor tenants or as migrant workers. And those now labeled "colored" are in the main descended from aboriginal African peoples such as the Khoi, the San, and the amaXhosa as well as from African and East Indian slaves. Within each of these groups of people, there are layers whose origins can be traced to specific needs or functions related to the labor process at a given time.

For reasons that are discussed elsewhere in this volume, the South African social formation came to be structured as a racial caste system, one where class, language, and other social markers were less salient than "race" or color. From the perspective of social psychology, where in the final analysis the fundamental shifts in "group consciousness" are recorded, the question I am addressing is whether and how the ingrained hierarchical white supremacist attitudes on the one hand and the debilitating slave mentality on the other hand can be attenuated and eventually eradicated. In a short, programmatic chapter such as this, I can do no more than raise some of the framing issues.

The Economic Sphere

Thus, to begin with we may ask: What should happen in the economic base of this society in order to ease the development of a nonracial ethos? And for the question to have any relevance at all to the subject under discussion, it has to be followed up with the corollary question: Is this happening or is it tending to happen?

It is common cause in South Africa that unless a radical redistribution of material resources is realized within the lifetime of the present generation, all the glib rhetoric of social transformation, national democratic revolution, and African renaissance will come to mock their authors and exponents in years to come. Even a relatively conservative commentator such as the Reverend Beyers Naude is quoted (in Murray 1997: p. 8) as having said that "'true reconciliation was only possible when we bridge the economic gulf, for you can't build a society of justice on the increasing gap between rich and poor.' Only if the government moved towards an equitable distribution of wealth, land property and income could the political 'miracle' begin to uproot the evil of racism which was 'deeply rooted in South Africa.'"

When we consider the continuing disparities between rich and poor, crudely, between white and black, we may well ask whether the new South Africa, in the words of Constitutional Court judge Albie Sachs, is doing anything more than legitimating inequality (see Murray 1997: p. 8). The statistics of poverty and wealth in South Africa are readily accessible (see, e.g., Wilson and Ramphele 1989; SALDRU 1994; Statistics South Africa 1998; Lam 1999). Most recently, the Poverty Hearings conducted by the South African NGO Coalition underlined the glacial tempo at which change is taking place, i.e., where it is taking place at all in the direction of ameliorating the conditions of life of the urban and the rural poor. The point is best made in the simple story of Mr. Maxwell Flekisi, a "petrol jockey" as well as "an archbishop in the Zionist Christian Church," as recounted in an installment of the *Cape Times* series entitled *One City, Many Cultures* on Friday, February 26, 1999. This father of three, sole breadwinner, earning R193 per week, gives vent to the feelings of disappointment that are eating up millions of South Africans today:

> [Since] the 1994 elections Maxwell has felt an increasing edge of desperation in his life. A desperation that renders all the freedoms and dignity guaranteed by the new political dispensation void. "I can say that the promises that were made by the ANC have not been kept," he

declares. "I can say things are much worse now than they have ever been. We are waiting to see what will happen with the next election because what does having freedom mean if you have no money?"

On what we may call broadly the left of the political spectrum, the prevailing view is that the neoliberal economic paradigm within which the transformation of the country is being tackled is a recipe for disaster at worst and for stagnation at best. The stark reality is that the political settlement of 1993–1994 was based on the retention of the status quo ante in respect of the fundamental economic relations and on the assumption of a more or less rapid trickle-down effect deriving from the "miraculous" increase in the rate of growth of the GDP, which most commentators and analysts foresaw as one of the main consequences of the end of the apartheid regime. It was assumed that there would be a constant and increasing inflow of foreign capital for direct investment in productive activities that, in turn, would lead to large-scale job creation, the renewal of the country's material infrastructure, upgrading of its transport and telecommunications systems, the provision of housing, better health and educational facilities for all.

Some of this has happened, of course. A romanticized version of the successes hitherto can be found in a pamphlet issued at the beginning of 1999 by the Government Communication and Information System, entitled *The Building Has Begun*, as well as in a more blatantly selective broadsheet entitled *Realising Our Hopes*. But only an apologist would pretend that that which everyone dreamt of has come true or even appears to be feasible in the present global and domestic conjuncture. The Growth, Employment and Redistribution (macroeconomic) strategy of the Mandela government, commonly known as GEAR, which, at bottom is a typical World Bank–IMF-style structural adjustment program, is undoubtedly not the panacea it is marketed to be by its supporters in government and big business. Concretely, there has been some "black empowerment" in the shape of co-opting individual black wannabees into the charmed circles of the ruling elites; there has been a measure of opportunities for small- and medium-scale entrepreneurs, as well as an ill-advised affirmative-action program in the civil service, itself the result of the compromise of 1993 at Kempton Park. Tap water has been brought closer to some urban and rural people who used to have to walk many miles in the past to get this basic necessity of life, and row after row of depressing, minimalist "housing units" are seen to be sprouting in the most arid of environments as shelter for those who under apartheid had nowhere to squat or were forced to live in infernal conditions of overcrowding. Among many people, these "RDP houses" have acquired the same stigma as the "toilets in the veld" of the apartheid government under P. W. Botha. There have also been some improvements in the health and educational sectors, even if they are often overshadowed in the public perception by negative developments in those self-same sectors.

These are indeed achievements and are considered to be such by the beneficiaries of these policies. But do they amount to much more than inadequate ad hoc attempts to deliver on the promises of the first flush of excitement? To draw any conclusions in this regard after a mere four years of implementation of the projected transformation, even if assessed in terms of its own assumptions and criteria of measurement, would be invidious. Consequently, our consideration of the issue has to be based on questioning the transformation paradigm itself. At worst, we might be proved wrong; at best, we might demonstrate that the promise of the pot of gold at the end of the rainbow is no more than an illusion.

The real situation is that hardly any change has taken place in the relations of economic power and control. Moreover, in the foreseeable future and in terms of the prevailing system, no such fundamental change is to be expected. All the sources of economic power remain in the hands that controlled them under apartheid. Again, the statistics are readily available. A recent detailed and extremely agonized analysis by one who remains a supporter of the ruling party puts the dilemma of the ANC government clearly. He cites the 1991 warning issued by then left-wing economist Stephen Gelb, who later became "one of the architects of GEAR," against

> an accumulation strategy which focuses on restructuring and regenerating the manufacturing sector in particular, by using "neo-liberal" (market-based) policies to alter cost structures and restore profitability and to expand markets for manufacturers, above all through exports . . . [a strategy that] would, in sum, reinforce and extend the dualistic structure of South African society.

He adds significantly:

> Yet that formulation captures the strategic direction adopted by the ANC government which, at the same time, claims commitment to a vision that states "we cannot rebuild our society at the expense of the standard of living of ordinary men and women. We cannot develop at the expense of social justice." (Marais 1998: p. 172)

The ANC's attempts to "balance the ideological books" has been traced with reference to biographical transformations undergone by leading members of the party and of its ally, the South African Communist Party, in a journalistic gem by John Matisonn (1998a and 1998b).

A glance at the land reform program shows beyond any shadow of doubt that delivery even in terms of the modest promises made is unlikely to occur to the satisfaction of those who have been deprived and marginalized. Indeed, some of the manifestations of "redistribution," "restitution," and "reform" are the exact opposite of what was promised. The security of labor tenants, for example, has led in many cases to tenants being evicted en masse and cheap labor of foreign origin being employed under the most vulnerable conditions of employment. It has become so obvious that even the modest land reform program adopted on the morrow of the 1994 elections is unattainable that recently senior officials of the Department of Land Affairs admitted this bluntly. Sharon Hammond and Justin Arenstein (1999: p. 1, supplement) wrote matter-of-factly:

> The government's land reform programme has failed dismally to redistribute a promised 30 percent of the country's agricultural land to 25.6 million landless black people by 1999. It has instead transferred land to just 0.6 percent, or an estimated 400,000 people since 1994. Land affairs officials said this week that the 30 percent target had always been unattainable and had been imposed on the department by political "unrealities."

They quote the director-general of the department, Geoff Budlender, as saying that "the government simply did not have the resources or capacity to meet its 30 percent target."

Job creation is another ever-shifting beacon of transformation that, like the reputed decoy beacon that caused the death of Samora Machel, is about to lead to the shooting down of the "flamingo scenario" in a rainbow spectacle of color. Four years after the founding elections of the new South Africa, the failure of the GEAR strategy to address this aspect of the economic problem gave rise belatedly to the oft-postponed "Job Summit," involving centrally government, business, and labor. The imminence of the first regular democratic elections, as well as the neo-Keynesian noises that were coming from the World Bank boffins in the wake of the crash landing of their famed structural adjustment strategies in East Asia and Latin America, made the summit not only possible but in fact essential. Among other things, the elections and the apparent rethink on the part of those who decide on global economic strategy had strengthened the leverage of the Congress of South African Trade Unions (COSATU) in the alliance that comprises what we call "the ANC." COSATU, at the formal level, had rejected (but not resisted the implementation of) GEAR ever since it became official government policy in June 1996.

What is beyond all doubt is that the macroeconomic strategy adopted by the ANC government, apparently without due consultation with its allies or even with the rank-and-file membership of the ANC, no longer has the unqualified sanction of those who can be said to have fathered it in the shadows of the political field of play. A shift has taken place in the strategies of the people who control the world economy. It is partly the result of the recent collapse of the East Asian and Latin American emerging markets, earth-shaking events that threaten to bring down the entire edifice of the global economy. Essentially, it is a move away from neoliberal toward what one might call neo-Keynesian economics. Joseph Stiglitz, a vice-president of the World Bank, during a recent visit to South Africa, captured the essentials of the change in strategic thinking in a newspaper interview. He found the prescriptions of "the Washington consensus" wanting on two fronts.

> One: they fail to take account of the complexities of the real world, where neither the market nor information is perfect. Two: together with World Bank president, James Wolfensohn, he has shifted the values on which economic policy should be measured. To look at gross domestic product is not enough, they argue—the key indicator of global and national economic well-being needs to be human development and equity. (Sole 1999)

All this, however, is what we might label domestic or household criticism, attempts at reforming and refining the existing structures and dynamics. It tries to deal with the software of the problem. What we have to do is to look at the hardware itself. The real question is whether the moral and political decision by which three hundred years of colonial plunder and rapine and half a century of apartheid, i.e., affirmative action based on "race" and "culture," are condoned, can constitute a viable platform from which to launch the rocket of transformation. It might seem to be unreasonable and unrealistic to demand at this late stage that that history of dispossession, expropriation, racist exploitation, and accumulation be revisited. However, the fact is that unless this is done, the logic of the capitalist system, as we know it, will simply reproduce the racial inequalities that have been programmed into the

South African social formation by the peculiarities of its history. That the leadership of the present government is aware of this can be inferred from numerous speeches, statements, and interviews. One of the most eloquent of these is a recent address by Deputy-President Thabo Mbeki (1998) at a session of the National Council of Provinces, in which he demonstrated clearly the difficulties within which those who want some genuine transformation are compelled to move.[1]

Whether the formulas for a postcapitalist dispensation can ever look like those that were on offer before the fateful year of 1989 is a question we cannot consider here, but whatever the formulas preferred, it is the honest thing to say that within the logic of an increasingly globalizing world-capitalist system, in which the so-called emerging markets constitute at best a second and at worst a third world, the promise of real change in the conditions of life of the urban and the rural poor is no more than the siren call that leads to disaster and devastation. Instead, we should be saying to the people of the new South Africa that we will institute every possible measure of reform as rapidly as possible, but in the end we shall have to align ourselves with those who want to build an entirely new world order.

In this connection, a few words have to be written about the significance of the Truth and Reconciliation Commission (TRC). Much has been and much more will be written on this unique attempt by a people at coming to terms with the past. Against the background of many similar half-hearted or ill-conceived experiments in dealing with the "sins of the fathers," it stands out. Its most positive achievements are without any doubt the way in which, for the first time ever, the voiceless masses were allowed to speak out not only to fellow South Africans but to the world at large, thanks to the wonders of the electronic media, and the related manner in which the African languages were for the first time ever in South Africa allowed to be heard in all their fullness and beauty on national television outside of a purely religious context. Within obvious limits, a certain measure of truth, understood as referring to the surface-level data of oppression and torture, was attained.

This is uncontroversial. But, it is equally obvious that the deep-level issues were hardly touched. The political leadership of the then ruling groups in government, business, the media, culture, and so on, got away virtually unscathed, and their foot soldiers, in the guise of the Eugene De Kocks, had to accept the stigma that should have been borne by all of them. The plain truth is that, given the compromise, only a blanket amnesty accompanied by a political tribunal involving all the main people who theorized, strategized, and funded apartheid could have dealt with the question preliminarily. The "truth" would have had to be found by other means, such as historical scholarship, detective work, and so forth. A public debate on the history, and especially on the historiography, of South Africa would have been much more capable of delivering "reconciliation," however we might wish to define this nebulous term.[2] In essence, the distorted Christian logic within which the TRC was conceived programmed it for failure. It was seized upon by people in the ruling party to give the impression to its disappointed, if not disillusioned, youth that a revolutionary victory was being "celebrated" through the ritual parading of the torturers of apartheid on the TV screens of the nation. In actual fact, as any serious political analyst must know, the TRC process has sown dragon's teeth that, like landmines, will require many years of toil and trouble to remove from the psyche of the people of the country.

The Political Sphere

Fundamental economic transformation is a necessary but not a sufficient condition for ensuring the prospect of a nonracial future in the new historical community that is emerging in South Africa. At the political level, it is essential that at least three other developments are initiated and consolidated for this objective to be realized. Even if the economic conditions I have referred to above were to be delayed for many decades, as seems likely at present, the political developments described below would have to be introduced if the vision of a nonracial democracy is to become more than a utopian mirage in a global desert of racial and ethnic conflict.

It has often happened in the history of peoples caught up in the many interconnected fields of social, economic, and technological force that fundamental change is triggered proximately by events in the political sphere. In this field also, the real situation looks very different from that which is projected onto TV screens and magazine covers. All South Africans have been enfranchised, and the country is blessed with "the most progressive constitution in the world." On paper, we live in paradise. On the ground, the security forces and the senior civil servants of the apartheid regime, "diversified" and made to look more "representative of the broad population" at the top levels by the odd melanin-rich face, continue to rule. As I have said elsewhere (see Alexander 1993), the ANC has come into office, not into power. This is perhaps no more than a witticism, but it spotlights a very real problem.

As intimated above, the continuity, coherence, and stability of the present political entity and the social order on which it is based—minus its racial faultline—have to be ensured. There can be no doubt that this is the most fundamental aspect of the strategy of the Mandela government. Without it, there can be no talk or hope of reform at any level or in any sector of the society. The avoidance of civil war and countering the threat of right-wing ("third-force") destabilization are the sine qua non of the political life of the Government of National Unity (GNU). Once the Mandela leadership had demonstrated its commitment to the principles of liberal democracy and the "free" market, the possibility of a reversion to a white supremacist minority government on the territory of South Africa became virtually nil. This was the real reason for the withdrawal of F. W. De Klerk's National Party from the GNU. This is also the basic reason for the perpetuation of the Inkatha Freedom Party as the junior partner inside the rump GNU.

There is no doubt that at this level, the efforts of the government have been met with a measure of success; indeed, given the forebodings of 1993–1994, they have been crowned with success beyond the expectations of most people. On the other hand, it is obvious that the tidal wave of organized and syndicated crime that is overwhelming the country at present, and which, next to job creation, is seen by most South Africans as the issue that should have the highest priority on the GNU agenda, is part of a surrogate low-intensity civil war. In terms of its effects, such as widespread feelings of insecurity, paranoia, intensified racial prejudice, and general pessimism, it leads many, especially young professionals and skilled artisans, to abandon all patriotism and noble intentions by choosing "the chicken run." The specter of the destabilizing implosive wars that have reduced much of the African continent to historical rubble and, in the case of Rwanda, led to the ultimate obscenity of ("black-on-black") genocide, haunts the regime and is an ever-present reminder to it that no "risky" social, economic, or political experiments should be undertaken. This explains the image of a relatively tame South African government, as which, paradoxically, it is seen in the world outside.

The second political condition that has to be sustained if stability and confidence are to be maintained is the present liberal democratic constitution with its multiparty system. This is particularly important because of the nervousness of the racially defined minorities—the whites, coloreds, and Indians. These groups, insofar as they have voted in elections, have in the main supported those parliamentary parties that operated during the apartheid era, the "New" National Party and the

Democratic Party. This has to change, and the social composition of these parties, if they survive the coming period of regroupment, will also have to change dramatically. The one-party dominant system that is emerging in South Africa and the tendency on the part of the ruling party to ignore or to deride the political positions of the parliamentary opposition are making it increasingly difficult for a spirit of tolerance and give-and-take to be proliferated. It is to be expected that this polarizing trajectory will strengthen the hand of those who believe that in a racially divided society such as South Africa, only a consociational form of democracy will succeed in damping down the fires of racial jealousy and hatred. Clearly, should this view become the prevailing one, racial identities will become the normal social condition and a nonracial future will by definition become impossible. It is clear to me that most political leaders do not have a lucid understanding of the interconnectedness of their discourse and the sociopolitical and socioeconomic behavior of their constituencies.

A last important political condition that will help to bring about a nonracial ethos is total transparency in regard to the policy of "corrective action." The evolving position in this regard is not very encouraging at all. In particular, the manner in which the Employment Equity Act and its counterpart for the public service are understood and implemented will determine whether "redress" will reinforce or undermine attempts at bringing about national consensus and some sense of a new South African identity. In a nutshell, it should be said that the only manner in which, under the difficult conditions of the transition, a policy of affirmative action can succeed is if it is clearly related to discrimination based on skin color (or gender or disability) in the past and if it is limited in time to, say, one or two generations. What this means in effect is that affirmative action should be viewed as a grand gesture accepted by those advantaged because of conquest, dispossession, racism, and exploitation, as an admittedly inadequate quid pro quo that does no more than demonstrate the willingness of the beneficiaries of past policies to concede some reparations. Beyond that point, affirmative action should no longer be based on the social categories of the past social order, i.e., race. Once it comes to be based on class or income groups, as is now apparently happening in the United States, it becomes difficult to distinguish it from ordinary poor relief or welfare measures.

In his excellent summary and analysis of the problematics of affirmative action in general and in the United States, South Africa, and Brazil in particular, john a. powell (Chapter 13 of this volume) concludes as follows:

among the ruling elites to try to keep the definitions of the black "ethnic groups" as fluid as the National Party ideologues had done in the case of their white constituency previously. By so doing, the cohesion of the majority of the oppressed and their common interest in national liberation, which constituted the ideological basis of the struggle against colonialism and apartheid, can be pressed into the service of those who are now in a position to inherit or to accumulate power in all relevant social spheres. The "minorities," which might once again be allowed to fragment themselves as much as they like, are accommodated within a model human rights charter and a genuine culture of tolerance. On this reading of the evolving situation, one or other version of an "Africanist" solution of the question of national and subnational identity appears to be in the offing. However, the actual boundaries of the dominant social category have not yet been drawn. An excellent illustration of the continuing fluidity of the concept "African" in the South African context is the lyrical extolling of his African being by Thabo Mbeki, the deputy-president of South Africa, in a recent, very significant speech in Parliament. It is also clear that the struggle over the definition of identities in South Africa has only just begun. It is in this area that the third set of conditions for a successful transition is to be found.

The Ethnic Danger

Already, the new democratic openness has created political and ideological spaces that all kinds of charlatans are trying to occupy in the quest for electoral power, which they perceive as the key to opening the door of opportunity for themselves. Suddenly, a Griqua, a Bushman, even an Indonesian identity is being marketed, and although all these purported groups refer to mere handfuls of people, the tendency to exploit them, as was done in many other African countries immediately after independence with dire consequences in most cases, is one that must be curbed if the Mandela (or the Mbeki) administration is not to be distracted from its main task of "reconstruction and development."

As against these ephemeral attempts to play the ethnic card, there are the very real facts of the Afrikaner Volksstaaters and the adherents of the Zulu kingdom. These two are without a doubt the most distinctive politicized ethnic identities to have been handed down to the present generation. While there are many other subnational identities in South Africa—based on religion, language, other cultural traits, and specific histories, as well as on perceived or reputed racial features—

none of these has been politicized in the recent past, or ever, for that matter. "English," "colored," "Malay," "Muslim," "Xhosa," "Tswana," "Jewish," or "Indian" South Africans have, with negligible exceptions in certain periods of our history, never mobilized themselves as such. Even the "Zulu-ness" of a party such as the Inkatha Freedom Party is denied by its leadership, which insists that it is nonracial in composition and transregional in its conception and in its organizational reach.

It is, therefore, a matter of some concern that the compromise in the constitution of South Africa that led to the establishment of the Commission for the Promotion and the Protection of the Rights of Cultural, Religious and Linguistic Communities of South Africa may inadvertently open the Pandora's box of ethnic, i.e., tribal, politics that has been one of the causes of the underdevelopment of many of the countries of postcolonial Africa. There is no doubt that this provision (Sections 185 and 186 of the constitution, which should be read together with the possibly fatal provision on territorial self-determination in Section 235) constitutionalizes ethnic politics in postapartheid South Africa. The best that can be said about this matter is that the government is obviously aware of the fact that it is not only a highly sensitive issue in every sense of the term but, more than that, that the wisest strategy is to hasten very slowly in the hope that the problem might just disappear of its own accord.

The Political Importance of Metaphors

One way or the other, there can be no doubt that South Africa has reached a watershed as far as identity politics is concerned. For this reason, it is vital that all journalists as well as political and cultural pacesetters consider deeply and carefully what metaphors and what social categories they create, support, reinforce, or, alternatively, counter, undermine, and discourage.

In recent writings in various newpapers and in speeches on various occasions, I have systematically raised the issue of the political importance of metaphors. It is axiomatic that metaphors born out of one set of conditions are not automatically appropriate to a different set of conditions. It is, therefore, problematical, to put it mildly, that so many South Africans are so ready to imitate other countries' jargon and discourse in order to describe the very different reality in which we are living. I cannot, for example, judge in any more than superficial ways, the appropriateness of the rainbow metaphor in the context of the United States,[3] but there is little doubt in my mind that it is arguably the worst metaphor with which to symbolize the destiny of the Republic of South Africa. Instead of the "foreign," color-centered image of coexisting racial groups, I have put forward the more "indigenous" image of the Gariep ("the great river"), which is the Khoe name for the Orange River, with its many tributaries that have their catchment areas in all parts of the country.

The essential notion behind this suggestion is that we have to conceive of the social categories in a more dynamic manner; we have to underline the *process* of identity formation rather than the *reified notions* of existing and inherited identities, even though the tenacity of such identities must not be underestimated.[4] In this conception, settler-colonial societies such as South Africa have been constituted, culturally speaking, by the confluence of different tributaries. There is, because of the colonially determined power relations, no hegemonic majority culture, unlike the situation in most former British dominions where the aboriginal populations had been largely wiped out in the genocidal wars that characterized much of European colonialism. There is, thus, no mainstream culture in the normal sense of that term. Instead, the different tributaries actually *constitute* the main stream, or the river, which by virtue of that fact is characterized by elements originating in all the tributaries. In South Africa itself, these tributaries are, very crudely, the African, the European, the Asian, and the modern "American." The tributaries are never washed away as in the assimilationist model that prevailed in the earlier part of this century in the United States. On the other hand, while they obviously affect the common cultural area in different ways, they are themselves influenced (through "interfluence") by backwash effects from the main stream. We can demonstrate the truth of this assertion by taking almost any domain of social life, such as sport, religion, music, language, and so forth.

These considerations have important implications for discourse of all kinds but especially for the discursive practices of the political- and the social-science domains. Among other things, they lead us to propose that concepts such as "culture" be disaggregated, as it were, rendered more fluid through verbalization instead of reification (nominalization). Thus, we would suggest the use of more "verbal" terminology, such as cultural practices, usages, traditions, customs—i.e., anything that suggests changeability as opposed to closure, fixity, rigidity, and so on. In the philosophy of language, this approach derives from the assumption that language does not merely *reflect*, it also *forms* (and, therefore, potentially *transforms*) reality.[5]

Concluding Remarks

Identities are in a state of flux in South Africa and will be for many decades to come. The socioeconomic and sociopolitical environment in which the transition is taking place is extremely unfavorable in many respects. Consequently, factors such as the competition for jobs, housing, land, education, and health care are prejudicial to a nation-building project. On the other hand, the commitment of the political leadership to the ideal of a nonracial democracy in which racial and ethnic conciousness is of secondary or even of no importance as far as the allocation of life-chances is concerned, as well as the fact that such a dispensation would serve the interests of the majority of the population, do mean that there is a real chance that a successful renegotiation of identities and significant social categories can take place. It remains true, as Hein Marais (1997: p. 74) stated, that

> South Africa's providence was that Mandela created a temporary recess in which a sense of nationhood could sink a few tenuous roots. The challenges that await resolution—in a nutshell, the redistribution of wealth, opportunity and resources—will test the firmness of Mandela's bedrock and the authenticity of the new South Africa. They cut to the heart of the liberation struggle. And they expose afresh the fault lines that fissure our society. The choreography of reconciliation can no longer disguise the turbulence of an incomplete transition.

Again, as so often when the national question is discussed in South Africa, we have to return to the clairvoyant vision of Olive Schreiner (1923: pp. 61–62, emphasis in original), which she penned at the end of the last century:

> Wherever a Dutchman, an Englishman, a Jew and a native are superimposed, there is that common South African condition through which no dividing line can be drawn. . . . South African unity is not the dream of a visionary, it is not even the forecast of genius, which makes clear and at hand that which only after ages can accomplish. . . . South African unity is a condition the practical necessity for which is daily and hourly forced upon us by the common needs of life: it is the one path open to us. For this unity all great men born in South Africa during the next century will be compelled directly or indirectly to labour; it is this unity which must precede the production of anything great and beautiful by our people as a whole. . . . It is the attainment of this unity which constitutes the problem of South Africa: *How from our political states and our discordant races, can a great, a healthy, a united, an organized nation be formed?*

At the end of the century she refers to, this question, clearly, remains on the agenda.

Notes

1. The following revealing anecdote shows the kind of resistance, even within the prevailing paradigm, with which the reformers have to deal:

> At a dinner in Sandton, foreign businessmen remark on the short-termism of SA's private sector. Besides the pressure for ever improving quarterly results . . . , there is a sense that assets are being kept liquid, they say. SA business is on the hop, limiting fixed investment in order to be able to leave quickly. (Laufer 1999)

2. As I was about to complete this chapter, Stephen Laufer (1999), the associate editor of the South African daily, *Business Day*, published a searching critique, from a very establishment position, of the notion of reconciliation. Instead of it, he proposes that in the post-Mandela period, the quest should be for what he calls "national consensus."

3. There seems to be increasing doubt in the United States itself about the usefulness of the metaphor, to judge by recent writings. (See, e.g., Mkhondo 1997.)

4. This is the reason why I consider the series, *One City, Many Cultures*, launched with much fanfare by the *Cape Times* and its backers on March 1, 1999, to be a strategic blunder of the worst kind.

5. In another paper prepared for the Comparative Human Relations Initiative, I have dealt with these issues in more detail. (See Alexander 1997.)

References

Alexander, N. 1993. *Some Are More Equal Than Others*. Cape Town: Buchu Books.

———. 1997. "The Role of Discourse in Anti-Racist Strategies in the Republic of South Africa, Brazil and the United States of America." Paper prepared for the Comparative Human Relations Initiative. Atlanta, USA. Unpublished mimeo.

Central Statistical Services. 1997. *RSA Statistics in Brief*. Pretoria: Central Statistical Services.

Friedman, R., and S. Gool. 1997. "Race Barriers Still Prevalent in South Africa: The Myth of the Rainbow Nation," *Cape Times*, April 25.

Hammond, S., and J. Arenstein. 1999. "Some Land Reform Projects Resemble Dumping Grounds," *Reconstruct: The Sunday Independent*, January 17.

Lam, D. 1999. "Schooling Inequality, Income Inequality, and Intergenerational Transmission of Human Capital in South Africa and Brazil." Paper prepared for the MacArthur Network Conference on Inequality in South Africa, Johannesburg, January 16. Unpublished mimeo.

Laufer, S. 1999. "A Society Divided Cannot Survive," *Business Day,* March 3.

Lawrence, P. 1997. "Our Growing Racial Divide," *Financial Mail,* August 15.

Marais, H. 1997. "Leaders of the Pack," *Leadership*, August.

———. 1998. *South Africa. Limits to Change. The Political Economy of Transformation*. London, New York, and Cape Town: Zed Books and University of Cape Town Press.

Matisonn, J. 1998a. "How the ANC Battled to Balance the Ideological Books," *Mail and Guardian*, November 6–12.

———. 1998b. "Taking a Stand, But How Could the ANC Deliver?" *Mail and Guardian*, November 13–19.

Mbeki, T. 1998. "End Degradation of the Black Majority," *Cape Times*, November 11.

Mkhondo, R. 1997. "Clinton Searches for 'One America': Race Issues Still Bedevil the US, Years After the Legal Battle Was Won," *Cape Argus*, August 6.

Murray, N., and M. Garrido. 1997. "Somewhere over the Rainbow: A Journey to the New South Africa." *Race and Class* 38, no. 3: 1–24.

Nicol, M. 1999. "This Isn't My Home. The Transkei Is," *Cape Times*, February 26.

powell, j. 2001. "Transformative Action: A Strategy for Ending Racial Hierarchy and Achieving True Democracy," Chapter 13 in this volume.

Republic of South Africa: Government Communication and Information System. 1999a. *The Building Has Begun. Government's Report to the Nation*. Pretoria: GCIS.

———. 1999b. *Realising Our Hopes*. Pretoria: GCIS.

SALDRU (Southern African Labour and Development Research Unit). 1994. *South Africans Rich and Poor: Baseline Household Statistics*. Cape Town: SALDRU.

Schreiner, O. 1923. "South Africa: Its Natural Features, Its Political Status: The Problem," in *Thoughts on South Africa*. London: T. Fisher Unwin Ltd.

Sole, S. 1999. "A Different Drum," *Saturday Argus*, January 16-17.

Statistics South Africa (SSA). 1998. *The October Household Survey*. Pretoria: SSA.

Wilson, F., and M. Ramphele. 1989. *Uprooting Poverty: The South African Challenge*. Report for the Second Carnegie Inquiry into Poverty and Development in Southern Africa. Cape Town: David Philip Publishers.

Response

Alex Boraine

Foundations for Nonracialism

While I appreciate the concerns that Alexander raises in his paper, I do not share his overall pessimism about our present situation.

We have a strong state and a stable government, unlike so many other countries—not only in Africa but in Europe, Latin America, and Asia. It is very much to the credit of the new government that they were willing to negotiate major concessions in order to create stability. This stability has been assisted further by the remarkably sophisticated succession from Mandela to Mbeki. The succession was not ad hoc but rather represents a collective thinking that produced an emerging leader in his own right.

In the brief five years of our new democracy, we have had elections at the national, provincial, and local government levels. Institutions are in place. Furthermore, to back up an excellent constitution we have a Constitutional Court that is sovereign to Parliament and thus guards the constitution. We have a Public Protector, a Human Rights Commission, a Gender Commission, and a Youth Commission. These institutions ensure that while Mandela is revered, the governance of South Africa is not dependent upon any one individual. We have the foundation necessary for us to build a human rights culture, to consolidate democracy and move toward a nonracial society.

While it is true that we have a conservative economic policy, when seen against the background of South Africa's position as an emerging market and the globalization of the economy, I do not think the government had any choice. Certainly there has been no financial collapse and no runaway inflation.

Of course there has been lack of delivery. The first promises made were wholly unrealistic but now have been acknowledged as such. There is an acceptance by government, in private and in public, that there is "unfinished business" that must be tackled by the new government.

I agree entirely that corruption is unacceptable and is very high, but it was the government that appointed the Heath Commission and a number of other inquiries that have been followed by suspensions and dismissals. If we bear in mind that the Olympic Games itself has been shot through with corruption, that the entire European Commission had to resign, we begin to see South Africa in some perspective. We have to surely acknowledge that within humankind there is a persistent perversity that calls for checks and balances and watchfulness at all times.

The crime level is alarmingly high and is not being countered successfully, despite all the new legislation and the attempts to reform our police force. But here too we should look at other countries in transition, notably Russia.

If we really want to be realistic about spiraling crime, then we should be grateful that we are not in the position of an ongoing civil war, as is the case in Angola and the Congo. The situation in Rwanda is perilous; Bosnia is hopelessly divided; Serbia and Kosovo have been the center of massive bombing by NATO forces.

We should be much more modest in our expectations, bearing in mind that we have come out of 300 years of racism and oppression. There is certainly no room for complacency, but we ought not to allow ourselves to be paralyzed by deep-seated pessimism.

Reconciliation and National Coexistence

I think we put too much burden on the word "reconciliation," and we focus too much on individual reconciliation rather than national coexistence. In Argentina they refuse to use the word "reconciliation" because the Catholic Church used it, which supported the dictatorship in that country, and the dictators themselves constantly used the word.

Ideally, it would be wonderful if we could change hearts and minds so that whites would start to look upon blacks as fellow citizens and neighbors, and blacks would begin to trust whites. We need to change structures, and this we are doing so that those who have oppressed for so long can change their behavior, and those who have been oppressed can do likewise. The pernicious superiority and inferiority interchange must change. But we should accept that this is not going to happen for a very long time. In the Czech Republic, after their transition, they said that it would take six months to write a new constitution, six years to get a good economic policy, and sixty years to change attitudes!

Let me offer an example of what I mean by structures bringing about changed behavior. In 1999 the Cape Town City Council passed its budget of R3.4 billion. It is an ANC-controlled council, but with substantial representation by the New National Party and the Democratic

Party. The former National Party together with the ANC passed it, and the majority of the budget was designated for areas that had formerly been totally ignored. They came to this decision through debate without bloodshed. This is the kind of approach we have to follow.

The Contribution of the
Truth and Reconciliation Commission

My strongest criticism of Alexander's paper is where he deals with the Truth and Reconciliation Commission. It seems almost as if he had dragged this in at the last moment. He makes a number of statements without any attempt to back them up.

In less than two pages, while acknowledging that the commission laid bare a certain measure of truth, in essence "the distorted Christian logic within which the TRC was conceived programmed it for failure." What on earth does this mean? How does he define Christian logic, bearing in mind that two critical elements of the Christian faith, namely repentance and forgiveness, play no part in the act that governs the commission? Worse, Alexander states that "the TRC process has sown dragon's teeth that, like landmines, will require many years of toil and trouble to remove from the psyche of the people of the country." Once again, a bald statement without any example or illustration.

After listening to victims tell their stories over a period of two and a half years, it is my experience that many of the more than 20,000 people who appeared before us spoke of a catharsis, a lightening of the load, of the end to sleepless nights, the relief of knowing at last what happened to their loved ones, and so on. The breaking of the silence was experienced not only by victims but, through radio and television, shared by millions of people in South Africa. I think the TRC planted seeds of hope, of new beginnings, of a more decent and gentler society, and I can back that up by the testimonies of thousands of people.

I regret very much that Alexander, in a paper on a nonracial future in South Africa, should dismiss so easily the work of the TRC. The commission demonstrated that human rights violations, suffering, courage, and hope are not defined by color but by the human condition. As South Africa discovers its common humanity, nonracialism becomes a real possibility.

Response

Mahmood Mamdani

I have ten minutes in which to convince you that my good friend Dr. Alexander is a good man, with good intentions, even though I do not entirely agree with what he writes in the paper before us.

I will disagree on two issues. The first concerns the question of black empowerment. The second concerns that of minority rights in light of majority aspirations.

Colonialism, Race and Ethnicity

We have a saying in my home university, Makerere University in Kampala: every time the right wins power, the left writes a good book. I used to like this saying until I realized what it meant. That the left is capable of a retrospective, but not a prospective. That it has hindsight, but it lacks foresight.

There is a genre of literature characteristic of this perspective. I remember reading a book by Perry Anderson, an English New Left author, about fifteen years ago. The book was called *Considerations on Western Marxism*. I wondered then what Anderson meant by "Western Marxism." He answered the question in the very first chapter. Western Marxism, he said, was that body of thought that tried to come to grips with why the proletariat in the West failed to make a revolution. I wondered about what it must mean to have an entire school of thought united, defined, by a nonevent. I was not surprised that the more this kind of literature grew, the more theological it became.

This kind of writing came to Africa after independence. It is now totally predictable. There runs a common theme through it: the revolution was betrayed! It is a lament about the revolution that was promised but not delivered, about the product that fell short of the advertisement.

The problem with focusing on what is *not* happening is that one tends to be blind to what *is* happening.

This is why I would like to begin with a comment on what is happening in South Africa today. I shall begin, as Dr. Alexander indeed does, with apartheid. But I will also begin with a disagreement with some of my fellow commentators on this panel who have spoken of the last 350 years as a history of racial discrimination: the last 350 years need to be understood as a period of colonial rule. Like every colonial rule on this continent, apartheid too turned around two core identities: race and ethnicity.

Race was an identity that united beneficiaries: Afrikaners, Dutch, English, Portuguese, Greeks, Germans, all were united into a common identity called "white." Ethnicity, in contrast, fragmented the victims of apartheid. For the victims were not brought together under a single identity called "black"; instead, they were fragmented into so many ethnic identities—Xhosa, Zulu, Venda, Pedi, and so on.

What the New Left in South Africa called "racial capitalism" should have been called "colonial capitalism." We would then have been in a position to draw some lessons from the experience of decolonization around this continent. The relevant lesson for our purposes is that nowhere was decolonization possible without deracialization. Even the most conservative form of decolonization required deracialization.

Black Empowerment

Conservative deracialization, narrow deracialization, was called Africanization around this continent. In South Africa, it is called black empowerment. I think it should properly be called black business empowerment.

Black business empowerment is an idea whose time has come. I mean this in the following sense: anyone who thinks you can have a predominantly white bourgeoisie in a predominantly black country, after independence, without a political upheaval, should have their heads examined.

I am not suggesting that the black bourgeoisie will necessarily be patriotic, or that it will not. All I am suggesting is that you cannot have political independence in this era without its consequence, capital accumulation among those colonized yesterday. Our choices lie not in whether or not there would be capital accumulation, but in its extent and nature and in the relationship of its beneficiaries to the state and to the bourgeoisie.

We cannot go away from black business empowerment, but we can go beyond it. The real question we need to focus on is: How do we broaden deracialization? In the economy, how do we go beyond benefiting a narrow elite tied to the bootstraps of the apartheid bourgeoisie to ensuring a dignified livelihood for the great mass of working people? And in society, how do we go beyond business, to deracializing education and culture, science and sports?

This is where I have my first disagreement with Dr. Alexander. He says in the paper that the real beneficiaries of the compromise of 1993–1994, the real social base of "rainbowism," are members of the rapidly growing black middle class. I disagree.

The beneficiaries of rainbowism include two groups. The first and the largest are most of the beneficiaries of apartheid, to whom rainbowism has given a fresh lease on life. The second is a smaller group comprised of some of the victims of apartheid to whom it has given a new life.

The beneficiaries of rainbowism among the victims of apartheid are too few. The social base of rainbowism among black people—even among the black middle class—is too narrow. Rainbowism involves too much of an embrace of inherited inequalities.

On the horizon, if I may speak as a university intellectual, is an impending clash between rainbowism and nationalism, between an embrace of inherited inequalities and a mobilization against it, between "reconciliation" ideology and "renaissance" ideology.

The relevant question is: Will this mobilization against inequality be rhetorical—even demagogic—or will it seek to reconnect with and rekindle the social and political movement that brought apartheid to an impasse?

Most likely, it will involve a mishmash of both. But the terms of that mishmash, and the direction in which it will flow, depends on initiative, our initiative.

Minority Rights and Majority Aspirations

The second issue I would like to focus on from Dr. Alexander's paper concerns his discussion of political identity, particularly in relation to minority rights.

When I first read Dr. Alexander's critique of the rainbow as a metaphor and his call that we replace it with another metaphor, that of the Gariep ("the great river"), I was delighted. My response was not mainly because the rainbow is an English word, and the Gariep a Khoi word. It was more so because the rainbow has no notion of a majority; there is no black in the rainbow! The Gariep, in contrast, is a metaphor that allows us to think of both the main stream and the streams that join it along the way and become part of it, with crosscurrents and undercurrents, backwashes alongside the thrust forward.

But then I read Dr. Alexander saying that the Gariep he has in mind has no cultural mainstream, that it comprises four minority streams: African, European, Asian, and modern "American." I disagree.

I would like to put a set of propositions to you. First, the question of identity in the public sphere is not really that of cultural identity. It is of political identity.

Second, political identity is about entitlements. Why is it that few or none of those who want to be defined as Africans today would not have stood up twenty years ago to say so? The answer is simple: to be considered an African today is to be entitled, whereas to be considered an African twenty years ago was to be stripped of any entitlement.

There is a lesson here. At the core of political identity is the question of entitlement. The question of entitlement is really that of social justice. If we do not address the question of justice forthrightly and swiftly, it will boomerang on us in the form of identity politics, whether racial or ethnic.

This means that so long as the legacy of apartheid is not addressed, the core identities created by apartheid will be reproduced. The core majority identity will be black, jelled around a demand for entitlement. And the core minority identity will be white. Dr. Alexander's Gariep will have a political mainstream.

This has a bearing on how we think of minority rights. At election time, it was depressing to see most of the opposition parties trying to fan minority fears and play on them. I did not hear any of them tell their constituency that the precondition—not the necessary condition, but the precondition—to safeguarding minority rights is to address majority aspirations. Let me state it differently: the key condition for the realization of a nonracial democracy is not the protection of minority rights but the realization of majority aspirations. To think otherwise, to ask minorities to think of their rights as opposed to majority aspirations, is to do them disservice. It is either to prepare them to fight back in the cause of an era gone by or to prepare them to leave the country!

Conclusion

Dr. Alexander is right that identities are fluid. But identities are also reproduced through institutions and crystallized as entitlements. This is why, if we want to deracialize identities, we have to deracialize institutions.

If you want a nonracial society, you cannot shut your eyes to racial inequality. The only viable road to nonracialism is deliberate, rapid, and sustained deracialization. In the specific context of postapartheid South Africa, there can be no deracialization without black empowerment.

I would like to close by reiterating that we need to broaden black empowerment in two ways. First, we need to go beyond black business empowerment to create a truly dynamic entrepreneurial class, not a narrow stratum of coupon clippers tied to the apron strings of big capital, and ensure a dignified livelihood for working people. Second, we need to broaden black empowerment beyond the economy to education and culture, science, and sports.

Response

Naledi Pandor

What is a useful basis from which a response to Dr. Alexander's paper can be pursued? Does the paper serve as a crisp and accurate reckoning with our context and the challenge of confronting racialism? And can it assist us as we take those painful and slow steps toward the crafting of a national identity? A harsh commentary on the paper is that it does not move us far beyond the present. A more accurate comment might be that it leaves several significant issues untouched.

This response cannot be the tabling of an alternative paper; it can, however, attempt to suggest issues for further debate and study.

First, the paper does not acknowledge the pervasive influence of racial bigotry in South Africa—an influence that has permitted the general perception that people who are white are somehow superior to all other races. The fact that twentieth-century developments and experiences have successfully challenged this racial myth is also left untouched. South Africa will over time also provide concrete evidence that the myth of white superiority is nothing but a myth. This has important implications for our future policies and programs. The paper does make scathing comments about some of the current attempts at ameliorating the condition of those who have experienced the worst excesses of exploitation, yet it falls short because, in a manner so recognizable as to be rather irritating, it identifies responsibility for this immense task as lying solely at the level of government delivery of basic social services. A range of policies and evidence clearly show change will have to go beyond government delivery of housing and water if we are to ditch the racial-superiority myth and begin social reconstruction. Many more institutions will have to be involved in that process.

A throwaway line on millions having access to water does not do justice to the immense project of change still confronting us. It would have been more useful to hear proposals for integrated strategies of development that might be encouraged within new water communities—strategies that would take off from access to water to tie in access to, for example, education for persons relieved of the water-bearing burden, and access to rural development programs that utilize water as a source of job and wealth creation.

The writer of the paper does touch on some of the "gains" and, interestingly, also on the constraints facing the ANC, but it is in laying all the failures at the door of the ANC that the paper seems to fall very short of what this theme requires. A question that arises from the paper is: Will economic policy and economic gain solve all our problems? Will nonracialism in South Africa come about if we adopt socialism as our approach to the economy? The paper is silent on these questions. Perhaps this was because the author of the paper has already tacitly accepted such a scenario and feels it does not require restating. He may be right. He does address several important issues as adjuncts to racism; they are in fact probably the most significant in our search for a national identity. In the short time available to me, I would like to introduce three issues that are not directly addressed in the paper. They may add a useful dimension to our consideration of the prospects for a nonracial South Africa.

These issues are democracy and its relationship to individuals and communities; liberalism and the humanist tradition—one that renders the individual as "icon" standing against the claims of the community; and capitalism and the protection of the community against individual greed and ambition.

Democracy and Its Relationship to Individuals and Communities

Through wide practice and various lobbies, the practice of democracy has come to mean the exercise of the individual right to elect governments. Most modern constitutions tend to confirm this guarantee of individual rights. Rights of communities such as language, cultural, and religious rights are often left untouched. Politicians view them as potential sources of conflict, and the general instinct of democracy is to ignore them and assert individuals over communities.

The South African Constitution is unusual in this regard: it guarantees individual rights while also giving status to communal rights of religion, language, and culture. This rather contradictory framing of the constitution poses challenging problems. The government and we as South Africans have accepted that we will seek to defend the individual against the tyrannies of their communities while also protecting small communities against big communities. The question arising from this is: In a country seeking to overcome a racial history, is such an agenda achievable? And if so, in what way?

Liberalism and the Humanist Tradition

Commentators have often criticized the African preference of community rights above individual rights. Our constitution, as already stated, does assert individual rights, but then it also creates the Commission for the Promotion of the Rights of Cultural, Religious and Linguistic Communities. Those with active access to government processes and programs will already be participants in the realization of this provision for the advancement of their communities' interests. The issue we need to confront is how to ensure that communities that have been marginalized by our context and history derive benefit and support from the commission once it is created. The national conference on the establishment of this commission that was held earlier this year had mainly male participants and presenters. Its most articulate participants were religious leaders; the cultural and the linguistic aspects were hardly touched. The impression conveyed there was that the rights of cultural, linguistic, and religious communities are held in male hands and it is they who will ensure their promotion. This does not augur well for the individual rights of women in particular communities or for the broader challenge of overcoming patriarchy and racialism. A further point to be noted is that the commission must not become a means for the advantaged to cling on to advantages that have links with our terrible past. The question arising from this is: Of what significance is the community focus of the commission to our objective of advancing nonracialism?

Capitalism and the Protection of the Community Against Individual Greed and Ambition

The paper presented this evening devotes a great deal of space to economic policy issues, but it does not clearly link that analysis to nonracialism. It perhaps lifts out economic matters because these are so inextricably a part of the solutions we need to find. Economic choices and models continue to be some of the most inflexible arenas of challenge for African societies. This is proving to be true for South Africa. Entry to the global economic arena has curtailed the number of options available to South Africa. This is because the economic favorites of the day are finance capitalism and service capitalism. The West has so arranged itself that trade favors the West and hardly notes the South. Our human resources, with the large reservoir of persons with little or no formal training, means we need to identify different forms of economic activity as the launch pad for our development. Manufacturing capitalism may have to become our focus, as opposed to finance and service capitalism.

Tied to this challenge of identifying coherent responses that synthesize the various strands that make up our problem is the challenge of creating an African bourgeoisie. Most of us tend to condemn the bourgeoisie wherever we find them, without acknowledging the instances where they have made a creative contribution to their societies. We need a responsive and creative African bourgeoisie. As one of my friends said, we need our own comrade capitalists.

In conclusion, it is true to say that the nineteenth-century ideal of "one nation, one language, one faith, one destiny" is not one that we have aspired to. Our preference is to seek nonracialism in a context that affirms multilingualism, multiethnicity, and multiculturalism.

Response

Mamphela Ramphele

I would like at the outset to establish points of agreement with Dr. Alexander. I agree with the centrality he establishes for the question: Under what conditions is the realization of a nonracial future for South Africa possible? This question becomes all the more central if one takes into consideration the supplementary question he implies: How does a society undo 350 years of affirmative action for white people, particularly white males? I am curious about Dr. Alexander's exclusion of gender as an important variable in the historical community he is exploring, given the intricate relationship between race, class, and gender in South Africa.

Critics of the post-1994 government do not always take sufficient cognizance of the enormous legacy of 350 years of advantaging a minority of the population at the expense of the majority. Many political activists in the wide spectrum of the liberation movement underestimated the extent to which the implementation of affirmative action for white people in this society was successful. The implications of this success were also underplayed. Part of the reason for the underestimation is the triumphalism that constituted essential fuel for a struggle waged against what often looked like an invincible foe. Faced with as powerful a force as apartheid South Africa, one had to resort to denial of the enormity of the power the regime had to shape both the history and the future of South Africa.

A second area of agreement relates to the affirmation of the capacity of South Africans to find solutions for the challenging problems they face. South Africans made Margaret Thatcher eat her words, uttered in the mid-1980s, that "anyone who thought the ANC could come to power in South Africa was living in cloud cuckoo land"—guess who lives there now! The question, however, remains: How effective are the solutions we are finding to our problems? This is an area I believe needs to be debated with greater rigor.

The third question of great importance Alexander poses is "whether and how the ingrained hierarchical white supremacist attitudes on one hand, and the debilitating slave mentality on the other hand, can be attenuated and eventually eradicated." At the heart of this problem is the ingrained group consciousness dominating social relationships even in postapartheid South Africa. The very use of the metaphor of the "rainbow nation" presupposes clear-cut and enduring differences between South Africa's people, like the colors of a rainbow that are distinct even though they reside alongside one another. The language of different "races" persists in spite of their nonexistence as scientific categories.

South Africans, both black and white, are caught up in essentialist views about the difference between being black and white without sufficient focus on the commonalties between black and white as, first and foremost, human beings.

Finally, I agree with Alexander's concern about the inadequate attention postapartheid South Africa has thus far paid to bridging the economic gulf as an essential building block for a just society. The latter is all the more surprising given the lengths to which the ANC went to include socioeconomic rights as an essential element of full citizenship. The Second Carnegie Enquiry into Poverty regarded uprooting poverty as a national priority and a major challenge. The authors of the report quoted the French philosopher Raymond Aron to make this point: "The existence of too great a degree of inequality makes human community impossible" (Wilson and Ramphele 1989: p. 4). The ANC government has yet to demonstrate its resolve to deal with this challenge effectively.

I part company with Alexander when he starts ascribing the failures of the postapartheid government to the "'neo-liberal economic paradigm within which the transformation of the country is being tackled." He regards such a paradigm as "a recipe for disaster at worst or stagnation at best." Alexander needs to come to terms with the hard reality that no ideological position is adequate to the task of socioeconomic development anywhere in the world, let alone in our poor country with its unenviable legacy.

The global economic environment is like a major snowstorm that demands adaptive behavior unfettered by ideological positioning. There is no choice in the matter of adaptation to the knowledge-driven competitive global environment. No economy in the world can survive by forging an isolationist stance. It has little to do with slavish following of the World Bank or IMF. It is the harsh reality out there. The nature of adaptation has to suit each country's needs and opportunities as well as take cognizance of its regional realities. Fortunately, Alexander's political stance is unlikely to gain sufficient dominance to subject us to the uncertainty of experimentation with his unspecified ideological position.

More rigorous analysis is required to get to the bottom of the gap between the ANC's pre-1994 commitments to nonracial, nonsexist egalitarianism and its performance over the last five years than has been offered by Alexander. Objective analysis would show that there have been major areas of success by the ANC-led government. Firm foundations have been laid for the envisaged future in a number of important areas. We have to take pride in the quality of our national Constitution of 1996; in the energy that has gone into the plethora of excellent social policies that have made a difference in the everyday lives of ordinary people; in the real courage to tackle issues that no other government in the history of this country dared to tackle, e.g., water and forestry, mining rights and their complementary responsibilities, and land restitution.

Whatever inadequacies the Truth and Reconciliation Commission had, it was a courageous attempt to record the legacy of human rights abuses. The TRC record has given victims a historical place for their stories and some restoration of their dignity. The TRC also forced our society to confront the depths of depravity to which some elements had descended in the service of defending white privilege as well as in the abuse of power among both the oppressed and oppressor groups. The biggest failure of the TRC is in having paid too little attention to redress for the victims. White South Africans who benefited from the inequities of the past got off very lightly. It would not have been too much to ask white South Africans who benefited so much from the inequities of the past to make a one-time payment in the form of a reconciliation tax to address some of the urgent redress needs of victims. Even the grossest abusers of human rights have been allowed to keep the fruits of looting the national purse.

Let us return to Alexander's other criticisms of the failures of the ANC-led government over the last five years. Why the gap between promise and delivery? There are three main reasons for this gap. First, the ANC promises were extravagant. There was no appreciation of the scale of development work that would be required to deliver all those wonderful promises. There may have been too much reliance on the success of the National Party government's model to deal with the problems of poor whites in the last fifty years. The two cases are radically different in both scale and context. Poor whites had the majority black population as a cushion against their poverty, whereas in the new South Africa everyone has rights under the national democratic constitution.

The emphasis on black economic empowerment, which focuses on enriching a few black males, is also a throwback to the post-1948 period during which English-speaking owners of capital sought to co-opt the new Afrikaner political elites. The co-option of a few black males is not sufficient to ward off the frustration of the majority who continue to live in grinding poverty without any visible path out. A wider spread of opportunity is essential to sustaining the hope that democracy will mean something in the everyday lives of ordinary South Africans. More strategic black economic empowerment is called for.

Second, there was a fundamental lack of appreciation by the new government of the extent to which the legacy of the past would continue to shape postapartheid South Africa and to haunt its future. To undo the planned inequality that characterized the system of government over 350 years is a mammoth task. Nothing short of a "Marshall Plan" would succeed in the short to medium term to redress the imbalances of the past.

Third, at the heart of the failure to deliver is lack of institutional capacity, which is an integral part of the legacy of the past. The capacity to govern and to pursue a national development strategy presupposes the existence of an efficient and effective machinery of governance. It is common knowledge that such a machinery had to be built from the rubble of a corrupt and fragmented system. The people who were to run government had to be trained from zero base in the case of the new elites, or to be retrained with respect to the old guard who were absorbed into the new system. Some members of the old guard spent all their energy resisting change, while a significant proportion showed a willingness to use their skills and experience to advance the course of the new South Africa.

The uneven performance in government ranks also reflects the unevenness of the human-resource capacity in the various sectors of government. Those areas blessed with capable leaders who were also confident enough to utilize available expertise and were willing to learn the basic principles of good management practice performed very well, e.g., water and forestry, transport, trade and industry, finance, and since July 1999, education under Kader Asmal. Others who lacked the basic understanding of governance or those who relied on ideological approaches to problem solving have not succeeded.

The most devastating aspect of the legacy of racism and sexism is the poor human and intellectual resource base our society has to contend with. We come last in the ranks of international competitiveness because of our poor performance on this score. Without skilled, properly motivated human resources one cannot succeed in running good public and private institutions. The inadequate institutional capacity in both the public and private sectors of South Africa is seriously hampering government's ability to deliver meaningful national development outcomes in a number of important areas. The most tragic area of poor performance is education. The inherited legacy of a disabling educational philosophy, poor quality of the teaching corps in many areas of South Africa where the majority of black people continue to live, as well as poor national and provincial leadership have perpetuated the inequalities of opportunities between the "haves" and the "have-nots."

I would also like to comment briefly on Alexander's concern about the possibility of transcending our racist past. South Africans have yet to face up to the depth of the superiority and inferiority complexes that are part of the legacy of 350 years of racism. There is a deep-seated, and in some cases not so deep-seated, view held by a significant proportion of white South Africans that black people have an inherent intellectual inferiority. This belief is shared by racists all over the world. But in the South African context, where there was an active national agenda to make black people fail, the everyday encounters between white and black people reinforced this view.

It is not surprising that a significant proportion of black people began to believe that they were inferior. How else does one explain to one's children that you fail to provide them with the most basic needs? That you are unable to stand up to white people abusing you and assaulting your dignity? That you are not knowledgeable about the most basic issues fundamental to everyday life in a modern society? But even more devastating over the long term is the subtle impact of "living under suspicion of intellectual inferiority" on those black people who are successful.[1] One's performance under such circumstances is undermined by the anxiety not to be seen as acting in line with the stereotypical view held by others of oneself. This "stereotype threat" puts a lot of pressure on many talented people, some of whom end up failing because the pressure ends up being too much. Even among those who succeed, paranoia prevents them from excelling because they cannot take criticism, the very lifeblood of excellence. Critical comment from peers is under circumstances of "stereotype threat" regarded as being driven by racism or lack of loyalty from one's black colleagues. We have seen many examples of this problem across the wide spectrum of our society over the last five years. We have to confront this cancer in our society if we are to have any chance of success.

To address racism will take an acknowledgment of the problem on both sides of the divide. There has to be a willingness to openly discuss it without the fudge of "rainbowism" and to do the hard work of confronting the racist culture in our midst. Both black and white people will have to be prepared to adopt new ways of looking at difference without enshrining it in essentialist notions. Deep-seated ethnocentric views also need to be confronted. In particular, the use to which difference has been employed to harness resources for one or another group has to be tackled vigorously.

At the end of the day, it is going to take a lot of soul-searching and hard work to unlearn the bad habits of a racist society. Higher-education institutions have to give leadership to South Africa in tackling this difficult issue. Psychological and intellectual liberation is essential to giving real meaning to political and economic liberation to all South Africans. The promotion of a science culture that encourages open dialogue about difficult subjects is an important step in the right direction. South Africa has a unique opportunity to give leadership in a global context in this area, not because we are wiser but because the consequences of our failure to resolve our racist past are too ghastly to contemplate for our own society.

Notes to Responses

1. See Claude Steele, *Atlantic Monthly* 69 (April 1992): 74.

17

It's in the Blood: Notes on Race Attitudes in Brazil from a Different Perspective

Elisa Larkin Nascimento

THE PURPOSE OF this chapter is to articulate considerations on the nature of race attitudes in Brazil that seem particularly relevant to the dialogues set in motion by the Southern Education Foundation's Comparative Human Relations Initiative (CHRI). It is intended for readers interested or involved in these dialogues. In the first section, we will approach from a critical standpoint three ideas: that antiracialism[1] has become intrinsic to the Brazilian social conscience; that color categories are neutral in Brazil; and that social movements advocating an inclusive definition of Afro-Brazilian identity are practicing black racialism. In the second and third sections, we will look at the historical grounding and popular expressions of racialism in Brazil; in the fourth and fifth sections, we will consider two areas where racialist attitudes continue to prevail: the systems of criminal justice and education. Consideration of these two areas is not intended to imply that similar phenomena are not relevant to others.

The notion that "racialism" can be effectively distinguished from "racism" is by no means immune to challenge. In this essay, the term *racialism* is used as a tool of convenience to denote biological theories of race. Such usage does not endorse the theoretical distinction between "racialism" and "racism." They are inextricably bound together as aspects of one and the same phenomenon.

Black Activism and the Social Category of Race

There is a broadly accepted consensus that since the publication of Gilberto Freyre's works in the 1930s, Brazil's social fabric and national personality absorbed not only the ideal of antiracialism but also a positive value change elevating the society's perception and acceptance of African descendants and their culture. An author who has made thoughtful contributions in the process of articulating useful approaches to the question of racial inequalities in Brazil, Antonio Sérgio Guimarães, states this consensus neatly in Chapter 6 of the present volume: "Brazilian modernity found a common national destiny in overcoming racialism and in valuing the cultural heritage of Brazilian blacks, mulattos, and *caboclos* [mixed-race persons of indigenous Brazilian and white ancestry]." He goes on to make the well-taken points that the national ideal of antiracialism is not incompatible with the existence of inequality and that it walks hand in hand with a systematic denial of racial discrimination in Brazil. Yet the fundamental importance he attributes to the building of the national identity on the basis of an antiracialist ideal expresses the basic tenet articulated by the social-science tradition whose history he so effectively records: that Brazilian society's repudiation of racialism is woven inextricably into the fabric of the national social order.

Correlative to this view is the assertion that there is a substantive and positive difference between race relations based on the color criterion that grounds the Brazilian "whitening" ideology and those based on the hypodescendancy criterion used in the United States that identifies on the basis of origin. An eloquent example in the CHRI context is Edith Piza's declaration at the outset of her essay on whiteness in Brazil (1999: p. 1): "I would like to alert the reader to the fact that everything we say here about color classification, denomination, and attributes in Brazil shall be screened inexorably by what Oracy Nogueira called the 'appearance rule,' as opposed to the 'origin rule' that prevails mainly in the United States."[2] Explanation of this distinction is accompanied by the observation that color in Brazil is determined also by a series of physical traits composing phenotype (texture of hair, shape of nose, lips, etc.), which are supposed to have no bearing in a society where discrimination is based on origin (e.g., the United States).

The line of research represented by Nogueira's work (1959, 1955) takes this distinction as its starting point in establishing the general rule that preference for whiteness and lighter color appearance in Brazil is purely an aesthetic one, devoid of racial connotation. Guimarães (Chapter 6, this volume, emphasis added) provides us with a succinct expression of this conclusion:

"Race" came to mean [for Brazilians] only "determination," "will power," or "character," but almost never "subdivisions of the human species"; these came to be designated only by a person's color: *branca* [white], *parda* [roughly, mulatto], *preta* [roughly dark black], and so on. These colors came to be considered objective, concrete, unquestionable realities *without moral or intellectual connotations . . . [which—when existing—]were rejected as "prejudice."*

Yet color is none other than the mark of origin. African, Native Brazilian Indian, or other nonwhite identity, as evidenced by color, is the target of prejudice and discrimination, which are based on the same ideology of white supremacism that moves other systems of racial exclusion. Guimarães himself elsewhere (1998: p. 5) notes several "misunderstandings" fomented by the line of thought that grew up around the color criterion and the appearance rule, among them the idea "that in Brazil there exist no races, but rather colors, as if the *idea* of race did not underlie that of 'color.'"

Nonetheless, taken generally as basic premises of most approaches to race relations in Brazil, such notions increasingly have been challenged by voices rising out of the Afro-Brazilian community[3] whose testimony indicates that the Afro-Brazilian experience of national social reality differs considerably from the postulates of social-science analysis, particularly with regard to the meaning and operation of the color criterion. For these critics, the antiracialist ideal is less a social reality than a pretense constructed as part and parcel of the "racial democracy" ideology that has served to obscure mechanisms of exclusion, reinforcing and contributing to the efficacy of racial domination. Indeed, this antiracist pretense has been effectively used as a tool to muffle the voice of Afro-Brazilian protest and to strengthen the whitening ideal. After all, what need is there to heed Afro-Brazilian protest if white society is already committed to the antiracist ideal, and what need is there for African Brazilians to articulate their own values and perspectives if the dominant intellectual milieu has already incorporated them?

Recent social-science research on inequality has joined Afro-Brazilian activists in rejecting the minutiae of color categories as analytically unworkable, partly because they are so subjective as to be essentially meaningless[4] and partly because, contrary to the appearance rule's prediction, it has been demonstrated that discrimination and inequalities are suffered by intermediate color groups (Lovell 1991; Hasenbalg and Silva, 1992; Silva 1999).[5] Accordingly, researchers and activists have reached a consensus largely accepted by the media[6] and increasingly by the general public that defines the sum of two official census groups—*pardos* and *pretos* (roughly meaning mulattos and very dark-skinned blacks, respectively)—as one category called *negros* (blacks) or *afro-descendentes* (African descendants).[7]

Such an inclusive criterion runs directly counter to the whitening ideal and has been branded as a return to racialism, an acceptance of biological theories condemned by social science and rejected by the Brazilian social milieu. It is not entirely clear why this criterion is seen to be based on biological rather than social constructs, while in contrast its inverse, the inclusion of persons with mixed ancestry in the "white" category, is considered devoid of biological implications and therefore not racialist. Guimarães (Chapter 6, this volume), remarks that "the great question is to understand why antiracialism has come under attack in the last few years, undergoing systematic criticism from black movements and from some social scientists."[8]

Black movements have directed their criticism not against antiracialism but against the false and self-serving nature of the racial democracy ideology with its antiracialist pretensions, based upon which, as Sueli Carneiro notes (1997: p. 225), "there developed in Brazil a sophisticated, perverse, and competent form of racism by means of which racial intolerance was masked as equality of rights on the discursive and legal plane and as the absolute inequality of opportunity on the level of concrete social relations."

If ambiguity reigns in Brazilian color-classification systems, it is much less present in the daily experienced reality of the political and socioeconomic order. As Oliveira, Lima, and Santos observe (1998: pp. 53, 56), "racial stratification by power and prestige is clear, well delineated and extremely rigid. . . . whites are at the top . . . and *pretos* and *pardos* are excluded."[9] They go on to point out that black movements in Brazil "have sought to define who is black by political and socio-economic criteria: *Pardos* are being grouped with *pretos* because they also suffer racial discrimination and not simply because they have a drop of black blood in their veins."

In addition to the shared experience of discrimination, the inclusive "black" category is based on specific historical and cultural experience (Nascimento 1980: p. 270). Whether or not individuals who could potentially belong to this group choose to declare themselves black, inequalities and specific life circumstances based in history and culture are shared by them. The fact that few Brazilians choose to class themselves as *pretos* or *negros* confirms the stigmatization of blackness and the efficacy of the whitening ideal, but in no way obviates the need for public policy to address racial inequalities.[10]

The idea that postulation of a broad social category of blacks is based on biological criteria or that black activists endorse biological notions of race is not sustained by the work of any Afro-Brazilian intellectual or activist of which I am aware, and none of their writings are cited to support that idea.[11] Yet it is not only recently that they have been labeled black racialists; this response to denunciation of racial inequality has long been the norm. Accustomed already in the 1950s to accusations that claims to black identity were based on biological notions of race, longtime activist Abdias Nascimento underscored the need for emphasis in the following lines written some twenty-five years ago (1980: pp. 270, 272): "I warn the intriguers, the malicious ones, those quick to judge: the word *race*, in the sense used here, is defined only in terms of history and culture, and not of biological purity. . . . I reiterate here the warning to the intriguers, the malicious ones, the ignorant, the racists: in this book the word *race* has exclusively historical-cultural meaning. Biologically pure race does not exist and never did." Indeed, it could be said that in this statement Nascimento harked forward to the idea of social construction of race now in vogue in the social sciences (Frankenberg 1994).

The racial democracy ideology created a taboo identifying the unmasking of its antiracialist pretense as a reverse racist attack on antiracialism. This phenomenon has an effect of supreme importance to the maintenance of the status quo: it robs those excluded of the legitimacy of their protest against discrimination, placing on their shoulders the onus of the very racism that operates their exclusion. Herein lies the perversity of this system of domination, and the reason why some activists have deemed it more pernicious than the outright rejection and explicit segregation that have characterized other racist societies.

Historical Groundings of Racialism in Brazil

While it is true that the pretense of antiracialism has become deeply entrenched in the national consciousness,[12] that pretense is accompanied closely by a parallel and equally entrenched, but generally nonexplicit, undercurrent of racialist ideas born of long tradition. Historically, this phenomenon is a result of the fact that in Brazil, African descendants constituted the great majority of the population over four-fifths of the country's existence.[13] Whitening of this racial stock was essential to the building of a state worthy of acceptance into the company of civilized nations, but scientific race theory prevailing at the time condemned race mixture as a process of inevitable biological degeneration. The solution was to create a new, nationally constructed theory exalting race mixture to justify the dilution of the inferior racial stock by means of incentive to massive European immigration and miscegenation. In 1911, the Brazilian delegate to the Universal Races Congress announced that by the year 2012 this process would have eliminated all vestiges of the African and mulatto presence from the population (as cited in Skidmore 1974: p. 66), attaining the desired white-only population, a goal amply and eloquently expressed in the literature of the time (Skidmore 1974).

Miscegenation was elevated to the status of a national ideal, then, not as an antiracialist proposal but as a tool of social engineering based precisely on the racialist notion of biological inferiority of Africans and their descendants. Social pressure to "improve the blood" motivated millions to see that their children would be lighter in color. The principle of eugenics was formally inscribed in the 1934 Constitution. Immigration law promulgated in 1945[14] maintained the criterion that had regulated entry into the country since the nineteenth century: "The need to preserve and develop in the ethnic composition of the population the more desirable characteristics of its European ancestry." As for Afro-Brazilian culture, its religious entities were required to register with the police until 1974, and were so much the constant objects of repression that the police museums of Rio de Janeiro and Bahia are replete with Afro-Brazilian worship objects confiscated during police raids. Gilberto Freyre himself made clear (1976: p. 7) that recognition of African cultural values would take place "without ever signifying a repudiation of the predominance of European cultural values in Brazilian development."

Racialist principles are perfectly compatible with the "racial democracy" ideology, for if, as this ideology posits, Brazilian society offers equal opportunities and black people nevertheless remain at the bottom of the socioeconomic scale, a "logical" explanation becomes evident to the lay person: their innate incapacity to compete for higher status. Thus, while the popular consciousness hotly defends its own nonracialism and that of the social order, it also retains notions of subdivisions of the human race, translating them into color categories that rarely, if ever, are neutral in social practice. Indeed, whatever the notions of social-science tradition, intellectual and moral connotations are associated intimately with these categories,[15] particularly in the workings of criminal justice and education considered below.

Perhaps the following observation of a prominent specialist in Brazilian history, Thomas E. Skidmore (1976: p. 211), best sums up the compatibility of the "racial democracy" ideology with a continuum of racialist tradition: "The practical value of [Gilberto Freyre's] analysis did not lie, however, in promoting racial egalitarianism. His analysis served, principally, to reinforce the ideal of whitening." Whitening epitomizes racialist notions about subdivision of the human species.

Popular Expression of Racialist Notions

The weight of the racialist tradition is translated in popular culture and everyday life in the repeated images, scenes, and language of black subordination, stereotype, and subservience to be found in schools, in commerce, in the workplace, in social relations, and particularly in police repression.

While it is true that the word "race" has come to denote determination, character, and will power in Brazil, this does not mean that the popular consciousness is entirely divorced from the inclusive idea of race as identity. Over the last few years, the magazine *Raça Brasil*, billed as the "Brazilian black people's magazine," has sold tens of millions of copies; its portrayal of "black people" graphically includes light-skinned persons of mixed ancestry.

On the other hand, the popular consciousness expresses racialist notions in several forms, one of them being by way of a certain preoccupation with the question of what is "in the blood," a theme clearly left over from the earlier concern with whitening promoted by the state—it was, after all, the massive infusion of "vivacious, energetic, and healthy Caucasian blood" (Joaquim Nabuco, as cited in Chiavenato 1980) that was to improve the nation's inferior racial stock.

In my own first experience of Brazil, as a U.S. exchange student living in São Paulo, it was explained to me that, differently from my country, in Brazil there was no discrimination against blacks. When I asked why, then, the rich young men who frequented the São Paulo Yacht Club were almost all blond and blue-eyed second-generation Europeans while beggars on the city streets, sharecroppers, and landless peasants were black, the answer was unforgettable: "There's nothing to be done about that, it's in the blood."[16]

Twenty-five years later (most of them lived in Rio de Janeiro), I was obliged to carry out major repair work in my apartment. There was a need for rather advanced plumbing service, and the specialist called in was a blond and blue-eyed Scandinavian-looking type. Admiring the quality of the work in progress, he addressed the technician in charge of the repairs, a fair-skinned Portuguese gentleman, while directing a glance of complicity to the white mistress of the house: "Of course. You don't get quality work unless there is European blood in the veins."[17]

Stereotypes of black, Indian, and Northeastern regional[18] laziness, indolence, intellectual backwardness, criminal tendencies, and so on, are often couched in terms of such characteristics lurking "in the blood" of these populations, just as special talent and vocation for rhythm, samba, and soccer are deemed generally to flow "in the blood" of African descendants.

Finally, the idea of "cleaning the race" is one that has weighed heavily on the consciousness of young black women, for whom the admonition operated at least well into the 1970s as a veritable call to social responsibility.[19] Perhaps less frequently now, black women are still called upon to take care that they have "clean wombs," i.e., lighter progeny.

The Living Lombrosian Heritage

Hédio Silva Jr. (1998)[20] provides us with a succinct portrait of the continued legacy of the racialist tradition in criminology, whose efficient use in the 1930s won the Criminal Identification Office of the Federal District (then Rio de Janeiro) a coveted award: the Lombroso Criminal Anthropology Prize, conferred by Italy's Royal Academy of Medicine in 1933 (Gomes 1995).

It is no news to students of the evolution of pseudo-scientific theories of racism that the Lombrosian tradition of criminal anthropology[21] — involving the measuring of skulls and identification of physical traits betraying the "suspect" racial origin of elements in custody and their belonging to certain criminal "types" — develops the essence of biological notions of inferiority in concrete social policy. What may be a novelty to those unfamiliar with the operation of such ideas in Brazil is the work of Lombroso's Brazilian apostle, Nina Rodrigues, a mulatto physician from Maranhão whose name proudly identifies Bahia's Institute of Legal Medicine. In his major work,[22] Rodrigues states the tenor of this tradition: "Aryan civilization is represented in Brazil by a fragile minority of the white race to whom is left the burden of defending it, not only against the anti-social acts—the crimes—of its own representatives, but also against the anti-social acts of the inferior races." On the crime of vagrancy, he noted: "The indolence of the mestizo population is perhaps one of the facts that will merit the least discussion in Brazil. . . . The latest Penal Code, correct along with the general consensus in finding in mestizos' indolence a manifestation of free will in not wanting to work, has come quickly to the rescue with Article 399, to remedy this harm."

Not content merely to transpose his master's ideas to the tropics, Rodrigues introduced into the Brazilian array of techniques identifying "criminal types" a new and audacious standard. To the measurements of cranium, length of middle finger, forearms, and so on, Rodrigues added measurement of the width of the suspect's nostrils (Silva Jr. 1998: p. 77).

The continuing impact of the Lombrosian heritage in criminology is registered, as Silva Jr. notes, in numerous contemporary studies on the discriminatory workings of the criminal justice system (e.g., Adorno 1995; Pinheiro 1994; Barcellos 1992; Ribeiro 1995). Blacks, often well-dressed and driving fancy cars—therefore not necessarily poor—are far more frequently arrested arbitrarily. They are also more frequently convicted and by far the favorite victims of police brutality, persecution, and torture. In an open letter to the police commissioner of Rio de Janeiro in 1950, Abdias Nascimento (1968: p. 59) made a statement that is valid still today: "One would say that the police consider men of color born criminals and are creating the criminal offense of being black."

Silva Jr. shows that Nina Rodrigues's theoretical legacy is present also in the writings of contemporary criminal jurists. One example, published in 1996, is this excerpt explaining the reasons why criminality among blacks and mulattos is "comparatively much higher than that of the white population":[23]

> A century after this abolition [of slavery], the Negro has not adjusted to social standards and our *mestizo,* our *caboclo,* is generally indolent, has a propensity to alcoholism, makes his living from primary tasks and very rarely is able to prosper in life. This is the *type* that normally . . . ends up involved in marginality and crime. (Silva Jr. 1998: p. 86, emphasis added)

In another text, this one published in 1995, the authors state that "Africans and Indians conserve their habits and customs and make of them an insoluble amalgam with new ones. In their actions, there must be a powerful influence of conscious or unconscious reminiscences of the savage life of yesterday, very poorly counterbalanced by the new emotional acquisitions of the civilization that was imposed on them."[24]

Stunning indeed is the 1996 declaration of then commander of the metropolitan police force of São Paulo Colonel Élio Proni, on police training in that city: "There is no preference for stopping blacks, because there are no suspect persons, but rather suspect situations." Frequently cited by the Military Police Academy as an example of the "suspect situation," he goes on to say, is that of "four black men [*crioulos*] inside a car."[25]

The Racialist Legacy in Education

In education, the racialist legacy is perpetuated implicitly in various forms but largely remains unarticulated in a nevertheless eloquent undercurrent. The effect of omission and of silence in race relations in the school as well as in educational literature is to underscore and reinforce the stereotypes created by racialist notions of biological inferiority.

First and foremost in this context are the differentiated expectations that teachers tend to entertain of their pupils. Educators specializing in the matter (Silva 1991; Silva and Barbosa 1997; Figueira 1993) agree that, in general, the Afro-Brazilian student is seen by most teachers as one lacking potential to learn. Formal knowledge, book learning, and writing are not considered talents innate to blacks. One teacher, interviewed by researchers from the State University of Santa Catarina (Neli Goes Ribeiro and Paulino de Jesus F. Cardoso, in Lima and Romão 1997: p. 44), said candidly of Afro-Brazilian children: "They can't learn, they're not disciplined, they're lazy and they give up soon. All they want is soccer and samba. It's in the blood." While it is relatively rare in Brazil to find such explicit endorsement of this stereotype, differentiated expectations of students are common. Black students are often seen as ones who will soon drop out, give up, or fail; teachers are apt to dedicate less time and energy to them.

Secondly, the silence of teachers and the failure of school authorities to act in the face of racist behavior targeting black children or their parents legitimizes and reinforces the posture of submission traditionally expected of them according to racialist standards. While it is true that Afro-Brazilian children protest in different and sometimes enigmatic ways against racist attitudes they sense or experience in school, the institution and its authority figures generally do nothing to support them in this protest or to arrest those attitudes. If anything, the behavior is condoned or even encouraged by the general understanding that the children are "just kidding" and that jokes are harmless.

Finally, the stereotypes reproduced in children's literature and textbooks reflect racialist ideas engrained in Brazilian culture (Rego 1981; Nosella 1981; Rosemberg 1984; Negrão 1987; Larkin-Nascimento 1993; Silva and Barbosa 1997). The animalization of black people depicted in school texts, their presentation devoid of family relations and in subordinate social positions, their exclusion from drawings or photos of large groups of Brazilians in public places and from illustrations of general interest, the omission of African civilizations, and the depiction of enslaved Africans as docile and submissive—all these stereotypes, and others, derive from racialism and reinforce its implicit continuing presence. Such stereotypes are so entrenched in the Brazilian general consciousness that in most cases they are seen as "natural" and people are genuinely shocked and surprised to be advised of their racist connotations. The pretense to antiracialism makes more difficult their unmasking as racist stereotypes.

Conclusion

The notions of an antiracialist national identity and of color categories unrelated to racial origin are indeed entrenched in the national consciousness and articulated in national discourse. However, they exist side by side with a battery of racialist notions that are silenced, obscured, and denied but which operate concretely in daily social practice. Invisible and unheard, racialist notions walk hand in hand with the stridently broadcast denial of racism in Brazil, forming a largely unrecognized part of the racial democracy ideology. With this ideology, the fear of the black majority that enunciated creation of whitening policies could give way to indignant denial of racism in Brazilian society and invocation of miscegenation as "proof" of its absence. The appeal of this image and its success were enormous. Thus, as Anani Dzidzienyo observed (1971), Brazilian society achieved apparently *without tension* the same social results of domination that segregationist racism achieved in the United States, the difference being that in Brazil the dominated group was more than half the population as opposed to a minority of little over 12 percent.

The set of ideas articulated by the racial-democracy theory has been constructed, reinforced, and legitimized in the interests of the well-entrenched elite that presides over a rigidly hierarchical social, economic, and political order reflected in the halls of the academy. That this elite has disciples of all colors who adopt its tenets shall be no news to those accustomed to the sinuous contours of any racist society. But there is an important contrast between Brazil and the United States, where the academic world has incorporated the persons, voices, and ideas of black activist intellectuals and they have gained substantial legitimacy. That victory is the result of a long, hard road walked by the U.S. African-American community, made possible by that community's cohesion and sense of identity in confronting racial exclusion. In Brazil, the pretense to antiracialism, reinforced by discourse around the color criterion and the appearance rule, not only has obscured domination and created obstacles to group cohesion, identity, and articulation of interests but also has prevented the formation of a tradition of interracial civil rights activism in which white allies march in significant numbers with black activists in the antiracist struggle. Those Brazilian allies who participate in this Comparative Human Relations Initiative are commendably part of an extremely minute group. Voices that seek to express Afro-Brazilian interests and points of view most often are muffled or branded racist.

The importance of the Comparative Human Relations Initiative is that it offers a forum for those voices to emerge. As Sueli Carneiro (1997: p. 225) observed, it is indeed a novelty that "we are here exercising the possibility of seeing Brazil in a different light, seeing it comparatively and from our perspective."

Notes

1. "Racialism" has been distinguished by some sociologists from the broader category of racism. It is defined as being the set of notions built around the assertion of race as a biological phenomenon (Appiah 1992).

2. While Piza is no apologist of the "racial democracy" ideology, the emphasis she places on this distinction is worthy of the major writers of that tradition.

3. The list is long; a few representative examples are Gonzalez 1986; Nascimento 1968, 1980, 1989; Gonzalez and Hasenbalg 1982; Santos 1994; Bairros 1988; Lovell 1991; Carneiro 1997; Silva 1998; Lima and Romão 1997; Oliveira, Lima, and Santos 1998.

4. In the oft-cited National Domicile Sample Survey (PNAD) of 1976, carried out by the Brazilian Geography and Statistics Institute (IBGE), the questionnaire left it to the respondent to define his/her color and 135 categories

were mentioned. In a similar but more recent survey by Fohla de São Paulo/ DataFolha (1995), sixty-two color categories were cited. However, Oliveira, Lima, and Santos (1998: p. 55) point out that six main color classifications correspond to 94 percent of the responses in both surveys.

5. A symbolic example arose in 1993, when Ana Flávia Peçanha de Azeredo, the very light-skinned daughter of African-Brazilian politician Albuíno Azeredo, then governor of Espírito Santo state, was directed to the service entrance of a middle-class building and protested that she was the victim of illegal racial discrimination. Quite a visible media event, this incident placed the sociologists' insistence on the appearance rule severely in question. Not only did Ana Flávia identify herself and not only was she treated as black, contradicting the appearance rule, but this event was seen as only one among countless instances of discrimination against light-skinned black people that refute its validity.

6. In the case of Ana Flávia, the media (*Veja* magazine gave the incident prominent coverage in its July 7, 1993 issue) did not hesitate to identify her as black, a fact that raised the eyebrows of social scientists such as Peter Fry (1995–1996), who came out in defense of the color criterion and the appearance rule.

7. Less frequently, the term "nonwhite" is used for this group.

8. It is surprising indeed to find this discourse advanced by an author whose analysis of the role of black social movements in Brazil and whose work on affirmative action have helped to build an intellectual base of support for the articulation of meaningful actions against racial inequalities in Brazil.

9. In the highest levels of government there are no African descendants except when Pelé was Extraordinary Minister of Sports (1995–1998). Of 594 members of Congress, 13 are African descendants. In public universities (those with highest prestige in Brazil), *pardo* professors are rare; *preto* professors almost nonexistent. Among judges there are almost no blacks, although white women are now the majority of new young judges (*Jornal do Brasil* 27.06 [1999]). In the Brazilian appellate courts there were no black justices until 1998, when one minister, Carlos Alberto Reis de Paula, took a seat on the Higher Labor Tribunal. Oliveira, Lima, and Santos (1998: pp. 52–53).

10. Once again, we are surprised to find an author like Guimarães (Chapter 6 of this volume) citing survey results on self-identification to support the notion that the black movement is on the verge of having to opt between "majority" and "minority" identity politics and that "the struggle for affirmative action for blacks must forcibly benefit those 7 percent of the population that identify themselves as *pretos* or *negros*."

11. On the contrary, African-Brazilian intellectuals and activists have written eloquent indictments of racialism and its operation in the history of Brazilian social relations (Ramos 1957; Nascimento 1968; Carneiro 1997; Gomes 1995; Silva Jr. 1998; Silva 1998).

12. Sueli Carneiro notes (1997: p. 225) that the country's "social imagination assimilated the romantic version of race relations in Brazil."

13. According to famous intellectual and diplomat Rio Branco (as cited in Nascimento 1968: p. 31), in 1822 there were about 2 million *pretos*, five hundred thousand *mulatos*, and 1 million whites. In 1872, the census counted more than 6 million *pretos* and *pardos* as opposed to 3.8 million whites.

14. Law Decree no. 7967 of September 14, 1945.
15. Edith Piza (1999) notes the moral connotations associated with blackness by white women interviewed in her research.
16. "Isso não tem jeito, está no sangue."
17. "Não se faz um trabalho bem feito sem sangue europeu nas veias."
18. In the poor Northeast region of Brazil, there is a very large majority proportion of African descendants and varied but mostly very dark-complexioned people of mixed heritage, especially Native Brazilian Indian and African. Northeasterners, who have migrated in enormous numbers to the major urban centers, are subjected to general racial inequalities and also to specific stereotyping as "Northeastern regionals."
19. This fact emerges in interviews this author has conducted with several black women, mostly educators, as part of a research project carried out in Rio de Janeiro.
20. Unless otherwise specified, the information contained in this section is taken from Silva's essay.
21. Cesare Lombroso (1835–1909) was the founder of the Italian school of criminological positivism, responsible for the scientific legitimation of ideas such as the existence of "born criminals" and "criminal types," the association of phenotype and racial identity with individuals' tendency to crime, criminal atavism, and so on.
22. Nina Rodrigues, *The Human Races and Penal Responsibility in Brazil* (1894: pp. 112, 124, 141–142), as cited in Silva 1998.
23. João Farias Jr., *Manual de Criminologia*, 2d. ed. (Curitiba: Juruá, 1996), pp. 74–76, as cited in Silva Jr. (1998: p. 86).
24. Roberto Lyra and João Marcello Araújo Jr., *Criminologia*, 4th ed. (Rio de Janeiro: Forense, 1995), pp. 130–133, as cited in Silva Jr. (1998: p. 87).
25. Published in *Veja* magazine, February 7, 1996.

References

Adorno, Sérgio. 1995. "Discriminação racial e Justiça Criminal." *Novos Estudos Cebrap* 43 (November).

Appiah, K. Anthony. 1992. *In My Father's House*. New York and London: Oxford University Press.

Bairros, Luíza. 1988. "Pecados no paraíso racial: o negro na força de trabalho na Bahia, 1950–1980," in João Reis, ed., *Escravidão e invenção da liberdade*. São Paulo: Editora Brasiliense.

Barcellos, Caco. 1992. *Rota 66—A História da Polícia que Mata*. 5th ed. São Paulo: Editora Globo.

Carneiro, Sueli. 1997. "Raça, Classe e Identidade Nacional." *Thoth: Pensamento dos Povos Afro-descendentes* 2 (May-August): 221–233. (Journal published and distributed gratuitously by the office of Senator Abdias Nascimento, Federal Senate, Brasília.)

Chiavenato, Júlio José. 1980. *O Negro no Brasil*. 3d. ed. São Paulo: Editora Brasiliense.

Dzidzienyo, Anani. 1971. *The Position of Blacks in Brazilian Society*. London:

The Minority Rights Group.

Figueira, Vera Moreira. 1993. "O Preconceito Racial na Escola," in Larkin-Nascimento, ed., 1993.

Folha de São Paulo/ DataFolha. 1995. *Racismo Cordial.* São Paulo: Folha de São Paulo.

Frankenberg, Ruth. 1994. *White Women, Race Matters: The Social Construction of Whiteness.* Minneapolis: University of Minnesota Press.

Freyre, Gilberto. 1976. "Aspectos da Influência Africana no Brasil." *Cultura* (journal of the Brazilian Ministry of Education and Culture) 6, no. 23 (October-December).

Fry, Peter. 1995–1996. "O que a Cinderela Negra tem a dizer sobre a 'Política Racial' no Brasil." *Revista USP* 28 (São Paulo, December-February): 122–135.

Gomes, Olívia. 1995. "1933: Um Ano em que Fizemos Contatos." *Revista USP* 28 (*Dossiê Povo Negro 300 Anos*) (São Paulo, December-February): 142–163.

Gonzalez, Lélia. 1986. "Mulher Negra." *Afrodiáspora* 6-7 (Rio de Janeiro: IPEAFRO).

González, Lélia, and Carlos Hasenbalg. 1982. *Lugar de Negro.* Rio de Janeiro: Editora Marco Zero.

Guimarães, Antonio Sérgio. 1998. "Race and the Study of Race Relations in Brazil." Essay contributed to the Southern Education Foundation's Initiative on Comparative Human Relations: Brazil, South Africa, United States.

Hasenbalg, Carlos. 1979. *Discriminação e desigualdades raciais no Brasil.* Rio de Janeiro: Editora Graal.

Hasenbalg, Carlos, and Nelson do Valle Silva. 1992. *Relações raciais no Brasil.* Rio de Janeiro: Editora Rio Fundo.

Larkin-Nascimento, Elisa, ed. 1993. *A África na Escola Brasileira.* 2d. ed. Rio de Janeiro: SEAFRO.

Lima, Ivan Costa, and Jeruse Romão, eds. 1997. *Negro e Currículo.* Florianópolis: Núcleo de Estudos Negros.

Lovell, Peggy, ed. 1991. *Desigualdade Racial no Brasil Contemporâneo.* Belo Horizonte: CEDEPLAR-FACE-UFMG.

Nascimento, Abdias. 1989. *Mixture or Massacre.* 2d. ed. Dover, MA: The Majority Press.

———. 1980. *O Quilombismo.* Petrópolis: Editora Vozes.

———. 1968. *O Negro Revoltado.* Rio de Janeiro: GRD.

Nascimento, Abdias, and Elisa Larkin-Nascimento. 1992. *Africans in Brazil: A Pan-African Perspective.* Trenton, NJ: Africa World Press.

Negrão, Esmeralda V. 1987. "Preconceitos e discriminações raciais em livros didáticos infanto-juvenis," in *Diagnóstico sobre a situação de negros (pretos e pardos) no Estado de São Paulo.* Belo Horizonte, Brazil: Fundação Carlos Chagas.

Nogueira, Oracy. 1959. "Skin Color and Social Class," in Department of Cultural Affairs, Division of Science Development, Social Science Monographs 7, *Plantation Systems of the New World.* Washington, DC: Pan-American Union.

———. 1955. "Preconceito de marca e preconceito racial de origem," in *Anais do XXXI Congresso Internacional de Americanistas* 1. São Paulo: Editora Anhembi, pp. 409–434.

Nosella, Maria de Lourdes Chagas Deiró. 1981. *As Belas Mentiras: As Ideologias Subjacentes aos Livros Didáticos*. São Paulo: Moraes.

Oliveira, Djaci D. de, Ricardo B. Lima, and Sales A. dos Santos, eds. 1998. *A Cor do Medo: Homicídios e Relações Raciais no Brasil*. Brasília: Editora UnB/ Editora UFG/ MNDH.

Pinheiro, Paulo Sérgio. 1994. *Escritos Indignados*. São Paulo: Editora Brasiliense.

Piza, Edith. 1999. "Whites in Brazil? Nobody's Heard of Them, Nobody's Seen Them." Mimeo. Contribution to the Southern Education Foundation's Initiative on Comparative Human Relations.

Ramos, Guerreiro. 1957. *Introdução Crítica à Sociologia Brasileira*. Rio de Janeiro: Editorial Andes.

Rego, Maria Filomena. 1981. *O Aprendizado da Ordem*. Rio de Janeiro: Achiamé.

Ribeiro, Carlos Antonio Costa. 1995. *Cor e Criminalidade: Estudo e Análise da Justiça no Rio de Janeiro,1900–1930*. Rio de Janeiro: Universidade Federal do Rio de Janeiro.

Rosemberg, Fúlvia. 1984. *Literatura infantil e ideologia*. São Paulo: Global Editora.

Santos, Hélio. 1994. "Uma teoria para a questão racial do negro brasileiro. A trilha do círculo vicioso." *São Paulo em Perspectiva: Revista da Fundação SEADE* 8, no. 3.

Silva, Jorge da. 1998. *Violência e Racismo no Rio de Janeiro*. Niterói: Fluminense Federal University Press.

Silva, Maria José Lopes da. 1991. *Fundamentos Teóricos da Pedagogia Multirracial*. Rio de Janeiro. Mimeo.

Silva, Nelson do Valle. 2000. "Extensão e Natureza das Desigualdades Raciais no Brasil," in Guimarães and Huntley, eds., Tirando A Máscara. São Paulo: Paz e Terra.

Silva, Petronilha Beatriz Gonçalves, and Lúcia Maria de Assunção Barbosa, eds. 1997. *O Pensamento Negro em Educação no Brasil*. São Carlos: UFSCar.

Silva Jr., Hédio. 1998. "Crônica da Culpa Anunciada," in Oliveira, Lima, and Santos, eds., 1998.

Skidmore, Thomas E. 1974. *Black into White: Race and Nationality in Brazilian Thought*. London and New York: Oxford University Press.

— — —. 1976. *Preto no Branco: Raça e Nacionalidade no Pensamento Brasileiro*. Rio de Janeiro: Paz e Terra.

Interview with Sérgio Adorno

Antonio Sérgio Alfredo Guimarães

Antonio Sérgio Guimarães: Professor Sérgio Adorno, how did you become interested in the Brazilian black population?

Sérgio Adorno: First of all because the issue of racism entered into the discussion of crime, violence, and human rights. Maybe that was the starting point. For a long time we had a feeling that people that are accused of a crime, people that are suspected of having committed a crime, if they are black, are treated in a harsher way by the justice system—specifically, by the police, courts, prison administrations—than if they are white. To my knowledge, there were no studies evaluating or measuring this. What existed was a bit of information here, a general feeling. Human-rights issues began to be discussed, as was citizenship. When equality entered the discussion, racism automatically came to the surface, in connection with violence and crime.

Guimarães: Was this something spontaneous or was it a response to a demand?

Adorno: It was not spontaneous. The struggle for respect of human rights was for the longest time, especially at the end of the 1960s and all through the 1970s, connected to the struggle against the dictatorship, the authoritarian regime, for the return of voting rights. So the human rights cause is born of the struggle against power, against violence by the state against political dissidence.

At the end of the 1970s and all through the 1980s, when the struggle began to be victorious and, as political violence began to subside given the advance of the democratic process, it became apparent the problem of violence in Brazil was not limited to dictatorships. Paulo Sérgio Pinheiro played a very important role in the process. Through research studies, he demonstrated that the Brazilian state, often with segments of the political elite, used all sorts of resources to repress, be it the claims of the working class or cultural manifestations. Today there are many studies that demonstrate the [historical] persecution of the working class, of the Afro-Brazilian religious cults, of alternate medicinal practices. All these phenomena were considered threats to a civilized nation, to a country on its way to civilization.

In my research, I sought to demonstrate that there was a preference by the police and the legal apparatus to punish suspects who were black. It became very clear that violence and violations of human rights were not necessarily related to political dissidence. Violence had deeper roots. I would say that at the end of the 1970s and through the 1980s, that which was not a public issue became one. In other words, everybody became aware of the following dilemma: How can we build a democratic society based on (the exercise of) citizenship, based on fundamental rights of the human person, if there is deep inequality in the legal treatment that is dispensed to poor citizens, especially to black citizens? The big theme became inequality of justice. How can you build a modern society, a democratic state, if we have not secured equality of justice? What I'm trying to say here is that the democratization process in Brazil has accumulated a debt, that of securing civil rights for everyone, regardless of economic conditions, racial differences, age, origin, socioeconomic condition. You cannot imagine a humane society if, for example, the fundamental right to life is not shared by everyone.

Today, studies have shown us that in terms of violence-related deaths, blacks are much more vulnerable than the whites. Therefore, we have a society in which the right to life has not been distributed evenly to all. One cannot say that this is a consolidated democracy, we cannot say that a social contract exists, that it is guaranteed. I believe that there are a few state-nation–related tasks [state-nation understood as being the eighteenth- and nineteenth-century model we have inherited] that still need to be implemented by Brazilian society. It seems to me that this is a challenge, but at the same time, we are undergoing a very deep process of transformation with regard to the state. I would say the following: all the fundamental transformations that have been taking place since the beginning of this century, that intensified after World War II, that have to do with the unification of markets, with this process of technological development, have brought all cultures closer together and at the same time drawn them further apart—a process of globalization and fragmentation. All of this points to problems related to differences of identity with an intensity never before experienced. So this fact of unequal treatment in the administration of justice has become a problem, the importance of which is greater now, perhaps, than in the past.

Guimarães: There are arguments, which I hear, that say that this citizenship model that you referred to is an extinct model, one that is typical of affluent capitalism, and that today we are living in a different era, not only one of globalization of markets, but, more importantly, one of deterioration of basic premises of citizenship that only make sense to certain, central countries. Something similar to Lenin's theory about the English aristocracy and the English working class, that English workers had a certain standard of living that was only possible because England owned the world. In a way, the central countries, because they own the world, can provide citizenship to all, to all of their nationals, obviously. Continuing this line of thought, this model of citizenship is deteriorating, both in the central and more peripheral countries. In this sense, we are advanced in terms of society. Our disrespect of citizens would then be much more advanced than the protection of citizenship. How do you react to this type of logic?

Adorno: I think Brazil is in a dilemma because as a nation it has not completed the steps of the previous model and is facing the problems of an emerging model. I think that is the big problem. In other words, it is one thing to be living through a process of deconstruction of citizenship in societies where citizenship has been consolidated to a certain extent, either through laws or political culture. It is another thing to talk about the deconstruction of citizenship in societies that haven't even minimally achieved the consolidation of a societal model based on the contract, on civil rights, on universal citizenship. This is a very complicated problem, because you haven't finished one task and already you have to face the challenges of another one that has not been defined.

To think that we are in a position to take a shortcut in a process is a mistake, because while in these other countries the process may seem to be one in which a return path is being taken, there has been an experience in construction, whereas here, what we have is an unfinished road.

Let me try to say this another way, using crime, which I have researched, as an example. The justice system of Brazil is historically backlogged. Crime rates began to rise, the profile of crimes began to change, crimes started becoming more violent and increasingly organized. Today, you have organized crime that has been colonizing other forms of crime. Look at contraband, bank robberies, kidnappings that before were specialist-type activities; now these have been colonized because the activities must produce money so that the drug-business machine can function. This is not a Brazilian problem—the whole world is facing this. What makes the problem more complicated in Brazil is that while crime is rapidly growing and becoming more violent and organized, we have a justice system that copies the liberal model but that has not completed the steps of the liberal model. The liberal model is structured upon the ideal of penal and individual responsibility but is increasingly faced with responsibilities that are collective in nature, without knowing what that is. What happens? What has to change? What really has to change is the role of violence-repression agents.

We have to change the physiognomy of the judicial power and change the place of the judicial system within the architecture of the state. For us, this isn't a task [that needs to be done]; this is a complicated bulldozing action plan. What does the state do? How does the state face the situation? In the worse possible way—it is undoing a structure that was not able to establish fundamental rights. In other words, today you have an enormous disorganization of the liberal justice system. We cannot give a qualitative jump and build another justice model that will be able to deal with the situation out there.

I think that with respect to human rights, under which you place the issue of racism, the case is not very different. In other words, the profile of human rights has changed; one thing is human rights as defined in the 1789 declaration and the 1948 translation of that, that results in the United Nations. The rights in that sense are based on individual rights. The individual is a reasonable being, has qualifications. Today, this concept of individual has changed. We have another understanding. We cannot take for granted that reason is a normal attribute of human beings, that human beings have a [shared] nature. Increasingly, human beings simply reflect their social dimension.

In my opinion, this means that this model of power, this model of nation-state that we inherited from the nineteenth century, cannot embrace the complexity of today's problems, especially the emerging social conflicts of the end of the twentieth century. Conflicts are increasingly less centered around the individual. The representation of individuals confronting each other and of individuals confronting the state is a very weak one. The presence of groups that are organized in corporations, civil organizations, nongovernmental organizations, alas, groups that confront other collective organizations and that confront parts of the state structure, and that are connected in different ways to civil society, this type of presence is more potent today.

I think that the image we once had of a very clear distinction between civil society and the state—that is, agents that are organized and that are articulated with other agents and the state—all of that has been surpassed. In relation to crime, for example, some believe in the need for negotiation, that there is need to create courts that are parallel to the state. There is a need to unload the state, the state cannot be the only agent that is responsible for order. The big problem is that the state is not capable of providing order in a complex network of relationships. Therefore, you have to have subsidiary mechanisms.

So, in order to answer your question, if the situation of Brazil is favorable, let me say the following. Whether the issue is civil rights or citizenship, because several steps should have been taken through time and haven't, we today find ourselves before a preeminent process that requires that we deconstruct institutions that should be seminal but have not been consolidated. One can, for instance, build an entire racial issue in Europe, based on the fact that there has been a past experience of consolidation of certain rights and guarantees of equality. When you try to discuss this in a society like the Brazilian one, which has not experienced equality, the challenge is more complex. I have the sensation that those whose citizenship has been fragile will become even more so.

Guimarães: Do you think that individual rights are still the basis for any type of rights, despite the emergence of collective rights?

Adorno: No. I would not say that. What I would say, in the Brazilian case, is that the task of making individual rights universal was not completed. I believe that those rights were the basis of citizenship. Today, they are no longer. My concern is what happens to these countries in which basic rights have not been ascertained but that no longer form the base for citizenship?

Guimarães: I'm asking this question because, in the Brazilian case, as opposed to the case of the United States and Europe, the biggest problem is not in the new collective groups, immigrants, for instance, that do not have the same rights as nationals. Here in Brazil, our rights are not recognized. Period. We do not have a democratic state in which individuals may compete on equal terms. We lack something that precedes the collective individual, something that goes beyond collective recognition. In Brazil, our international immigration is minimal, a few Paraguayans, a few Peruvians, other Latin American minorities in São Paulo and in the Southeast, and so forth. The nucleus of the Brazilian population is suffering from the absence of recognition that has nothing to do with the legal representation of collective groups, such as immigrants. It has to do with the basic understanding that individuals have certain rights.

Adorno: The base has not been consolidated. I agree with you entirely. I believe that the era for the consolidation of these types of individual rights has passed. The problem is that the countries that are in this position find themselves, as I see it, in a difficult situation. I do not know if they are going to have the historical chance to make up for the lost opportunity. That's the problem.

Guimarães: Are equal rights not part of systems of domination, of accumulation?

Adorno: Yes, but they can be overlooked. They are overlooked although I do believe that from the standpoint of the groups that are dominated, individual rights continue to be a basic. That's the challenge. The process of modernization of the country is not taking this into consideration. In a society such as ours, this is all very complicated because the process is so alarmingly fast, and this alarming speed means, in truth, that you have to step over these basic rights that have never been consolidated and would need to be consolidated.

Guimarães: What creative strategies can we develop toward that? For example, would the affirmative-action policies that were developed in the United States be a way to go? How do you feel about this situation in which public policies must be implemented in order to compensate or counteract the historical tendencies that you have just described?

Adorno: I think that we have unfinished business to take care of. We must cultivate this business. It will not be finished immediately, but I think we must proceed with it. The job is to insist in moral indignation. Brazilian society is one that does not become indignant because of racial discrimination, because of racism. I think that there is a very privileged social arena that would be ideal for the development of indignation: schools. I mean, we cannot accept that there be discrimination in schools. That is important. There is more. We must continue, through research, using the press . . . we must embark on a sort of crusade. We must continue to denounce racist situations in the justice system, in schools, in the workplace. But we must not just denounce, because denouncement is qualified by indignation. I mean, it is not ennobling to any country, to any population or nationality, to know that one's country accepts, tolerates, and even feels that racial discrimination is normal. So I think there needs to be a mobilization process. It must be done. We know this [racial discrimination] exists, but it [the absurdity] has not been realized by the Brazilian population. I don't think people are ashamed to be Brazilians because they live in a racist and discriminatory country. This has to change.

Guimarães: Before we design strategies, we must develop indignation?

Adorno: It makes sense, people must feel uncomfortable. Race and ethnic origin cannot be the basis for inequality. I must become accustomed; I must respect people who share the same spaces with me; I must accept people despite their differences. These differences cannot be the source of social inequality, an arbitrary way of establishing a hierarchy of people.

Guimarães: You will agree with me that after a while, indignation becomes a sort of convention and that it is necessary to use ingenuity and develop efficient ways to counteract the existing situation.

Adorno: I agree. This can happen and will happen. But when it does happen, I'd say, "good," because that means that people are convinced that this is something that bothers them. People will eventually become convinced that racial difference is not a premise for inequality. What I am trying to say is a little different. It is that indignation should precede any minimally consistent formulation of policies. It is not enough for people to be indignant and then just say, all right, we are convinced. Once they are convinced, you have an open field upon which to advance in terms of civil rights. We must think of efficient and successful policies. It is important that people believe that such policies are right and that institutions work well, that institutions are instruments that protect rights and not instruments that discriminate in the application of rights.

In order for this to happen, you need a consensus that discrimination is intolerable, and you need policies that show citizens in a concrete way that discrimination is intolerable. We mustn't only insist on a sense of indignation. But indignation is a basic premise. We have to contaminate society with that feeling. Of course, things cannot be left at that. We must develop policies that guarantee that whites and blacks have equal access to goods and services such as schools, justice, security institutions, etc. That is to say, we need the guarantee that color, ethnicity, and race are not instruments of discrimination. I must feel indignant because I must convince myself that discrimination makes me unsafe. I can only be sure that I will be secure if a minimum level of security is ascertained for all.

Guimarães: What do you feel about impact strategies, such as that of suing the Brazilian government for the practice of slavery in the past and the demand for vacancies [for blacks] at the University of São Paulo, for instance?

Adorno: If [such programs are] well controlled, if well formulated, that's fine. In the end we will be educating the whites about the world of the blacks. But there is a danger here. If these strategies do not eliminate the problem of domination, if they do not touch on the divisive culture of society . . . if, instead, they buffer, humanize the hierarchy or the divisions amongst humans in any way . . . then . . . I don't mean to say that these policies imply these types of effects. But I do feel that, politically, they may be appropriated by different groups within society and used for that purpose. Toward a new philanthropy. I think that's a new phenomenon. It is a new phenomenon that we must analyze to understand its reach. It is a philanthropy that is informed by a notion of rights. However, I can't say that the promotion of rights, in a philanthropic sense, is something new. The so-called philanthropic socialism, created in the beginning of the twentieth century . . . well, we saw what happened to that. It turned into a type of solidarity the basis of which, in the end, was the idea of a society where each had and recognized the place the other belonged. People needed to be civilized in order to know their place. So I think we've got to be careful here, to look where these things may lead us.

Guimarães: We live in the richest state of Brazil, São Paulo, that concentrates 70 percent of the national riches. In a way, the society of São Paulo is a model of exclusion. So let me ask you, do you think that affirmative-action strategies that would enable the black population to share in this wealth would promote this philanthropic effect?

Adorno: I would say two things. In principle, I am favorable to the idea of affirmative policies. I think that the opening of institutions to citizens of different classes, races, ethnic background, color, gender, generations, that's democratic. That is part of the democratic package. I am entirely in favor of any mechanism that society may create to overcome barriers of access to institutions, that promote well-being and justice.

But parallel to that comes the regulation of who can and who cannot benefit from these mechanisms, sometimes in explicit, other times in subtle ways. This is very complicated, this thing of classifying who is black, who is going to have the right to the job, to get into a school, to leisure, to justice. This is complicated. One thing is to regulate the forms of access, another is to qualify who has the right and who does not have the right in a society like the Brazilian one, and especially in São Paulo, a historically very segregated society, with a very weak public structure.

From the point of view of democratic prerogatives, I believe that any mechanism that seeks to enhance competition, that seeks placement in managerial positions those representing the social groups that are competing, I am entirely supportive of that. I truly believe that the São Paulo bourgeoisie must be challenged. The bourgeoisie must realize that there are other groups in society with whom it must share rights; that doesn't mean that everyone has to sit down at the same table, but it means that the bourgeoisie cannot ask for security for themselves when the problem of security is broader than their neighborhood. It must realize that violence affects the citizens who live on the periphery of the city much more than those who live in the more central areas. I think it very unjust that people claim things for their own neighborhoods, feel there are too many assaults, when the citizen who lives on the outskirts of town opens his/her front door and every other day finds a body lying across the threshold. There has been research that shows that children from the periphery that are four or five years old find death a normal occurrence. They see death as a daily phenomenon. That is, they wake up early and see the same thing every day: dead bodies lying out on the street. One can't live in this type of situation. This is absence of social democracy. That the bourgeoisie must face the rights of others is absolutely fundamental. Now, new philanthropy? Possibly it is a new phase of philanthropy. I have nothing against philanthropy itself. I think that it is historically a two-way street. It can follow the domination path or the promotion of civil rights. In Europe there was a moment at which the bourgeoisie was confronted with social movements—the workers movement and the social movements—and it had to decide: either the progressive segments had to go ahead and create philanthropic policies that were consistent—right to work, school, protection, and assistance in the workplace—or their heads would be cut off. So, in my understanding, it is possible that we are at a turning point of a new philanthropy. I think that this is a struggle. I cannot see this differently. We must refuse. I think that this is a space for struggle. The agencies are there . . . groups must compete.

Guimarães: Are you disqualifying philanthropic efforts?

Adorno: No. If you study the history of philanthropy, you cannot disqualify philanthropy. But it is very clear that the charitable philanthropies that come from the Catholic, Christian tradition do not see the problem as I do. It is more like, "If I'm not charitable, I do not go to heaven." The problem is another one. The other is a type of hygienic philanthropy. The one that wants to clean up the city and impose order. That is progressive philanthropy.

Today, business philanthropy has also renounced charity. The idea of charity may even be present, but charity is not the source. The basic concept is that society cannot function if there is disorder. So, what does disorder mean? It means anything from disturbance of the peace to unbearable inequalities. It is very difficult today to sustain a white elite, as happened a century ago, for example, in South Africa or even in Latin American countries, sovereign reigns that worked by way of very efficient models of unquestioned domination. Today this is not possible, one cannot live in a white enclave. . . .

Guimarães: But in Brazil, the so-called white elite is not that white. They are mixed individuals who have a light tone, yet you still have the enclave. What do you think of the presence of a mestiço elite with regard to the fight for citizenship and civil rights . . . does this complicate matters, simplify matters?

Adorno: I believe that affirmative-action policies are the only mechanisms for overcoming enclaves and situations of inequality, but if it is the only mechanism that expresses differences, then I think it is a terrible form of integration. What will be happening is that you will only be co-opting black citizens to live the world of the white folk.

I have an example, something that has happened within my own family experience: a person was raised in a white world and lives in the white world. She is protected, and evidently she does not identify with blacks. I find that something terrible. Now, if you have other mechanisms of confrontation, of struggle, etc., then this begins to become another issue. It is legitimate that black citizens want to ascend socially, become bourgeoisie, businessmen/women. That's legitimate. What I do not think is legitimate is that it become the vital nerve. Ethnicity that hasn't yet been constructed culturally is defined by the state. That's what I think the problem is, that of running the risk of falling into an authoritative path, a nondemocratic one. Now, when you have an open space and there are other alternatives to complete the picture, then I don't see any problem.

Guimarães: Wrapping up here . . . do you think that democracy is a basic precondition for any advancement of the black person?

Adorno: It is citizenship in the sense of a social democracy, more than a political democracy. The recognition that differences are legitimate but that they must not be principles for social inequality. It is a fact that we live in a society in which men and women are different; blacks and whites are different; homosexuals and heterosexuals are different; children and adults are different. This can serve as the prerequisite for the creation of a hierarchy of subordination. That is why democracy is fundamental. I think that the recognition of the legitimacy of differences and not the conversion of differences into inequalities, that is at the heart of a political democracy. There must be a space where these differences can coexist. And this space is the public space. My idea is like that of Arendt: there must be spaces where you must address yourself and where you find people with whom to make exchanges.

The problem in Brazil is absence of democracy. We are all the time strengthening mechanisms of political participation, but we are not fortifying the public spaces where exchanges take place. So you have a situation whereby there is a democracy that is considered legitimate and a social sphere where the exchanges are savage. This is a Portuguese tradition that became implanted in Brazil: the nonregulation of the public sphere and the recognition that people have rights. The tradition has been one in which the civil space where family, property are involved, that's not meddled with. That's where it gets complicated.

Guimarães: Please make a quick evaluation of the role of feminism and the gay movement in Brazil in the fight against racism. Also, what should these movements have done and haven't?

Adorno: In truth, I do not study these movements, I observe them, I read about them. I think these movements were extremely important for Brazil. I think they brought to the public sphere matters that up to then had been dealt with in the private sphere. If you take crime, for instance, people will generally say that there is more crime before than now. I don't know if this is true or not; my historical studies have not been able to establish that.

Now, what I can say is that the subject of crime has entered the public debate in the last few decades. Previously, crimes were domestic conflicts, conflicts that related to the private sphere. They were situations that were not publicly debated. The greatest importance of these movements was to make existing differences explicit and to reveal that Brazil is a violent and authoritarian society, that we don't live here in a sea of tranquility. There was an image/idea of Brazil: that old image that in Brazil there are thieves, yes, but Brazil is a generous country no longer sustains itself. On the contrary. Increasingly, one observes more and more people involved in violence, in corruption, etc., and destruction of nature. I think the social movements played a very important role by slowly changing this self-complacent image that Brazilians had of living in a paradise.

My problem with these movements is that I do not see their meeting at points of convergence, to discuss their differences and similarities. In my opinion it would be very hard for the black movement to sit with the gay and lesbian movement and discuss where each are coming from and where to go from here. On the contrary, one often has the sensation that these movements are fighting with each other. That is one of the reasons why I sought Geledés out to work on a project. I am very fond of Geledés, this organization that works with the black woman. We were discussing women, black women, not just women, not just black people. One very interesting discovery I made in the research project we carried out with Geledés was the presence of racism in the judicial system. The probability of condemnation of whites is lower than that of blacks. However, when you take gender into consideration, the study showed that the white woman is more protected than the black man and the black woman. In other words, the sequence is as follows: white man, white woman, black man, black woman.

We're faced here with two issues: gender and race. It is at this point that we must see how things balance out. You see a mix of types of discrimination that contribute to create a system of inequality that is much more complex than we had imagined. I don't see the different movements collaborating amongst each other, I don't. When we worked with the National Movement for Human Rights, our report was made up in parts, segments. The demands were very segmented. It was hard to interrelate things. Some demands were common, such as right to life. Well, we know that black men are victims more often than white men. But I believe that the right to life must overcome this issue. The right to life is basic, should not be discussed. This cannot be negotiated, no matter what the circumstances. These are the types of things that are common in every movement. There should be an institution capable of uniting the common goals of all these movements. I don't know if that would be the university, different fora, the movements themselves. I don't know. But they all should gather somewhere. . . .

Guimarães: What do you think you should do, not as an intellectual but as an activist, as someone who is committed to his work? What type of legacy do you want to leave for another generation?

Adorno: I have to combine two things: subjective indignation and intervention in public debates, using my experience as a researcher, as a university professor. Let's start with the most subjective part. I become very indignant when I see any type of discrimination. The other day I went to a bread store near my house, it's sort of a bread boutique, and when I arrived, there was an older black woman ahead of me. There was also another woman from Perdizes, a middle-class district of São Paulo city. The attendant was helping this blond lady from Perdizes. When he finished helping the blond lady, he turned to me and said, "You, sir." I told him, "No, this lady is ahead of me," and he said, "No, she can wait a little." I became furious. I said, "Why?" and I turned to her and said, "Have you been helped?" When she responded she hadn't, I said, "Alright, then you will be helped next." I turned to the guy and said, "I don't want to come here and have somebody be helped ahead of me if I'm waiting in line. Why aren't you helping her?" She looked very humble, was black. What made me more irritated was that the attendant was black himself, and yet he was being courteous to a white person at the cost of a black person who was in line. He probably identified the woman as a domestic worker from the area. As a citizen, I must become very indignant with this type of thing. I would like to see more people publicly manifest their indignation. I didn't say anything about race [color] because I wasn't sure how people would react. My argument was the order of the line, which was fundamental. I remember that Martins, our colleague in the department, experienced a similar situation in England. He was waiting in line to use a public phone. He was third in line, and when it was his turn, he put in one, then two, then another coin, just like in Brazil. A lady said, "It's not that way. What happened? Let's go to the phone company and complain, because if we don't, the phone company will never fix this and who will suffer the consequences? Everyone who passes this way and needs a public phone. I will go with you to make the complaint."

This may seem extraordinary, but the moment something causes indignation, it is a sign that rights are being demanded. I would like indignation to spread. I would like people to demand their rights in traffic. Now, I am convinced that my research has an important consequence. It is militant research. I know that I can intervene in public debates and in the formulation of public policies. Not all of my research is militant, some of it is pure research, development of theories, methodologies, etc. But a large part of my research practice is as a citizen researcher. I do not produce neutral knowledge. I produce knowledge, data that is geared toward the construction of a democratic society, the recognition and legitimacy of differences and toward the strengthening of institutions that protect rights. This is fundamental to me.

With regard to the racial issue, I am going to continue to research the legal system; I want to continue the research we began about racism in the legal system because the first part was very superficial. I identified a relationship between the type of sentences and racism. However, I was not able to identify the relationship between the process and racism. That's another research project. I would have to conduct the research in another manner. I'd have to research the training process of the operators of the legal system, if that training [educational] process favors discrimination or not. Is the racial question regarded as an important issue in law schools? Does this have a weight in the cultural education of lawyers? Do people [in their training process] take into consideration that they are citizens, men and women, black and white? Are they invested in power? I want to carry out work regarding the training of lawyers, and I am sure I can be of help.

Interview with
Friar David Raimundo Santos

Antonio Sérgio Alfredo Guimarães

Guimarães: Friar, to begin with I would ask you to think a little about the current context of a world that is increasingly globalized in terms of capital flows, fluxes of people, of information. . . . How does the fight against racism fit into this environment?

Friar David Raimundo Santos: This question is broad and rich, because we Brazilian-African descendants are more and more aware that globalization brings new challenges and requires different positions than the ones we have taken up to now. This demands from all of us African descendants a new way of thinking about the economic question, meaning that we can't try to change the reality of Brazilian blacks without concerning ourselves with their lack of economic power. This is why, in the last few years, we have made great efforts to broaden the alternatives open to African descendants. This also depends on increasing their access to the university campus, to the academy, to higher education, so that with better academic qualifications, they can have better chances of competing for a place in the world of knowledge, which makes and generates the riches of society and the world. This concern is greater if we consider, for example, that the black population of South Africa between the ages of twenty-five and twenty-nine has a national average of nine years of schooling, while in Brazil, African descendants in the same age bracket have an average of 3.8 years in school. Clearly, this shows that Brazilian-African descendants will enter the third millennium at a disadvantage, unprepared because of this poorly resolved, very inhuman and oppressive history. In other words, for many years, Brazilian-African descendants will still continue to be the cheap labor force of the Brazilian system.

Guimarães: Just for curiosity's sake, how did you arrive at this position, making access to the labor market through access to the university a major priority. How did that happen?

Santos: In the first place, it was an option that came from our hearts as a family. It is due to my family life history as the son of a black man and a white woman, people who had a middle-class life but whose family was sacrificed by the violent economic crisis of the 1960s. In the 1970s, my family was hit by an even worse economic crisis and we ended up in a *favela* [Brazilian shantytown]. The second big family crisis was its breakdown: father abandoned the home and mother had to be the man and the woman of the family all at once. . . living in a *favela* with seven children . . . all of them undernourished. . . . This miserably poor and moreover illiterate woman planted in her heart and put into her plans the determination that all of her children would finish their higher education. This woman would not rest until we were all graduated. She washed a lot of clothes in the washtub for pay, to make money and make it possible for all her children to go to school.

Looking back on my family's life, rereading it, the decisive role of education to help turn *favela*-dwellers into middle-class citizens becomes clear. Today, my brothers and sisters are all married, well off in life compared to the average Brazilian-African descendant. Very well off, with a place on the beach, a car, a house in the city, an easy job . . . they're all fine. Looking back on this history, I realized that over and above having a mother who was decisive, a strong woman in the family, there was the university's role in this process.

In the second place, we can evaluate data researched by IPEA:[1] individuals with eight years of schooling have, on the average, 38 percent more income than those with four years' education. People with secondary-school diplomas have, on the average, 173 percent more income than people with eight years of school. And according to the same institute, persons with higher educations earn, on the average, 517 percent more than those who completed only the secondary level. These data show that one of the ways to get the African-descendant population out of its situation of miserable poverty is by taking the university path.

In the third place, consider this: according to DataFolha,[2] 59 percent of the Brazilian population is African-descended, but according to the IBGE [Brazilian Institute of Geography and Statistics] only 2 percent of the African descendant population are in public universities.[3] If you include private universities, the percentage is a little higher. Now, it is a scandalous crime, an attack on national dignity, to maintain this situation. In other words, the Afro-Brazilian population is 59 percent of the nation—and yet only 2 percent attend public universities.

There was another factor that made us create this alternative called Ethnic College Entrance Examination Preparatory Courses. They are a formidable tool to revolutionize, transform, and illuminate the reality of African descendants. This other factor was the realization that all public secondary schools in all of Brazil, especially the Baixada Fluminense, where I work, are horrible in quality. African descendants are enrolled in these schools. Whether this was or was not a government plan we don't know; the fact is that African descendants are the real victims of the abysmal quality of education in Brazilian schools. This situation made the experience of Ethnic College Entrance Examination Preparatory Courses come to life. It began in 1992, in the style that still prevails today, where groups of fifty or more young African descendants, and poor people, some of them whites, meet intensively on the weekends, from 8:00 in the morning until 8:00 at night, with ten volunteer teachers who take turns, hour by hour, going over preparatory courses for university admissions exams: Portuguese, chemistry, math, biology, physics. We also include a special subject called "culture and citizenship," which has the same class time as the other subjects. Our dream, our goal, is not only to put blacks into the university. It is to place in the university black people who carry a certain baggage, including reflections on social injustice and the ability to be indignant, people who will help change this reality. In the culture and citizenship classes, we go very deeply into race issues because we want every black person and every white person who participates in this project to be aware of how injustice takes place in Brazilian race relations. We want to prepare blacks for the third millennium. We are preparing the black people of future generations, aware of their social reality, who communicate with others to see it, analyze it, and put their professions at the service of recovering the dignity of the African-descended population.

Guimarães: I can't help but ask you a question. Listening to you now, I hear an agenda very close to the one that was called Liberation Theology in the [Latin American Catholic] Church in the 1970s and 1980s. In that context, Christians full of moral indignation came out of the theology schools believing in rationality and work to change an unjust reality, to fight against injustice. The highest Church authorities forced a change in the direction of strengthening faith and other Christian values, discarding more rational or material attitudes. The College Entrance Preparatory program is pastoral work, done in the context of today's Church. Now, how is it seen, how is it received by the high Church authorities? Is there still some contradiction between Christian faith and political action, in the Church?

Santos: Yes . . . I would say that the activism of Catholic blacks, and also of those blacks who are not Catholic in Brazilian society, has gone through two stages. From the 1970s until the 1990s, we had a radical stand against all structures and against the government in general, and particularly against the Church structures. We had a radical critique. Personally, I began my activism in 1976. It's been almost fifteen years.

In the 1990s, evaluating in concrete terms what exactly was left of our actions, we were taken by surprise: we saw that we had actually built very little, in reality. We had done a lot of theorizing, criticized the structures, hitting them hard . . . and we asked ourselves: What have we achieved? We saw that almost nothing had gone forward, and this made us engage in a lot of discussion, criticizing our own practice. Among the people with whom we sat down to speak to and think out our practice was Friar Leonardo Boff, the Liberation Theology theorist and intellectual. In these dialogues with Leonardo Boff, one thing strongly influenced my position as an activist, as a priest, and as a black person. When I spoke to him of my anguish about fifteen useless years of work, fifteen years that bore no fruits, he said something that influenced me: "We must reconsider our practice. If we are not making changes with this practice, we have to change our paradigm. Why not drive a wedge into the cracks in those structures, the cracks in power, and from inside power positions, using the power structures, see that possibilities are created for the community to raise itself up, for the community to recover the rights it has been denied and its dignity?" And I started to ask myself: As a priest, as a black person, how can I do that? That was when I made a big change in my life, I stopped seeing the central goal as being to denounce the Church's mistakes [those mistakes go on], and I began to see that structure from a different angle: how can I put the Church at my people's service? That was how the College Entrance Exams Prep Course was born.

Guimarães: Still on the College Entrance Exam Preparatory Course for Blacks and the Poor, to make it more clear what this movement is, why do you say "blacks and the poor"? I'm asking this question because often in the black movement, the term "black" is considered enough. And there are those who criticize the black movement and say what is important is precisely the "poor." So you set up a movement for blacks and the poor, what does this mean?

Santos: This is another new paradigm to be brought out. We saw that, for the great revolution that we want, we have to count on people's solidarity, and we discovered that the problem of black people was not generated by black people. It was not black people who created slavery here in Brazil, it was not blacks who created laws barring black people's access to schools, it was not black people who passed the Land Property Law that barred black people's access to land. So we discovered this: it would be very mean on our part, to ourselves, to leave the whole task of undoing the evil that was done just to black people alone. We know that this evil done to black people can only be undone when people become aware of the evil done, and we concluded that it was essential to count on people's solidarity, so we thought it was important to open this movement also to poor whites, to teach them solidarity with our cause. This way, we destroy one of the weapons our opposers forged against us, saying that we were practicing reverse racism. By putting poor whites in the process, we collapsed the main criticism against the movement, and with that—I don't know if I am exaggerating, but I would not be afraid to say that we created a nationally unanimous idea, the College Admissions Preparatory Course for Blacks and the Poor. This way, we also gave back to white people the mission of helping undo the evil and helping, with their own hands, to bring in a new reality. So, for example, we have in the College Admissions Prep Course for Blacks and the Poor, in its various local branches, several white teachers, even though, in principle, we had intended to carry out this job only through black organizations. But helping black people get out of poverty is not a task just for black organizations. We started to invest in the idea of challenging society to commit itself to creating the conditions for blacks and poor whites to get out of miserable poverty by means of education. With this change in methodology, we drove a wedge into one of the cracks in the major media, and we got a lot of press. By doing this, we took to the four corners of Brazil this new intuitive idea. What is that idea? It is precisely to help poor African descendants and poor whites to break the barriers of access to the university. Between 1992 and 1999, we managed to create about seven hundred local branches of community university entrance exam preparatory courses in Brazil. The name varies from place to place. In Rio Grande do Sul it is the Zumbi dos Palmares University Admissions Preparatory Course. In Victoria, Espirito Santo State, it has another name. In Rio de Janeiro, it is the University Admissions Preparatory Course for Blacks and the Poor. Here in São Paulo, it is called EDUCAFRO—Education and Citizenship for African Descendants and the Poor. The name changes, but the intuitive idea is the same. It is this: that poor blacks and poor whites are coming together in all of Brazil. We are now counting on the solidarity of white people too. Before, we only accepted black teachers, but we have brought down that practice.

Guimarães: Friar, I am going to ask you a personal question, you can answer if you want to. Both you and I are mixed people, people who have whites and blacks in their ancestry. You had a black father; I, one of my grandparents. You were born in Rio de Janeiro, and I was born in Bahia; they are very miscegenated areas, so neither of us would be called "black" in these places. . . .

Santos: I was born in Minas Gerais.

Guimarães: That's also a very mixed area. I am asking the following: normally, in Brazil, people of our color identify themselves as whites and they use precisely this mixture, light skin, white features, straight or curly hair, this "good appearance" . . . they use this good appearance to climb higher in life and forge their path identifying themselves as whites. I don't recall anyone in my family ever identifying themselves as black. The most I heard, from my mother, was to say she was a light-skinned mulatto and that my grandfather was mulatto. So what is the reason for your racial identification? You must know, by personal experience, that even among black people a lot of value is given to color.

Santos: I would say this: the new generation of activists considers all African descendants who opted to make our people a sector of society, regardless of miscegenation, to be black. There was a moment in my life when I reconsidered my option, when I overturned my own table—the fact of being an African descendant, a mixed person, a *mestiço*—and built my activism and discourse out of black community experience, this was the result of conflicts, considerable ones. I went into the Franciscan seminary with a very clear awareness of self, in which there was no space for race issues. Until then, it had never been a problem for me. Even though I had a black father and a white mother, I had always been raised thinking I was white, and I was accepted that way. The fact that my color was a little different was resolved in my mind as being a consequence of going to the beach. I was born in Minas Gerais [a landlocked state], but I was raised in Victoria, Espirito Santo State, which is a region with lots of beaches. I always saw myself as "tanned by the sun," so I would say to myself, "I'm not black, not at all. . . ." But then, a very serious incident happened in the seminary that made me fall apart. I entered seminary in March 1976. Two months later, on May 13th, the white seminary students, most of them of German or Italian descent, decided to celebrate the Golden Law [the slavery abolition decree]. And so they decorated a table in the cafeteria, they made that table a slave ship. All the nonwhites, all the African descendants, all the blacks were supposed to sit on that table and, during lunch, they would receive "honors"—kidding, fun, jokes, and things like that. Well, since I had never imagined myself to be black, I sat at the side table with the other whites. The jokes began, and those with more pigmentation, who couldn't walk through the free area, were obliged to sit at the center table. They walked by us, like all blacks do, humbly, all bent over, to sit at the center table. When the jokes officially began, someone yelled:

"Hey, there's an empty chair, someone's missing. Who's missing?" And then, half a dozen "German" and "Italian" seminarians came over to where I was sitting, took me by force and pulled me over to the center table. Now, that was one of the greatest insults I had ever suffered in my whole life: they called me black in public. As soon as they sat me down on the table and let me go, my reaction was none other than to knock the glass water jar over with my arm, break the dishes on the table, and leave the cafeteria for my dormitory to pack my bags and leave. At that point the conflict was set up and that conflict burst out unexpectedly, and someone went running to tell the highest authority, the seminary president. The president came up to find me packing my bag. He asked: "What happened?" "They called me black," I said bitterly, "they called me black, they insulted me, they called me black." And then the president said: "If you want to leave, you have the right to do so, you can go. But in your first interview with me, you said you wanted to be a Franciscan to help the poor, to fight for justice, to forgive, to help the world be happy, to create a climate of peace on earth. Now, David, on your first test you did not find it in yourself to forgive. Either you weren't truthful with me in the interview, when you said you wanted to be a Franciscan, to forgive, to help the poor, or you are not well." And so he convinced me that, for my own good, I should stay there another one or two days, looking straight in the eyes of the people who had insulted me, forgive those people, and *then* leave, and go away with my heart healed and not go away with that open wound. I saw that I was in a corner, I was in a very unusual situation, with no options. "If you run the beast will get you, if you stay the beast will eat you." I decided to stay. That evening, he scheduled me to participate in community volunteer service with the team that was going to gather fruit in the orchard, and, coincidentally or not, most of the team was made up of those who had pulled me over by force and taken me to the center of the cafeteria. And even then it was a very hard test for me to have to look them in the face. I worked all afternoon with them, sulkily, and without my knowing it, the president was watching me from afar. When the volunteer work was over, he called me and said: "David, you haven't been able to forgive your colleagues." Then he said: "I will be home after dinner. Look me up and we will talk a little, is that all right?" "Okay, all right. I'll talk to you." After dinner, I went to his room. He asked, "Which soccer team do you root for?" I said, "Flamengo." So he started to talk about Flamengo, the good players, and as soon as he saw that I was completely relaxed and calm, he asked: "Do you have a picture of your mother?" I said yes, I did. I took out my wallet and the picture of my mother and showed him, in a tremendous rush. He looked at the photo and exclaimed: "Your mother is white?" I answered, "Of course, I'm white, my mother has to be white." He saw that things were getting complicated, so he changed the subject. . . . "So you live in Victoria, Espirito Santo, lots of beaches. . . ." I said yes, Friar, there are a lot of beaches, that's why I'm tan from the beach, like this. He changed the subject, spoke of the beach, spoke of . . . and all of a sudden he asked, "Do you have a picture of your father there?" I said no, I didn't. He asked, "Why don't you have a photo of your father? Why not?" And I gave an excuse: "I do have one, but it's in my suitcase." Look at the place of blackness in my life: . . . inside the suitcase, very far away, well guarded under seven locks. And he said: "Look David, you're leaving tomorrow, how about if you go to your suitcase and get the photo of your father and bring it here for me to see. After all, you're leaving, I won't have a chance to meet your family, let me meet them at least by photograph." I said: "Friar, the suitcase is closed, it will be such a bother to open the suitcase, take out . . . I don't know if I can find that picture." "Do me this one favor, try to find it, go ahead." So I went, humiliated, ashamed. I got the photograph of my father and brought it; terribly embarrassed, my arm all weak, I held it out for him to see, and he exclaims, "Congratulations, your father is black!" When he said, "Your father is black," it shocked me, I stood still, shocked, like when someone finds you stealing something, or you have a very deep secret you should keep under lock and key. . . . He said: "Your father is black." And then something short-circuited in me. He saw that things were getting serious, he went and got water, gave me water, told me to sit down, and said to me, "David, you are suffering from a serious illness, it's an illness you are not aware of, you have not looked for it, but society passed this illness on to you. The name is a very strange name, you might not understand it. You suffer from the illness called 'whitening ideology.'" So he explained what that is. I started to cry. I had no more identity, I wasn't white anymore, I couldn't be black because I didn't accept being black, I didn't exist anymore, my world had ended. A huge hole opened up in front of me. I sweated cold, I cried, it was truly a fall to the bottom of the well. For those who know a little of the Bible, where it tells about Paul's fall from the horse, for me it was a little like that fall. Right there, my world had ended. He could see that I was broken, and he began to explain to me that this wasn't any evil of mine, that it was important to me not to be black because society treats black people badly, and I had grown up wanting to be white. He gave me a very deep lesson in cultural reconstitution. . . . I listened to all that and I made a decision: it is impossible to go home now, I don't exist any more, I'm broken, I don't know who I am. I came here whole, I will go back broken. No, I am going to stay here until I am reconstituted, then I'll go back. The next day, my first deed was to go to the seminary library and search for books on my black people. Then I had my first experience of exclusion of a people. In all the large shelves of that library, there was not one book about the black people. Then I went to my superior and said, "Friar, I wanted so much to read about the black people, the people I deny. But I found hundreds of books in our library about Germans; hundreds of books about the Italians, the French, the English . . . and I couldn't find anything about my African people and their descendants, Afro-Brazilians." The friar answered: "You know, you're right. Let's go to the city and buy some books." And that was where my change began, my existential reconstitution. Right there, I would say that I changed my whole vocational drive. While up until then I had wanted to be a priest to fight against injustice, to do good, to forgive, now I wanted to be a priest in order to help black people recover their identity. I decided, in my prayers before God, in front of the altar, that it would only make sense to be ordained a priest if I were to dedicate my whole life to this cause. In sum, that is the story in the background.

Guimarães: Friar David, by way of this college admissions preparations movement, you have been the protagonist and the creator of a very important strategy to recover the dignity and improve the opportunities of black people in Brazil. What other strategies do you see that can also be done?

Santos: Other strategies to recover the dignity of black people . . . I see the following. First, the Brazilian black community must overcome its mistrust of government and become active in political parties. That will slowly put the political party structure at the service of our cause. For example, in Brizola's administration in the Rio de Janeiro state government, a group of black people made the choice of accepting power and placing the power structures at the service of the cause. Unfortunately, some of them lost sight of their goals, which prejudiced the quality of that strategy. Right now, in the Garotinho and Benedita Rio de Janeiro state government administration, there is a team of blacks with a different posture, but the tactic is the same: to place the power structure at the service of black people. It won't do any good to get an education, find a home, get used to privileges, earn and keep your salary, if you don't propose to create strategies and offer possibilities to the black people as a whole. That is why, currently, in the Rio de Janeiro state government, we have thirty black men and women in important government posts who are creating various new situations, for example, with public policy geared to African descendants. This group of black people, together with the vice-governor [Benedita da Silva] and with Governor Garotinho's full support, is going to sign a law that will make the teaching of *capoeira* a physical-education alternative in the state public-school system. This experience has already been put into practice, on a smaller scale, in the municipality I live in, in Nilopolis. . . . We, as organized blacks, brought pressure on the city government and won the creation of a law making *capoeira* a physical-education alternative. And the experiment worked. This experience is catching on in more and more areas. This group of black people is also promoting debates and events on black people, their social problems, and the public policies that might benefit blacks. One idea, for example, is to challenge all state public schools to create community university admissions preparation programs, which this team would coordinate, and the state university—UERJ—would provide the teachers, who could very well be students themselves and would participate as interns. If this idea works, it will be a great revolution. Not only will UERJ itself have opened a college admissions prep branch, but UERJ would be encouraging schools to open college admissions prep branches, where the state university provides the teachers, final-year interns—biology, history, math. . . . They would do their internship and the school would give them a certificate. I thought that idea was fantastic and simply revolutionary: this is public policy geared to blacks and the poor.

As for strategy, I think it is important to intensify the exchange of experiences among black communities of different countries, I think this is fundamentally important.

For example, in my few visits to the United States, and in the contacts I have had with the North American black community, I came to the following conclusion. Of every ten black North American leaders who are active in the political field, about nine were trained in the churches. They are people who woke up to social struggle, to the civil rights movement, in churches in general. In Brazil, before the year 1990, out of every ten black leaders active in Brazilian society not one came out of the religious camp. What did we do? The new factor is this: today, in Brazil as a whole, the number of black leaders coming into the churches is very large. And in the next generation, I believe sometime around the year 2005, out of every ten Brazilian black leaders, five will come out of ecclesiastical work. It's a vision. We have intensified black consciousness training in church areas. It is our strategy for the next generations. Another one is to start to challenge some very consensual ideas in the nonconscious black community, where the idea prevails that the best way for a black man to get anywhere in life is to be a soccer player. When we open up the possibility of a university option, we are questioning the place society has reserved for blacks. According to recent research that will be made public soon, here in Brazil 5 percent of African-descended professional soccer players earn less than two times the value of the minimum wage[4] per month. What a pittance! Ninety percent earn two to five minimum wages per month, which is a little better but still a pittance. And only 5 percent of Brazilian soccer players, African descendants, earn over five times the value of the minimum wage. These numbers are trying to show the black community that it has to change its paradigm. The male black community needs to forget soccer as a way to get somewhere in life, they need to free themselves from this illusion created by TV images. That is why we are proposing in-depth discussion in the black community on the natural options of black Brazilians. We want to challenge them to change their view.

Guimarães: I liked your agenda very much in terms of education, in terms of politics, in terms of religion. I want to ask a question but don't take it as an insult. A criticism that I have heard, coming out of the black community itself, is that the college prep programs are no more than a Band-Aid, they are serious and important, but they don't go to the bottom of the problem. As you said at the beginning, the biggest crime committed against black children in Brazil is the extremely poor primary and secondary education offered to them, which means that most of these children will not manage, as adolescents, even to think about getting through a college admissions preparation program. In other words, education is so bad, teaching conditions are so humiliating, that dropout rates are very high. Well, I have heard this criticism from radical types, just as one hears conservative sectors say that all affirmative-action programs only work for the elites. How do you react to this criticism?

Santos: Those who make this criticism are right, but only partially right; they should have had the opportunity to discuss the question more with the people organizing the process. Why? Because we know that the Brazilian black community, in all age brackets, is broken, miserably poor, destroyed, hopeless. The better question would be: Are we going to invest in people who are fifty years old, to give them a better life's end? Shall we invest in those who are being born now so they can have more dignity? How are we going to invest for a fast return? And we concluded that in any investment field you have to have money and a lot of it. Well, we have no money in our black community, but a lot of us have determination and a dream that we can turn into prophetic energies. We concluded that the age bracket where we would have the fastest return would be youth. They are strategic decisions, looking at how fast we could create something new. And then we saw this: we have to invest in the dream. You can do reasonable work with those youth who have finished secondary school and haven't gone any further, but who now have the great desire to get into a university. In the second year of our project's experience we opened the course for 100 students and 716 people signed up to compete for 100 places. This was just in the Baixada Fluminense, with hardly any publicity at all. This huge demand confirmed our prediction; we had a prediction but we didn't have the practice. This is what we call practice—we saw that there are really a very large number of blacks who have finished secondary school, however long ago, and we saw that this was the path. So we are investing in this group, giving this group a chance, and demanding from this group the commitment to continue the struggle. As soon as they go on to college, they will open up new local branches or be an assistant teacher, a classroom monitor, or whatever. And this strategy was excellent and the results are there to see. Here in São Paulo, for example, the experience was introduced in a more active way in 1998, and in 1999 we had planned to reach thirty local branches. In April 1999, we already had the thirty local branches, so for us the strategy is a success, it is working. As for those who say that the college prep courses will only benefit a few privileged individuals, I would say that is a partial reading. It is not the privileged group but those whose hopes the system has not yet destroyed. Those who still hope to win are the ones who are with us. And that isn't privilege, it's hope. Any just nation always maintains its children's hope. Any nation that does not honor its people begins to destroy the hope of youth. And this is what Brazil did to the young black community. This is what we are fighting against, so that the number of young people killing themselves with drugs and killing each other will get smaller, or so that it won't happen anymore. We have lots of examples of people in the *favelas* who had every reason to be one more criminal and who are now in college because of this project. So we are aware that we are doing our part, within the range of our possibilities. Now the organization that popped up in the four corners of

Brazil is turning to society and demanding from society and from government, public policies designed for African descendants.

Guimarães: During the course of your life, you gave yourself over to a task, a mission, that grew as you carried it out, and this mission is more or less set out in your words. What would you like to see done but is no longer your mission, because your life is short? What is left for future generations to do? What is the agenda of the future?

Santos: My great anguish is not having placed in action black people's fight for land. As much as we may have struggled, we can see the great weakness of blacks in the struggle for land. And we know that the areas that bring a little bit of dignity and opportunity for economic success for blacks are access to academic knowledge and access to land ownership. We are sad because in the Landless Workers' Movement there are not many black people, particularly black people with consciousness. We are sad because, in Brazil, there exist more than a thousand Quilombo community areas, and these lands are semiabandoned by the public authorities and also by the conscious black movement. Not by meanness. The black community is too worn down. Black people, in this current crisis in Brazil, are concerned with their own skins. And if our presence was already tenuous in these frontline battles, it will stay weak for another ten years or so. So, in my view, the great struggle for land, which black people will have to launch into, will unfortunately be left for later, it's not a fight for now. Nevertheless, I am absolutely convinced that the fight for black people's access to the university will grow so much that a lot of novelties will come around. I am sure that in three years we are going to have big changes in black people's action, in their fight for education. Who knows, maybe other areas of struggle will open up, as they have in other countries, like opportunity for small- and medium-sized black business?

Notes to the Interviews

1. The Institute of Applied Economic Research (IPEA) is an official government research institute.

2. Research survey institute owned by the *Folha de São Paulo*, one of Brazil's major daily newspapers.

3. Public university education is free (admitted students pay no tuition), while private colleges and universities charge high tuition. During the military dictatorship (1964–1985), public education was largely left without investment while private faculties, colleges, and universities were encouraged to flourish, with state subsidies, for profit. Public secondary schools became far inferior by

virtue of the state policy of underinvestment The university entrance system is based on a single entrance exam administered by each university, and this process favors well-to-do students' admission to tuition-free public schools, since they are generally better prepared for the single exam. Poor and working-class students, educated at the inferior public schools, pay high tuition for second-rate education at private colleges.

4. At this writing, the value of the monthly minimum wage is equivalent to about US$75.00.

18

"Bluebeard's Castle": An American Fairy Tale*

Derrick Bell

LIFE SEEMS TO favor those in power, while it seldom rewards with triumphs good works. Defeat, disgrace, and sometimes death are often the fate of the righteous who must rely on their faith that truth and justice were worth championing. "Bluebeard's Castle" (*Encyclopedia Britannica* 1977, vol. 2: p. 97) is a French fairy tale about a nobleman who marries a succession of women and escorts them to his castle, where they disappear and are never heard from again.[1] The Hungarian composer, Bela Bartok, working from a variation of the story, composed a darkly beautiful opera about Bluebeard's fourth wife, Judith, who ignores her family's warnings and marries the strange and awe-inspiring man whose great power she hopes to humanize with her devotion, with her love.

Bartok's opera is stark. Even though written in 1911, the harmonies sound strange and dissonant; symbolism fills both text and music. We know at the outset that Judith is doomed, and yet she intrigues us with the increasingly dangerous risks she takes to fulfill her vision of her ideal life with Bluebeard. As she pushes him to provide her with an openness he is unable to give, we can gain a revelatory perspective from which to review the unkept promises of racial justice made to black people throughout U.S. history.

Upon entering his foreboding, windowless fortress, Judith realizes that the sun can never enter. The walls are not simply musty but wet.[2] She sings ominously: "Darkness rules within your castle. Oozing

---

waters! Bluebeard, tell me. Can it be that stone is weeping? Can a castle feel its sadness?" Along the somber corridor she detects seven locked doors, and seeking light and some understanding of her husband's life, she urges Bluebeard to allow her to open all of them: "That the stone be done with weeping/ That the air once more be live." He refuses urging her to accept him on faith and not look behind the doors: "Life you are and light, my Judith. Love me, trust me, ask me nothing."

Judith knows that in the midst of devastation, neither love nor life can be sustained on unearned trust. Despite the ominous signs, she wants to believe her marriage will succeed. Surely, the symbols of reassurance for happiness and acceptance she seeks must lie behind those doors. With great effort, Judith gains from Bluebeard one key at a time. She opens each door in expectation, but finds increasingly horrifying sustenance for her fears. Bluebeard's torture weapons are in one chamber, his armaments, his gold, and his jewels are in another. One door opens to a scene of his vast land holdings, another to a beautiful flower garden. Each scene, however, is stained with blood.

Bluebeard declares his love for his newest wife and urges her not to unlock the seventh door. Judith, her hope gone, and expecting the worse, nevertheless insists on opening that door. In a haunting aria she sings:

> Now I know what waits behind it, Now I know its fatal secret! Blood is on your gems and weapons; blood besmears your flower garden. Over your domain's expanses Blood encroaches like a shadow. Now I know whose tears of sorrow Fill the lake with mournful silence: There lie all your former wives, They lie in blood, the blood of murder! Woe! How true were my forebodings!

With trembling hands Judith opens the final door. Inside, stand Bluebeard's three former wives. He has not murdered them. Rather, they are living, very beautiful, but quite pale as they advance in single file, splendidly adorned with mantles, crowns, and jewels.

Bluebeard approaches Judith. Despite her pleas for mercy, he arrays her, as the others, with a mantle, crown, and jewels. Sadly, she follows her predecessors through the door, which closes after her. The stage darkens. The curtain falls.

The fairy tale, as analyzed in a study of that literary genre by Robert Damton (1984), is far more than an amusing narrative for children. Originating from folktales, fairy tales did not always have happy endings, but primarily reflected the harsh experiences of the peasants' lives. The peasant versions "undercut the notion that virtue will be rewarded or that life can be conducted according to any principle other than basic mistrust" (p. 33). Surely, the oppressive experiences of American blacks, so much a part of the spirituals, the blues, and gospel music, are not unlike the harsh existence of early eighteenth-century French peasants, as reflected in their fairy tales.

I know of no exact parallels in American folk literature to Bluebeard, who sought to find in a new wife a symbol through which he might extirpate his evil past. His goal eludes him, however, because Judith, try as she might to become the instrument of his liberation, is unable to move him beyond his desire for dominance. Her commitment to him is insufficient because only Bluebeard can take the step that could bring sunlight to his castle, salvation to his soul. That step, the transformation of corruptive power for cooperative sharing is analogous to American society, which periodically produces a symbol of redemption in the wake of unspeakable cruelty or crippling racial discrimination. At the national level, the symbol is usually a policy with liberating potential: the Emancipation Proclamation (1863), the post–Civil War amendments (Amendment 14, 1868; Amendment 13, 1865), the decision in *Brown v. Board of Education*, the Civil Rights Acts of 1964, the Voting Rights Act of 1965,[3] and, of course, the affirmative-action movement. Actually, there are many more lesser ones, but these six policies, while fashioned out of the honest commitment of some and the selfish self-interest of many, contain the potential to expunge this nation's Bluebeard image: the dark stain of slavery and racism. Without looking closely at the motives behind these long-sought policies, black Americans have accepted the language of their redemptive promise and have urged their fulfillment. Like Judith, they have urged white America to: "Let in sunlight, light completely Flood the darkness from your castle, Let the Breeze in! Let the sun in! Soon, O soon, The air itself will ring with blessings!"

After much effort, a door is opened, but after a brief period of hope, blacks again find themselves trapped in the darkness of a new and more subtle set of subordinating social shadows. They cry out in petition and prayer for the light of racial justice. For many, despair is displayed in antisocial, self-destructive behavior. Society's response can be summarized in Bluebeard's answer to Judith, who pleaded that he let in the wind, the sun, the light: "Nothing can enlight this castle."

If the contemporary economic distress of so many black Americans represented the first time their expectations had been dashed by conditions over which they possessed no control, it would still be no less a disaster. As with any natural catastrophe, one would at least expect that nature's devastation would not strike the same place time and time again. History indicates, though, that from the very beginning, the subordination of blacks has been tied at least as closely to economic factors as it has been to the simple belief in white superiority.[4] Indeed, the latter belief, functioning in the face of the most basic biological facts, is nurtured and sustained by a fertilization process that is economic rather than intellectual.

As Bluebeard's wives were doomed to suffer imprisonment, blacks seem foreordained to endure one racial disaster after another. The tableau changes with the times, but its structure and final outcome never change. Each reconciliation is a wedding feast, rich with exchanged promises of freedom for blacks and forgiveness for whites. Forgiving and extending themselves in reliance on the promises of a new day, blacks discover all too soon that the new relationship, while seeming better than the one they risked so much to escape, has placed them in a different but still subordinate posture. Each time, the symbol of the new relationship ends up behind a new and more imposing door, constructed of current economic needs and secured with a racism that is no less efficient because some blacks are able to slip by the barriers of class, wealth, and bigotry.

Using the idiom of "Bluebeard's Castle," let us examine the carnage of hopes beyond six doors, each of which until opened held out the promise of black freedom.

Door 1: The Emancipation Proclamation

When Abraham Lincoln signed the executive order purporting to free the slaves in Confederate-held territory, it electrified the world and ensured that the North would triumph in the Civil War.[5] Responding to the emancipation order with unbounded enthusiasm, slaves disrupted southern work forces, destroying property and escaping in ever-swelling numbers. Nearly 200,000 blacks enlisted in the Union Army and made the decisive difference for the North in many battlefield victories.

Although the Emancipation Proclamation, bolstered by the 13th Amendment, undermined the legal claims of slave masters, it created no substantive rights in the slaves themselves. The freedom document left them defenseless against resubjugation under the notorious Black Codes, race riots, and widespread white terror and intimidation.[6] Congress, for its part, never granted the much-touted Freedman's Bureau the authority to provide reparations for the years of free labor stolen from the slaves. When congressional resolve foundered on the economic rock of expropriating the plantations of Confederate whites and using the proceeds to provide blacks with "forty acres and a mule" (Bennett 1961), blacks were left with neither the money nor the means necessary for survival in a still racially hostile world.

Door II: The Post–Civil War Amendments

Radical Republicans committed to the abolitionist cause pushed for the passage of the post–Civil War amendments, which were designed to secure citizenship for the former slaves and to provide them with voting rights. Other statesmen realized that unless they acted to legitimate the freedman's status, Southerners would use violence to force blacks back into slavery, and the economic dispute that had precipitated the Civil War would surface again.

In an effort to avoid another conflict and to secure Republican control of the Southern states, Congress enacted the 13th, 14th, and 15th Amendments and the Civil Rights Acts of 1870–1875. Registering to vote in great numbers, blacks helped. But within a decade Southern planters rendered the 13th Amendment obsolete by exercising raw economic power and using naked violence to establish a sharecropping system that provided them with the same labor benefits as slavery without the minimum obligations inherent in the slave-master's role.

Although blacks had gained the right to vote, the federal government failed to enforce the 15th Amendment for almost a century after its enactment. The 14th Amendment, not passable as a specific protection for black rights, was finally enacted as a general guarantee of life, liberty, and property for all "persons." Following a period of judicial ambivalence, corporations were deemed persons under the 14th Amendment and for several generations received far more judicial protection than blacks. Indeed, blacks became the victims of judicial interpretations of the 14th Amendment and of legislation construed so narrowly as to render the promised protection virtually meaningless.

Door III: Desegregation

Black people believed that *Brown v. Board of Education* was the greatest Supreme Court decision of all time. Certainly, it was a freedom symbol without equal in the long struggle for racial equality. Even though its promise of equality emanated more from its language than from its holding,[7] as they had with earlier symbols, blacks read the opinion for all it was worth and hoped for the best.

But the promise has proven elusive. *Brown*, like its predecessors, is fading into the gloom, its message unfulfilled, its language of lime use when pitted against the economic barriers that seriously dilutes its potential. Good schools and decent housing remain beyond the financial reach of most of those who were the intended beneficiaries. In short, *Brown* and its judicial and legislative progeny have opened the door toward middle-class success for many, but have not touched those blacks still needing the modern-day equivalent of "forty acres and a mule."

Door IV: The Civil Rights Acts of 1964

The civil rights protest movement of the early 1960s developed out of the realization that court-mandated changes in the interpretation of the Constitution would not alone bring an end to racial segregation. Responding to the moral pressure exerted by courageous civil rights activists whose peaceful protests both embarrassed the nation and disrupted business in hundreds of cities and towns, Congress enacted legislation in 1964 to provide enforceable remedies for victims of racial discrimination in voting, employment, and access to public accommodations.

While the obnoxious "Colored" and "White" segregation signs slowly disappeared, racial discrimination in voting, employment, and even in access to public accommodations continued in forms both simplistic and sophisticated.

Door V: The Voting Rights Act of 1965

Southern states' determination to prevent blacks from exercising the basic citizenship right of suffrage remained firm despite the reform pressures of new federal laws. A massive effort by the Reverend Martin Luther King Jr.'s followers in Alabama and the vicious response of police officials, much of it documented on television, sparked congressional action. The Voting Rights Act of 1965, signed by President Lyndon Johnson and quickly approved by the Supreme Court, provided civil rights lawyers with effective enforcement tools that, despite continuing resistance, resulted in thousands of new black voters whose ballots quickly increased the numbers of black elected officials.

Resistance, though, did not end. Southern states show their defense from barring black voters in a host of techniques designed to dilute the black vote. The remedy that evolved over several years and dozens of voting-rights cases required establishment of majority black voting districts. Under this process, many more blacks were elected to Congress and to state legislatures, but a conservative Supreme Court again jeopardized black political gains by finding these districts in violation of the Constitution.

Door VI: Affirmative Action

Frustration with the slow pace of desegregation in inner cities across the nation led to a series of urban rebellions in the late 1960s and early 1970s. While the heavy damage and loss of life was mainly confined to predominantly black areas, corporate, government, and institutional leaders, fearing more widespread disruption, instituted a series of efforts to bring more blacks to college and employment opportunities that had been either closed to blacks or where only token numbers had been admitted. Under these "affirmative action" policies, as they came to be known, some of these programs worked better than others, but as the job market tightened and anxiety about their well-being increased, more and more whites opposed these programs—whatever their effectiveness. This opposition was encouraged by politicians at every level quite willing to win elections by blaming the nation's malaise on affirmative-action programs. The Supreme Court's early support of these measures evaporated as public opposition grew.

Even the most determined pessimist must acknowledge the change in the racial landscape over the last century. But each door opened has revealed another barrier, less foreboding but still impenetrable. In a generation that promised the beginning of the golden age of opportunity for all blacks, their share of not only the good things, but also the essentials of life, has been drastically reduced for all but the most fortunate among them.

Thus, despite breakthroughs, we find ourselves in the midst of an increasingly grim national scene. As black people sink ever deeper into the misery of unemployment, crime, broken families, and out-of-wedlock births—all indicators of an exploited, colonized people. These multitudes are without jobs, decent homes, and adequate education. Ironically, these same black people are protected by more expansive civil rights laws than any of their black ancestors.

Because poor blacks remain outcasts in the United States, the progress made by better-off blacks is placed in jeopardy. The gap between the economic statistics for blacks and whites is hardly greater than that which exists between upper-class blacks and their poverty-level brethren. Blacks who have and those who have not are increasingly separated by neighborhood, schooling, employment, recreation, and even place of worship. Both groups are caught in the gap of an economic segregation as structured, and as harmful, as the law-enforced segregation that plagued their lives a generation ago.

Dr. King, in his last book (1967: p. 12), recognizing that civil rights progress had been slowed by a white backlash, urban riots, and other problems of the late 1960s, sought to reassure blacks with the explanation that:

> The line of progress is never straight. For a period a movement may follow a straight line and then it encounters obstacles and the path bends. It is like curving around a mountain when you are approaching a city. Often it feels as though you were moving backward, and you lose sight of your goal; but in fact you are moving ahead, and soon you will see the city again, closer by.

It is a beautiful thought, elegantly expressed. But Dr. King's reassurance is now more than three decades old, and its continued applicability to the current condition of black people cannot ease our fears. The goal of equal opportunity that once loomed on the horizon like a heavenly city is now seldom visible.

In the version of "Bluebeard's Castle" that Charles Perrault published, Judith's relatives arrive in time and slay Bluebeard. No possibility of a similar happy ending seems to exist in my analogous use of the fairy tale to gain an understanding of American racial policy. For here, the nation, like Bluebeard, is a mixture of all the evil in its history with all the potential for good in its national ideals. Neither Bluebeard nor the United States is able to suppress the belief that, somehow, redemption may be gained without surrendering or even acknowledging spoils obtained through the most pernicious evil.

Bartok's *Bluebeard's Castle* manifests this hope for redemption without contrition in the opera's final scene. When Judith opens the seventh door and learns that Bluebeard has not murdered his former wives, they advance, proudly and slowly, in single file, splendidly adorned with their crowns and jewels. They stop in front of Bluebeard. Then he, and not they, sinks to his knees. As in a dream and with open arms, he sings:

> Lovely visions! Beauty tend you:
> Live in beauty, never ending!
> You have gathered all my riches;
> Wrought the fragrance of my garden;
> Brought me land and armed my power;
> Yours is my domain and being!

Bluebeard's seeming homage to his wives is actually a reassertion of his power. Similarly, the Emancipation Proclamation and the other documents of black freedom, simulate a nation's concern about racial discrimination. Actually, the civil rights laws and policies are the fortuitous fallout of initiatives and policies that are important in the maintenance of white dominance.

And just as there is little reason to believe Judith will be Bluebeard's last attempt to regain his humanity through symbolic marriage and the inhumane sacrifice of another bride, I can find little basis for hope, either from history or by analogy from the fairy tale, that the racial pattern of freedom symbols for blacks and preservation of substantive power for whites will change anytime soon.

America too has a seventh door. Behind it there is the potential for self-revelation for whites as well as blacks. Salvation for all is possible if its light can reveal the destructiveness of "whiteness"—can provide an antidote to its corrupting influence, a corrective for its mesmerizing hypnotic spell. The door will not be opened until blacks become insistent or political or economic conditions dictate this long-overdue revelation.

And if the door of racial revelation is thrown open, there is certainly reason to expect that blacks and whites will be wary of what they learn from the light, will hesitate to risk reaching out and embracing the truth about a racial history that changes form but never alters its racial advantage for whites. Perhaps behind this door, too, we will find a betrayal of our dreams for an end to this racial bondage. Disappointed, resigned to our fate, we will watch as it too, like Bluebeard's Judith, is retired to some somber chamber while the stage grows dark and the curtain falls.

Notes

1. The tale is attributed to Charles Perrault, a seventeenth-century French poet, prose writer, and storyteller. He was a prominent member of the Academie Française and wrote fairy stories, actually updated versions of half-forgotten folk stories, to amuse his children. In addition to "Bluebeard's Castle," his stories include "Little Red Riding Hood," "The Sleeping Beauty," and "Puss-n-Boots."

2. See Bartok 1963; the quoted text is from the libretto.

3. Civil Rights Act of 1964, Pub. L. No. 88-352, 78-Stat. 241 (codified as amended in scattered section of 42 U.S.C.); Voting Rights Act of 1965, Pub. L. No. 89-110, 79 Stat. 437 (codified as amended in scattered sections of 42 U.S.C.); Fair Housing Act of 1968, Pub. L. No. 90-284, 82 Stat. 81 (codified as amended in scattered sections of 42 U.S.C.); *Brown v. Board of Education*, 349 U.S. 294 (1955).

4. See, e.g., Allen 1969 (racism used to maintain black America as a domestic colony of white America); Berry 1975 (maintaining that the 13th Amendment was prompted less by the desire to free blacks generally than the necessity of placating and then disarming large numbers of black troops recruited during the period); Morgan 1975 (a study of slavery in early colonial Virginia, indicating that elements of both prejudice and profit were present in the slavery equation, with emphasis on the latter); Zilversmit 1967 (reviewing the economic factors that undergirded efforts to abolish slavery in the northern states in the years following the Revolutionary War); "Land, Slavery and the Founding Fathers" (1968: p. 119, reflecting the founding fathers' debate over slavery and their inability to overcome the sense that a nation conceived to protect property should not destroy property interests in slaves). All the above authorities and more are collected and discussed in Bell 1980.

5. See generally, Franklin 1963 (tracing the history of the Emancipation Proclamation); Dillard (1963: p. 23, discussing Lincoln's motivations and frank subordination of slaves' interest in freedom to his changing perceptions of the nation's needs).

6. See *United States v. Price*, 383 U.S. 787, 804 (1966) (in 1868 organizations with romantic titles launched a wave of murders and assaults, including assassinations, designed to keep Negroes from the polls); *Monroe v. Pape*, 365 U.S. 167, 175 (1961) (quoting the speeches of congressmen detailing atrocities); Ginsburg 1969 (newspaper excerpts of lynchings of five thousand blacks since 1859); Woodson and Wesley 1922 (providing an almost contemporary report of violence and killings perpetrated against blacks in the post-Reconstruction period).

7. The Court's dramatic opinion ended more than a decade of litigation over whether a particular state school was "separate but equal" by broadening the issue: "Does segregation of children in public schools solely on the basis of race, even though the physical facilities and other 'tangible' factors may be equal, deprive the children of the minority group of equal educational opportunities? We believe that it does." 347 U.S. at 483 (1954).

Taking cognizance of the psychological damage done to black children by segregation, the Court abandoned the half-century-old precedent in *Plessy v.*

Ferguson (163 U.S. 537), concluding "that in the field of public education the doctrine of 'separate but equal' has no place." 347 U.S. at 495.

Having raised the hopes of blacks to heavenly levels, the Court then deferred relief until further arguments could be held, a departure from the usual process of granting immediate relief for the violation of personal constitutional rights. The following year, the Court rejected NAACP petitions for immediate relief and returned the cases to the district courts with instructions requiring that "defendants make a prompt and reasonable start toward full compliance with our May 17, 1954, ruling," *Brown v. Board of Education* (1955: p. 300).

References

Allen, Robert L. 1969. *Black Awakening in Capitalist America*. Garden City, NY: Doubleday.

Bartok, Bela. 1963. *Bluebeard's Castle*. Columbia Records recording.

Bell, Derrick A. 1973. *Race, Racism, and American Law*. Boston: Little, Brown.

― ― ― . 1998. *Afrolantica Legacies*. Chicago: Third World Press.

Bennett, Lerone. 1962. *Before the Mayflower*. Chicago: Johnson Publishing Co.

Berry, Mary F. 1975. *Toward Freedom and Civil Rights for the Freedom: Military Policy Origins of the Thirteenth Amendment and the Civil Rights Act of 1866*. Pamphlet provided by the Department of History, Howard University.

Brown v. Board of Education. 1955. 349 U.S. 294.

Civil Rights Act of 1964. Pub. L. No. 88-352, 78-Stat. 241 (codified as amended in scattered section of 42 U.S.C.).

Damton, Robert. 1984. *The Great Cat Massacre and Other Episodes in French Cultural History*. New York: Basic Books.

Dillard, Irving. 1963. "The Emancipation Proclamation in the Perspective of Time." *Law in Transition* 23: 95.

Drimmer, Melvin. 1968. "Land, Slavery and the Founding Fathers," in Melvin Drimmer, ed., *Black History*. Garden City, NY: Doubleday.

Emancipation Proclamation. 1863. 12 Stat. 1268 (No. 17).

Fair Housing Act of 1968. Pub. L. No. 90-284, 82 Stat. 81 (codified as amended in scattered sections of 42 U.S.C.).

Franklin, John Hope. 1963. *The Emancipation Proclamation*. Garden City, NY: Doubleday.

Ginzburg, Ralph. 1962. *One Hundred Years of Lynchings*. New York: Lancer Books.

King Jr., Martin Luther. 1967. *Where Do We Go from Here: Chaos or Community?* Boston: Beacon Press.

Monroe v. Pape. 1961. 365 U.S. 167.

Morgan, Edmund Sears. 1975. *American Slavery, American Freedom*. New York: W. W. Norton.

Perrault, Charles. 1798. *Fairy Tales, or Histories of Past Times*. New York: John Harrison Publishers.

Plessy v. Ferguson. 1896. 163 U.S. 537.

United States Constitution, Amendment 13. 1865 (ratified December 18).

——— , Amendment 14. 1868 (ratified July 28).

United States v. Price. 1966. 383 U.S.787.

Voting Rights Act of 1965. Pub. L. No. 89-110, 79 Stat. 437 (codified as amended in scattered sections of 42 U.S.C.).

Woodson, Carter, and Charles Wesley. 1962. *The Negro in Our History*. Washington, DC: Associated Publishers.

Zilversmit, Arthur. 1967. *The First Emancipation: The Abolition of Slavery in the North*. Chicago: University of Chicago Press.

Reflections on "Bluebeard's Castle"

What follows are excerpts from a panel discussion, facilitated by Charles Hamilton and organized by Lynn Huntley, on the relevance of the fairy tale "Bluebeard's Castle" on race relations in the United States. Participants included Derrick Bell, Richard Delgado, Andrew Hacker, Jennifer Hochschild, Kathryn Rodgers, Kenneth Roth, Catharine Stimpson, and Jack Tchen.

Derrick Bell: Analysis is not prophecy. Those of us who have studied and are concerned with racial issues may be gifted with energy and insight but not necessarily prophetic power. Like many of you, I began my career after law school with a desire to become a civil rights lawyer. After graduation, I had a conversation with Judge William Hastie, who said of my aspiration, "Well, son, it's very praiseworthy, but it's 1957, the *Brown* decision has been made, and I'm afraid that while there's a little mopping up to be done, basically you were born fifteen years too late." That was an optimistic analysis but not very prophetic.

I've been attracted to literary parallels as a means of trying to decode where we are in the effort to overcome racism and discrimination. I was particularly attracted to the fairy tale of "Bluebeard's Castle." Bela Bartok's opera focuses on one revealing part of the Bluebeard story. Like so many artists, Bartok was recognized and applauded much more after his death than before. Both his life and music in this piece parallel the race situation in America in interesting ways. He seems to be writing about the potential for spiritual victory in political defeat.

I have written that racism is permanent. This view is criticized as despairing, and yet portions of truth seem to lie in that direction when you look at history and what keeps the American economy, with all its disparities, relatively stable. You see the role that race has played in that stability. It seems very difficult to imagine maintaining this society without this anchor of the "Other"—the group on the bottom—without the recognition or understanding of the property right in "whiteness" held by some people. The Bluebeard story provides a means to help us explore this terrain.

Judith tries to see something of value in this man and to bring that goodness out, using the power of love and right. In my piece [above], the doors represent our efforts to overcome racism with the Emancipation Proclamation, the civil rights statutes coming out of our

Reconstruction era, the *Brown* decision, the Voting Rights Act, and finally, affirmative action. All of these seem to be opportunities to move us beyond where we're stuck. Judith thinks that behind each of these doors, there is going to be salvation. But she finds, as she unlocks and opens each door, only cause for disappointment, not reason for hope.

Her plight is so much like that of African Americans because often we grasp and embrace these new remedies as "the way." Only afterward do we recognize that these remedies would not even have come into being save for the fact that at least some whites in policymaking positions saw within them a potential for self-interest. That's not how it's promoted. Whites say: "Oh, we're doing this because it's the right thing to do." But when the interest changes, as it did in the 1870s, you see that whites weren't really thinking about blacks at all.

The failure doesn't invalidate the attempt. Judith did what she felt had to be done. It just didn't work for her. So she finally passes from the scene, as I sometimes think we will finally pass from the scene, at least in the way that we now perceive ourselves. But that is not the end. It was not the end of the story of Bluebeard nor Bartok's music. Bartok continues to live through his music.

Race in America has been an evil, but those who have been condemned by race have made tremendous contributions. The spiritual victory is in sight, the political defeat not yet certain. There is still some chance, still some hope. Our challenge is to recognize exactly where we are so as to try to maximize the potential for political victory, without undermining or corrupting or selling out that which is spiritual.

Richard Delgado:[1] Why did Derrick Bell choose a French fairy tale to illustrate a point about African-American history and experience? Perhaps to illustrate a universal truth about raised hopes and their cynical deployment by empowered groups to keep the peasantry in line. Perhaps, too, Bell was drawn to the story of "Bluebeard's Castle" because he saw himself in Judith, whose transformation from besotted idealist to disillusioned bride mirrors Bell's own path. As the opera's curtain rises, Judith entertains a vision of an ideal life with Bluebeard and, despite warnings, takes risks to achieve that life. When finally allowed access to the castle, she recognizes it for what it is—just as Bell, despite his hopes, also recognizes the bleak reality of a persistently racist country.

Notice how, despite her growing realization, Judith clings to the belief that her marriage will succeed, just as civil rights scholars once clung to the hope for a better future for communities of color. Eventually, this enthusiasm wanes. On seeing the reality of Bluebeard's castle firsthand, Judith resigns herself to her fate. But being the seeker after truth that she is, she wants to confirm her destiny. "Judith," Bell writes, "her hope gone and expecting the worse, nevertheless insists on opening that door." Is this where Bell is in his thinking today?

The force behind the story of Bluebeard lies in its use of repetition. The seven doors not only allow for a chronological presentation of black history but also serve to highlight the maddening similarity of each historical step. The likeness of each door and the repeat cycle of curiosity, hope, revelation, and disappointment mirror the repetitive and unchanging nature of blacks' predicament on these shores. Similarly, the eerie image of the imprisoned bride, comalike in her consciousness, is made more dramatic through repetition. Three, now four, seemingly identical pale imprisoned brides are a powerful image of the fate of people of color who fail to grasp their situation—or who listen to the siren song of conservatives of color who preach that all is well.

Bell ends the essay with the apocalyptic words: "And the stage grows dark and the curtain falls." Like the fairy tale, Bell is issuing a warning—to America that mere symbols of redemption are not enough, and to blacks to watch their backs.

[Bartok's] *Bluebeard's Castle* is easily read as an allegory for gender power disparity. Indeed, Bell sets the stage for a feminist reading of the opera through the line: "Judith, try as she might to become the instrument of his liberation, is unable to move him beyond his desire for dominance." Bell does not follow up on this possibility, however, even though at Harvard he was a voice for "women's equality" and elsewhere recognizes that oppression, for many black women, is twofold.

A second latent possibility also goes unexplored. Bell reminds us that favorable judicial decisions like *Brown v. Board of Education* are followed by great celebrations and dancing in the streets—after which they are invariably cut back by narrow judicial interpretations, administrative foot-dragging, and delay. He might have noted that in some respects they leave us even worse off than before. Conservatives, believing that the legal system has given away the store to undeserving minorities, redouble their resistance, while our friends, the liberals, believing the problem has been solved, go on to something else, such as saving the whales. Psychologists know that a variable reinforcement schedule is the surest way to hook someone, so that the law's intermittent bestowal of breakthroughs, followed by a train of regressive decisions, is exactly what is needed to keep us coming back for more.

Bell ought to take a closer look, as well, at the architecture of that castle, its arrangement of rooms, and the relationships they set up among Bluebeard's four wives. Like an Eastern potentate with a harem, Bluebeard may be playing his wives off against each other, maintaining everything nicely in control. Recall how *Brown v. Board of Education* announced a ringing breakthrough for black schoolchildren, just at the same time that Congress was ordering Operation Wetback, a massive roundup of Chicanos, many of them American citizens, for deportation to Mexico. Only a few years earlier, a presidential decree had ordered all Japanese Americans living on the West Coast to wartime detention centers, many losing farms and businesses in the process. In Mississippi, planters refused to rehire the newly freed blacks, instead bringing in Mexicans and Asians. In the wake of *Brown*, school authorities in Texas certified certain schools as desegregated on the grounds that they had arranged it so that they were 50 percent Mexican and 50 percent black. Ignoring how society racializes one group, say blacks, at the expense of others, say Chicanos, Asians, or Indians, then, can end up positively injuring the other. To understand when one is out of favor or being used to manipulate someone else, each ethnic group must struggle to understand the full texture of race and not be content with a particular binary, say black-white or brown-white. Castle doors may open and shut in a more complex sequence than we know, if we only focus on the fortunes of one group.

Had Bell followed through with this larger exploration, the desperate urgency that he illustrated through the Bluebeard analogy would gain even more force. Not only would he be able to show that what we saw as advances actually moved us closer to the forfeiture of our dreams, but he would show how the dominant society intended and schemed it so. Like Judith, then, we would learn to be skeptical because "neither love nor life can be sustained on unearned trust." This is even more so because the tyrannical Bluebeard rationalizes that he did his bedecked, bejeweled, but imprisoned wives a favor.

Jennifer Hochschild: It seems to me that there are three themes that are going to run through the next century in a really complicated way. Where all of this will end up, given the interaction among them, is almost unpredictable. The only thing one can predict is that they are going to occur.

First, black exceptionalism: African Americans have always been different and will for the foreseeable future be treated differently. Middle-class African Americans are increasingly angry and frustrated with the "American Dream" story, and many African Americans are still left out of the recent dramatic economic improvement. This story is going to continue in the future, but in different ways.

Question: Exceptionalism, nationally or internationally?

Jennifer Hochschild: I'm only thinking nationally. Probably I would also say internationally, but I haven't thought about that. I think it will play out differently in different countries, but my general sense is that there will be some variant of that at least in the three countries [South Africa, Brazil, and the United States] that this group is focused on.

Question: Would that be contested or maintained?

Jennifer Hochschild: I think it has always been and will continue to be contested, ranging from what it means to be black, to what it means to be exceptional, to what the relationship is. All of those components have been and will continue to be contested. In the other countries, probably more than in the United States, the whole question of "who counts" as "black" and what the variant and gradations are, is more salient than it is here, but it could possibly become more salient here. The general point is that much of what Derrick Bell is arguing will continue. But that is in context with two other things.

Second, class has been and will continue to be increasingly important within the nation as a whole and the black population. What it means to be African American is in some very important ways different for people with relatively high incomes, occupations, and educational status than for people with very low incomes, occupations, and educational status. Thirty, forty, fifty years ago, that was much less true. That is much more true now and will continue to be. If you look at the evidence, there is a growing polarization in the black population, and my guess is that that is going to continue. That is why I started with the black exceptionalism point. It is not to say that middle-class African Americans are moving into an integrated, assimilated, and comfortable society—I don't think that's the case at all. But what it means to be black for the relations between blacks and whites is going to be different and increasingly different for the "best-off" third from the "worst-off" third, and the middle third will muddle around.

The third point that is absolutely essential is demography. Demography is completely predictable, which is a virtue that no other discipline has. What we know is that, assuming no dramatic changes in immigration laws take effect, the Hispanic population is going to be twice as large as the black population; the Asian population is going to be almost as large; and the white majority is going to stop being the majority. Sometime in the twenty-first century, the demographics are going to move in that direction. That changes politics in a big and complicated way. To sum up my point in one sentence, I would say that the critical question is how those populations that are neither white in conventional understanding, nor black, are going to position themselves and are going to be positioned politically. My guess is that Hispanics and Asians are going to look like turn-of-the-century white, ethnic immigrants. Which is to say that, with some exceptions, and predominantly dark-skinned exceptions, they both are going to try to, and will over the next two generations, assimilate into a more conventional or mainstream (that is, white-dominated) society. This is a prediction, which I don't want to be held to necessarily, but that's my guess.

Poor, recently arrived, and dark-skinned immigrants are going to look more like African Americans, but the bulk of immigrants are going to look more like and are going to try to become more like assimilated whites. For example, if you look at survey data, intermarriage rates, political-party affiliations, efforts at residential mobility, occupational data, you see that at least second-generation Hispanics are trying very hard to become "like whites." Asian Americans are also very rapidly intermarrying, moving into predominantly mainstream institutions and largely being accepted in a way that seems to be extraordinary, given the experiences of fifty years ago.

My prediction is that demography is going to complicate politics in unpredictable ways. It will force an increase in black exceptionalism rather than decrease it. I think you are less likely to see a "rainbow coalition" of people of color and more likely to see an assimilation into the mainstream, with the exception of blacks and dark-skinned recent immigrants. Then class will muddle the whole thing in very complicated ways.

Catharine Stimpson: I'd like to say to Derrick Bell that it is wonderful to have brought in art in two ways: Art is a sign of spiritual celebration and an achievement, and art is a way of understanding our situation. Of course, the difficulty with using art as a way of understanding our situation is that we tend to do reductive interpretations. Reductionism simply has to be repudiated.

After reading [Bell's] essay again, I wondered about the situation for white women, especially, white women of a certain class. Like Judith, we both own the jewels and wear the jewels. It is terribly important for others to understand this duality, if they are to understand their relations to justice.

A question for us all is: When we speak of defeat, how would we measure success? What would it look like? When could we declare victory, insofar as one could ever in the face of history declare victory? What would it mean to be able to say, we don't have to do this anymore? What would be the criteria to say that this has been won? It has been difficult, it has been bloody, and it has been awful, but has this been won?

An important part of Derrick Bell's [essay] is that what seem to be victories, turned out not to be. The victory is illusory. What would it mean to say: yes, people have done this? How would we know this and when would we know this?

Kenneth Roth: What struck me was that the series of victories have all been legal. What have we won? I think one of the problems is that we've tended to view victory in purely legal terms. We have won many legal victories, and it clearly hasn't been anything close to enough.

I believe there is a need to move on to the next stage. Many, if not most, of the legalized forms of discrimination have been ended, and we still have a long way to go. One can ask sociologically why it is that in this country we are so likely to judge progress in legal terms; that clearly is our culture, and the civil rights movement has not escaped it.

There is too much of a disjunction between, on the one hand, the eradication of one form of de jure discrimination after another and, on the other hand, the impact on the way people actually lead their lives— what you might call de facto discrimination. I'm not even sure you can define the problem wholly in discriminatory terms, instead of simply saying that there is a large segment of society that has been left behind and is not being helped sufficiently by these legal victories.

Being a lawyer, I have a hard time escaping the legal paradigm. So I tend to think of this problem in terms of an international treaty that my organization, Human Rights Watch, has been trying to uphold. The treaty is the UN Convention Against Racial Discrimination, which has a legal tool in it that is akin to what was once understood to be in the civil rights legislation of the 1960s but was judicially carved out. That is to say, the focus of the treaty is not simply on intentional discrimination but also on discrimination in fact. There was a brief period in the United States when we legally were allowed to speak in those terms, but the conservative courts wiped out that possibility with time. What we do have, though, is a brand new treaty that the Clinton administration has now formally ratified. One of the interesting things is that the treaty requires any new country that has ratified it to report to the United Nations in one year about its success in meeting the terms of the treaty. In this case, that should include a discussion not only of efforts to eradicate intentional discrimination but also efforts to eradicate discriminatory results.

I think this focus on what one might call the "unintentional fact" of discrimination is important because a lot of racial problems today are problems that you have a hard time proving were created intentionally to hold back African Americans. Just to give you one example of an issue that my organization is working on: we did a study recently that found that 13 percent of African-American males across the country are disenfranchised—that is to say that they are denied the right to vote because they have been convicted of a felony. In some states, such as Florida, over one-third of the African-American male population formally, legally, cannot vote. Now, you may ask, why is that? We have had felony disenfranchisement rules for eons. You can debate why they were adopted in the first place, and there may well have been a racial component to it at one time. But at this stage, those laws are so engrained in our culture that it is hard to say that they are intentionally designed to disenfranchise African-American males. But that clearly is the effect. So if you want to move beyond the paradigm of intentional discrimination to one of discrimination in fact, you have to ask the hard question: is there any adequate rationale for such laws to justify their devastating political weakening of a population very much in need of every vote it can get? As a corollary, one must also ask why so many African-American males find themselves behind bars, and why are they behind bars for such lengthy periods of time?

You can look at things like the crack-cocaine distinction—the far more severe penalty imposed for the use of crack than for the use of cocaine. Is this because blacks tend to use crack and whites tend to use cocaine, or is that just the effect? If one takes the "effect" approach, though, the intent doesn't matter so much; one still must show that this discriminatory treatment is justified.

Similarly, mandatory minimum sentences or those outrageously long sentences for relatively minor nonviolent crimes tend to have the effect of putting huge proportions of the African-American male population behind bars. You end up devastating communities with relatively little justification. I see the need to move beyond a focus on intentional discrimination—to look at some of the effects of these laws and practices to see if we can justify their differential treatment.

One of the political lessons that this leaves me with is that not only do we need to start looking factually at the effects of various practices—and it's not coincidental that conservative forces in this country are right now trying to prevent even the collection of racial data in many areas—but also we need to talk about broader alliances.

If our greatest concern is no longer intentional discrimination, but rather the fact that a combination of policies and practices has left behind segments of the population, it may be that alliances could be built between African Americans and others, based on class or other common interests, in overcoming barriers to securing decent education, jobs, housing, medical care, or other needs. It is not necessary to be couched in terms of the legacy of discrimination or the legacy of slavery, although they could be. What is at stake is a basic question of fairness—whether it is right that such a large segment of our population, for whatever reason, is being left out and has so little prospect of joining the mainstream of society.

Jack Tchen: The one term that hasn't been mentioned so far is "culture." If we're to look at intentions between the present, the past, and the future, and how stubborn some of these patterns appear to be, I think one of the ways to describe the pattern beyond law, beyond art, narrowly, is really culture. There's obviously a culture to law and the history of law, as well as a culture to the history of race relations. Just to stick with the door analogy: if we were to begin to reject the linear notion of progress and therefore the linear notion of doors—one, two, three, and four in that order—and instead, to open up that process and to think about doors behind doors, then we would begin to approximate the complex histories and trajectories of different racial ethnic groups coming into contact with this new world.

There were colonization efforts of which clearly the African-American enslavement is principal. But at the same time, we need to consider questions of land policy in relation to Native Americans, Chicanos, and Hispanics. And, however we want to describe it, we must consider luxury. Luxury is something we tend to drop out of this whole equation. The first explorers were looking for the luxuries of the "Orient." When Columbus was trying to find the Orient and ran into the Caribbean, he kept asking local natives where Japan was. He couldn't understand their replies, and he thought they were saying "the next island over." So we are already talking about a process of globalization.

The United States was founded with many types of hierarchical arrangements in mind, derived from being a capitalist state. Different groups regionally, and later internationally, get brought into that complex hierarchy. So, if we're going to talk about the "doors" and this complex history, then we begin to approximate something that, on one hand, doesn't dismiss or dilute the importance of the black-white power dynamic but gets also to the history of "whiteness" and "otherness" in its multiple configurations.

Clearly now, in terms of globalization and its effects—everything we pick up now is made in China, Asia, Latin America, or the

Caribbean, but not so much Africa—we're talking about a complex
stage of development of international political economies. Think about
Nike and Michael Jordan, who's making those sneakers, to *Lethal
Weapon IV*, in which the buddies are black and white cops, and the evil
one coming in is Jet Lee. I'm not saying this is the new paradigm, but
for this moment, in terms of how globalization is working, in many
ways the peasant women in Asia and elsewhere who are going into
these shoe factories, are clearly the proletarian slave, semislaved laborers in this international, global system. Where does that, in the U.S.
context, place the hierarchy of race relations? So we're talking about
very complex relationships that need to be taken into account without at
the same time forgetting about the importance of addressing particulari-
ties of black-white relations.

Clearly, there are complex gender, racial, sexual characteristics in
all of these things. Consider these cartoons I'm passing around that feature a mix of stereotypic East Asian characters. These stereotypes and
hierarchies are deeply entrenched. They keep on coming back just when
we think they're gone.

This is connected to the accusations of Asians and in particular
Chinese being spies. I just pulled down from the web an article that
appeared in the *Los Angeles Times* in which 400 lab researchers in the
auditorium of Livermore National Laboratory met with Bill Richardson
last Friday. They were talking honestly about how Asian Americans,
professionals who are considered "success stories," are in deep and
constant fear of harassment and being charged as spies. We've seen this
pattern before. It can be argued that maybe this is a temporary aberra-
tion and that maybe Asians, like Jews, are going to continue to
advance. But I suspect, especially with global capitalism, it's not so
simple.

Kathy Rodgers: We cannot ignore the intersections of race and gender. Kate talked about white women being both the owner and wearer of
jewels. For women of color, it is the other end of the spectrum.

The notion that men should have all the power and dominance cuts
across races. That becomes very complicated when you examine all the
roles women play in our society. But, if you look at economic measures,
you will find that women of color come out at the bottom of virtually
every measure. We have to constantly interject the notion of the intersection of race and gender in any discussion as we move into the future.
We haven't yet done that adequately.

We also need to look at some new models and ideas. Speaking of
our culture, one of its foundations is the emphasis on and importance of

individual rights. That is something that has been a cornerstone of the civil rights movement as well. It's something that has been at the cornerstone of the women's rights movement. But it's much too limiting. It should not be exclusive of a notion of social responsibility and social good. Some things we have to do collectively. It's better for all of us.

Something that I'm thinking a lot about right now is child care and caregiving. This is the one important service function that is still basically unpaid, still performed almost completely by women, still relegated to women as individuals in the small family unit. We need to develop the idea that this is a social responsibility, like public education. There is a social good for all of us if we work together and find solutions for child care so that women can move into the paid economy. Doing that would have an enormous impact, not just on white women but on women of color who predominate in the service industries.

Question: We're all good at exhortation of what we need. We're not good at figuring how to get there from here. Do you think that making that argument frequently, visibly, publicly, with the appropriate art, anecdotes, history, whatever, is going to persuade people? Or do we have to move to a self-interest model where employers are going to lose their female workers unless they do a better job of child care? How do we do it? Is it a political question of coalitions of people of color? How do we get there from here?

Kathy Rodgers: I think the way we get there is to develop new models. We can use new language or we can resurrect some language that we gave up, like "social responsibility." One of the most important things we have to do is clarify what our messages are and repeat them over and over and over again, so that they begin to sink into the psyche of the nation. This is something that conservatives in the last fifteen or twenty years have done very, very successfully. I have no problem taking a page out of that book.

I would also say that we have to work differently in our coalitions. On the whole issue of affirmative action, for example, our coalitions have not been very successful. And we have allowed opponents of affirmative action to define this as strictly a race issue. It's clearly an issue for women as much as it is for people of color, but we allowed them to call it primarily a "black issue." At the same time, we were too timid to come up with some new terms, new models, and better ways to admit to the limitations as well as strengths of affirmative action. What we really want is fair outcomes. The laws may not be the way to structure that. We may need to change the culture and the practices in our businesses. We haven't had that conversation among ourselves, and we shouldn't be so timid. We need to face the complexities of these issues and then say "this is what we want." What we're after is the outcome, and the old legal structures may not be the best way to get there.

Catharine Stimpson: How do we admit error? How do we talk to each other about mistakes or limitations? Here, I think, affirmative action is a perfect case study. I supported affirmative action from the beginning, but when I administered affirmative action at a state university, I began to see some of its difficulties, and there was no way around them. I gave a public lecture about some of the difficulties and did an early version of "let's mend, not end," and I thought the applause was polite, but that's putting it politely.

We speak of "allowing" the conservatives to do this and the conservatives to do that, as if we were in control of things. Part of the difficulty with affirmative action is that those of us who were supporters did not find a way to talk about what was wrong with it so we could talk to each other first. We didn't look at its clumsiness; we didn't look at the difficulties before it was too late. One of the virtues of small gatherings like this, if the tape recorder were not on, would be to have honest, modest discussions about what is not working.

The issue is not just race; it is not just gender. If we are indeed in a global society, in an international society, it's also nationality. That will, of course, create tensions and difficulties. I think the Chinese *were* spying, and I don't think I'm being anti-Asian to say that. The Americans were spying on the Chinese—I don't think I'm being unpatriotic to say that. It is a difficult, power-driven world, and of course the "Chinese government" was up to no good in our labs. I think we have to be able to look at the political configurations, as well as the economic configurations of the global society, because there are some very nasty things that can create conflict. I am an American woman. For better or for worse, I am patriotic, and I feel my little old back getting up if I think anyone is going against my national self-interest. That can be done simultaneously with national critique.

Jack Tchen: Part of the problem lies in us accepting the fact that all nations are spying on each other, including European nations who are allies and part of the mutual pact, and why at some particular point in time is there such a controversy? Just ten years ago, when the Japan bashing was going on, and all of that stuff was coming out about who owns New York City, and all the newspapers were saying the Japanese, in point of fact, the Canadians owned much more of New York City than the Japanese. We need a deeper analysis of why that kind of scrutiny is happening now.

The position of Asian Americans is distinct and has its own peculiar traits. All groups have such distinctive markings. Asian Americans have always been seen as foreigners and not accepted as full U.S. citizens. So, in the case of Chinese Americans, the head of Raytheon (in the Democratic National Party scandal that happened a few years ago) was caught by the people in the CIA, who asked how long he'd been a U.S. citizen. That kind of racialization, that particular twist is what I'm trying to get at. So, in fact, all Asian Americans continue to be vulnerable, especially East-Asian Americans. If we look at South-Asian Americans, who often have darker complexions, it gets more complicated, because there are many middle-class and elite South Asians who are here as well, not simply the kind of garment workers whom we tend to think of.

Andrew Hacker: Asian Americans have essentially been in this country in the current way for less than twenty years. These are new immigrants. New immigrants have never been promised a suite at the hotel. And yet, in the twenty years, at Berkeley and UCLA, the flagship campuses, Chinese, Koreans, and Japanese now outnumber whites on merit. You have plenty of white parents who say, "We pay taxes. We built UCLA and Berkeley, but my kid can't get into UCLA and Berkeley. They've got to go to Santa Cruz. Why? Because some recent immigrant is taking my daughter's place." By the way, when I mentioned UCLA, you know what some people say "UCLA" now stands for, given the figures just mentioned? "Unhappy Caucasians Lost Among Asians." Many whites feel this way.

I'm not going to worry about Asian Americans. By the way, "Asian" is very interesting—this odd thing that combines people from Bangladesh with people from Korea. We used to have a term called "yellow," which we don't use anymore, nor do we use the term "oriental" anymore. It's almost as if we whites are saying that we need Chinese, Japanese, and Koreans because whites are not reproducing themselves. For a group or nation to reproduce itself, every 100 women must have 212 children. Among whites, every 100 women are now only having 175 children, which is well below reproduction. Black Americans are slightly over the rate. Mexicans, 345 per 100—doing just fine. By the way, Chinese, Japanese, Koreans are where the whites are—about 180. They're having either one or two children. So, we, whites, need numbers. This is why we are prepared to co-opt particularly Chinese, Japanese, Koreans.

Out in Queens where I teach, virtually all of the Chinese, Japanese, Korean, and other Asian students were born and raised with Asian first names. Very soon, about the age of five or six, they pick an Anglo first name: Charles, Mary, Vincent, Charlotte, and their parents don't object—no way. And this is a sign that Charlotte, Mary, and so on are ready to be co-opted, and they know this. They know how to pass the telephone test—they speak with a better Anglo diction than most of my American-born kids out of Queens, and they're ready.

We made up the term "Hispanics" for a reason. I believe that whites use the test of whether someone calls him- or herself "Hispanic" versus "Latino" to form judgments: If they call themselves "Latino," that's a foreign word and that means that you still have one foot in the Dominican Republic or wherever. But if you call yourself "Hispanic," that shows that you're ready to join "us."

As far as class is concerned—one of my projects in time is looking for the white poor. We whites have been pretty good at abolishing white poverty. We did it for the aged, and while we still have "trailer trash," interestingly, the people in the trailers get jobs. They have pals in their gun clubs who get them jobs as garage mechanics. Even when they go to Arkansas state prison, when a white guy comes out, you don't see him begging on the streets of Little Rock the way you do in New York. His pals get him a job. So we have a white sub-working class but not many white poor. In fact, what we've done in a sense is make sure that black Americans and certain Hispanic Americans are the big clump of the poor so that very few whites would join the coalition and say, "Hey, I'm a poor white guy, joining with others." Toqueville noticed this, James Madison noticed this—it's been part of the white American plan.

Just one more thing. Jennifer, you used the term "exceptionalism" of blacks. That's too academic for me. I know what you mean. The big problem, of course, here and maybe elsewhere too, is Africa. Which is to say that not just Europe but all other continents have wanted to distance themselves from Africa in every possible way. And what black Americans represent here is Africa within the United States. Africa was brought here for a purpose, served it for 250 years, and what white Americans are uneasy about is Africa remaining within the United States. African Americans are, as you say, "exceptional."

Last comment: gender. Of the bachelor's degrees awarded last year nationwide, 55 percent were to women, 45 percent to men. There's been a huge dropout among men. And it's not as if these guys who are high school graduates are going into construction and computers. Very few of them are. There's a kind of "white group," it's not totally an underclass, that's falling behind because they don't like schoolwork, they're not good at it, whereas the girls are. Girls get better grades. At Johns

Hopkins, Yale, and Stanford medical schools, currently the entering class has more women than men, again on merit. So I'm not going to shed too many tears for women. What women have to decide, if they really want to become CEOs, is if they want to be that assertive. If so, they can adopt the Margaret Thatcher model. You can be as tough as a guy if you want to—I can give you names: Oprah Winfrey, Barbara Streisand, who've got this. So, in the coming century, women and girls are going to take care of themselves. And increasingly, by the way, white women are going to find, as black women have found, not enough men measure up to their standards, even with the latest pharmaceuticals.

Comment: You certainly see more women in law school. When I went to law school, there were no women. Now, in my class, there are not only more women, but they're more impressive overall.

Jennifer Hochschild: There are two points that I want to bring back to the table. One is this question of coalitions among people of color. This is critically important because there are relatively few poor whites. We know from eons back that the odds of them allying with other people according to economic interests are close to zero. There are and will be more and more relatively poor people who are neither white nor black. Arguably, that is the group that is going to make a big difference on issues of distributive justice—child care, education, jobs, housing, crime, police brutality—pick your issue. They are going to make the difference in at least half a dozen states and ten to fifteen of the biggest cities. These are the people who are going to make a difference in how the politics play out. And I think that Hispanics or Latinos are, in some sense, "up for grabs," politically and ideologically in terms of availability for coalitions.

Latinos, as a group, are relatively poor, relatively inclined to accept and encourage governmental help. They are also deeply Catholic, culturally conservative, suspicious of African Americans, and typically don't have a lot of patience for claims about historic discrimination and uniqueness and exceptionalism. It's a tricky coalitional possibility. I would say that roughly the same thing holds for Asian Americans, although in general at a higher-class level, partly because educational attainment is usually higher. But again, if you look at surveys, the evidence suggests that Asian Americans are probably the most libertarian group in the sense of some suspicion of government. This means that they're in favor of "women's right to choose," but they're also often opposed to governmental intervention in the economy or society. So they are an interesting potential coalitional partner because they don't break down neatly into either liberal/conservative or Democratic/ Republican. It seems we need a lot of discussion, which could only be begun here, about how to think about what these coalitional possibilities are, the language and models to use, and who is the "we" we are talking about? Are we talking about local economic development groups, national advocacy groups, or candidates for city council? Over the next twenty to fifty years, it's going to be absolutely critical to think hard about such questions.

My fear is that once again blacks are going to be left out. Why would anyone want to enter a coalition with people in the bottom 20 percent if they have the possibility of entering a coalition with people in the middle or upper 20 percent? The answer to this simple and straight-forward starting point needs to be thought about very hard and clear-headedly.

I also want to bring the question of class back to the table. We've talked about nationality, we've talked about gender, we've talked about race, we've talked about university students and business professionals, but we have not talked as much as I think we need to about community colleges, high school, and child care. Setting aside the global question, if you look at survey data or political coalitions on the ground, what you see is relatively less concern about discrimination either on grounds of gender, race, or nationality, or anything else, and a lot more concern about child care, about jobs. People are worried about getting their kids to school safely, getting their son out of jail. Arguably, elites are more attentive (elites being the top third of the population, the best educated, and most professionally successful third of the population) to questions of racial or ethnic or gender discrimination and slights. Correctly or not. The poorest third of the population seem to be more concerned with questions of making it through the day and making a chance for their children to make it through the day. So, in a sense, I think the coalitional possibilities are greater among the poor than among the wealthy.

Kathy Rodgers: What we're interested in is fair outcomes. Women of whatever race should have the same economic opportunities. I'd like to respond to the use of statistics. It's very easy to fall into traps and not address the argument. I'm not so interested in doctors and lawyers because they are such a small percentage of the population. I want it to be fair for them, but they don't reflect what is happening to the vast majority of women in the country. We need to have more discussion beyond the elites. What we tend to look at all the time when we talk about women is the elites. For example, the number of black women on welfare is a much higher proportion of the black population than the proportion of white women on welfare is to the whole white female population. That may be in fact the more important measure than whether there are more black or white women on welfare in absolute numbers. That is my point. We need to look at the full array of numbers and see what they tell us.

Richard Delgado: I'd like to address the Hispanic/Latino population and call attention to the so-called immigrant model that one or two of you might subscribe to in the back of your minds. It seems to me that to believe that folks like me will follow the pattern of the Irish or Jews, right up the ladder, really requires about as much faith as Judith does. Consider some of the differences: We have been here, many of us, a very long time. We were here first. The immigrant model is not particularly apt. We're not moving into the middle class very rapidly at all. Many of us hang on to loyalty to our countries of origin (Mexicans at least). One statistic that just came out is that about 10 percent of Latinos in the state of California plan to naturalize. Talk about disenfranchisement. Even larger numbers of those who are U.S. citizens are planning to take advantage of Mexico's new law allowing dual citizenship, to acquire or reacquire citizenship in that country. Latinos' high school dropout rate is greater than 50 percent, the highest of the ethnic groups. Latinos' rate of earning Ph.D.s is the lowest of all the ethnic groups. We have almost no Hispanic caucus and very few big-city mayors, unlike other groups. It seems to me that if you are worried that Latinos are active and play coalition politics with whites against blacks, I'm not sure that's a realistic fear. To many of my Latino buddies, it looks like other groups have cut better deals with the white power structure than we.

Question: Can you identify who you mean?

Richard Delgado: Yes, groups with a better rate of entry into the middle class, better records of school success, records of entry into politics, judgeships, commissionerships. It's a mental checklist. I would ask all of you to think of the names of two Latino law professors other than me. Do you know any? At any rate, I think that the immigrant analogy is inapt in one or two ways. Some of us do indeed immigrate here from south of the border, but it's lazy scholarship and it leads to the wrong sort of thinking if you believe that we're like the Irish and Italians.

Andrew Hacker: What are the intermarriage rates?

Richard Delgado: I believe less than for Japanese and Chinese, and higher than for blacks. Somewhere in the middle.

Andrew Hacker: And once you have intermarriage and the children of the marriage . . .?

Richard Delgado: They tend to identify with the Latino side.

Kenneth Roth: I want to come back to affirmative action. While affirmative action has been very useful in building gradually an African-American middle class, to take the racial aspect of it for a moment, there has been a political cost to it, which I would like to articulate in terms of the broader themes that we have been discussing today.

First of all, I'm afraid that in some respects affirmative action has been a diversion in that it has encouraged people to focus on providing opportunities to a few relatively well-off minorities without looking at whether the vast majority of African Americans or other minorities are given the basic capacity ever to take advantage of those opportunities. It fits very much into the individual paradigm—if you are already virtually capable and need only a little help, then you can walk through the door. Great, but the vast majority of African Americans might not have the educational background to go to Berkeley or UCLA, and we're not doing anything to give them that background. We're not improving our public schools, we're not providing better day care, we're not building better housing; all the basic needs are ignored as we focus on simply giving a relative handful of individuals an opportunity to advance.

Richard Delgado: But it does help them get jobs as firefighters and clerks and other advancements, right?

Kenneth Roth: My point is that where people are in a position to actually walk through a door, yes, when they've had a basic education, when their basic needs are met, affirmative action does open doors for them.

Jennifer Hochschild: Through the classic model of individual upward mobility rather than through structural change, with all its virtues and defects.

Kenneth Roth: Yes, I think that affirmative action has allowed us to avoid talking sufficiently about meeting the basic needs of the broader population. And those needs in the case of African Americans are quite acute, not to mention those in the case of Latinos and others. Also, I'm afraid that affirmative action works against coalition politics. It reinforces the sense of fighting for your own group's access. That's inherent in the concept: as soon as you're going to advance by virtue of your racial or ethnic identity, there's a tendency to reinforce that identity rather than to reach out and mobilize around poverty issues that may indeed cross racial or ethnic barriers. It also has tended to play into the conservative argument about whether a particular individual deserves extra benefits. He or she may not have been the immediate victim of discrimination. The historical legacy of slavery seems far off. Those kinds of arguments have resonated quite widely with the American public.

I think there's another way of going at the underlying problems. You could call it distributive justice, although even that I don't think quite gets at it, because people are going to say: "I made this money, why should I give it to somebody else?" I think it's more a matter of basic fairness. You could almost use a kind of Rawlsian model here: what basic resources should every individual have in terms of education, in terms of housing, in terms of child care? That's a kind of appeal to fairness that I think would resonate among Americans and would resonate more than purely redistributive arguments. But we've been relatively locked into the "hand-out model"—allowing people to ask: Why do you deserve a handout?—rather than asking what basic resources does everybody deserve? What responsibility do we as a nation have to each person here to make sure that he or she has the basic capacity to go out and make it on his or her own? My sense is that we've lost track of that conversation. We've been diverted into a very conservative version of the conversation, which we're losing.

Catharine Stimpson: I would like to remind us all of what affirmative action was because I would disagree with Ken's characterization of it, and maybe others at this table would say that I've got it wrong. It was not a practice for the professional leagues. It was, at heart, a practice for blue-collar as well as white-collar employment. Affirmative action was to apply to construction, to firefighters, to police. It was a way of getting people into good blue-collar as well as white-collar positions.

So how did the practice of it or the politics of it change so much? Some of the worst cases were about construction, but not now. The contemporary fight about affirmative action is now admission to the professional leagues, but affirmative action was and still is an employment policy. Second, there were the opportunities for coalition work because the overarching rubric was underrepresented groups. You could argue about what underrepresentation meant, but it met in many ways the basic conditions for coalition. To me, the best writing about coalition politics is still that wonderful essay by Berenice Johnson Regan, in which she says that the condition of coalition politics is each group, however defined, sets up its survival issues. You say: if you respect my survival issue, I'll respect your survival issue and whatever common survival issues we have. Affirmative action gave us a common survival issue, which is enough income to be able to eat. And third, affirmative action really was the fairness model because what affirmative action promised was equal access and equal opportunity. So, at its source, affirmative action fits straight into some of the deepest and most attractive parts of the American ethos, which was the possibility of having a chance, the possibility of leveling the playing field. So, to me, Ken, the question is not what was affirmative action, but how did it get so quickly distorted? What happened there in terms of the public relations of affirmative action that made it get distorted?

Part of the difficulty was that it was such cumbersome apparatus. This enormous machinery got set up, and the machinery obscured the hope of affirmative action. But I'd like to answer Jennifer and her question of what is coalition politics. We're supposed to be talking about race/gender relations. Well, of course, we're all a race and we're all a gender, so our problem in part is to keep reminding ourselves that we are both, as well as everything else.

But what is the coalition issue that I think will matter the most? It is education. Charter schools are an interesting sideshow now. But it seems to me that public education, good public education, is the best coalition issue now. Get people working together on good public education, and they then can begin to have the difficult conversations about race and gender relations. In my experience, things have worked best where we have a common task. If we just sit down as strangers and say, "Hi, what do you think about race and gender?" everybody gets artificial and phony. But we can learn to trust each other over a common task. It seems to me that a coalition task is public education.

Interestingly, your choice of the issue goes right to what the basic resources are that people really need to be able to walk in the door and do the job. Education is clearly one of the most critical.

The common survival means is exactly what I'm driving at. I think that whatever happened to the origins of affirmative action, it is now understood very differently. I think that there's a need to go back to identifying what the basic resources are that everyone should have in a just society.

What is the nature of that curriculum? What constitutes the curriculum? Who's teaching? What languages? These are all part of the basic issues that we continue to debate and contest.

Jack Tchen: Different points have been made. I do agree that "nationalism" continues to be an incredibly salient issue; I do fully understand your point about UCLA and Irvine. In fact, Irvine has an even greater percentage of Asian-American students—I think 60–70 percent—and I agree with the point about class. But part of the reason for these phenomena goes back to historical reasons. So, if we're to just go back for one moment to the nature of the Chinese Exclusion Act of 1882, it was, besides being racialized, largely a class-based act. In other words, merchants and scholars, those considered part of the "court culture," were exempt. It was really the "heathen" workers, those cast about as heathens and racialized in very particular ways, that were excluded.

This political culture has always had a bifurcating effect on attitudes toward Asia and Asians. On the one hand, the luxuries of the court culture of Confucius, of the "good Asians," and on the other, those masses that everyone is afraid of. We are talking about a global system in which class, racialization, nationalism, ethnicization, all of these things are operating. I think we have to talk about this honestly and then talk about how many of these Asians, who come out of that system and do well and get jobs, often are quite conservative in their views of race and gender and affirmative-action politics in this country.

Now, what roles do we have as educators? The education system has a critical role in making sure that these issues related to history and race, affirmative action, and hierarchy are put before us all. Asian-American students need to understand this more, if not as much, as many other students. A counterpart to "whiteness," there are complex dynamics in play that do not make Asians "white"; I perhaps disagree with you in that sense, but they are becoming a part of a new kind of elite that perhaps we don't have the terms for. It is an elite that has its international characteristics, and it is also tied into certain elites of Europe in this country. Now that doesn't mean that all Asians are that way by any means. The great majority of Asians are of other kinds of middle-class and other kinds of working-class and many of them are of rural, peasant backgrounds.

How can we understand how the larger system is going to work in terms of competition for resources? I don't mean to say this as a way to make ethnocentric claims, but I think the days of talking about coalitions uncritically are past. We need to address how power works. As a historian, I always have to go back to that racial/ethnic hierarchy of the nineteenth century and eighteenth century that talked about some Asians as "somewhat civilized" and others as "primitives." That continues to hold to this day. Asians are not seen as necessarily being on top of the hierarchy, of having that forehead that allows for the proper rationality, but as good mimics, good traders in a certain way, etc. Asians are not seen as necessarily among the elite. How have these patterns changed?

Jennifer Hochschild: The paradigm is shifting very quickly, and there is the lack of evidence. There was one national survey of Latino Americans done a decade ago—which is the one that everyone uses because it's the only one that exists. It's a good survey but it's a decade old. There has been no national survey of Asian Americans ever. I've been looking for this for years, and there isn't one. There are good regional surveys. The *Los Angeles Times* has terrific surveys. There are two or three people in Texas who do terrific surveys; the National Conference (NCCJ) has a good survey. The *Washington Post* did a good survey, so for public opinion surveys, it's scattered and incomplete.

Once you're beyond public-opinion data on the grounds that they are superficial and broad but not very deep, you don't really know what the evidence is telling you. Then you're talking about individual case studies of particular cities. There are very few comparative cases across cities. You've got historians who have done excellent in-depth historical work on particular groups, but typically, it is for a particular period, a particular region, a particular group, and a particular part of the social or cultural configuration.

Andrew Hacker: Let's suppose, as some people have been saying, that we have affirmative action based on economic need regardless of say, race. What would happen then is that all the places that we're talking about, say education, would go to poorer whites. In particular, the biggest clump of poorer whites who are eligible are children being raised by their divorced moms. Dad is off with a new, younger wife; Mom is still out in the suburbs where the kids were raised; the kids are going to suburban schools, but their cashmere sweaters are a bit tattered. They will take up all the affirmative-action places for the so-called needy, and they'll all be white. So, bear that in mind.

From the beginning, we've been using the word "racism." I do a bit of talking on questions dealing with race in this country, and very frequently, the audience, say at college or elsewhere, is predominantly white. I've discovered that if I'm to get anything across to this audience, I cannot use the word "racism." Once I use the word "racism" or "racist," every white freezes and won't listen anymore. What they'll say is: "I'm not racist, I'm not bigoted, I'm not prejudiced, I have black friends." They also tell you that on surveys: "I have black friends." Somebody once remarked that with all these white people having all these black friends, there must be 400 million black friends out there. Nobody's a racist. Strom Thurmond or anyone else will say: "Hey, the other day I was chatting with my friend, Clarence Thomas." So, in this sense, it's not so much the liberalization, it's the fact that now even conservatives know how to respond to this.

Now, I know that something called "racism" is real. I talk about it, I write about it, but without using the term. Whites want to be declared "innocent" of any transgressions: "Hey, I wasn't here, that was my great-grandparents." This is a big hump to get over. The late Erving Goffman invented a phrase: "presentation of self." All of us—liberal, conservative, black, white, fascist, whatever—want to project, present a "self" who is a good self, a moral self, a progressive self.

Charles Hamilton: On the matter of coalitions, which everyone has talked about considerably, where do you expect in the near term the leadership for these varying coalitions will come from? I have a notion, but it's no more provocative than Andrew Hacker has been this morning. That is to say, I posit that blacks can't lead these social-justice coalitions anymore. Or they can't be prominently in front. I think that whites won't follow blacks' leadership on these kinds of even "universal" issues. I think whites have to lead these coalitions, and I'm very serious about that. I think that the Jim Hightowers of this country must take the leadership role. They must mobilize whites. The problem is not mobilizing blacks for these universalistic coalitions. It has not been historically or otherwise, even with the intervention of black power, which was seen as "separatist." That has not been the problem politically. Since the turn of the century with the populist movement, the problem has been mobilizing and sustaining and leading whites into viable coalitions. I'd be interested in a word or two on that.

Finally, I'm very concerned and am intrigued by Catharine's earlier point: How do we measure success? When do we start saying we don't have to do this anymore? Is this an interminable thing, we just keep going and going and going? That's very interesting.

What about leadership?

Catharine Stimpson: I have been looking for leaders. I have been inspired, even heartened by this. I just came back from Santa Clara, California, where I met the leader of a Mexican-American group. Extraordinary work. Much more grass-roots energy out there than we know. There are more leaders than we realize—who may or may not be recognized.

This may be an example of white—not innocence—white ignorance. I reacted very badly to your comment that blacks can't lead these coalitions, whites have to do it. Where I agree with you is that whites have to act and have to be far more conscious of their own color and the consequences of their own color. I wonder if we can develop—and I think the women's model is a good one—can we develop joint leadership? Can we move away from the notion of one leader for all time for one cause and have rotating leaders, joint leaders, co-chairs—look for multiracial leadership configurations? That's a fancy way of saying: let's have more than one president, have more than one person in the presidency but make sure that this is a rotating leadership without becoming dysfunctional.

I also see a role for the established organizations to play in terms of identification of leaders. I'm looking at what Girls Inc. does, what the Ys do. I'm looking at what church groups do. I think that in our metropolitan secularism, we are apt to overlook what some of the traditional organizations are doing at the local level in terms of leadership training programs.

You asked about education and about art as a form of education. I insist that a great work of art has more than one interpretation. I really think that for kids to see art, hear art, read stories, see tapes of dancing is also a form of education.

Jennifer Hochschild: Another possible answer to the leadership question: roughly, neither blacks nor whites are going to have enough trust to lead coalitions. The leadership for some of these multirace coalitions—wherever it's going to come from, I think your instinct is right—ought to be neither black nor white, which is to say it should be Chicano, Asian American, Native American, mixed race, etc. It feels to me that whites are in general so sensitive about being accused of being racist, or are so incapable of not having a position of leadership, that they're not going to follow black leaders very much, very far. Black activists are sufficiently suspicious of white leaders—the suspicion levels are very high among activists on either side. Therefore, I'm reaching for several terms, which could be "rotating leaders." For example, Berkeley's Chancellor Tien, the Asian-American educator who has been defending affirmative action, regardless of whether you think he should have gone to the wall on affirmative action—that was a very interesting political phenomenon. That broke up for a moment conventional assumptions about who's on what side. What I would like to see is people who are not in any particular identifiable group, who are not automatically assumed to be an X or a Y because of their race, move into positions where they're taking counterintuitive stances. Chicano leaders of multiracial coalitions. Where these people come from, how they make it work, I don't know.

Kenneth Roth: This answers the question in slightly different terms. I want to go back to something that I said at the beginning. The leaders of the future coalitions cannot be oriented to the courtroom. I think we have gone as far as we're going to get in the courtroom. What we need now is a different legal strategy. Clearly there are roles for legislation. But what we need, first, is to collect the relevant data and, second, to change the intellectual atmosphere in which these issues are discussed, something that the right has done very effectively and the left has fallen behind on. When people talk about race and about affirmative action, any of the topics we've been discussing today, the discussion tends to trigger reactions that are working against us now. We need to change that, and it's going to take a concerted effort through doing the right kind of surveys and polling, publishing op-eds, actively getting out there and changing the intellectual environment.

The work that has gone into writing briefs for the courts has now got to go into writing in journals, magazines, and newspapers to shift public opinion.

Kathy Rodgers: There are many forms of leadership. We need more than one form. It can vary with the nature of the tasks that need to be done, as well as the issues. We also need to separate out the role of leader from that of spokesperson or messenger. The leadership of a movement may not be the ones you choose to be a messenger to this group or that group. We should keep a very flexible mind about what leadership is and what we mean.

On the question of success, it seems that we will have success when everyone really is treated with equal respect, has the resources they need, and can take advantage of opportunities in their way, based on the resources that they have. I think we are probably at least a century away from that. We are so far away from it that I don't want us to confuse progress with success. And I don't want us to desire so much to have something done and over with that we lose our energy. We must keep focused on digging deeper into these issues.

Richard Delgado: It's important to keep in mind that coalition politics presupposes mutual respect. That, in turn, requires hard study and coming to grips with the differences of that other group. It is not a dismissal of their patterns and their loyalties and their cultures. One area in which white folks can exercise leadership, and they alone can do it, is dealing with "white privilege," the bundle of assumptions, gratuities, benefits, courtesies, and so on that come to people based on their whiteness. They align themselves with white values, white baselines, and even white standards of beauty and sociability. It seems to me that that's an area in which whites can undoubtedly achieve leadership and do a great deal of good to the applause of all the other subjugated groups.

Derrick Bell: I agree with Charles on the need for leadership. As we talked, I concluded that I brought you the wrong story. In the same

Afrolantica Legacies (Bell 1998), I imagined that my heroine, Geneva, had gotten to President Clinton, and instead of the things he has said about race, gets him to say the things that need to be said. Part of the reason for getting him to do that is because of my conclusion: that whites have to do this. We need whites. Beverly Tatum, in her book *Why Do All the Black Children Sit Together in the Cafeteria?*, asks her class members to name some outstanding whites with regard to leadership in this area. One suggests Martin Luther King. The fact is they can't come up with an answer.

There is that need. It seems like so much self-serving when we do it. Yet the potential is there, not only to talk about white privilege and to get folks to see the privileges that they have, whether they want them or not, but also the costs of those privileges, the burdens that go along with them. It builds into the self-interest theme. Happily, the story goes on to find that there really are white groups that work along this line: the "race traitors" Noel Ignatiev is working with. Much more needs to be done, but that is going to be a very important part of it.

As to success, we're talking about fundamental issues that go all the way back through history. And to assume that any particular coalition or approach or strategy or some good fortune is going to enable us to declare success is tough. I think it is worthwhile to raise the question: How do you measure success? It is also appropriate, perhaps essential, to conclude that success is when I recognize that this is what I'm going to do as long as I have breath.

Note on the Reflections

1. Copyright 1999 by Richard Delgado. Used by permission of the author.

19

Concluding Note

Charles V. Hamilton

THE FOCUS OF this book has been on the causes and consequences of racism in three countries on three continents, and on efforts to deal with these issues. Each country has racial problems in varying dimensions and complexities, and the chapters in this book have not presumed the existence of a uniform, cross-national set of remedies or solutions. Racism may well have common features wherever it exists in the world, but different historical experiences and sociopolitical and economic contexts inevitably lead to different approaches to minimizing its impact.

One might suggest, nonetheless, at least three ways of examining the problem of racism in the different countries. First, the matter of sheer demography. Second, the political institutional structures and ideologies charged with the responsibility of producing policies—legal, economic, and so on—necessary to protect against racism. Third, the function of "education," formally understood as mass literacy and the development of a high level of widespread intellectual and technological capacity, commonly called "human capital."

The Significance of Numbers

The sheer size of an identifiable racial or ethnic group in a society is important. It might not be determinative, but a large majority group cannot for too long be ignored. Thus, black South Africans constituting approximately 76 percent of the population have a resource that (coupled with other factors) permitted them to negotiate an agreement that finally overturned formal apartheid and install a new democratic government in 1994. The blacks could then assume many governmental posts and begin to be a legitimate voice in their society.

This is quite different from the status of black Americans, who are only 13 percent of the population and will likely not come close to being even a sizeable minority. Black Americans cannot look forward to having "group" power over political decisionmaking institutions, except in some local cities and counties. Having influence is not the same thing as having power, especially when socioeconomic problems require national resources, decisions, and solutions.

The U.S. situation also means that blacks must first negotiate alliances with others before they can think effectively of obtaining needed and legitimate public policies. Such coalitions always mean, of course, sharing power, hopefully among coequals, in alliances where compromise is more often than not necessary to accomplish virtually anything of value. This is so because no one group has the sole power to achieve its goals on its own. Therefore, the stronger the coalition, the greater the potential outcome for each of its members. But basically, U.S.-style political coalitions are self-interested, issue-driven arrangements that are not intended to be permanent. They exist as long as they are functional to the interests involved. (James Madison's Federalist Paper No. 10 was clear on this point, and astute American political observers have absorbed this lesson well.) Therefore, black Americans, more than many other groups without the prospect of "taking over" government and having relatively little to bring to a viable coalition, must resort to persuasion (moral and political), pleading, and juridical arguments to make their case. (Episodically, the threat of internal disruption through civil mass protest is seen as a potential bargaining weapon, but this is hardly a resource of lasting validity.)

This demographic factor is important even where the government espouses equal opportunity and justice for all. In a black majority situation, *how* to achieve those goals is easier to conceptualize, put on the agenda, and debate, if not (as we shall see) to immediately obtain. Likewise, once certain goals are obtained—in various forms and stages—the results are less likely to be reversed or substantially muted, as has occurred in some instances in the United States. Derrick Bell's chapter in this volume underscores this point. The black American minority by necessity is more vulnerable, even in the most favorable circumstances. It can look forward to being influential in some policymaking forums as part of a viable coalition, but the prospect of being a dominant factor in most (or many) instances is slim to nil.

A permanent minority status means that while the group cannot be constitutionally or legally excluded, it cannot expect to have the agenda-setting, issue-defining capacity enjoyed by a black majority. The minority can, indeed, initiate and participate, but its interests must never be understood as incompatible with that of the majority. Whereas the majority (whether whites in the United States or blacks in South Africa) will always have the prerogative of defining what is ultimately in the national (read: overall) interest. This, after all, is what majorities do in democratic societies, sometimes wisely, sometimes to the discomfort of the minority. But, hopefully, never to the constant disregard and detriment of the minority.

In demographic terms, ironically, the whites in South Africa are in a position similar to that of blacks in the United States. In this sense, both groups must face certain political realities and expect to make certain accommodations as minorities that majority status does not require. There are other important factors to consider that sharply differentiate the two groups, however.

How does this "demographic" conceptualization work in Brazil? One might respond, candidly, "uneasily." In that country, unlike in South Africa and the United States, there was never an official recognition of the existence of a racist problem in the first place. Thus, the initial prerequisite to "transformation" was never met, namely, societal agreement that there was a need to do so. This meant that talking in terms of a racial group "majority" or "minority" had no meaning in a country where "race" was presumed (at least since the abolition of slavery) to be politically irrelevant.

To the extent that there appear to be signs of a different, more realistic understanding of race and color in Brazil, one might conclude that those who see themselves as "black" (*preto*, 6 percent of the population) will be in the statistical situation of black Americans. The *pardos* (38 percent) in Brazil are the ones, it seems, who will be critical in determining how this demographic scenario plays out in that country.

The Constraints on Political
Victory in Democratic, Capitalist Societies

There is no question that in democratic politics numbers are important, especially when carefully mobilized to win electoral campaigns for governmental office. But, as could be expected, the matter is far more complicated than simply capturing office. In the United States, African Americans have made remarkable strides in electoral politics over the last thirty years. The number of black officeholders at all levels of government has increased dramatically from a few hundred in the mid-1960s to over 8,000 at the end of the century. In a sense, these victories have illustrated the success of one important component of the civil rights movement. For decades, blacks concentrated considerable effort on overcoming official and unofficial racist barriers to voting. In an inspiring speech on May 17, 1957, before a rally in Washington, D.C., Martin Luther King Jr. articulated the hopes and aspirations of that effort:

> Give us the ballot . . . and we will transform salient misdeeds of bloodthirsty mobs into the abiding good deeds of orderly citizens.
> Give us the ballot . . . and we will fill our legislative halls with men of good will, and send to the sacred halls of Congress men who will not sign a southern manifesto [favoring states' rights and the racial status quo] because of their devotion to the manifesto of justice.
> Give us the ballot . . . and we will place judges on the benches of the South who will "do justly and love mercy," and we will place at the head of the southern states governors who have felt not only the tang of the human but the glow of the Divine.

Clearly noble sentiments. But gaining the right to vote (and using the franchise to the fullest) could not lead, in the most optimistic circumstances, to such laudable results. Two important systemic/institutional constraints make this evident.

First, the U.S. democratic political system is a complex structure of checks and balances whereby, at the national level, there is a separation of powers between the executive, legislature, and judiciary. These have interlocking powers of "veto" in various forms over each other. The officeholders serve different terms and are elected from different constituencies (states, congressional districts), with the federal judiciary being appointed for life. This was no accident. The framers of the Constitution deliberately designed the institutions to guard against the tyranny of a permanent majority. They firmly believed that government, if left unchecked, would abuse its powers and diminish the freedoms of the (white) citizens. In addition to diffusing power centers and pitting them as checks against each other, different size majorities are required for different purposes: simple majority for some legislative measures; two-thirds for others; still three-quarters of the states for amending the Constitution.

Therefore, sheer *voting* by the electorate is only a first step in an intricate policymaking process designed to make government move cautiously, incrementally, and only with a reasonably broad consensus behind its actions. Such a system is quite satisfactory (and has proven to be so over a long period of time) for those in the society fortunate enough to have their status, economic and political, rather well secured. Maintenance of the status quo or, at least, patient, conservative change is highly preferred. And anything that potentially threatens this condition is eschewed.

Second, perhaps the most sacrosanct economic concern in U.S. society is the preference for a market economy—a capitalist society. Leading from the first point, namely, a fragmented decisionmaking structure, this preference is stated in the maxim: "That government is best which governs least." The intent is clear: the government should not interfere with the private-sector market any more than is absolutely necessary and then only for regulatory purposes, hardly ever for purposes of imposing ownership. Such a strong ideological preference obviously has implications for public policy concerning the issues raised in this book.

In all three countries, evidence is presented of the need for more resources to be distributed to those most in need. But for government to do that would require political control over vast resources that does not now exist, even in the affluent United States. Americans would have to support higher taxes, or a redistribution of current projected budget surpluses, or at least accept no current reduction in taxes. At the beginning of the twenty-first century, this is precisely the fiscal policy debate in the country. And this discussion should be seen as intimately related to the subject of this book, namely, effective ways to overcome racism and the legacy of past racism.

Civil rights advocates in the United States have, indeed, been successful in obtaining important civil and political rights. Those victories *are* real, but they are not—and never should have been seen as—panaceas. What blacks gained mainly in the political arena were the right to vote and protection against de jure segregation and discrimination. Steps were made in providing economic support directly from government and from the private sector, but these have been far from sufficient given the need still existing.

Importantly, this issue is faced by all three countries, as many chapters in this volume point out, notwithstanding the big differences in economic wherewithal. The common feature is that while these societies are politically democratic, they are also market-capitalist economics, and in a highly competitive global economy such systems are not automatically inclined to put expenditures on "human capital" too high on the policy priority list.

The only thing that can conceivably alter this inclination is a persuasive argument supporting *society's* interest in doing so. Which leads to the third point.

Education: The Predominate Independent Variable

Intentionally, this book has presented a wide selection of analytical and prescriptive articles dealing with racism in the three countries. The editors did not presume there would be a rank-order of priorities in terms of "solutions." Such would be unnecessary, as well as unwise and unrealistic. Precisely because the issue of racism in these societies is intertwined with so many economic, political, and social phenomena, one would hardly expect any but a complex set of ideas and proposals to emerge: total societal "transformation" (powell); preferential reallocation of economic resources; resort to international human rights agencies, official and nongovernmental (McDougall); intracountry reconciliation and coalition building (Wolfe); and many more. All have merit in some context or another.

At the risk of oversimplification, this editorial summary focuses attention on what is arguably the single most important factor (short and long term) to address. That is the matter of substantially raising the formal educational level of masses of those people subject to the legacy and persistence of racism. This is the crucial independent variable that will impact the outcome of all other efforts at progress in all three countries. For every conceivable goal sought—high productive employment, good health and housing, political participation, effective enforcement of antidiscrimination laws—the ultimate enjoyment of these goals requires an educated mass society. Comparative statistics indicate the dimensions of the problem in terms of illiteracy rate and education attained. Data shows quite clearly the advantage whites have, notwithstanding their minority status in South Africa, and this renders them, as a minority, to have much more power than their minority counterpart in the United States. (This, combined with white control of the economy, per the discussion in the previous section, further distinguishes the minority status of the groups in their respective societies.) Precisely because of apartheid in both countries historically, one group—white South Africans—is a highly privileged minority, the other group—black Americans—is a highly disadvantaged minority. Both are minorities, but otherwise noncomparable in their relationship to their respective societies.

In all three countries, there is official commitment to end racism and to assure "equal opportunity." But achieving these goals will be frustrated if there remain wide educational disparities. An uneducated populace cannot function intelligently in a democratic society and will remain susceptible to political demagogy. Unskilled workers cannot compete for high-technology jobs, thus diminishing the international competitive advantage of domestic industries. And the emphasis has to be on education not only of the elite but the masses of the citizenry. Elites—those who for various reasons have or are readily able to acquire skills and training—will and should take advantage of the immediate opportunities brought on by the new legal and political dispensations. But this should never be the end result of viable social movements. The masses of people must be able to benefit from social transformation, and this can only be secured if they have the human capital to facilitate their competitive participation in the governance and economic productivity of the total society.

The fight against racism and the legacy of racism must center on helping those who will not be able to benefit without the help other prior beneficiaries have received under more closed systems. This special, targeted help should be as unapologetically deliberate as it was earlier when policies were designed successfully (and maliciously) to exclude people and to benefit a privileged few. Now, such policies must be consciously designed to *include* people, in the interest of all society. In various manifestations, this would appear to be a matter common to all three countries, with the societal interest of each readily apparent. Concentrating on substantially raising the level of mass formal education might be a simplistic way to formulate the issue, but one cannot question its predominate value. It does not guarantee social progress, but it is difficult to imagine such without it.

The Contributors

Sérgio Adorno (Sérgio França Adorno de Abreu) is a professor of sociology in the School of Philosophy and adjunct director in the Center for the Study of Violence at the University of São Paulo. He has published two books and has written numerous articles and chapters. He has served as assistant editor for the *Brazilian Review of Social Sciences* (*Revista Brasileira de Ciências Sociais*) and was president of the Brazilian Society of Sociology for four years. He obtained his undergraduate degree in social science and his Ph.D. in human science from the University of São Paulo.

Neville Alexander is the director of the Project for the Study of Alternative Education in South Africa at the University of Cape Town. He has been the director of the Cape Town Centre of the South African Committee on Higher Education and the executive secretary of the Health, Education and Welfare Society of South Africa. He has received several bachelors' degrees and a master's degree from the University of Cape Town and a Ph.D. from the University of Tübingen.

Derrick Bell was dean of the University of Oregon law school and law professor at both Harvard Law School and New York University. He served as both executive secretary and staff attorney for the NAACP Legal Defense and Educational Fund. He is a member of the bar of the District of Columbia and of the states of New York, Pennsylvania, California, the U.S. Supreme Court, the U.S. Courts of Appeals for 4th, 5th, 6th, 8th, and 10th circuits, and several federal district courts. He is the author of *Confronting Authority: Reflections of an Ardent Protester*; *Race, Racism and American Law*; *And We Are Not Saved, The Elusive Quest for Racial Justice*; *Faces at the Bottom of the Well: The*

Permanence of Racism; and *Afrolantica Legacies*. He received his
bachelor's degree from Duquesne University and his law degree from
the University of Pittsburgh Law School.

Nancy Birdsall is senior associate of the Carnegie Endowment for
International Peace, where she directs the economics programs. She
was the executive vice president of the Inter-American Development
Bank from 1993 until 1998. She is the author of numerous publications
on economic development issues. Her most recent work is on the causes
and effects of inequality in a globalizing world. She holds a master's
degree in international relations from the Johns Hopkins School of
Advanced International Studies and a doctorate in economics from Yale
University.

Alex Boraine is visiting professor to the Global Law School at New
York University. In 1996, President Nelson Mandela appointed him as
vice chairperson of the Truth and Reconciliation Commission of South
Africa. In 1970, he served as the youngest minister ever elected as president of the Methodist Church of South Africa and later cofounded the
Institute for Democracy in South Africa. Boraine has published widely
on issues of democracy and reconciliation.

Emmett D. Carson is the president and chief executive officer of the
Minneapolis Foundation. He has been an adjunct lecturer at the
University of Maryland at College Park, a project director for the Joint
Center for Political and Economic Studies, a program officer for the
Ford Foundation's Rights and Social Justice Program, and a program
officer for Ford's Governance and Public Policy Program. He designed
and directed the first national comparative study of the charitable giving
and volunteer behavior of black and white Americans. He has a bache-
lor's degree in economics from Morehouse College and an MPA and a
Ph.D. from Princeton University.

Richard Delgado is a leading commentator on race in the United
States. He has appeared on *Good Morning America*, the *MacNeil-
Lehrer Report*, PBS, NPR, and Canadian National Public Radio. He has
written over a hundred law review articles and eleven books. His work
has been reviewed in *The Nation*, the *New Republic*, the *New York
Times*, the *Washington Post*, and the *Wall Street Journal*. His books
have won eight national awards.

George M. Fredrickson is the Edgar E. Robinson Professor of United
States History at Stanford University and past president of the

Organization of American Historians. He is the author of *The Inner Civil War: Northern Intellectuals and the Crisis of the Union*; *The Black Image in the White Mind: The Debate on Afro-American Character and Destiny, 1817-1914*; and *White Supremacy: A Comparative Study in American and South African History*. He was a Fulbright scholar at the University of Oslo and a Fulbright professor of American history at Moscow University. He received his bachelor's degree and his Ph.D. from Harvard University.

Antonio Sérgio Alfredo Guimarães holds a doctorate from the University of Wisconsin–Madison and is professor of sociology at the University of São Paulo. Dr. Guimarães specializes in the study of race relations in Brazil, focusing on racism and the construction of racial and national identities. He has published two books on race relations in Brazil (*Racismo e Anti-Racismo no Brazil*; and *Preconceito e discriminação*) and several articles in academic journals. He was also president of the Brazilian Society of Sociology from 1996 until 1998.

Andrew Hacker teaches political science at Queens College in New York City. Prior to that, he served as a professor of government at Cornell University. His writings include a book entitled *The End of the American Era*. He has written extensively for scholarly journals, as well as publications including the *New York Review of Books*, *Time*, *Newsweek*, *Harper's*, *Atlantic*, the *Wall Street Journal*, and *Fortune*. He has a Ph.D. from Princeton University.

Charles V. Hamilton is Wallace S. Sayre Professor Emeritus of Government at Columbia University. He taught political science and government for over forty years at Tuskegee University, Roosevelt University, Rutgers University, Lincoln University, and Columbia University. Among other works, he coauthored *Black Power* and *The Dual Agenda: Race and Social Welfare Policies of Civil Rights Organizations*. He has a bachelor's degree from Roosevelt University in Chicago and a law degree from Loyola University School of Law. He has an M.A. and a Ph.D. from the University of Chicago.

Jennifer Hochschild is a professor of government and Afro-American studies at Harvard University. Until December 2000, she was the William Stewart Tod Professor of Public and International Affairs at Princeton University, with a joint appointment in the Department of Politics and the Woodrow Wilson School of Public and International Affairs. She is the author of *Facing Up to the American Dream: Race, Class, and the Soul of the Nation*; *The New American Dilemma: Liberal*

Democracy and School Desegregation; *What's Fair: American Beliefs About Distributive Justice*; and a coauthor of *Equalities*. She is coeditor of *Social Policies for Children*. Her forthcoming book is tentatively entitled *Madison's Constitution and Identity Politics*. Professor Hochschild is a fellow of the American Academy of Arts and Sciences, a former vice-president of the American Political Association, and a member of the Board of Trustees of the Russell Sage Foundation. She received a B.A. with high honors from Oberlin College and a Ph.D. from Yale University.

Lynn Walker Huntley is executive vice president of the Southern Education Foundation and director of the Comparative Human Relations Initiative. She previously served as director of the Ford Foundation's Rights and Social Justice Program. Huntley served as deputy assistant attorney general and section chief in the Civil Rights Division of the U.S. Department of Justice, staff counsel at the NAACP Legal Defense and Educational Fund, and general counsel to the NYC Commission on Human Rights. She is a member of the National Bar Association and has been admitted to the bar for the District Court for the Southern District of New York, the U.S. States Court of Appeals for 2nd and 5th circuits, and is a member of the New York State Bar. She is a graduate of Barnard College and Columbia University Law School.

Wilmot G. James is an associate editor at Independent Newspapers Cape and a professor at the University of Cape Town. Previously he served as dean of the Institute for Democracy in South Africa. He was a contributing author and coeditor of *After the TRC: Reflections on Truth and Reconciliation in South Africa; Now that We are Free: The Coloured Communities in a Democratic South Africa; Angry Divide: Social and Economic History of the Western Cape;* and *Crossing Boundaries: Mine Migrancy in a Democratic South Africa.* He is the author of *Our Precious Metal: African Labour in South Africa's Gold Industry.* He holds a Ph.D. in sociology from the University of Wisconsin-Madison and a bachelor's (honors) degree from the University of the Western Cape.

Jeffrey Lever works with the Impumelelo Innovation Awards Programme in Cape Town, South Africa, and has taught at various South African universities, including the University of Stellenbosch, the University of Cape Town, and most recently, the University of the Western Cape. Lever has published articles on various aspects of the social and political life of South Africa and on social theory. He holds a Ph.D. in sociology.

Mahmood Mamdani is the Herbert Lehman Professor of Government in the Departments of Anthropology and Political Science, and director of the Institute of African Studies in the School of International and Public Affairs at Columbia University. He was formerly the A.C. Jordan Professor for African Studies and director of the Centre for African Studies, at the University of Cape Town. He is president of the Council for the Development of Social Research in Africa. He holds a bachelor's degree from the University of Pittsburgh, an M.A. and an M.A.L.D. from the Fletcher School of Law and Diplomacy in Tufts, Massachusetts, and a Ph.D. from Harvard University.

Gay McDougall is executive director of the International Human Rights Law Group and serves as independent expert on the United Nations treaty body that oversees the International Convention on the Elimination of All Forms of Racial Discrimination (CERD). Ms. McDougall was the first American elected to this body of eighteen international experts who oversee compliance by governments worldwide. With the International Human Rights Law Group, Ms. McDougall oversees human-rights projects in Africa, Asia, Europe, Latin America, and the United States. Ms. McDougall is a graduate of Yale Law School and the London School of Economics.

Abdias do Nascimento, organizer of the Afro-Campineiro Congress (1938), the National Convention of Brazilian Blacks (1946), and the First Congress of Brazilian Blacks (1950), created the Black Experimental Theater (1944) and the Black Arts Museum (1968) in Rio de Janeiro. A Pan-African activist, he organized the Third Congress of Black Culture in the Americas (São Paulo, 1982). He holds postgraduate degrees from the Superior Institute of Brazilian Studies and the Institute of Ocean Studies. He is professor emeritus at the State University of New York at Buffalo, where he founded the chair in African Culture in the New World. He was the first Afro-Brazilian congressman to champion black people's human and civil rights in the national legislature (1983–1987). He was also in the federal senate. His paintings have been exhibited throughout the United States, in Brazil, and in Europe. He is the author of *Brazil: Mixture or Massacre?*; *Sortilege (Black Mystery)*; and *Orishas: The Living Gods of Africa in Brazil*, among other works.

Elisa Larkin Nascimento is cofounder and director of the Afro-Brazilian Studies and Research Institute, which organized the Third Congress of Black Culture in the Americas (São Paulo, 1982). Organizer of the Sankofa teachers' training courses (Rio de Janeiro,

1985–1995), she served as founding director of curriculum development at the African and African-American Studies Program, State University of Rio de Janeiro. She holds master's and J.D. degrees from the State University of New York and a Ph.D. from the University of São Paulo. Coeditor of the journal *Afrodiaspora*, she is the author of *Pan-Africanism and South America*; editor of *Sankofa: Matrizes Africanas da Cultura Brasileira*; and coauthor of *Africans in Brazil: A Pan-African Perspective*, among other works.

Lesley O'Connell is a consultant for the Inter-American Development Bank, specializing in the development of social programs in Latin America. She has worked on various upper primary and lower secondary education projects and labor training programs in Central America. Her research interests and publications focus on the linkages between education, labor market performance, and poverty reduction. She received a master's degree in Public Policy from the Kennedy School of Government, Harvard University, and specialized in Latin American studies at Georgetown University's School of Foreign Service.

Melvin L. Oliver is vice president of the Asset Building and Community Development (Assets) Program at the Ford Foundation. He previously was a professor of sociology at the University of California–Los Angeles. He has published widely in the areas of race and ethnic relations, poverty and inequality, and urban studies. He is most recently coeditor with Lawrence D. Bobo, James H. Johnson Jr., and Abel Valenzuela Jr. of *Prismatic Metropolis: Inequality in Los Angeles*.

Naledi Pandor is chairperson of the National Council of Provinces in South Africa. She was elected to Parliament following the nation's first democratic election in 1994. She became deputy chief whip of the majority party in 1995. She also served as convenor of the subcommittee on higher education in the Education Portfolio Committee. In August 1998, Ms. Pandor joined the National Council of Provinces.

john a. powell is the Sonosky Professor of Law at the University of Minnesota Law School. He is the founder and director of the Institute on Race and Poverty created in 1993. He was an attorney with the Seattle Public Defender's Office and national legal director of the American Civil Liberties Union. Professor powell has also served as consultant to the government of Mozambique. He has taught at Columbia University School of Law, Harvard Law School, University of Miami School of Law, American University, and the University of San Francisco School of Law. Professor powell holds a bachelor's degree from Stanford University and a J.D. from the University of California at Berkeley.

Mamphela Ramphele is the managing director of the World Bank, with responsibility for human development and the use of information technology to tackle development challenges. She was the vice-chancellor at the University of Cape Town during 1996–2000. She has worked as a doctor, a civil-rights leader, an academic researcher, and a university administrator. She has served on the boards of major corporations and nongovernmental organizations. She has been with the University of Cape Town since 1986, first as a research fellow, then in 1991 as a deputy vice-chancellor, and in 1996 stepped into the vice-chancellor's position, becoming the first black woman to hold this post at the University of Cape Town. She is the author of two books and coauthor of several more. She holds a Ph.D. in social anthropology from the University of Cape Town, a B.com. degree in administration from the University of South Africa, and diplomas in tropical health and hygiene and public health from the University of Witwatersrand. She holds nine honorary doctoral degrees from universities in the United States, Europe, and South Africa.

Kathryn J. Rodgers is the president of NOW Legal Defense and Education Fund (NOW Legal Defense). Before NOW Legal Defense, she spent fourteen years at Barnard College as its general counsel, as vice president for nonacademic students' services and in 1993–1994, as acting president. She also taught a political science colloquium on civil rights and women's issues. Prior to joining Barnard, she was an associate at Poletti Freidin Prashker Feldman & Gartner, where she specialized in labor relations law. She is a graduate of Columbia University School of Law and Smith College.

Kenneth Roth is the executive director of Human Rights Watch, a position he has held since 1993. From 1987 to 1993, he served as the organization's deputy director. He is a former federal prosecutor for the U.S. Attorney's Office for the Southern District of New York and the Iran-Contra investigation in Washington. He has also worked in the private sector as a litigator. Mr. Roth has conducted human rights investigations in some twenty countries worldwide. He has written extensively on a range of human rights topics for the *New York Times*, the *Washington Post*, *Foreign Affairs*, *The Nation*, and the *New York Review of Books*. He has frequent media appearances on NPR, the BBC, CNN, PBS, ABC, NBC, and CBS. He is a graduate of Yale Law School and Brown University.

Friar David Raimundo Santos was born in Minas Gerais. He and six siblings were raised by his mother in a *favela* in Espirito Santo. He entered Franciscan Seminary in March 1976, and as a priest he has lived and done his pastoral work in Nilópolis, a township in the Rio de Janeiro metropolitan area. He is one of the founders of the University Admissions Preparatory Course for Blacks and the Poor, which began in Nilópolis in 1992 and by 1999 had 700 local branches all over Brazil. Currently, he works with Educafro (Education and Citizenship for African Descendants and the Poor) in São Paulo, where he is completing his master's degree in theology.

Melissa Steyn is the director of the Institute for Intercultural and Diversity Studies of Southern Africa, University of Cape Town. As a Fulbright scholar, Ms. Steyn studied intercultural communication at Arizona State University. Her major interest is Whiteness Studies, although she has published on various aspects of diversity, including race, culture, gender, and sexuality. Her books include *Whiteness Just Isn't What It Used to Be: The Master's Narrative and the New South Africa*, and the coedited *Cultural Synergy in South Africa: Weaving Strands of Africa and Europe*. She is currently working on another coedited collection, *The Prize and the Price: Shaping Sexualities in the New South Africa*.

Catharine Stimpson is professor and dean of the Graduate School of Arts and Science at New York University. She formerly served as director of the Fellows Program at the MacArthur Foundation in Chicago and was dean of the graduate school and vice provost for graduate education at Rutgers, the State University of New Jersey at New Brunswick. Before that, she taught at Barnard College and was the first director of its Women's Center. She has written a book entitled *Class Notes* and has edited numerous volumes. She has published over 150 monographs, essays, stories, and reviews. She was educated at Bryn Mawr College, Cambridge University, and Columbia University. She holds honorary degrees from ten colleges and has won Fulbright and Rockefeller Humanities fellowships.

John Kuo Wei Tchen is the founding director of the Asian/Pacific/American Studies Program and Institute at New York University and associate professor of history. Before NYU, Dr. Tchen was director of the Asian/American Center at Queens College of the City University of New York, as associate professor of the Department of Urban Studies at Queens College, and on the Ph.D. faculty in sociology at the Graduate

Center (CUNY). He cofounded the New York Chinatown History Project, recently renamed the Museum of Chinese in the Americas. He is the author of *New York Before Chinatown* and *Genthe's Photographs of San Francisco's Old Chinatown*; and editor of *The Chinese Laundryman: A Study of Social Isolation.*

Francis Wilson has taught for thirty years in the School of Economics at the University of Cape Town, where he founded and directs the Southern African Labour and Development Research Unit (SALDRU). He was chairman of the Council of the University of Fort Hare from 1990 to 1999 and also first chairman, 1996–1998, of the National Water Advisory Council. In 1989, he coauthored with Mamphela Ramphele *Uprooting Poverty: The South African Challenge.*

Leslie R. Wolfe is the president of the Center for Womens Policy Studies, a Washington-based national, independent, multiethnic feminist policy research and advocacy institute, founded in 1972. Prior to coming to the center, Dr. Wolfe was director of the Project on Equal Education Rights of the NOW Legal Defense and Education Fund. Before that she was director of the Women's Educational Equity Act Program in the U.S. Department of Education. She has served as deputy director of the Women's Rights Program at the U.S. Commission on Civil Rights and as special assistant to the assistant secretary of education in the former U.S. Department of Health, Education, and Welfare.

Jonas Zoninsein holds a Ph.D. in economics from the New School for Social Research and teaches International Political Economy at James Madison College of Michigan State University. He has published a book entitled *Monopoly Capital Theory* and multiple articles on development economics and political economy in Brazil, Germany, Japan, Mexico, South Korea, and the United States. His most recent research work addresses the roles of civil society and the nation-state in promoting a bottom-up process of globalization. His latest article on "International Labor Standards and Growth Policy" will be published in Erik Borg, ed., *Globalization, Nations and Markets* (Cambridge University Press, 2002). Professor Zoninsein has taught at the Federal University of Rio de Janeiro, Catholic University of Chile, and Brown University.

Index

About the Book

This provocative comparative study explores issues of race, racism, and strategies to improve the status of people of African descent in Brazil, South Africa, and the United States.

What constitutes "race"? Is Brazil in fact a "great racial democracy"? What is the significance of color in postapartheid South Africa? How will the changing U.S. demographics affect efforts to combat discrimination? The authors provide in-depth information about each country, together with probing analyses of crosscutting themes and trends. They present a rich collage of ideas and information designed to encourage critical thinking—about race relations, human rights, democratization, national development, and other equally crucial topics.